NITRIC OXIDE IN HEALTH AND DISEASE
Therapeutic Applications in Cancer and Inflammatory Disorders

NITRIC OXIDE IN HEALTH AND DISEASE

Therapeutic Applications in Cancer and Inflammatory Disorders

Edited by

LUCIA MORBIDELLI, PhD
Department of Life Sciences, University of Siena, Siena, Italy

BENJAMIN BONAVIDA, PhD
Department of Microbiology, Immunology and Molecular Genetics, David Geffen School of Medicine, Jonsson Comprehensive Cancer Center, University of California at Los Angeles, Los Angeles, CA, United States

JORDI MUNTANÉ, PhD
Department of Medical Physiology and Biophysics, Institute of Biomedicine of Seville (IBiS), Seville, Spain

ELSEVIER

ACADEMIC PRESS
An imprint of Elsevier

Academic Press is an imprint of Elsevier
125 London Wall, London EC2Y 5AS, United Kingdom
525 B Street, Suite 1650, San Diego, CA 92101, United States
50 Hampshire Street, 5th Floor, Cambridge, MA 02139, United States
The Boulevard, Langford Lane, Kidlington, Oxford OX5 1GB, United Kingdom

Notices
Knowledge and best practice in this field are constantly changing. As new research and experience broaden our
understanding, changes in research methods, professional practices, or medical treatment may become
necessary.

Practitioners and researchers must always rely on their own experience and knowledge in evaluating and using
any information, methods, compounds, or experiments described herein. In using such information or methods
they should be mindful of their own safety and the safety of others, including parties for whom they have a
professional responsibility.

To the fullest extent of the law, neither the Publisher nor the authors, contributors, or editors, assume any liability
for any injury and/or damage to persons or property as a matter of products liability, negligence or otherwise, or
from any use or operation of any methods, products, instructions, or ideas contained in the material herein.

ISBN 978-0-443-13342-8

For information on all Academic Press publications
visit our website at https://www.elsevier.com/books-and-journals

Publisher: Stacy Masucci
Senior Acquisition Editor: Linda Versteeg-Buschman
Editorial Project Manager: Samantha Allard
Production Project Manager: Punithavathy Govindaradjane
Cover Designer: Vicky Pearson

Typeset by STRAIVE, India

Working together
to grow libraries in
developing countries

www.elsevier.com • www.bookaid.org

Contents

I

Development of NO donors and derivatives, and new delivery formations

1. Nitric oxide and derivatives: Molecular insights and translational opportunities

Braian Ledesma, Fakiha Firdaus,
Maria Silena Mosquera, Katherine Campbell,
Farah Rahman, Maria Camila Suarez Arbelaez,
and Himanshu Arora

2. Biomedical applications of polymeric nitric oxide (NO) donors

Soumya Paul, Manish Kumar, Arindam Mukherjee,
and Priyadarsi De

II

Nitric oxide pathway and cancer progression and therapy

3. Therapeutic potential for coxib-nitric oxide releasing hybrids in cancer treatment

Antonio Giordani, Giovanna Poce, Sara Consalvi,
Samuele Maramai, Mario Saletti, Antonietta Rossi,
Paola Patrignani, Mariangela Biava,
and Maurizio Anzini

4. Targeting dimethylarginine dimethylaminohydrolase 1 to suppress vasculogenic mimicry in breast cancer: Current evidence and future directions

Arduino A. Mangoni, Julie-Ann Hulin, Lashika Weerakoon,
and Sara Tommasi

III

Nitric oxide donors and cardiovascular and metabolic diseases

IV

Nitric oxide derivatives
in ocular diseases

Contributors

Eda Acikgoz Department of Histology and Embryology, Faculty of Medicine, Van Yuzuncu Yil University, Van, Turkey

Maurizio Anzini Department of Biotechnology, Chemistry, and Pharmacy, University of Siena, Siena, Italy

Maria Camila Suarez Arbelaez Desai Sethi Urology Institute, Miller School of Medicine, University of Miami, Miami, FL, United States

Bhaskar Arora Chitkara College of Pharmacy, Chitkara University, Rajpura, Punjab, India

Himanshu Arora Desai Sethi Urology Institute; John P Hussman Institute for Human Genomics; The Interdisciplinary Stem Cell Institute, Miller School of Medicine, University of Miami, Miami, FL, United States

Zahra Bahadoran Nutrition and Endocrine Research Center, Research Institute for Endocrine Sciences, Shahid Beheshti University of Medical Sciences, Tehran, Iran

Lorenzo Berra Harvard Medical School; Department of Anesthesia, Critical Care and Pain Medicine, Massachusetts General Hospital; Respiratory Care Department, Massachusetts General Hospital, Boston, MA, United States

Mariangela Biava Department of Chemistry and Technologies of Drug, Sapienza University of Rome, Rome, Italy

Benjamin Bonavida Department of Microbiology, Immunology and Molecular Genetics, David Geffen School of Medicine, Jonsson Comprehensive Cancer Center, University of California at Los Angeles, Los Angeles, CA, United States

Katherine Campbell Desai Sethi Urology Institute, Miller School of Medicine, University of Miami, Miami, FL, United States

Antolín Cantó Department of Biomedical Sciences, Faculty of Health Sciences, Institute of Biomedical Sciences, Cardenal Herrera-CEU University, CEU Universities, Valencia, Spain

Bastien Cautain Department of Screening and Target Validation, Fundación MEDINA, Granada, Spain; Evotec – University Paul Sabatier Toulouse III, Toulouse, France

Carla Speroni Ceron Department of Biological Sciences, Institute of Exact and Biological Sciences, Federal University of Ouro Preto (UFOP), Ouro Preto, Minas Gerais, Brazil

Sara Consalvi Department of Chemistry and Technologies of Drug, Sapienza University of Rome, Rome, Italy

Francisco J. Corpas Group of Antioxidants, Free Radicals and Nitric Oxide in Biotechnology, Food and Agriculture, Estación Experimental del Zaidín, CSIC, Granada, Spain

Priyadarsi De Polymer Research Centre; Centre for Advanced Functional Materials, Department of Chemical Sciences, Indian Institute of Science Education and Research Kolkata, Mohanpur, Nadia, West Bengal, India

José Pérez del Palacio Department of Screening and Target Validation, Fundación MEDINA, Granada, Spain

Aleyna Demir Department of Histology and Embryology, Faculty of Medicine, Ege University, Izmir, Turkey

Caridad Díaz Department of Screening and Target Validation, Fundación MEDINA, Granada, Spain

Gabriel Tavares do Vale Minas Gerais State University (UEMG), Passos, Minas Gerais, Brazil

Bijan Safaee Fakhr Department of Emergency and Intensive Care, San Gerardo Hospital, Monza, Italy

Fakiha Firdaus   Desai Sethi Urology Institute, Miller School of Medicine, University of Miami, Miami, FL, United States

Asghar Ghasemi   Endocrine Physiology Research Center, Research Institute for Endocrine Sciences, Shahid Beheshti University of Medical Sciences, Tehran, Iran

Stefano Gianni   Department of Anesthesia and Intensive Care Medicine, Niguarda Ca' Granda Hospital, Milan, Italy

Antonio Giordani   Formerly Rottapharm (Monza, Italy) at the Present Consultant, Pavia, Italy

Salvador González-Gordo   Group of Antioxidants, Free Radicals and Nitric Oxide in Biotechnology, Food and Agriculture, Estación Experimental del Zaidín, CSIC, Granada, Spain

Amarjot Kaur Grewal   Chitkara College of Pharmacy, Chitkara University, Rajpura, Punjab, India

Julie-Ann Hulin   Discipline of Clinical Pharmacology, College of Medicine and Public Health and Flinders Health and Medical Research Institute, Flinders University, Adelaide, SA, Australia

Khosrow Kashfi   Department of Molecular, Cellular, and Biomedical Sciences, Sophie Davis School of Biomedical Education, City University of New York School of Medicine, New York, NY, United States

Heena Khan   Chitkara College of Pharmacy, Chitkara University, Rajpura, Punjab, India

Manish Kumar   Polymer Research Centre; Centre for Advanced Functional Materials, Department of Chemical Sciences, Indian Institute of Science Education and Research Kolkata, Mohanpur, Nadia, West Bengal, India

Braian Ledesma   Desai Sethi Urology Institute, Miller School of Medicine, University of Miami, Miami, FL, United States

Brayden K. Leyva   Department of Physiological Sciences, David Geffen School of Medicine, Jonsson Comprehensive Cancer Center, University of California at Los Angeles, Los Angeles, CA, United States

Katie Lin   Department of Microbiology, Immunology and Molecular Genetics, David Geffen School of Medicine, Jonsson Comprehensive Cancer Center, University of California at Los Angeles, Los Angeles, CA, United States

Rosa López-Pedraja   Department of Biomedical Sciences, Faculty of Health Sciences, Institute of Biomedical Sciences, Cardenal Herrera-CEU University, CEU Universities, Valencia, Spain

Arduino A. Mangoni   Discipline of Clinical Pharmacology, College of Medicine and Public Health and Flinders Health and Medical Research Institute, Flinders University; Department of Clinical Pharmacology, Flinders Medical Centre, Southern Adelaide Local Health Network, Adelaide, SA, Australia

Samuele Maramai   Department of Biotechnology, Chemistry, and Pharmacy, University of Siena, Siena, Italy

Javier Martínez-González   Department of Biomedical Sciences, Faculty of Health Sciences, Institute of Biomedical Sciences, Cardenal Herrera-CEU University, CEU Universities, Valencia, Spain

María Miranda   Department of Biomedical Sciences, Faculty of Health Sciences, Institute of Biomedical Sciences, Cardenal Herrera-CEU University, CEU Universities, Valencia, Spain

Parvin Mirmiran   Department of Clinical Nutrition and Human Dietetics, Faculty of Nutrition Sciences and Food Technology, National Nutrition and Food Technology Research Institute, Shahid Beheshti University of Medical Sciences, Tehran, Iran

Maria Silena Mosquera   Center for Fetal Research, Children's Hospital of Philadelphia, Philadelphia, PA, United States

Arindam Mukherjee   Centre for Advanced Functional Materials, Department of Chemical Sciences, Indian Institute of Science Education and Research Kolkata, Mohanpur, Nadia, West Bengal, India

Gulperi Oktem   Department of Histology and Embryology, Faculty of Medicine, Ege University, Izmir, Turkey

José M. Palma Group of Antioxidants, Free Radicals and Nitric Oxide in Biotechnology, Food and Agriculture, Estación Experimental del Zaidín, CSIC, Granada, Spain

Paola Patrignani Department of Neuroscience, Imaging and Clinical Sciences, and Center for Advanced Studies and Technology (CAST), School of Medicine, G. D'Annunzio University, Chieti, Italy

Soumya Paul Polymer Research Centre; Centre for Advanced Functional Materials, Department of Chemical Sciences, Indian Institute of Science Education and Research Kolkata, Mohanpur, Nadia, West Bengal, India

Bruna Pinheiro Pereira Federal University of Alfenas (UNIFAL), Alfenas, Minas Gerais, Brazil

Giovanna Poce Department of Chemistry and Technologies of Drug, Sapienza University of Rome, Rome, Italy

Simone Regina Potje Minas Gerais State University (UEMG), Passos, Minas Gerais, Brazil

Farah Rahman Desai Sethi Urology Institute, Miller School of Medicine, University of Miami, Miami, FL, United States

Carmen Ramos Department of Screening and Target Validation, Fundación MEDINA, Granada, Spain

Emanuele Rezoagli School of Medicine and Surgery, University of Milano-Bicocca; Department of Emergency and Intensive Care, San Gerardo Hospital, Monza, Italy

Marta Rodríguez-Ruiz Group of Antioxidants, Free Radicals and Nitric Oxide in Biotechnology, Food and Agriculture, Estación Experimental del Zaidín, CSIC, Granada, Spain

Antonietta Rossi Department of Pharmacy, School of Medicine and Surgery, "Federico II" University of Naples, Naples, Italy

Mario Saletti Department of Biotechnology, Chemistry, and Pharmacy, University of Siena, Siena, Italy

Amparo Sánchez-Fideli Department of Biomedical Sciences, Faculty of Health Sciences, Institute of Biomedical Sciences, Cardenal Herrera-CEU University, CEU Universities, Valencia, Spain

Thakur Gurjeet Singh Chitkara College of Pharmacy, Chitkara University, Rajpura, Punjab, India

Claudiu T. Supuran University of Florence, Neurofarba Department, Section of Pharmaceutical and Nutraceutical Chemistry, Florence, Italy

Aysegul Taskiran Department of Histology and Embryology, Faculty of Medicine, Ege University, Izmir, Turkey

Sara Tommasi Discipline of Clinical Pharmacology, College of Medicine and Public Health and Flinders Health and Medical Research Institute, Flinders University; Department of Clinical Pharmacology, Flinders Medical Centre, Southern Adelaide Local Health Network, Adelaide, SA, Australia

Francisca Vicente Department of Screening and Target Validation, Fundación MEDINA, Granada, Spain

Lashika Weerakoon Discipline of Clinical Pharmacology, College of Medicine and Public Health and Flinders Health and Medical Research Institute, Flinders University, Adelaide, SA, Australia

About the Editors

Prof. Lucia Morbidelli's present position is Associate Professor of Pharmacology at the Department of Life Sciences, University of Siena, Italy.

Prof. Morbidelli's research experience is within the pharmacology of angiogenesis and microcirculation by means of a plethora of in vitro and in vivo models. Her background is based around the definition of the role of nitric oxide and prostanoid pathways in the process of physiological and tumor angiogenesis. She contributed to characterizing the activity of synthetic molecules and natural bioactives as pro- or antiangiogenic strategies. In the last decade, she has focused her attention on the gaseous transmitters nitric oxide and hydrogen sulfide by characterizing their activity in the maintenance of endothelial survival and functionality or as antitumor agents.

Prof. Morbidelli is author of over 170 scientific publications in peer reviewed journals, reviews, and chapters in books on the molecular, biochemical, and cellular aspects of angiogenesis and endothelial pharmacology.

Prof. Morbidelli was Guest Editor of the Special Issue of Pharmacological Research "Drugs and druggable signaling in angiogenesis" and of the Special Issue of Molecules on "Natural products as preventive or therapeutic tools for angiogenesis related diseases." Together with Dr. Benjamin Bonavida, she was editor of the book "Therapeutic Application of Nitric Oxide in Cancer and Inflammatory Disorders," published by Elsevier. In 2021, she edited the book "Antiangiogenic drugs as chemosensitizers in cancer therapy" by AP/Elsevier.

In addition to her scientific production, Prof. Morbidelli's international collaborations are related to participation in the COST Action BM1005 European Network on Gaseoustransmitters (2012–2015) and as member responsible for pharmacological countermeasures of the ESA topical team "Tissue Healing in Space: Techniques for promoting and monitoring tissue repair and regeneration" (since 2017) and "Pharmacological Countermeasures" (since 2021).

Prof. Morbidelli's current research topics are related to: (1) defining new targets within the tumor microenvironment responsible for the control of tumor angiogenesis; (2) the identification of drugs and medical devices (natural extracts, nutraceuticals) to recover endothelial and tissue function following injury, or disease conditions related to inflammation and oxidative stress, or unloading conditions.

Dr. Benjamin Bonavida, PhD, is currently a distinguished research professor at the University of California, Los Angeles (UCLA). His research career, thus far, has focused on basic immunochemistry and cancer immunobiology. His research investigations have ranged from the mechanisms of cell-mediated killing, sensitization of resistant tumor cells to chemo-/immunotherapy, characterization of resistant factors in cancer cells, cell signaling pathways mediated by therapeutic anticancer antibodies, and characterization of a dysregulated NF-κB/Snail/YY1/RKIP/PTEN loop in many cancers, which regulates cell survival, proliferation, invasion, metastasis, and resistance. He has also investigated the role of nitric oxide in cancer and its potential antitumor activity. Many of the above studies are centered on the clinically challenging features of cancer patients' failure to respond to both conventional and targeted therapies. The development and activity of various targeting agents, their modes of action, and their resistance are highlighted in many refereed publications.

Prof. Jordi Muntané's scientific career has been devoted to the study of the relevance of oxidative and nitrosative stress in cell proliferation and death in different experimental models and clinical settings involving acute hepatocellular injury and hepatocellular carcinoma. He studied the time-, dose-, and compartment-dependent impact of nitric oxide (NO) in cell death, as well as its involvement in the cytoprotective properties of classical antioxidants, prostanoids, and alpha-tocopherol in liver injury. The antitumoral properties of NO has also been demonstrated using NO-donors and nitric oxide synthase type III (NOS3) overexpression in in vivo and in vitro models. The NO-dependent posttranslational protein modifications induced by NOS3 overexpression was related to a drastic alteration of redox status and reduction of cell proliferation and induction of apoptosis in liver cancer cells. The relevance of NO-dependent posttranslational downregulation of cell death receptors to the antitumoral properties of the recommended molecular therapies for patients with advanced hepatocellular carcinoma, such as the tyrosine kinase inhibitor sorafenib, has also been studied. Furthermore, sorafenib altered the redox cellular status and reduced Nrf2-regulated genes such as *thioredoxin-1* that appear to play a relevant role during the induction of caspase-3 in HepG2 cells.

Prof. Muntané coorganized with Prof. Benjamin Bonavida the Fourth International Workshop on "Nitric Oxide in Cancer" held in Sevilla, March 13–14, 2015. The meeting addressed various topics, including NO, mutagenesis, carcinogenesis, tumor promotion and tumor growth; NO regulation of cell death pathways; NO and proliferation and epithelial-mesenchymal transition; regulation of immune response by NO; antitumoral activity of NO-based releasing strategies: preclinical studies; and antitumoral activity of NO-based releasing strategies: clinical trials.

The Second International Conference "Therapeutic Applications of Nitric Oxide in Cancer and Inflammatory-related Diseases" was held on March 3–5, 2022, in Seville, Spain, coorganized by Prof. Jordi Muntané, Prof. Lucia Morbidelli, and Prof. Benjamin Bonavida. The state of the art in new applications of NO and derivatives was reported, as well as the engineering of various NO complexes that showed specific targeting.

Preface

Special issue "Therapeutic applications of nitric oxide and derivatives"

Nitric oxide (NO) is a small and gaseous signaling molecule that plays a vital role in numerous physiological processes, the disturbances of which are involved in different pathologies. The regulation of NO generation has important clinical applications. The different approaches for the therapeutic applications of NO are described in this volume. The chapter by Ledesma et al. [1] describes the impact of NO derivatives such as diazeniumdiolates (NONOates), S-nitrosothiols, NO hybrid drugs, NO-NSAIDs, S-nitroso-hybrid drugs, and zoolites, the effectiveness of which is actually tested in nearly 100 clinical trials. All dimensions of healthcare can be affected or potentially improved by the discovery of NO-based strategies, and highly relevant to this is the development of suitable carriers allowing tight dosage and target-specific NO delivery. The chapter by Paul et al. [2] reports that the polymeric NO donors are more advantageous than small molecular NO donors, as they provide additional control, including multifunctionality and stimuli-based NO release.

The tumor microenvironment results from the pivotal cross-talks among tumor cells, stromal cells, and the altered extracellular matrix, which functionally impacts the induction or progression of cancer cells. During the last three decades an increasing body of evidence has supported the involvement of chronic inflammation in all stages of tumorigenesis, tumor growth, and spread. In this regard, Giordani et al. [3] highlight the relevance of cyclooxygenase-2 (COX-2) and PGE2-derived products regarding tumor growth and tumor immune evasion. NO-donor COX-2 inhibitors can be effective therapeutic agents for cancer treatment, either in combination with immune checkpoint (PD-1/PD-L1) inhibitors or with standard chemotherapy. The pathophysiological and clinical significance of vasculogenic mimicry, an alternative neovascularization process involving the formation of vessel-like networks directly by the tumor cells, is especially important in triple negative breast cancer. Mangoni et al. [4] describe the promising agents being developed to inhibit dimethylarginine dimethylaminohydrolase (DDAH1), which is responsible for the removal of endogenous NO synthase (NOS) inhibitors, thus allowing vasculogenic mimicry in triple negative breast cancer.

Taskiran et al. [5] reported that cancer stem cells (CSCs) present in the tumor microenvironment are thought to be the main reason for the ineffectiveness of conventional cancer therapies including surgery, radiotherapy, and chemotherapy. The regulation of CSC-derived NO can be a suitable approach for regulating chronic inflammation in the tumor microenvironment, pro-tumorigenic activities of cancer-associated fibroblast (CAFs), drug resistance, invasion, and metastasis. Leyva et al. [6] reported on the unbalanced pro-oncogenic and pro-immunosuppressive activities of inflammatory cells that impact tumor progression. Moreover, the polarization of gamma delta T ($\gamma\delta$-T) cells from anti- to immunosuppressive Th17 phenotype largely related to

NOS2 overexpression might be successfully regulated by NOS2 or NO inhibitors, promoting antitumor activities and the inhibition of tumor growth.

Lin et al. [7] discussed the development of immune checkpoint regulators that have been a vital breakthrough in cancer therapy. The use of the FDA-approved monoclonal antibodies directed against PD-L1 or PD-1 to block the inactivation of CD8 T cells results in significant killing of tumor cells and tumor inhibition. Interestingly, the expression of inducible NOS2 is related to PD-L1 overexpression in tumor cells. They also suggest that NO-based therapeutic interventions may restore the activity of the antitumor CD8 T cells. Fruits and vegetables contain bioactive compounds, such as vitamins, polyphenols, carotenoids, terpenoids, and alkaloids. Their content is, in most cases, improved during ripening or through the treatment of fruits with exogenous NO gas. Consequently, numerous fruits and vegetables can be considered, not only as nutritional vehicles, but also as nutraceutical foods, as discussed by Palma et al. [8].

NO is a key vascular mediator that allows adequate functional homeostasis of all organs and tissues. In particular, NO dysfunction is associated with alteration of renal hemodynamics. The review by Tavares Do Vale et al. [9] contributes to the understanding of the therapeutic potential of NO-regulatory drugs in the regulation of kidney function and derived diseases. Bahadoran et al. [10] review cardiovascular dysfunctions that are widely associated with chronic diseases that impact the survival of patients. The lack of responsiveness to NO of myocardium, vasculature, platelets, skeletal muscle, and vascular smooth muscle is a major risk for the development of cardiovascular events. They propose that nitroxyl (HNO) can circumvent the NO resistance associated with type 2 diabetes mellitus. The infusion of NO is also useful to treat neonates with persistent pulmonary hypertension and as a rescue strategy for the treatment of severe hypoxemia as a consequence of chronic pulmonary hypertension.

The study by Stefano et al. [11] defines the clinical conditions of treatments and the monitoring of blood oxygenation and methemoglobin concentration during NO infusion in order to ensure an adequate tissue oxygenation. Bijan et al. [12] review cost-effective methods to produce infused NO. The methods primarily used to measure the amount of infused NO delivered to the patient are very relevant in the clinical setting. Their proposal is to make it more cost-effective, making the procedure available worldwide. The impact of NO donors and/or inhibitors regulating oxidative stress and inflammatory response during acute brain damage during ischemic stroke is also addressed in the study by Arora et al. [13].

NO modulates visual transduction and maintains a normal visual function in the retina, also acting positively as a vasodilator agent implicated in ocular blood flow control under normal situations. Altered NO generation is related to different pathologies. Moreover, low NO generation is related primarily to glaucoma, while an excess of NO is related to retinitis pigmentosa, as reviewed by Cantó et al. [14]. In this setting, although drugs interfering with aqueous humor secretion (e.g., adrenergic agonists/antagonists, carbonic anhydrase inhibitors) and with its outflow from the eye (e.g., prostaglandin analogs, Rho kinase inhibitors and NO donors) are in clinical use, Supuran [15] reviews the recently approved prostaglandin-NO donor hybrids (such as latanoprostene bunod) and the Rho kinase inhibitors that have allowed the advancement of new therapeutic opportunities for the pharmacological management of this disease.

In conclusion, the volume "Therapeutic Applications of Nitric Oxide and Derivatives" provides a comprehensive description of new advancements at the frontier of knowledge that will allow a greater understanding of the impact of NO and its effectiveness for the management of patients suffering from cancer, stroke, cardiovascular diseases, and visual alterations.

Jordi Muntané

References

[1] Ledesma B., Firdaus F., Mosquera S., Campbell K., Farah Rahman M.P.H., Reddy R., Arora H. Nitric oxide and derivatives: molecular insights and translational opportunities.

[2] Paul S., Kumar M., Mukherjee A., De P. Biomedical applications of polymeric nitric oxide (NO) donors.

[3] Giordani A., Poce G., Consalvi S., Maramai S., Saletti M., Rossi A., Patrignani P., Biava M., Anzini M. Therapeutic potential for coxib-nitric oxide releasing hybrids in cancer treatment.

[4] Mangoni A.A., Hulin J.-A., Weerakoon L., Tommasi S. Targeting dimethylarginine dimethylaminohydrolase-1 to suppress vasculogenic mimicry in breast cancer: current evidence and future directions.

[5] Taskiran A., Demir A., Acikgoz E., Oktem G. Cancer stem cells and nitric oxide.

[6] Leyva B.K., Bonavida B. Inducible nitric oxide synthase 2 (NOS2) and anti-tumor γδ-T cells.

[7] Lin K., Bonavida B. The regulation of the programmed death ligand 1 (PD-L1) by nitric oxide in breast cancer: immuno-therapeutic implication.

[8] Palma J.M., del Palacio J.P., Rodríguez-Ruiz M., González-Gordo S., Díaz C., Ramos C., Cautain B., Vicente F., Corpas F.J. Pepper fruit as a nutraceutical food with anti-proliferative activity against tumor cells potentiated by nitric oxide (NO).

[9] Do Vale G.T., Pereira B.P., Potje S.R. Ceron C.S. Nitric oxide (NO) donors in kidney damage and diseases.

[10] Bahadoran Z., Mirmiran P., Kashfi K., Ghasemi A. Nitric oxide resistance in type 2 diabetes: potential implications of HNO donors.

[11] Stefano G., Berra L., Emanuele R. Inhaled nitric oxide (iNO) administration in intubated and non-intubated patients: delivery systems, interfaces, dose administration, and monitoring techniques.

[12] Bijan S.F., Berra L., Emanuele R. Inhaled nitric oxide (iNO): clinical applications in critical care medicine, delivery devices and measuring techniques.

[13] Arora B., Khan H., Grewal A.K., Singh T.G. Mechanistic insights on role of nitric oxide in ischemia-reperfusion injury.

[14] Cantó A., Martínez-González J., López-Pedraja R., Sánchez-Fideli A., Miranda M. Effect of nitric oxide inhibitors in retinitis pigmentosa.

[15] Supuran C.T. Advances in the discovery of novel agents for the treatment of glaucoma: the role of nitric oxide donors.

Highlights of the II international conference "therapeutic applications of nitric oxide in cancer and inflammatory-related diseases"

It was with great pleasure and honor that we welcomed the II International Conference "Therapeutic Applications of Nitric Oxide in Cancer and Inflammatory-Related Diseases" that was held at the Institute of Biomedicine of Seville on March 3–5, 2022. The meeting was organized within the activities of the International Society for NO and Cancer (ISNOC, https://isnoc.org). Over 45 international scientists, either on-site or on-line, participated in this meeting and fostered with their expertise the current progress in the field of therapeutic applications of nitric oxide (NO).

The aim of the conference was to promote quality research and discuss the latest developments and innovations in NO-based drugs or NO-generating systems in the treatment of cancer and other inflammatory-related disorders. The workshop also expands on its translational implications in the diagnosis, prognosis and therapy of diseases. Briefly, the conference was organized to meet the following goals that, in our opinion, were achieved successfully:

(1) To discuss novel biochemical and molecular advances of NO implications in the pathophysiology of cancer and other diseases and their response to various treatments.

(2) To explore different options that could be employed to materialize the potential of targeting NO signaling for novel therapies.

(3) To facilitate scientific and collaborative interactions among the participants and encourage the establishment of lasting professional relationships among researchers investigating the role of NO in physiopathology.

Although each participant gave a special input to the success of the congress, undoubtedly, the contributions of the world-renowned experts on NO-based therapeutics have fulfilled the above goals.

Dr. Dennis J. Stuehr (Department of Inflammation and Immunity, Lerner Research Institute, The Cleveland Clinic, Cleveland, United States), in his keynote lecture entitled "Hemeproteins, NO, and their relationships in cancer," presented an update on what is known about the intracellular heme trafficking during hemeprotein maturation, including his laboratory's investigations in identifying the proteins involved in heme delivery, their mechanisms of action, and how the processes may be regulated. Different aspects of cancer are influenced by several hemeproteins, including the NO synthases, soluble guanylyl cyclase, NADPH oxidases, tryptophan and indoleamine dioxygenases, myoglobin, and hemoglobin. A new role for NO in regulating the intracellular heme allocations was presented.

Dr. David A. Wink (National Cancer Institute, Frederick, United States), in the keynote lecture "NO-based therapeutic intervention in cancer," discussed the role of NO in tumor biology at the chemical, biochemical, and cellular levels to explore potential new strategies, based on the assumption that NO and other small redox-reactive molecules promote cancer progression. His research goals are focused on the identification of redox-related mechanisms and biomarkers expressed during chronic inflammation as they relate to cancer progression and poor clinical outcome.

Other highlights of the conference included the following advances that are briefly discussed below:

- Myoglobin-dependent decreased NO bioavailability and regulation of metabolism result in the attenuation of pro-tumorigenic signaling. Ongoing studies are delineating the exact mechanisms by which myoglobin regulates metabolic signaling and may offer a potential therapeutic avenue to attenuate tumor progression (presented by Dr. Sruti Shiva, University of Pittsburgh, Pittsburgh, United States).
- Up-to-date findings regarding NO signaling in cardiovascular health and disease were discussed. Some of the latest paradigms underlying the successes (or failures) of clinical applications of NO-based therapeutics in cardiovascular diseases were reported, highlighting the interest in measurements of nitrosylated hemoglobin as a biomarker for diagnostics and treatment tailoring (presented by Dr. Jean-Luc Balligand, Institut de Recherche Experimentale et

Clinique (IREC) and Cliniques Universitaires Saint-Luc, Université Catholique de Louvain, Brussels, Belgium).

- Different polymeric nanoparticles that have been specifically designed to deliver anticancer drugs and to image specific tissues were discussed for their advanced applications. The delivery of NO was presented using these nanoparticles for the treatment of liver fibrosis and neuroblastoma, demonstrating a synergistic effect when NO is combined with chemotherapeutic drugs for the treatment of multidrug resistance in cancer. Further, the synthesis of new hybrid organic/inorganic nanomaterials, based on iron oxide, gold, and gadolinium, were reported for use as MRI contrast agents (presented by Dr. Cyrille Boyer, Australian Centre for NanoMedicine or CAN, and Centre for Advanced Macromolecular Design or CAMD, School of Chemical Engineering, University of New South Wales, Sydney, Australia).
- Photoresponsive polypeptide nanomedicines were discussed regarding their rational design for efficient NO gas delivery and cancer therapy (presented by Dr. Chang-Ming Dong, School of Chemistry and Chemical Engineering, Shanghai Jiao Tong University, Shanghai, China).
- Dimethylarginine dimethylaminohydrolase, a metabolic enzyme responsible for the processing of endogenous inhibitors of the NOS pathway, is essential for triple negative breast cancer cells to undertake vasculogenic mimicry, a hallmark of malignancy and therapy escape. The current evidence and future directions related to targeting dimethylarginine dimethylaminohydrolase isoform 1 to

suppress vasculogenic mimicry in cancer were discussed (presented by Dr. Arduino A. Mangoni, Department of Clinical Pharmacology, Flinders Medical Centre and Flinders University, Bedford Park, Australia).

- The advances in the discovery of novel agents for the treatment of glaucoma, a neuropathic disease characterized by increased intraocular pressure, were presented. NO donors play a relevant role in developing novel antiglaucoma agents, due to the involvement of this gas-transmitter in relevant ocular physiological processes, affording interesting new opportunities for the pharmacological management of this disease (presented by Dr. Claudiu T. Supuran, Department of Neuroscience, Psychology, Drug Area and Child Health University of Florence, Florence, Italy).

- The role of the gasotransmitter hydrogen sulfide was demonstrated by analyzing the value of sulfur nutraceuticals against cardiovascular inflamm-aging, a condition characterized by features common to many cardiovascular diseases accompanied by endothelial dysfunction. Experimental data were presented on erucin, the isothiocianate deriving from *Eruca sativa Mill.*, which showed protective cardiovascular effects against vascular inflammation, endothelial dysfunction, and hypertension (presented by Dr. Alma Martelli, Department of Pharmacy, University of Pisa, Italy).

- The roles of NO in retinal pathologies were reported in relation to the high reactive tissue environment. Three different retinal degenerative disorders were considered: diabetic retinopathy (DR), age-related macular degeneration (AMD), and retinitis pigmentosa (RP). Although the data are contrasting, the experimental use of NOS inhibitors seems protective (presented by Dr. María M. Miranda, Department of Biomedical Sciences, University CEU Cardenal Herrera, Alfara del Patriarca, Valencia, Spain).

- The modulation of neurovascular coupling (NVC) in the brain by NO and its relationship with cognitive enhancement were addressed. By developing innovative tools for in vivo assessment of NVC, it was shown that neuronal NO along the NMDA receptor-nNOS-NO pathway acts as a direct mediator of the communication between neurons and local microvessels. The functionality of NVC is key for cognitive performance and becomes impaired during aging and age-associated neurodegeneration, notably Alzheimer's disease. In vivo experimental data support that the redox interaction of nitrite/ascorbate/NO functionally coupled to neuronal activation in NVC, and rescue from impaired NVC, results in enhancement of cognitive performance (presented by Dr. João Laranjinha, Center for Neuroscience and Cell Biology, University of Coimbra, Coimbra, Portugal).

- The role of iNOS and NO in regulating inflammation in neurodegenerative disease was reported. Nitration strongly increased Abeta's propensity to aggregate and also made it harder to degrade and digest by microglia. In in vivo seeding models of cerebral amyloidosis, NO-mediated nitration of the Abeta increased overall deposition. Data were provided suggesting that NO may also exert harmful effects during the course of neurodegenerative disease. Its use as a therapeutic or its inhibition should be titrated in time, dose, and site of action (presented by Dr. Michael T. Heneka, Luxembourg Centre for Systems

Biomedicine-LCSB, University of Luxembourg, Luxembourg).

- NO-mediated neuroinflammatory pathways have been considered as treatment targets in neurodegeneration. In addition to nitration reactions, nonenzymatic and irreversible glycation signaling has been implicated as an underlying pathway that promotes protein (i.e., Abeta) misfolding via the generation of advanced glycation end-products (AGE). Following activation of specific receptors recognizing AGEs (RAGE), further oxidative stress and production of cytokines induce an upregulation of inflammatory mediators. The direct interactions between NO-mediated neuroinflammation and RAGE signaling pathways were documented (presented by Dr. Joern R. Steinert, Division of Physiology, Pharmacology and Neuroscience, Faculty of Medicine and Health Sciences, University of Nottingham, United Kingdom).
- NOS and COX inhibition augment immune polarization and improve survival in radiotherapy. The possibility that NSAIDs and NOS inhibitors could be new approaches to improve radiation and immunotherapy efficacy was discussed (presented by Dr. Lisa A. Ridnour, National Cancer Institute, Frederick, United States).
- The state of the art and future directions of nanomedicine allied to NO donors in cancer therapy was discussed. NO-releasing engineered nanoparticles can have direct toxic effects on tumor cells, or can promote cancer cell sensitization for traditional cancer treatments, with reversion of multidrug resistance. The recent progress in the cytotoxicity (tumoral and nontumoral cell lines) of NO-releasing nanomaterials and the

in vivo biocompatibility of NO-releasing nanoparticles were highlighted and discussed (presented by Dr. Amedea B. Seabra, Nanomedicine Research Unit, Federal University of ABC, Santo André, Brazil).
- The role of NO in macrophage immunometabolism was dissected. The elevated lactate levels in tumors can transcriptionally reprogram tumor-associated macrophages into immunosuppressive cells, promoting tumor growth and progression. The expression, signaling, and function of receptors expressed by innate immune cells in the context of cancer was discussed in relation to immunometabolism. Data showing the dissection of the biochemical mechanisms underlying activation-induced metabolic changes in innate immune cells were demonstrated (presented by Dr. Daniel W. McVicar, National Cancer Institute, Frederick, United States).
- The fascinating hypothesis of a fourth gasotransmitter, selenium and hydrogen selenide, besides being an essential micronutrient, was demonstrated, opening up research to new frontiers (presented by Dr. Alex Dyson, Institute of Pharmaceutical Science, and Centre for Pharmaceutical Medicine Research King's College London, London, United Kingdom).
- The active principles present in pepper fruits during their maturation were characterized, along with the role of NO in fruit ripening. Based on the potential therapeutic effects of pepper fruit bioactive principles, the question arises whether NO could potentiate the antitumoral activity of pepper fruit extracts (presented by Dr. José M. Palma, Department of Biochemistry, Molecular and Cell Biology of Plants, Estación

Experimental del Zaidín, CSIC, Granada, Spain).

- The design of conventional anticancer drugs complexed with a NO-releasing moiety was verified. NO-releasing gemcitabine was experimentally demonstrated to work as a new weapon against pancreatic cancer (presented by Dr. Chiara Riganti, Department of Oncology, University of Torino, Torino, Italy).

The last session of the meeting included a roundtable in which speakers presented their opinions on the aspects highlighted in the meeting regarding the impact of NO and the NO-based drugs for the management of patients in cancer and related-inflammatory diseases.

As a closing remark, we, as organizers, sincerely hope that this symposium served as an international platform for meeting researchers from all around the world, widened professional interactions, and created new opportunities for research collaborations. We have set high expectations on this series of NO meetings to be established on a regular basis and that it will attract global participants intent on sharing, exchanging, and exploring new avenues of the NO implications in human diseases and the latest developments in novel therapies.

Lucia Morbidelli (co-organizer)

The symposium program is enclosed in the following pages.

MIMG, David Geffen School of
Medicine, UCLA, CA

SECOND INTERNATIONAL CONFERENCE
Therapeutic Applications of Nitric Oxide in Cancer and Inflammatory-related Diseases
(on-site and virtual)

Institute of Biomedicine of Seville
March 3-5, 2022, Seville, Spain

Dear Colleagues,

We are delighted you attend the Second International Conference "Therapeutic Applications of Nitric Oxide in Cancer and Inflammatory-related Diseases" (on-site and virtual) in Seville (Spain) from the March 3 to 5, 2022. The conference is held in the Institute of Biomedicine of Sevilla (IBiS) that includes researchers from different biomedical disciplines into an active and innovative research atmosphere.

The First International Conference on "Therapeutic Application of Nitric Oxide in Cancer and Inflammatory Disorders" was organized by Dr. Lucia Morbidelli and Dr. Benjamin Bonavida in Siena (Italy) on October 4-5, 2018. Since then, the field has significantly progressed and we, Dr. Lucia Morbidelli, Dr. Benjamin Bonavida and myself are co-organizing this Second International Conference on "Therapeutic Applications of Nitric Oxide in Cancer and Inflammatory-related Diseases". The main focus of the conference is an update with presentations and discussions regarding the impact of nitric oxide-based drugs or nitric oxide-generating systems, under basic laboratory investigations or in clinical trials, with the overall objective to treat particularly cancer and inflammatory human diseases.

The present workshop is divided into six sessions specifically focused on the "Development of nitric oxide donors in targeting disease management", "Nitric oxide disturbances in metabolic and cardiovascular disorders", "Nitric oxide in hypertensive-related diseases", "Nitric oxide and neurodegeneration" and "Acute and chronic inflammatory-related diseases". Each session includes conferences presented by well-known researchers in the field, as well as young investigators presenting their data. In addition, two keynote lectures entitled "Hemeproteins, nitric oxide, and their relationships in cancer" by Dr. Dennis J Stuehr and "Nitric oxide-based therapeutic intervention in cancer" by Dr. David A Wink are included in the program. All registered researchers will have the opportunity to submit original research manuscripts, methods or graphical issues or full review articles to be published in a special book edited by Elsevier.

We hope that the workshop will allow scientific exchanges among researchers from different fields with an opportunity for valuable scientific discussions, initiating new research links and friendships as well as enjoying the culture of Sevilla, Andalucía and Spain.

I gratefully acknowledge the financial support received from the International Society of Nitric Oxide and Cancer (ISNOC), Institute of Biomedicine of Seville (IBiS), Elsevier/AP Publishing Company, University of Seville and the Società Italiana di Farmacologia (SIF). I would also to thank the members of my research group Elena Navarro, Patricia de la Cruz, Carlotta Pranzo and Thaissa Marins who have greatly help me during the meeting, as well as the secretariat of IBiS and Viajes Atlanta for their effectiveness.

Sincerely yours,

Jordi Muntané, Ph.D.   Benjamin Bonavida, Ph.D.   Lucia   Morbidelli,   Ph.D.
Professor of Physiology   *Research Professor, UCLA*   *Professor of Pharmacology*

Organizing Committee:

Jordi Muntané, PhD
Associate Professor
Department of Medical Physiology and Biophysics
University of Seville

Lucia Morbidelli, Ph.D
Professor of Pharmacology
Department of Life Sciences
University of Siena

Benjamin Bonavida, Ph.D
Professor
Department of Microbiology, Immunology,
and Molecular Genetics
University of California

Meeting link: https://isnoc.org/ii-therapeutic-application-of-no-in-cancer-and-inflammatory-diseases/

ISNOC link: https://isnoc.org/

Secretariat:
Viajes Atlanta (congresssvq@atlanta.es)

Main sponsors:
International Society of Nitric Oxide and Cancer (ISNOC)
Institute of Biomedicine of Seville (IBiS)
Elsevier/AP Publishing Company
University of Seville
Società Italiana di Farmacologia (SIF)

PROGRAM

Day 1: March 3, 2022

16:00-16:15
Welcome and opening the meeting from the authorities
Rafael Fernández Chacón (Scientific Director of the Institute of Biomedicine of Seville) (ON-SITE)
Benjamin Bonavida (International Society of Nitric Oxide and Cancer, University of California) (ZOOM)
Jordi Muntané (Local Organizing Committee, Institute of Biomedicine of Seville) (ON-SITE)

OPENING SESSION I
KEYNOTE LECTURE 1
Moderator: Dr. Ben Bonavida (ZOOM)
(University of California, USA)

16:15-17:00 (ON-SITE)
Dennis J Stuehr (Department of Inflammation and Immunity, Lerner Research Institute, The Cleveland Clinic, Cleveland, USA)
Hemeproteins, NO, and their Relationships in Cancer

17:00-17:30 *Coffee break*

SESSION 2
DEVELOPMENT OF NITRIC OXIDE DONORS IN TARGETING DISEASE MANAGEMENT
Moderator: Dr. Lucia Morbidelli (ON-SITE)
(University of Siena, Italy)

17:30-18:00 (ZOOM)
Sruti Shiva (University of Pittsburgh, Pittsburgh, USA)
Regulation of mitochondria and metabolism by NO and myoglobin in cancer and inflammation

18:00-18:30 (ZOOM)
Alia Shatanawi (School of Medicine, The University of Jordan, Amman, Jordan)
The role of the arginase-Nitric Oxide pathway in vascular dysfunction and inflammation

18:30-19:00 (ON-SITE)
Jean-Luc Balligand (Institut de Recherche Experimentale et Clinique (IREC) and Cliniques Universitaires Saint-Luc, Université Catholique de Louvain, Brussels, Belgium)
Nitric oxide signaling in cardiovascular health and disease

<u>19:00-19:30</u>
Young investigator session (10+5 min)

The metal-nonoate Zn(PipNONO)Cl exhibit antitumor activity through inhibition of epithelial and endothelial mesenchymal transitions (EMT and EndMT) (ZOOM)
<u>Valerio Ciccone</u>[1,2], Carlotta Pranzo[1], Arianna Filippelli[1], Enrico Monzani[3], Lucia Morbidelli[1]
[1]Department of Life Sciences, University of Siena, Siena, Italy; [2]Department of Experimental Medicine, University of Campania "Luigi Vanvitelli", Naples, Italy; and [3]Department of Chemistry, University of Pavia, Pavia, Italy

Interactions between Nitric Oxide and Hemin and their Implications in the Nitration of Proteins (ZOOM)
<u>Amir Alsharabasy</u>[1], Sharon Glynn[1,2], Pau Farràs[1,3], Abhay Pandit[1]
[1]CÚRAM, SFI Research Centre for Medical Devices; [2]Discipline of Pathology, Lambe Institute for Translational Research, School of Medicine, [3]School of Biological and Chemical Sciences, Ryan Institute, National University of Ireland, Galway

<u>19:30-23:00</u> *Dinner*

Day 2: March 4, 2022

SESSION 3
NITRIC OXIDE DISTURBANCES IN METABOLIC AND CARDIOVASCULAR DISORDERS
Moderator: Dr. Sharon Glynn (ON-SITE)
(National University of Ireland, Ireland)

<u>8:00-8:30 (ZOOM)</u>
Cyrille Boyer (Australian Centre for NanoMedicine or CAN, and Centre for Advanced Macromolecular Design or CAMD, School of Chemical Engineering, University of New South Wales, Sydney, Australia)
Engineering Polymeric NanoParticles for Advanced Applications

<u>8:30-9:00 (ZOOM)</u>
Chang-Ming Dong (School of Chemistry and Chemical Engineering, Shanghai Jiao Tong University, Shanghai, China)
Photoresponsive polypeptide nanomedicines: from rational design to efficient NO gas delivery and cancer therapy

<u>9:00-9:30 (ZOOM)</u>

Arduino A. Mangoni (Department of Clinical Pharmacology, Flinders Medical Centre and Flinders University, Bedford Park, Australia)
Targeting dimethylarginine dimethylaminohydrolase to suppress vasculogenic mimicry in cancer: current evidence and future directions

9:30-10:00
Young investigator session (10+5 min)

Nitric oxide as an activator of HER2 in breast cancer (ZOOM)
Ciara O'Neill[1], Eoin Dervan[1], Jake McAuliffe[1], Suguna Sundararaman[1], Sharon Glynn[1]
[1]Discipline of Pathology, Lambe Institute for Translational Research, National University of Ireland Galway

Oxidative stress-induced endothelial dysfunction and decreased vascular nitric oxide in COVID-19 patients (ZOOM)
Virginie Montiel[1,2], Irina Lobysheva[2], Ludovic Gérard[1,3], Marjorie Vermeersch[4], David Perez-Morga[4], Thomas Castelein[1], Jean-Baptiste Mesland[1], Philippe Hantson[1], Christine Collienne[1], Damien Gruson[5], Marie-Astrid van Dievoet[5], Alexandre Persu[6,7], Christophe Beauloye[6,7], Mélanie Dechamps[1,7], Leïla Belkhir[8], Annie Robert[9], Marc Derive[10], Pierre-François Laterre[1], A.H.J Danser[11], Xavier Wittebole[1], Jean-Luc Balligand[2]
[1]Intensive Care Unit, Cliniques Universitaires Saint-Luc, Brussels, Belgium; [2]Institute of Experimental and Clinical Research, Pole of Pharmacology and Therapeutics, Université catholique de Louvain, Brussels, Belgium; [3]Institute of Experimental and Clinical Research, Pole of Pneumology, ENT and Dermatology, Université catholique de Louvain, Brussels, Belgium; [4]Center for Microscopy and Molecular Imaging, Université Libre de Bruxelles, Gosselies, Belgium; [5]Department of Laboratory Medicine, Cliniques Universitaires Saint-Luc, Brussels, Belgium; [6]Institute of Experimental and Clinical Research, Pole of Cardiovascular Research, Université catholique de Louvain, Brussels, Belgium; [7]Department of Cardiology, Cliniques Universitaires Saint-Luc and Université catholique de Louvain, Brussels, Belgium; [8]Department of Internal Medicine, Cliniques Universitaires Saint-Luc and Université catholique de Louvain, Brussels, Belgium; [9]Institute of Experimental and Clinical Research, Pole of Epidemiology and Biostatistics (EPID), Université catholique de Louvain, Brussels, Belgium; [10]Inotrem SA, Vandoeuvre-les-Nancy France, France; [11]Department of Internal Medicine, Erasmus MC, Rotterdam, the Netherlands

10:00-10:30 *Coffee break*

SESSION 4
NITRIC OXIDE IN HYPERTENSIVE-RELATED DISEASES
Moderator: Dr. Stéphanie Plenchette (ON-SITE)
(EPHE PSL-University of Burgundy, France)

10:30-11:00 (ZOOM)
Claudiu T. Supuran (Department of Neuroscience, Psychology, Drug Area and Child Health University of Florence, Florence, Italy)
Advances in the discovery of novel agents for the treatment of glaucoma

11:00-11:30 (ZOOM)
Alma Martelli (Department of Pharmacy, University of Pisa, Pisa, Italy)
The value of sulfur nutraceuticals for the cardiovascular inflamm-ageing: possible role of hydrogen sulfide

11:30-12:00 (ON-SITE)
María M. Miranda (Department of Biomedical Sciences, University CEU Cardenal Herrera, Alfara del Patriarca, Valencia, Spain)
Nitric oxide roles in retinal pathologies

12:30-13:00
Young investigator session (10+5 min)

Excessive *S*-nitrosylation induced by GSNOR deficiency increases malignancy in rhabdomyosarcoma (ZOOM)
Costanza Montagna[1], Chiara Pecorari[2], Paola Giglio[1], Valeria Fiorentini[1], Salvatore Rizza[2], Giuseppe Filomeni[1,2,3]
[1]Department of Biology, University of Rome Tor Vergata, Rome, Italy; [2]Redox Biology Group, Danish Cancer Society Research Center, Copenhagen, Denmark. [3]Center for Healthy Aging, University of Copenhagen, Denmark

Unraveling the role of AKR1A1 in renal and hepatocellular carcinoma progression (ON-SITE)
Chiara Pecorari[1], Giuseppe Filomeni[1,2]
[1]Redox Biology Group, Danish Cancer Society Research Center, Copenhagen, Denmark; [2]Department of Biology, University of Rome Tor Vergata, Rome, Italy

13:00-15:00 *Lunch*

SESSION 5
NITRIC OXIDE AND NEURODEGENERATION
Moderator: Dr. Giuseppe Filomeni (ON-SITE)
(Danish Cancer Society Research Center, Denmark)

15:00-15:30 (ZOOM)
João Laranjinha (Center for Neuroscience and Cell Biology, University of Coimbra, Coimbra, Portugal)

Modulation of neurovascular coupling in the brain by nitric oxide and cognitive enhancement

15:30-16:00 (ON-SITE)
Michael T Heneka (Luxembourg Centre for Systems Biomedicine-LCSB, University of Luxembourg, Luxembourg)
Inflammation in neurodegenerative disease: Role of iNOS and nitric oxide

16:00-16:30 (ON-SITE)
Joern R Steinert (Division of Physiology, Pharmacology and Neuroscience. Faculty of Medicine and Health Sciences, University of Nottingham, UK)
NO-mediated neuroinflammatory pathways as treatment targets in neurodegeneration

16:30-17:00 *Coffee break*

SESSION 6
ACUTE AND CHRONIC INFLAMMATORY-RELATED DISEASES
Moderator: Dr. Khosrow Kashfi (ON-SITE)
(The City College of New York, USA)

17:00-17:30 (ZOOM)
Lisa A Ridnour (National Cancer Institute, Frederick, USA)
NOS and COX Inhibition Augments Immune Polarization and Improves Survival in Radiotherapy: Are NSAIDs and NOS inhibitors a New Approach to Immunotherapy?

17:30-18:00 (ZOOM)
Amedea B Seabra (Nanomedicine Research Unit, Federal University of ABC, Santo André, Brazil)
Nanomedicine allied to nitric oxide donors in cancer: Where are we and where can we go?

18:00-18:30 (ZOOM)
Daniel W McVicar (National Cancer Institute, Frederick, USA)
Nitric Oxide in Macrophage Immunometabolism: Evidence for HNO-mediated inhibition of PHD during activation

SESSION 7
KEYNOTE LECTURE 2
Moderator: Dr. Jordi Muntané (ON-SITE)
(Institute of Biomedicine of Seville, Spain)

<u>18:30-19:15 (ZOOM)</u>
David A Wink (National Cancer Institute, Frederick, USA)
NO-based therapeutic intervention in cancer

<u>19:15-23:00</u> *Dinner*

Day 3: March 5, 2022

SESSION 8
PROTECTIVE EFFECTS OF NUTRACEUTICALS: FOCUS ON NITRIC OXIDE AND OTHER GASOTRANSMITTERS
Moderator: Dr. Valentina Rapozzi (ON-SITE)
(University of Udine, Italy)

<u>8:00-8:30 (ON-SITE)</u>
Alex Dyson (Institute of Pharmaceutical Science, and Centre for Pharmaceutical Medicine Research King's College London, London, UK)
Selenium and hydrogen selenide: essential micronutrient and the fourth gasotransmitter?

<u>8:30-9:00 (ON-SITE)</u>
José M Palma (Department of Biochemistry, Molecular and Cell Biology of Plants, Estación Experimental del Zaidín, CSIC, Granada, Spain)
Does nitric oxide potentiate the anti-tumoral activity of pepper fruit extracts?

<u>9:00-9:30 (ZOOM)</u>
Chiara Riganti (Department of Oncology, University of Torino, Torino, Italy)
Nitric oxide-releasing gemcitabine: a new weapon against pancreatic cancer?

<u>9:30-10:00</u> *Coffee break*

<u>10:00-11:00</u>
Young investigator session (10+5 min)

Unraveling the role and regulation of S-nitrosoglutathione reductase in breast cancer progression (ON-SITE)
Valeria Fiorentini[1], Salvatore Rizza[1,2], Fiorella Faienza[1], Paola Giglio[1], Gennaro Pepe[1], Giuseppe Filomeni[1,2]
[1]Department of Biology, University of Rome Tor Vergata, Rome, Italy; [2]Redox Biology Group, Danish Cancer Research Center, Copenhagen, Denmark

TRAP1 regulation by NO and ROS highlight its potential role as a mitochondrial redox Sensor (ZOOM)

Fiorella Faienza[1], Salvatore Rizza[2], Chiara Pecorari[2], Valeria Fiorentini[1], Paola Giglio[1], Claudio Laquatra[3], Carlos Sanchez-Martin[3], Giovanni Chiappetta[4], Francesca Pacello[1], Andrea Battistoni[1], Elena Papaleo[5], Andrea Rasola[3], Giuseppe Filomeni[1,2,6]
[1]Department of Biology, University of Rome Tor Vergata, Rome, Italy. [2]Redox Biology Group, Danish Cancer Society Research Center, Copenhagen, Denmark. [3]Department of Biomedical Sciences, University of Padova, Padova, Italy. [4]Laboratory of Proteomics and Biological Mass Spectrometry, USR, CNRS - ESPCI Paris, Paris, France. [5]Computational Biology Laboratory, Danish Cancer Society Research Center, Copenhagen, Denmark. [6]Center for Healthy Aging, University of Copenhagen, Denmark.

The induction of peroxynitrite generation by Sorafenib plays a relevant role during mitochondrial dysfunction in liver cancer cells (ON-SITE)

Elena Navarro-Villarán[1,2,3], Patricia de la Cruz-Ojeda[1,2,3], Jordi Muntané[1,2,3]
[1]Institute of Biomedicine of Seville (IBiS), Hospital University "Virgen del Rocío"/CSIC/University of Seville, Spain. [2]Biomedical Research Center for Hepatic and Digestive Diseases (CIBERehd), Madrid, Spain. [3]Department of Medical Physiology and Biophysics, University of Seville, Seville, Spain.

Investigating the role of NO in cancer stem cell pathophysiology (ZOOM)

Giasemi Eptaminitaki[1], Benjamin Bonavida[2], Stavroula Baritaki[1]
[1]Laboratory of Experimental Oncology, Division of Surgery, Medical School, University of Crete, Heraklion 71003, Crete, Greece; [2]Department of Microbiology, Immunology and Molecular Genetics, University of California, Los Angeles, USA.

ROUND TABLE SESSION 9

11:00-12:00
Round Table (ON-SITE)
NO-based therapeutic strategies in diseases
Dennis J Stuehr
Jean-Luc Balligand
María M. Miranda
Michael T Heneka
Alex Dyson
José M Palma

CLOSING SESSION 10

<u>12:00-13:00</u>
Concluding remarks, awards for the best three communications
Jordi Muntané (Local Organizing Committee, Institute of Biomedicine of Seville)
Lucia Morbidelli (Local Organizing Committee, University of Siena)
Khosrow Kashfi (International Society of Nitric Oxide and Cancer, New York, USA)

The best three communications will be for the presenting authors (predoctoral or postdoctoral researchers under 40 years-old). All three winners will receive the amount of 100 Euros, free registration to the meeting, and one-year ISNOC membership 2022.

<u>13:00-15:00</u>: *Lunch and farewell of attendees*

PART I

Development of NO donors and derivatives, and new delivery formations

Nitric oxide and derivatives: Molecular insights and translational opportunities

Braian Ledesma[a], Fakiha Firdaus[a], Maria Silena Mosquera[b], Katherine Campbell[a], Farah Rahman[a], Maria Camila Suarez Arbelaez[a], and Himanshu Arora[a,c,d]

[a]Desai Sethi Urology Institute, Miller School of Medicine, University of Miami, Miami, FL, United States [b]Center for Fetal Research, Children's Hospital of Philadelphia, Philadelphia, PA, United States [c]John P Hussman Institute for Human Genomics, Miller School of Medicine, University of Miami, Miami, FL, United States [d]The Interdisciplinary Stem Cell Institute, Miller School of Medicine, University of Miami, Miami, FL, United States

Abstract

Nitric oxide (NO), a small, gaseous signaling molecule, plays a vital role in numerous processes such as hemodynamic maintenance, immune responses, and neurotransmission. Synthesized by nitric oxide synthase (NOS) in human tissue, NO can act as an electron donor or acceptor and thus participate in physiologic redox reactions. At low concentrations, NO plays a role in the regulation of immune responses with downstream effects including inducing inflammation, propagation of the cellular immune response, and direct cytotoxicity. Overproduction of NO at high concentrations results in DNA damage, inhibition of DNA repair, excess proliferation, and angiogenesis. Thus, at the genetic level, NO can either be cytoprotective or be cytotoxic, allowing scientists to harness the power of NO as an agent of future therapeutic strategy in cancer, cardiovascular disease, epilepsy, type II diabetes and others. The promising pharmaceutical future of NO is demonstrated in the fact that there are nearly 100 clinical trials focusing on NO as the primary target of interest. While NO may be minuscule in nature, it's roles, activities, and implications seem to be a microcosm of discovery waiting for the scientific community to understand.

Abbreviations

ACE	angiotensin-converting enzyme
ADMA	asymmetric dimethylarginine
BCG	Bacillus Calmette-Guerin
ECAM	endothelial cell adhesion molecule
Hb	hemoglobin

HPLC	high-performance liquid chromatography
IL-1i	interleukin 1
L-NAME	L-N^G-nitro arginine methyl ester
LPS	lipopolysaccharides
MDSC	myeloid-derived suppressor cell
N$_2$O$_3$	dinitrogen trioxide
NF-kB	nuclear factor kappa-beta
NO	nitric oxide
NO$_2^-$	nitrite
NO$_3^-$	nitrate
NONOate	diazeniumdiolates
NOS	nitric oxide synthase
NSAIDs	nonsteroidal antiinflammatory drugs
ONOO$^-$	peroxynitrite
oxyHb	oxyhemoglobin
PAD	peripheral artery disease
PCD	primary ciliary dyskinesia
RBC	red blood cell
RSNO	*S*-nitrosothiol adducts
SNOAlb	*S*-nitrosoalbumin
SNO-Cap	*S*-nitrosocaptopril
SOD	superoxide dismutase
TGF-β	transforming growth factor-β
TNF	tumor necrosis factor

Conflict of interest

No potential conflicts of interest were disclosed.

Introduction

Nitric oxide (NO) serves a multifaceted role in signaling and is implicated in a multitude of physiological mechanisms, including but not limited to hemodynamic homeostasis, immune responses, and retrograde neurotransmission [1,2]. This molecule also influences innumerable pathologic processes in the human body, from the mechanism of vasoconstriction and vasodilation to diseases and cancer. The versatility of nitric oxide can, in part, be attributed to its chemical properties: It is small, reactive, uncharged, and a free radical [3].

The history of nitric oxide (NO) traces back to Joseph Priestley in 1772, who first documented the gas in his experiment involving iron and brimstone [4]. Notably, Louis Ignarro, Robert F. Furchgott, and Ferid Murad won a Nobel Prize for their discoveries of NO as a molecular messenger in the cardiovascular system, paving a new path for therapeutics.

Aside from the functions that NO holds in physiology, this molecule can also be utilized as a therapeutic agent. Inhaled NO has been clinically employed in the management of a spectrum of cardiopulmonary diseases, including pulmonary hypertension in children and adults [5]. Furthermore, derivatives of NO, such as nitrogen dioxide and peroxynitrite, have been utilized for anticancer purposes [6]. In this chapter, we discuss the metabolism of NO, its role in physiological regulation, its use in ongoing clinical trials, and future potential avenues for this heterodiatomic molecule.

Bioavailability/biotransformation of NO

Nitric oxide (NO) is a gaseous signaling molecule synthesized in various mammalian organs by nitric oxide synthase (NOS). To date, three distinct isoforms have been identified, namely neuronal NOS (type I), inducible NOS (type II), and endothelial NOS (type III). Various cofactors critically influence NO synthesis like tetrahydrobiopterin, flavin mononucleotide, and flavin adenine dinucleotide, reduced thiols, endogenous NOS inhibitor asymmetric dimethylarginine (ADMA), and substrate availability. Additionally, NOS I and III depend on calmodulin and Ca^{2+}. The clearance of NO depends on its concentration. NO may react electrostatically to its target by electron gain or loss to form the nitrosyl anion NO^- or NO^+, the nitrosonium ion, respectively. The conversion of NO to NO^+ is contributed by numerous factors, such as heme proteins like guanylate cyclase, enzymes such as catalase, xanthine oxidase and superoxide dismutase along with hemoglobin (Hb), or any high-energy free radicals such as the hydroxyl radical. NO is presumably charge neutral, which facilitates its free infusibility in aqueous solution and across cell membranes to travel significant distances via blood vessels.

The major immediate breakdown product of NO in human plasma is nitrite (NO_2^-). RBCs could take up plasma NO_2^-, where it is oxidized in a Hb-dependent manner to nitrate (NO_3^-), which may subsequently redistribute into plasma [7]. Another potential decomposition pathway for NO is its rapid interaction with superoxide anions to produce the potent oxidant peroxynitrite ($ONOO^-$). $ONOO^-$ is thought to oxidize thiols or thioethers, nitrating tyrosine residues, nitrating and oxidizing guanosine, degrading carbohydrates, initiating lipid peroxidation, and cleaving DNA. The $ONOO^-$ in excess decomposes to yield NO_3^-. Alternatively, NO can react with O_2 to yield reactive intermediates. It is well appreciated that the autoxidation of NO in an aqueous environment leads to the formation of reactive nitrogen oxide species such as dinitrogen trioxide (N_2O_3) [8]. This intermediate can nitrosate and oxidize different substrates to yield either nitrosamines or S-nitrosothiol adducts (RSNO). In vivo studies have revealed that redox-active thiols, which are abundantly present in plasma, can incorporate NO and transport it throughout the mammalian circulation in the form of bioactive RSNOs [9,10]. Plasma RSNOs are divided into low-molecular-weight (S-nitroso-glutathione and S-nitrosocysteine) and high-molecular-weight [S-nitrosoalbumin (SNOAlb)] nitroso thiols.

Although there is no doubt as to its existence in vivo, mechanisms of formation and subsequent release of NO from SNOAlb and other RSNOs are poorly understood.

The RBCs represent the second major compartment for NO metabolism in blood. NO is metabolized in the RBCs by direct interaction with Hb. Depending on the oxygenation state of the heme protein, three routes of NO interactions are envisioned. In aqueous solution, NO reacts rapidly with oxyhemoglobin (oxyHb) to form NO_3^- and methemoglobin [10]. Alternatively, NO may bind to the heme group of deoxyhemoglobins (deoxyHb) to form nitrosylhemoglobin (NOHb) [11]. The latter has been detected in the blood of patients receiving nitroglycerin or inhaling NO gas and may interconvert, by reaction with the sulfhydryl group of the Cys93 of the β-Hb chains, to form S-nitrosylated Hb (SNOHb) [11,12] or slowly degrade to NO_2^- [13].

ADMA has been characterized as an endogenous, competitive inhibitor of NOS [13]. In young hypercholesterolemic patients, elevated plasma ADMA concentrations were associated with an impaired endothelium-dependent vasodilation and reduced urinary NO_3^- excretion as surrogate parameters of NO bioavailability. Others reported a significant correlation between raised ADMA concentrations and intima media thickness in apparently healthy, middle-aged individuals [14]. Moreover, plasma ADMA concentrations in hemodialysis patients were recently identified as a strong and independent predictor of mortality and cardiovascular outcome. These studies provide increasing evidence that plasma ADMA levels are related to endothelial dysfunction and represent a risk indicator for the development of cardiovascular diseases in patients with chronic renal failure. However, direct evidence for a link between NO bioavailability and plasma ADMA concentrations in human circulation is lacking. However, various NOS-independent factors influence plasma NO_3^- levels, including dietary NO_3^- intake, saliva formation, bacterial NO_3^- synthesis within the bowels, denitrifying liver enzymes, inhalation of atmospheric gaseous nitrogen oxides, and renal function.

In general, NO production is unlikely to be determined at the luminal surface of the endothelium in vivo. However, stable reaction products formed in relation to NO may serve as an index of NO availability. Recently, to overcome the problem of NO assessment has been overcame by measuring the NO-related amino acids L-arginine and L-citrulline, and, in particular, the stable intermediate compound NOHA in the plasma of healthy volunteers by using high-performance liquid chromatography (HPLC) [15]. Plasma concentrations from different regions were similar and showed no gender- or age-related differences. In contrast, in patients with metabolic syndrome, a disease state known to be associated with endothelial dysfunction and reduced NO availability, plasma concentrations of NOHA were significantly reduced, whereas the plasma concentrations of the NO precursor L-arginine and the end product L-citrulline were unchanged. So, it was suggested that this is either caused by a decreased NOS III activity or by an increased breakdown of NOHA by pathways independent of NOS, resulting in a reduced availability of NOHA for NO synthesis.

It has recently been proposed that NO is stabilized by covalent binding with thiols such as glutathione, cysteine, albumin, and Hb [16]. These low- and high-molecular-weight RSNOs are believed to play a role in stabilizing and delivery of NO to the vascular bed, where NO may modify vascular tone. Stamler et al. [12] have proposed that the binding of oxygen to heme irons in Hb promotes the binding of NO to the specific cysteine residue located in the β-subunits of Hb, forming SNOHb [17]. An allosteric transition accompanies deoxygenation in SNOHb that releases the NO group. Therefore, SNOHb has been proposed to participate in the regulation of blood flow [17] and platelet aggregability. However, although suggested to have a potential vital role in transport and delivery of NO, neither qualitative nor quantitative measurements of RSNOs, NOHb, or SNOHb have been demonstrated to represent an index of NO availability in human blood.

Different NO donors available, their specific role, differences, and similarities

Diazeniumdiolates (NONOates)

Diazeniumdiolates (NONOates) have been labeled NO donors for several years. An adduct of diethylamine and NO was first synthesized in 1960 [18]. The NO donor properties of diazeniumdiolates were considered in biological settings in the 1990s. These compounds contain a diolate group [N(O—)N=O] connected to a nucleophile adduct (primary or secondary amine or polyamine) with a nitrogen atom [19]. This class of compounds has specific features, which makes them popular. The amount of NO generated in vitro is closely correlated to biological activities, such as vasodilatation [19,20], inhibition of platelet aggregation [21,22], inhibition of blood coagulation [23], and inhibition of VSMC proliferation [24]. These compounds experience a lack of tolerance, which could be accounted for by the lack of tissue requirement for NO release [25].

NONOates have been experimentally tested in cardiovascular disease models, although they still have to be used in clinical settings. Depending on the design of the nucleophile adduct, various NONOates have shown to decrease pulmonary vascular resistance, with or without [26] decreasing systemic vascular resistance. NONOates can increase blood flow to the penis [27], to treat erectile dysfunction.

S-Nitrosothiols

S-Nitrosothiols contain a broad range of compounds that carry one chemical bond between a thiol (sulfhydryl) group (R-SH) and the NO moiety. The metabolic environment of the parent thiol strongly influences the activity of S-nitrosothiols. The chemistry of NO release from basic S-nitrosothiol allows these compounds to be biologically available. Several factors, like light, heat, transition metals thiols, superoxide, and enzymes such as xanthine oxidase [28], superoxide dismutase [29], protein disulfide isomerase [30], and various dehydrogenases, can release NO from S-nitrosothiols. These nitrosothiols have more usual metabolic requirements than other classes of NO donors. This could be the reason that these do not create any tolerance issues [31,32].

S-Nitrosothiols have advantages over other classes of NO donors. Firstly, these are tissue-selective, as they have a different hemodynamic profile of action compared to classical organic nitrates. This is due to the fact that they are selective for arteries over veins. Second, since S-nitrosothiols are potent antiplatelet agents, they can inhibit aggregation at doses that do not influence vascular tone [33]. Additionally, S-nitrosothiols can directly transfer NO^+ species, which allows biological activity to be passed through a chain of other thiols, preventing the release of free NO. Through this mechanism of bioactivation, NO moiety is protected from attack by oxygen-centered free radicals, which makes S-nitrosothiols less susceptible to oxidative stress. GSNO has the potential to simultaneously boost intracellular levels of the endogenous antioxidant, GSH, which could suggest that S-nitrosothiols could act as antioxidants conferred by the parent thiol. Data from multiple studies suggest that S-nitrosothiols are unlikely to carry significant cytotoxicity and pharmacologically relevant concentrations.

NO hybrid drugs

Hybrid NO donor drugs allow for an approach to the design of NO-releasing compounds.

This group contains a range of established drugs with structural modifications to incorporate NO-containing molecules. The goal of this method is to synthesize drugs with the biological abilities of NO, but also to retain the pharmacological activity of the parent compound. It is important that NO release is balanced to provide enough activity within the concentration range of the parent compound [34].

NO-NSAIDs

Drugs such as aspirin have become invaluable in various clinical fields due to the high efficacy and low cost of nonsteroidal antiinflammatory drugs (NSAIDs) to treat mild and severe inflammatory conditions. Aspirin causes the loss of protective prostanoids, which can be counteracted by the effects of NO in the gastrointestinal tract. Increase in secretion of protective gastric mucus, increase in blood flow to the gastric mucosa, promotion of repair and removal of toxins, decrease in interaction of neutrophils with the gastric microcirculation, and promotion of healing gastric ulcers can all be accomplished with NO [35,36]. Thus, integrating NO-releasing properties in NSAIDs could reduce the gastric side effects of drugs such as aspirin.

S-Nitroso-hybrid drugs

Inhibitors of angiotensin-converting enzyme (ACE) have been assigned a hybrid approach. ACE inhibitor, captopril, contains a SH group which can be nitrosated, which produces S-nitrosocaptopril (SNO-Cap) [37]. Long-lasting hypotensive effect in vivo can be caused by intravenous SNO-Cap. Similar to S-nitrosothiols, SNO-Cap is less susceptible to intolerance.

Zeolites

NO storage and delivery using ion-exchanged zeolites has been recently accepted [38]. Ion-exchanged zeolites are microporous insoluble materials that form a meshwork consisting of metal ions that can bind NO. To bind NO to metal ions within the pores, the solid needs to be exposed to NO gas. This facilitates highly efficient packing of NO in the solid. In the anhydrous state, these types of NO zeolites are stable, although water displaces the NO upon immersion into an aqueous environment. These materials have a high capacity for storage of NO. Also, by changing the porosity of zeolite, the metal ion in the framework, and the composition and nature of the binder, the rate of NO release can be modulated [38]. This large amount of flexibility allows for several NO donor materials for different purposes. This can range from fast-acting antimicrobial coatings for urinary catheters and wound dressings, to durable, slow-acting, antithrombotic coatings for stents, bypass tubing, cannulas, and catheters. This approach represents site-selective delivery of NO, which improves the benefits of NO as a local mediator.

Role of NO in regulating inflammation and other functions during normal physiological activities

Inflammation is the complex biological process that occurs in response to tissue damage and is characterized by heat, pain, redness, swelling, and loss of function. In response to harmful stimuli, microcirculatory changes to vascular permeability, leukocyte recruitment, and inflammatory mediatory release occur in order to destroy invading organisms and initiate tissue repair [17,39,40]. In particular, in response to microbial products or pro-inflammatory cytokines such as tumor necrosis factor (TNF) and interleukin 1 (IL-1), nuclear factor kappa-beta (NF-kB) is activated [41]. Subsequently, NF-kB potentiates the immune response by regulating inflammatory gene expression and modulating the activity of ECAMS, the surface glycoproteins responsible for movement of immune cells to sites of injury.

Nitric oxide plays a key role in the regulation of NF-kB and thus the regulation of the immune response. By inducing a conformational change in the monomeric G protein p21ras, NO is responsible for increased activity of NF-kB [42]. Contrastingly, NF-kB has been shown to block interaction of NF-kB with its DNA binding site [43,44]. NO also directly nitrosylates transcription factors through JAK/STAT pathways to modulate immune signaling cascades [45]. Lastly, NO may block interaction of the transcription factor Sp1 to interfere with its DNA-binding properties [46]. Thus, NO can affect immune function in the absence of chemokine and cytokine changes.

Additionally, NO inhibits the expression of genes that encode cytokines and adhesion molecules responsible for potentiation of the immune response [46]. Constitutively produced NO works primarily to vasodilate and increase vascular permeability through a cGMP-dependent pathway [47,48]. During an acute inflammatory reaction, iNOS-derived NO kills microorganisms through redox reactions that cause DNA damage, LDL oxidation, and inhibition of mitochondrial respiration [49].

NO also appears to play a role in the immune response at a cellular level. Exogenous NO has been shown to downregulate ECAM expression in vitro, thus blocking immune cell migration [50]. At low concentrations, endogenous constitutive NOS including nNOS has been shown to inhibit the cellular pathways that lead to chemokine synthesis, leukocyte adhesion, and transmigration [51]. Paradoxically, high concentrations of NO generated primarily by iNOS can inhibit the inflammatory cascade [51]. Thus, NO appears to have both pro-inflammatory and antiinflammatory functions.

Constitutively produced NO may also be involved in T helper cell proliferation and cytokine production [52]. Studies in iNOS knockout mice indicate altered Th1 response to infection, thus driving an increased Th2 response (29). NO also appears to inhibit IgE-mediated histamine release from mast cells [53,54].

In addition to its direct impact on the immune response, nitric oxide is present in high quantities in inflamed tissue. Nitric oxide is generated by activated macrophages during immunologic reactions as a part of nonspecific immunity [55]. Once released, nitric oxide exerts its effect on cells through cytotoxic mechanisms such as inhibition of mitochondrial respiratory chain and nuclear DNA synthesizing enzymes [56–58].

Given the potentially damaging effects of NO on tissue and cells, it is imperative that human cells have protective mechanisms to counter excess oxidative damage and stress. These antioxidant systems include enzymatic systems like superoxide dismutase (SOD) and catalase, metabolic antioxidants such as lipoic acid and coenzyme Q10, and nutrient antioxidants like vitamins E, C, and beta carotene [59,60]. They primarily function through inhibition of the generation of oxidative stress and by scavenging free radicals [61]. Though NO, and its downstream pro-inflammatory effects, has been shown to increase oxidative stress, NO has also been shown to have strong antiinflammatory properties even at exceptionally low concentrations [61].

I. Development of NO donors and derivatives, and new delivery formations

Role of NO during inflammatory diseases, tumor microenvironment, and cancers progression

Nitric oxide (NO) houses a diverse role in the physiological function of vasodilation, smooth muscle relaxation, neurotransmission, and immune modulation. To understand the relationship between NO and the progression from physiological function to pathological disease state and eventual malignancy, we must refer back to the pathway of NO production. L-Arginine undergoes oxidation to L citrulline through a family of enzymes called nitric oxide synthases (NOSs) [59]. There are three isoforms of NOS, nNOS in the nervous system, eNOS found in the endothelium, and iNOS expressed in several cell types [60,61]. NNOS and eNOS are constitutively produced and are responsible for exquisitely lesser amounts of NO (nanomolar) that may last for seconds to minutes, exerting a time-limited effect.

Meanwhile, iNOS is produced by the induction of inflammatory cytokines, lipopolysaccharides (LPSs), or foreign pathogens, and releases significant amounts of NO (micromolar), which last for hours. This difference in concentration and duration of exposure is essential to the role each NOS plays in physiological harmony. The large amount of NO produced by iNOS helps in defending the host against invading pathogens and is critical in maintaining a proper inflammatory and immune response. However, overexpression and dysregulation of iNOS may have detrimental effects on the host. In animal models, elevated levels of NO production are noted to contribute to septic and cardiogenic shock [62]. In human models, prominent levels of NO and iNOS activity are noted in septic shock, neuronal damage, diabetes, pain, and a myriad of cancers [63]. The theme of NO concentration and duration of exposure are fundamental to understanding latent downstream effects of NO in disease and malignancy.

Initially found in macrophages, iNOS has now been isolated in hepatocytes, smooth muscle cells, chondrocytes, glial cells, astrocytes, neurons, and cardiomyocytes [64]. The main inducers of iNOS expression are TNF alpha, IL-1B, IFN gamma, and LPS [65]. In addition to cytokines and LPS, viruses and parasites can also induce the expression of iNOS. Upregulation of iNOS in human cells has been noted in the presence of human immunodeficiency virus, hepatitis b virus, and plasmodium falciparum [66–69], underlining that NO is a vital compound in immune defense against a large quantity of pathogens.

Over the years, research has demonstrated an important linkage between nitric oxide (NO)/iNOS with malignant pathology, including many cancers such as colon, bladder, breast, melanoma, pancreatic, and lung [70,71]. The mechanisms by which NO and its downstream derivatives induce carcinogenesis include the induction of DNA damage, inhibition of DNA repair, posttranslational modification of proteins, excess proliferation, promotion of angiogenesis, metastasis, and inhibition of apoptosis. The vast network of potential pathways of carcinogenesis demonstrates the intricate balance NO must maintain in the human body.

When examining the role of NO in cancer biology, scientists should look through the lens of NO concentration. At low concentrations, NO exerts a cytoprotective effect on cancer cells and stimulates carcinogenesis through the activation of several oncogenic pathways. However, at high concentrations, NO has been shown to produce cytotoxic effects within cancer cells and induce apoptosis [72]. Examples of this effect are seen in keratinocytes, which increase proliferation at low concentrations of NO (0.01–0.25 mM), but demonstrate cytostasis at NO concentrations >0.5 mM [73]. Additionally, demonstrated within pheochromocytomas

PC12 cells, elevated levels of proliferation at low concentrations of NO (25 to 50 µM), whereas high concentrations of NO inhibited the proliferation [74]. Other examples of cell proliferation at low NO levels are seen again in breast cancer cells, choriocarcinoma, and ovarian carcinoma. Conversely, at high concentrations of NO, there is tumor regression. The duality of pro- and antitumor effects of NO allows one molecule to modulate both metastatic and apoptotic processes within cancer biology.

Another facet of NO-mediated cancer progression is the mechanism of angiogenesis. Depending on the concentration and duration, NO can either promote or inhibit angiogenesis. While the mechanism is intricate and complex, the basic understanding is angiogenic factors such as endothelial growth factor, sphingosine-1-phosphate, angiopoietins, and estrogen, which promote the release of endothelial NO via the upregulation of NOS3 [75]. Conversely, NO secondary to sodium nitroprusside and L arginine has been noted to inhibit angiogenesis in in vivo models [76].

Lastly, it is important to understand the mechanism by which NO can induce apoptosis in cells. Similar to the concepts of proliferation and angiogenesis, whether NO induces or inhibits apoptosis is dependent on the source, concentration, and duration of exposure to NO. Low levels of NO inhibit the pathways of apoptosis by activating guanylyl cyclase and inhibiting apoptotic proteins such as Bax [76]. While at a high concentration of NO, apoptosis is induced via receptors such as FAS, death receptor 5, and TNFR1 [77].

As discussed thus far, the bimodal nature of NO allows scientists to use NO signaling as a therapeutic strategy against malignancy. Current classes of NO derivatives used for their anticancer properties include glyceryltrinitrate, isosorbidedinitrate, *S*-nitroso-*N*-acetylpenicillamine, and *S*-nitrosoglutathione [78]. All of these have demonstrated antineoplastic impacts on different malignancies. However, some tumors overexpress iNOS, and the utilization of iNOS inhibitors would be a more appropriate therapy. Examples of this include ER-negative breast cancer and triple-negative breast cancer. INOS inhibitors used in mouse models have demonstrated decreased tumor growth and metastasis [78]. Beyond the scope of cancer, researchers are exploring iNOS inhibition as a tangible therapeutic option for a wide catchment of diseases. While the specifics of therapeutic discovery are beyond the scope of this book chapter, it is important to know current iNOS inhibition is being investigated within the realm of epilepsy, type II diabetes, and obesity-associated insulin resistance.

The role of NO varies from physiological to pathological and eventual malignancy. Research over the years has demonstrated a clear relationship between the concentration of NO, duration of exposure, source, and eventual downstream effect. With the whole microenvironment in mind, scientists can now manipulate NO for therapeutic gain. Once tumor environments are determined to be NO-dependent or independent, modulating NO and NO derivatives can create cytotoxic effects on cancerous cells. Beyond cancer treatment, the role of NO-derived therapies is also being explored in the treatment of epilepsy, type II diabetes, and obesity-related insulin resistance.

Current clinical trials of NO

Nitric oxide (NO) is a critical topic for investigation. From its first discovery as a gas in 1772 [79], until nowadays, significant added information continues to be found on this subject. NO is a very adaptable metabolite that regulates and takes part in several reactions of the human body. Considering its versatility, multiple fields of medicine tried to find solutions to some fundamental questions via NO. The most recent examples emerged during the COVID-19 pandemic in 2020 [80,81]. Throughout that particular period, thousands of studies associating transmission, duration, outcome, and complications of COVID-19 with NO were published. Some studies concluded with more encouraging results than others, but all of them demonstrated one more time the importance of understanding the basic function and metabolisms of NO in order to comprehend and find a response to contemporary interrogations [82,83].

Currently, there are nearly 100 clinical trials that have NO as their primary interest topic. From cardiology to neurology, endocrinology, and orthopedics, all dimensions of health care can be affected or potentially improved by the discovery of new roles of NO.

As an illustration, at the present time, the recruitment process has just started over a clinical trial that is trying to use nasal NO testing to improve primary ciliary dyskinesia (PCD) management. PCD is a rare genetic disease, and its pathophysiologic mechanism consists of immotile cilia causing recurrent otologic, sinus, and pulmonary diseases [84–86]. Diagnosis of this condition improved in the last decades, after finding its relation with low nasal nitric oxide production [87,88]. But now, investigators from the Arkansas Children's Hospital want to examine how the NO test results correlate with other tests done to make the diagnosis of this pathology. This can potentially lead to some answers and future guidelines in the management of these considered "rare" diseases. Simultaneously, on the same theme, another investigation group from the University of Texas is trying to discover what effect a NO-rich dietary supplement would have in patients with a diagnosis of PCD [89,90]. This example perfectly reflects how NO versatility can be exploited in various aspects of management of even the same disease.

Remitting to the cardiovascular system, some lines of investigation are being directed toward the relationship between NO and peripheral artery disease (PAD). PAD is the manifestation of atherosclerotic disease in the lower extremities. Presentation ranges from asymptomatic to severe symptoms and complications such as claudication, ulcers, and gangrene, among others [91,92]. Investigators from the University of Massachusetts are testing if the ATLAS therapy (based on L-arginine, tetrahydrobiopterin, and L-ascorbate) in patients with PAD leads to an increase in the production of NO, and if that correlates with an improvement in pain-free walking distance and overall physical activity [93,94]. This would offer alternative approaches to the management of classical diseases.

Diabetes is a chronic disease characterized by insulin resistance or impaired insulin production that leads to a chronic hyperglycemic state in the organism. It is one of the most common diseases among the US population, with more than 37.3 million Americans affected [95]. Diabetes can lead to macro- and microvascular complications throughout life. Microvascular complications refer specifically to retinopathy, nephropathy, and neuropathy. The latter is a contributor to the development of diabetic foot ulcers [95]. Nitric oxide insufficiency is a well-known contributor to poor healing in diabetic foot ulcers. A research team from the Achilles Foot Health Centre in Canada is testing if a nitric oxide solution, delivered as a footbath, could act as a treatment for patients with a diabetic foot ulcer compared with placebo [96].

These examples demonstrate, once again, the major potential of NO in predominant and nonpredominant conditions and offer expectations on future changes in the paradigms of diagnosis, treatment, and management of diseases.

Ying and Yang of nitric oxide studies: Immunosuppressive tumor microenvironment induced by the nitric oxide production

The success of BCG immunotherapy for BC requires a competent host immune system [97,98], where CD8+ and NK cells are fundamental participants, since their depletion has been associated with loss of BCG antitumor activity [99]. Also, it was shown that BCG is not effective in athymic mice [99]. On the other hand, Treg and MDSC inhibit immune cytotoxic cells slowing the removal of tumor cells and promoting tumor growth [100–102]. Recent studies showed that bladder tumors secreted chemokines that recruit regulatory cells and BCG was not able to modify this effect [103]. Among others, the expression of immunosuppressive molecules such as iNOS and S100A9 was described [104,105]. These molecules could contribute to BCG therapeutic failure, generating an immunosuppressive tumor microenvironment. It was demonstrated that about 50% of patients with BC present iNOS tumor expression, associated with worse prognosis [106], and linked to BCG failure [107]. Langle et al., first evaluated the association between iNOS and S100A9 expression in human bladder tumors. They found that iNOS-positive tumors were related with the expression of S100A9, not only at tumor cells, but also in tumor-infiltrating cells. These results raised the hypothesis that iNOS expression could be generating an immunosuppressive tumor microenvironment. If this idea is correct, inhibitors of NO production combined with BCG may reverse the immunosuppression and contribute to control tumor growth. To test this hypothesis, they used a preclinical MB49 BC model that constitutively expresses iNOS, closely related to human pathology [108,109]. Results showed that in the heterotopic model, BCG, L-NAME, and its combination reduced MB49 tumor growth. However, only L-NAME alone or combined with BCG reduced orthotopic tumor growth and incidence. In the subcutaneous model, it was observed that the inhibition of NO production by L-NAME was enough to reduce S100A9 expression. This protein can be produced either by immune cells or by tumor cells [110–112] and has been associated with an immunosuppressive microenvironment, inducing suppressor cells differentiation (Treg and MDSC) and inhibiting cytotoxic cells [113]. S100A9 binding to its receptors on different cells from tumor microenvironment leads a variety of different responses [114]. It has been shown that in tumor cells, S100A9 induces its proliferation, since its inhibition leads to a reduction in tumor growth [115]. On the other hand, in immune cells, S100A9 is a potent inducer of MDSC differentiation and expansion. Thus, S100A9 is a prominent participant in tumor growth and in the immunosuppression developed. Similar to that observed in human bladder tumors, in their murine BC model, they found that iNOS and S100A9 were associated, while the inhibition of NO production not only reduces S100A9, but also recruits CD8+-infiltrating tumor cells. One candidate protein that could link the relation between iNOS and S100A9 is the immunosuppressive factor TGF-β. TGF-β is usually expressed to protect and prevent the normal tissue damage in response to chronic

I. Development of NO donors and derivatives, and new delivery formations

inflammation process induced by iNOS activity [116]. Tumors also use this protein as a growth factor to proliferate and to evade the immune response, inhibiting cytotoxic cells and inducing Tregs and MDSC. Furthermore, it was described that TGF-β expressed in tumor microenvironment is capable induce S100A9 expression, associated with the recruiting of suppressor cells [117]. Reinforcing this idea, they observed that in their murine BC model, MB49 tumors present high TGF-β expression and BCG and LNAME (alone or combined with BCG) reduced this factor. This inhibition in TGF-β pathway by all treatments may contribute to revert the tumor immunosuppressive microenvironment. Other authors demonstrated that tumor TGF-β production induces a systemic immune suppression and inhibits host immunosurveillance. Similar to Langle's team, they also observed that its neutralization increases the infiltration of inflammatory immune cells and enhances the antitumor immune response mediated by CD8+ and NK cytotoxic cells [118]. Langle's evaluation of immune populations also showed that CD8+ and NK cytotoxic effectors were decreased in periphery (spleen and DLN) of SC and orthotopic MB49 TBM. An increase in suppressor cells Treg and MDSC was also observed. These results indicate that MB49 iNOS-expressing tumors generate a systemic immunosuppressive profile, similar to that observed in other iNOS-expressing tumors [119]. BCG treatment combined with L-NAME changed the immune profile, increasing cytotoxic effectors cells and decreasing suppressor immune cells. It was previously shown that MB49 tumors express iNOS, produce NO, and that BCG induces both iNOS and NO production [120]. These results, added to current ones, indicate that iNOS expression generates either, systemic and tumor immunosuppressive microenvironment. Moreover, a recent study showed that NO inhibition in iNOS-expressing tumors downregulates suppressive immune response and enhances other immunotherapies based on checkpoint blockade [121]. As shown in the orthotopic model, NO inhibition with L-NAME reduced bladder tumor growth and incidence and induced specific spleen cytotoxicity against MB49 tumor cells. BCG treatment increased specific cytotoxicity, but this response was not enough to significantly reduce bladder tumor growth. However, BCG+L-NAME induced a similar spleen-specific MB49 cytotoxicity that was observed for BCG or L-NAME alone, while it did reduce bladder tumor growth. Globally, the combined treatment of BCG+L-NAME presented a higher orthotopic tumor growth inhibition and a powerful systemic change of the immune profile. Their findings agree with data from other author, who showed that BCG therapy induced the immune cytotoxic activation, but it was not able to completely downregulate the suppressive response induced in human bladder tumors.

Conclusion

Nitric oxide's role in physiologic and pathologic metabolism and normal human functioning is complex but crucial to appreciate. NO activity widely depends on the enzymatic process, cell type, and nature of the reaction, among other factors. There is enthralling evidence that NO plays an indispensable role in the protection against free radicals, regulation of inflammation, fat cell metabolism, and mitochondrial dynamics, all factors contributing to chronic and age-related diseases. As the prevalence of chronic diseases continues to increase in the developed world, efforts should be focused on understanding the complex pathophysiological contribution of NO in these diseases to find some explanation, and, optimistically, answers. It is worth clarifying that the mechanisms of these complex diseases are multifactorial rather than restricted to some metabolite specifically and depend on more factors than just NO. Thus, the path ahead will require continued identification and incorporation of new discoveries into the extended system of NO activity in the body.

References

[1] Tuteja N, et al. Nitric oxide as a unique bioactive signaling messenger in physiology and pathophysiology. J Biomed Biotechnol 2004;2004(4):227–37.

[2] Bryan NS, Bian K, Murad F. Discovery of the nitric oxide signaling pathway and targets for drug development. Front Biosci (Landmark Ed) 2009;14(1):1–18.

[3] Lancaster Jr JR. Nitric oxide: a brief overview of chemical and physical properties relevant to therapeutic applications. Future Sci OA 2015;1(1):FSO59.

[4] West JB. Joseph Priestley, oxygen, and the enlightenment. Am J Physiol Lung Cell Mol Physiol 2014;306(2): L113–7.

[5] Ichinose F, Roberts JD, Zapol WM. Inhaled nitric oxide. Circulation 2004;109(25):3107–9.

[6] Kamm A, et al. Nitric oxide and its derivatives in the cancer battlefield. Nitric Oxide 2019;93:102–4. Böger RH, Bode-Böger SM, Szuba A, Tsao PS, Chan JR, Tangphao O, Blaschke TF, Cooke JP. Asymmetric dimethylarginine (ADMA): a novel risk factor for endothelial dysfunction. Its role in hypercholesterolemia. Circulation 1998;98:1842–7.

[7] Cannon III RO, Schechter AN, Panza JA, Ognibene FP, Pease-Fye ME, Waclawiw MA, Shelhamer JH, Gladwin MT. Effects of inhaled nitric oxide on regional blood flow are consistent with intravascular nitric oxide delivery. J Clin Invest 2001;108:279–87.

[8] Garlichs CD, Beyer J, Zhang H, Schmeisser A, Plötze K, Mügge A, Schellong S, Daniel WG. Decreased plasma concentrations of l-hydroxy-arginine as a marker of reduced NO formation in patients with combined cardiovascular risk factors. J Lab Clin Med 2000;135:419–25.

[9] Gladwin MT, Ognibene FP, Pannell LK, Nichols JS, Pease-Fye ME, Shelhamer JH, Schechter AN. Relative role of heme nitrosylation and β-cysteine 93 nitrosation in the transport and metabolism of nitric oxide by hemoglobin in the human circulation. Proc Natl Acad Sci USA 2000;97:9943–8.

[10] Kelm M. Nitric oxide metabolism and breakdown. Biochim Biophys Acta 1999;1411:273–89.

[11] Miyazaki H, Matsuoka H, Cooke JP, Usui M, Ueda S, Okuda S, Imaizumi T. Endogenous nitric oxide synthase inhibitor. A novel marker of atherosclerosis. Circulation 1999;99:1141–6.

[12] Stamler JS, Jaraki O, Osborne J, Simon DI, Keaney J, Vita J, Singel D, Valeri CR, Loscalzo J. Nitric oxide circulates in mammalian plasma primarily as an S-nitroso adduct of serum albumin. Proc Natl Acad Sci USA 1992;89:7674–7.

[13] Stamler JS, Jia L, Eu JP, McMahon TJ, Demchenko IT, Bonaventura J, Gernert K, Piantadosi CA. Blood flow regulation by S-nitrosohemoglobin in the physiological oxygen gradient. Science 1997;276:2034–7.

[14] Vallance P, Leone A, Calver A, Collier J, Moncada S. Accumulation of an endogenous inhibitor of nitric oxide synthesis in chronic renal failure. Lancet 1992;339:572–5.

[15] Wennmalm A, Benthin G, Edlund A, Jungersten L, Kieler-Jensen N, Lundin S, Westfelt UN, Petersson AS, Waagstein F. Metabolism and excretion of nitric oxide in humans. An experimental and clinical study. Circ Res 1993;73:1121–7.

[16] Zoccali C, Bode-Boeger SM, Mallamaci F, Benedetto FA, Tripepi G, Malatino LS, Cataliotti A, Bellanuova I, Fermo I, Frölich JC, Böger RH. Plasma concentration of asymmetrical dimethylarginine and mortality in patients with end-stage renal disease: a prospective study. Lancet 2001;358:2113–7.

[17] Ferrero-Miliani L, Nielsen OH, Andersen PS, Girardin SE. Chronic inflammation: importance of NOD2 and NALP3 in interleukin-1beta generation. Clin Exp Immunol 2007;147(2):227–35. https://doi.org/10.1111/j.1365-2249.2006.03261.

[18] Drago RS, Paulik FE. The reaction of nitrogen (II) oxide with diethylamine. J Am Chem Soc 1960;82:96–8.

[19] Maragos CM, Morley D, Wink DA, Dunams TM, Saavedra JE, Hoffman A, et al. Complexes of ·NO with nucleophiles as agents for the controlled biological release of nitric oxide. Vasorelaxant effects. J Med Chem 1991;34:3242–7.

[20] Morley D, Maragos CM, Zhang XY, Boignon M, Wink DA, Keefer LK. Mechanism of vascular relaxation induced by the nitric oxide (NO)/nucleophile complexes, a new class of NO-based vasodilators. J Cardiovasc Pharmacol 1993;21:670–6.

[21] Diodati JG, Quyyumi AA, Hussain N, Keefer LK. Complexes of nitric oxide with nucleophiles as agents for the controlled biological release of nitric oxide: antiplatelet effect. Thromb Haemost 1993;70:654–8.

[22] Sogo N, Magid KS, Shaw CA, Webb DJ, Megson IL. Inhibition of human platelet aggregation by nitric oxide donor drugs: relative contribution of cGMP-independent mechanisms. Biochem Biophys Res Commun 2000;279:412–9.

[23] Nielsen VG. Nitric oxide decreases coagulation protein function in rabbits as assessed by thromboelastography. Anesth Analg 2001;92:320–3.

[24] Mooradian DL, Hutsell TC, Keefer LK. Nitric oxide (NO) donor molecules: effect of NO release rate on vascular smooth muscle cell proliferation in vitro. J Cardiovasc Pharmacol 1995;25:674–8.

[25] Brilli RJ, Krafte-Jacobs B, Smith DJ, Roselle D, Passerini D, Vromen A, et al. Intratracheal instillation of a novel NO/nucleophile adduct selectively reduces pulmonary hypertension. J Appl Physiol 1997;83:1968–75.

[26] Talukdar A, Wang PG. In: Wang PG, Cai TB, Taniguchi N, editors. N-Nitroso compounds nitric oxide donors. Weinheim: Wiley-VCH; 2005. p. 55–89.

[27] Trujillo M, Alvarez MN, Peluffo G, Freeman BA, Radi R. Xanthine oxidase-mediated decomposition of S-nitrosothiols. J Biol Chem 1998;273:7828–34.

[28] Jourd'heuil D, Laroux FS, Miles AM, Wink DA, Grisham MB. Effect of superoxide dismutase on the stability of S-nitrosothiols. Arch Biochem Biophys 1999;361:323–30.

[29] Ramachandran N, Root P, Jiang XM, Hogg PJ, Mutus B. Mechanism of transfer of NO from extracellular S-nitrosothiols into the cytosol by cell-surface protein disulfide isomerase. Proc Natl Acad Sci USA 2001;98:9539–44.

[30] Hanspal IS, Magid KS, Webb DJ, Megson IL. The effect of oxidative stress on endothelium-dependent and nitric oxide donor-induced relaxation: implications for nitrate tolerance. Nitric Oxide 2002;6:263–70.

[31] Miller MR, Roseberry MJ, Mazzei FA, Butler AR, Webb DJ, Megson IL. Novel S-nitrosothiols do not engender vascular tolerance and remain effective in glyceryltrinitrate-tolerant rat femoral arteries. Eur J Pharmacol 2000;408:335–43.

[32] Ramsay B, Radomski M, De Belder A, Martin JF, Lopez-Jaramillo P. Systemic effects of S-nitroso-glutathione in the human following intravenous infusion. Br J Clin Pharmacol 1995;40:101–2.

[33] Bandarage UK, Chen L, Fang X, Garvey DS, Glavin A, Janero DR, et al. Nitrosothiol esters of diclofenac: synthesis and pharmacological characterization as gastrointestinal-sparing prodrugs. J Med Chem 2000;43:4005–16.

[34] Hallas J, Dall M, Andries A, Andersen BS, Aalykke C, Hansen JM, et al. Use of single and combined antithrombotic therapy and risk of serious upper gastrointestinal bleeding: population-based case–control study. Br Med J 2006;333:726.

[35] Ma L, Wallace JL. Endothelial nitric oxide synthase modulates gastric ulcer healing in rats. Am J Physiol Gastrointest Liver Physiol 2000;279:G341–6.

[36] Loscalzo J, Smick D, Andon N, Cooke J. S-Nitrosocaptopril. I. Molecular characterization and effects on the vasculature and on platelets. J Pharmacol Exp Ther 1989;249:726–9.

[37] Wheatley PS, Butler AR, Crane MS, Fox S, Xiao B, Rossi AG, et al. NO-releasing zeolites and their antithrombotic properties. J Am Chem Soc 2006;128:502–9.

[38] Frost MC, Reynolds MM, Meyerhoff ME. Polymers incorporating nitric oxide releasing/generating substances for improved biocompatibility of blood-contacting medical devices. Biomaterials 2005;26:1685–93.

[39] Chertov O, Yang D, Howard OM, Oppenheim JJ. Leukocyte granule proteins mobilize innate host defenses and adaptive immune responses. Immunol Rev 2000;177:68–78.

[40] Chen L, Deng H, Cui H, Fang J, Zuo Z, Deng J, et al. Inflammatory responses and inflammation-associated diseases in organs. Oncotarget 2018;9(6):7204–18.

[41] Colasanti M, Persichini T. Nitric oxide: an inhibitor of NF-kappaB/Rel system in glial cells. Brain Res Bull 2000;52(3):155–61.

[42] Laroux FS, Pavlick KP, Hines IN, Kawachi S, Harada H, Bharwani S, et al. Role of nitric oxide in inflammation. Acta Physiol Scand 2001;173(1):113–8.

[43] Park SK, Lin HL, Murphy S. Nitric oxide regulates nitric oxide synthase-2 gene expression by inhibiting NF-kappaB binding to DNA. Biochem J 1997;322(Pt 2):609–13.

[44] Bogdan C. Nitric oxide and the regulation of gene expression. Trends Cell Biol 2001;11(2):66–75.

[45] Ignarro LJ. Signal transduction mechanisms involving nitric oxide. Biochem Pharmacol 1991;41(4):485–90.

[46] Lugnier C, Keravis T, Eckly-Michel A. Cross talk between NO and cyclic nucleotide phosphodiesterases in the modulation of signal transduction in blood vessel. J Physiol Pharmacol 1999;50(4):639–52.

[47] Guzik TJ, Korbut R, Adamek-Guzik T. Nitric oxide and superoxide in inflammation and immune regulation. J Physiol Pharmacol 2003;54(4):469–87.

[48] Coleman JW. Nitric oxide in immunity and inflammation. Int Immunopharmacol 2001;1(8):1397–406.

[49] Man MQ, Wakefield JS, Mauro TM, Elias PM. Regulatory role of nitric oxide in cutaneous inflammation. Inflammation 2022;45(3):949–64.

[50] Eastmond NC, Banks EM, Coleman JW. Nitric oxide inhibits IgE-mediated degranulation of mast cells and is the principal intermediate in IFN-gamma-induced suppression of exocytosis. J Immunol 1997;159(3):1444–50.

[51] Masini E, Di Bello MG, Pistelli A, Raspanti S, Gambassi F, Mugnai L, et al. Generation of nitric oxide from nitrovasodilators modulates the release of histamine from mast cells. J Physiol Pharmacol 1994;45(1):41–53.

[52] Moncada S. The 1991 Ulf von Euler lecture. The L-arginine: nitric oxide pathway. Acta Physiol Scand 1992;145(3):201–27.

[53] Marletta MA, Yoon PS, Iyengar R, Leaf CD, Wishnok JS. Macrophage oxidation of L-arginine to nitrite and nitrate: nitric oxide is an intermediate. Biochemistry 1988;27(24):8706–11.

[54] Moncada S, Higgs A. The L-arginine-nitric oxide pathway. N Engl J Med 1993;329(27):2002–12.

[55] Pham-Huy LA, He H, Pham-Huy C. Free radicals, antioxidants in disease and health. Int J Biomed Sci 2008;4(2):89–96.

[56] Bendich A. Physiological role of antioxidants in the immune system. J Dairy Sci 1993;76(9):2789–94.

[57] Joshi MS, Ponthier JL, Lancaster Jr JR. Cellular antioxidant and pro-oxidant actions of nitric oxide. Free Radic Biol Med 1999;27(11–12):1357–66.

[58] Hummel SG, Fischer AJ, Martin SM, Schafer FQ, Buettner GR. Nitric oxide as a cellular antioxidant: a little goes a long way. Free Radic Biol Med 2006;40(3):501–6.

[59] Abu-Soud HM, Gachhui R, Raushel FM, Stuehr DJ. The ferrous-dioxy complex of neuronal nitric oxide synthase. J Biol Chem 1997;272(28):17349–53.

[60] Kone BC, Kuncewicz T, Zhang W, Yu Z-Y. Protein interactions with nitric oxide synthases: controlling the right time, the right place, and the right amount of nitric oxide. Am J Physiol Renal Physiol 2003;285(2):F178–90.

[61] Titheradge MA. Nitric oxide in septic shock. Biochim Biophys Acta Bioenerg 1999;1411(2–3):437–55.

[62] Sharma JN, Al-Omran A, Parvathy SS. Role of nitric oxide in inflammatory diseases. Inflammopharmacology 2007;15(6):252–9.

[63] Cinelli MA, Do HT, Miley GP, Silverman RB. Inducible nitric oxide synthase: regulation, structure, and inhibition. Med Res Rev 2019;40(1):158–89.

[64] Cinelli MA, Do HT, Miley GP, Silverman RB. Inducible nitric oxide synthase: regulation, structure, and inhibition. Med Res Rev 2020;40(1):158–89.

[65] Saha RN, Pahan K. Regulation of inducible nitric oxide synthase gene in glial cells. Antioxid Redox Signal 2006;8(5–6):929–47.

[66] Liu X, Jana M, Dasgupta S, Koka S, He J, Wood C, et al. Human immunodeficiency virus type 1 (HIV-1) TAT induces nitric-oxide synthase in human Astroglia. J Biol Chem 2002;277(42):39312–9.

[67] Majano PL, García-Monzón C, López-Cabrera M, Lara-Pezzi E, Fernández-Ruiz E, García-Iglesias C, et al. Inducible nitric oxide synthase expression in chronic viral hepatitis. Evidence for a virus-induced gene upregulation. J Clin Investig 1998;101(7):1343–52.

[68] Cramer JP, Mockenhaupt FP, Ehrhardt S, Burkhardt J, Otchwemah RN, Dietz E, et al. iNOS promoter variants and severe malaria in Ghanaian children. Trop Med Int Health 2004;9(10):1074–80.

[69] Vannini F, Kashfi K, Nath N. The dual role of iNOS in cancer. Redox Biol 2015;6:334–43.

[70] Grimm EA, Ellerhorst J, Tang C-H, Ekmekcioglu S. Constitutive intracellular production of iNOS and NO in human melanoma: possible role in regulation of growth and resistance to apoptosis. Nitric Oxide 2008;19(2):133–7.

[71] Korde Choudhari S, Chaudhary M, Bagde S, Gadbail AR, Joshi V. Nitric oxide and cancer: a review. World J Surg Oncol 2013;11(1).

[72] Krischel V, Bruch-Gerharz D, Suschek C, Kröncke K-D, Ruzicka T, Kolb-Bachofen V. Biphasic effect of exogenous nitric oxide on proliferation and differentiation in skin derived keratinocytes but not fibroblasts. J Investig Dermatol 1998;111(2):286–91.

I. Development of NO donors and derivatives, and new delivery formations

[73] Bal-Price A, Gartlon J, Brown GC. Nitric oxide stimulates PC12 cell proliferation via cGMP and inhibits at higher concentrations mainly via energy depletion. Nitric Oxide 2006;14(3):238–46.

[74] Sessa WC. eNOS at a glance. J Cell Sci 2004;117(12):2427–9.

[75] Pipili-Synetos E, Papageorgiou A, Sakkoula E, Sotiropoulou G, Fotsis T, Karakiulakis G, et al. Inhibition of angiogenesis, tumour growth and metastasis by the no-releasing vasodilators, isosorbide mononitrate and dinitrate. Br J Pharmacol 1995;116(2):1829–34.

[76] Johlfs MG, Fiscus RR. Protein kinase G type-iα phosphorylates the apoptosis-regulating protein bad at serine 155 and protects against apoptosis in N1E-115 cells. Neurochem Int 2010;56(4):546–53.

[77] Huerta S, Chilka S, Bonavida B. Nitric oxide donors: novel cancer therapeutics (review). Int J Oncol. 2008; 33(5):909–27.

[78] Walsh EM, Keane MM, Wink DA, Callagy G, Glynn SA. Review of triple negative breast cancer and the impact of inducible nitric oxide synthase on tumor biology and patient outcomes. Crit Rev Oncog 2016;21(5–6):333–51.

[79] Gillman MA. Mini-review: a brief history of nitrous oxide (N2O) use in neuropsychiatry. Curr Drug Abuse Rev 2019;11(1):12–20.

[80] Winchester S, John S, Jabbar K, John I. Clinical efficacy of nitric oxide nasal spray (NONS) for the treatment of mild COVID-19 infection. J Infect 2021;83(2):237–79.

[81] Dominic P, Ahmad J, Bhandari R, Pardue S, Solorzano J, Jaisingh K, Watts M, Bailey SR, Orr AW, Kevil CG, Kolluru GK. Decreased availability of nitric oxide and hydrogen sulfide is a hallmark of COVID-19. Redox Biol 2021;43:101982.

[82] Green SJ. Covid-19 accelerates endothelial dysfunction and nitric oxide deficiency. Microbes Infect 2020; 22(4–5):149–50.

[83] Frostell CG, Hedenstierna G. Nitric oxide and COVID-19: Dose, timing and how to administer it might be crucial. Acta Anaesthesiol Scand 2021;65(5):576–7.

[84] Knowles MR, Zariwala M, Leigh M. Primary ciliary dyskinesia. Clin Chest Med 2016;37(3):449–61.

[85] Shapiro AJ, Davis SD, Polineni D, Manion M, Rosenfeld M, Dell SD, Chilvers MA, Ferkol TW, Zariwala MA, Sagel SD, Josephson M, Morgan L, Yilmaz O, Olivier KN, Milla C, Pittman JE, Daniels MLA, Jones MH, Janahi IA, Ware SM, Daniel SJ, Cooper ML, Nogee LM, Anton B, Eastvold T, Ehrne L, Guadagno E, Knowles MR, Leigh MW, Lavergne V. Diagnosis of primary ciliary dyskinesia. An official American Thoracic Society clinical practice guideline. Am J Respir Crit Care Med 2018;197(12):e24–39.

[86] Arkansas Children's Hospital Research Institute, Ghazala Z. Use of nasal nitric oxide testing in improving primary ciliary dyskinesia clinical care; 2021. June 14–2025 June. Identifier: NCT05287022.

[87] Knowles MR, Daniels LA, Davis SD, Zariwala MA, Leigh MW. Primary ciliary dyskinesia. Recent advances in diagnostics, genetics, and characterization of clinical disease. Am J Respir Crit Care Med 2013;188(8):913–22.

[88] Walker WT, Jackson CL, Lackie PM, Hogg C, Lucas JS. Nitric oxide in primary ciliary dyskinesia. Eur Respir J 2012;40(4):1024–32.

[89] The University of Texas Health Science Center, Mosquera RA. The effect of a dietary supplement rich in nitric oxide in patients diagnosed with primary ciliary dyskinesia; 2019. July 31–2022 August 1. Identifier: NCT04489472.

[90] Kullo IJ, Rooke TW. Peripheral artery disease. N Engl J Med 2016;374(9):861–71.

[91] Campia U, Gerhard-Herman M, Piazza G, Goldhaber SZ. Peripheral artery disease: past, present, and future. Am J Med 2019;132(10):1133–41.

[92] University of Massachusetts, Worcester MLM. The effects of ATLAS (arginine tetrahydrobiopterin L-ascorbate) therapy on nitric oxide bioavailability and pain-free walking in patients with intermittent claudication; 2021. June 15, 2023 February Identifier: NCT04800692.

[93] Centers for Disease Control and Prevention. National diabetes statistics report website, https://www.cdc.gov/diabetes/data/statistics-report/index.html. [Accessed 26 August 2022].

[94] Chatterjee S, Khunti K, Davies MJ. Type 2 diabetes. Lancet 2017;389(10085):2239–51.

[95] Achilles Foot Health Centre, Schumacher S. Safety & efficacy of topical nitric oxide releasing solution (NORS) delivered as an adjunctive footbath treatment as compared to placebo in the management of diabetic foot ulcers; 2021. February 23–2022 December 30. Identifier: NCT04755647.

[96] Knott AB, Bossy-Wetzel E. Impact of nitric oxide on metabolism in health and age-related disease. Diabetes Obes Metab 2010;12:126–33.

[97] Morales A, Eidinger D, Bruce AW. Intracavitary Bacillus Calmette-Guerin in the treatment of superficial bladder tumors. J Urol 1976;116:180–3.

[98] Kamat AM, Li R, O'Donnell MA, Black PC, Roupret M, Catto JW, et al. Predicting response to intravesical Bacillus Calmette Guerin immunotherapy: are we there yet? A systematic review. Eur Urol 2018;73:738–48.

[99] Pettenati C, Ingersoll MA. Mechanisms of BCG immunotherapy and its outlook for bladder cancer. Nat Rev Urol 2018;15:615–25.

[100] Zhang H, Ye YL, Li MX, Ye SB, Huang WR, Cai TT, et al. CXCL2/MIF-CXCR2 signaling promotes the recruitment of myeloid-derived suppressor cells and is correlated with prognosis in bladder cancer. Oncogene 2017;36:2095–104.

[101] Lin CR, Wei TY, Tsai HY, Wu YT, Wu PY, Chen ST. Glycosylation-dependent interaction between CD69 and S100A8/S100A9 complex is required for regulatory T-cell differentiation. FASEB J 2015;29:5006–17.

[102] Rabinovich GA, Conejo-Garcia JR. Shaping the immune landscape in cancer by galectin-driven regulatory pathways. J Mol Biol 2016;428:3266–81.

[103] Muthuswamy R, Wang L, Pitteroff J, Gingrich JR, Kalinski P. Combination of IFNalpha and poly-I:C reprograms bladder cancer microenvironment for enhanced CTL attraction. J Immunother Cancer 2015;3:6.

[104] Bronte V, Zanovello P. Regulation of immune responses by L-arginine metabolism. Nat Rev Immunol 2005;5:641–54.

[105] Wu AA, Drake V, Huang HS, Chiu S, Zheng L. Reprogramming the tumor microenvironment: tumor-induced immunosuppressive factors paralyze T cells. Onco Targets Ther 2015;4:e1016700.

[106] Sandes EO, Faletti AG, Riveros MD, Vidal Mdel C, Gimenez L, Casabe AR, et al. Expression of inducible nitric oxide synthase in tumoral and non-tumoral epithelia from bladder cancer patients. Nitric Oxide 2005;12:39–45.

[107] Mitropoulos D, Petsis D, Kyroudi-Voulgari A, Kouloukoussa M, Zervas A, Dimopoulos C. The effect of intravesical Bacillus Calmette-Guerin instillations on the expression of inducible nitric oxide synthase in humans. Nitric Oxide 2005;13:36–41.

[108] Sandes EO, Lodillinsky C, Langle Y, Belgorosky D, Marino L, Gimenez L, et al. Inducible nitric oxide synthase and PPARgamma are involved in bladder cancer progression. J Urol 2012;188:967–73.

[109] Belgorosky D, Langle Y, Mc Prack B, Cormick L, Colombo E, Sandes AME. Inhibition of nitric oxide is a good therapeutic target for bladder tumors that express iNOS. Nitric Oxide 2014;36:11–8.

[110] Ye Y, Liu S, Wu C, Sun Z. TGF-beta modulates inflammatory cytokines and growth factors to create premetastatic microenvironment and stimulate lung metastasis. J Mol Histol 2015;46:365–75.

[111] Zhao F, Hoechst B, Duffy A, Gamrekelashvili J, Fioravanti S, Manns MP, et al. S100A9 a new marker for monocytic human myeloid-derived suppressor cells. Immunology 2012;136:176–83.

[112] Langle Y, Sandes EO, Belgorosky D, Balarino N, Mc Prack B, Cormick LM, et al. La expresión de S100A9 vinculada con el óxido nítrico, es un marcador de mal pronóstico en pacientes con cáncer de vejiga, siendo su inhibición un posible blanco terapéutico. Rev Argent Urol 2014;79:64–70.

[113] Letterio JJ, Roberts AB. Regulation of immune responses by TGF-beta. Annu Rev Immunol 1998;16:137–61.

[114] Shabani F, Farasat A, Mahdavi M, Gheibi N. Calprotectin (S100A8/S100A9): a key protein between inflammation and cancer. Inflamm Res Off J Eur Histamine Res Soc 2018;67:801–12.

[115] Ichikawa M, Williams R, Wang L, Vogl T, Srikrishna G. S100A8/A9 activate key genes and pathways in colon tumor progression. Mol Cancer Res 2011;9:133–48.

[116] Cabrie A, Guittet O, Tomasini R, Vincendeau P, Lepoivre M. Crosstalk between TAp73 and TGF-beta in fibroblast regulates iNOS expression and Nrf2-dependent gene transcription. Free Radic Biol Med 2019;134:617–29.

[117] Cheng P, Corzo CA, Luetteke N, Yu B, Nagaraj S, Bui MM, et al. Inhibition of dendritic cell differentiation and accumulation of myeloid-derived suppressor cells in cancer is regulated by S100A9 protein. J Exp Med 2008;205:2235–49.

[118] Yang L, Pang Y, Moses HL. TGF-beta and immune cells: an important regulatory axis in the tumor microenvironment and progression. Trends Immunol 2010;31:220–7.

[119] Nagaraj S, Gupta K, Pisarev V, Kinarsky L, Sherman S, Kang L, et al. Altered recognition of antigen is a mechanism of CD8+ T cell tolerance in cancer. Nat Med 2007;13:828–35.

[120] Alvarez V, Lodillinsky C, Umerez S, Sandes E, Eijan AM. Inhibition of bacillus Calmette-Guerin-induced nitric oxide in bladder tumor cells may improve BCG treatment. Int J Mol Med 2005;16:565–71.

[121] Connolly EC, Freimuth J, Akhurst RJ. Complexities of TGF-beta targeted cancer therapy. Int J Biol Sci 2012;8:964–78.

I. Development of NO donors and derivatives, and new delivery formations

Biomedical applications of polymeric nitric oxide (NO) donors

Soumya Paul[a,b], *Manish Kumar*[a,b], *Arindam Mukherjee*[b], *and Priyadarsi De*[a,b]

[a]Polymer Research Centre, Department of Chemical Sciences, Indian Institute of Science Education and Research Kolkata, Mohanpur, Nadia, West Bengal, India [b]Centre for Advanced Functional Materials, Department of Chemical Sciences, Indian Institute of Science Education and Research Kolkata, Mohanpur, Nadia, West Bengal, India

Abstract

Nitric oxide (NO), a potential diatomic radical-based gasotransmitter, exerts a spectrum of concentration-dependent physiological effects by binding to receptors. Over the past decades, the advancement in NO-related research uncloaked its potential in wound healing, anticancer, and antibacterial activities. However, it is essential to release a specific dosage depending on the action needed, thus warranting the fabrication of suitable carriers for target-specific NO delivery. The polymeric NO donors are more advantageous than small molecular NO donors in such circumstances, as they can be designed to provide additional control, including multifunctionality and stimuli-based NO release. In this chapter, the discussion is initiated by disseminating the biological pathway of NO production followed by the advantages of different types of NO donors and the future perspectives of the present research topic. We then provide a comprehensive insight into the state-of-the-art studies on the design, synthesis, and biological applications of various polymeric NO donors. The discussion encompasses stimuli-responsive behavior and pharmacodynamics after treating with polymeric NO donors. We anticipate that the article would provide a foundation to sketch the next-generation polymeric NO donors for suitable biological applications.

Abbreviations

Bcl-2	B-cell lymphoma-2
BH4	tetrahydrobiopterin
bNOS	bacterial nitric oxide synthase
Ca^{2+}	calcium ion
CaM	calmodulin
CD	cyclodextrin
CD31	cluster of differentiation 31

c-di-GMP   cyclic-diguanylate-guanosine monophosphate
Cip   ciprofloxacin
cMOATs   canalicular multispecific organic anion transporters
CO   carbon monoxide
COF   covalent organic framework
COX   cyclooxygenase
DAF   diaminofluorescein
DMMA   dimethyl maleic anhydride
DOX   doxorubicin
EDRF   endothelial-derived relaxing factor
eNOS   endothelial nitric oxide synthase
EPR   enhanced permeation and retention
EPS   extracellular polymeric substance
FAD   flavin adenine dinucleotide
FMN   flavin mononucleotide
GSH   glutathione
H_2S   hydrogen sulfide
Hb   hemoglobin
HCPT   10-hydroxycamptothecin
HNO_2   nitrous acid
IL   interleukin
iNOS   inducible nitric oxide synthase
LPS   lipopolysaccharide
MDR   multidrug resistance
metHb   methemoglobin
MOF   metal organic framework
MRSA   methicillin-resistant *S. aureus*
N_2O_3   dinitrogen trioxide
N_2O_4   dinitrogen tetroxide
NADPH   nicotinamide adenine dinucleotide phosphate
NIR   near-infrared
NMR   nuclear magnetic resonance
nNOS   neuronal nitric oxide synthase
NO   nitric oxide
NO_2   nitrogen dioxide
NO_2^*   excited-state nitrogen dioxide
NO_2^-   nitrate
NOHA N^ω-hydroxy-L-arginine
NONOates   *N*-diazeniumdiolates
NOS   nitric oxide synthase
NSAID   nonsteroidal antiinflammatory drug
NTC   nitrate trimethylene carbonate
O_2   oxygen
O_3   ozone
$ONOO^-$ peroxynitrite
oxyHb   oxyhemoglobin
PBMC   peripheral blood mononuclear cell
PDT   photodynamic therapy
PEG   polyethylene glycol
P-gP   P-glycoprotein
PTT   photothermal therapy
RNS   reactive nitrogen species
ROS   reactive oxygen species

RSNOs	*S*-nitrosothiols
shRNA	short-hairpin RNA
siRNA	small interfering RNA
TNF-α	tumor necrosis factor-α
α-SMA	α-smooth muscle actin

Conflict of interest

No potential conflicts of interest were disclosed.

Introduction

Nitric oxide (NO), a short-lived diatomic compound, was first discovered in 1772. It took more than 200 years to understand this omnipotent molecule's physiological relevance and therapeutic importance. In the late 20th century, the significant discoveries by Furchgott [1], Murad [2], Palmer [3], and Ignarro [4] enlightened the salient roles of NO in the biological system. They recognized NO as an endothelial-derived relaxing factor (EDRF), which plays a pivotal role in smooth muscle vasodilation [5]. In 1998, this ground-breaking discovery led to a Nobel Prize, awarded to Robert Furchgott, Ferid Murad, and Louis Ignarro. This sparked the research into this burgeoning field and established prominent roles of NO in immunological systems, cardiovascular, respiratory, and neurological activities [6].

NO resides in a free radical form with a bond length of ca. 1.15 Å and an unpaired electron in its π^* molecular orbital (Fig. 1A). This unpaired electron governs its affinity toward transition metals and potentially reactive molecules. Due to its electronic configurations, NO is unstable and exceedingly reactive toward biomolecules, especially certain metalloproteins.

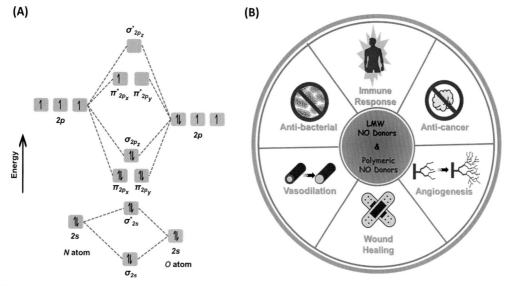

FIG. 1 (A) Molecular orbital diagram of NO. (B) Various therapeutic applications of NO donors. *Reproduced with the permission from Paul S, Pan S, Mukherjee A, De P. Nitric oxide releasing delivery platforms: design, detection, biomedical applications and future possibilities. Mol Pharmaceutics 2021;18:3181–205. Copyright (2021) American Chemical Society.*

I. Development of NO donors and derivatives, and new delivery formations

NO can bind with the ferrous form of hemoglobin (Hb) to form iron nitrosyl Hb [7]. NO also reacts with oxyhemoglobin (oxyHb) and transforms it into methemoglobin (metHb) which may be used as a tool to detect NO quantitatively [8].

The emerging studies of the last two decades uncloaked several therapeutic applications of NO [9], providing deeper insight into its role in the homeostasis in the cardiovascular system, apoptosis, platelet aggregation and adhesion, inflammation and neurotransmission [10]. Typically, the NO generated by endothelial cells retains the blood flow and blood pressure in the cardiovascular system by impeding the thrombus formation. Significant evidence also found that the NO exhibits anticancer activity, wound-healing properties, and antibacterial properties at higher concentrations (Fig. 1B) [11,12]. It is crucial to note that functions of NO may seem paradoxical as they can act in opposite fashion depending on the concentration. Pico- to nanomolar concentrations of NO govern most of the biological activities, and the release takes place for a shorter period. Whereas the NO release for an extended period with micro-molar concentration can be lethal for the cell and the biological milieu, this phenomenon is primarily observed in immunological responses. A higher concentration of NO can react with reactive oxygen species (ROS) and produce reactive nitrogen species (RNS) (e.g., nitrogen dioxide (NO_2), peroxynitrite ($ONOO^-$)), to cause cell and DNA damage. NO can exhibit antitumor properties or tumor-promoting activity depending on its local concentration [13], and the same is true for anti- or proinflammatory activity [10]. Detailed studies also showed that NO plays a significant role in neurodegenerative disorders like Alzheimer's and Parkinson's diseases [14].

In the recent past, gasotransmitters like NO, hydrogen sulfide (H_2S), and carbon monoxide (CO) were extensively probed for various therapeutic applications [15,16]. The spurring research led to the FDA-approved commercial use of nitroglycerin and sodium nitroprusside to treat angina and blood pressure. However, due to both genotoxic and angiogenic effects of NO, it is crucial to design delivering molecules capable of target-specific controlled NO release. Several NO-delivering platforms have been reported that can be broadly categorized into two classes: small-molecule NO donors and polymeric NO donors [17,18]. Both have their benefits and flaws. However, in this chapter, the discussion will be mostly focused on polymeric NO donors and their therapeutic applications.

NO donor motifs like N-diazeniumdiolates (NONOates) [19], S-nitrosothiols (RSNOs) [20], and N-nitrosamines [21] are well studied. They mostly release NO in the presence of suitable exogenous (e.g., light, ultrasound) or endogenous (e.g., pH, glutathione (GSH)) triggers [22], which makes them preferable for target-specific delivery. NONOates are type of NO donors that release NO spontaneously in an aqueous medium. They possess short half-lives, and the polymeric systems are required to entrap these molecules in the core for the target-specific delivery. Synthetic RSNOs, commonly used as a vasodilator and angiogenic agents, are a class of molecules similar to endogenous NO-delivering motifs. On the other hand, N-nitrosamines have been used to eradicate bacterial cells and inhibit tumor growth. In vivo applications of NO-releasing motifs depend on factors like sustainable release, fewer side effects, biocompatibility, and systemic clearance from the body that must be addressed.

Among the multiple aspects of NO, in this chapter, we start with a brief deliberation on NO release mechanism of various small-molecule NO-donating motifs, followed by a more detailed discussion on various types of recently reported (2010-present) NO-delivering polymers for anticancer, antibacterial, and wound-healing activities.

Nitric oxide detection

The detection and measurement of NO became a crucial aspect of NO research since estimating its concentration is important to gain insight into the type of activity promoted. It is evident that NO concentration plays a pivotal role in therapeutic applications though the activity of NO in the biological system is not exhaustively understood. Continuous monitoring of NO in the biological milieu may provide a fascinating insight. Many techniques are available to detect NO directly or indirectly [23,24]. Griess assay is one of the oldest and a reliable methods to identify NO quantitatively [25]. This technique detects the concentration of nitrite (NO_2^-) generated in solution from the released NO. The NO_2^- reacts with the different constituents of the Griess reagent and generates an azo-dye having absorption at ca. 540 nm in an aqueous medium (Fig. 2). Another well-known technique is the fluorometric assay using certain *ortho*-diaminobenzene compounds. NO (or dinitrogen trioxide, N_2O_3 formed from the released NO) forms a triazole compound by reacting with these

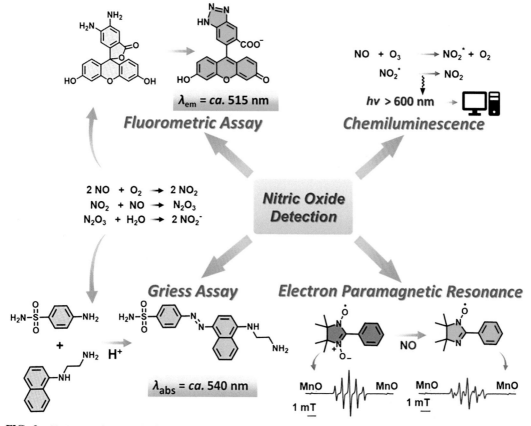

FIG. 2 Various techniques to detect NO in the biological system and solution phase. The electron paramagnetic resonance spectra were reproduced with the permission from *Duan Y, Wang Y, Li X, Zhang G, Zhanga G, Hu J. Light-triggered nitric oxide (NO) release from photoresponsive polymersomes for corneal wound healing. Chem Sci 2020;11:186–94.* Copyright (2020) Royal Chemical Society.

compounds [26]. The diaminofluorescein (DAF) is one such compound often used to trace NO in the cell (Fig. 2) [27]. Chemiluminescence analysis is also a convenient method for NO detection [11]. Along with the measurement of the NO concentration, this technique can determine the NO flux released from the NO donor. In general, the NO released from the NO donor reacts with the ozone (O_3) gas and produces excited-state nitrogen dioxide (NO_2^*), which returns to the ground state by releasing a photon. This technique quantifies the NO concentration by assessing the photon count (Fig. 2) [28]. Several other promising methods, viz. electron paramagnetic resonance spectroscopy, electrooxidation, and electroreduction, are also available to identify NO [23,29].

NO production in human body

It is noteworthy that all aspects of NO biosynthesis are not precisely understood yet. It is certain that the production and release rate of NO is modulated by intrinsic factors like autoinhibitory loop, extended C-terminus, CaM binding, heme involvement, and extrinsic factors, such as phosphorylation and interaction with various other proteins. L-arginine is the primary amino acid to produce NO in the mammalian body. The bioproduction of NO is catalyzed by nitric oxide synthase (NOS) and a panel of other factors like nicotinamide adenine dinucleotide phosphate (NADPH), tetrahydrobiopterin (BH4), flavin adenine dinucleotide (FAD), flavin mononucleotide (FMN), etc. [30]. The L-arginine generates NO and transforms into L-citrulline with the assistance of these substituents, NOS, and oxygen (O_2). The NOSs exist in many isoforms in the body and are categorized into two classes: constitutive and inducible. The constitutive NOS includes endothelial nitric oxide synthase (eNOS or NOS III) and neuronal nitric oxide synthase (nNOS or NOS I), whereas inducible nitric oxide synthase (iNOS or NOS II) is an example of the other class.

The eNOS is expressed mainly in the membrane of the endothelial cells, hippocampal pyramidal cells, and cardiac myocytes [31]. It promotes angiogenesis and vasodilation in smooth muscle cells and inhibits platelet aggregation. The nNOS is found in skeletal muscle cells and neurons, and primarily produces NO for neurotransmission. The iNOS can be expressed in many types of cells because of the immune response and is regulated by IL-1β (IL = interleukin), cytokines, tumor necrosis factor-α (TNF-α), lipopolysaccharide (LPS), etc. All the isoforms of NOS have 50%–60% similarities in their amino acid sequences [32]. The eNOS and nNOS have an autoinhibitory loop and extended C-terminus, which is absent in iNOS. All the NOS isoforms demand similar cofactors for their activation and NO production; however, the calcium ion (Ca^{2+})/calmodulin (CaM)-dependent activity is more prominent among the NOS. For example, the constitutive NOSs typically exhibit Ca^{2+}/CaM-dependent NO release, whereas the release from iNOS is Ca^{2+}/CaM independent. With the elevation of the Ca^{2+} concentration in the cell, Ca^{2+} binds to CaM, followed by the binding of Ca^{2+}/CaM to NOS. Thus, CaM plays a vital role in NO production from NOS, and the rate significantly decreases when CaM is absent. Primarily, it facilitates the electron transfer between the two domains of NOS and helps to reduce heme [32]. On the other hand, the iNOS has a higher affinity to bind with CaM, which is not Ca^{2+} dependent. Moreover, the NO release from constitutive NOS is lower than the concentration of NO released from the iNOS.

The NOS enzyme has two domains, oxygenase, and reductase, which are connected via a linker where the Ca^{2+}/CaM binding occurs. The oxygenase domain holds L-arginine, BH4, and tetracoordinate Zn^{2+}. On the other hand, the reductase domain has binding sites for FAD, FMN, and NADPH [32]. The generation of NO is typical P450 chemistry by which two monooxygenation reactions occur. In the first monooxygenation reaction, L-arginine produces N^{ω}-hydroxy-L-arginine (NOHA); and in the other, L-citrulline and NO production occur from NOHA (Fig. 3A). The detailed mechanism of NO production (Fig. 3B) is not precise and speculated based on specific evidence. For example, various experimental studies suggested the oxyferrous complex formation, donation of one electron by BH4 to the iron center of the heme, and NO release from ferrous NO complex occurs during the NO production by NOS [33]. In the first step, the iron center is activated by electron reduction, binds with the O_2, and produces oxyferryl porphyrin radical cation. Later, the BH4 donates one electron to the iron and eventually makes the peroxo-heme complex. It is anticipated that this complex abstracts the proton from the substrate, which acts as a driving force of the first monooxygenation reaction and yields NOHA [34]. The second monooxygenation reaction follows a similar pathway, and the NOHA produces ferrous NO complex and L-citrulline. Afterward, the reduction of BH4 takes place, and NO is released from the iron center. Typically, the NO release flux from the endothelial cells is $\sim(0.5\text{–}4) \times 10^{-10}\,mol\,cm^{-2}\,min^{-1}$ [10]. Since depending on the concentration of NO, the effect varies, researchers have focused on NO-releasing molecules spanning continuous release, burst release, and stimuli-based release.

NO-releasing small molecules

The modulation of NO concentration via controlled release is indispensable since various biomedical applications require different amounts of NO concentrations. Such variation may be achieved with NO donors of well-understood NO release profile. The most commonly studied small-molecule NO donors are NONOates, RSNOs, and N-nitrosamines (Fig. 4A) [35]. Besides, there are other familiar donors, viz. metal nitrosyl complexes, oximes, organic nitrates, and nitrites (Fig. 4A) useful for therapeutic applications and fabricating future generation NO-releasing drugs. This section discusses their design, synthesis, release process, and fate in the biological milieu.

N-diazeniumdiolates

The diazen-1-ium-1,2-diolates, commonly known as NONOates, can bind with various atoms, such as C, N, O, and S. They have attractive potential in NO-releasing efficacy. Typically, the NONOates are synthesized with secondary amines and gaseous NO at high pressure [36] (Fig. 4A). They often exhibit thermal and photodegradation in solution, but are stable in solid form. The NONOates readily release two equivalents of NO at physiological conditions. The release rate also increases in acidic conditions. The half-lives of these NO donors are dependent on the chemical configuration to a great extent. For example, the half-lives of proline-NONOate and diethylenetriamine-NONOate are 1.8 s and 20 h, respectively

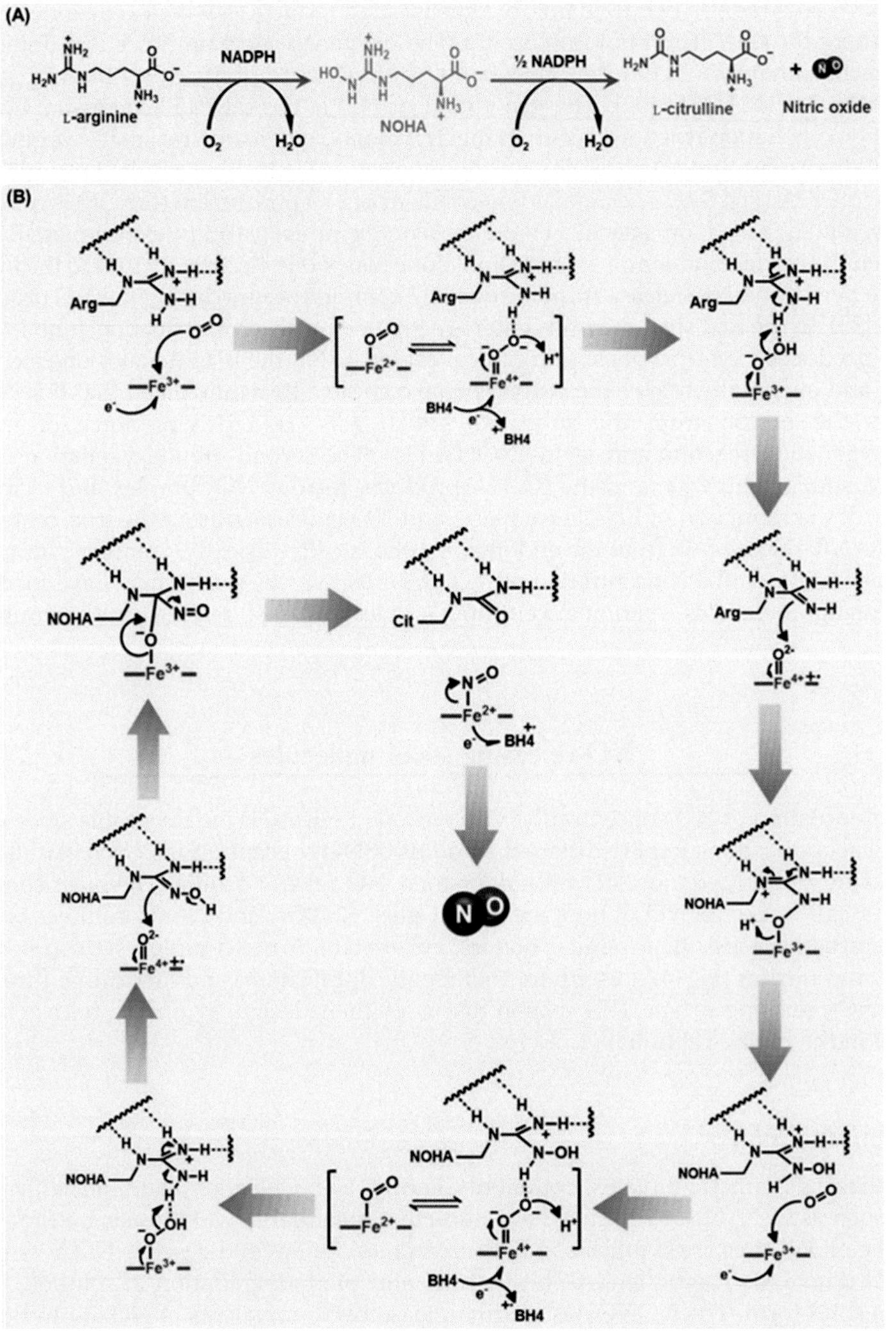

FIG. 3 (A) Overall NO production reaction from L-arginine; (B) plausible NO release mechanism in nitric oxide synthase (NOS).

(A)

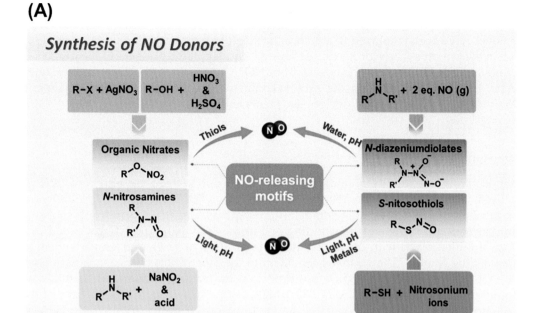

(B)

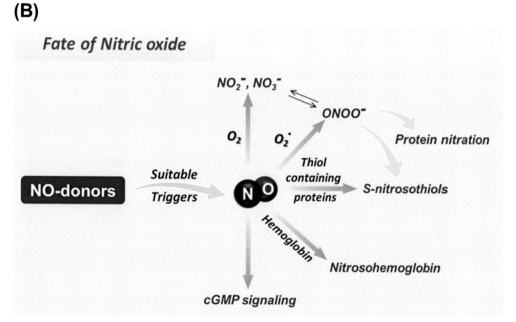

FIG. 4   (A) Synthetic strategies of different NO-releasing motifs and their triggers for NO release; (B) fate of NO in the biological systems.

I. Development of NO donors and derivatives, and new delivery formations

[36,37]. The two-terminal amine groups of diethylenetriamine-NONOate stabilize the NONOate motif with hydrogen bonding and cease the rapid degradation. Various suitable techniques have been employed to enhance the stability by introducing O^2-alkyl protecting group in these motifs. These protecting groups get cleaved in the presence of the triggers like enzymes or GSH [38,39]. The NO release from NONOates is proton-driven, and the release rate can be tuned by changing the proton abundance in the solution. Nevertheless, the NONOates are used in medical devices like stents and grafts.

S-nitrosothiols

Nitrosothiols, a naturally abundant NO donor in our system, are also conventionally employed for effective therapeutic applications. The endogenous RSNOs, viz. S-nitrosoalbumin, S-nitrosohemoglobin, S-nitrosoglutathione, and S-nitrosocysteine, are mainly helpful in storing and transporting NO in the body [40]. The NO generated in the biological milieu reacts with the thiol-containing proteins or GSH, and converts them into corresponding RSNOs. They transfer the NO into the other thiols by transnitrosation reactions [41]. Synthetically, the RSNOs are produced by reacting corresponding thiols with nitrosonium ions (e.g., nitrous acid (HNO_2), NO_2, N_2O_3, N_2O_4) (Fig. 4A) [42]. Many of these RSNOs are thermal- or photodegradable, and readily form disulfide compounds. However, some exceptions are S-nitrosoglutathione, S-nitroso-N-acetylpenicillamine, trityl thionitrite, and S-nitroso-L-cysteine. These artificially synthesized RSNOs are primarily red, pink, or green in color. They are generally characterized by nuclear magnetic resonance (NMR) and UV-Vis spectroscopy. The stability and NO-releasing properties of RSNOs depend on the chemical substituent of the α and β carbon atoms. The tertiary RSNOs are generally more stable than the primary ones [43] with a few exceptions. The NO release from these compounds is further facilitated upon exposure to various triggers like pH, light, heat, heavy metals, etc.

N-nitrosamines

This class of NO donors has achieved prosperity in recent years because of their stimuli-responsive behavior [44]. N-nitrosamines were first reported in the 19th century, and synthesized by the reaction between secondary amines and nitrosating agents (Fig. 4A). The commonly employed nitrosating agents are HNO_2, NOCl, N_2O_3, N_2O_4, $NO^+BF_4^-$, etc. [17]. Early findings implicated that the N-nitrosamines are genotoxic and cause DNA alkylation. Thus, this class of compounds was unexplored for many years. Later on, it was entrenched that these molecules exhibit NO-delivering property in the presence of light and pH. They are also competent in anticancer and antimicrobial activities [45,46] through DNA alkylating mechanism. The oxidases and oxygenase enzymes in the body convert N-nitrosamines to α-hydroxy-N-nitroso compounds. These compounds decompose and form diazonium intermediates, which causes DNA alkylation [17]. The stability of N-nitrosamines depends on the chemical configuration of the corresponding amines. Except for the heterocyclic and aromatic N-nitrosamines, the aliphatic N-nitrosamines are rarely stable [47]. They release NO through homolytic or heterolytic cleavage of the N–NO bond. However, the homolytic cleavage is more favored under photoirradiation.

Organic nitrates

The most famous molecule in this category is a simple one, nitroglycerin, a clinical drug. It is mostly used to treat angina pectoris and anal fissure [48,49]. Interestingly, this drug's NO-releasing property was unrevealed until the late 20th century. Organic nitrates are artificially synthesized by the reaction between the alkyl halide and silver nitrate or alcohols and nitric acid in the presence of sulfuric acid [11] (Fig. 4A). They exhibit both enzymatic and nonenzymatic stimuli-responsive release. A primary trigger for the NO release is thiol, which converts the organic nitrates into corresponding alcohol and releases NO. The cytochrome P450-related enzymes also induce these donors to release NO. Unfortunately, these donors develop "nitrate tolerance" in the body after repetitive utilization, and as a result, the influence of the drug gets attenuated [17]. Organic nitrates also show antiviral activity against the herpes simplex virus and vaccinia virus [50].

Other donors and the fate of NO

Apart from the above common NO donors, many different delivery platforms are reported that are competent enough for therapeutic applications. Among them, oxime [51], furoxans [52], organic nitrites [53], and metal nitrosyls [54] are in continuous development where proper design enables capability of stimuli-responsive release. The major drawback of the aforementioned type of NO donors is their low stability and tedious synthetic strategies. The comprehensive details of these NO donors are summarized in Table 1.

TABLE 1   Different types of NO donors, their triggers and therapeutic applications.

NO donors	Triggers	Applications	References
NONOates	Water and acidic pH	Antibacterial activity, wound healing activity, anticancer activity, vasodilation, etc.	[11,37,39]
RSNOs	Light, heat, metals (Cu^+, Fe^{2+})	Anticancer activity, inhibition of platelet aggregation, etc.	[11]
N-nitrosamines	pH, light	Primarily used for anticancer and antimicrobial activities because of their DNA alkylation property	[46]
Organic nitrates	Thiols	Treatment for anal fissure, angina, antiviral, and antiinflammatory activity; nitroglycerin is a commercially available drug	[48–50]
Metal nitrosyls	Mostly light	Treatment of blood pressure, heart failure, and plant physiology; sodium nitroprusside is another commercial drug from this class	[11,54]
Oximes	Thiols	Antimicrobial and anticancer activity	[51]

NO has a very short half-life; after being released from these delivery agents, it is transformed into various by-products (Fig. 4B). In the solution phase, NO readily reacts with the molecular O_2 and forms different nitrogen oxide derivatives (e.g., NO_2, N_2O_3, NO_2^-, NO_3^-, etc.). It also generates RNS by reacting with peroxy radicals. In the biological milieu, it readily binds with Hb and modifies proteins through nitrosylation reaction of thiol components. Although there are small-molecule NO donors with which it is possible to achieve NO release at various concentrations, target-specific release is scarce, thus opening the scope to control release and introduce target specificity by fabricating multifunctional polymeric NO-delivering vehicles. Such tailored molecules would also be crucial to understand the in vivo and in vitro mechanism of NO actions.

Polymeric NO donors

In the past two decades, scientists have been more concerned with syntheses of polymeric NO donors, which can exhibit burst, slow, or fast release via different triggers at specific targets to overcome the limitations of small-molecule NO donors. However, the small molecules are superior in contributing to the mechanism of release and fate of NO in the biological milieu. On the other hand, the polymeric NO donors have relatively high half-lives and shelf-lives [10]. In addition, introducing various desired functionality into these systems is beneficial for the targeted delivery of NO. For example, incorporating polyethylene glycol (PEG) in the polymer can enhance the biocompatibility and the solubility of the system in the biological environment.

Many macromolecular systems employed to deliver NO (Fig. 5) are broadly classified into inorganic and organic polymeric NO donors. The inorganic NO donors contain inorganic nanoparticles, metal-organic frameworks (MOFs), zeolites, etc. [55]. On the other hand, the organic polymeric NO donors include branched polymers, dendrimers, micelles, vesicles, liposomes, organic gels, and so on. Earlier, the fumed silica particles were employed to deliver NO. The surfaces of the fumed particles were functionalized with suitable amines and thiols, and the NONOate or RSNO motifs were synthesized [56,57]. These platforms had a higher half-life than the similar small-molecule NO donors. However, the size of these fumed particles was in the micrometer range. To overcome this issue, nanoparticles were fabricated mostly with silica [58], gold [59], and iron [60]. Primarily, these nanoparticles were used to prepare NONOate and RSNO-based NO-releasing platforms. Later on, nitrobenzene derivative-based motifs were also incorporated onto the nanoparticle surface, and they exhibited NO release through nitro to nitrite rearrangement under photoirradiation [61]. Albumin-based silica nanoparticles were reported where the vasodilatory compound linsidomine was incorporated into the system [62]. In the presence of GSH, linsidomine-conjugated silica nanoparticles underwent a self-immolative fragmentation reaction and released NO. They also exhibited cytosol selective NO release and tumor-specific cytotoxicity.

Among the inorganic macromolecular scaffolds, MOFs play a vital role because of their various interesting properties like catalysis, gas adsorption, and separations. In most cases, the NO adducts with the metal center of the MOFs, and the release takes place in suitable conditions [63]. The light-triggered NO-releasing MOFs were also fabricated with

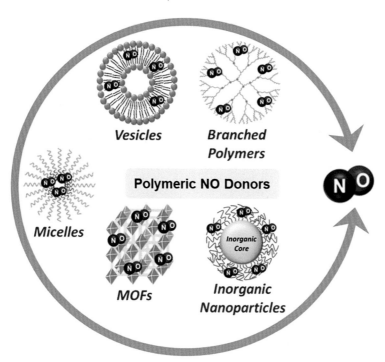

FIG. 5 Suitable macromolecular platforms for the NO delivery.

nitroimidazole derivatives, which showed NO release [64]. The nitroimidazole derivatives are generally less photoreactive; however, the reactivity is enhanced when they are organized in a crystalline framework. They are stable in ambient conditions, and under photoirradiation, the nitro group of the nitroimidazole derivatives was converted into nitrite. The NO release takes place due to the cleavage of the nitrite bond. NO-releasing motifs can be synthesized in the linker of the MOFs to achieve further enhancement in half-life and NO storing capacity [65].

Organic polymeric NO donors are another category of macromolecular NO donors with wide therapeutic applications. This class of NO delivery agents has high half-lives and payload. They are easily tuneable for targeted delivery. The codelivery of NO and drug molecules is also possible with these architectures. The first organic polymeric NO donor was reported by Parzuchowski et al. [66]. They prepared various copolymers with secondary amine-based monomers and methyl methacrylate. The secondary amine positions were functionalized with NONOates that had half-lives between 30 and 60 min. Apart from the NONOates, other NO donating motifs were installed on these polymers with minimal modifications.

Recent endeavors have led to polymeric stimuli-responsive NO donors to avoid premature NO leakage. Among them, light-triggered NO release gained much attention [67,68]. For example, our group has synthesized N-nitrosamine-based NO donors, PxNO, by modifying the PEG-conjugated styrene and maleic anhydride alternating copolymer [68] (Fig. 6). Typically, the styrene and maleic anhydride form alternating copolymers [69], and this NO-conjugated

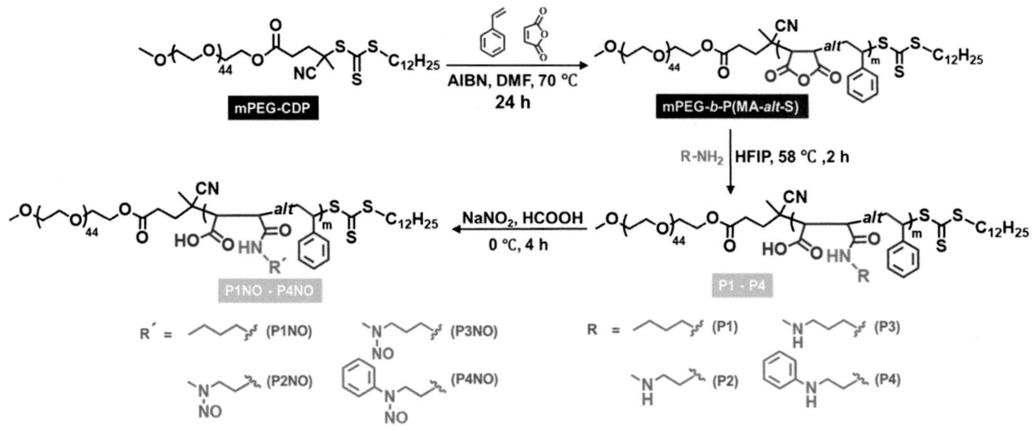

FIG. 6 Synthesis of various *N*-nitrosamine-based polymeric NO donors using reversible addition-fragmentation chain transfer (RAFT) polymerization technique. *Reproduced with the permission from Paul S, Pan S, Chakraborty A, De P, Mukherjee A. Ultraviolet light- or pH-triggered nitric oxide release from a water-soluble polymeric scaffold. ACS Appl Polym Mater 2021;3:2310–5. Copyright (2021) American Chemical Society.*

polymeric system releases NO in the presence of UV light and acidic pH. The release also showed temperature dependence. This study implicated that aromatic *N*-nitrosamines are much more stable and capable of the steady release of NO as compared to aliphatic *N*-nitrosamines.

Biomedical applications

The previous section discussion elucidates that the macromolecular NO donors, especially the organic polymeric NO-releasing platforms, are more beneficial for biomedical applications. Herein, we will discuss a few major applications of these systems where significant outcomes were perceived.

Anticancer

Cancer has one of the highest morbidity and mortality rate in the human population. Chemotherapy is a technique to fight this situation. Drugs like doxorubicin (DOX) and paclitaxel are used to eradicate cancer cells. Polymeric systems [70,71] and metal-based complexes [72] are also employed in anticancer therapeutics. However, many existing therapeutic techniques are impeded by the emergence of multidrug resistance (MDR) apart from toxic side effects. The plausible cause for the MDR is the overexpression of multidrug resistance-associated proteins (e.g., P-glycoprotein (P-gP), MDR1, canalicular multispecific organic anion transporters (cMOATs)) in the cancer cell. These proteins enhance the efflux of compounds sent from external sources inside the cells, viz. commercial drugs. Small interfering RNA (siRNA) or short-hairpin RNA (shRNA) therapy is a viable way to decrease the P-gP expression in cancer cells, which results in the reversal of MDR [73]. An alternate way is to inhibit P-gP and reverse MDR using NO therapy. NO can cause the nitrification of specific amino acids of the P-gP and inhibit their functions. Furthermore, a higher concentration of NO can be lethal for cancer cells. NO promotes the enhanced permeation and retention (EPR) effect by enhancing vasodilation in blood vessels. Thus, a higher amount of NO can be accumulated in the tumor site. To date, various suitable NO donors are reported for this application, where stimuli mostly govern the release.

One of the common strategies is to synthesize a polymeric platform associated with protected NONOates, where the release takes place by the deprotection of that group [74]. Park et al. synthesized a protected NONOate-based polymeric system that releases NO in the presence of GSH and pH [39]. In particular, they have separately prepared an O_2-protected NONOate-based small molecule, P-NO, and a diblock copolymer with PEG and phenylboronic acid (Fig. 7A). The P-NO was incorporated into the polymeric system by molecular recognition between the diol of P-NO and pendant phenylboronic acid of the polymer. The molecular recognition between the P-NO and phenylboronic acid dissociates at endolysosomal pH (pH $\sim$5) in cancer cells and releases the P-NO. Eventually, the NO release occurred when the GSH deprotected the P-NO in the cytosol at pH 7.4. Further investigation indicated that the NO release was impeded in the presence of GSH at pH 5.0, which confirmed that the NO release took place in the cytosol of the cancer cells. The reasonable

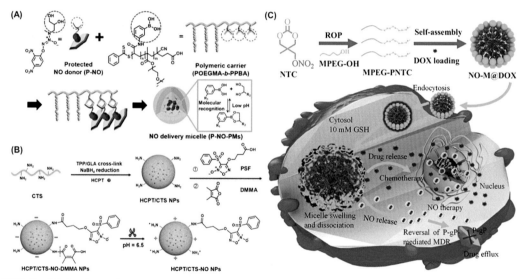

FIG. 7 (A) Synthesis of O_2-protected NONOate-based NO donor. Reproduced with the permission from Park D, Im S, Saravanakumar G, Lee YM, Kim J, Kim K, Lee J, Kim J, Kim WJ. A cyotosol-selective nitric oxide bomb as a new paradigm of an anticancer drug. Chem Commun 2019;55:14789–92. Copyright (2019) Royal Chemical Society. (B) Synthetic route of a chitosan-based HCPT loaded polymeric nanoparticle and its surface modification with dimethyl maleic anhydride (DMMA) and phenylsulfonyl furoxan. Reproduced with the permission from *Niu X, Cao J, Zhang Y, Gao X, Cheng M, Liu Y, Wang W, Yuan Z. A glutathione responsive nitric oxide release system based on charge-reversal chitosan nanoparticles for enhancing synergistic effect against multidrug resistance tumor. Nanomed Nanotechnol Biol Med 2019;20:1–12.* Copyright (2019) Elsevier. (C) Synthesis of PEG and nitrate trimethylene carbonate (NTC)-based block copolymer and their NO and DOX releasing property in the cancer cell. Reproduced with the permission from *Gao L, Dong B, Zhang J, Chen Y, Qiao H, Liu Z, Chen E, Dong Y, Cao C, Huang D, Chen W. Functional biodegradable nitric oxide donor-containing polycarbonate-based micelles for reduction-triggered drug release and overcoming multidrug resistance. ACS Macro Lett 2019;8:1552–8.* Copyright (2019) American Chemical Society.

explanation is that the nucleophilicity of the GSH decreases in acidic conditions; thus, it cannot deprotect the P-NO.

Recently, other types of NO donors, such as furoxan, were employed to construct the polymeric scaffold for GSH-responsive NO release [75]. A chitosan-based organic nanoparticle was prepared and loaded with an antitumor drug 10-hydroxycamptothecin (HCPT) in the system. The surface of the nanoparticles was modified with dimethyl maleic anhydride (DMMA) and phenylsulfonyl furoxan (Fig. 7B). The DMMA moiety gets cleaved at pH 6.5, and the nanoparticle showed charge reversal from negative to positive, aiming to enhance the cellular uptake of the nanoparticle. At the same time, the NO was released from phenylsulfonyl furoxan due to the intracellular GSH. This system also exhibited a significant cytotoxic effect against the MDR cancer cell line. The EPR effect and tumor regression efficacy of this organic nanoparticle were confirmed from the in vivo studies.

Since organic nitrate has the potential to release NO in the presence of GSH, a biodegradable organic nitrate-conjugated polymeric platform was prepared by Gao et al. [76] (Fig. 7C). They developed a polymer with PEG and nitrate trimethylene carbonate (NTC) using the ring-opening polymerization technique. Apart from stimuli-responsive NO release, they also incorporated DOX in the polymer to investigate the synergistic effect on tumor. The NO-delivering scaffolds exhibited conspicuous anticancer activity against the MDR cancer cell line by reducing the overexpression of P-gP and inhibiting the tumor growth. Following a similar strategy, another polymeric material was prepared where the cis-aconitine anhydride motif was introduced into the system [77]. Along with the DOX, they also encapsulated IR780, which is well known for photodynamic therapy (PDT) and photothermal therapy (PTT). A cis-aconitine anhydride motif is an acid-labile group that facilitates intracellular DOX release, and the NO delivery occurred due to GSH. The ROS generation by the IR780 under the near-infrared (NIR) laser irradiation boosted the anticancer activity of this system. In another study, Studenovsky et al. reported a set of organic nitrate-based NO donors, where the functional motifs were incorporated into the polymer architecture via postpolymerization modification reactions [78]. Primarily, they prepared a copolymer of N-(2-(hydroxypropyl) methacrylamide and 6-methacrylamidohexanohydrazide. Different organic nitrate compounds were prepared separately and attached to the polymer through a pH-sensitive hydrazone bond. The intracellular NO release was confirmed from fluorometric detection. It was also observed that the codelivery of NO and DOX significantly inhibited tumor growth in the mice model.

Another well-entrenched NO-releasing motif is RSNO. Although these motifs are mostly employed for cardiovascular applications, RSNO-based systems were recently reported for anticancer activities [79,80]. Deng and coworkers fabricated a block copolymeric system with PEG and polylysine with adamantane moiety [81]. Separately, the RSNO-conjugated β-cyclodextrin (β-CD) and Pt(IV) prodrug-conjugated β-CD were synthesized. The supramolecular nanoassemblies were prepared by the host-guest interaction between the block copolymer and modified β-CD moieties (Fig. 8A). The system released NO in the presence of GSH, and the Pt(II) drug was released due to the intracellular reduction. The release of NO in the cancer cell generated RNS, downregulating the abundance of glutathione, glutathione reductase, and xeroderma pigmentosum group A. This decreased the possibility of repairing the DNA damage by Pt(II) drugs or the sequestration and deactivation of the Pt(II) drugs by the thiols. The codelivery of NO and Pt(IV) prodrugs exhibited anticancer

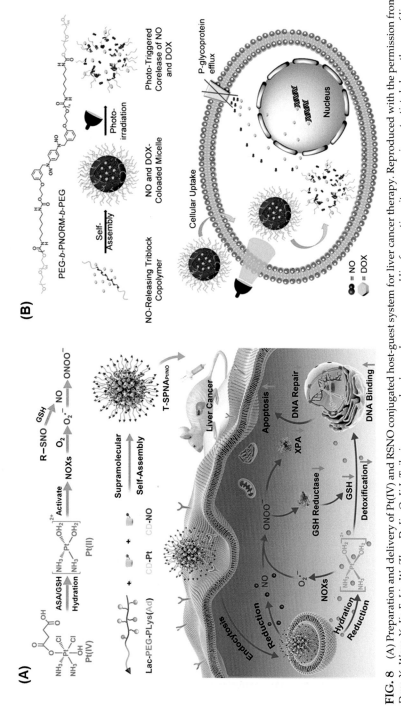

FIG. 8 (A) Preparation and delivery of Pt(IV) and RSNO conjugated host-guest system for liver cancer therapy. Reproduced with the permission from *Deng Y, Wang Y, Jia F, Liu W, Zhou D, Jin Q, Ji J. Tailoring supramolecular prodrug nanoassemblies for reactive nitrogen species-potentiated chemotherapy of liver cancer. ACS Nano 2021;15:8663–75.* Copyright (2021) American Chemical Society. (B) Synthesis of photoinducible N-nitrosamine-based polymeric NO donor and co-delivery of NO and DOX in the cancer cell for chemotherapeutic applications. Reproduced with the permission from *Ding Z, He K, Duan Y, Shen Z, Cheng J, Zhang G, Hu J. Photo-degradable micelles for co-delivery of nitric oxide and doxorubicin. J Mater Chem B 2020;8:7009–17.* Copyright (2020) Royal Chemical Society.

activity, and in vivo studies anticipated that these nanoassemblies could be beneficial for treating liver cancer.

Exogenous stimuli like light and ultrasounds were also proven potential triggers for cancer therapy. The small-molecular NO donors, when encapsulated in the core of the polymeric system, release NO after the stimuli-triggered degradation of the polymeric aggregates. BNN6, an *N*-nitrosamine-based small molecule, was incorporated in the polydopamine and PEG-based nanocarrier, which released NO in the presence of NIR irradiation [82]. They reported that the DOX-loaded nanocarrier and BNN6-loaded nanocarrier exhibited potential anticancer activity under NIR irradiation via downregulation of apoptotic inhibitory protein, B-cell lymphoma-2 (Bcl-2) and upregulation of apoptosis-promoting protein, Caspase-3. The high-intensity-focused ultrasound-responsive *N*-heterocyclic carbene-based NO donors were prepared by Kang et al. [83]. The moiety and DOX were encapsulated in a polymer fabricated with PEG and polycaprolactone. The synergistic effect of high-intensity-focused ultrasound stimulated NO and DOX, eventually inhibited tumor growth in the mice model. Ding et al. reported a triblock copolymer where the light-responsive *N*-nitrosamine-based NO donor was covalently attached to the polymer [84] (Fig. 8B). The polymer released NO under 410-nm light irradiation, and the release saturated after 30 min. The total amount of NO release was around 100 μM from 0.1 g/L polymer solution. The codelivery of NO and DOX exhibited MDR reversal in the cancer cell and antitumor activity. Thus, codelivery of NO with commercial drugs is more effective for chemotherapeutic applications, since NO also has a substantial effect in overcoming the MDR in cancer cells and in vasodilation to get more drug in the cancer cells. Although both the endogenous and exogenous stimuli for NO release were employed for anticancer therapy, there are a few limitations for endogenous triggers, such as less selectivity and slow NO release rate. Overall, introducing multi-desired motifs in polymeric systems and clever designing is useful to overcome the lacunae and generate better delivery vehicles for concomitant release of other drugs along with NO.

Antibacterial

Nitric oxide assists bacteria in building resistance to antibiotics and protects them from oxidative stress [85]. It may be synthesized in the bacterial cells from L-arginine via bacterial nitric oxide synthase (bNOS). The development of antibiotic resistance of bacterial cells provided the pace for designing an alternative way to eradicate the bacterial cells and the dispersal of biofilms. Although many cationic charge pendant polymeric systems were developed for this application [86], systematic studies imparted that delivering NO at higher concentrations can be a potential strategy. High concentration of exogenous NO renders bactericidal effect because of its RNS generation ability. The RNS, such as $ONOO^-$ and N_2O_3, react with the amine and thiol components of amino acids and cause nitrosation. The oxidative damage in bacterial DNA and damage to the cell membrane by inducing lipid peroxidation results in bacterial cell death [87].

Biofilm is an aggregate of microorganisms protected by extracellular polymeric substance (EPS) and resistant to most conventional antibacterial drugs. Thus, biofilm-related infections are hard to treat. Attachment, colonization, maturing, and dispersal are the four crucial stages of the biofilm life cycle [88] (Fig. 9A). Low NO concentration is employed for the biofilm dispersal. However, the mechanism of action is not yet clearly understood. Several studies supported that the intracellular second-messenger cyclic-diguanylate-guanosine monophosphate (c-di-GMP) plays a pivotal role in regulating biofilm formation. It is evident that the increase in the concentration of c-di-GMP enhances biofilm formation and the decrease in the intracellular concentration of c-di-GMP facilitates the dispersal of bacteria [89]. The low concentration of NO delivery on the biofilm activates bacterial phosphodiesterase, which halts the function of c-di-GMP. As a result, the bacteria go into the planktonic mode, and the codelivery of commercial drugs with NO can eradicate the bacterial cells.

Suitable NO-releasing multifunctional polymers showed potential for antibacterial activity. Sun et al. reported a series of poly(propyleneimine)-based NO-releasing dendrimers, where they had varied the generation number of dendrimer and exterior functionality [90]. The NO storing capacity of these systems was 1.1–3.8 μmol/mg, and the half-lives varied from 0.7 to 1.7 h. The NO-conjugated styrene oxide-functionalized dendrimers exhibited the highest antibacterial activity against Gram-positive *Staphylococcus aureus*, Gram-negative *Pseudomonas aeruginosa*, and methicillin-resistant *Staphylococcus aureus* (MRSA). The bactericidal effect was primarily observed because of NO release, the cationic charges of the dendrimer, and hydrophobicity due to the presence of styrene oxide. It was also evident that balanced hydrophilicity and lipophilicity were the main governing factors for the antibacterial activity of these cationic dendrimers. Similarly, poly-(amidoamine)-based NO-delivering dendrimers were also studied, where the chain end was tailored with propylene oxide, 1,2-epoxy-9-decene [91]. The NO payload of the NO-conjugated dendrimers was ~1 μmol/mg, and the half-lives were ~1 h. The balanced hydrophilic and hydrophobic modifications in these NO-conjugated dendrimers were proven beneficial in eradicating the planktonic and biofilm of *P. aeruginosa*. Later studies also supported that the propylene oxide-modified hyperbranched poly-(amidoamine) had significant antibacterial activity against Gram-negative periodontal pathogens and Gram-positive cariogenic bacteria [92]. The hyperbranched polyaminoglycosides-based NO-releasing platforms were also developed for similar applications [93].

Nguyen and coworkers have fabricated a polymeric system with the reversible addition-fragmentation chain transfer (RAFT) polymerization technique [94]. They coupled the antibiotic drug gentamicin in the pendant chains of the polymer, and the free amine groups of gentamicin were functionalized with NONOates (Fig. 9B). The codelivery of gentamicin and NO in the physiological conditions caused the eradication of *P. aeruginosa* biofilms and dispersed bacteria. In another study, an antibacterial polymer was prepared with hydrophobic aliphatic chain, PEG, and primary amine-containing moieties [95]. The NONOate functionalization was carried out on the primary amine moieties. Although these NONOates were less stable, freshly prepared NO-conjugated polymer exhibited antibacterial activity against *P. aeruginosa*, known to cause infection in hospital patients. A star polymer was also prepared using the RAFT polymerization technique for a similar purpose [96]. The NONOate functionalization was performed to incorporate these motifs into the core of star polymers to enhance the half-life of the NO release.

The other NO-releasing motifs, RSNOs, were not explored readily for antibacterial activities. In a few cases, small-molecular RSNOs were also incorporated into the polymeric matrix for such applications [97]. Pelegrino et al. synthesized a chitosan-based RSNO-conjugated

(A)

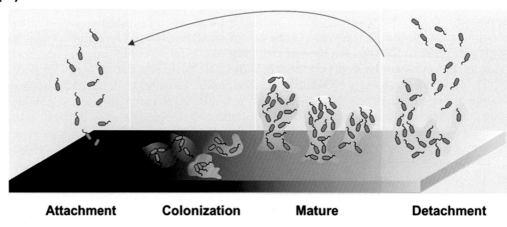

Attachment   **Colonization**   **Mature**   **Detachment**

(B)

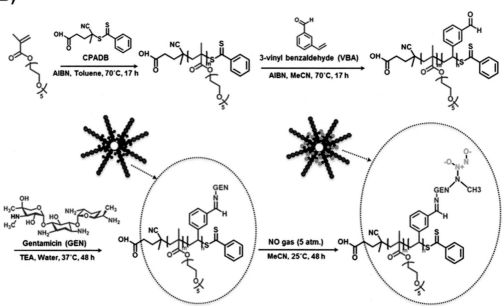

FIG. 9   (A) Different stages of biofilm formation by bacteria. Reproduced with the permission from *Wo Y, Brisbois EJ, Bartlett RH, Meyerhoff ME. Recent advances in thromboresistant and antimicrobial polymers for biomedical applications: just say yes to nitric oxide (NO). Biomater Sci 2016;4:1161–83.* Copyright (2016) Royal Chemical Society. (B) Synthetic strategy to prepare the Gentamicin-conjugated NONOate-based polymeric NO donor using RAFT polymerization technique. Reproduced with the permission from *Nguyen T-K, Selvanayagam R, Ho KKK, Chen R, Kutty SK, Rice SA, Kumar N, Barraud N, Duong HTT, Boyer C. Co-delivery of nitric oxide and antibiotic using polymeric nanoparticles. Chem Sci 2016;7:1016–27.* Copyright (2016) Royal Chemical Society.

I. Development of NO donors and derivatives, and new delivery formations

polymeric system that released NO at physiological conditions [98]. The antibacterial property was evaluated for chitosan, thiolated chitosan, and S-nitroso chitosan against *Escherichia coli*, *Staphylococcus aureus*, and *Streptococcus mutans*. The S-nitroso chitosan exhibited the highest antibacterial potency among all the polymers. In another study, S-nitroso-N-acetylpenicillamine covalently attached to the polyacrylonitrile fibers [99] showed antibacterial property by reducing the adhesion of *Staphylococcus aureus* bacteria.

Recently, N-nitrosamine-based polymeric materials have been broadly used for antibacterial applications. Shen et al. synthesized amphiphilic diblock copolymer with PEG and coumarin-coupled monomer to deliver NO and ciprofloxacin (Cip) [100]. The visible light (410nm) triggered NO and Cip release from the polymer, eradicated the bacterial strain of *P. aeruginosa*, and facilitated the biofilm dispersion. The same group also developed a visible light (410nm) triggered NO-releasing polymeric system with tetraphenylethylene for a similar purpose [101], exhibiting potential antibiofilm activity against *P. aeruginosa*. Another type of diblock copolymer was prepared (Fig. 10) for such application [102]. The NO release took place from the polymer in the presence of visible light (410nm). Afterward, the formaldehyde was also released due to the self-immolative degradation of the polymer system (Fig. 10B). The simultaneous release of NO and formaldehyde readily killed *E. coli* and *Staphylococcus aureus*.

Although significant development has been accomplished to prepare the antibacterial NO-releasing polymers with NONOates, they are less stable and cause premature leakage. However, the light-triggered N-nitrosamine-based polymeric NO donors and nitroaniline-based systems [103] were also exploited for antibacterial activity. The results suggest that stimuli-responsive NO-releasing polymers should be explored more to achieve desirable control over the NO release.

Wound healing

Wound healing is the reestablishment of tissue integrity after some injury or damage caused by any external forces or bacterial infections. This process includes many phases, viz. hemostasis, inflammation, proliferation, and remodeling [104]. Recent studies suggest that NO has unique effects on wound healing [105]; however, the mechanism of action is not explicit. Systematic studies unveiled that the iNOS expression is enhanced in the early phase of wound healing due to the inflammatory response or cytokine signaling [106]. It was showed that the treatment of NOS inhibitor at the wounded site impaired the wound repair [107]. Suitable NO concentration enhances collagen deposition, proliferation, and angiogenesis, the predominant factors for wound healing. The NO donor incorporation in the wound dressing facilitates healing and inhibits bacterial growth.

Kang et al. prepared the NO donors with Pluronic F127, and NONOate-conjugated branched polyethyleneimine [108]. They incorporated the NO donor into PEG ointment to enhance the half-life of the donor. The PEG ointment provides moisture to the wounded area and eventually improves the healing process. The NO storing capacity of this NO donor containing PEG ointment was 95.8nmol/mg. It was evident from the study that the system indeed accelerated the healing process through re-epithelialization, granulation formation, collagen deposition, and improved angiogenesis.

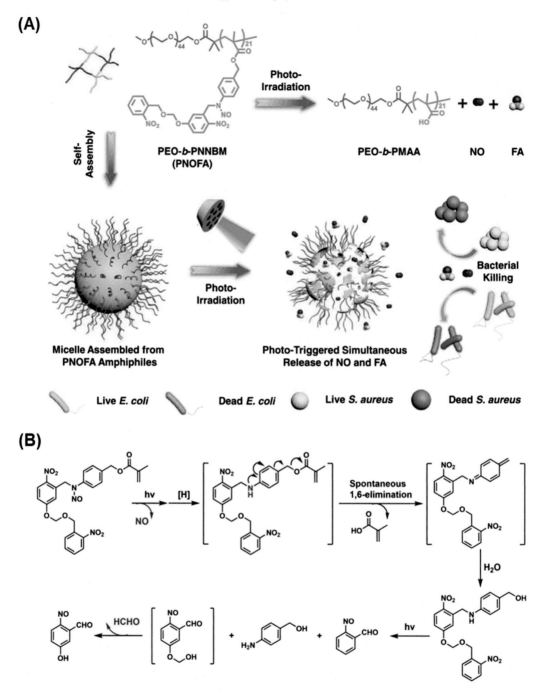

FIG. 10 (A) Representative diagram of antibacterial activity of *N*-nitrosamine-based amphiphilic diblock copolymer; (B) self-immolative degradation of the functional motif after photo-irradiation, which resulted in NO and formaldehyde release. *Reproduced with the permission from Duan Y, He K, Zhang G, Hu J. Photoresponsive micelles enabling codelivery of nitric oxide and formaldehyde for combinatorial antibacterial applications. Biomacromolecules 2021;22: 2160–70. Copyright (2021) American Chemical Society.*

I. Development of NO donors and derivatives, and new delivery formations

Similar work was carried out by Zhang et al., where NONOate-conjugated hyperbranched polymer was prepared with polyethyleneimine, having the NO payload of 0.57 μmol/mg [109]. The NO release from the polymer was tuned by varying the pH of the solution. This biocompatible polymer accelerated cutaneous wound healing when applied with PEG oint-ment. However, in most cases, the polymeric NO donors were prepared for antibacterial wound repairing. For example, hyaluronic acid biopolymer was modified with alkylamine moieties, and the NONOates motifs were functionalized on the secondary amine positions [110]. Hyaluronic acid is a polysaccharide of D-glucuronic acid and N-acetyl-D-glucosamine residues found in healthy tissues. The hyaluronic acid-based NO donors exhibited NO stor-ing capacity of 0.3–0.6 μmol NO/mg with the half-lives in the range of 5–75 min. These NO-conjugated biopolymers were proven potential antibacterial agents against common wound pathogens. The studies also emphasized that the polymer could accelerate the healing of *P. aeruginosa*-infected wounds.

Li and coworkers also prepared the RSNO-based polymeric platform for wound-healing applications [111]. They covalently attached the GSH or phytochelatins, a derivative of GSH, with the poly(vinyl methyl ether-*co*-maleic anhydride), and prepared the interpolymer complex with these modified polymer and poly(vinyl pyrrolidone). Typically, the RSNOs degrade and release NO in the presence of light, heat, and metals. However, their NO-conjugated interpolymer complex was stable and exhibited NO release for up to 10 days. The in vivo studies on diabetic mice supported the wound-healing property of the polymer.

In another study, Hu and coworkers prepared different NO carriers with PEG and poly-peptide [112]. The chlorin e6 and RSNO motifs were synthesized by modifying α-cyclodextrin (α-CD), and the modified α-CDs were then incorporated into the polymer via host-guest interactions (Fig. 11A). The RSNO motif showed NO release in the presence of GSH. The study implicated that the NO release and PDT, using chlorin e6, eradicated MRSA biofilms and accelerated the wound healing caused by MRSA biofilm. After the NO release, the RSNOs also decreased the local concentration of GSH by forming disulfide bonds (Fig. 11A), and eventually, PDT efficiency was improved.

Light-triggered *N*-nitrosamine-based NO-releasing polymers were also designed for wound repairing and mostly for recovering bacterial wounds. For example, Sun et al. synthe-sized covalent organic frameworks (COFs) with porphyrin units and 2,3,6,7,10,11-triphenylenehexol [113] (Fig. 11B). Further, *N*-nitrosamine-based small-molecular NO donor, BNN6, was encapsulated in the system, which shows light-triggered NO release. The porphyrin-based COF itself can be used for PDT and PTT under 635-nm red light irradiation. The synergistic effect of PDT, PTT, and NO delivery resulted in antibacterial ac-tivity against *E. coli* and *Staphylococcus aureus*. In addition, the NO recovered the *Staphylococ-cus aureus*-infected wound by upregulating α-smooth muscle actin (α-SMA), cluster of differentiation 31 (CD31), promoting collagen deposition and angiogenesis. In a separate study, coumarin-based *N*-nitrosamine was prepared in the polymeric system and applied for similar applications [114]. However, photoredox catalysis was used for NO generation in this case. Along with the coumarin-based NO donors, palladium(II) tetraphenyltetraben-zoporphyrin was also conjugated in the polymer. After the red light (630 or 700 nm) irradi-ation, the photoredox catalysis took place between the porphyrin derivative and NO-conjugated coumarin derivative, which resulted in NO release and showed wound-healing properties caused by bacterial infection. The same group also fabricated a *N*-nitrosamine-

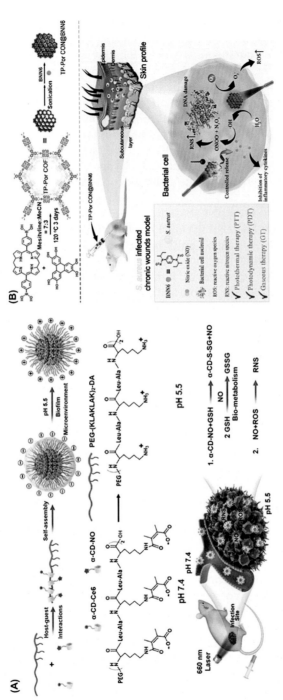

FIG. 11 (A) Synthetic diagram of NO delivering nanocarrier containing RSNO conjugated α-cyclodextrin (α-CD), chlorin e6 conjugated α-CD, and block copolymer of PEG and polypeptide; the charge reversal mechanism of the block copolymer; schematic representations of bacterial wound healing caused by MRSA. Reproduced with the permission from *Hu D, Deng Y, Jia F, Jin Q, Ji J. Surface charge switchable supramolecular nanocarriers for nitric oxide synergistic photodynamic eradication of biofilms. ACS Nano 2020;14:347–59.* Copyright (2020) American Chemical Society. (B) Schematic representations for synthesizing BNN6 encapsulated porphyrin-based COFs and their application in bacteria caused wound healing. Reproduced with the permission from *Sun B, Ye Z, Zhang M, Song Q, Chu X, Gao S, Zhang Q, Jiang C, Zhou N, Yao C, Shen J. Light-activated biodegradable covalent organic framework-integrated heterojunction for photodynamic, photothermal, and gaseous therapy of chronic wound infection. ACS Appl Mater Interfaces 2021;13:42396–410.* Copyright (2021) American Chemical Society.

based block copolymer with PEG, which showed NO release under 365-nm UV light irradiation and stimulated corneal wound healing [67].

Although the involvement of NO in the wound-healing process is evident from the above discussion, a clear picture of its mechanism is yet to be revealed. Most of the polymers were synthesized for repairing the bacterially infected wound. The studies reveal that NO significantly affects antibacterial activity, granulation tissue formation, collagen deposition, and angiogenesis. Hence, the NO-releasing polymer-blended dressing materials benefit topical wound healing and recovering bacterial wounds.

Antiinflammatory

In normal conditions, NO acts as an antiinflammatory agent in the body; however, the abnormal production of NO in adverse conditions exhibits proinflammatory activities [115]. Typically, nonsteroidal antiinflammatory drugs (NSAIDs) are used for inflammatory diseases, which inhibit the cyclooxygenase (COX) pathway and prostaglandin synthesis. The long-term use of NSAIDs may exhibit gastrointestinal, renal, and hepatic side effects [116]. NO has a significant role in increasing the renal blood flow and protecting the renal system. It also protects the stomach and decreases the gastrointestinal toxicity caused by NSAIDs. To combat such situations, the employment of NO-releasing NSAIDs is a potential alternative [117].

To establish the antiinflammatory activities of NO, various polymeric donors were prepared. For example, Oh et al. prepared a NONOate-based system with poly(lactic-*co*-glycolic acid) and branched polyethylenimine NONOates [118] (Fig. 12A). To impede the burst release from NONOate motifs, the branched polyethylenimine NONOates were encapsulated in the nanoparticles of poly(lactic-*co*-glycolic acid). The NO release was facilitated in acidic conditions, and the half-lives varied from 0.16 to 0.38 h. The antiinflammatory activity of the polymer was investigated in peripheral blood mononuclear cells (PBMCs). The treatment of these NO-releasing nanoparticles downregulated the expression of proinflammatory cytokines, such as IL-6 and TNF-α. The NO release flux of the nanoparticles in cells was $0.098 \, \text{nmol cm}^{-2} \, \text{min}^{-1}$, comparable to the NO flux from eNOS in normal conditions. Organic nitrate-terminated poly(amidoamine)-based dendrimers (Fig. 12B) were also used for such purpose, and the dendrimer exhibited NO release in the presence of cysteine [119]. In human THP-1 cells, the inflammatory cytokine IL-8 was produced by the stimulation with LPS. The dendrimer exhibited antiinflammatory activities in the concentration range of $(1.17-7.50) \times 10^4 \, \text{nM}$ of NO motif of the dendrimer by inhibiting the IL-8 secretion of 13.7%–27.9%. However, the monomer 3-nitroxypropylammonium nitrate exhibited proinflammatory activities over 62.5 nM concentration.

The NO displays paradoxical activities in inflammatory responses, and the effect solely depends on the NO concentration. Thus, more rigorous studies need to be carried out to establish the antiinflammatory activities of NO. The NO delivery along with the antiinflammatory drugs may be beneficial in such applications to overcome the side effects of these drugs.

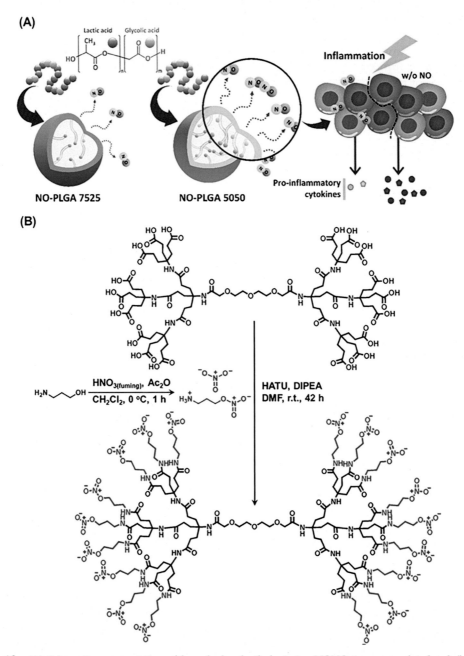

FIG. 12 (A) Schematic representation of branched polyethylenimine NONOates encapsulated poly(lactic-*co*-glycolic acid) nanoparticles and their NO release properties. Reproduced with the permission from *Oh Y, Jeong H, Lim S, Hong J. Controlled nitric oxide release using poly(lactic-co-glycolic acid) nanoparticles for anti-inflammatory effects. Biomacromolecules 2020;21:4972–9.* Copyright (2020) American Chemical Society. (B) Synthesis of organic nitrate terminated poly(amidoamine)-based dendrimers. Reproduced with the permission from *Porras AMG, Bertuzzi DL, Lucas K, Silva LCE, Oliveira MG, Ornelas C. Nitric oxide-releasing polyamide dendrimer with anti-inflammatory activity. ACS Appl Polym Mater 2020;2:2027–34.* Copyright (2020) American Chemical Society.

I. Development of NO donors and derivatives, and new delivery formations

Other effects

Apart from the aforementioned applications, NO-releasing materials can be employed for other purposes. For example, Mowery and coworkers prepared NO-releasing hydrophobic polymer with polyurethane and poly(vinyl chloride) to improve the thromboresistivity [120]. They prepared a series of NONOate-conjugated motifs and incorporated them into the polymer matrix through dispersion, covalent attachment, and ion-pairing approaches. The NONOate-based hydrophobic films prepared via dispersion and covalent attachment showed thromboresistant properties by inhibiting the platelet activation and adhesion.

Interestingly, NO was also employed as a mucolytic agent, i.e., reduction of elasticity and viscosity of the mucus. In various respiratory diseases, thick and highly viscous mucus is produced, which can cause choking of the airways and increase the possibilities of bacterial colonization. To mitigate the problem, Ahonen et al. prepared a series of biopolymers with secondary amine-functionalized low-molecular-weight alginates [121]. They coupled various secondary amines with the alginates and synthesized NONOate motifs. The NONOate-conjugated biopolymers had NO storing capacity of 0.3–0.5 μmol/mg with the half-lives in the range of 0.1–2.4 h. The study implicated that a higher NO concentration can cause more reduction of viscoelasticity of the mucus. However, a slow and sustained release of NO is needed for longer retention of the mucolytic effect.

In another study, furoxan-conjugated polymeric architectures were prepared, and the NO release was observed in the presence of thiols (e.g., cysteine and GSH) [122]. The furoxan derivatives were synthesized, and the PEG chain was conjugated with the furoxan moieties with a "click" reaction. Along with the thiols, the system also showed NO release in the presence of the cell lysate of murine macrophages. The antiproliferative activity of the compound was also investigated in human colon cancer cells, HT-29. The study revealed that minor enhancement in antiproliferative activity occurred when the HT-29 cells were treated with the furoxan-conjugated polymer and ibuprofen, a well-known NSAID. Although there are many other well-established applications of NO, few of them were investigated in the polymeric system. Numerous applications are related to the fabrication of medical devices [123]; however, in most cases, the small-molecular NO donors are bound to the polymeric materials to achieve the purposes.

Conclusion and future perspectives

We have discussed the role of the endogenous gasotransmitter NO in various biological phenomena. The plethora of the concentration-dependent activities discloses the paradoxical nature of opposite activity induced by alteration in NO concentration. A low NO concentration can decrease platelet aggregation or increase angiogenesis, proliferation, and tumor growth. On the other hand, the high concentration of NO can cause DNA damage, apoptosis, and increase oxidative stress. Several suitable NO-releasing small molecules were synthesized to achieve proper control of the local concentration of the delivered NO. Later, several polymeric NO donors were fabricated to overcome the limitation of target-specific delivery and shorter solution half-lives faced by small-molecule NO donors. The results showcased the effectiveness of the polymeric NO donors in various biomedical applications. The polymer-based NO donors stretched the NO storing capacity, half-lives, biocompatibility, and bioavailability. Further demand for better control on NO release led to the development of stimuli-responsive NO-releasing polymeric architectures with improved target-specific NO release in the biological milieu.

In addition to enhanced aqueous solubility and controllable molecular weight, polymeric scaffolds offer the establishment of multifunctionality in the system; thus, the release of a different class of drugs can take place along with NO simultaneously to enhance the efficacy. Various potential NO donors were synthesized, which displayed moderate-to-excellent anticancer, antibacterial, and wound-healing properties. Although many of the polymers showed excellent effectiveness in various biomedical applications, a considerable number of factors need to be clarified before their therapeutic applications.

First, the polymers synthesized for NO delivery are mostly NONOate- and RSNOs-based. More small-molecule donors capable of stimuli-responsive NO release are yet to be explored in conjugation with the polymeric system. The recent flourishment with stimuli-responsive NO-releasing motifs (e.g., organic nitrates, *N*-nitrosamines, etc.) attached to polymer architectures warrants more work to optimize the stimuli-responsive polymers with sustained NO release for biomedical applications. Second, the required NO concentrations for various biomedical applications are known, but a deeper and more precise understanding of the mechanism of action of NO is needed to tailor the needs of a particular application. Third, in most cases, the NO release profiles of the newly synthesized polymeric NO donors require more experimentation to avoid the adverse effect of NO, in in vitro or in vivo studies. Moreover, newer methodologies need to be explored to prevent premature leaching and loss of specificity while incorporating small-molecular NO donors in the polymer system. The target specificity of the polymer can be enhanced by exploiting the multifunctional nature of polymer chains used in synthesizing NO-delivering polymers. Fourth, improvements in NO detection techniques are required. Most of the detection methods measure the NO concentration indirectly. It is essential to design a detection method that will be cheap, selective toward NO, and could precisely measure the NO concentration directly.

Finally, apart from investigating new polymeric NO donors, it would also be beneficial to prepare some polymeric materials that would increase the endogenous NO production from its precursors at the target-specific site. It is evident that NO has excellent potential in various biomedical applications. Systematic studies, including pharmacokinetics and pharmacodynamics of the polymeric NO donors, and the employment of biopolymers and biodegradable polymers in their preparation, would increase the efficacy and help streamline the lab bench to clinical transformation to reduce the risks and permit future therapeutic applications.

Acknowledgment

SP acknowledges the Government of India for Prime Minister's Research Fellowship (PMRF). AM acknowledges SERB CRG/2021/001118.

References

[1] Furchgott RF, Zawadzki JV. The obligatory role of endothelial cells in the relaxation of arterial smooth muscle by acetylcholine. Nature 1980;288:373–6.

[2] Katsuki S, Arnold W, Mittal C, Murad F. Stimulation of guanylate cyclase by sodium nitroprusside, nitroglycerin and nitric oxide in various tissue preparations and comparison to the effects of sodium azide and hydroxylamine. J Cycl Nucl Prot Phosphoryl Res 1977;3:23–5.

[3] Palmer R, Ferrige A, Moncada S. Nitric oxide release accounts for the biological activity of endothelium-derived relaxing factor. Nature 1987;327:524–6.

[4] Ignarro LJ, Byrns RE, Buga GM, Wood KS. Endothelium-derived relaxing factor from pulmonary artery and vein possesses pharmacologic and chemical properties identical to those of nitric oxide radical. Circ Res 1987;61:866–79.

[5] Ignarro LJ, Buga GM, Wood KS, Byrns RE, Chaudhuri G. Endothelium-derived relaxing factor produced and released from artery and vein is nitric oxide. Proc Natl Acad Sci U S A 1987;84:9265–9.

[6] Lundberg JO, Weitzberg E, Gladwin MT. The nitrate-nitrite-nitric oxide pathway in physiology and therapeutics. Nat Rev Drug Discov 2008;7:156–67.

[7] Helms C, Kim-Shapiro DB. Hemoglobin-mediated nitric oxide signaling. Free Radic Biol Med 2013;61:464–72.

[8] Noack E, Kubitzek D, Kojda G. Spectrophotometric determination of nitric oxide using hemoglobin. Neuroprotocols 1992;1:133–9.

[9] Carpenter AW, Schoenfisch MH. Nitric oxide release: Part II. Therapeutic applications. Chem Soc Rev 2012;41:3742–52.

[10] Seabra AB, Justo GZ, Haddad PS. State of the art, challenges and perspectives in the design of nitric oxide-releasing polymeric nanomaterials for biomedical applications. Biotechnol Adv 2015;33:1370–9.

[11] Paul S, Pan S, Mukherjee A, De P. Nitric oxide releasing delivery platforms: design, detection, biomedical applications and future possibilities. Mol Pharm 2021;18:3181–205.

[12] Yang T, Zelikin AN, Chandrawati R. Progress and promise of nitric oxide-releasing platforms. Adv Sci 2018;5:1701043.

[13] Wink DA, Vodovotz Y, Laval J, Laval F, Dewhirst MW, Mitchell JB. The multifaceted roles of nitric oxide in cancer. Carcinogenesis 1998;19:711–21.

[14] Forstermann U, Sessa WC. Nitric oxide synthases: regulation and function. Eur Heart J 2012;33:829–37.

[15] Qian Y, Matson JB. Gasotransmitter delivery via self-assembling peptides: treating diseases with natural signaling gases. Adv Drug Deliv Rev 2017;110:137–56.

[16] Chun-tao Y, Li C, Shi X, Jacob JD, Xiang L, Ming X. Recent development of hydrogen sulfide releasing/stimulating reagents and their potential applications in cancer and glycometabolic disorders. Front Pharmacol 2017;8:1–16.

[17] Wang PG, Xian M, Tang XP, Wu XJ, Wen Z, Cai TW, Janczuk AJ. Nitric oxide donors: chemical activities and biological applications. Chem Rev 2002;102:1091–134.

[18] Jen MC, Serrano MC, Lith R, Ameer GA. Polymer-based nitric oxide therapies: recent insights for biomedical applications. Adv Func Mater 2012;22:239–60.

[19] Saavedra JE, Booth MN, Hrabie JA, Davies KM, Keefer LK. Piperazine as a linker for incorporating the nitric oxide-releasing diazeniumdiolate group into other biomedically relevant functional molecules. J Org Chem 1999;64:5124–31.

[20] Hou YC, Wu XJ, Xie WH, Braunschweiger PG, Wang PG. The synthesis and cytotoxicity of fructose-1-SNAP, a novel fructose conjugated S-nitroso nitric oxide donor. Tetrahedron Lett 2001;42:825–9.

[21] Karaki F, Kabasawa Y, Yanagimoto T, Umeda N, Firman UY, Nagano T, Otani Y, Ohwada T. Visible-light-triggered release of nitric oxide from N-pyramidal nitrosamines. Chem Eur J 2012;18:1127–41.

[22] Fan W, Yung BC, Chen X. Stimuli-responsive NO release for on-demand gas sensitized synergistic cancer therapy. Angew Chem Int Ed 2018;57:8383–94.

[23] Hetrick EM, Schoenfisch MH. Analytical chemistry of nitric oxide. Annu Rev Anal Chem 2009;2:409–33.

[24] Coneski PN, Schoenfisch MH. Nitric oxide release: Part III. Measurement and reporting. Chem Soc Rev 2012;41:3753–8.

[25] Tsikas D. Analysis of nitrite and nitrate in biological fluids by assays based on the Griess reaction: appraisal of the Griess reaction in the L-arginine/nitric oxide area of research. J Chromatogr B 2007;851:51–70.

[26] Yang M, Fan J, Du J, Peng X. Small-molecule fluorescent probes for imaging gaseous signaling molecules: current progress and future implications. Chem Sci 2020;11:5127–41.

[27] Kojima H, Nakatsubo N, Kikuchi K, Kawahara S, Kirino Y, Nagoshi H, Hirata Y, Nagano T. Detection and imaging of nitric oxide with novel fluorescent indicators: diaminofluoresceins. Anal Chem 1998;70:2446–53.

[28] Bates JN. Nitric oxide measurement by chemiluminescence detection. Neuroprotocols 1992;1:141–9.

[29] Privett BJ, Shin JH, Schoenfisch MH. Electrochemical nitric oxide sensors for physiological measurements. Chem Soc Rev 2010;39:1925–35.

[30] Luiking YC, Engelen MPKJ, Deutz NEP. Regulation of nitric oxide production in health and disease. Curr Opin Clin Nutr Metab Care 2010;13:97–104.

[31] Bonavida B, Khineche S, Huerta-Yepez S, Garban H. Therapeutic potential of nitric oxide in cancer. Drug Resist Updat 2006;9:157–73.

[32] Roman LJ, Martasek P, Masters BSS. Intrinsic and extrinsic modulation of nitric oxide synthase activity. Chem Rev 2002;102:1179–89.

[33] Stuehr DJ, Santolini J, Wang ZQ, Wei CC, Adak S. Update on mechanism and catalytic regulation in the NO synthases. J Biol Chem 2004;279:36167–70.

[34] Daff S. NO synthase: structures and mechanisms. Nitric Oxide 2010;23:1–11.

[35] Miller MR, Megson IL. Recent developments in nitric oxide donor drugs. Br J Pharmacol 2007;151:305–21.

[36] Hrabie JA, Keefer LK. Chemistry of the nitric oxide-releasing diazeniumdiolate ("nitrosohydroxylamine") functional group and its oxygen-substituted derivatives. Chem Rev 2002;102:1135–54.

[37] Saavedra JE, Southan GJ, Davies KM, Lundell A, Markou C, Hanson SR, Adrie C, Hurford WE, Zapol WM, Keefer LK. Localizing antithrombotic and vasodilatory activity with a novel, ultrafast nitric oxide donor. J Med Chem 1996;39:4361–5.

[38] Saavedra JE, Billiar TR, Williams DL, Kim YM, Watkins SC, Keefer LK. Targeting nitric oxide (NO) delivery in vivo. Design of a liver-selective NO donor prodrug that blocks tumor necrosis factor-α-induced apoptosis and toxicity in the liver. J Med Chem 1997;40:1947–54.

[39] Park D, Im S, Saravanakumar G, Lee YM, Kim J, Kim K, Lee J, Kim J, Kim WJ. A cyotosol-selective nitric oxide bomb as a new paradigm of an anticancer drug. Chem Commun 2019;55:14789–92.

[40] Giustarini D, Milzani A, Colombo R, Dalle-Donne I, Rossi R. Nitric oxide and S-nitrosothiols in human blood. Clin Chim Acta 2003;330:85–98.

[41] Smith BC, Marletta MA. Mechanisms of S-nitrosothiol formation and selectivity in nitric oxide signaling. Curr Opin Chem Biol 2012;16:498–506.

[42] Williams DLHA. Chemist's view of the nitric oxide story. Org Biomol Chem 2003;1:441–9.

[43] Roy B, d'Hardemare AM, Fontcave M. New thionitrites: synthesis, stability, and nitric oxide generation. J Org Chem 1994;59:7019–26.

[44] Zhang Z, Wu J, Shang Z, Wang C, Cheng J, Qian X, Xiao Y, Xu Z, Yang Y. Photocalibrated NO release from N-nitrosated napthalimides upon one-photon or two-photon irradiation. Anal Chem 2016;88:7274–80.

[45] He H, Xia Y, Qi Y, Wang HY, Wang Z, Bao J, Zhang Z, Wu FG, Wang H, Chen D, Yang D, Liang X, Chen J, Zhou S, Liang X, Qian X, Yang Y. A water-soluble, green-light triggered, and photo-calibrated nitric oxide donor for biological applications. Bioconjug Chem 2018;29:1194–8.

[46] Sarkar A, Karmakar S, Bhattacharyya S, Purkait K, Mukherjee A. Nitric oxide release by N-(2-chloroethyl)-N-nitrosoureas: a rarely discussed mechanistic path towards their anticancer activity. RSC Adv 2015;5:2137–46.

[47] Miura M, Sakamoto S, Yamaguchi K, Ohwada T. Influence of structure on N-NO bond cleavage of aliphatic N-nitrosamines. Tetrahedron Lett 2000;41:3637–41.

[48] Munzel T, Daiber A, Mulsch A. Explaining the phenomenon of nitrate tolerance. Circ Res 2005;97:618–28.

[49] Fenton C, Wellington K, Easthope SE. 0.4% nitroglycerin ointment: in the treatment of chronic anal fissure pain. Drugs 2006;66:343–9.

[50] Naimi E, Zhou A, Khalili P, Wiebe LI, Balzarini J, Clercq ED, Knaus EE. Synthesis of 3′- and 5′-nitrooxy pyrimidine nucleoside nitrate esters: "nitric oxide donor" agents for evaluation as anticancer and antiviral agents. J Med Chem 2003;46:995–1004.

[51] Aziz HA, Moustafa GAI, Abuo-Rahma GEA, Rabea SM, Hauk G, Krishna VS, Sriram D, Berger JM, Abbas SH. Synthesis and antimicrobial evaluation of new nitric oxide-donating fluoroquinolone/oxime hybrids. Arch Pharm (Weinheim) 2021;354, e2000180.

[52] Li X, Wang X, Xu C, Huang J, Wang C, Wang X, He L, Ling Y. Synthesis and biological evaluation of nitric oxide-releasing hybrids from gemcitabine and phenylsulfonyl furoxans as anti-tumor agents. Med Chem Commun 2015;6:1130–6.

I. Development of NO donors and derivatives, and new delivery formations

[53] Ghosh SM, Kapil V, Fuentes-Calvo I, Bubb KJ, Pearl V, Milsom AB, Khambata R, Maleki-Toyserkani S, Yousuf M, Benjamin N, Webb AJ, Caulfield MJ, Hobbs AJ, Ahluwalia A. Enhanced vasodilator activity of nitrite in hypertension. Hypertension 2013;61:1091–102.

[54] Filippou P, Antoniou C, Fotopoulos V. The nitric oxide donor sodium nitroprusside regulates polyamine and proline metabolism in leaves of Medicago truncatula plants. Free Radic Biol Med 2013;56:172–83.

[55] Riccio DA, Schoenfisch MH. Nitric oxide release: Part I. Macromolecular scaffolds. Chem Soc Rev 2012;41:3731–41.

[56] Zhang H, Annich GM, Miskulin J, Stankiewicz K, Osterholzer K, Merz SI, Bartlett RH, Meyerhoff ME. Nitric oxide-releasing fumed silica particles: synthesis, characterization, and biomedical application. J Am Chem Soc 2003;125:5015–24.

[57] Frost MC, Meyerhoff ME. Synthesis, characterization, and controlled nitric oxide release from S-nitrosothiol-derivatized fumed silica polymer filler particles. J Biomed Mater Res 2005;72A:409–19.

[58] Shin JH, Schoenfisch MH. Inorganic/organic hybrid silica nanoparticles as a nitric oxide delivery scaffold. Chem Mater 2008;20:239–49.

[59] Rothrock AR, Donkers RL, Schoenfisch MH. Synthesis of nitric oxide-releasing gold nanoparticles. J Am Chem Soc 2005;127:9362–3.

[60] Seabra AB, Pasquoto T, Ferrarini ACF, Santos MC, Haddad PS, Lima R. Preparation, characterization, cytotoxicity, and genotoxicity evaluations of thiolated- and S-nitrosated superparamagnetic iron oxide nanoparticles: implications for cancer treatment. Chem Res Toxicol 2014;27:1207–18.

[61] Kandoth N, Vittorino E, Sortino S. Gold nanoparticles decorated with a photoactivable nitric oxide donor/cyclodextrin host/guest complex. New J Chem 2011;35:52–6.

[62] Kim T, Suh J, Kim J, Kim WJ. Lymph-directed self-immolative nitric oxide prodrug for inhibition of intractable metastatic cancer. Adv Sci 2022;9:1–13.

[63] Bloch ED, Queen WL, Chavan S, Wheatley PS, Zadrozny JM, Morris R, Brown CM, Lamberti C, Bordiga S, Long JR. Gradual release of strongly-bound nitric oxide from $Fe_2(NO)_2(dobdc)$. J Am Chem Soc 2015;137:3466–9.

[64] Diring S, Wang DO, Kim C, Kondo M, Chen Y, Kitagawa S, Kamei K, Furukawa S. Localized cell stimulation by nitric oxide using a photoactive porous coordination polymer platform. Nat Commun 2013;4:2684–92.

[65] Nguyen JG, Tanabe KK, Cohen SM. Postsynthetic diazeniumdiolate formation and NO release from MOFs. CrystEngComm 2010;12:2335–8.

[66] Parzuchowski PG, Frost MC, Meyerhoff ME. Synthesis and characterization of polymethacrylate-based nitric oxide donors. J Am Chem Soc 2002;124:12182–91.

[67] Duan Y, Wang Y, Li X, Zhang G, Zhanga G, Hu J. Light-triggered nitric oxide (NO) release from photoresponsive polymersomes for corneal wound healing. Chem Sci 2020;11:186–94.

[68] Paul S, Pan S, Chakraborty A, De P, Mukherjee A. Ultraviolet light- or pH-triggered nitric oxide release from a water-soluble polymeric scaffold. ACS Appl Polym Mater 2021;3:2310–5.

[69] Bag S, Ghosh S, Paul S, Khan MEH, De P. Styrene-maleimide/maleic anhydride alternating copolymers: recent advances and future perspectives. Macromol Rapid Commun 2021;42:2100501.

[70] Saha B, Haldar U, De P. Polymer-chlorambucil drug conjugates: a dynamic platform of anticancer drug delivery. Macromol Rapid Commun 2016;37:1015–20.

[71] Saha B, Bhattacharyya S, Mete S, Mukherjee A, De P. Redox-driven disassembly of polymer-chlorambucil polyprodrug: delivery of anticancer nitrogen mustard and DNA alkylation. ACS Appl Polym Mater 2019;1:2503–15.

[72] Chatterjee R, Bhattacharya I, Roy S, Purkait K, Koley TS, Gupta A, Mukherjee A. Synthesis, characterization and cytotoxicity of morpholine-containing Ru(II)-p-cymene complexes. Inorg Chem 2021;60:12172–85.

[73] Wu M, Lin X, Tan X, Li J, Wei Z, Zhang D, Zheng Y, Zheng A, Zhao B, Zeng Y, Liu X, Liu J. Photo-responsive nanovehicle for two independent wavelength light-triggered sequential release of P-Gp shRNA and doxorubicin to optimize and enhance synergistic therapy of multidrug-resistant cancer. ACS Appl Mater Interfaces 2018;10:19416–27.

[74] Duan S, Cai S, Yang Q, Forrest ML. Multi-arm polymeric nanocarrier as a nitric oxide delivery platform for chemotherapy of head and neck squamous cell carcinoma. Biomaterials 2012;33:3243–53.

[75] Niu X, Cao J, Zhang Y, Gao X, Cheng M, Liu Y, Wang W, Yuan Z. A glutathione responsive nitric oxide release system based on charge-reversal chitosan nanoparticles for enhancing synergistic effect against multidrug resistant tumor. Nanomed Nanotechnol Biol Med 2019;20:1–12.

[76] Gao L, Dong B, Zhang J, Chen Y, Qiao H, Liu Z, Chen E, Dong Y, Cao C, Huang D, Chen W. Functional biodegradable nitric oxide donor-containing polycarbonate-based micelles for reduction-triggered drug release and overcoming multidrug resistance. ACS Macro Lett 2019;8:1552–8.

I. Development of NO donors and derivatives, and new delivery formations

[77] Liu Z, Zhong Y, Zhou X, Huang X, Zhou J, Huang D, Li Y, Wang Z, Dong B, Qiao H, Chen W. Inherently nitric oxide containing polymersomes remotely regulated by NIR for improving multi-modal therapy on drug resistant cancer. Biomaterials 2021;277:1–10.

[78] Studenovsky M, Sivak L, Sedlacek O, Konefal R, Horkova V, Etrych T, Kovar M, Rihova B, Sirova M. Polymer nitric oxide donors potentiate the treatment of experimental solid tumours by increasing drug accumulation in the tumour tissue. J Control Release 2018;269:214–24.

[79] Kim J, Francis DM, Sestito LF, Archer PA, Manspeaker MP, O'Melia MJ, Thomas SN. Thermosensitive hydrogel releasing nitric oxide donor and anti-CTLA-4 micelles for anti-tumor immunotherapy. Nat Commun 2022;13:1–13.

[80] Jiang W, Dong W, Li M, Guo Z, Wang Q, Liu Y, Bi Y, Zhou H, Wang Y. Nitric oxide induces immunogenic cell death and potentiates cancer immunotherapy. ACS Nano 2022;16:3881–94.

[81] Deng Y, Wang Y, Jia F, Liu W, Zhou D, Jin Q, Ji J. Tailoring supramolecular prodrug nanoassemblies for reactive nitrogen species-potentiated chemotherapy of liver cancer. ACS Nano 2021;15:8663–75.

[82] Wei G, Yang G, Wei B, Wang Y, Zhou S. Near-infrared light switching nitric oxide nanoemitter for triple-combination therapy of multidrug resistant cancer. Acta Biomater 2019;100:365–77.

[83] Kang Y, Kim J, Park J, Lee YM, Saravanakumar G, Park KM, Choi W, Kim K, Lee E, Kim C, Kim WJ. Tumor vasodilation by N-heterocyclic carbene-based nitric oxide delivery triggered by high-intensity focused ultrasound and enhanced drug homing to tumor sites for anti-cancer therapy. Biomaterials 2019;217:1–11.

[84] Ding Z, He K, Duan Y, Shen Z, Cheng J, Zhang G, Hu J. Photo-degradable micelles for co-delivery of nitric oxide and doxorubicin. J Mater Chem B 2020;8:7009–17.

[85] Gusarov I, Shatalin K, Starodubtseva M, Nudler E. Endogenous nitric oxide protects bacteria against a wide spectrum of antibiotics. Science 2009;325:1380–4.

[86] Mukherjee I, Ghosh A, Bhadury P, De P. Matrix assisted antibacterial activity of polymer conjugates with pendant antibiotics, and bioactive and biopassive moieties. J Mater Chem B 2019;7:3007–18.

[87] Rong F, Tang Y, Wang T, Feng T, Song J, Li P, Huang W. Nitric oxide-releasing polymeric materials for antimicrobial applications: a review. Antioxidants 2019;8:556–87.

[88] Wo Y, Brisbois EJ, Bartlett RH, Meyerhoff ME. Recent advances in thromboresistant and antimicrobial polymers for biomedical applications: just say yes to nitric oxide (NO). Biomater Sci 2016;4:1161–83.

[89] Arora DP, Hossain S, Xu Y, Boon EM. Nitric oxide regulation of bacterial biofilms. Biochemistry 2015;54:3717–28.

[90] Sun B, Slomberg DL, Chudasama SL, Lu Y, Schoenfisch MH. Nitric oxide-releasing dendrimers as antibacterial agents. Biomacromolecules 2012;13:3343–54.

[91] Lu Y, Slomberg DL, Shah A, Schoenfisch MH. Nitric oxide-releasing amphiphilic poly(amidoamine) (PAMAM) dendrimers as antibacterial agents. Biomacromolecules 2013;14:3589–98.

[92] Yang L, Wang X, Suchyta DJ, Schoenfisch MH. Antibacterial activity of nitric oxide-releasing hyperbranched polyamidoamines. Bioconjug Chem 2018;29:35–43.

[93] Yang L, Schoenfisch MH. Nitric oxide-releasing hyperbranched polyaminoglycosides for antibacterial therapy. ACS Appl Bio Mater 2018;1:1066–73.

[94] Nguyen T-K, Selvanayagam R, Ho KKK, Chen R, Kutty SK, Rice SA, Kumar N, Barraud N, Duong HTT, Boyer C. Co-delivery of nitric oxide and antibiotic using polymeric nanoparticles. Chem Sci 2016;7:1016–27.

[95] Namivandi-Zangeneh R, Sadrearhami Z, Bagheri A, Sauvage-Nguyen M, Ho KKK, Kumar N, Wong EHH, Boyer C. Nitric oxide-loaded antimicrobial polymer for the synergistic eradication of bacterial biofilm. ACS Macro Lett 2018;7:592–7.

[96] Duong HTT, Jung K, Kutty SK, Agustina S, Adnan NNM, Basuki JS, Kumar N, Davis TP, Barraud N, Boyer C. Nanoparticle (star polymer) delivery of nitric oxide effectively negates Pseudomonas aeruginosa biofilm formation. Biomacromolecules 2014;15:2583–9.

[97] Liu Q, Singha P, Handa H, Locklin J. Covalent grafting of antifouling phosphorylcholine-based copolymers with antimicrobial nitric oxide releasing polymers to enhance infection-resistant properties of medical device coatings. Langmuir 2017;33:13105–13.

[98] Pelegrino MT, Pieretti JC, Nakazato G, Goncalves MC, Moreira JC, Seabra AB. Chitosan chemically modified to deliver nitric oxide with high antibacterial activity. Nitric Oxide 2021;106:24–34.

[99] Workman CD, Hopkins S, Pant J, Goudie M, Handa H. Covalently bound S-nitroso-N-acetylpenicillamine to electrospun polyacrylonitrile nanofibers for multifunctional tissue engineering applications. ACS Biomater Sci Eng 2021;7:5279–87.

[100] Shen Z, He K, Ding Z, Zhang M, Yu Y, Hu J. Visible-light-triggered self-reporting release of nitric oxide (NO) for bacterial biofilm dispersal. Macromolecules 2019;52:7668–77.

[101] He K, Shen Z, Chen Z, Zheng B, Cheng S, Hu J. Visible light-responsive micelles enable codelivery of nitric oxide and antibiotics for synergistic antibiofilm applications. Polym Chem 2021;12:6344–54.

[102] Duan Y, He K, Zhang G, Hu J. Photoresponsive micelles enabling codelivery of nitric oxide and formaldehyde for combinatorial antibacterial applications. Biomacromolecules 2021;22:2160–70.

[103] Marino N, Perez-Lloret M, Blanco AR, Venuta A, Quaglia F, Sortino S. Photo-antimicrobial polymeric films releasing nitric oxide with fluorescence reporting under visible light. J Mater Chem B 2016;4:5138–43.

[104] Oliver S, Pham TPP, Li Y, Xu F-J, Boyer C. More than skin deep: using polymers to facilitate topical delivery of nitric oxide. Biomater Sci 2021;9:391–405.

[105] Luo J, Chen A. Nitric oxide: a newly discovered function on wound healing. Acta Pharmacol Sin 2005;6:259–64.

[106] Witte MB, Barbul A. Role of nitric oxide in wound repair. Am J Surg 2002;183:406–12.

[107] Lee RH, Efron D, Tantry U, Barbul A. Nitric oxide in the healing wound: a time-course study. J Surg Res 2001;101:104–8.

[108] Kang Y, Kim J, Lee YM, Im S, Park H, Kim WJ. Nitric oxide-releasing polymer incorporated ointment for cutaneous wound healing. J Control Release 2015;220:624–30.

[109] Zhang Y, Tang K, Chen B, Zhou S, Li N, Liu C, Yang J, Lin R, Zhang T, He W. A polyethylenimine-based diazeniumdiolate nitric oxide donor accelerates wound healing. Biomater Sci 2019;7:1607–16.

[110] Maloney SE, McGrath KV, Ahonen MJR, Soliman DS, Feura ES, Hall HR, Wallet SM, Maile R, Schoenfisch MH. Nitric oxide-releasing hyaluronic acid as an antibacterial agent for wound therapy. Biomacromolecules 2021;22:867–79.

[111] Li Y, Lee PI. Controlled nitric oxide delivery platform based on *S*-nitrosothiol conjugated interpolymer complexes for diabetic wound healing. Mol Pharm 2010;7:254–66.

[112] Hu D, Deng Y, Jia F, Jin Q, Ji J. Surface charge switchable supramolecular nanocarriers for nitric oxide synergistic photodynamic eradication of biofilms. ACS Nano 2020;14:347–59.

[113] Sun B, Ye Z, Zhang M, Song Q, Chu X, Gao S, Zhang Q, Jiang C, Zhou N, Yao C, Shen J. Light-activated biodegradable covalent organic framework-integrated heterojunction for photodynamic, photothermal, and gaseous therapy of chronic wound infection. ACS Appl Mater Interfaces 2021;13:42396–410.

[114] Shen Z, Zheng S, Xiao S, Shen R, Liu S, Hu J. Red-light-mediated photoredox catalysis enables self-reporting nitric oxide release for efficient antibacterial treatment. Angew Chem Int Ed 2021;60:20452–60.

[115] Sharma JN, Al-Omran A, Parvathy SS. Role of nitric oxide in inflammatory diseases. Inflammopharmacology 2007;15:252–9.

[116] Shoman ME, Abdel-Aziz M, Aly OM, Farag HH, Morsy MA. Synthesis and investigation of anti-inflammatory activity and gastric ulcerogenicity of novel nitric oxide-donating pyrazoline derivatives. Eur J Med Chem 2009;44:3068–76.

[117] Koc E, Kucukguzel SG. Medicinal chemistry and anti-inflammatory activity of nitric oxide-releasing NSAI drugs. Med Chem 2009;9:611–9.

[118] Oh Y, Jeong H, Lim S, Hong J. Controlled nitric oxide release using poly(lactic-co-glycolic acid) nanoparticles for anti-inflammatory effects. Biomacromolecules 2020;21:4972–9.

[119] Porras AMG, Bertuzzi DL, Lucas K, Silva LCE, Oliveira MG, Ornelas C. Nitric oxide-releasing polyamide dendrimer with anti-inflammatory activity. ACS Appl Polym Mater 2020;2:2027–34.

[120] Mowery KA, Schoenfisch MH, Saavedra JE, Keefer LK, Meyerhoff MK. Preparation and characterization of hydrophobic polymeric films that are thromboresistant *via* nitric oxide release. Biomaterials 2000;21:9–21.

[121] Ahonen MJR, Hill DB, Schoenfisch MH. Nitric oxide-releasing alginates as mucolytic agents. ACS Biomater Sci Eng 2019;5:3409–18.

[122] Wang T, Vlies AJ, Uyama H, Hasegawa U. Nitric oxide-releasing polymeric furoxan conjugates. Polym Chem 2015;6:7737–48.

[123] Frost MC, Reynolds MM, Meyerhoff ME. Polymers incorporating nitric oxide releasing/generating substances for improved biocompatibility of blood-contacting medical devices. Biomaterials 2005;26:1685–93.

I. Development of NO donors and derivatives, and new delivery formations

PART II

Nitric oxide pathway and cancer progression and therapy

Therapeutic potential for coxib-nitric oxide releasing hybrids in cancer treatment

Antonio Giordani[a], Giovanna Poce[b], Sara Consalvi[b], Samuele Maramai[c], Mario Saletti[c], Antonietta Rossi[d], Paola Patrignani[e], Mariangela Biava[b], and Maurizio Anzini[c]

[a]Formerly Rottapharm (Monza, Italy) at the Present Consultant, Pavia, Italy [b]Department of Chemistry and Technologies of Drug, Sapienza University of Rome, Rome, Italy [c]Department of Biotechnology, Chemistry, and Pharmacy, University of Siena, Siena, Italy [d]Department of Pharmacy, School of Medicine and Surgery, "Federico II" University of Naples, Naples, Italy [e]Department of Neuroscience, Imaging and Clinical Sciences, and Center for Advanced Studies and Technology (CAST), School of Medicine, G. D'Annunzio University, Chieti, Italy

Abstract

In the last three decades, several experimental evidences pointed out the involvement of chronic inflammation in promoting the development of cancer, supporting all stages of tumorigenesis, tumor growth, and spread. In addition, the importance of the tumor microenvironment, an indispensable participant for tumor establishment and growth, turned out by highlighting the important role that stromal and inflammatory cells have in orchestrating the promotion of tumor cells proliferation, survival, and migration. The relationship between inflammation and cancer, the underlying mechanisms, the cells involved, as well as the corresponding crosstalks are, herein, briefly reviewed.

In particular, the effects mediated by cyclooxygenase-2 (COX-2) and corresponding product prostaglandin (PG) E2 on tumor growth and tumor immune evasion are discussed along with corresponding molecular mechanisms.

Immunotherapy has become a milestone in cancer treatment, strikingly improving life expectancy of patients with a broad variety of malignancies while dramatically reducing the side effects of the therapy. The progresses obtained with immunotherapy (in particular with Programmed cell deth protein 1 (PD-1)/programmed cell death ligand 1 (PD-L1) inhibitors) in cancer treatment are briefly reviewed along with the underlying mechanisms. The effects exerted by the $COX-2/PGE_2$ axis on PD-1/PD-L1 expression, and more in general on the immune system, are discussed.

The clinical investigations on cancer prevention of nonsteroidal antiinflammatory drugs and corresponding results are herein commented along with the side effects that hampered the clinical trials. The outcome obtained with NO-releasing drugs in overcoming these side effects is commented in comparison with the corresponding results obtained with the NO-donor COX-2 inhibitors that we have developed. Moreover, the effect that NO release may have on tumor initiation, growth, and metastasis as well as in controlling immunosuppression is briefly reviewed.

Taking into account the issues discussed above, we think that the NO-donor COX-2 inhibitor (**12e**) (**VA694**) and corresponding backups can be good candidates for further studies as therapeutic agents for cancer treatment, either in combination with immune checkpoint (PD-1/PD-L1) inhibitors or with standard chemotherapy.

Abbreviations

15R-HETE	15R-hydroxyeicosatetraenoic acid
AA	arachidonic acid
ADC	lung adenocarcinoma
AP-1	activator protein-1
ASA	acetyl salicylic acid
ATLs	aspirin-triggered lipoxins
BC	breast cancer
CINODs	COX-inhibiting nitric oxide donors
COX	cyclooxygenase
CTL	cytotoxic T-lymphocyte
CTLA4	T-lymphocyte antigen 4
CV	cardiovascular
DAMPs	damage-associated molecular patterns
DCs	dendritic cells
DHA	docosahexaenoic acid
diHETE	dihydroxy-eicosatetraenoic acid
EETs	epoxy-eicosatrienoic acids
EGF	epidermal growth factor
EGFR	epidermal growth factor receptor
EMT	epithelial-mesenchymal transition
EP1-4	prostaglandin receptors
EPA	eicosapentaenoic acid
ERK	extracellular signal-regulated kinase
ETEs	eicosatetraenoic acids
FGF	fibroblast growth factor
GBM	glioblastoma
GI	gastrointestinal
GM-CSF	granulocyte-macrophage colony-stimulating factor
GPCRs	G protein-coupled receptors
GSK3β	glycogen synthase kinase-3β
HEPE	hydroxyeicosapentaenoic acid
HIF-1	hypoxia-inducible factor-1
HLA-G	human leukocyte antigen G
ICAM-1	intercellular adhesion molecule-1
ICIs	immune checkpoint inhibitors
IDO1	indoleamine 2,3-dioxygenase
IL	interleukin
INF-γ	interferon-γ
iNOS	inducible nitric oxide synthase
JAK-STAT	Janus kinase-signal transducer and activator of transcription
JNK	Jun-N-terminal kinase
LAG-3	lymphocyte-activation gene-3
LC	lung cancer
LCLC	large-cell lung carcinoma

LOX	lipoxygenase
LPS	lipopolysaccharide
LTs	leukotrienes
LXs	lipoxins
MAPKs	mitogen-activated protein kinases
MCs	mast cells
MDSCs	myeloid-derived suppressor cells
MMPs	matrix metalloproteinases
MOX	monooxygenase
mPGES1	microsomal prostaglandin E synthase-1
NF-κB	nuclear factor-κB
NKs	natural killer cells
NO	nitric oxide
NOBA	4-(nitrooxy)butanol
NSAIDs	nonsteroidal antiinflammatory drugs
NSCLC	nonsmall-cell lung cancer
ODQ	quinoxalin-1-one
PAMPs	pathogen-associated molecular patterns
PD-1	programmed cell death protein 1
PD-L1	programmed cell death ligand 1
PGHS	prostaglandin H synthase
PGs	prostaglandins
PRRs	pattern recognition receptors
ROS	reactive oxygen species
Rv	resolvin
SAR	structure-activity relationship
SCLC	small-cell lung cancer
SHRs	young male spontaneous hypertensive rats
SPMs	specialized proresolving lipid mediators
SQSLC	squamous cell lung cancer
STAT-3	signal transducer and activator of transcription-3
TAMs	tumor-associated macrophages
TANs	tumor-associated neutrophils
TCR	T-cell receptor
TGF-β	transforming growth factor-β
TLR	Toll-like receptor
TME	tumor microenvironment
TNF-α	tumor necrosis factor-α
t-**NSAIDs**	traditional-NSAIDs
TXA2	thromboxane A2
VCAM-1	vascular cell adhesion molecules
VEGF	vascular endothelial growth factor
WHB	whole-blood assays

Conflict of interest

No potential conflicts of interest were disclosed.

Introduction

Inflammation

Inflammation is an evolutionary conserved defense process, developed not only to counteract pathogens infection or tissue damage and promote tissue repair, but also to enforce the

II. Nitric oxide pathway and cancer progression and therapy

defense of the organism in order to properly face adverse environmental factors [1]. When exposed to molecules bearing pathogen-associated molecular patterns (PAMPs) or damage-associated molecular patterns (DAMPs), the innate immune system quickly reacts [2]. As a response to PAMPs/DAMPs, the pattern recognition receptors (PRRs) [3] trigger the activation of sentinel cells (macrophages, dendritic cells, and mast cells) giving rise to the recruitment of neutrophils at the inflammatory site [4].

Neutrophil activation leads to the release of inflammatory lipid mediators like prostaglandins (PGs), leukotrienes (LTs), and inflammatory cytokines such as tumor necrosis factor-α (TNF-α), interleukin (IL)-1β (IL-1β) and (IL-6) to eliminate the pathogens and repair tissue damages. After neutrophil recruitment, also monocytes and lymphocytes (NK cells, T-cells and B cells) reach the site of inflammation, where they not only amplify the inflammatory process, clear foreign particles, and host debris, but also release cytokines in order to configure the following adaptive immune response [5].

During normal inflammatory processes, there is a balance between the production of inflammatory cytokines (TNF-α, IL-1β and IL-6) and the production of immune suppressive factors such as IL-10 and transforming growth factor-β (TGF-β) that give rise to inflammation dampening [6].

The acute inflammatory response consists of two phases: initiation and resolution, followed by the reestablishment of homeostasis. In addition to cytokines, products of arachidonic acid (AA) metabolism (eicosanoids), including PGs, LTs, lipoxins (LXs) (Fig. 1), and resolvins (Rvs) (Fig. 2), critically regulate both inflammation and its resolution [7].

In the past, the resolution of inflammation was thought to be a passive ending process; more recently, it turned out to be an active reprogramming of the immune environment, mediated by the endogenous specialized proresolving lipid mediators, a class of lipid mediators acting as "brake signals," in order to turn off inflammation and stimulate tissue regeneration [8]. Insufficient pathogen clearance, recurring tissue damage, long-lasting inflammatory

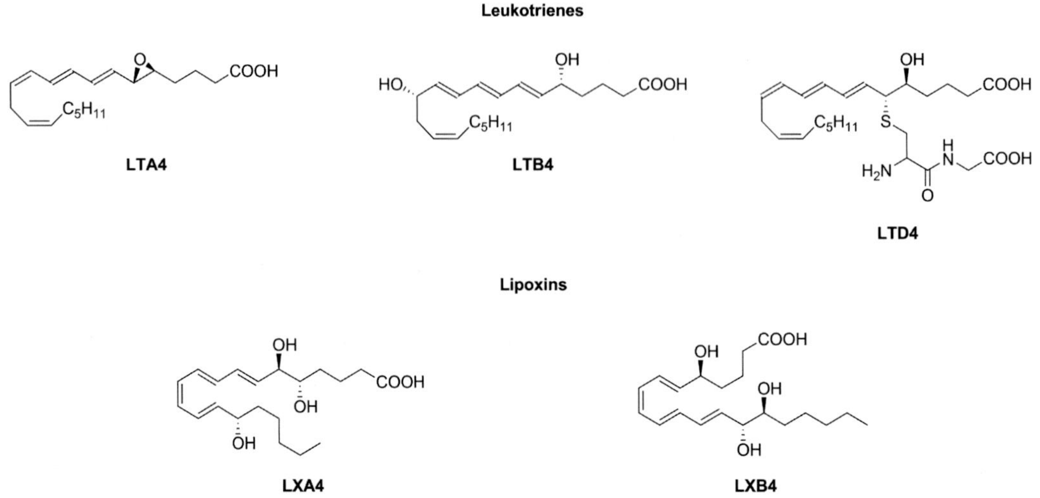

FIG. 1   Structures of leukotrienes and lipoxins.

II. Nitric oxide pathway and cancer progression and therapy

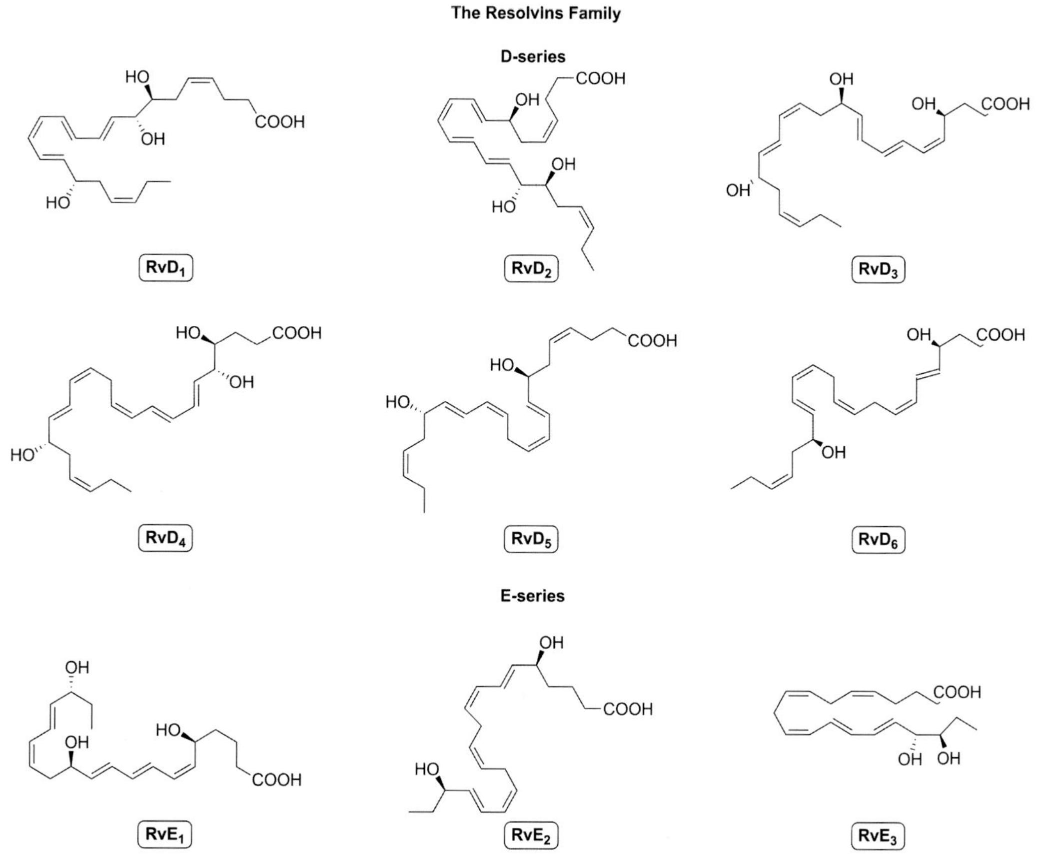

FIG. 2   The Resolvins family.

signaling, and failure to regenerate homeostasis by antiinflammatory natural mechanisms may lead to deregulation of the control systems for the acute inflammatory process giving rise to chronic inflammation [9].

Inflammation and cancer

Both preclinical and epidemiological studies support the assumption that chronic inflammation predisposes to various types of cancer and underpins tumor development, as well as these studies highlight a preventive/therapeutic effect exerted by antiinflammatory agents on cancer development [10]. Moreover, the impact of inflammation in cancer was recently highlighted by a clinical study on atherosclerosis. In this study, patients who received canakinumab, an IL-1β blocker for treatment of systemic inflammatory diseases, pointed out a reduced incidence of lung cancer as well as cancer-related mortality [11].

Interestingly, a relationship between inflammation and cancer was firstly suggested in 1863, when Rudolf Virchow, the founder of cellular pathology, speculated about a possible link between inflammation and cancer, due to the recurrent presence of leukocytes within tumors along with the observation that inflammation from tissue injury stimulated cell proliferation [12]. However, the evidence that inflammation is closely associated with carcinogenesis, tumor development, and metastasis, along with the understanding of underlying molecular mechanisms, has been consolidated only more recently [13]. Thus, while in the past, the mechanisms of carcinogenesis have been focused on genotoxic activity of compounds or radiations as the cause for mutations [14], more recently nongenotoxic mechanisms such as chronic inflammation and oxidative stress have been proven to be effective in promoting cellular proliferation, genotoxicity, carcinogenesis, tumor growth, and metastatic spread [15].

As a matter of fact, chronic inflammation giving rise to the overexpression of inflammatory cytokines, chemokines, and other inflammatory mediators (PGs and LTs), along with the recruitment of inflammatory cells [macrophages, neutrophils, T-cells and mast cells (MCs)] destabilizes the local tissue homeostasis, leading to a sustained and continuous production of inflammatory mediators that can induce tissue and DNA damage, generating a microenvironment that predisposes to cancer, promoting cell proliferation, carcinogenesis, angiogenesis, and metastasis [16].

According to H.F. Dvorak, "cancer is a wound that does not heal"; this statement is based on the similarity of the cell types and mechanisms involved in wound healing and tissue regeneration (occurring at the end of the inflammatory process) with those involved in cancer [17]. In fact, in both cases, similar programs are activated, including increased vascular permeability, extravasation of plasma, formation of a provisional stroma by extravascular fibrin gel deposition, induction of angiogenesis, fibrin degradation, and replacement with highly vascularized connective tissue (desmoplasia). However, while in wound healing the above tissue-remodeling process is able to reestablish homeostasis, during cancer development the inflammatory response is nonresolving. Indeed, the tumor prevents the inflammation dampening, by reprogramming the immune cells toward a protumorigenic phenotype, which maintain production of inflammatory mediators and blocks the resolution of inflammation [18]. According to Mantovani et al., cancer and inflammation are connected by two pathways: the intrinsic pathway and the extrinsic pathway [10]. A genetic event such as a mutation leading to oncogene activation as well as chromosomal rearrangement or amplification, along with the inactivation of tumor-suppressor genes, gives rise to the neoplasia in the intrinsic pathway. Thus, genotoxic substances induce cancer by binding to DNA via adduct formation, which leads to mutations. For example, DNA adducts of aflatoxin B1 lead to genetic modifications linked with a specific mutational pattern in the hepatocyte of human hepatocellular carcinoma [19]. In this case are the mutated cells that generate the inflammatory mediators, which trigger the inflammatory microenvironment able to support tumor establishment and growth. This cancer-related inflammation which is effective in promoting carcinogenesis, tumor progression, and immune system evasion is due to several mechanisms acting in the tumor microenvironment (TME) [20]. Both tumor and stromal cells release chemotactic factors in order to recruit macrophages and neutrophils, and, in addition, tumor growth produces tissue damages and consequently DAMPs which activate granulocytes. These recruited immune cells, in concert with tumor and stromal cells, release cytokines and reactive oxygen species (ROS) that amplify inflammation, give rise to epigenetic alterations in premalignant lesions, silence tumor suppressor genes, and establish the inflammatory microenvironment required for tumor development.

Conversely, in the extrinsic pathway, inflammatory conditions are the key factor in the development of cancer. Thus, while in the intrinsic pathway, mechanisms of carcinogenesis are based on genotoxic activity which induces mutations that lead to inflammation, in the extrinsic pathway, nongenotoxic mechanisms such as inflammation and the consequent oxidative stress are the promoters of genotoxicity, mutations, and uncontrolled proliferation [21]. The DNA damages generated during the inflammatory process under oxidative stress conditions, caused by the interaction of reactive electrophilic molecules with nuclear DNA, although necessary, are not sufficient for cancer development [22]. Indeed, inflammatory cells and mediators can destabilize the cancer cell genome by means of several mechanisms that, in addition to the direct DNA damage, include downregulation of the pathways for DNA repair, dysregulation of cell cycle checkpoints, and inhibition of apoptosis leading to the proliferation of cells with random genetic alterations. Thus, inflammation can contribute to carcinogenesis and cancer progression also by genetic destabilization of cancer cells [23]. Indeed, the high degree of genetic heterogeneity in tumor cells points out genomic instability as an important feature for tumor development, selecting an heterogenous population of tumor cells according to their ability to proliferate, spread through the organism, and evade host defenses [24].

From a mechanistic point of view, in tumor cells, both intrinsic and extrinsic pathways converge in the activation of transcription factors, mainly nuclear factor-κB (NF-κB) [25], signal transducer, and activator of transcription-3 (STAT-3) [26], activator protein-1 (AP-1) [27], and hypoxia-inducible factor-1 (HIF-1) [28]. These transcription factors control the expression of genes involved in both innate and adaptive immunities that activate the synthesis and release of inflammatory mediators, including cytokines, (TNF-α, IL-1β, and IL-6), chemokines, as well as the induction of cyclooxygenase-2 (COX-2), which give rise to the production of eicosanoids, including PGs and LTs. These mediators activate the same transcription factors in various immune cells, stromal and tumor cells, giving rise to the inflammatory environment which characterizes the TME. Thus, extracellular signals and cross talks among several cells contribute to the shaping of the TME to support tumor growth and survival [29].

Nontumor cells present within the tumor microenvironment

Almost all tumors are characterized by a leukocyte infiltrate along with modifications in the surrounding stroma. Initially, these infiltrations of immune cells and stroma alterations were thought to be the consequence of the immune reaction of the host to the tumor's presence. Thus, in inflammatory responses, immune cells secrete inflammatory mediators [cytokines, PGs, LTs, and nitric oxide (NO)] that activate defense mechanisms that contribute to the killing of invading organisms. Only recently, it was understood how for tumor development, progression, and fate, it is important to appropriately reshape its environment [29].

The tumor cells modify their environment through the secretion of various cytokines, chemokines, and other factors, that lead to a reprogramming of the surrounding cells (endothelial cells and fibroblasts), along with the recruitment of immune cells such as macrophages, neutrophils, myeloid-derived suppressor cells (MDSCs) [30], MCs, dendritic cells (DCs), natural killer cells (NKs), and adaptive immune system cells (T and B cells) to lead to the TME. Tumor-associated macrophages (TAMs) and neutrophils (TAN) are important components of the leukocyte infiltrate of solid tumors, and several studies support their relevance to tumor progression [31].

II. Nitric oxide pathway and cancer progression and therapy

TAMs and TANs instead of eliminating tumors exert protumoral functions, fostering tumor cell invasion, extracellular matrix remodeling, angiogenesis, metastasis, and inhibit the antitumoral immune reaction [32]. Based on their adaptability (plasticity) in response to the signals of the environment, macrophages can modify their phenotype, switching from the classical cytotoxic M1 phenotype to the immunosuppressive M2 phenotype, which promotes tumor growth, tissues remodeling, angiogenesis, and suppress the immune reactions. This dualism in the M1/M2 phenotypes is a simplification originated by in vitro studies, because in vivo macrophages can acquire a wide spectrum of different phenotypes and functions (where M1-M2 represents the extremes). In particular, macrophage stimulation with TGF-β, IL-10, glucocorticoids, or immune complexes leads to the M2-polarized subtypes that are specific (M2-like) and different from the "classical" M2 phenotype induced by IL-4 or IL-13 [33].

Physiologically, this macrophage polarization switch from M1 to M2 is due to a self-protection mechanism. Indeed, in order to reduce the tissue-damaging effects of the M1 macrophage action, after pathogen clearance, macrophages undergo apoptosis or switch into an antiinflammatory M2 phenotype, that minimize the inflammatory response, fostering tissue remodeling, and wound healing.

Tumor cells are able to take advantage of this self-protection mechanism in order to skew or "hijack" macrophages leading to a protumoral effect and evading the immunosurveillance [34]. In the TME, M2-type macrophages exert a relevant immunosuppressive role, not only by secreting IL-10, TGF-β, and human leukocyte antigen G (HLA-G), but also interacting with MDSCs and suppressing T-cell-mediated antitumor responses, by increasing the expression of programmed cell death ligand 1 (PD-L1) [35] and T-lymphocyte antigen 4 (CTLA4) [36,37].

Moreover, M2 macrophages can directly have an impact on cancer cell proliferation by secretion of TGF-β, fibroblast growth factor (FGF) and epidermal growth factor (EGF). Due to tumor immunogenicity, the immune system is able to discriminate between healthy and malignant cells and to give rise to immune responses (innate or adaptive) able to stop tumor growth and to clear it [38]. Among the immune cells involved in tumor suppression, in addition to macrophages and neutrophils, T lymphocytes are important players of the adaptive immune system, especially considering their antigen-directed cytotoxicity [39].

T-cells can be distinguished from other immune cells by the expression of the T-cell receptor (TCR) on their cellular membrane. Antigen stimulation of the TCR gives rise to T-cell activation and proliferation, but an additional signaling or costimulation by another membrane protein (CD28) is necessary to fully activate T-cell functions [40].

Two broad subtypes of differentiated T-cells, with different mechanisms and functions in controlling and organizing the immune response, are characterized by the expression of additional coreceptors, CD4 and CD8, respectively. T-cells recognize peptide antigens derived from nonself-proteins degraded intracellularly and loaded onto the cell surface MHC molecules. CD4 + T-cells ("helper" T-cells) detect antigen in the context of MHC class II molecules, and secrete various cytokines with chemotactic and proinflammatory properties enhance the capacity of DCs to induce CD8 + T-cell responses and to eliminate tumor cells. CD8 + T-cells (killer T-cells) detect antigen in the context of MHC class I molecules and give rise to direct cytotoxic reactions that kill tumor cells, secrete interferon-γ (IFN-γ), and TNF-α. For tumor suppression, the mutual relationship between CD4 and CD8 T-cells that require antigen experience for both T-cell populations to trigger antitumor immunity is an important function within the adaptive immune system [41].

Another distinct population of T-cells is represented by the regulatory T-cells (Treg) or "suppressor" T-cells that provide tolerance, preventing immune cells to react against "self" cells giving rise to an "autoimmune" reaction. These Treg cells are recruited in the TME in order to prevent the immune response against tumor cells [42].

Another mechanism to provide tolerance is the production of the inhibitory molecules CTLA-4 and PD-1 that are expressed during immune responses and represent a "checkpoint" to avoid T-cell hyperactivation. This mechanism is also exploited by the tumor to evade immune reaction, and its blockade with antibodies against CTLA-4 or PD-1 induces tumor remissions and durable responses (see "Immunotherapy and immune checkpoint inhibitors" section for more details) [43].

Signaling involved in cancer-related inflammation

As outlined in the previous paragraphs, inflammation turned out as an important factor in carcinogenesis and tumor development, owing to the exposure of the TME to proinflammatory mediators (cytokines, chemokines, prostanoids) along with the overactivation of signaling pathways mediated by the transcription factors NF-κB, STAT3, AP-1, and HIF-1. Activated inflammatory cells (macrophages, neutrophils, dendritic cells, mast cells, and T-cells) that produce proinflammatory mediators are crucial tumor promoters. These proinflammatory mediators not only play a role in the TME but also exert a direct action on tumor cells, stimulating their proliferation, activating their antiapoptotic mechanisms, and evading immunosurveillance.

Transcription factors

The NF-κB pathway can be activated by a large number of extracellular stimuli, such as cytokines (TNF-α and IL-1), through the signaling pathways activated by corresponding receptors (TNFR and IL-1R), or by PAMPs and DAMPs, through the Toll-like receptor (TLR) signaling pathway, or by antigens through TCR activation, or by signaling induced by the EGF receptor (EGFR) [44].

NF-κB is a key player in both innate and adaptive immunities, since it regulates (through PI3K/Akt/mTOR signaling pathway) several genes involved in the differentiation, activation, and survival of immune cells of the innate system as well as T-cells [45]. Indeed, NF-κB has crucial roles in inflammation since it induces the expression of several proinflammatory genes, including those for cytokines (TNF-α, IL-1, IL-6,), chemokines, matrix metalloproteinases (MMPs), COX-2 intercellular adhesion molecules (ICAM-1), and vascular cell adhesion molecules (VCAM-1) [46].

Moreover, NF-κB represents a mechanistic link between inflammation and tumorigenesis, because NF-κB is a major factor in the regulation of apoptosis, which is at the basis of tumor immune surveillance, tumor angiogenesis, and invasiveness; mutations in components of the signaling cascade as well as effects of inflammatory factors in the TME give rise to NF-κB activation in cancer [47].

Interestingly, NF-κB does not only mediate tumorigenesis but also exert antitumorigenic effects both in the TME and in tumor cells [48].

Despite that TNF-α is considered a proinflammatory cytokine, its dual role in carcinogenesis depends on concentration; low TNF-α levels can induce tumorigenesis by the NF-kB pathway and the generation of ROS, but high TNF-α concentrations trigger an antitumor response [49].

The cooperation of both NF-κB and STAT-3 is crucial for cancer-related inflammation and consequent support to tumorigenesis [50]. Thus, while NF-κB signaling contributes to inflammation-driven carcinogenesis, STAT-3 gives rise to cancer-promoting inflammation and prevents antitumor immune responses mediated by cytotoxic cytokines; in addition, it regulates cell proliferation, survival, and apoptosis [51]. Other kinases that interact with the NF-κB pathway are mitogen-activated protein kinases (MAPKs) including Jun-N-terminal kinase (JNK), extracellular signal-regulated kinase (ERK), and p38 [52].

STAT-3, Janus kinase-signal transducer and activator of transcription (JAK-STAT) signaling, controls almost all immune regulatory processes, including those involved in tumor cell recognition and those that mediate tumor immune escape [26]. The JAK/STAT signaling pathway is an intracellular signal transduction pathway that regulates cell proliferation, differentiation, apoptosis, in addition to immune regulation. Though the mechanism of JAK/STAT signaling is not complex, the biological consequences of its activation are complicated owing to its cross talk with other signaling pathways. Moreover, the persistent activation of the JAK/STAT signaling pathway seems to give rise to many immune and inflammatory diseases. Within the STAT family of proteins (1–6), STAT3 and STAT 5 have been widely linked to cancer cell survival, immunosuppression, and inflammation in the TME.

The transcription factor, known as AP-1, is constituted of a group of proteins involved in T-cell activation, differentiation, and functions along with several other cellular processes including proliferation and survival, and is among the critical regulators of the immune response in cancer. It is also one of the downstream targets of the MAPK signaling [27].

HIF-1 (α or β) is the main transcription factor activated in hypoxic conditions. In the hypoxic TME, HIF-1 signaling suppresses the immune responses by stimulating the epithelial-mesenchymal transition, inducing the expression of immunosuppressive factors such as VEGF, PGE_2, and immune checkpoint molecules (PD-1/PD-L1). In addition, HIF-1 promotes cancer cell survival, proliferation, and motility [28].

Cytokines

IL-6 is an inflammatory cytokine that activates STAT-3, plays a key role in promoting oncogenesis and tumor growth, and inhibits apoptosis. IL-6 signaling, after interaction with the IL-6 receptor (IL-6R), is mediated by the JAK/STAT pathway. In addition to IL-6, other cytokines such as IL-10 and IL-17 activate STAT-3 along with other factors such as TGF-β, vascular endothelial growth factor (VEGF), and granulocyte-macrophage colony-stimulating factor (GM-CSF). STAT-3 activation, in several human tumors, leads to the expression of antiapoptotic genes, activates cell transformation controlled by the Src oncogene, blocks the expression of IL-12 and INF-γ, and suppresses macrophages, DCs, and T-cells antitumor effects [53].

IL-1 is a cytokine which triggers and amplifies the inflammatory response controlling the innate immune response [54]. IL-1 also plays a crucial role in promoting cancerogenesis and cancer progression, since it is upregulated in several types of tumors including lung, breast, colon, head and neck, pancreas, and melanoma. IL-1 can be produced and secreted by cancer cells, leading to the recruitment within the TME of protumor immune cells leading to immunosuppression [55].

Though at the present are known 11 members of the IL-1 family, all related with inflammatory processes and cancer, the more studied members are IL-1α and IL-1β, acting through the same receptor IL-1R. Both IL-1α and IL-1β are proinflammatory cytokines, players of the innate immune system, where they are the response to PAMPs or DAMPs. IL-1α is constitutively expressed at a low level by several types of cells, including macrophages, DCs, T-cells, endothelial and epithelial cells along with fibroblasts. These cells release IL-1α in response to stress-associated factors, DAMPs, and PAMPs, thus acting as an alarmin. But when the inflammatory response is initiated, the expression of IL-1α increases remarkably.

IL-1β is a cytokine expressed by cells of myeloid origin in response to inflammatory stimuli. IL-1β activates innate immune cells with a polarization aimed at resolving acute inflammation. In addition, it upregulates COX-2 with an increase of PGs that mediate MDSCs propagation. Overexpression of IL-1α and IL-1β has been shown to promote tumor growth and metastasis by inducing the expression of angiogenic genes and growth factors. In particular, IL-1β produced by TAM promotes angiogenesis and MDSCs propagation, as well as leads to antiapoptotic signaling in tumor cells [56].

IL-17 A-F is a family of proinflammatory cytokines involved in the control of several activities, including host defense, inflammation, and tissue repair [57]. Though it is known that IL-17 is mainly produced by Th17 (a CD4 + T-cell), also other immune and nonimmune cells can release IL-17. This cytokine is an important player of innate immunity since its activity is tightly connected with T-cells and its deregulation leads to autoimmunity and allergic diseases. Analogously to the TLR and IL-1R, IL-17 signaling activates transcription factors that lead to gene expression mediated by NF-κB and MAPK pathways. Moreover, IL-17 interacts synergistically with other ligands such as TNFα, lipopolysaccharide (LPS) for the activation of NF-κB, with IFN-γ for activation of STAT1 and with TGF-β. IL-17 promotes tumorigenesis both by activation of transcription factors (such as NF-κB, STAT, AP-1 as well as activation of MAPK pathways) which result in cancer cell stimulation, and by an immunosuppressive effect in the TME [58]. TGF-β is a potent immuno-suppressive and antiinflammatory factor that has a role in embryogenesis, cell differentiation, and proliferation, as well as apoptosis [59]. TGF-β is released within the TME by tumor cells, immune cells, and fibroblasts, and it promotes tumor growth, metastasis, and immuno-suppression. TGF-β's function during cancer development is complex and depends on both the involved cell type and the stage of tumorigenesis. In the early steps of tumorigenesis, TGF-β promotes tumor suppression, inhibiting the progression of the cell cycle and activating apoptosis, but later it promotes the epithelial-mesenchymal transition (EMT) by increasing invasion and metastasis. Currently, TGF-β is considered an interesting target for cancer therapy [60].

IL-10 is a powerful antiinflammatory cytokine, produced by almost all the cells of the immune system (both myeloid and lymphoid cells), but also by cancer cells. Macrophages and DCs activated by TLR and MAPK are the key players in regulating IL-10 expression [61].

II. Nitric oxide pathway and cancer progression and therapy

Through the activation of STAT3 mediated by MAPK, IL-10 leads to a protumorigenic effect, due to upregulation of Bcl-2 and activation of resistance to apoptosis. IL-10 inhibits NF-kB and consequently downregulates the expression of proinflammatory cytokines. IL-10 affects macrophages and DCs maturation and differentiation, and inhibits cytokine production and IFN-γ secretion by T-cells, thus allowing tumor cells to evade immunosurveillance [62].

Eicosanoids

In response to cancer-related inflammation, in addition to cytokines and chemokines, also proinflammatory eicosanoids are released by epithelial and immune cells in order to create the TME.

As highlighted by several in vitro and in vivo studies, PGs and LTs (AA [63] bioactive metabolites known as eicosanoids) [64] are not only endowed with a key role in promoting inflammation and in establishing the TME, but they are also involved in the cross talk among tumor cells, immune cells, and stromal cells. One example of PGs/cytokines cooperation in the amplification of inflammation is the synergistic activation of NF-κB to induce the expression of inflammatory genes, including COX-2, which gives rise to a positive feedback loop. Another example is the induction of expression of the cytokine receptors, as observed for T-cell differentiation or Th17 cell expansion. Several prostanoids, including PGE$_2$, highly expressed in tumor tissues, suppress antitumor immune reaction [65].

Phospholipase A2 releases AA from the cellular membrane in response to stimuli, such as LPS, cytokines, growth factors, stress, and other physiological stimuli. Free intracellular AA is metabolized to eicosanoids, by COX isoforms (mainly COX-1 and COX-2) leading to PGs and thromboxane A2 (TXA2), or lipoxygenases (5-, 8-, 12-, and 15-LOX) leading to LTs, or cytochrome P450-dependent monooxygenase (MOX) leading to epoxy-eicosatrienoic acids (EETs), dihydroxy-eicosatetraenoic acid (diHETE), eicosatetraenoic acids (ETEs), and LXs (Fig. 1) [66].

Eicosanoids act locally by binding to specific G-protein-coupled receptors (GPCRs), and can either give rise to inflammatory responses or resolve inflammation [67]. In particular, PGH$_2$, produced by COX, is converted by cell-specific PG synthases into biologically active PGs: PGD$_2$, PGE$_2$, PGF$_{2\alpha}$ prostacyclin (PGI$_2$), and TXA$_2$; these mediators have a half-life ranging from seconds to minutes [68]. PGs activate a family of GPCRs that propagate the signal through distinct downstream pathways. For example, the major inflammatory mediator PGE$_2$ activates EP1, EP2, EP3, and EP4 receptors; EP2 and EP4 receptors activate cyclic adenosine monophosphate (cAMP) signaling and PI3K pathway; and EP3 inhibits cAMP signaling while EP1 activates the PKC and Ca^{2+} pathways [69].

Inflammatory cells including leukocytes, macrophages, and mast cells synthesize LTs through the LOX pathway [64]. In contrast to the fast cleared PGs, LTs have a half-life up to 4 h. LTA$_4$, LTB$_4$, and LTD$_4$ are inflammatory mediators synthesized by the 5-LOX pathway.

Inflammation-associated cancers overexpress COX-2 and LOX (5- and 12-), and the importance of these enzymes in carcinogenesis is supported by several clinical trials and animal experiments [70].

The corresponding eicosanoid products can support tumor progression through several mechanisms, either by directly activating their receptors on the tumor cells to activate cell proliferation, suppress apoptosis, and promote migration and invasion, or by inducing cells of the normal microenvironment to support tumor growth creating the TME [71].

PGE$_2$ induces proliferation by activating at least two signaling pathways Ras-Erk and glycogen synthase kinase-3β (GSK3β); in addition, it promotes tumor cell survival by activating the PI3K/Akt/mTOR pathway. Inhibition of apoptosis by PGE$_2$ is thought to be due to upregulation of BCL-2, an antiapoptotic factor, and activation of NF-κB [72]. PGE$_2$ controls tumor-related immunosuppression through T-cells, Treg, DCs, and MDSCs. The immunosuppressive action of PGE$_2$, which is responsible for the switch of cytotoxic T-cells into protumoral T helper cells, is due to the downregulation of the release of TNFα, IFN-γ, and the upregulation of the release of IL-10 and IL-6 exerted by PGE$_2$ on the T-cells [73]. Moreover, PGE$_2$ promotes tumor progression by recruiting MDSCs, promoting their expansion, and stabilizing the phenotype [74].

Conversely, PGD2 exhibits antitumorigenic activity in various experimental models [75]. In colon tumor cells, LTB4 promotes cell proliferation and survival by activation of the BLT1-Erk pathway, while in pancreatic cancer cells, it promotes cell proliferation by activation of both the Mek-Erk and PI3K/Akt pathways [76]. COX-2 induction by means of LTD$_4$, as well as PGE$_2$ production, strongly suggest a cross talk between the 5-LOX and COX-2 pathways. Indeed, dual COX/5-LOX inhibitors are being developed and are more potent in several tumor models in inducing cancer cells apoptosis than inhibiting either eicosanoid pathway alone [77]. The human 5-LOX pathway, which can be induced by proinflammatory stimuli, is involved in the carcinogenesis and in tumor progression of several cancers (including lung, breast, and prostate), while inhibition of 5-LOX reduces tumorigenesis and cancer cell proliferation.

Both 5-HETE and 12-HETE are also products of LOX and are responsible for tumor growth and progression. 5-HETE can stimulate the proliferation of cancer cells and act as a survival factor, whereas the inhibition of its formation gives rise to apoptosis of cancer cells. Moreover, 5-HETE has a critical role in angiogenesis, in the motility of the tumor cell, in tumor cell-vasculature interactions, and metastasis [78]. Also, 12-LOX, the enzyme that in human biosynthesizes 12-HETE, is involved in both proliferation and survival of cancer cells, and inhibition of this enzyme decreases proliferation and induces apoptosis [79].

In the resolution phase of inflammation, PGE$_2$ and PGD$_2$ induce the production of nonimmunosuppressive mediators, such as LXs and resolvins that act as both antiinflammatory and proresolving agents activating specific mechanisms to promote homeostasis [80]. LXs, which are eicosanoids secreted during the resolution of inflammation, have been demonstrated to be antitumorigenic. The two most potent mediators of the resolution of inflammation LXA$_4$ and LXB$_4$ (Fig. 1) stop neutrophil infiltration, stimulate macrophages to clear cellular debris and apoptotic neutrophils, and inhibit the release of proinflammatory mediators/ROS [81].

Interestingly, aspirin triggers the formation of carbon-15 epimeric LXs, known as aspirin-triggered lipoxins (ATLs). This is due to the effect of COX-2 acetylation, which blocks prostanoid biosynthesis switching its activity in the conversion of AA into 15R-hydroxyeicosatetraenoic acid (15R-HETE), and this transformation occurs at the level of vascular endothelial cells/epithelial cells. 15R-HETE in neutrophils is in turn transformed by 5-LOX into the 15-R-epimers of LXs (ATLs). ATLs displayed strong antiinflammatory activity and have been proved to be effective agents in promoting resolution of inflammation in a number of animal models and in some clinical trials [82].

II. Nitric oxide pathway and cancer progression and therapy

Recently discovered new endogenous antiinflammatory and proresolving lipid mediators are resolvins, which are derived from metabolism of the omega-3 polyunsaturated fatty acids: eicosapentaenoic acid (EPA, E-series) and docosahexaenoic acid (DHA, D-series) [83]. The E-series Rv include RvE_1, RvE_2, RvE_3, and RvE_4, all of them are involved in resolving inflammation (Fig. 2).

The D-series consists of RvD_1 and 17R-RvD_1 that potently stimulate macrophage phagocytosis of tumor cell debris, promote resolution of inflammation, and are tissue protective; RvD_2 promotes the clearance of tumor cell debris, suppresses tumor growth, and is tissue protective; RvD_3 and 17R-RvD_3 are potent regulators of leukocyte activation with anticancer activity; RvD reduces the release of neutrophil extracellular traps and controls thrombosis; RvD5 controls bacterial infections and stimulates phagocytosis performed by M1 macrophages [84]. Moreover, Rv effectively regulates the release of TNFα, IL-6, IL-8, and other cytokines/chemokines from macrophages stimulated by cancer cell debris, thus further reducing inflammation [85]. The biosynthesis of E-series Rv starts from EPA and proceeds via the production of 15- or 18-hydroperoxy-eicosapentaenoic acid, in turn converted into 15- or 18-hydroxy-eicosapentaenoic acid (HEPE). These precursors can be biosynthesized by the action of P-450 enzymes in epithelial cells followed by the sequential action of 5-LOX and 15-LOX enzymes to lead to Rv [86].

Also in this case, acetylation of COX-2 by aspirin inhibits the PGs biosynthesis but does not impair its ability to produce 18R-HEPE starting from EPA, thus leading to RvE1 and RvE2, while direct EPA processing by 15-LOX gives rise to RvE3, and EPA conversion into 15-S-HEPE by 15-LOX followed by 5-LOX action provides RvE4 [87]. D-series Rv are produced through successive actions of 15-LOX and 5-LOX on DHA; also in this case, acetylated COX-2 leads to the R-epimer (namely 17-R epimer).

COX-2 and cancer

The discovery of the relationship between chronic inflammation and cancer prompted to investigate the effects on cancer prevention or treatment exerted by antiinflammatory drugs. Therefore, a great deal of preclinical and clinical research was focused on the use of the well-known nonsteroidal antiinflammatory drugs (NSAIDs) for cancer prevention or treatment. Many of these investigations were epidemiologic studies, where the impact of NSAIDs use on the risk reduction in the development of several types of cancer, such as breast, colorectal, lung, head and neck, prostate and ovarian cancer, was assessed [88].

NSAIDs exert their antiinflammatory effect by inhibition of PGs synthesis, and in addition to the antiinflammatory effect, they are endowed with antipyretic and analgesic properties and are among the most commonly prescribed drugs worldwide [89]. Examples of NSAIDs include aspirin, naproxen, ibuprofen, nimesulide, meloxicam, diclofenac, and celecoxib, all these drugs inhibit COX. As discussed in "Eicosanoids" section, free intracellular AA is metabolized to eicosanoids by enzymes such as COXs, LOXs, and CYP. Among them, PGH synthase (PGHS) (COX) catalyzes the conversion of AA into PGG_2, which is in turn converted into PGH_2 by a peroxidase activity. Then, cell-specific syntheses convert PGH_2 into PGD_2, PGE_2, $PGF_{2\alpha}$, PGI_2, and TXA_2 [90].

PGHS is then an enzyme that catalyzes two coupled reactions: an initial cyclo-oxygenation reaction followed by hydroperoxide formation; since drugs that inhibit PGs formation generally inhibit the first cyclo-oxygenation reaction, PGHS is generally described as COX. Thus, COX is the rate-limiting step enzyme for the production of PGE_2 and other PGs. For COX two isoforms (COX-1 and COX-2) and a splice variant (COX-3) [91] have been reported so far. Among these isoforms, COX-1 is constitutively expressed in a wide range of tissues, where it works as a housekeeping enzyme, it is involved in maintaining tissue homeostasis, in platelet function, and in gastrointestinal (GI) cytoprotection, and it is responsible for the physiological production of prostanoids; involvement of COX-1 in cancer has been recently reviewed [92].

COX-2 is an enzyme whose expression is upregulated in several cells during the inflammatory processes, leading to the synthesis of PGE_2 (along with PGF2α and TXA_2) [93]. In addition, though COX-2 expression is usually negligible in normal cells, a basal expression is reported in kidney, stomach, central nervous system, and female reproduction system [94]. Moreover, COX-2 is frequently overexpressed in several types of cancers, including GI, lung, breast, head and neck, pancreatic and hepatocellular cancer, and associated with poor prognosis [95].

COX-1 and COX-2 enzymes are characterized by about 60% sequence identity and by similar three-dimensional structures, but there are differences in the active sites (COX-2 binding site is more flexible and with a side pocket not present in COX-1) that allowed the development of "selective" COX-2 ligands [96]. As the matter of fact, all NSAIDs, in a concentration-dependent mode, can inhibit both COX-1 and COX-2; for COX-2 selectivity, it is intended the ratio between the 50% inhibitory concentration (IC_{50}) values for COX-1 and COX-2. Selective COX-2 inhibitors have been named coxibs, while COX inhibitors with scanty selectivity for COX-2 are referred to as traditional NSAIDs (t-NSAIDs). Namely, an IC_{50} ratio > 1 indicates that the drug is preferentially selective for COX-2; conversely, a ratio < 1 indicates that the drug is more selective for COX-1. For example, COX-1/COX-2 ratios for naproxen and ibuprofen are 0.49 and 0.56, respectively, while coxibs that have a ratio > 1 include meloxicam, diclofenac, celecoxib, etoricoxib, and rofecoxib.

Therapy with t-NSAIDs gives rise to side effects, such as GI erosions (GI side effect) as well as renal side effects (renal insufficiency and even renal failure in severe cases). Such critical adverse reactions are mostly dependent on COX-1 inhibition [97]. Coxibs were developed to overcome these GI and renal side effects [98]. However, several studies of clinical pharmacology and epidemiology performed on coxibs highlighted that preferential inhibition of COX-2 leads to cardiovascular (CV) hazard, due to an increased risk of coronary events related to a diminished restraining effect of endothelial PGI_2 on platelet activation [99].

Interestingly, an analysis of the outcome of a clinical trial in high-risk CV patients, which compared the CV risk of celecoxib, ibuprofen, and naproxen, pointed out that the use of both t-NSAIDs and coxibs, dose dependently, may increase the CV risks (increased risks of elevated blood pressure, heart attack or stroke as well as an increased risk of thrombotic events) [100]. Thus, coxibs CV hazard is shared with t-NSAIDs (excepted aspirin) through the same mechanism, and it could be more relevant as higher is the COX-2 selectivity of the drug, even though there is still an open debate about this issue [101].

Despite the interesting clinical data on cancer prevention along with the evidences about COX-2 involvement in cancer, the side effects found with both t-NSAIDs and coxibs strongly

II. Nitric oxide pathway and cancer progression and therapy

impacted the clinical investigations on NSAIDs effects in oncology [102]. However, owing to the striking data about the cancer-protective effects of NSAIDs in many types of tumors, many experimental studies aimed at exploring the underlying mechanisms of the anticancer effects exerted by NSAIDs have been carried out mainly in cell lines or in animal models.

COX-2 and colorectal cancer

Colorectal cancer (CRC) is the third common fatal cancer in developed countries, and it could be caused by factors such as genetic alterations, smoking, alcohol drinking, obesity, diet and lifestyle, as well as chronic inflammation (IBD/colitis-associated CRC) [103] and elevated COX-2 expression levels [104]. Historically, the attention was firstly focused on the role played by PGs and COX in cancer, since it was discovered that colonic polyps in patients with familial adenomatous polyposis almost completely disappeared by long-term therapy with sulindac [105].

Indeed, overexpression of COX-2 mRNA was found in almost 80% of the CRC patients, suggesting that COX-2 expression could be a biomarker for CRC risk, and a promising drug target [106]. As previously discussed, deregulated inflammation is among the key drivers for tumor initiation and development. In the intestine, inflammation takes place when the balance between external pathogens pressure and intestinal barrier defense collapses; if the homeostasis is not reestablished infiltrated immune cells and fibroblast promote tumorigenesis and cancer development. In this context, COX-2/PGE_2/EPs signaling plays a crucial role since PGE_2 regulates several functions in immune cells, and COX-2 overexpression is observed in the early phases of CRC development [107]. Indeed, increased PGE_2 levels not only promote CRC stem-like cells [108] expansion and metastasis, but also promote tumor immune evasion, inducing the differentiation of macrophages in the M2 phenotype, inhibiting NK cells and DCs proliferation, inducing the switch of cytotoxic T-cells into Treg, and finally increasing IL-10 release [109].

As discussed in "Eicosanoids" section, COX-2/PGE_2 signaling is mediated by PGE_2 receptors (EP1-4), each coupled to different intracellular signaling pathways. The studies on CRC provided more insights about the underlying mechanisms linking COX-2/PGE_2 axis to carcinogenesis and tumor progression. PGE_2 signaling by the EP4 receptor is involved in the CRC stem cells expansion and hence in colorectal tumorigenesis owing to the activation of the downstream PI3K/Akt/mTOR pathway [110]; in addition, the concomitant activation of Ras-MAPK (ERK1) pathway by PGE_2-EP4 signaling allows maintenance and proliferation of stem cells [111]. Downstream of EP4 receptor, both PI3K and MAPK pathways are independent; however, both pathways are required for NF-κB activation by PGE_2, thus pointing out a mechanistic link between chronic inflammation and CRC. Moreover, PGE_2 signaling through EP2 and EP4 activates not only the PI3K/Akt/mTOR survival pathway, but also β-catenin signaling that promotes COX-2 transcription which in turn induces an amplification loop leading to CRC cells migration and metastasis [112].

Antagonists or knockdown of EP4 receptor, inhibitors of PI3K, ERK, and NF-κB suppress PGE_2-induced stimulation and proliferation of CRC cells as well as formation of metastasis. Knockdown of ERK1 or PI3K also reduced PGE_2-triggered NF-κB activation. In human Caco-2 cell line, PGE_2-EP4 axis also inhibits apoptosis through the PI3K/Akt/mTOR pathway and p38 MAPK activation [113].

Interestingly, recent studies about the resistance to immunotherapy, and in particular to PD-1/PD-L1 antagonists, highlighted the COX-2 colocalization of PD-1 receptor in the TME of the peripheral CRC cells. In addition, it was found that PD-1 expression, in macrophages and T-cells, was increased by COX-2-PGE$_2$ activation due to binding of NFκB to the PD-1 promoter, via the EP4-PI3K-Akt signaling pathway. Accordingly, silencing COX-2 mRNA reduced PD-L1 expression by 86% in CRC cells, and COX-2 inhibitors significantly decrease PD-L1 expression in CRC lesions as well as PD-1 expression in Tregs. These findings point out an important PGE$_2$ role in tumor immune evasion and open new therapeutic opportunities for EP4 antagonists and coxibs in counteracting resistance to PD-1/PD-L1 immunotherapy (see "Immunotherapy and immune check points inhibitors" and "COX-2/PGE2/EPs signaling and immunotherapy" sections for more details) [114].

Overexpression of COX-2 has been also documented in gastric cancer (GC) patients, and COX-2 inhibitors demonstrated chemotherapeutic potentials in GC. GC is mainly due to *Helicobacter pylori* infection, which triggers immune responses by TLRs activation which in turn induces COX-2/PGE$_2$ pathway through NF-κB activation [115].

COX-2 and breast cancer

The use of COX-2 inhibitors in the management of breast cancer (BC), along with analysis of the mechanisms responsible for the anticancer effect of COX-2 inhibitors, has been reviewed [116].

An elevated chemo-preventive effect of coxibs on BC development (about 70% risk reduction) is supported by epidemiological studies that highlight a relationship between COX-2 selectivity and protective effect, as well as point out a correlation among COX-2 overexpression (occurring in 40%–50% BC patients) tumor progression and metastasis [117]. Studies in animal models evidenced how COX-2 overexpression and consequent massive PGE$_2$ production is sufficient by itself for breast tumor initiation, progression, and metastasis, and is linked to poor patient prognosis [118].

As discussed in "Eicosanoids" section, COX-2/PGE$_2$ signaling is mediated by PGE$_2$ receptors (EP1-4), each coupled to different intracellular signaling pathways. Among EP receptors, EP2 and EP4 seem to be involved in BC progression and angiogenesis. In particular, EP2 overexpression in BC cells gives rise to VEGF (C and D) upregulation via a cAMP/PKA-dependent pathway, EP2 plays a role in the oncogenesis induced by TGF-β during BC development, and stimulation of EP2 resulted in an increase of aromatase expression; this last effect is also mediated by EP4 activation and also mediated by cAMP/PKA pathway for both receptors [118].

Transcription of aromatase induced by PGE$_2$ leads to enhanced estrogen levels, which in turn evokes growth factors release leading to cell proliferation. On the other hand, EP4 activation stimulates migration of BC cells, metastasis, and angiogenesis through activation of cAMP/PKA and PI3K/Akt pathways. The expression of iNOS which supports tumor invasiveness is also upregulated in BC cells, owing to COX-2 expression and PGE$_2$/EP4 signaling through the cGMP/PKG pathway [69].

COX-2/EP4 activation, through PI3K/Akt/Notch/Wnt axis, also promotes BC progression by inducing stem-like cells which plays an important role in BC initiation, metastasis, and in resistance to chemotherapy and radiotherapy [119].

A further driving factor for tumor progression is represented by MDSCs owing to their immunosuppressive properties, and in addition, they resulted among the main limiting factors for the efficacy of immunotherapy. MDSCs are induced by PGE_2 activation of EP2 and EP4 receptors expressed on myeloid cells, and activation of these receptors inhibits the maturation of MDSCs in cytotoxic T-cells or dendritic cells [120]. Inhibition of COX-2 in myeloid cells inhibited human M2 macrophage differentiation and switched the TAM phenotype from M2 to M1 [121].

The emergence of endocrine resistance in estrogen receptor-positive BC patients is a relevant issue in the BC therapy with tamoxifen. It was demonstrated how TAMs can be associated with endocrine resistance in BC by increasing the expression of COX-2, which in turn increases PGE_2 concentration that leads to tamoxifen resistance through the activation of the PI3K/Akt/mTOR signaling pathway [122].

Interestingly, it was found in clinical studies that the treatment with COX-2 inhibitors can prevent the development of resistance to chemotherapy with paclitaxel, doxorubicin, or other cytotoxic drugs in BC patients; this effect is likely due to the inhibition of COX-2-mediated upregulation of the efflux pumps critical for multidrug resistance [123].

COX-2 and lung cancer

Lung cancer is the leading cause of cancer-related death worldwide. It is classified into four main subtypes: small-cell lung cancer (SCLC), lung adenocarcinoma (ADC), squamous cell lung cancer (SCLC), and large-cell lung carcinoma (LCLC): last three represent the class of nonsmall-cell lung cancer (NSCLC) [124]; in particular, NSCLC accounts for 80%–85% of LC cases while SCLC accounts for the remaining 15%–20% and is more aggressive [125].

Clinical and epidemiological studies have suggested a strong correlation among chronic infection, inflammation, and the LC pathogenesis. In addition, a correlation between elevated circulating levels of C-reactive protein, an inflammation marker, and elevated LC risk has been widely documented [126]. Though one of the main causes for LC seems to be cigarette smoking, several studies suggested an increased risk also in patients with inflammatory lung diseases as well as infections (tuberculosis or pneumonia). Other studies highlighted a connection between LC risk and genetic polymorphisms in the inflammation pathway and hence in the modulation of the inflammatory response [127].

As previously discussed, also for LC, a deregulated inflammatory response promotes tumor progression, by releasing proangiogenic and immunosuppressive factors in the TME, that lead to proliferation and survival of malignant cells, resistance to apoptosis, and metastasis [128].

Epidemiological studies and metaanalysis indicated that prolonged use of t-NSAIDs reduces LC risk, and that these chemo-preventive properties are related to the COX inhibitory activity of NSAIDs [129]. Indeed, COX-2 is overexpressed in 70% to 90% of NSCLC (particularly in ADC and SCLC) and is associated with poor prognosis [130]. COX-2 overexpression and the related high PGE_2 concentration lead to the proinflammatory environment which plays a striking role in both initiation and growth of LC. Approximately 80% of LCs are connected to cigarette smoking; in fact, benzo(a)pyrene along with other carcinogens derived from tobacco smoke can induce COX-2 expression and raise the PGE_2 level.

The survival-promoting and proproliferative properties of the PGE$_2$/EP4 axis are due to several different molecular mechanisms also in LC.

In NSCLC cells, PGE$_2$ activates the PI3K/Akt/mTOR pathway [131], which has a key role in the initiation and progression of the disease, by promoting cell proliferation, invasion, metastasis, and angiogenesis, as well as in preventing apoptosis. Moreover, also in LC, the PI3K/Akt/mTOR activation gives rise to a feedback loop which leads to COX-2 expression, thus amplifying the response; inhibiting the pathway using a PI3K inhibitor abrogates the PGE$_2$-induced protumor effect, as well as a synergistic action in reducing LC cell proliferation and migration was highlighted when combining a PI3K inhibitor with a COX-2 inhibitor [132].

The Wingless-type protein (Wnt)/β-catenin pathway turned out to be among the main signaling pathways involved in lung homeostasis, and its deregulation is associated with increased carcinogenic potential since it is involved in maintaining LC stem cells population, at the same time promoting cell proliferation and differentiation [133]. The Wnt/β-catenin signaling pathway has an important role in LC tumorigenesis and development especially when it is activated in the presence of KRAS mutations that leads to constitutive activation of the KRAS (missense mutations), thus leading to KRAS and Wnt-jointed activation [134]. In NSCLC cells, Wnt is also involved in the control of apoptosis and in the induction of PD-1, as well as in controlling angiogenesis [135].

Preclinical data highlight that sulindac suppresses β-catenin expression in LC cells and inhibits proliferation by downregulating transcriptional targets of β-catenin. In addition, it was shown that in LC cells inhibition of COX-2/Wnt/β-catenin signaling pathway significantly promoted apoptosis and inhibited the tumor growth [136]. A close correlation between COX-2-PGE$_2$ axis and Wnt/β-catenin signaling pathway turned out in several studies, and nowadays, it is known how COX-2/PGE$_2$ modulates Wnt/β-catenin pathway. PGE$_2$ activation of EP-2 and EP-4 on one side leads to PKA activation by increasing cAMP, and on the other side through c-Src-mediated EGFR signaling activates Ras/MAPKs and PI3K/Akt pathways. Akt activation gives rise to β-catenin pathway control through GSK3β, preventing β-catenin degradation. Accordingly, activation of COX-2 leads to significantly elevated transcriptional/translational levels of the key gene β-catenin in Wnt/β-catenin signaling pathway, and COX-2 inhibition strikingly decreased these transcriptional/translational levels [137].

Aberrant activation of the COX-2/Wnt/β-catenin pathway has been reported to promote survival and proliferation of cancer stem cells not only in LC but also in other tumors such as glioblastoma, gastric, colorectal, breast and prostate cancer [138]. An increase in cellular c-Src tyrosine kinase protein level and activity is correlated to promotion of metastasis, and c-Src inhibition decreases tumor cell migration and invasion. Finally, PGE$_2$ activates ERK phosphorylation in ADC lung cells, thus promoting cell migration [139].

Preclinical experiments in animal models of LC highlighted a tumor reduction when COX-2 inhibitors were combined with chemotherapeutic drugs. These findings prompted several clinical trials to evaluate the effects of COX-2 inhibitors combined with chemotherapy or radiation therapy in patients with advanced NSCLC. In addition, celecoxib, in lung tumors implanted in mice, delayed the LC growth and improved the chemotherapy effects, suggesting that celecoxib at the higher doses could prevent the development of the tumors in LC patients [140].

II. Nitric oxide pathway and cancer progression and therapy

Despite similar trials with rofecoxib in murine LC models gave analogous results, the GECO phase III trial in the therapy for advanced NSCLC demonstrated that the combined administration of rofecoxib with gemcitabine did not increase overall survival and highlighted CV toxicity. A remarkable CV toxicity also turned out in the clinical trials aimed at assessing the efficacy of rofecoxib in CRC. This serious side effect limited the COX-2 inhibitor clinical dose and discouraged further trials [141].

Though celecoxib displayed a better clinical profile in terms of CV toxicity, several randomized clinical trials have been carried out in LC in combination with standard chemotherapy or radiotherapy, and evidences of a significant improvement in survival indices were not found, as supported by the metaanalysis carried out on these trials [142]. In addition to LC, celecoxib clinical trials were also carried out on the treatment of CRC, BC, prostate, stomach, head and neck cancers, as well as premalignant lesions such as familial adenoma polyposis; the best outcome was observed in CRC, BC, prostate, and head and neck cancers [143]. Thus, in the treatment of NSCLC as well as other cancers, the efficacy of COX-2 inhibitors alone or in combination with therapy remains controversial, and it is difficult to understand whether the failures till now encountered may be due to the limits in the dosage or to other factors.

COX-2 and the immune system

Some of the effects exerted by the COX-2/PGE$_2$/EP pathway on the immune system have been mentioned in previous paragraphs; however, considering the therapeutic potential this pathway may have in the modulation of the immune system, in several kind of cancers, and in particular in the overcoming of the resistance found in cancer immunotherapy with immune checkpoint inhibitors (ICIs), more details are discussed herein.

Immunotherapy and immune checkpoint inhibitors

Over the past 10 years, the clinical application of immunotherapy has revolutionized cancer treatments; in particular, targeting the immune checkpoints, programmed cell death protein I (PD-1), or CTLA4 with blocking antibodies (immune checkpoint inhibitors, ICIs) resulted in a milestone for cancer treatment, giving rise to unprecedented and durable responses in several types of cancers [144]. However, this therapy is still refractory for a significant number of patients, since many of them fail to respond to ICIs or acquire resistance to the therapy; thus, overcoming resistance to ICIs has become a relevant medical need [145].

The immune checkpoint receptor PD-1 is a type I transmembrane protein (size 50–55 kDa) expressed as coinhibitory receptor in several hematopoietic cells and widely expressed in immune cells (macrophages, T-cells, DC, B cells), and it acts as a negative regulator of immune functions. The specific ligands for PD1 are PD-L1 and PD-L2, and these are type I transmembrane proteins with almost overlapping functions, expressed in both lymphoid tissue and nonlymphoid tissue, in immune cells, and usually overexpressed in almost all kind of tumor cells [146].

PD-1 and PD-L1/PD-L2, along with CTLA-4, become important drug targets in order to develop new immune cancer therapies based on immune checkpoint blockade. From 2011 onward, several monoclonal antibodies acting as ICIs have been approved by FDA and EMA. After the approval of ipilimumab (anti-CTLA4), ICIs targeting the PD-1/PD-L1 axis (such as nivolumab, pembrolizumab, and cemiplimab, PD-1 inhibitors; atezolizumab, avelumab, and durvalumab, PD-L1 inhibitors) were also approved to treat a broader range of cancers. Despite CTLA-4-targeting immunotherapy was the first approach that helped to explore the anticancer effects of ICIs, the clinical application of the blockade for the PD-1/PD-L1axis gave overall better results than CTLA4-based therapies, since the PD-1/PD-L1 approach demonstrated, in the treatment of a wide range of cancers, important therapeutic efficacies and long-lasting responses along with relatively limited side effects.

PD-1/PD-L1 and CTLA-4 exert quite different functions in antitumor immune response, since CTLA-4 regulates T-cell proliferation and activation, mainly in lymph nodes, at an early stage of the T-cell immune response, whereas PD-1 acts on T-cells at a later stage of the immune response, mainly in peripheral tissues [147].

Notably, upon activation, T-cells undergo a metabolic reprogramming to fulfill the high energy needs due to the transition between resting, activation, and differentiation states. Thus, in order to obtain the required energy, they skip from the lipid degradation, typical for quiescent T-cells, to the aerobic glycolysis. When PD1 is engaged by PD-L1 or PD-L2, an ERK and PI3K/Akt/mTOR-mediated suppression of oxygen consumptions takes place, aerobic glycolysis is stopped, and the cell metabolism goes back to fatty-lipid oxidation as the main energy source; this prompts T-cells to enter in a quiescent state or become apoptotic [148].

In physiological conditions, the role of PD-1/PD-L1 axis is the fine-tuning of the immune response, in particular for T-cells; it inhibits their proliferation, cytokine production, and cytolytic function (by TCR downmodulation) in order to maintain tolerance, and prevent excessive responses and auto-immune reactions [149]. This mechanism is exploited by tumor cells to evade the immune response, since PD-1/PD-L1 expression can be induced by pro-tumorigenic pathways activated in cancer cells during cancer progression. Since lymphocyte infiltration in tumors mainly consists in memory T-cells specific for tumor antigens, the binding of PD-L1/PD-L2 to PD-1 inhibits the activity and proliferation of CD8+ T-cells, induces their apoptosis, and leads to tumor immune evasion. Conversely, blockade of PD-1/PD-L1 axis triggers anticancer immunity by increasing the number of infiltrated CD8+ memory T-cell and corresponding cytotoxic activity, and promotes immune responses against the cancer cells.

Several molecular mechanisms (previously discussed in "Signaling involved in cancer-related inflammation" section) have been involved in the regulation of PD-L1 expression by cancer cells, such as activation of mitogenic and prosurvival pathways including MAPK and PI3K/AKT/mTOR, increased activity of transcriptional factors HIF-1, STAT-3, NF-κB, and AP-1. The PI3K/Akt pathway is associated in a variety of cells with proliferation and apoptosis, whereas the mTOR pathway is involved in the regulation of the innate and adaptive immune systems and an increase in its activity has been reported in cancers. The PI3K/AKT/mTOR pathway controls the nutritional intake and energy production of CD8+ T-cells, controlling their activation of and is responsible for regulating the biological effects of immune cell stimulation. The association between the PD-1/PD-L1 axis and the MAPK pathway has been reported for metastatic melanoma, NSCLC, CRC, in hepatocellular and renal cell carcinoma, Hodgkin's lymphoma. The inhibition of MAPK pathway increases antigen presentation from tumor cells, potentiates MHC I expression, suppresses Treg expansion, and increases proliferation and activation of tumor-infiltrating cytotoxic T-cells [150]. In

II. Nitric oxide pathway and cancer progression and therapy

preclinical studies, combination therapies aimed at inactivating MAPK jointly with ICIs have recently highlighted a promising synergy [151].

The functional cross talk between Wnt/β-catenin signaling and PD-L1 expression has been widely documented as well as the effects promoted by inhibitors of Wnt pathway on the potentiation of ICIs immunotherapy. The Wnt/β-catenin signaling both controls PD-L1 expressions and impairs CD8+ T-cell infiltration in the TME. For example, glioblastoma (GBM) responds poorly to PD-1 ICIs due to insufficient infiltration of immune cells. Wnt/β-catenin pathway activation in GBM decreases the infiltration of CD8+ T-cells, whereas blockade of Wnt/β-catenin signaling inhibits GBM cells growth and potentiates the response to PD-1 ICIs immunotherapy. Thus, combined treatment with PD-1 ICIs and Wnt/β-catenin signaling inhibitors led to better antitumor immunity than either treatment alone [152]. The JAK/STAT pathway has also been demonstrated to be involved in the control of PD-L1 expression in several cancers such as CRC, pancreatic cancer, NSCLC, and brain metastatic melanoma [153].

The involvement of NF-κB in the induction of PD-L1 expression has been reported in gastric cancer where infiltrated macrophages release cytokines TNF-α and IL-6, which induced PD-L1 expression in tumor cells through TLR and NF-κB signaling. An analogous relationship has also been found in BC, CRC, and melanoma cell lines, where NF-κB inhibitors suppressed INF-γ-induced PD-L1 expression [154].

The transcription factor AP-1, a downstream target of the MAPK pathway, is known to induce the expression of PD-1/PD-L1, but also to regulate Treg differentiation and functions [27].

HIF-1 in the hypoxic TME suppresses the immune responses by stimulating EMT inducing the expression of immunosuppressive including PGE_2 and PD-1/PD-L1 molecules. In addition, HIF-1 promotes cancer cell survival, proliferation, and motility. Recent data suggested that the combination of HIF inhibitors and ICIs may synergize to inhibit tumor development both by potentiating antitumor immunity and inhibiting cancer cell proliferation and survival [155].

COX-2/PGE₂/EPs signaling and immunotherapy

Several preclinical studies have documented the regulation of PD-L1 expression by COX-2, in different types of cancer cells including melanoma, LC, BC, and CRC, but also in immune system cells [156]. These studies highlighted how PGE_2 in the TME promotes tumor immune evasion and how COX-2-PGE_2-EPs signaling pathway contributes to escape the antitumor host immune responses leading to poor responses or even resistance to cancer immunotherapy [157]. In addition, recent retrospective clinical studies highlighted that t-NSAIDs may enhance the overall response rate and time to progression of cancer patients (NSCLC or metastatic melanoma) in treatment with ICIs [158]. For example, the immune system plays an important role in eradicating melanoma cells, and several clinical trials demonstrated that the ICIs approach increases the overall survival of metastatic melanoma patients with or without BRAF/NRAS mutations. However, tumor cells develop immune escape mechanisms that reduce the response rate to ICIs immunotherapy to about 50%. COX-2 is overexpressed in malignant melanomas, and PGE_2 is reported to enhance carcinogenesis, tumor progression, and to support immunosuppression whereas its inhibition may prevent melanoma progression. In addition, melanoma cancer cells that express high levels of COX-2 also coexpressed high PD-L1 levels, and inhibition of COX-2 activity by celecoxib downregulated PD-L1 expression in vitro and prolonged the time-to-progression in clinical trials with ICIs and enhances the response to the therapy with ICIs even reversing resistance [159]. It has been reported that in BC cells, COX-2 suppresses immunosurveillance by inhibiting cytotoxic CD8 + T-cells (cytotoxic T-lymphocyte, CTL) function likely through the PD-1/PD-L1 axis. Remarkably, the mechanism of evading the immune surveillance of CTL by expressing PD-L1 is common to several types of cancer cells [160].

CRC initiation and development occurs under inflammatory conditions related with upregulation of immune checkpoint proteins. Recently, it was reported that in CRC cells, regulation of PD-L1 is dependent on COX-2 expression, and that COX-2 inhibitors (celecoxib and naproxen) decrease the expression of PD-L1 and positively impact the number and the activity of tumor-infiltrating CTLs, significantly decreasing the tumor growth. Studies on the immune modulation promoted by NSAIDs (celecoxib and naproxen) in CRC cell lines highlighted that silencing COX-2 mRNA dramatically reduced PD-L1 expression while a negligible effect on PD-L1 expression was found silencing COX-1. Notably, COX-2 inhibitors not only impacted tumor PD-L1 expression but also reduced the expression of PD-1 and lymphocyte-activation gene-3 (LAG-3) (another coinhibitor receptor) [161] on regulatory T-cells. Importantly, both decrease of PD-L1 expression and increase of CTLs are associated with the inhibition of COX-2/PGE$_2$ pathway. These data clearly suggest that NSAIDs can regulate the immune response in TME by multiple ways, including suppression of expression of PD-1/PD-L1 and regulation of immune cells infiltration and activity [162].

It is known how the continuous challenge with chronic antigen may lead to the failure of tumor-specific immune response due to "exhaustion" of CTLs following the activation of immunosuppressive pathways (PD-1/PD-L1; TGF-β; IL-10) that inhibit the ability of CTLs to produce key cytokines, to maintain memory, and to effectively exert tumor-suppressive function. In in vitro and ex vivo studies, carried out on tumor-infiltrated CTLs, the role of COX-2-PGE$_2$-EPs signaling pathway in depressing CTLs function and survival was further assessed. It was demonstrated that inhibition of COX-2 reversed the ability of cancer cells to suppress CTLs proliferation and functions. In addition, it was found that the combined blockade of PD-1/PD-L1 and COX-2-PGE$_2$-EPs pathway increased the number of infiltrated CTLs with normal effector functions reversing the immunosuppression present in tumor-derived CTLs, thus confirming that the simultaneous inhibition of PGE$_2$/PD-1 pathways is an effective way to rescue CTLs from exhaustion triggered by chronic antigen exposure. The synergy of COX-2 inhibition with ICIs (PD-1/PD-L1) in improving the antitumor immunity was also demonstrated in animal models. Remarkably, since it has been reported that the biological actions of PGE$_2$ involved in the induction of exhausted CTLs are mediated by EP2 and EP4 receptors, it was demonstrated that an EP-2/EP-4 receptor antagonist suppresses tumor growth and restores the immune response toward an antitumorigenic condition as obtained with a COX-2 inhibitor [163].

The approach of blocking both PD-1 and COX-2 has been evaluated in terms of efficacy and safety with a clinical study in CRC (NCT03926338, ongoing) using toripalimab as PD-1 blocker and celecoxib as COX-2 inhibitor, though preliminary data on the combination seem to be promising and long-term data are not available yet [164].

The finding that the antagonism at EPs receptors (in particular EP-4) may lead to the same results obtained with COX-2 inhibitors, in terms of both immunomodulation and reversal of resistance to ICIs, but without CV safety concerns, prompted a series of in-depth studies

II. Nitric oxide pathway and cancer progression and therapy

about this issue [165]. EP-4 receptors are expressed on the surface of tumor cells, immune cells, fibroblasts, and the other tumor stroma cells. EP-4 is upregulated in CRC, LC, BC, prostate, and ovary cancer cells. In vitro and ex vivo studies demonstrated that EP4 antagonists dose-dependently increased the population of intratumoral effector CTLs, suppressed macrophages M2-like polarization, induced the reprogramming to M1-like phenotype, reversed the immunosuppressive effects exerted by PGE_2 on DCs and NK cells, and inhibited MDSCs activation and infiltration in TME. Animal experiments in tumor models, with selective EP-4 antagonists, or experiments of EP-4 gene silencing confirmed in vivo the involvement of EP4 receptor in immunosuppression and tumor growth. In addition, the therapeutic potential of the dual blockade of PD-1/PD-L1 with ICIs and EP4 with small-molecule antagonists was assessed in animal cancer models, highlighting higher antitumor efficacies, decreased tumor volume, and prolonged survival in comparison with each therapy alone [166].

These evidences pointed out how specific inhibition of EP-4 receptor, instead of COX-2 inhibition, might substitute NSAIDs in the therapy of the immune suppression and resistance to ICIs induced by tumors, as discussed above.

Several pharmaceutical companies are currently conducting clinical trials on the combination of EP-4 selective antagonists with ICIs for cancer therapy, particularly the combination of grapiprant and pembrolizumab in patients with advanced CRC (NCT03658772, active), grapiprant and pembrolizumab in patients with advanced or metastatic NSCLC (NCT03696212, terminated), and BMS-986310 administered alone and in combination with nivolumab in patients with advanced solid tumors (NCT03661632, completed). Corresponding results and activity data are not yet available in literature.

mPGES1 inhibitors

Another approach to overcome the COX-2/PGE_2-mediated tumor escape from immune system that targets the PGE_2 pathway downstream of COX-2 consists in the inhibition of microsomal prostaglandin E synthase-1 (mPGES1). This inducible enzyme situated downstream of COX-2 completes the conversion of AA into PGE_2 and is considered a more specific and potentially less toxic target than COX-2 [167]. Overexpression of mPGES1 has been reported in several types of cancer including CRC, GI cancer, BC, NSCLC, pancreatic, kidney, head and neck, and ovary cancer. It has been reported that mPGES1, in terms of evasion of immunity, mediates most of the effects previously mentioned for COX-2/PGE_2 axis. Indeed, current available data highlight mPGES1 as an important factor in controlling CTLs and DCs infiltration in the TME. Moreover, inhibition of PGE_2 formation, using mPGES1 inhibitors resulted in reduced PD-L1 expression in cancer cells and in tumor-infiltrating myeloid cells. Finally, long-lasting tumor regression was observed in mice bearing mPGES1 knockout tumors treated with anti-PD-1 therapy [168].

Clinical trials in inflammatory diseases with mPGES1 inhibitors highlighted a higher inhibition of PGE_2 synthesis than celecoxib, without the suppression of PGI_2 or TXA_2 synthesis; trials using coadministration of mPGES1 inhibitors with ICIs have not carried out till now [169].

IDO1 immunosuppressive action

Another immunosuppressive mechanism in the TME which plays in concert with COX-2 is mediated by indoleamine 2,3-dioxygenase 1(IDO1) [170]. Metabolism of the essential amino acid tryptophan into kynurenine and other metabolites has emerged as an important factor orchestrating tumor immune evasion. Aberrant tumoral expression of IDO1 has been reported for a wide series of cancer cells (including acute myeloid leukemia, melanoma, CRC, BC, NSCLC, and ovarian cancer), and high IDO1 expression is correlated with a poor prognosis and shorter overall survival. In addition to tumor cells, IDO1 is expressed by endothelial cells, fibroblasts, mesenchymal stromal cells, and immune system cells (DCs and macrophages). IDO1 supports the inflammatory process in TME and plays a relevant role in the development of immune tolerance to tumor antigens in immune cells, since its activity suppresses CTLs and NK cells, and promotes the differentiation of Treg and the activation of MDSCs. Thus, IDO1 is traditionally viewed as a general suppressor of T-cell activation, but it also supports tumor growth in the context of chronic inflammation.

In vitro testing demonstrated how the TME, owing to IDO1 activation, is constituted of very low concentration of tryptophan and is enriched in kynurenine, which is immunosuppressive by itself and causes T-cell apoptosis as well as differentiation in Tregs, whereas tryptophan shortage induces an arrest of T-lymphocyte proliferation and reduces intratumoral T-cell infiltration.

Notably, IFN-γ induces IDO1 expression in myeloid cells, since IFN-γ is produced by T-cells at the peak of their response, and the physiological role of IDO1 might be a negative feedback control for the T-cell response, aimed at modulating the immune reaction. IDO-inhibiting drugs for treatment of cancer have been designed and developed, and some of them are presently in clinical development [171].

Recently, it was demonstrated that IDO1 expression was dependent by COX-2/PGE$_2$/EPs axis, which activates PI3K and PKC pathways, that in turn leads to IDO1 transcription in a wide range of human cancers. Moreover, in animal cancer models, COX-2 inhibition translates into downregulation of IDO1 expression at the tumor sites, decreased levels of kynurenine in TME and increased CTLs infiltration and activity, decreased Treg activation, thus avoiding immune surveillance escape of malignant cells. Accordingly, a COX-2 inhibitor could be used instead of an IDO1 inhibitor in immunomodulation and in overcoming resistance to ICIs, because the combined therapy with ICIs and IDO1 inhibitors was found to be effective in potentiating the antitumor response, due to the antiimmunosuppressive effects of IDO1 inhibitors, including an increased infiltration of CTLs in TME [172].

Hybrid drugs: NO-releasing COX inhibitors

COX-inhibiting NO donors and safety

As previously discussed in "COX-2 and cancer" section, all t-NSAIDs can inhibit both COX-1 and COX-2, in a concentration-dependent fashion and with different selectivity for COX-2. Therapy with t-NSAIDs is hampered by some side effects, including damage in the upper and lower GI tracts (GI side effects) and renal insufficiency. These adverse reactions are mainly dependent on COX-1 inhibition [173].

COX-inhibiting nitric oxide donors (CINODs) were a class of drugs initially developed to combine the pharmacological action of a COX inhibitor with the protective action of NO, with the aim of reducing the GI toxicity and improving the renal safety profile of the drug, while retaining its analgesic and antiinflammatory effects [174].

With the discovery of the COX-2 related CV side effects, it was speculated that t-NSAIDs endowed with NO-releasing properties could also mitigate the corresponding CV hazard related to COX-2 inhibition. Because NO is endowed with remarkable CV protective actions, being involved in vascular smooth muscle relaxation, platelet aggregation, thrombosis inhibition, modulation of the platelets, and leucocytes adhesion to the endothelium [175].

Within the CINODs group of compounds, naproxcinod, also referred to as NO-naproxen, was the most investigated drug, and its dual action was obtained by adding to the parent NSAID, via an ester linkage, a NO-releasing moiety (4-(nitrooxy)butanol; NOBA) (Fig. 3).

The combination of a balanced inhibition of the two main COX isoforms, along with the NO release, reduced the GI toxicity while maintaining the potent antiinflammatory activity of naproxen. In animal and clinical studies in osteoarthritis patients, naproxcinod displayed analgesic and antiinflammatory effects comparable to naproxen, but with improved GI safety. In addition, renal-sparing effects have been reported for naproxcinod in comparison with the parent drug, both in animal models of renal failure and in clinical trials. The CV safety of naproxcinod was assessed in a clinical trial on osteoarthritis patients, compared to placebo naproxcinod that showed a similar blood pressure profile, whereas naproxen increased the blood pressure [176]. However, the FDA review of the naproxcinod new drug application [177], though considering of interest the approach, did not consider the provided data enough

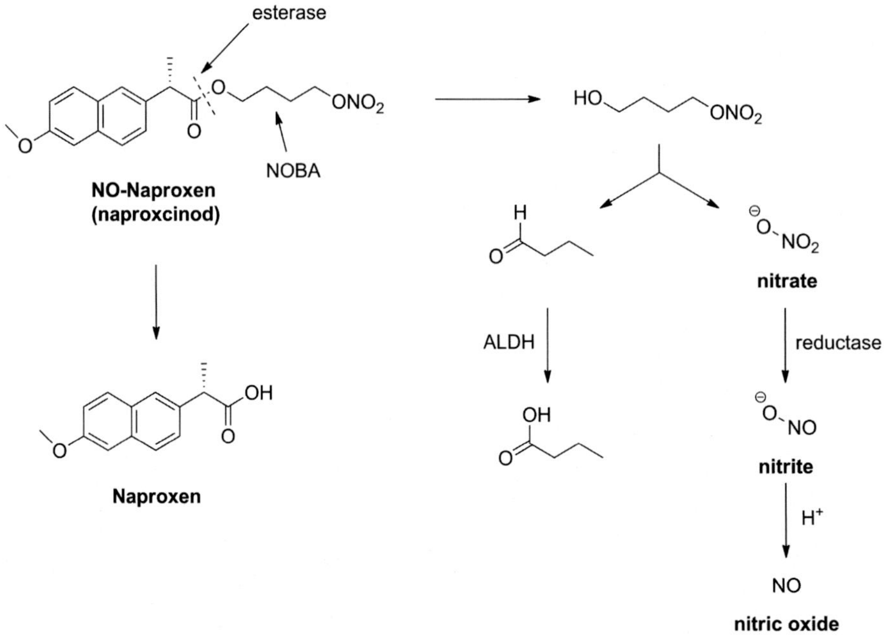

FIG. 3   Metabolic pathways of NO-naproxen (naproxcinod).

to approve naproxcinod as a drug with improved CV safety in comparison with naproxen and requested further long-term CV safety studies, in order to provide robust data about the significance of the difference in CV safety between the two drugs [178].

Taking into account that naproxcinod is the ester of naproxen with NOBA (Fig. 3), despite the fact that metabolic conversion of the nitrooxy derivatives into NO may be complex, the pathway (either enzymatic or not) converting NOBA nitroester into the corresponding hydroxylated derivative is widely considered to be the usual metabolic destiny of organic nitrates [179]. For naproxcinod and related CINODs that utilize the ester bond between the NSAID and NOBA, the esterase-mediated hydrolysis into the NSAID scaffold and NOBA, followed by further metabolic conversion of the NOBA into NO, was proved to be the major metabolic pathway [180]. In this case, the hydrolysis is fast and occurs mainly in the GI tract, rather than in the blood and tissues, and rapidly converts the most of the CINOD into the t-NSAID and NOBA, that can be absorbed and circulate separately. Moreover, most of the NOBA is metabolized in the liver rather than in the peripheral tissues [181].

We thought that this pharmacokinetic profile was unfavorable to optimize the protective and therapeutic effects of the NO release that should be slow and occur mainly in the peripheral tissues, where both the COX inhibitor and the NO donor moiety should jointly exert their action. It is likely that this issue was the main factor that determined the scanty performance of naproxcinod in terms of CV safety. Accordingly, among the possible approaches for "hybridization" of the t-NSAID scaffold, we preferred to focus on those leading to a metabolically more stable link between the nitroester-bearing moiety and the COX-2 inhibitor (see "NO-coxibs based on diarylpyrrole scaffold" section for details). The pharmacokinetics of the compounds and the NO-releasing properties were also optimized in order to provide compounds with the appropriate duration of action along with a relatively slow NO release.

Coxibs were developed to overcome the GI and renal side effects associated with the use of t-NSAIDs; however, they displayed CV hazards shared with t-NSAIDs [182]. In order to obtain COX-2-selective inhibitors with improved CV safety, NO-releasing coxibs have been synthesized by several groups [183]. We synthesized a wide group of compounds endowed with both NO-releasing and COX-2-selective inhibiting properties, some of them have been progressed in advanced preclinical development [184]. Interestingly, in these compounds, both the nitroester and the corresponding hydroxyl derivative metabolite were selective COX-2 inhibitors, some of them with remarkable and long-lasting antiinflammatory effects, as characterized by in-depth studies. The CV beneficial effects of selected compounds were assessed in vitro to evaluate the kinetics of NO release in hepatic homogenate and in the blood, confirming they were slow NO donors and that the NO release was enzymatic. The NO-mediated relaxant effects were evaluated in the vascular smooth muscle. Moreover, the chronic oral administration of the selected candidate to young spontaneously hypertensive rats significantly slowed down the age-related development of hypertension, and led to a significant improvement of coronary flow and a significant reduction of endothelial dysfunctions (details in "NO-coxibs based on diarylpyrrole scaffold" section) [185]. These works demonstrated that an appropriate approach to the design of NO-releasing COX-2-selective inhibitors, at least in animal models, remarkably mitigates the CV risks related with the therapy with coxibs.

NO-releasing hybrid drugs and cancer

NO plays important roles in tumor initiation, growth, and metastasis. Most of the NO effects in cancer are discussed in depth in the other chapters of this book as well as in recent reviews [186]. Aberrant inducible NO synthase (iNOS) expression has been reported for several types of cancers and iNOS-derived NO has been associated with the several phases of cancer progression. Indeed, increased amount of NO has been found along with significantly higher levels of iNOS expressions, in patients with CRC, GI, lung, breast, cervical and ovarian cancers.

The role of NO in cancer is biphasic since it can act either as a proneoplastic molecule or as an antineoplastic agent, depending on both its concentration in the TME and the type of the tumor. Generally, low NO levels inhibit apoptosis, activate oncogenic pathways, and promote genomic instability, immunosuppression, tumor growth, migration, angiogenesis and metastasis, while higher levels (e.g., those generated by activated macrophages) are cytotoxic for tumor cells, giving rise to growth arrest, apoptosis, and sensitize tumors to conventional therapies [187].

An approach to establish ranges for low and high NO concentrations was reported by Vannini et al.; they established that the tissue NO concentration of 50–100nM (low) corresponds to those that usually stimulates cancer cell progression and metastasis, and intermediate NO levels (100–400nM) led to HIF-1 stabilization, whereas for levels of 400–1000nM, an antitumor cytotoxic action is expected [188]. This dual effect complicates the development of cancer treatments based on the release of NO in the TME, since in vivo it is difficult to establish the NO concentration at the tumor site, as well as the proper half-life necessary to lead to effective anticancer properties, owing to NO instability under physiological conditions.

Among the several approaches exploiting NO in cancer therapy, the one based on immunotherapy has recently attracted a great deal of attention. The importance of immunotherapy has gained in the treatment of cancer as well as the need to overcome resistance mechanisms have been previously discussed in "COX-2 and the immune system" section. It has been reported that the NO released by NO donors can sensitize many types of tumors to immunotherapy, chemotherapy and radiotherapy. In particular, it was shown how NO donors inhibited cancer cells activities also by inhibiting PD-L1 expression [189].

In addition, as previously discussed in "Nontumor cells present within the tumor microenvironment" section, macrophages in response to external stimuli polarize into the M1-like proinflammatory or the antiinflammatory M2-like phenotypes. TAMs preferentially behave as the M2-like phenotype, secreting protumoral signaling molecules such as growth factors, cytokines, chemokines, and other mediators that promote angiogenesis and metastasis, and inhibit antitumor immune response, whereas M1-like macrophages activate iNOS and NO production, inhibit cell proliferation, induce oxidative stress, apoptosis, and activate NK cells. Thus, due to their plasticity, macrophages represent a promising target for immunotherapy, and reprogramming M2-like into M1-like phenotype represents an asset to optimize antitumor immune response. In addition to the effects on PD1/PD-L1 axis, macrophage polarization, as previously described for the COX-2/PGE$_2$/EPs axis, can be also modulated by iNOS-derived NO that impacts TAMs activity by repolarizing them to antitumor M1-type phenotype [190].

As discussed above, the immune response mediated by T-cells plays an important role in eradicating the tumor. This immune response is regulated by various effector cells and mechanisms, and one of them is mediated by iNOS-derived NO, that is involved in the regulation and differentiation of various cells including macrophages and CD8 T-cells. Also in this case, different NO concentrations and time of exposure exert different effects on T-cells, including enhancement of their cytotoxic activity, inhibition of Treg induction, and downregulation of PD-L1. However, NO can also exert protumoral effects on T-cells by inhibiting their proliferation and activation [191].

Accordingly, NO donors are a potential new asset for overcoming the resistance to immunotherapy (PD-1/PD-L1 ICIs). Due to the promising antitumor effects of NO, numerous NO-releasing agents have been developed as antitumor drugs, and these are mainly organic nitrates (also other NO-donating groups have been reported, such as furoxans, hydroxylamines, peroxynitrites, S-nitrosothiols, and N-diazeniumdiolates), which have appropriate half-life, bioavailability, and relatively low toxicity [192].

In particular, NO-NSAIDs were expected to overcome the NSAIDs side effects and to display promising properties in cancer therapy.

It has been clinically proven that the daily administration of low doses of aspirin reduces the CV risks (heart attacks and strokes), but can also lead to severe damage to the GI tract owing to the inhibition of cytoprotective PGs synthesis. Thus, modified versions of aspirin (acetyl salicylic acid, ASA) that release NO were designed in order to protect the heart without GI side effects. Two nitrooxy derivatives of aspirin (NO-aspirin; NCX-4016 and NCX-4040) have been reported by Nicox. They consist of ASA bound, by an ester linkage, to a ((nitrooxy)methyl)phenyl group acting as NO donor. NCX 4016 and NCX 4040 are positional isomers (*meta* and *para*, respectively) with respect to the $-CH_2ONO_2$ group on the benzene ring (Fig. 4).

Notably, the two drugs have similar but not overlapping pharmacological effects. In preclinical and clinical testing, NO aspirin (both isomers) retained the analgesic, antiinflammatory and antithrombotic activity of aspirin (with potentiation in some cases), but in addition, they highlighted no toxicity for the GI tract and protected gastric mucosa from noxious stimuli. In in vitro and animal models, NO aspirin (NCX 4016) inhibited platelet activation more effectively than aspirin, protected endothelial cells, and displayed blood flow modulation properties. Moreover, NO aspirin (NCX 4016) reduced the blood pressure in animal models of hypertension, protected from platelet thromboembolism, prevented restenosis in atherosclerosis-prone

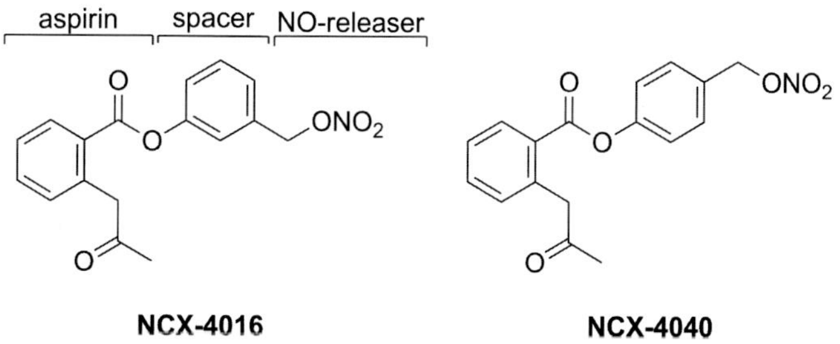

NCX-4016   **NCX-4040**

FIG. 4   Structures of NO-aspirins.

animals, and displayed protective effects in the heart ischemia/reperfusion model [193]. As expected, NO aspirin (NCX 4016) displayed protective activity on the GI tract owing to the mucosal defense properties of NO [194]. In vitro studies highlighted that CINODs such as NO-aspirin, NO-sulindac, NO-naproxen, and NO-ibuprofen reduced the growth of CRC cell lines more effectively than the corresponding NSAIDs [195]. Several animal studies in CRC models confirmed the preventive effect exerted by NO-aspirin on carcinogenesis, tumor development, and metastasis. Thus, both in vitro and in vivo experiments with NO-aspirin highlighted an inhibition of colorectal and GI carcinogenesis more potent than that elicited by aspirin; later on, the same effect was also reported for the other NO-NSAIDs [196].

In an in vitro study on the proliferation of cisplatin-resistant human ovarian cancer cells, it was found that the cell growth inhibition exerted by NO-aspirin (NCX 4016) was due to downregulation of EGFR/PI3K/STAT3 signaling and Bcl-2 modulation, that trigger cell cycle arrest and apoptosis [197].

Interestingly, in a rat pharmacokinetic study (100 mg/kg, p.o., 0–24 h) focused on the metabolism of NO-aspirin (NCX 4016), the unchanged drug was not detectable in plasma at any time, but aspirin and bioactive forms of NO (S-nitrosothiols) (peak at 4 h coincident with aspirin peak) as well as nitrites/nitrates. In myocardial tissue, neither the drug nor NO/bioactive forms levels were detected (0–24 h). Conversely, after i.p. administration, a fast delivery of the unchanged drug was detected in the myocardial tissue along with appreciable levels of NOx (up to 2 h). In the blood, the peak of NOx and its bioactive forms were reached faster (1–2 h) and still in coincidence with the aspirin peak. Interestingly, in this case, a metabolite of the parent still bearing the nitro-ester was found. This points out that after oral administration, a fast metabolism occurs at the ester linkage (despite the ester was found to be stable in the stomach) [198]. The metabolism of the nitroester in nitro-aspirin (NCX 4016) was studied also in humans; after p.o. administration, the presence of plasma levels of NOx and S-nitrosothiols as well as of nitrate/nitrites, consistent with the nitro ester metabolism of the drug, confirmed that also in humans, the nitroester is metabolized to NO and its bioactive forms [199].

Surprisingly, aspirin, in human whole blood and isolated human monocytes, resulted 70-fold less potent than NO-aspirin (NCX 4040) in inhibiting PGE_2 release and did not impact on COX-2 expression and cytokine release, whereas NCX 4040, but not NCX 4016, affected COX-2 expression and cytokine generation (IL-1β, TNF-α, IL-10, and IL-18). These further antiinflammatory effects of NCX 4040 were ascribed to inhibition of NF-κB activation [200]. In addition, NCX 4040 inhibited cell proliferation more potently than NCX 4016, being the corresponding IC50 for cell growth inhibition, respectively, 1–5 and 200–500 μM. This difference in potency between NCX 4040 and NCX 4016 was confirmed by in vivo CRC models, where NCX 4040 displayed approximately twice as high potency than NCX 4016 in decreasing the CRC cells proliferation [201].

Interestingly, the metabolism of NCX 4040 was found to be different from the one of NCX 4016, since for NCX 4040, the metabolic hydrolysis of the ester produced salicylic acid and a transient intermediate which led to nitrate, (hydroxymethyl)phenol, and a conjugate of the spacer with glutathione [202]. It was also demonstrated that NCX 4040, in CRC cells, induces apoptosis by consuming glutathione reserves due to formation of glutathione conjugate by NCX 4040 metabolism. The reduced glutathione availability induced oxidative stress, which in turn leads to apoptosis activating the intrinsic apoptosis pathways. NCX 4040 also interferes with Wnt/β-catenin pathway [203].

Further works reported that the potent antitumor activity of NCX 4040 was not mediated by NO release, but in contrast could be due to the quinone methide formed after carboxylic ester hydrolysis. Moreover, further studies confirmed that NO does not contribute to the NCX 4040 biological activity and that this NO-aspirin isomer does not act as NO donor, but rather by enzymatic hydrolysis of the ester bond, it gives rise to nitrates and to the electrophile quinone methide intermediate, responsible for the biological activity found. The formation of this reactive metabolite confers to NCX 4040 a genotoxic potential higher than NCX 4016 as confirmed by the Comet assay [204]. Though a similar mechanism was suggested also for NCX 4016, the results obtained by pharmacokinetics and in vitro studies about NO formation along with the ones highlighted by the Comet assay did not strongly support the hypothesis.

In addition to NO-aspirin, as previously mentioned, also other CINODs displayed antitumoral properties. It should be taken into account that these NO-releasing agents do not contain the ((nitrooxy)methyl)phenyl group as NO-donor moiety; thus, they cannot share the NCX 4040 mode of action. Taking into account the reduced GI and CV toxicity, also naproxcinod was evaluated as anticancer agent since naproxen, in preclinical models, resulted highly effective in preventing colon, urinary bladder, and skin cancer. Naproxcinod resulted effective in reducing the development of large urinary bladder tumors and colon tumors, but resulted ineffective in controlling mammary carcinogenesis. These activities have been related to NF-kB inhibition [205].

Also, NO-sulindac, NO-ibuprofen, and NO-indomethacin were tested on CRC cells, prostate, and lung cancer cells for inhibition of cell proliferation. All these CINODs inhibited cancer cell growth and induced apoptosis with potencies higher than that of the corresponding NSAIDs.

In order to obtain celecoxib derivatives acting as antitumoral drugs but without CV toxicity, nitrooxymethyl-substituted derivatives of celecoxib were prepared [206]. These derivatives were found to be metabolized in whole human blood into the corresponding alcohols and displayed NO-dependent vasodilatory activity. Notably, the derivative [207] obtained by simultaneous substitution of both the methyl and the aminosulfonyl moiety in the celecoxib structure with the nitrooxymethyl group, despite less potent than celecoxib, resulted endowed with high COX-2 selectivity and a long duration of action ($t_{1/2}$: 30 h). This compound displayed a remarkable antitumoral activity on CRC cells inducing a relevant cell growth reduction, induction of apoptosis along with the inhibition of the ERK-MAPK cascade. In order to get more insights on the role played by NO on this activity, the effect on cancer cell proliferation was assessed in the presence of benzyl nitrate alone, or by coadministering celecoxib and benzyl nitrate. Only the coadministration caused the remarkable decrease of cancer cell survival obtained with NO-celecoxib, whereas benzyl nitrate alone had no effect. In addition, it was found that NO-celecoxib inhibited ERK activation whereas benzyl nitrate alone had no effect. Moreover, celecoxib as well as NO-celecoxib inhibited PI3K and Akt activation. Though the same effect was mimicked by the coadministration of celecoxib and benzyl nitrate, benzyl nitrate alone had no effect on PI3K and Akt activation. It is to take into account that PI3K/Akt signaling is involved in the induction of apoptosis.

Recently, a new group of pyrazole derivatives acting as COX-2 inhibitors and NO donors was reported to inhibit Hela cell proliferation and induce apoptosis, demonstrating antitumoral properties also in animal models [208].

NO-coxibs based on diarylpyrrole scaffold

In the past, we developed a new class of potent and selective coxibs based on the diarylpyrrole scaffold [209–211]. Later, with the aim to obtain compounds characterized by a better CV safety profile, we developed the corresponding NO-releasing coxibs (NO-coxibs) with antiinflammatory properties, endowed with considerable antithrombotic and cardioprotective effects [184a,b,c]. The pharmacokinetics and NO-release properties of these compounds were then optimized with the aim to provide compounds with appropriate duration of action and slow NO-release properties [185,212,213]. In the same time frame, an interesting NO-releasing prodrug of rofecoxib (1) [214] has been reported, as well as nitrooxy-substituted 1,5-diarylimidazoles [215] and corresponding celecoxib analogs (2) (Fig. 5) [216].

CINOD structures are characterized by a central heterocyclic nucleus responsible for COX-2 inhibition linked to an NO-donor moiety. Many years ago, the starting point of our project, focused on selective COX-2 inhibitors, was to synthesize 1,5-diarylpyrrole-3-acetic acid and esters (3) which showed high inhibitory potency and selectivity on COX-2 and promising anti-inflammatory and antinociceptive activity in animal models [209–211]. Based on previous studies, suitable substituents were selected in both N1 and C5 phenyl rings for best results. In details, H, 3-F, 4-F, and 4-OMe were introduced in N1 while the p-(methylsulfonyl)-phenyl moiety was preferred in the C-5 of the pyrrole ring (Fig. 6).

The manipulation of position 3 of the pyrrole nucleus allowed to maintain the inhibitory properties of COX-2 and to introduce the NO-donor alkyl chains of different lengths (4a–h) [209]. The COX-2 inhibitory activity of the corresponding hydroxyl derivatives (5a–h) as possible active metabolites was also considered (Fig. 7).

All compounds were evaluated for in vitro COX-1 and COX-2 potency and selectivity in J774 murine macrophage cell line. The best compounds were also evaluated in the human whole-blood assays (WHB) [184a]. The NO-releasing properties for the compounds (4a–h) were evaluated assessing their efficacy and potency in determining NO-vasorelaxant responses, in a model of vascular smooth muscle relaxation (endothelium denuded rat aortic rings) [184a].

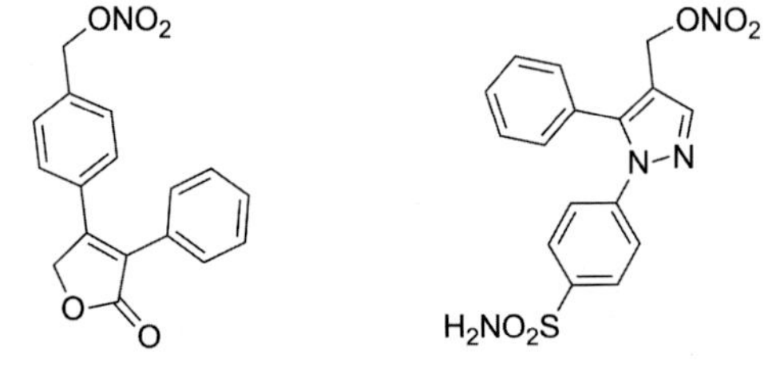

1
NO-releasing rofecoxib

2
NO-releasing celecoxib

FIG. 5   Structures of NO-coxibs (1) and (2).

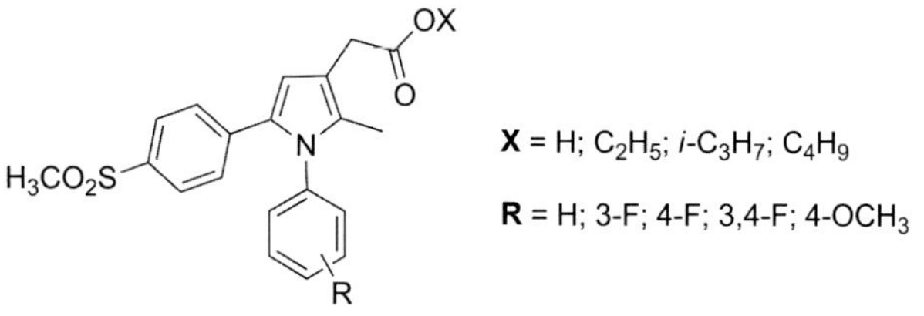

FIG. 6   COX-2 inhibitors: 1,5-diarylpyrrole-3-acetic esters (3).

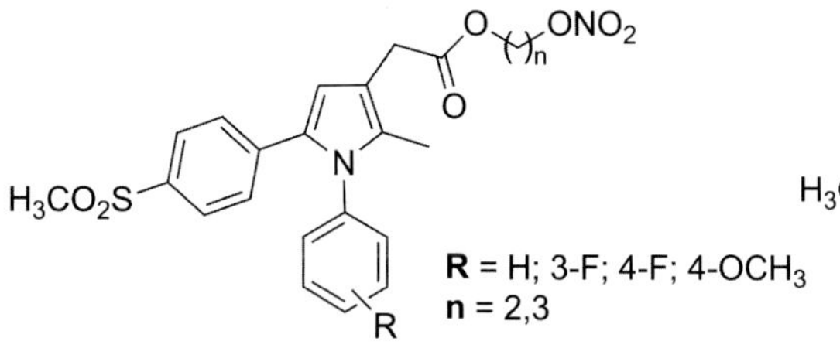

FIG. 7   NO-releasing coxibs: nitrooxyalkyl esters (4a–h) and their metabolites (5a–h).

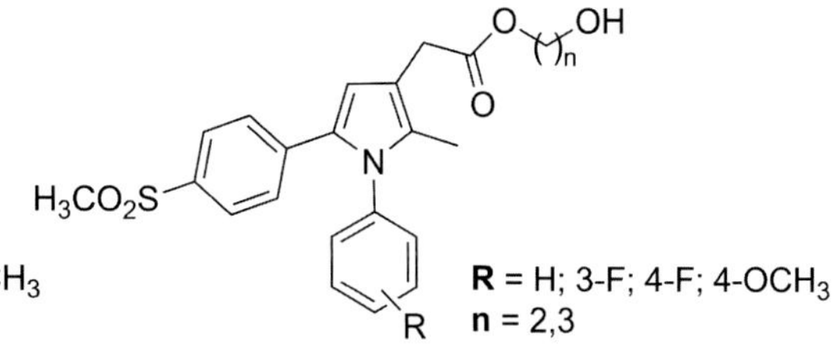

In order to confirm that the vasorelaxant effects were due to the NO release, the experiments were also carried out in the presence of the guanylate cyclase inhibitor 1H-[1,2,4]-oxadiazole [4,3-a] quinoxalin-1-one (ODQ). This test confirmed that these vasorelaxant effects were due to the NO-release. The total loss of vasorelaxant activity of the hydroxylated derivatives (5a–h), to be considered as the metabolites, further supported the absence of contribution from other moieties of the molecule to the CV effect. Compounds (4) showing to be efficacious NO donors were then evaluated in vivo for both antiinflammatory and antinociceptive activities in animal models of inflammation, by means of the chemical visceral inflammatory model (writhing test), along with the carrageenan-induced inflammatory pain model [184a,217,218]. Dependence on the side-chain length with the COX-2 inhibition potency was highlighted in this series, as well as in determining NO-dependent vasorelaxant responses. Hydroxylated derivatives (5a–h) displayed a similar trend.

Starting from high inhibitory potency and selectivity of COX-2 of the esters (4a–h), and considering their enzymatic liability, the corresponding NO-amides (6a–d, 7a–d), (8a–d, 9a–d), (10a–b, 11a–b) (Fig. 8), and NO-ethers (12a–f, 13a–f) were also synthesized Fig. 9, with the aims to obtain more active and selective compounds, showing better pharmacokinetic in terms of enzymatic stability. Among them, NO-ethers (12a–f) proved to be the best ones in terms of activity and selectivity (Fig. 9).

NO-esters

Despite the higher in vitro potency, nitrooxy esters (4a–h) and (5a–h) (Fig. 7) in vivo were less potent than celecoxib, though similar effects could be obtained at higher doses. Findings

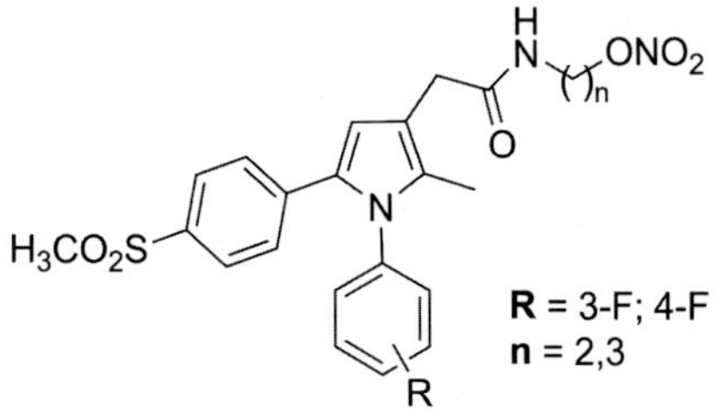

FIG. 8   NO-releasing coxibs: nitrooxyalkyl amides (**6a–d**, **8a–d**, **10a–b**) and their metabolites (**7a–d**, **9a–d**, **11a–b**).

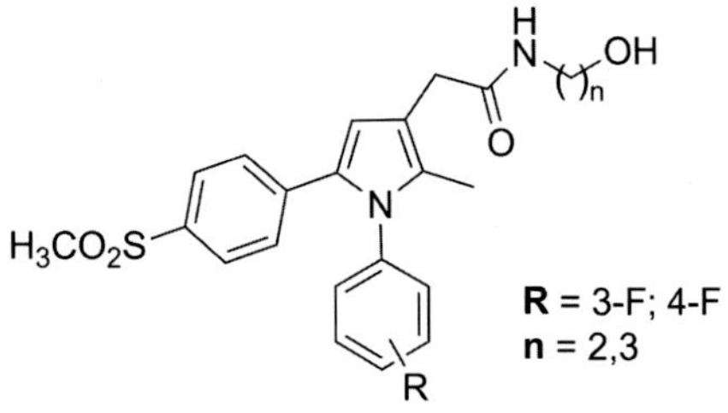

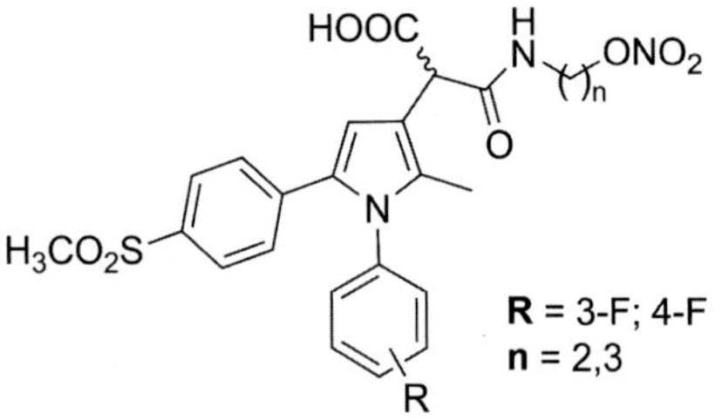

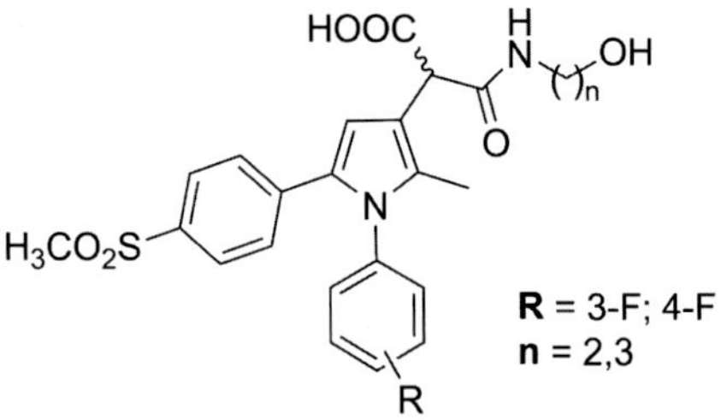

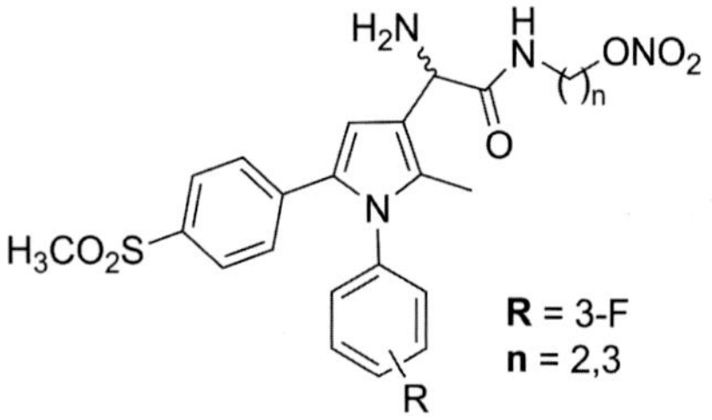

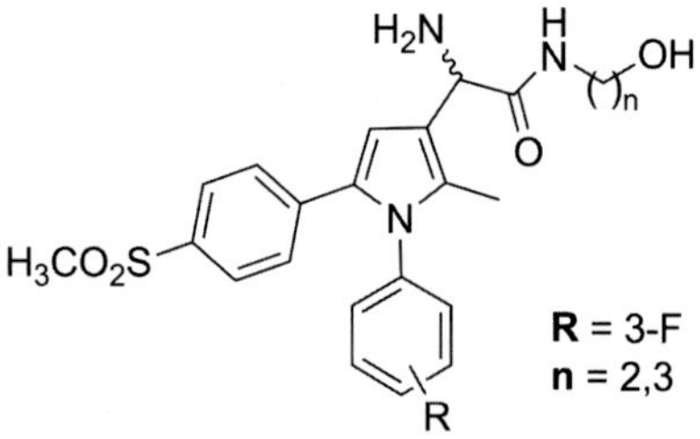

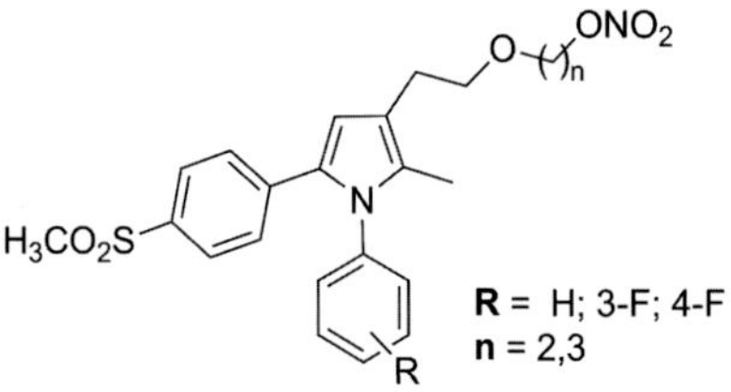

FIG. 9   NO-releasing coxibs: nitrooxyalkyl ethers (**12a–f**) and their metabolites (**13a–f**).

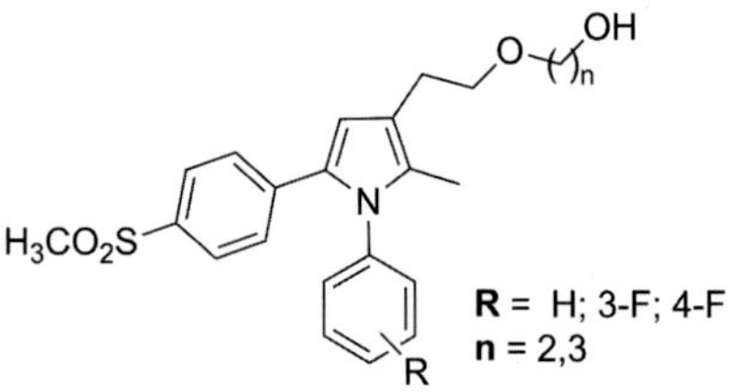

II. Nitric oxide pathway and cancer progression and therapy

reported for carrageenan-induced hyperalgesia and edema showed that all compounds were endowed with a satisfactory activity.

Overall, the activity of the compounds was remarkable, albeit not comparable to celecoxib. Noteworthy, compound (4c, R = 3-F, $n = 2$) (COX-2 inhibition: $IC_{50} = 0.019\,\mu M$), which in vitro showed to be more active than celecoxib (COX-2 inhibition: $IC_{50} = 0.061\,\mu M$) was less effective and had a shorter duration of action in the in vivo test. The shorter duration of the pharmacological effect suggested a possible metabolic deactivation for compound (4c) and/or other pharmacokinetic issues. Moreover, since these molecules were characterized by low solubility, that in turn could heavily affect their absorption; in order to increase solubility, an amino group was introduced at the α-position of the acetic side chain, since previous structure-activity relationship (SAR) studies highlighted this as a favorable position for such a change [210]. Unfortunately, the best compounds in the series, in general, proved to be less active than corresponding compound (4c), in the carrageenan test, with a duration of action still shorter than celecoxib, pointing out the presence of a metabolic issue as well.

NO-amides

As for NO-naproxen (naproxcinod) and related CINODs, the esterase-mediated hydrolysis into the parent NSAID scaffold (naproxen) and NOBA (nitrooxybutyl alcohol) (Fig. 3), followed by further metabolic conversion of the nitroester into NO and hydroxybutyl alcohol, proved to be the major metabolic pathway [180]. Accordingly, the hydrolysis of alkyl esters into the corresponding acid and nitrooxy alcohol could be expected also for ester derivatives. Since the enzymatic liability of the esters was considered to be a remarkable factor, different groups of compounds were generated through replacement of the ester moiety with the amide group, in order to address the structural issues impacting both stability and solubility [184c,213].

Firstly, a class of "simple" amides (6a–d) and their metabolites (7a–d) (Fig. 8) obtained through the replacement of the ester moiety with the amide group was explored. The diarylpyrrole-3-acetic scaffold was retained, and the substitution pattern as well as the side-chain length were based on the previous SAR.

In the second group of compounds (8a–d) and (9a–d) (Fig. 8) in addition to the replacement of the ester moiety with amide group, a carboxylate group was added to the α-position of the acetic moiety in order to increase solubility [213]. Hydroxylated derivatives (9a–d) were in general more potent in COX-2 inhibition than the corresponding derivatives (8a–d), with IC_{50} ranging from 0.14 to 1.6 μM, while the corresponding hydroxylated derivatives were effective in the range IC_{50} 0.068–0.16 μM. However (8a–d), produced unsatisfactory vasorelaxant effects, probably due to the presences of the unfavorable carboxylate moiety.

In the third group of compounds, (10a–b, 11a–b) (Fig. 8), in addition to the introduction of the amide group, an amino group was added to the α-position of the acetic moiety to increase solubility.

A good activity for COX-2 inhibition was found for these compounds with the higher potency for (10a, R = 3-F, $n = 2$) ($IC_{50} = 0.054\,\mu M$). Interestingly, corresponding hydroxylated derivative (11a) lacked any relevant COX inhibitory activity, while (11b, R = 3-F, $n = 3$), where there is an extra carbon in the side chain, was effective ($IC_{50} = 0.047\,\mu M$). The introduction of

II. Nitric oxide pathway and cancer progression and therapy

the amino group did not compromise the NO-mediated vasorelaxant effects. Compounds (10a) and (10b) exhibited high levels of vasorelaxant efficacy and good potencies, with $pIC_{50} = 6.38$ for both compounds. ODQ significantly antagonized the vasorelaxant activity.

The replacement of the ester functionality with the amide moiety provided in general more soluble molecules. The best solubility profile was displayed by the NO-amides (10a–b). Comparative stability studies of the esters with amides revealed the liability of the esters to hydrolysis in comparison with amides.

All the nitrooxyamides (6a–d), (8a–d), and (10a–b) were tested in the writhing test, and highlighted a good and dose-dependent activity [213]. The most representative derivatives (6c, R = 4-F, $n = 2$) and (10a, R = 3-F, $n = 2$) were endowed with the higher potency, displaying, respectively, 77% and 79% of reduction at 20 mg/kg, respectively. Moreover, compound (10a) displayed writhes reduction of 56% at the dose of 10 mg/kg. The most active nitrooxy compounds (6c) and (10a) were also evaluated for their activity in the carrageenan-induced edema and hyperalgesia [213]. The carrageenan-induced inflammation test showed that 9c was associated with a good but not outstanding activity. Conversely, compound (10a) was proved to be highly active, with a reduction of hyperalgesia at 10 mg/kg of 80% after 30 min. The activity was maintained for 60 min (70%), and even after 90 min, a satisfactory activity (50%) was still found.

The pharmacokinetics of the best-performing compounds were assessed in rats after p.o. and i.v. administration at 10 mg/kg [213]. After i.v. administration, (6c) was detected in plasma up to 6 h, characterized by moderate-to-high rate of clearance and high volume of distribution. Compound (6c) showed absolute bioavailability (24%) higher than derivative (10a) (9%).

NO-ethers

As mentioned above, the side chain manipulation of 1,5-diarylpyrrole scaffold allowed us to disclose two different series NO-esters (4) and NO-amides (6), (8), and (10) as new chemical entities endowed with a hybrid behavior resulting efficacious NO donors and selective COX-2 inhibitors. So, with the aim to enlarge the family of our NO-coxibs and in order to further increase the stability of the linker between the 1,5-diarylpyrrole scaffold and the NO-releasing moiety, the corresponding NO-ethers (12a–f) along with their metabolites (13a–f) [184b] were prepared (Fig. 9) (Table 1).

The transformation of the nitrooxyalkyl ester of (4) into the nitrooxyalkyl ether moiety (12) of 1,5-diarylpyrrole scaffold gave potent COX-2 inhibitors (J774 cells assay). Some of these compounds showed good NO-donating properties (Table 2) [184b] along with significant and selective COX-2 inhibitory activity ranging from low nanomolar-to-micromolar values. Most of NO-ethers (12a–f), highlighted a better COX-2 inhibitory activity with respect to their metabolites (13), being as active as corresponding NO-esters (4). Compounds (12a, R = H, $n = 2$), (12b, R = H, $n = 3$), (12c, R = 3-F, $n = 2$), (12d, R = 3-F, $n = 3$) emerged as low nanomolar COX-2 inhibitors. Compounds (12a), (12c), and (12e) also referred to as VA694 (R = 4-F, $n = 2$) demonstrated better NO-vasorelaxant responses in comparison with the other compounds of the group (Table 2), confirming what previously shown in terms of dependence of the activity with side chain length. Experiments run in the presence of ODQ confirmed that the vasorelaxant effects were due to the NO release.

TABLE 1 COX-1 and COX-2 inhibitory activity compounds **12a–f**, **13a–f**, and celecoxib.

Compd.	R	n	X	COX-1 inhibition IC_{50} (µM)[a]	COX-2 inhibition IC_{50} (µM)[a]	Selectivity index[b]
12a	H	2	NO$_2$	>10	0.017	>588.2
12b	H	3	NO$_2$	>10	0.015	>666.7
12c	3-F	2	NO$_2$	>10	0.027	>357.1
12d	3-F	3	NO$_2$	2.9	0.023	126.1
12e	4-F	2	NO$_2$	>10	0.014	>714.3
12f	4-F	3	NO$_2$	>10	0.190	>52.6
13a	H	2	H	>10	0.027	>370.4
13b	H	3	H	>10	8.990	1.11
13c	3-F	2	H	>10	0.046	>217.4
13d	3-F	3	H	3.7	0.240	15.4
13e	4-F	2	H	>10	0.089	>112.3
13f	4-F	3	H	>10	0.940	>10.6
Celecoxib				3.84	0.061	>63

[a] Results are expressed as the mean (n = 3 experiments) of the % inhibition of PGE$_2$ production by test compounds with respect to control samples, and the IC$_{50}$ values were calculated by GraphPad Instat program; data fit was obtained using the sigmoidal dose-response equation (variable slope) (GraphPad software).
[b] In vitro COX-2 Selectivity Index [IC$_{50}$ (COX-1)/IC$_{50}$(COX-2)].

TABLE 2 Efficacy and potency in determining NO-dependent vasorelaxing responses of **12a–f** and GTN.[a]

Compd.	E_{max}[b]	pIC_{50}[c]
12a	65 ± 3	5.22 ± 0.03
12b	48 ± 5	≤5
12c	60 ± 4	5.32 ± 0.05
12d	ND	–
12e	58 ± 5	5.47 ± 0.07
12f	41 ± 2	≤5
GNT	93 ± 2	6.90 ± 0.07

[a] GTN, glyceryl trinitrate.
[b] E_{max} represents the vasorelaxing efficacy, expressed as a % of the vasoconstriction induced by the preadministration of KCl.
[c] Parameter of potency is expressed as pIC$_{50}$, representing −log of the molar concentration capable of inducing a vasorelaxing effect = 50% of E$_{max}$.

In addition, HWB assay for compounds (12e) and its metabolite (13e) [184a] allowed to assess their COX-2 inhibition. Concentration-response curves for inhibition of COX-1 and COX-2 in HWB showed that compound (12e) and its hydroxyethyl derivative (13e) inhibited LPS-induced PGE_2 generation (COX-2 assay) in a concentration-dependent fashion with IC_{50} values, respectively, of 0.64 and 0.44 μM. Compounds (12e) and (13e) also showed comparable IC_{80} values (2.26 and 2.31 μM, respectively). These results pointed out that NO-ether (12e) and its metabolite (13e) gave a comparable and potent inhibitory effect on COX-2 activity in HWB. Compounds (12) and corresponding hydroxylated derivatives (13) were also evaluated in vivo, both in the writhing test and in the carrageenan-induced inflammatory pain model [184a]. In the writhing test, the minimal dose able to revert the painful condition was 10 mg/kg p.o. for (12a), (12e), and (13a), 20 mg/kg for (12b), (13b), and 40 mg/kg for (12c) and (13e). In the carrageenan inflammatory pain model, all the tested molecules were effective in the range between 40 and 20 mg/kg p.o., at 120 min., and a significant paw edema decrease was observed 60 min after the administration for all the investigated compounds [184b]. At the higher tested dose, the antihyperalgesic activity lasted up to 120 min for all the compounds, except for (12a) and (12b).

A negligible formation of nitrites and nitrates (3.2 ± 0.7 and 0.24 ± 0.24 μM, respectively, at 120 min) was observed after the incubation of (12e) in rat plasma, while the corresponding experiment with naproxcinod showed a massive formation of nitrate [185]. The incubation of (12e) in liver homogenate was followed by a slow and time-dependent production of nitrites and nitrates; after 120 min of incubation, the recorded concentrations were 4.6 ± 0.5 μM and 26.9 ± 3.4 μM, respectively. So, naproxcinod showed a more rapid accumulation of larger amounts of these metabolites (28.0 ± 6.0 μM of nitrites and 340.1 ± 5.0 μM of nitrates, at 120 min) [185]. Therefore, (12e) exhibited the feature of "NO-reservoir," stable in plasma and slowly converted to NO by the cell metabolism (liver, vascular smooth muscle, endothelium, etc.). The (12e) NO-releasing properties were confirmed by the endothelium-independent vasorelaxant effects evoked in aortic rings of normotensive rats; these effects were antagonized by ODQ. In order to determine the NO generation in vivo and its possible effects on the progression of systolic blood pressure (SBP), (12e) (20 mg/kg/day) was chronically administered to young male spontaneous hypertensive rats (SHRs) [185]. The effect of the metabolite (13e) was studied as well. The coxib-associated CV adverse effects are increased when other CV disorders are already present; therefore, (12e) effect was studied when chronically administered to SHRs, a suitable experimental model of heavy alteration of the CV function. Indeed, in young SHRs, an age-related progression of blood pressure is always observed, and highly selective COX-2 inhibitors, such as rofecoxib, accelerate and worsen it. After 1 month of pharmacological treatments of SHRs, serum concentrations of nitrites and nitrates were measured [185]. Though, treatment with (13e) did not influence the levels of plasma nitrites and nitrates; in the (12e)-treated animals, the concentration of nitrites was not significantly changed, but a significant increase in nitrates concentration was observed. In the Langendorff-perfused isolated hearts of vehicle-treated SHRs, the coronary flow was like that recorded in normotensive animals. The coronary flow in SHR rats treated with (13e) was significantly increased while the one of (12e)-treated animals was not significantly changed. The SBP development in (12e)-treated SHRs was completely equivalent to that of vehicle-treated SHRs, while treatment with (13e) (devoid of NO releasing properties) did not accelerate the age-related increase of SBP in young SHRs. Overall, this indicates that the NO-releasing property of (**12e**) can significantly improve the overall CV function and thus is a useful complementary aspect for coxibs.

Conclusions

A close relationship between inflammation and cancer has emerged in the last three decades. Indeed, several lines of evidence have pointed out inflammation as a key process underpinning carcinogenesis, tumor development, and metastasis. The inflammatory process giving rise to overexpression of cytokines, chemokines, and other inflammatory mediators, along with the recruitment of inflammatory cells, especially when persistent, can destabilize the local tissue homeostasis, leading to oxidative stress, tissue damage, and cell genome destabilization. Thus, a chronic inflammatory process cannot only induce a direct DNA damage, but also downregulates the pathways for DNA repair, impairs the regulation of cell cycle checkpoints, and inhibits apoptosis leading to the proliferation of a heterogeneous population of cancer cells.

In addition to cell genome destabilization, inflammatory cells and mediators are key players in shaping the inflammatory microenvironment which is fundamental for supporting tumor establishment, growth, and spread. Indeed, the tumor cells modifying their environment by secretion of various cytokines/chemokines and other inflammatory factors give rise to a reprogramming of both the surrounding cells (endothelial cells and fibroblasts) and of the infiltrated immune cells (macrophages, neutrophils, MDSCs, and adaptive immune system cells) to generate a TME, which predisposes to cancer development, promoting cancer cell proliferation, angiogenesis, and metastasis along with the escape from immune response. In this scenario, the recruited immune system cells have a central role, since instead of eliminating the tumor, they exert protumoral functions, fostering tumor cell invasion, extracellular matrix remodeling, angiogenesis, metastasis, and promotes the immune escape.

Recent research has provided several experimental evidences about the crucial role played by the COX-2/PGE_2/EPs axis in establishing the TME, in promoting tumor cell proliferation, and in fostering tumor immune evasion, thus providing with a robust rationale the great deal of preclinical and clinical data about the effects exerted by NSAIDs (either *t*-NSAIDs or coxibs) in reducing the risk for the development of several types of cancer.

Despite the interesting clinical data on cancer prevention, along with the experimental evidence about COX-2 overexpression in cancer and its involvement in carcinogenesis and cancer progression, both *t*-NSAIDs and coxibs failed to provide clinical evidences for an increased overall survival, when administered in combination with standard antitumoral therapy (cytotoxic drugs). The reason/s of this is/are at present unclear, but a relevant factor could be due to the clinical dose limitation, owing to the remarkable side effects found for both *t*-NSAIDs and coxibs.

CINODs was a class of drugs initially developed to combine the pharmacological action of a COX inhibitor with the protective action of NO, with the aim of reducing its GI and renal toxicity as well as to improve its CV safety while retaining COX-1/2 inhibitory properties.

We demonstrated, in animal models, that our NO-releasing coxibs, based on a metabolically stable link between the nitroester bearing moiety and the COX-2 inhibitor, are endowed with an appropriate pharmacokinetic and suitable NO-releasing properties. In particular, the clinical candidate (**VA694**) was able to significantly slow down the SHR age-related development of hypertension, and to lead to a significant improvement of coronary flow and a significant reduction of endothelial dysfunction.

Thus, demonstrating an appropriate design of NO-releasing COX-2-selective inhibitors in animal models remarkably mitigates the CV risks related with the therapy with coxibs, while retaining an appropriate potency and selectivity in COX-2 inhibition. Accordingly, we think that these NO-releasing coxibs could be good candidates to investigate more in-depth the effects of COX-2 inhibition in cancer, also taking into account that in addition to conferring a safer CV profile, the NO-donor moiety could synergize with COX-2 in terms of antitumor action.

Considering the complexity of the disease, a drug acting through multiple mechanisms may provide benefits. This task can be achieved either using a multitarget drug or a drug combination [219].

Notably, it was discussed how tumors can evade T-cells immune-mediated eradication exploiting the PD-1/PD-L1 immune checkpoint mechanism. Thus, in the last decade, immunotherapy targeting PD-1/PD-L1 axis with inhibitory antibodies (ICIs) has become the most promising approach for the treatment of several types of tumors, since treatments with ICIs provided significant improvement in overall survival versus chemotherapy, limited side effects, and in some cases even tumor remission.

Despite therapy with ICIs that changed the outcomes for many patients, a significant proportion of them still suffers lack of response (primary resistance), and some tumors which initially responded to ICI treatment later developed mechanisms of acquired resistance.

Several preclinical studies have documented the regulation of PD-L1 expression by COX-2, in several types of cancer cells as well as in immune system cells. These studies not only highlighted how PGE_2 in the TME promotes tumor immune evasion through the COX-2-PGE_2-EPs signaling pathway, but also that celecoxib and other NSAIDs downregulated PD-L1 expression in vitro and prolonged the time-to-progression in clinical trials with ICIs, enhancing the response to the therapy with ICIs and reversing resistance. Comparable effects were found by silencing COX-2 mRNA. Clinical studies on the effects exerted by simultaneous blockade of PD1/PD-L1 axis along with COX-2-PGE_2-EPs pathway are ongoing mainly with EP-4 antagonists, in order to avoid the side effects related with COX-2 inhibition. We believe that the NO-releasing COX-2-selective inhibitors herein described, in particular (**12e**) **VA694**, coadministered with ICIs could provide an interesting asset for cancer therapy.

References

[1] Medzhitov R. The spectrum of inflammatory responses. Science 2021;374(6571):1070–5. https://doi.org/ 10.1126/science. abi5200 [Epub 2021 Nov 25] 34822279.

[2] (a) Murao A, Aziz M, Wang H, Brenner M, Wang P. Release mechanisms of major DAMPs. Apoptosis 2021;26 (3–4):152–62. https://doi.org/10.1007/s10495-021-01663-3 [Epub 2021 Mar 13] 33713214. PMCID: PMC8016797. (b) Newton K, Zindel J, Kubes P. DAMPs, PAMPs, and LAMPs in immunity and sterile inflammation. Annu Rev Pathol 2020;15:493–518. https://doi.org/10.1146/annurev-pathmechdis-012419-032847 [Epub 2019 Nov 1] 31675482.

[3] Li D, Wu M. Pattern recognition receptors in health and diseases. Signal Transduct Target Ther 2021;6(1):291. https://doi.org/10.1038/s41392-021-00687-0. 34344870. PMCID:PMC8333067.

[4] Gong T, Liu L, Jiang W, Zhou R. DAMP-sensing receptors in sterile inflammation and inflammatory diseases. Nat Rev Immunol 2020;20(2):95–112. https://doi.org/10.1038/s41577-019-0215-7 [Epub 2019 Sep 26] 31558839.

[5] (a) Demaria O, Cornen S, Daëron M, Morel Y, Medzhitov R, Vivier E. Harnessing innate immunity in cancer therapy. Nature 2019;574(7776):45–56. https://doi.org/10.1038/s41586-019-1593-5 [Epub 2019 Oct 2]. (b) Sun L, Wang X, Saredy J, Yuan Z, Yang X, Wang H. Innate-adaptive immunity interplay and redox regulation in immune response. Redox Biol 2020;37:101759. https://doi.org/10.1016/j.redox.2020.101759. 33086106. PMCID: PMC7575795 [Epub 2020 Oct 10].

[6] Propper DJ, Balkwill FR. Harnessing cytokines and chemokines for cancer therapy. Nat Rev Clin Oncol 2022; 19(4):237–53. https://doi.org/10.1038/s41571-021-00588-9 [Epub 2022 Jan 7] 34997230.

[7] Calder PC. Eicosanoids. Essays Biochem 2020;64(3):423–41. https://doi.org/10.1042/EBC20190083. 32808658.

[8] Panigrahy D, Gilligan MM, Serhan CN, Kashfi K. Resolution of inflammation: an organizing principle in biology and medicine. Pharmacol Ther 2021;227:107879. https://doi.org/10.1016/j.pharmthera.2021.107879 [Epub 2021 Apr 27] 33915177.

[9] Furman D, Campisi J, Verdin E, et al. Chronic inflammation in the etiology of disease across the life span. Nat Med 2019;25:1822–32. https://doi.org/10.1038/s41591-019-0675-0.

[10] (a) Mantovani A, Allavena P, Sica A, Balkwill F. Cancer-related inflammation. Nature 2008;454(7203):436–44. https://doi.org/10.1038/nature07205. 186509.

[11] Ridker PM, JG MF, Thuren T, Everett BM, Libby P, Glynn RJ, CANTOS Trial Group. Effect of interleukin-1β inhibition with canakinumab on incident lung cancer in patients with atherosclerosis: exploratory results from a randomised, double-blind, placebo-controlled trial. Lancet 2017;390(10105):1833–42. https://doi.org/10.1016/S0140-6736(17)32247-X [Epub 2017 Aug 27] 28855077.

[12] Balkwill F, Mantovani A. Inflammation and cancer: back to Virchow? Lancet 2001;357(9255):539–45. https://doi.org/10.1016/S0140-6736(00)04046-0. 11229684.

[13] (a) Fishbein A, Hammock BD, Serhan CN, Panigrahy D. Carcinogenesis: failure of resolution of inflammation? Pharmacol Ther 2021;218:107670. https://doi.org/10.1016/j.pharmthera.2020.107670 [Epub 2020 Sep 3] 32891711. PMCID: PMC7470770. (b) Galdiero MR, Marone G, Mantovani A. Cancer inflammation and cytokines. Cold Spring Harb Perspect Biol 2018;10(8):a028662. https://doi.org/10.1101/cshperspect.a028662. 28778871. PMCID:PMC6071493. (c) Colotta F, Allavena P, Sica A, Garlanda C, Mantovani A. Cancer-related inflammation, the seventh hallmark of cancer: links to genetic instability. Carcinogenesis 2009;30(7):1073–81. https://doi.org/10.1093/carcin/bgp127 [Epub 2009 May 25] 19468060.

[14] Luch A. Nature and nurture—lessons from chemical carcinogenesis. Nat Rev Cancer 2005;5(2):113–25. https://doi.org/10.1038/nrc1546. 15660110.

[15] (a) Khandia R, Munjal A. Interplay between inflammation and cancer. Adv Protein Chem Struct Biol 2020;119:199–245. https://doi.org/10.1016/bs.apcsb.2019.09.004 [Epub 2019 Nov 26] 31997769. (b) Bogen KT. Inflammation as a cancer co-initiator: new mechanistic model predicts low/negligible risk at noninflammatory carcinogen doses. Dose Response 2019;17(2). https://doi.org/10.1177/1559325819847834. 1559325819847834 31205456. PMCID:PMC6537503.

[16] Senga SS, Grose RP. Hallmarks of cancer the new testament. Open Biol 2021;11(1):200358. https://doi.org/10.1098/rsob.200358 [Epub 2021 Jan 20] 33465324. PMCID:PMC7881179.

[17] Dvorak HF. Tumors: wounds that do not heal-redux. Cancer Immunol Res 2015;3(1):1–11. https://doi.org/10.1158/2326-6066.CIR-14-0209. 25568067. PMCID: PMC4288010.

[18] Digifico E, Balinzo S, Belgiovine C. The dark side of the force: when the immune system is the fuel of tumor onset. Int J Mol Sci 2021;22(3):1224. https://doi.org/10.3390/ijms22031224. 33513730. PMCID: PMC7865698.

[19] Chawanthayatham S, Valentine 3rd CC, Fedeles BI, Fox EJ, Loeb LA, Levine SS, Slocum SL, Wogan GN, Croy RG, Essigmann JM. Mutational spectra of aflatoxin B_1 in vivo establish biomarkers of exposure for human hepatocellular carcinoma. Proc Natl Acad Sci USA 2017;114(15):E3101–9. https://doi.org/10.1073/pnas.1700759114 [Epub 2017 Mar 28] 28351974. PMCID:PMC5393230.

[20] (a) Grivennikov SI, Karin M. Inflammation and oncogenesis: a vicious connection. Curr Opin Genet Dev 2010;20 (1):65–71. https://doi.org/10.1016/j.gde.2009.11.004 [Epub 2009 Dec 25] 20036794. PMCID:PMC2821983. (b) Reuter S, Gupta SC, Chaturvedi MM, Aggarwal BB. Oxidative stress, inflammation, and cancer: how are they linked? Free Radic Biol Med 2010;49(11):1603–16. https://doi.org/10.1016/j.freeradbiomed.2010.09.006 [Epub 2010 Sep 16] 20840865. PMCID:PMC2990475.

II. Nitric oxide pathway and cancer progression and therapy

[21] Greten FR, Grivennikov SI. Inflammation and cancer: triggers, mechanisms, and consequences. Immunity 2019;51(1):27–41. https://doi.org/10.1016/j.immuni.2019.06.025. 31315034. PMCID:PMC6831096.

[22] Nilsson R, Liu N-A. Nuclear DNA damages generated by reactive oxygen molecules (ROS) under oxidative stress and their relevance to human cancers, including ionizing radiation-induced neoplasia part II: relation between ROS-induced DNA damages and human cancer. Radiat Med Prot 2020;1(4):196–204. ISSN 2666-5557 https://doi.org/10.1016/j.radmp.2020.11.003.

[23] (a) Torgovnick A, Schumacher B. DNA repair mechanisms in cancer development and therapy. Front Genet 2015;6:157. https://doi.org/10.3389/fgene.2015.00157. 25954303. PMCID: PMC4407582. (b) Andor N, Maley CC, Ji HP. Genomic instability in cancer: teetering on the limit of tolerance. Cancer Res 2017;77(9):2179–85. https://doi.org/10.1158/0008-5472.CAN-16-1553 [Epub 2017 Apr 21] 28432052. PMCID:PMC5413432.

[24] Turajlic S, Sottoriva A, Graham T, Swanton C. Resolving genetic heterogeneity in cancer. Nat Rev Genet 2019;20 (7):404–16. https://doi.org/10.1038/s41576-019-0114-6 [Erratum in: Nat Rev Genet 2020;21(1):65] 30918367.

[25] NF-kB: nuclear factor kappa-light-chain-enhancer of activated B cells; Mitchell S, Vargas J, Hoffmann A. Signaling via the NFκB system. Wiley Interdiscip Rev Syst Biol Med 2016;8(3):227–41. https://doi.org/10.1002/wsbm.1331 [Epub 2016 Mar 16] 26990581. PMCID:PMC8363188.

[26] STAT-3: Signal Transducer and Activator of Transcription-3; Owen KL, Brockwell NK, Parker BS. JAK-STAT signaling: a double-edged sword of immune regulation and cancer progression. Cancers (Basel) 2019;11 (12):2002. https://doi.org/10.3390/cancers11122002. 31842362. PMCID:PMC6966445.

[27] Atsaves V, Leventaki V, Rassidakis GZ, Claret FX. AP-1 transcription factors as regulators of immune responses in cancer. Cancers (Basel) 2019;11(7):1037. https://doi.org/10.3390/cancers11071037. 31340499. PMCID: PMC6678392.

[28] Hayashi Y, Yokota A, Harada H, Huang G. Hypoxia/pseudohypoxia-mediated activation of hypoxia-inducible factor-1α in cancer. Cancer Sci 2019;110(5):1510–7. https://doi.org/10.1111/cas.13990 [Epub 2019 Mar 23] 30844107. PMCID:PMC6501028.

[29] Hinshaw DC, Shevde LA. The tumor microenvironment innately modulates cancer progression. Cancer Res 2019;79(18):4557–66. https://doi.org/10.1158/0008-5472.CAN-18-3962 [Epub 2019 Jul 26] 31350295. PMCID: PMC6744958.

[30] Myeloid-derived suppressor cells are a heterogeneous population of non-defined myeloid cells, not present in healthy individuals, that are expanded during inflammation and cancer, giving rise to immune suppression, promoting angiogenesis and metastases. Gabrilovich DI. Myeloid-derived suppressor cells. Cancer Immunol Res 2017;5(1):3–8. https://doi.org/10.1158/2326-6066.CIR-16-0297. 28052991. PMCID:PMC5426480.

[31] (a) Pathria P, Louis TL, Varner JA. Targeting tumor-associated macrophages in cancer. Trends Immunol 2019;40 (4):310–27. https://doi.org/10.1016/j.it.2019.02.003 [Epub 2019 Mar 17] 30890304. (b) Mantovani A, Bottazzi B, Colotta F, Sozzani S, Ruco L. The origin and function of tumor-associated macrophages. Immunol Today 1992;13(7):265–70. https://doi.org/10.1016/0167-5699(92)90008-U. 1388654. (c) Tolle F, Umansky V, Utikal J, Kreis S, Bréchard S. Neutrophils in tumorigenesis: missing targets for successful next generation cancer therapies? Int J Mol Sci 2021;22(13):6744. https://doi.org/10.3390/ijms22136744. 34201758. PMCID: PMC8268516.

[32] See Ref. [13b].

[33] (a) Macrophage stimulation with IFN-γ, TNF-α, PAMP, DAMP leads to the differentiation into an M1 phenotype (classically activated macrophages). M1 Macrophages exert a strong cytotoxic and anti-proliferative activity due to the production of ROS and nitric oxide along with the inflammatory cytokines: IL-1, TNF-α, IL-6, IL-12, IL-23. Wynn TA, Chawla A, Pollard JW. Macrophage biology in development, homeostasis and disease. Nature 2013;496(7446):445–55. https://doi.org/10.1038/nature12034. 23619691. PMCID: PMC3725458. (b) Locati M, Curtale G, Mantovani A. Diversity, mechanisms, and significance of macrophage plasticity. Annu Rev Pathol 2020;15:123–47. https://doi.org/10.1146/annurev-pathmechdis-012418-012718 [Epub 2019 Sep 17] 31530089. PMCID:PMC7176483. (c) Boutilier AJ, Elsawa SF. Macrophage polarization states in the tumor microenvironment. Int J Mol Sci 2021;22(13):6995. https://doi.org/10.3390/ijms22136995. 34209703. PMCID: PMC8268869.

[34] Monocyte recruitment involves several chemotactic molecules released in TME such as: CCL2, CCL5, vascular endothelial growth factors (VEGFs), and macrophage colony stimulating factor (M-CSF). In addition to chemotactic effects these molecules contribute to the polarization of macrophages toward specific M2 phenotypes. Olingy CE, Dinh HQ, Hedrick CC. Monocyte heterogeneity and functions in cancer. J Leukoc Biol

2019;106(2):309–22. https://doi.org/10.1002/JLB.4RI0818-311R [Epub 2019 Feb 18] 30776148. PMCID: PMC6658332.

[35] Ghosh C, Luong G, Sun Y. A snapshot of the PD-1/PD-L1 pathway. J Cancer 2021;12(9):2735–46. https://doi.org/10.7150/jca.57334. PMID: 33854633; PMCID: PMC8040720.

[36] Van Coillie S, Wiernicki B, Xu J. Molecular and cellular functions of CTLA-4. Adv Exp Med Biol 2020;1248:7–32. https://doi.org/10.1007/978-981-15-3266-5_2. 32185705.

[37] Kim J, Bae JS. Tumor-associated macrophages and neutrophils in tumor microenvironment. Mediators Inflamm 2016;2016:6058147. https://doi.org/10.1155/2016/6058147 [Epub 2016 Feb 4] 26966341. PMCID: PMC4757693.

[38] Hillion S, Arleevskaya MI, Blanco P, Bordron A, Brooks WH, Cesbron JY, Kaveri S, Vivier E, Renaudineau Y. The innate part of the adaptive immune system. Clin Rev Allergy Immunol 2020;58(2):151–4. https://doi.org/10.1007/s12016-019-08740-1. 31154567.

[39] Waldman AD, Fritz JM, Lenardo MJ. A guide to cancer immunotherapy: from T-cell basic science to clinical practice. Nat Rev Immunol 2020;20(11):651–68. https://doi.org/10.1038/s41577-020-0306-5 [Epub 2020 May 20] 32433532. PMCID:PMC7238960.

[40] (a) Kumar BV, Connors TJ, Farber DL. Human T-cell development, localization, and function throughout life. Immunity 2018;48(2):202–13. https://doi.org/10.1016/j.immuni.2018.01.007. 29466753. PMCID:PMC5826622. (b) Azuma M. Co-signal molecules in T-cell activation: historical overview and perspective. Adv Exp Med Biol 2019;1189:3–23. https://doi.org/10.1007/978-981-32-9717-3_1. 31758529.

[41] (a) van den Broek T, Borghans JAM, van Wijk F. The full spectrum of human naive T-cells. Nat Rev Immunol 2018;18(6):363–73. https://doi.org/10.1038/s41577-018-0001-y. 29520044. (b) Philip M, Schietinger A. CD8+ T-cell differentiation and dysfunction in cancer. Nat Rev Immunol 2022;22(4):209–23. https://doi.org/10.1038/s41577-021-00574-3 [Epub 2021 Jul 12] 34253904.

[42] (a) Grover P, Goel PN, Greene MI. Regulatory T-cells: regulation of identity and function. Front Immunol 2021;12:750542. https://doi.org/10.3389/fimmu.2021.750542. 34675933. PMCID:PMC8524049. (b) Ohue Y, Nishikawa H. Regulatory T (Treg) cells in cancer: can treg cells be a new therapeutic target? Cancer Sci 2019;110(7):2080–9. https://doi.org/10.1111/cas.14069 [Epub 2019 Jun 18] 31102428. PMCID:PMC6609813.

[43] Sun C, Mezzadra R, Schumacher TN. Regulation and function of the PD-L1 checkpoint. Immunity 2018;48 (3):434–52. https://doi.org/10.1016/j.immuni.2018.03.014. 29562194. PMCID:PMC7116507.

[44] (a) Hoesel B, Schmid JA. The complexity of NF-κB signaling in inflammation and cancer. Mol Cancer 2013;12:86. https://doi.org/10.1186/1476-4598-12-86. 23915189. PMCID:PMC3750319. (b) Taniguchi K, Karin M. NF-κB, inflammation, immunity and cancer: coming of age. Nat Rev Immunol 2018;18(5):309–24. https://doi.org/10.1038/nri.2017.142 [Epub 2018 Jan 22] 29379212. (c) Another pathway for NF-kB activation referred to as "non canonical" is also known, the noncanonical NF-κB pathway cooperates with canonical NF-κB pathway in the fine tuning of some functions of the adaptive immune system. Sun SC. The non-canonical NF-κB pathway in immunity and inflammation. Nat Rev Immunol 2017;17(9):545–58. https://doi.org/10.1038/nri.2017.52 [Epub 2017 Jun 5] 28580957. PMCID:PMC5753586.

[45] (a) Mulero MC, Huxford T, Ghosh G. NF-κB, IκB, and IKK: integral components of immune system signaling. Adv Exp Med Biol 2019;1172:207–26. https://doi.org/10.1007/978-981-13-9367-9_10. 31628658. (b) Hayden MS, Ghosh S. NF-κB in immunobiology. Cell Res 2011;21(2):223–44. https://doi.org/10.1038/cr.2011.13 [Epub 2011 Jan 18] 21243012. PMCID:PMC3193440. (c) Hagemann T, Lawrence T, McNeish I, Charles KA, Kulbe H, Thompson RG, Robinson SC, Balkwill FR. "Re-educating" tumor-associated macrophages by targeting NF-kappaB. J Exp Med 2008;205(6):1261–8. https://doi.org/10.1084/jem.20080108 [Epub 2008 May 19] 18490490. PMCID:PMC2413024.

[46] Intercellular adhesion molecule 1 (ICAM-1), vascular cell adhesion molecule 1 (VCAM-1); roles of these molecules in inflammation and cancer have been recently reviewed: Bui TM, Wiesolek HL, Sumagin R. ICAM-1: a master regulator of cellular responses in inflammation, injury resolution, and tumorigenesis. J Leukoc Biol 2020;108(3):787–99. https://doi.org/10.1002/JLB.2MR0220-549R [Epub 2020 Mar 17] 32182390. PMCID: PMC7977775.

[47] (a) Zinatizadeh MR, Schock B, Chalbatani GM, Zarandi PK, Jalali SA, Miri SR. The nuclear factor kappa B (NF-kB) signaling in cancer development and immune diseases. Genes Dis 2020;8(3):287–97. https://doi.org/10.1016/j.gendis.2020.06.005. 33997176. PMCID:PMC8093649. (b) Baud V, Karin M. Is NF-kappaB a good target for cancer therapy? Hopes and pitfalls. Nat Rev Drug Discov 2009;8(1):33 40. https://doi.org/10.1038/

II. Nitric oxide pathway and cancer progression and therapy

nrd2781. 19116625. PMCID:PMC2729321. (c) Dolcet X, Llobet D, Pallares J, Matias-Guiu X. NF-kB in develop-ment and progression of human cancer. Virchows Arch 2005;446(5):475–82. https://doi.org/10.1007/s00428-005-1264-9 [Epub 2005 Apr 27] 15856292.

[48] Verzella D, Pescatore A, Capece D, Vecchiotti D, Ursini MV, Franzoso G, Alesse E, Zazzeroni F. Life, death, and autophagy in cancer: NF-κB turns up everywhere. Cell Death Dis 2020;11(3):210. https://doi.org/10.1038/s41419-020-2399-y. 32231206. PMCID:PMC7105474.

[49] Pires BRB, Silva RCMC, Ferreira GM, Abdelhay E. NF-kappaB: two sides of the same coin. Genes (Basel) 2018;9 (1):24. https://doi.org/10.3390/genes9010024. 29315242. PMCID:PMC5793177.

[50] Fan Y, Mao R, Yang J. NF-κB and STAT3 signaling pathways collaboratively link inflammation to cancer. Pro-tein Cell 2013;4(3):176–85. https://doi.org/10.1007/s13238-013-2084-3 [Epub 2013 Mar 13] 23483479. PMCID: PMC4875500.

[51] Yu H, Kortylewski M, Pardoll D. Cross talk between cancer and immune cells: role of STAT3 in the tumor mi-croenvironment. Nat Rev Immunol 2007;7:41–51.

[52] Schulze-Osthoff K, Ferrari D, Riehemann K, Wesselborg S. Regulation of NF-κB activation by MAP kinase cas-cades. Immunobiology 1997;198:35–49.

[53] (a) Johnson DE, O'Keefe RA, Grandis JR. Targeting the IL-6/JAK/STAT3 signalling axis in cancer. Nat Rev Clin Oncol 2018;15(4):234. https://doi.org/10.1038/nrclinonc.2018.8. 48. PMCID: PMC5858971. [Epub 2018 Feb 6]. (b) Gu Y, Mohammad IS, Liu Z. Overview of the STAT-3 signaling pathway in cancer and the development of specific inhibitors. Oncol Lett 2020;19(4):2585. https://doi.org/10.3892/ol.2020.11394. 32218808. 94. PMCID: PMC7068531 [Epub 2020 Feb 13]. (c) Zhou J, Qu Z, Sun F, Han L, Li L, Yan S, Stabile LP, Chen L-F, Siegfried JM, Xiao G. Myeloid STAT3 promotes lung tumorigenesis by transforming tumor immunosurveillance into tumor-promoting inflammation. Cancer Immunol Res 2017;5:257–68.

[54] Mantovani A, Dinarello CA, Molgora M, Garlanda C. Interleukin-1 and related cytokines in the regulation of inflammation and immunity. Immunity 2019;50(4):778–95. https://doi.org/10.1016/j.immuni.2019.03.012. 30995499. PMCID: PMC7174020.8.

[55] (a) Mantovani A, Barajon I, Garlanda C. IL-1 and IL-1 regulatory pathways in cancer progression and therapy. Immunol Rev 2018;281(1):57–61. https://doi.org/10.1111/imr.12614. 29247996. PMCID: PMC5922413. (b) Zhang W, Borcherding N, Kolb R. IL-1 signaling in tumor microenvironment. Adv Exp Med Biol 2020;1240:1–23. https://doi.org/10.1007/978-3-030-38315-2_1. 32060884. (c) Malik A, Kanneganti TD. Function and regulation of IL-1α in inflammatory diseases and cancer. Immunol Rev 2018;281(1):124–37. https://doi.org/10.1111/imr.12615. 29247991. PMCID: PMC5739076.

[56] Bent R, Moll L, Grabbe S, Bros M. Interleukin-1 beta-a friend or foe in malignancies? Int J Mol Sci 2018;19 (8):2155. https://doi.org/10.3390/ijms19082155. 30042333. PMCID:PMC6121377.

[57] (a) Miossec P, Kolls JK. Targeting IL-17 and TH17 cells in chronic inflammation. Nat Rev Drug Discov 2012;11 (10):763–76. https://doi.org/10.1038/nrd3794. 23023676. (b) Gu C, Wu L, Li X. IL-17 family: cytokines, recep-tors and signaling. Cytokine 2013;64(2):477–85. https://doi.org/10.1016/j.cyto.2013.07.022 [Epub 2013 Sep 3] 24011563. PMCID:PMC3867811.

[58] (a) Gorczynski RM. IL-17 signaling in the tumor microenvironment. Adv Exp Med Biol 2020;1240:47–58. https://doi.org/10.1007/978-3-030-38315-2_4. 32060887. (b) Vitiello GA, Miller G. Targeting the interleukin-17 immune axis for cancer immunotherapy. J Exp Med 2020;217(1):e20190456. https://doi.org/10.1084/jem.2019045. 31727783. PMCID: PMC7037254. (c) Li X, Bechara R, Zhao J, McGeachy MJ, Gaffen SL. IL-17 receptor-based signaling and implications for disease. Nat Immunol 2019;20(12):1594–602. https://doi.org/10.1038/s41590-019-0514-y [Epub 2019 Nov 19] 31745337. PMCID: PMC6943935. (d) Bastid J, Dejou C, Docquier A, Bonnefoy N. The emerging role of the IL-17B/IL-17RB pathway in cancer. Front Immunol 2020;11:718. https://doi.org/10.3389/fimmu.2020.00718. 32373132. PMCID: PMC7186465.

[59] Morikawa M, Derynck R, Miyazono K. TGF-β and the TGF-β family: context-dependent roles in cell and tissue physiology. Cold Spring Harb Perspect Biol 2016;8(5):a021873. https://doi.org/10.1101/cshperspect.a021873. 27141051. PMCID:PMC4852809.

[60] (a) Hao Y, Baker D, Ten Dijke P. TGF-β-mediated epithelial-mesenchymal transition and cancer metastasis. Int J Mol Sci 2019;20(11):2767. https://doi.org/10.3390/ijms20112767. 31195692. PMCID:PMC6600375. (b) Liu S, Ren J, Ten Dijke P. Targeting TGFβ signal transduction for cancer therapy. Signal Transduct Target Ther 2021;6(1):8. https://doi.org/10.1038/s41392-020-00436-9. 33414388. PMCID:PMC7791126. (c) Gómez-Gil

V. Therapeutic implications of TGFβ in cancer treatment: a systematic review. Cancers (Basel) 2021;13(3):379. https://doi.org/10.3390/cancers13030379. 33498521. PMCID:PMC7864190.

[61] (a) Ouyang W, O'Garra A. IL-10 family cytokines IL-10 and IL-22: from basic science to clinical translation. Immunity 2019;50(4):871–91. https://doi.org/10.1016/j.immuni.2019.03.020. 30995504. (b) Saraiva M, O'Garra A. The regulation of IL-10 production by immune cells. Nat Rev Immunol 2010;10(3):170–81. https://doi.org/10.1038/nri2711 [Epub 2010 Feb 15] 20154735.

[62] Saraiva M, Vieira P, O'Garra A. Biology and therapeutic potential of interleukin-10. J Exp Med 2020;217(1): e20190418. https://doi.org/10.1084/jem.20190418. 31611251. PMCID: PMC7037253.

[63] AA: arachidonic acid, all-cis-5, 8, 11, 14-eicosatetraenoic acid; Martin SA, Brash AR, Murphy RC. The discovery and early structural studies of arachidonic acid. J Lipid Res 2016;57(7):1126–32. https://doi.org/10.1194/jlr.R068072 [Epub 2016 May 3] 27142391. PMCID:PMC4918860.

[64] Wang D, Dubois RN. Eicosanoids and cancer. Nat Rev Cancer 2010;10(3):181–93. https://doi.org/10.1038/nrc2809. 20168319. PMCID:PMC2898136. [Epub 2010 Feb 19]. See also Ref. [7].

[65] (a) Johnson AM, Kleczko EK, Nemenoff RA. Eicosanoids in cancer: new roles in immunoregulation. Front Pharmacol 2020;11:595498. https://doi.org/10.3389/fphar.2020.595498. 33364964. PMCID:PMC7751756. (b) Boniface K, Bak-Jensen KS, Li Y, Blumenschein WM, McGeachy MJ, McClanahan TK, McKenzie BS, Kastelein RA, Cua DJ, de Waal MR. Prostaglandin E2 regulates Th17 cell differentiation and function through cyclic AMP and EP2/EP4 receptor signaling. J Exp Med 2009;206(3):535–48. https://doi.org/10.1084/jem.20082293 [Epub 2009 Mar 9] 19273625. PMCID:PMC2699124.

[66] (a) Wang B, Wu L, Chen J, Dong L, Chen C, Wen Z, Hu J, Fleming I, Wang DW. Metabolism pathways of arachidonic acids: mechanisms and potential therapeutic targets. Signal Transduct Target Ther 2021;6(1):94. https://doi.org/10.1038/s41392-020-00443-w. 33637672. PMCID:PMC7910446. (b) Murakami M, Nakatani Y, Atsumi GI, Inoue K, Kudo I. Regulatory functions of phospholipase A2. Crit Rev Immunol 2017;37(2–6):127–95. https://doi.org/10.1615/CritRevImmunol.v37.i2-6.20. 29773019.

[67] (a) Dennis EA, Norris PC. Eicosanoid storm in infection and inflammation. Nat Rev Immunol 2015;15(8):511–23. https://doi.org/10.1038/nri3859 [Epub 2015 Jul 3. Erratum in: Nat Rev Immunol. 2015;15(11):724] 26139350. PMCID:PMC4606863. (b) Serhan CN, Chiang N, Van Dyke TE. Resolving inflammation: dual anti-inflammatory and pro-resolution lipid mediators. Nat Rev Immunol 2008;8(5):349–61. https://doi.org/10.1038/nri2294. 18437155. PMCID:PMC2744593.

[68] Seo MJ, Oh DK. Prostaglandin synthases: molecular characterization and involvement in prostaglandin biosynthesis. Prog Lipid Res 2017;66:50–68. https://doi.org/10.1016/j.plipres.2017.04.003 [Epub 2017 Apr 7] 28392405.

[69] Ching MM, Reader J, Fulton AM. Eicosanoids in cancer: prostaglandin E2 receptor 4 in cancer therapeutics and immunotherapy. Front Pharmacol 2020;11:819. https://doi.org/10.3389/fphar.2020.00819. 32547404. PMCID: PMC7273839.

[70] (a) Jara-Gutiérrez Á, Baladrón V. The role of prostaglandins in different types of cancer. Cell 2021;10(6):1487. https://doi.org/10.3390/cells10061487. 34199169. PMCID:PMC8231512. (b) Rådmark O, Werz O, Steinhilber D, Samuelsson B. 5-lipoxygenase, a key enzyme for leukotriene biosynthesis in health and disease. Biochim Biophys Acta 2015;1851(4):331–9. https://doi.org/10.1016/j.bbalip.2014.08.012 [Epub 2014 Aug 22] 25152163. (c) Hashemi Goradel N, Najafi M, Salehi E, Farhood B, Mortezaee K. Cyclooxygenase-2 in cancer: a review. J Cell Physiol 2019;234(5):5683–99. https://doi.org/10.1002/jcp.27411 [Epub 2018 Oct 20] 30341914.

[71] Fishbein A, Hammock BD, Serhan CN, Panigrahy D. Carcinogenesis: failure of resolution of inflammation? Pharmacol Ther 2021;218:107670. https://doi.org/10.1016/j.pharmthera.2020.107670 [Epub 2020 Sep 3] 32891711. PMCID:PMC7470770.

[72] Sobolewski C, Cerella C, Dicato M, Ghibelli L, Diederich M. The role of cyclooxygenase-2 in cell proliferation and cell death in human malignancies. Int J Cell Biol 2010;2010:215158. https://doi.org/10.1155/2010/215158 [Epub 2010 Mar 17] 20339581. PMCID:PMC2841246.

[73] Sreeramkumar V, Fresno M, Cuesta N. Prostaglandin E2 and T-cells: friends or foes? Immunol Cell Biol 2012;90 (6):579–86. https://doi.org/10.1038/icb.2011.75 [Epub 2011 Sep 27] 21946663. PMCID:PMC3389798.

[74] Obermajer N, Wong JL, Edwards RP, Odunsi K, Moysich K, Kalinski P. PGE (2)-driven induction and maintenance of cancer-associated myeloid-derived suppressor cells. Immunol Invest 2012;41(6–7):635–57. https://doi.org/10.3109/08820139.2012.695417. 23017139.

II. Nitric oxide pathway and cancer progression and therapy

[75] Jara-Gutiérrez Á, Baladrón V. The role of prostaglandins in different types of cancer. Cell 2021;10(6):1487. https://doi.org/10.3390/cells10061487. 34199169. PMCID:PMC8231512.

[76] Jeon WK, Choi J, Park SJ, Jo EJ, Lee YK, Lim S, Kim JH, Letterio JJ, Liu F, Kim SJ, Kim BC. The proinflammatory LTB4/BLT1 signal axis confers resistance to TGF-β1-induced growth inhibition by targeting Smad3 linker region. Oncotarget 2015;6(39):41650–66. https://doi.org/10.18632/oncotarget.6146. 26497676. PMCID: PMC4747179.

[77] (a) Meshram MA, Bhise UO, Makhal PN, Kaki VR. Synthetically-tailored and nature-derived dual COX-2/5-LOX inhibitors: structural aspects and SAR. Eur J Med Chem 2021;225:113804. https://doi.org/10.1016/j.ejmech.2021.113804 [Epub 2021 Aug 27] 34479036. (b) Goossens L, Pommery N, Hénichart JP. COX-2/5-LOX dual acting anti-inflammatory drugs in cancer chemotherapy. Curr Top Med Chem 2007;7(3):283–96. https://doi.org/10.2174/156802607779941369. 17305571. (c) Hang J, Tang N, Fang Q, Zhu K, Liu L, Xiong X, Zhu Z, Zhang B, Zhang M, Tao J. Inhibition of COX-2 and 5-LOX regulates the progression of colorectal cancer by promoting PTEN and suppressing PI3K/AKT pathway. Biochem Biophys Res Commun 2019;517(1):1–7. https://doi.org/10.1016/j.bbrc.2018.01.061 [Epub 2018 Jan 13] 29339153.

[78] Moore GY, Pidgeon GP. Cross-talk between cancer cells and the tumor microenvironment: the role of the 5-lipoxygenase pathway. Int J Mol Sci 2017;18(2):236. https://doi.org/10.3390/ijms18020236. 28125014. PMCID:PMC5343774.

[79] Greene ER, Huang S, Serhan CN, Panigrahy D. Regulation of inflammation in cancer by eicosanoids. Prostaglandins Other Lipid Mediat 2011;96(1–4):27–36. https://doi.org/10.1016/j.prostaglandins.2011.08.004.

[80] Basil MC, Levy BD. Specialized pro-resolving mediators: endogenous regulators of infection and inflammation. Nat Rev Immunol 2016;16(1):51–67. https://doi.org/10.1038/nri.2015.4 [Epub 2015 Dec 21] 26688348. PMCID: PMC5242505.

[81] (a) Chandrasekharan JA, Sharma-Walia N. Lipoxins: nature's way to resolve inflammation. J Inflamm Res 2015;8:181–92. https://doi.org/10.2147/JIR.S90380. 26457057. PMCID:PMC4598198. (b) Chen Y, Hao H, He S, Cai L, Li Y, Hu S, Ye D, Hoidal J, Wu P, Chen X. Lipoxin A4 and its analogue suppress the tumor growth of transplanted H22 in mice: the role of antiangiogenesis. Mol Cancer Ther 2010;9(8):2164–74. https://doi.org/10.1158/1535-7163.MCT-10-0173 [Epub 2010 Aug 3] 20682645.

[82] (a) Romano M, Cianci E, Simiele F, Recchiuti A. Lipoxins and aspirin-triggered lipoxins in resolution of inflammation. Eur J Pharmacol 2015;760:49–63. https://doi.org/10.1016/j.ejphar.2015.03.083 [Epub 2015 Apr 18] 25895638. (b) Fierro IM, Colgan SP, Bernasconi G, Petasis NA, Clish CB, Arita M, Serhan CN. Lipoxin A4 and aspirin-triggered 15-epi-lipoxin A4 inhibit human neutrophil migration: comparisons between synthetic 15 epimers in chemotaxis and transmigration with microvessel endothelial cells and epithelial cells. J Immunol 2003;170(5):2688–94. https://doi.org/10.4049/jimmunol.170.5.2688. 12594298.

[83] (a) Serhan CN, Levy BD. Resolvins in inflammation: emergence of the pro-resolving superfamily of mediators. J Clin Invest 2018;128(7):2657–69. https://doi.org/10.1172/JCI97943 [Epub 2018 May 14] 29757195. PMCID: PMC6025982. (b) Chiang N, Serhan CN. Specialized pro-resolving mediator network: an update on production and actions. Essays Biochem 2020;64(3):443–62. https://doi.org/10.1042/EBC20200018. 32885825. PMCID: PMC7682745.

[84] Chiang N, Serhan CN. Specialized pro-resolving mediator network: an update on production and actions. Essays Biochem 2020;64(3):443–62. https://doi.org/10.1042/EBC20200018. 32885825. PMCID: PMC7682745.

[85] Sulciner ML, Serhan CN, Gilligan MM, Mudge DK, Chang J, Gartung A, Lehner KA, Bielenberg DR, Schmidt B, Dalli J, Greene ER, Gus-Brautbar Y, Piwowarski J, Mammoto T, Zurakowski D, Perretti M, Sukhatme VP, Kaipainen A, Kieran MW, Huang S, Panigrahy D. Resolvins suppress tumor growth and enhance cancer therapy. J Exp Med 2018;215(1):115–40. https://doi.org/10.1084/jem.20170681 [Epub 2017 Nov 30] 29191914. PMCID:PMC5748851.

[86] Serhan CN, Chiang N, Dalli J. New pro-resolving n-3 mediators bridge resolution of infectious inflammation to tissue regeneration. Mol Aspects Med 2018;64:1–17. https://doi.org/10.1016/j.mam.2017.08.002 [Epub 2017 Sep 1] 28802833. PMCID:PMC5832503.

[87] Serhan CN, Libreros S, Nshimiyimana R. E-series resolvin metabolome, biosynthesis and critical role of stereochemistry of specialized pro-resolving mediators (SPMs) in inflammation-resolution: preparing SPMs for long COVID-19, human clinical trials, and targeted precision nutrition. Semin Immunol 2022;101597. https://doi.org/10.1016/j.smim.2022.101597 [Epub ahead of print] 35227568. PMCID:PMC8847098.

[88] (a) Zappavigna S, Cossu AM, Grimaldi A, Bocchetti M, Ferraro GA, Nicoletti GF, Filosa R, Caraglia M. Anti-Inflammatory drugs as anticancer agents. Int J Mol Sci 2020;21(7):2605. https://doi.org/10.3390/ijms21072605. 32283655. PMCID: PMC7177823. (b) Dierssen-Sotos T, Gómez-Acebo I, de Pedro M, Pérez-Gómez B, Servitja S, Moreno V, Amiano P, Fernandez-Villa T, Barricarte A, Tardon A, Diaz-Santos M, Peiro-Perez R, Marcos-Gragera R, Lope V, Gracia-Lavedan E, Alonso MH, Michelena-Echeveste MJ, Garcia-Palomo A, Guevara M, Castaño-Vinyals G, Aragonés N, Kogevinas M, Pollán M, Llorca J. Use of non-steroidal anti-inflammatory drugs and risk of breast cancer: the Spanish multi-case-control (MCC) study. BMC Cancer 2016;16(1):660. https://doi.org/10.1186/s12885-016-2692-4. 27542890. PMCID:PMC4992258. (c) Friis S, Riis AH, Erichsen R, Baron JA, Sørensen HT. Low-dose aspirin or nonsteroidal anti-inflammatory drug use and colorectal cancer risk: a population-based, case-control study. Ann Intern Med 2015;163(5):347–55. https://doi.org/10.7326/M15-0039. 26302241. (d) Shi J, Leng W, Zhao L, Xu C, Wang J, Chen X, Wang Y, Peng X. Nonsteroidal anti-inflammatory drugs using and risk of head and neck cancer: a dose-response meta-analysis of prospective cohort studies. Oncotarget 2017;8(58):99066–74. https://doi.org/10.18632/oncotarget.21524. 29228752. PMCID: PMC5716792. (e) Doat S, Cénée S, Trétarre B, Rebillard X, Lamy PJ, Bringer JP, Iborra F, Murez T, Sanchez M, Menegaux F. Nonsteroidal anti-inflammatory drugs (NSAIDs) and prostate cancer risk: results from the EPICAP study. Cancer Med 2017;6(10):2461–70. https://doi.org/10.1002/cam4.1186 [Epub 2017 Sep 21] 28941222. PMCID:PMC5633590. (f) Trabert B, Ness RB, Lo-Ciganic WH, Murphy MA, Goode EL, Poole EM, Brinton LA, Webb PM, Nagle CM, Jordan SJ, Australian Ovarian Cancer Study Group, Australian Cancer Study (Ovarian Cancer), Risch HA, Rossing MA, Doherty JA, Goodman MT, Lurie G, Kjær SK, Hogdall E, Jensen A, Cramer DW, Terry KL, Vitonis A, Bandera EV, Olson S, King MG, Chandran U, Anton-Culver H, Ziogas A, Menon U, Gayther SA, Ramus SJ, Gentry-Maharaj A, Wu AH, Pearce CL, Pike MC, Berchuck A, Schildkraut JM, Wentzensen N, Ovarian Cancer Association Consortium. Aspirin, nonaspirin nonsteroidal anti-inflammatory drug, and acetaminophen use and risk of invasive epithelial ovarian cancer: a pooled analysis in the ovarian cancer association consortium. J Natl Cancer Inst 2014;106(2):djt431. https://doi.org/10.1093/jnci/djt431. 24503200. PMCID: PMC3924755.

[89] Rao P, Knaus EE. Evolution of nonsteroidal anti-inflammatory drugs (NSAIDs): cyclooxygenase (COX) inhibition and beyond. J Pharm Pharm Sci 2008;11(2):81s–110s. https://doi.org/10.18433/j3t886. 19203472.

[90] (a) Ricciotti E, FitzGerald GA. Prostaglandins and inflammation. Arterioscler Thromb Vasc Biol 2011;31(5):986–1000. https://doi.org/10.1161/ATVBAHA.110.207449. 21508345. PMCID:PMC3081099. (b) Hanna VS, Hafez EAA. Synopsis of arachidonic acid metabolism: a review. J Adv Res 2018;11:23–32. https://doi.org/10.1016/j.jare.2018.03.005. 30034873. PMCID:PMC6052663.

[91] (a) Przybyła GW, Szychowski KA, Gmiński J. Paracetamol—an old drug with new mechanisms of action. Clin Exp Pharmacol Physiol 2020. https://doi.org/10.1111/1440-1681.13392 [Epub ahead of print] 32767405. (b) Schwab JM, Schluesener HJ, Meyermann R, Serhan CN. COX-3 the enzyme and the concept: steps towards highly specialized pathways and precision therapeutics? Prostaglandins Leukot Essent Fatty Acids 2003;69 (5):339–43. https://doi.org/10.1016/j.plefa.2003.07.003. 14580368.

[92] (a) Fitzpatrick FA. Cyclooxygenase enzymes: regulation and function. Curr Pharm Des 2004;10(6):577–88. https://doi.org/10.2174/1381612043453144. 14965321. (b) Pannunzio A, Coluccia M. Cyclooxygenase-1 (COX-1) and COX-1 inhibitors in cancer: a review of oncology and medicinal chemistry literature. Pharmaceuticals (Basel) 2018;11(4):101. https://doi.org/10.3390/ph11040101. 30314310. PMCID:PMC6316056. (c) Vitale P, Panella A, Scilimati A, Perrone MG. COX-1 inhibitors: beyond structure toward therapy. Med Res Rev 2016;36 (4):641–71. https://doi.org/10.1002/med.21389 [Epub 2016 Apr 25] 27111555.

[93] Simon LS. Role and regulation of cyclooxygenase-2 during inflammation. Am J Med 1999;106(5B):37S–42S. https://doi.org/10.1016/s0002-9343(99)00115-1. 10390126.

[94] Zidar N, Odar K, Glavac D, Jerse M, Zupanc T, Stajer D. Cyclooxygenase in normal human tissues is COX-1 really a constitutive isoform, and COX-2 an inducible isoform? J Cell Mol Med 2009;13(9B):3753–63. https://doi.org/10.1111/j.1582-4934.2008.00430.x [Epub 2008 Jul 24] 18657230. PMCID:PMC4516524.

[95] (a) Hashemi Goradel N, Najafi M, Salehi E, Farhood B, Mortezaee K. Cyclooxygenase-2 in cancer: a review. J Cell Physiol 2019;234(5):5683. https://doi.org/10.1002/jcp.27411. 99. [Epub 2018 Oct 20] 30341914. (b) Wang D, Cabalag CS, Clemons NJ, DuBois RN. Cyclooxygenases and prostaglandins in tumor immunology and microenvironment of GI cancer. Gastroenterology 2021;161(6):1813. https://doi.org/10.1053/j.gastro.2021.09.059. 29. [Epub 2021 Oct 2] 34606846. (c) Nagaraju GP, El-Rayes BF. Cyclooxygenase-2 in GI malignancies. Cancer 2019;125(8):1221. https://doi.org/10.1002/cncr.32010. 27. [Epub 2019 Feb 12] 30747998. (d) Zhan P, Qian Q, Yu

II. Nitric oxide pathway and cancer progression and therapy

LK. Prognostic value of COX-2 expression in patients with non-small cell lung cancer: a systematic review and meta-analysis. J Thorac Dis 2013;5(1):40. https://doi.org/10.3978/j.issn.2072-1439.2013.01.02. 23372950. 7. PMCID: PMC3547998. (e) Chen EP, Smyth EM. COX-2 and PGE2-dependent immunomodulation in breast cancer. Prostaglandins Other Lipid Mediat 2011;96(1–4):14–20. https://doi.org/10.1016/j.prostaglandins.2011.08.005 [Epub 2011 Aug 31] 21907301. PMCID: PMC4031099. (f) Frejborg E, Salo T, Salem A. Role of cyclooxygenase-2 in head and neck tumorigenesis. Int J Mol Sci 2020;21(23):9246. https://doi.org/10.3390/ijms21239246. 33287464. PMCID: PMC7731111.

[96] Rayar AM, Lagarde N, Ferroud C, Zagury JF, Montes M, Sylla-Iyarreta VM. Update on COX-2 selective inhibitors: chemical classification, side effects and their use in cancers and neuronal diseases. Curr Top Med Chem 2017;17(26):2935–56. https://doi.org/10.2174/1568026617666170821124947. 28828990.

[97] (a) García-Rayado G, Navarro M, Lanas A. NSAID induced GI damage and designing GI-sparing NSAIDs. Expert Rev Clin Pharmacol 2018;11(10):1031–43. https://doi.org/10.1080/17512433.2018.1516143. (b) Ungprasert P, Cheungpasitporn W, Crowson CS, Matteson EL. Individual non-steroidal anti-inflammatory drugs and risk of acute kidney injury: a systematic review and meta-analysis of observational studies. Eur J Intern Med 2015;26(4):285–91. https://doi.org/10.1016/j.ejim.2015.03.008. [Epub 2015 Apr 8 25862494. (c) Drożdżal S, Lechowicz K, Szostak B, Rosik J, Kotfis K, Machoy-Mokrzyńska A, Białecka M, Ciechanowski K, Gawrońska-Szklarz B. Kidney damage from nonsteroidal anti-inflammatory drugs-myth or truth? Review of selected literature. Pharmacol Res Perspect 2021;9(4):e00817. https://doi.org/10.1002/prp2.817. 34310861. PMCID:PMC8313037.

[98] Ferrer MD, Busquets-Cortés C, Capó X, Tejada S, Tur JA, Pons A, Sureda A. Cyclooxygenase-2 inhibitors as a therapeutic target in Inflammatory diseases. Curr Med Chem 2019;26(18):3225–41. https://doi.org/10.2174/0929867325666180514112124.

[99] (a) Tacconelli JS, Bruno A, Grande R, Ballerini P, Patrignani P. Nonsteroidal anti-inflammatory drugs and cardiovascular safety - translating pharmacological data into clinical readouts. Expert Opin Drug Saf 2017;16 (7):791–807. https://doi.org/10.1080/14740338.2017.1338272. (b) Patrono C. Cardiovascular effects of cyclooxygenase-2 inhibitors: a mechanistic and clinical perspective. Br J Clin Pharmacol 2016;82(4):957–64. https://doi.org/10.1111/bcp.13048.

[100] Ruschitzka F, Borer JS, Krum H, Flammer AJ, Yeomans ND, Libby P, Lüscher TF, Solomon DH, Husni ME, Graham DY, Davey DA, Wisniewski LM, Menon V, Fayyad R, Beckerman B, Iorga D, Lincoff AM, Nissen SE. Differential blood pressure effects of ibuprofen, naproxen, and celecoxib in patients with arthritis: the PRECISION-ABPM (prospective randomized evaluation of celecoxib integrated safety versus ibuprofen or naproxen ambulatory blood pressure measurement) trial. Eur Heart J 2017;38(44):3282–92. https://doi.org/10.1093/eurheartj/ehx508. 29020251. PMCID:PMC8139400.

[101] (a) Schjerning AM, McGettigan P, Gislason G. Cardiovascular effects and safety of (non-aspirin) NSAIDs. Nat Rev Cardiol 2020;17(9):574–84. https://doi.org/10.1038/s41569-020-0366-z [Epub 2020 Apr 22] 32322101. (b) Grosser T, Ricciotti E, FitzGerald GA. The cardiovascular pharmacology of nonsteroidal anti-inflammatory drugs. Trends Pharmacol Sci 2017;38(8):733–48. https://doi.org/10.1016/j.tips.2017.05.008 [Epub 2017 Jun 23] 28651847. PMCID:PMC5676556. (c) Gunter BR, Butler KA, Wallace RL, Smith SM, Harirforoosh S. Nonsteroidal anti-inflammatory drug-induced cardiovascular adverse events: a meta-analysis. J Clin Pharm Ther 2017;42(1):27–38. https://doi.org/10.1111/jcpt.12484 [Epub 2016 Dec 26] 28019014.

[102] (a) Ramos-Inza S, Ruberte AC, Sanmartín C, Sharma AK, Plano D. NSAIDs: old acquaintance in the pipeline for cancer treatment and prevention structural modulation, mechanisms of action, and bright future. J Med Chem 2021;64(22):16380–421. https://doi.org/10.1021/acs.jmedchem.1c01460 [Epub 2021 Nov 16] 34784195. (b) Wong RSY. Role of nonsteroidal anti-inflammatory drugs (NSAIDs) in cancer prevention and cancer promotion. Adv Pharmacol Sci 2019;2019:3418975. https://doi.org/10.1155/2019/3418975. 30838040. PMCID: PMC6374867. (c) Hawk E, Maresso KC, Brown P. NSAIDs to prevent breast cancer recurrence? An unanswered question. J Natl Cancer Inst 2018;110(9):927–8. https://doi.org/10.1093/jnci/djy049. 29554350. PMCID: PMC6136929.

[103] IBD: Inflammatory Bowel Disease, Yao D, Dong M, Dai C, Wu S. Inflammation and inflammatory cytokine contribute to the initiation and development of ulcerative colitis and its associated cancer. Inflamm Bowel Dis 2019;25(10):1595–602. https://doi.org/10.1093/ibd/izz149. 31287863.

[104] (a) Dekker E, Tanis PJ, Vleugels JLA, Kasi PM, Wallace MB. Colorectal cancer. Lancet 2019;394(10207):1467–80. https://doi.org/10.1016/S0140-6736(19)32319-0. 31631858. (b) Sheng J, Sun H, Yu FB, Li B, Zhang Y, Zhu YT.

The role of cyclooxygenase-2 in colorectal cancer. Int J Med Sci 2020;17(8):1095–101. https://doi.org/10.7150/ijms.44439. 32410839. PMCID:PMC7211146.

[105] Friend WG. Sulindac suppression of colorectal polyps in Gardner's syndrome. Am Fam Physician 1990;41(3):891–4. Mar 2305666.

[106] (a) Kunzmann AT, Murray LJ, Cardwell CR, McShane CM, McMenamin UC, Cantwell MM. PTGS2 cyclooxygenase-2 expression and survival among colorectal cancer patients: a systematic review. Cancer Epidemiol Biomarkers Prev 2013;22(9):1490–7. https://doi.org/10.1158/1055-9965.EPI-13-0263 [Epub 2013 Jun 27] 23810915. (b) Wang D, Dubois RN. The role of COX-2 in intestinal inflammation and colorectal cancer. Oncogene 2010;29(6):781–8. https://doi.org/10.1038/onc.2009.421 [Epub 2009 Nov 30] 19946329. PMCID: PMC3181054.

[107] Mizuno R, Kawada K, Sakai Y. Prostaglandin E2/EP signaling in the tumor microenvironment of colorectal cancer. Int J Mol Sci 2019;20(24):6254. https://doi.org/10.3390/ijms20246254. 31835815. PMCID:PMC6940958.

[108] Stem-like cells are a tumor cells subpopulation endowed with a plastic phenotype, with the ability to self-renew, to reconstitute the tumor or sustain new tumor growth, to be resistant to chemotherapy and radiotherapy Mathonnet M, Perraud A, Christou N, Akil H, Melin C, Battu S, Jauberteau MO, Denizot Y. Hallmarks in colorectal cancer: angiogenesis and cancer stem-like cells. World J Gastroenterol 2014;20(15):4189–96. https://doi.org/10.3748/wjg.v20.i15.4189. 24764657. PMCID:PMC3989955.

[109] (a) Wang D, Cabalag CS, Clemons NJ, DuBois RN. Cyclooxygenases and prostaglandins in tumor immunology and microenvironment of GI cancer. Gastroenterology 2021;161(6):1813–29. https://doi.org/10.1053/j.gastro.2021.09.059 [Epub 2021 Oct 2] 34606846. (b) Nanda N, Dhawan DK. Role of cyclooxygenase-2 in colorectal cancer patients. Front Biosci (Landmark Ed) 2021;26(4):706–16. https://doi.org/10.2741/4914. 33049690.

[110] Phosphoinositide 3-kinase (PI3Ks) is a member of intracellular lipid kinases and involved in the regulation of cellular proliferation, differentiation and survival. Overexpression of the PI3K/Akt/mTOR signalling has been reported in various forms of cancers, especially in CRC. PI3K/Akt/mTOR signalling is an important event in colorectal carcinogenesis Narayanankutty A. PI3K/Akt/mTOR pathway as a therapeutic target for colorectal cancer: a review of preclinical and clinical evidence. Curr Drug Targets 2019;20(12):1217–26. https://doi.org/10.2174/1389450120666190618123846. 31215384.

[111] ERK: extracellular signal-regulated kinases; the ERKs signaling pathway is crucial for carcinogenesis, cancer cell proliferation, migration, and invasion, in several cancers including CRC Fang JY, Richardson BC. The MAPK signalling pathways and colorectal cancer. Lancet Oncol 2005;6(5):322–7. https://doi.org/10.1016/S1470-2045(05)70168-6. 15863380.

[112] (a) Wang D, Fu L, Sun H, Guo L, DuBois RN. Prostaglandin E2 promotes colorectal cancer stem cell expansion and metastasis in mice. Gastroenterology 2015;149(7):1884–1895.e4. https://doi.org/10.1053/j.gastro.2015.07.064 [Epub 2015 Aug 7] 26261008. PMCID:PMC4762503. (b) Hsu HH, Lin YM, Shen CY, Shibu MA, Li SY, Chang SH, Lin CC, Chen RJ, Viswanadha VP, Shih HN, Huang CY. Prostaglandin E2-induced COX-2 expressions via EP2 and EP4 signaling pathways in human LoVo colon cancer cells. Int J Mol Sci 2017;18(6):1132. https://doi.org/10.3390/ijms18061132. 28587064. PMCID:PMC5485956.

[113] Leone V, di Palma A, Ricchi P, Acquaviva F, Giannouli M, Di Prisco AM, Iuliano F, Acquaviva AM. PGE2 inhibits apoptosis in human adenocarcinoma Caco-2 cell line through Ras-PI3K association and cAMP-dependent kinase a activation. Am J Physiol Gastrointest Liver Physiol 2007;293(4):G673–81. https://doi.org/10.1152/ajpgi.00584.2006 [Epub 2007 Jul 19] 17640974.

[114] (a) Cecil DL, Gad EA, Corulli LR, Drovetto N, Lubet RA, Disis ML. COX-2 inhibitors decrease expression of PD-L1 in colon tumors and increase the influx of type I tumor-infiltrating lymphocytes. Cancer Prev Res (Phila) 2022;15(4):225–31. https://doi.org/10.1158/1940-6207.CAPR-21-0227. 34987061. PMCID:PMC8983455. (b) Wei J, Zhang J, Wang D, Cen B, Lang JD, DuBois RN. The COX-2-PGE2 pathway promotes tumor evasion in colorectal adenomas. Cancer Prev Res (Phila) 2022;15(5):285–96. https://doi.org/10.1158/1940-6207.CAPR-21-0572. 35121582. PMCID:PMC9064954.

[115] (a) Hu Z, Hu Y, Jiang H. Overexpression of COX-2 and clinicopathological features of gastric cancer: a meta-analysis. Transl Cancer Res 2020;9(4):2200–9. https://doi.org/10.21037/tcr.2020.03.52. 35117580. PMCID:PMC8798741.

[116] (a) Regulski M, Regulska K, Prukała W, Piotrowska H, Stanisz B, Murias M. COX-2 inhibitors: a novel strategy in the management of breast cancer. Drug Discov Today 2016;21(4):598–615. https://doi.org/10.1016/j.drudis.2015.12.003. Apr. [Epub 2015 Dec 23] 26723915. (b) Ristimäki A, Sivula A, Lundin J, Lundin M, Salminen

II. Nitric oxide pathway and cancer progression and therapy

T, Haglund C, Joensuu H, Isola J. Prognostic significance of elevated cyclooxygenase-2 expression in breast cancer. Cancer Res 2002;62(3):632–5. 11830510.

[117] Hawk E, Maresso KC, Brown P. NSAIDs to prevent breast cancer recurrence? An unanswered question. J Natl Cancer Inst 2018;110(9):927–8. https://doi.org/10.1093/jnci/djy049. 29554350. PMCID:PMC6136929.

[118] Walker OL, Dahn ML, Power Coombs MR, Marcato P. The prostaglandin E2 pathway and breast cancer stem cells: evidence of increased signaling and potential targeting. Front Oncol 2022;11:791696. https://doi.org/10.3389/fonc.2021.791696. 35127497. PMCID:PMC8807694.

[119] (a) Dittmer J. Breast cancer stem cells: features, key drivers and treatment options. Semin Cancer Biol 2018;53:59–74. https://doi.org/10.1016/j.semcancer.2018.07.007 [Epub 2018 Jul 27] 30059727. (b) Majumder M, Xin X, Liu L, Tutunea-Fatan E, Rodriguez-Torres M, Vincent K, Postovit LM, Hess D, Lala PK. COX-2 induces breast cancer stem cells via EP4/PI3K/AKT/NOTCH/WNT Axis. Stem Cells 2016;34(9):2290. https://doi.org/10.1002/stem.2426. 305. [Epub 2016 Jun 27 27301070.

[120] (a) Tomić S, Joksimović B, Bekić M, Vasiljević M, Milanović M, Čolić M, Vučević D. Prostaglanin-E2 potentiates the suppressive functions of human mononuclear myeloid-derived suppressor cells and increases their capacity to expand IL-10-producing regulatory T-cell subsets. Front Immunol 2019;10:475. https://doi.org/10.3389/fimmu.2019.00475. 30936876. PMCID:PMC6431635. (b) Li K, Shi H, Zhang B, Ou X, Ma Q, Chen Y, Shu P, Li D, Wang Y. Myeloid-derived suppressor cells as immunosuppressive regulators and therapeutic targets in cancer. Signal Transduct Target Ther 2021;6(1):362. https://doi.org/10.1038/s41392-021-00670-9. 34620838. PMCID: PMC8497485.

[121] Na YR, Yoon YN, Son DI, Seok SH. Cyclooxygenase-2 inhibition blocks M2 macrophage differentiation and suppresses metastasis in murine breast cancer model. PLoS One 2013;8(5):e63451. https://doi.org/10.1371/journal.pone.0063451. 23667623. PMCID:PMC3646746.

[122] Li D, Ji H, Niu X, Yin L, Wang Y, Gu Y, Wang J, Zhou X, Zhang H, Zhang Q. Tumor-associated macrophages secrete CC-chemokine ligand 2 and induce tamoxifen resistance by activating PI3K/Akt/mTOR in breast cancer. Cancer Sci 2020;111(1):47–58. https://doi.org/10.1111/cas.14230 [Epub 2019 Dec 19] 31710162. PMCID: PMC6942430.

[123] (a) Zatelli MC, Molè D, Tagliati F, Minoia M, Ambrosio MR, degli Uberti E. Cyclo-oxygenase 2 modulates chemoresistance in breast cancer cells involving NF-kappaB. Cell Oncol 2009;31(6):457–65. https://doi.org/10.3233/CLO-2009-0490. 19940361. PMCID:PMC4619115. (b) Liu B, Qu L, Tao H. Cyclo-oxygenase 2 upregulates the effect of multidrug resistance. Cell Biol Int 2009;34(1):21–5. https://doi.org/10.1042/CBI20090129. 20001974.

[124] NSCLC: Not Small Cell Lung Cancer; within the NSCLC are: lung adenocarcinoma (lung ADC), SCLC, LCLC Rodak O, Peris-Díaz MD, Olbromski M, Podhorska-Okołów M, Dzięgiel P. Current landscape of non-small cell lung cancer: epidemiology, histological classification, targeted therapies, and immunotherapy. Cancers (Basel) 2021;13(18):4705. https://doi.org/10.3390/cancers13184705. 34572931. PMCID:PMC8470525.

[125] (a) Hirsch FR, Scagliotti GV, Mulshine JL, Kwon R, Curran Jr WJ, Wu YL, Paz-Ares L. Lung cancer: current therapies and new targeted treatments. Lancet 2017;389(10066):299–311. https://doi.org/10.1016/S0140-6736(16)30958-8 [Epub 2016 Aug 27] 27574741. (b) Bade BC, Dela Cruz CS. Lung cancer 2020: epidemiology, etiology, and prevention. Clin Chest Med 2020;41(1):1–24. https://doi.org/10.1016/j.ccm.2019.10.001. 32008623.

[126] Allin KH, Nordestgaard BG. Elevated C-reactive protein in the diagnosis, prognosis, and cause of cancer. Crit Rev Clin Lab Sci 2011;48(4):155–70. https://doi.org/10.3109/10408363.2011.599831. 22035340.

[127] Engels EA. Inflammation in the development of lung cancer: epidemiological evidence. Expert Rev Anticancer Ther 2008;8(4):605–15. https://doi.org/10.1586/14737140.8.4.605. 18402527.

[128] Gomes M, Teixeira AL, Coelho A, Araújo A, Medeiros R. The role of inflammation in lung cancer. Adv Exp Med Biol 2014;816:1–23. https://doi.org/10.1007/978-3-0348-0837-8_1. 24818717.

[129] (a) Bittoni MA, Carbone DP, Harris RE. Ibuprofen and fatal lung cancer: a brief report of the prospective results from the Third National Health and Nutrition Examination Survey (NHANES III). Mol Clin Oncol 2017;6 (6):917–20. https://doi.org/10.3892/mco.2017.1239 [Epub 2017 May 5] 28588790. PMCID:PMC5451865. (b) VA MC, Hung RJ, Brenner DR, Bickeböller H, Rosenberger A, Muscat JE, Lazarus P, Tjønneland A, Friis S, Christiani DC, Chun EM, Le Marchand L, Rennert G, Rennert HS, Andrew AS, Orlow I, Park B, Boffetta P, Duell EJ. Aspirin and NSAID use and lung cancer risk: a pooled analysis in the International Lung Cancer Consortium (ILCCO). Cancer Causes Control 2011;22(12):1709–20. https://doi.org/10.1007/s10552-011-9847-z [Epub 2011 Oct 11] 21987079. PMCID:PMC3852431.

II. Nitric oxide pathway and cancer progression and therapy

[130] (a) Laga AC, Zander DS, Cagle PT. Prognostic significance of cyclooxygenase 2 expression in 259 cases of non-small cell lung cancer. Arch Pathol Lab Med 2005;129:1113–7. (b) Mascaux C, Martin B, Verdebout JM, Ninane V, Sculier JP. COX-2 expression during early lung squamous cell carcinoma oncogenesis. Eur Respir J 2005;26(2):198–203. https://doi.org/10.1183/09031936.05.00001405 [Erratum in: Eur Respir J. 2005;26(4):753] 16055866.

[131] (a) Sanaei MJ, Razi S, Pourbagheri-Sigaroodi A, Bashash D. The PI3K/Akt/mTOR pathway in lung cancer; oncogenic alterations, therapeutic opportunities, challenges, and a glance at the application of nanoparticles. Transl Oncol 2022;18:101364. https://doi.org/10.1016/j.tranon.2022.101364. 35168143. PMCID:PMC8850794. [Epub 2022 Feb 12]. (b) Peng Y, Wang Y, Zhou C, Mei W, Zeng C. PI3K/Akt/mTOR pathway and its role in cancer therapeutics: are we making headway? Front Oncol 2022;12:819128. https://doi.org/10.3389/fonc.2022.819128. 35402264. PMCID:PMC8987494.

[132] Yang J, Wang X, Gao Y, Fang C, Ye F, Huang B, Li L. Inhibition of PI3K-AKT signaling blocks PGE2-induced COX-2 expression in lung adenocarcinoma. Onco Targets Ther 2020;13:8197–208. https://doi.org/10.2147/OTT.S263977. 32904445. PMCID: PMC7455753.

[133] Rapp J, Jaromi L, Kvell K, Miskei G, Pongracz JE. WNT signaling—lung cancer is no exception. Respir Res 2017;18(1):167. https://doi.org/10.1186/s12931-017-0650-6. 28870231. PMCID:PMC5584342.

[134] Pacheco-Pinedo EC, Morrisey EE. Wnt and Kras signaling-dark siblings in lung cancer. Oncotarget 2011;2(7):569–74. https://doi.org/10.18632/oncotarget.305. 21753228. PMCID:PMC3248175.

[135] Dejana E. The role of wnt signaling in physiological and pathological angiogenesis. Circ Res 2010;107(8):943–52. https://doi.org/10.1161/CIRCRESAHA.110.223750. 20947863.

[136] Han A, Song Z, Tong C, Hu D, Bi X, Augenlicht LH, Yang W. Sulindac suppresses beta-catenin expression in human cancer cells. Eur J Pharmacol 2008;583(1):26–31. https://doi.org/10.1016/j.ejphar.2007.12.034 [Epub 2008 Feb 5.] 18291362. PMCID:PMC2350231.

[137] (a) Buchanan FG, DuBois RN. Connecting COX-2 and Wnt in cancer. Cancer Cell 2006;9(1):6–8. https://doi.org/10.1016/j.ccr.2005.12.029. 16413466. (b) Goessling W, North TE, Loewer S, Lord AM, Lee S, Stoick-Cooper CL, Weidinger G, Puder M, Daley GQ, Moon RT, Zon LI. Genetic interaction of PGE2 and Wnt signaling regulates developmental specification of stem cells and regeneration. Cell 2009;136(6):1136–47. https://doi.org/10.1016/j.cell.2009.01.015. 19303855. PMCID:PMC2692708. (c) Zheng C, Qu YX, Wang B, Shen PF, Xu JD, Chen YX. COX-2/PGE2 facilitates fracture healing by activating the Wnt/β-catenin signaling pathway. Eur Rev Med Pharmacol Sci 2019;23(22):9721–8. https://doi.org/10.26355/eurrev_201911_19534. 31799638.

[138] (a) Wu M, Guan J, Li C, Gunter S, Nusrat L, Ng S, Dhand K, Morshead C, Kim A, Das S. Aberrantly activated Cox-2 and Wnt signaling interact to maintain cancer stem cells in glioblastoma. Oncotarget 2017;8(47):82217–30. https://doi.org/10.18632/oncotarget.19283. 29137258. PMCID:PMC5669884. (b) Zheng BY, Gao WY, Huang XY, Lin LY, Fang XF, Chen ZX, Wang XZ. HBx promotes the proliferative ability of HL-7702 cells via the COX-2/Wnt/β-catenin pathway. Mol Med Rep 2018;17(6):8432–8. https://doi.org/10.3892/mmr.2018.8906 [Epub 2018 Apr 20] 29693167. (c) Che D, Zhang S, Jing Z, Shang L, Jin S, Liu F, Shen J, Li Y, Hu J, Meng Q, Yu Y. Macrophages induce EMT to promote invasion of lung cancer cells through the IL-6-mediated COX-2/PGE2/β-catenin signalling pathway. Mol Immunol 2017;90:197–210. https://doi.org/10.1016/j.molimm.2017.06.018 [Epub 2017 Aug 21. Erratum in: Mol Immunol. 2020; 126:165–166] 28837884.

[139] Kim JI, Lakshmikanthan V, Frilot N, Daaka Y. Prostaglandin E2 promotes lung cancer cell migration via EP4-betaArrestin1-c-Src signalsome. Mol Cancer Res 2010;8(4):569–77. https://doi.org/10.1158/1541-7786.MCR-09-0511 [Epub 2010 Mar 30] 20353998. PMCID:PMC2855782.

[140] (a) Krysan K, Reckamp KL, Sharma S, Dubinett SM. The potential and rationale for COX-2 inhibitors in lung cancer. Anticancer Agents Med Chem 2006;6(3):209–20. https://doi.org/10.2174/187152006776930882. 16712449. (b) Kim ES, Hong WK, Lee JJ, Mao L, Morice RC, Liu DD, Jimenez CA, Eapen GA, Lotan R, Tang X, Newman RA, Wistuba II, Kurie JM. Biological activity of celecoxib in the bronchial epithelium of current and former smokers. Cancer Prev Res (Phila) 2010;3(2):148–59. https://doi.org/10.1158/1940-6207.CAPR-09-0233 [Epub 2010 Jan 26] 20103722. PMCID:PMC4028718.

[141] (a) Tanaka T, Delong PA, Amin K, Henry A, Kruklitis R, Kapoor V, Kaiser LR, Albelda SM. Treatment of lung cancer using clinically relevant oral doses of the cyclooxygenase-2 inhibitor rofecoxib: potential value as adjuvant therapy after surgery. Ann Surg 2005;241(1):168–78. https://doi.org/10.1097/01.sla.0000149427.84712.d9. 15622005. PMCID:PMC1356860. (b) Gridelli C, Gallo C, Ceribelli A, Gebbia V, Gamucci T, Ciardiello F, Carozza F, Favaretto A, Daniele B, Galetta D, Barbera S, Rosetti F, Rossi A, Maione P, Cognetti F, Testa A, Di Maio M, Morabito A, Perrone F, GECO Investigators. Factorial phase III randomised trial of rofecoxib and prolonged

II. Nitric oxide pathway and cancer progression and therapy

constant infusion of gemcitabine in advanced non-small-cell lung cancer: the GEmcitabine-COxib in NSCLC (GECO) study. Lancet Oncol 2007;8(6):500–12. https://doi.org/10.1016/S1470-2045(07)70146-8. 17513173. (c) Kerr DJ, Dunn JA, Langman MJ, Smith JL, Midgley RS, Stanley A, Stokes JC, Julier P, Iveson C, Duvvuri R, CC MC, VICTOR Trial Group. Rofecoxib and cardiovascular adverse events in adjuvant treatment of colorectal cancer. N Engl J Med 2007;357(4):360–9. https://doi.org/10.1056/NEJMoa071841. 17652651.

[142] (a) Dai P, Li J, Ma XP, Huang J, Meng JJ, Gong P. Efficacy and safety of COX-2 inhibitors for advanced non-small-cell lung cancer with chemotherapy: a meta-analysis. Onco Targets Ther 2018;11:721–30. https://doi.org/10.2147/OTT.S148670. 29440919. PMCID:PMC5804138. (b) Zhou YY, Hu ZG, Zeng FJ, Han J. Clinical profile of cyclooxygenase-2 inhibitors in treating non-small cell lung cancer: a meta-analysis of nine randomized clinical trials. PLoS One 2016;11(3):e0151939. https://doi.org/10.1371/journal.pone.0151939. 27007231. PMCID:PMC4805232. (c) Hou LC, Huang F, Xu HB. Does celecoxib improve the efficacy of chemotherapy for advanced non-small cell lung cancer? Br J Clin Pharmacol 2016;81(1):23–32. https://doi.org/10.1111/bcp.12757 [Epub 2015 Nov 2] 26331772. PMCID:PMC4693572. (d) Groen HJ, Sietsma H, Vincent A, Hochstenbag MM, van Putten JW, van den Berg A, Dalesio O, Biesma B, Smit HJ, Termeer A, Hiltermann TJ, van den Borne BE, Schramel FM. Randomized, placebo-controlled phase III study of docetaxel plus carboplatin with celecoxib and cyclooxygenase-2 expression as a biomarker for patients with advanced non-small-cell lung cancer: the NVALT-4 study. J Clin Oncol 2011;29(32):4320–6. https://doi.org/10.1200/JCO.2011.35.5214 [Epub 2011 Oct 11] 21990410. (e) Koch A, Bergman B, Holmberg E, Sederholm C, Ek L, Kosieradzki J, Lamberg K, Thaning L, Ydreborg SO, Sörenson S, Swedish Lung Cancer Study Group. Effect of celecoxib on survival in patients with advanced non-small cell lung cancer: a double blind randomised clinical phase III trial (CYCLUS study) by the Swedish Lung Cancer Study Group. Eur J Cancer 2011;47(10):1546–55. https://doi.org/10.1016/j.ejca.2011.03.035 [Epub 2011 May 10] 21565487. (f) Edelman MJ, Wang X, Hodgson L, et al. Phase III randomized, placebo-controlled, double-blind trial of celecoxib in addition to standard chemotherapy for advanced Non-Small-Cell Lung Cancer with cyclooxygenase-2 overexpression: CALGB 30801 (Alliance). J Clin Oncol 2017;35:2184–92. https://doi.org/10.1200/JCO.2016.71.3743 [Epub 2017 May 10] 28489511. PMCID:PMC5493050.

[143] (a) Tołoczko-Iwaniuk N, Dziemiańczyk-Pakieła D, Nowaszewska BK, Celińska-Janowicz K, Miltyk W. Celecoxib in cancer therapy and prevention - review. Curr Drug Targets 2019;20(3):302–15. https://doi.org/10.2174/1389450119666180803121737. 30073924. (b) Kerr DJ, Chamberlain S, Kerr RS. Celecoxib for stage III colon cancer. JAMA 2021;325(13):1257–8. https://doi.org/10.1001/jama.2021.2651. 33821916.

[144] (a) Bie F, Tian H, Sun N, Zang R, Zhang M, Song P, Liu L, Peng Y, Bai G, Zhou B, Gao S. Research progress of anti-PD-1/PD-L1 immunotherapy related mechanisms and predictive biomarkers in NSCLC. Front Oncol 2022;12:769124. https://doi.org/10.3389/fonc.2022.769124. 35223466. PMCID:PMC8863729. (b) Pardoll DM. The blockade of immune checkpoints in cancer immunotherapy. Nat Rev Cancer 2012;12(4):252–64. https://doi.org/10.1038/nrc3239. 22437870. PMCID:PMC4856023. (c) Alsaab HO, Sau S, Alzhrani R, Tatiparti K, Bhise K, Kashaw SK, Iyer AK. PD-1 and PD-L1 checkpoint signaling inhibition for cancer immunotherapy: mechanism, combinations, and clinical outcome. Front Pharmacol 2017;8:561. https://doi.org/10.3389/fphar.2017.00561. 28878676. PMCID:PMC5572324.

[145] (a) Schoenfeld AJ, Hellmann MD. Acquired resistance to immune checkpoint inhibitors. Cancer Cell 2020;37 (4):443–55. https://doi.org/10.1016/j.ccell.2020.03.017. 32289269. PMCID:PMC7182070. (b) Shergold AL, Millar R, Nibbs RJB. Understanding and overcoming the resistance of cancer to PD-1/PD-L1 blockade. Pharmacol Res 2019;145:104258. https://doi.org/10.1016/j.phrs.2019.104258 [Epub 2019 May 4] 31063806.

[146] (a) Ghosh C, Luong G, Sun Y. A snapshot of the PD-1/PD-L1 pathway. J Cancer 2021;12(9):2735–46. https://doi.org/10.7150/jca.57334. 33854633. PMCID:PMC8040720. (b) Latchman Y, Wood CR, Chernova T, Chaudhary D, Borde M, Chernova I, Iwai Y, Long AJ, Brown JA, Nunes R, Greenfield EA, Bourque K, Boussiotis VA, Carter LL, Carreno BM, Malenkovich N, Nishimura H, Okazaki T, Honjo T, Sharpe AH, Freeman GJ. PD-L2 is a second ligand for PD-1 and inhibits T-cell activation. Nat Immunol 2001;2(3):261–8. https://doi.org/10.1038/85330. 11224527.

[147] Buchbinder EI, Desai A. CTLA-4 and PD-1 pathways: similarities, differences, and implications of their inhibition. Am J Clin Oncol 2016;39(1):98–106. https://doi.org/10.1097/COC.0000000000000239. 26558876. PMCID:PMC4892769.

[148] (a) Patsoukis N, Bardhan K, Chatterjee P, Sari D, Liu B, Bell LN, Karoly ED, Freeman GJ, Petkova V, Seth P, Li L, Boussiotis VA. PD-1 alters T-cell metabolic reprogramming by inhibiting glycolysis and promoting lipolysis

and fatty acid oxidation. Nat Commun 2015;6:6692. https://doi.org/10.1038/ncomms7692. 25809635. PMCID: PMC4389235. (b) Franco F, Jaccard A, Romero P, Yu YR, Ho PC. Metabolic and epigenetic regulation of T-cell exhaustion. Nat Metab 2020;2(10):1001–12. https://doi.org/10.1038/s42255-020-00280-9 [Epub 2020 Sep 21] 32958939.

[149] (a) The mechanism of T-cell activation is complex, and requires: interaction of an antigen with MHC molecule and a second interaction of the CD28 protein on the T-cell with ligands present on the antigen presenting cell. The binding of PD-1 to PD-L1 inhibits the TCR/CD28 signal transduction Shah K, Al-Haidari A, Sun J, Kazi JU. T-cell receptor (TCR) signaling in health and disease. Signal Transduct Target Ther 2021;6(1):412. https://doi.org/10.1038/s41392-021-00823-w. 34897277. PMCID:PMC8666445. (b) Chamoto K, Al-Habsi M, Honjo T. Role of PD-1 in immunity and diseases. Curr Top Microbiol Immunol 2017;410:75–97. https://doi.org/10.1007/82_2017_67. 28929192.

[150] (a) Zerdes I, Matikas A, Bergh J, Rassidakis GZ, Foukakis T. Genetic, transcriptional and post-translational regulation of the programmed death protein ligand 1 in cancer: biology and clinical correlations. Oncogene 2018;37 (34):4639–61. https://doi.org/10.1038/s41388-018-0303-3 [Epub 2018 May 16] 29765155. PMCID:PMC6107481. (b) Lamberti G, Sisi M, Andrini E, Palladini A, Giunchi F, Lollini PL, Ardizzoni A, Gelsomino F. The mechanisms of PD-L1 regulation in non-small-cell lung cancer (NSCLC): which are the involved players? Cancers (Basel) 2020;12(11):3129. https://doi.org/10.3390/cancers12113129. 33114576. PMCID:PMC7692442.

[151] Wang Y, Liu S, Yang Z, Algazi AP, Lomeli SH, Wang Y, Othus M, Hong A, Wang X, Randolph CE, Jones AM, Bosenberg MW, Byrum SD, Tackett AJ, Lopez H, Yates C, Solit DB, Ribas A, Piva M, Moriceau G, Lo RS. Anti-PD-1/L1 lead-in before MAPK inhibitor combination maximizes antitumor immunity and efficacy. Cancer Cell 2021;39(10):1375–1387.e6. https://doi.org/10.1016/j.ccell.2021.07.023 [Epub 2021 Aug 19] 34416167. PMCID: PMC9126729.

[152] (a) Galluzzi L, Spranger S, Fuchs E, López-Soto A. WNT signaling in cancer immunosurveillance. Trends Cell Biol 2019;29(1):44–65. https://doi.org/10.1016/j.tcb.2018.08.005 [Epub 2018 Sep 13] 30220580. PMCID: PMC7001864. (b) Takeuchi Y, Tanegashima T, Sato E, Irie T, Sai A, Itahashi K, Kumagai S, Tada Y, Togashi Y, Koyama S, Akbay EA, Karasaki T, Kataoka K, Funaki S, Shintani Y, Nagatomo I, Kida H, Ishii G, Miyoshi T, Aokage K, Kakimi K, Ogawa S, Okumura M, Eto M, Kumanogoh A, Tsuboi M, Nishikawa H. Highly immunogenic cancer cells require activation of the WNT pathway for immunological escape. Sci Immunol 2021;6(65): eabc6424. https://doi.org/10.1126/sciimmunol.abc6424 [Epub 2021 Nov 12] 34767457. (c) Zhang H, Bi Y, Wei Y, Liu J, Kuerban K, Ye L. Blocking Wnt/β-catenin signal amplifies anti-PD-1 therapeutic efficacy by inhibiting tumor growth, migration, and promoting immune infiltration in glioblastomas. Mol Cancer Ther 2021;20 (7):1305–15. https://doi.org/10.1158/1535-7163.MCT-20-0825 [Epub 2021 May 17] 34001635.

[153] (a) Li P, Huang T, Zou Q, Liu D, Wang Y, Tan X, Wei Y, Qiu H. FGFR2 promotes expression of PD-L1 in colorectal cancer via the JAK/STAT3 signaling pathway. J Immunol 2019;202(10):3065–75. https://doi.org/10.4049/jimmunol.1801199 [Epub 2019 Apr 12] 30979816. (b) Doi T, Ishikawa T, Okayama T, Oka K, Mizushima K, Yasuda T, Sakamoto N, Katada K, Kamada K, Uchiyama K, Handa O, Takagi T, Naito Y, Itoh Y. The JAK/STAT pathway is involved in the upregulation of PD-L1 expression in pancreatic cancer cell lines. Oncol Rep 2017;37(3):1545–54. https://doi.org/10.3892/or.2017.5399 [Epub 2017 Jan 23] 28112370. (c) Ritprajak P, Azuma M. Intrinsic and extrinsic control of expression of the immunoregulatory molecule PD-L1 in epithelial cells and squamous cell carcinoma. Oral Oncol 2015;51(3):221–8. https://doi.org/10.1016/j.oraloncology.2014.11.014 [Epub 2014 Dec 12] 25500094. (d) Becco P, Gallo S, Poletto S, Frascione MPM, Crotto L, Zaccagna A, Paruzzo L, Caravelli D, Carnevale-Schianca F, Aglietta M. Melanoma brain metastases in the era of target therapies: an overview. Cancers (Basel) 2020;12(6):1640. https://doi.org/10.3390/cancers12061640. 32575838. PMCID:PMC7352598.

[154] Ju X, Zhang H, Zhou Z, Chen M, Wang Q. Tumor-associated macrophages induce PD-L1 expression in gastric cancer cells through IL-6 and TNF-α signaling. Exp Cell Res 2020;396(2):112315. https://doi.org/10.1016/j.yexcr.2020.112315 [Epub 2020 Oct 5] 33031808.

[155] (a) You L, Wu W, Wang X, Fang L, Adam V, Nepovimova E, Wu Q, Kuca K. The role of hypoxia-inducible factor 1 in tumor immune evasion. Med Res Rev 2021;41(3):1622–43. https://doi.org/10.1002/med.21771 [Epub 2020 Dec 11] 33305856. (b) Shurin MR, Umansky V. Cross-talk between HIF and PD-1/PD-L1 pathways in carcinogenesis and therapy. J Clin Invest 2022;132(9):e159473. https://doi.org/10.1172/JCI159473. 35499071. PMCID: PMC9057611.

[156] (a) Botti G, Fratangelo F, Cerrone M, Liguori G, Cantile M, Anniciello AM, Scala S, D'Alterio C, Trimarco C, Ianaro A, Cirino G, Caracò C, Colombino M, Palmieri G, Pepe S, Ascierto PA, Sabbatino F, Scognamiglio

II. Nitric oxide pathway and cancer progression and therapy

G. COX-2 expression positively correlates with PD-L1 expression in human melanoma cells. J Transl Med 2017;15(1):46. https://doi.org/10.1186/s12967-017-1150-7. 28231855. PMCID:PMC5324267. (b) Cecil DL, Gad EA, Corulli LR, Drovetto N, Lubet RA, Disis ML. COX-2 inhibitors decrease expression of PD-L1 in colon tumors and increase the influx of type I tumor-infiltrating lymphocytes. Cancer Prev Res (Phila) 2022;15 (4):225–31. https://doi.org/10.1158/1940-6207.CAPR-21-0227. 34987061. PMCID:PMC8983455.

[157] Pu D, Yin L, Huang L, Qin C, Zhou Y, Wu Q, Li Y, Zhou Q, Li L. Cyclooxygenase-2 inhibitor: a potential combination strategy with immunotherapy in cancer. Front Oncol 2021;11:637504. https://doi.org/10.3389/fonc.2021.637504. 33718229. PMCID:PMC7952860.

[158] Wang SJ, Khullar K, Kim S, Yegya-Raman N, Malhotra J, Groisberg R, Crayton SH, Silk AW, Nosher JL, Gentile MA, Mehnert JM, Jabbour SK. Effect of cyclo-oxygenase inhibitor use during checkpoint blockade immunotherapy in patients with metastatic melanoma and non-small cell lung cancer. J Immunother Cancer 2020;8(2): e000889. https://doi.org/10.1136/jitc-2020-000889. 33020239. PMCID:PMC7537331.

[159] Botti G, Fratangelo F, Cerrone M, Liguori G, Cantile M, Anniciello AM, Scala S, D'Alterio C, Trimarco C, Ianaro A, Cirino G, Caracò C, Colombino M, Palmieri G, Pepe S, Ascierto PA, Sabbatino F, Scognamiglio G. COX-2 expression positively correlates with PD-L1 expression in human melanoma cells. J Transl Med 2017;15 (1):46. https://doi.org/10.1186/s12967-017-1150-7. 28231855. PMCID:PMC5324267.

[160] (a) Markosyan N, Chen EP, Evans RA, Ndong V, Vonderheide RH, Smyth EM. Mammary carcinoma cell derived cyclooxygenase 2 suppresses tumor immune surveillance by enhancing intratumoral immune checkpoint activity. Breast Cancer Res 2013;15(5):R75. https://doi.org/10.1186/bcr3469. 24004819. PMCID:PMC3979159. (b) Schoenfeld AJ, Hellmann MD. Acquired resistance to immune checkpoint inhibitors. Cancer Cell 2020;37 (4):443–55. https://doi.org/10.1016/j.ccell.2020.03.017. 32289269. PMCID:PMC7182070.

[161] Maruhashi T, Sugiura D, Okazaki I, et al. LAG-3: from molecular functions to clinical applications. J Immunother Cancer 2020;8:e001014. https://doi.org/10.1136/jitc-2020-001014.

[162] (a) Cecil DL, Gad EA, Corulli LR, Drovetto N, Lubet RA, Disis ML. COX-2 inhibitors decrease expression of PD-L1 in colon tumors and increase the influx of type I tumor-infiltrating lymphocytes. Cancer Prev Res (Phila) 2022;15(4):225–31. https://doi.org/10.1158/1940-6207.CAPR-21-0227. 34987061. PMCID:PMC8983455. (b) Rao CV. Anti-inflammatory drugs decrease the PD-L1 expression and increase the CD8+ T-cell infiltration. Cancer Prev Res (Phila) 2022;15(4):209–11. https://doi.org/10.1158/1940-6207.CAPR-22-0052. 35373258.

[163] (a) Miao J, Lu X, Hu Y, Piao C, Wu X, Liu X, Huang C, Wang Y, Li D, Liu J. Prostaglandin E2 and PD-1 mediated inhibition of antitumor CTL responses in the human tumor microenvironment. Oncotarget 2017;8(52):89802–10. https://doi.org/10.18632/oncotarget.21155. 29163789. PMCID:PMC5685710. (b) Pio R, Ajona D, Ortiz-Espinosa S, Mantovani A, Lambris JD. Complementing the cancer-immunity cycle. Front Immunol 2019;10:774. https://doi.org/10.3389/fimmu.2019.00774. 31031765. PMCID: PMC6473060.

[164] (a) Hu H, Kang L, Zhang J, Wu Z, Wang H, Huang M, Lan P, Wu X, Wang C, Cao W, Hu J, Huang Y, Huang L, Wang H, Shi L, Cai Y, Shen C, Ling J, Xie X, Cai Y, He X, Dou R, Zhou J, Ma T, Zhang X, Luo S, Deng W, Ling L, Liu H, Deng Y. Neoadjuvant PD-1 blockade with toripalimab, with or without celecoxib, in mismatch repair-deficient or microsatellite instability-high, locally advanced, colorectal cancer (PICC): a single-centre, parallel-group, non-comparative, randomised, phase 2 trial. Lancet Gastroenterol Hepatol 2022;7(1):38–48. https://doi.org/10.1016/S2468-1253(21)00348-4 [Epub 2021 Oct 22] 34688374.

[165] (a) Ching MM, Reader J, Fulton AM. Eicosanoids in cancer: prostaglandin E_2 receptor 4 in cancer therapeutics and immunotherapy. Front Pharmacol 2020;11:819. https://doi.org/10.3389/fphar.2020.00819. 32547404. PMCID:PMC7273839. (b) Take Y, Koizumi S, Nagahisa A. Prostaglandin E receptor 4 antagonist in cancer immunotherapy: mechanisms of action. Front Immunol 2020;11:324. https://doi.org/10.3389/fimmu.2020.00324. 32210957. PMCID:PMC7076081.

[166] (a) Sajiki Y, Konnai S, Cai Z, Takada K, Okagawa T, Maekawa N, Fujisawa S, Kato Y, Suzuki Y, Murata S, Ohashi K. Enhanced immunotherapeutic efficacy of anti-PD-L1 antibody in combination with an EP4 antagonist. Immunohorizons 2020;4(12):837–50. https://doi.org/10.4049/immunohorizons.2000089. 33443026. (b) Wang Y, Cui L, Georgiev P, Singh L, Zheng Y, Yu Y, Grein J, Zhang C, Muise ES, Sloman DL, Ferguson H, Yu H, Pierre CS, Dakle PJ, Pucci V, Baker J, Loboda A, Linn D, Brynczka C, Wilson D, Haines BB, Long B, Wnek R, Sadekova S, Rosenzweig M, Haidle A, Han Y, Ranganath SH. Combination of EP_4 antagonist MF-766 and anti-PD-1 promotes anti-tumor efficacy by modulating both lymphocytes and myeloid cells. Oncoimmunology 2021;10 (1):1896643. https://doi.org/10.1080/2162402X.2021.1896643. 33796403. PMCID:PMC7993229. (c) Karpisheh V, Joshi N, Zekiy AO, Beyzai B, Hojjat-Farsangi M, Namdar A, Edalati M, Jadidi-Niaragh F. EP4 receptor as

a novel promising therapeutic target in colon cancer. Pathol Res Pract 2020;216(12):153247. https://doi.org/10.1016/j.prp.2020.153247 [Epub 2020 Oct 19] 33190014.

[167] Bergqvist F, Morgenstern R, Jakobsson PJ. A review on mPGES-1 inhibitors: from preclinical studies to clinical applications. Prostaglandins Other Lipid Mediat 2020;147:106383. https://doi.org/10.1016/j.prostaglandins.2019.106383 [Epub 2019 Nov 4] 31698145.

[168] Prima V, Kaliberova LN, Kaliberov S, Curiel DT, Kusmartsev S. COX2/mPGES1/PGE2 pathway regulates PD-L1 expression in tumor-associated macrophages and myeloid-derived suppressor cells. Proc Natl Acad Sci USA 2017;114(5):1117–22. https://doi.org/10.1073/pnas.1612920114 [Epub 2017 Jan 17] 28096371. PMCID:PMC5293015.

[169] Wang Q, Li Y, Wu M, Huang S, Zhang A, Zhang Y, Jia Z. Targeting microsomal prostaglandin E synthase 1 to develop drugs treating the inflammatory diseases. Am J Transl Res 2021;13(1):391–419. 33527033. PMCID: PMC7847505.

[170] (a) Song X, Si Q, Qi R, Liu W, Li M, Guo M, Wei L, Yao Z. Indoleamine 2,3-dioxygenase 1: a promising therapeutic target in malignant tumor. Front Immunol 2021;12:800630. https://doi.org/10.3389/fimmu.2021.800630. 35003126. PMCID:PMC8733291. (b) Kim M, Tomek P. Tryptophan: a rheostat of cancer immune escape mediated by immunosuppressive enzymes IDO1 and TDO. Front Immunol 2021;12:636081. https://doi.org/10.3389/fimmu.2021.636081. 33708223. PMCID:PMC7940516.

[171] (a) Ricciuti B, Leonardi GC, Puccetti P, Fallarino F, Bianconi V, Sahebkar A, Baglivo S, Chiari R, Pirro M. Targeting indoleamine-2,3-dioxygenase in cancer: scientific rationale and clinical evidence. Pharmacol Ther 2019;196:105–16. https://doi.org/10.1016/j.pharmthera.2018.12.004 [Epub 2018 Dec 4] 30521884. (b) Tang K, Wu YH, Song Y, Yu B. Indoleamine 2,3-dioxygenase 1 (IDO1) inhibitors in clinical trials for cancer immunotherapy. J Hematol Oncol 2021;14(1):68. https://doi.org/10.1186/s13045-021-01080-8. 33883013. PMCID: PMC8061021.

[172] (a) Lee SY, Choi HK, Lee KJ, Jung JY, Hur GY, Jung KH, Kim JH, Shin C, Shim JJ, In KH, Kang KH, Yoo SH. The immune tolerance of cancer is mediated by IDO that is inhibited by COX-2 inhibitors through regulatory T- MAURIZIO NON corrggere questi perchè sono come scritto nerl titolo, controlla su ubmed da cui sono presi I riferimenti; ANCHE SOTTOcells. J Immunother 2009;32(1):22. https://doi.org/10.1097/CJI.0b013e31818ac2f7. 8 19307990. (b) Hennequart M, Pilotte L, Cane S, Hoffmann D, Stroobant V, Plaen ED, et al. Constitutive IDO1 expression in human tumors is driven by cyclooxygenase-2 and mediates intrinsic immune resistance. Cancer Immunol Res 2017;5(8):695. https://doi.org/10.1158/2326-6066.CIR-16-0400.

[173] García-Rayado G, Navarro M, Lanas A. NSAID induced GI damage and designing GI-sparing NSAIDs. Expert Rev Clin Pharmacol 2018;11(10):1031–43. https://doi.org/10.1080/17512433.2018.1516143 [Epub 2018 Sep 20] 30139288.

[174] (a) This class of drugs includes: NO-aspirin, NO-naproxen, NO-ibuprofen, NO-indomethacin, NO-sulindac; Rigas B, Kashfi K. Nitric-oxide-donating NSAIDs as agents for cancer prevention. Trends Mol Med 2004;10(7):324–30. https://doi.org/10.1016/j.molmed.2004.05.004. 15242680. (b) Stefano F, Distrutti E. Cyclooxygenase (COX) inhibiting nitric oxide donating (CINODs) drugs: a review of their current status. Curr Top Med Chem 2007;7(3):277–82. https://doi.org/10.2174/156802607779941350. 17305570.

[175] Muscará MN, Wallace JL. COX-inhibiting nitric oxide donors (CINODs): potential benefits on cardiovascular and renal function. Cardiovasc Hematol Agents Med Chem 2006;4(2):155–64. https://doi.org/10.2174/187152506776369917. 16611049.

[176] (a) Nitronaproxen: AZD 3582, HCT 3012, naproxen nitroxybutylester, NO-naproxen. Drugs R D 2006;7(4):262–6. https://doi.org/10.2165/00126839-200607040-00007. 16784252. (b) Geusens P. Naproxcinod, a new cyclooxygenase-inhibiting nitric oxide donor (CINOD). Expert Opin Biol Ther 2009;9(5):649–57. https://doi.org/10.1517/14712590902926071. 19392579.

[177] NDA: New Drug Application: the file for registration of a new drug with FDA.

[178] (a) Geusens P. Naproxcinod, a new cyclooxygenase-inhibiting nitric oxide donor (CINOD). Expert Opin Biol Ther 2009;9(5):649–57. https://doi.org/10.1517/14712590902926071. 19392579. (b) Schnitzer TJ, Kivitz A, Frayssinet H, Duquesroix B. Efficacy and safety of naproxcinod in the treatment of patients with osteoarthritis of the knee: a 13-week prospective, randomized, multicenter study. Osteoarthritis Cartilage 2010;18(5):629. https://doi.org/10.1016/j.joca.2009.12.013. 39. [Epub 2010 Feb 16] 20202489. (c) White WB, Schnitzer TJ, Bakris GL, Frayssinet H, Duquesroix B, Weber M. Effects of naproxcinod on blood pressure in patients with osteoarthritis. Am J Cardiol 2011;107(9):1338–45. https://doi.org/10.1016/j.amjcard.2010.12.046 [Epub 2011 Mar 2]

21371681. (d) Huerta S. Nitric oxide for cancer therapy. Future Sci OA 2015;1(1):FSO44. https://doi.org/10.4155/fso.15.44. 28031862. PMCID:PMC5137992.

[179] Li H, Liu X, Cui H, Chen YR, Cardounel AJ, Zweier JL. Characterization of the mechanism of cytochrome P450 reductase-cytochrome P450-mediated nitric oxide and nitrosothiol generation from organic nitrates. J Biol Chem 2006;281(18):12546–54. https://doi.org/10.1074/jbc.M511803200 [Epub 2006 Mar 9] 16527817.

[180] Govoni M, Casagrande S, Maucci R, Chiroli V, Tocchetti P. In vitro metabolism of (nitrooxy)butyl ester nitric oxide-releasing compounds: comparison with glyceryl trinitrate. J Pharmacol Exp Ther 2006;317(2):752–61. https://doi.org/10.1124/jpet.105.097469 [Epub 2006 Jan 19. Erratum in: J Pharmacol Exp Ther. 2007;320 (1):497] 16424150.

[181] (a) Shi X, Shang W, Wang S, Xue N, Hao Y, Wang Y, Sun M, Du Y, Cao D, Zhang K, Shi Q. Simultaneous quantification of naproxcinod and its active metabolite naproxen in rat plasma using LC-MS/MS: application to a pharmacokinetic study. J Chromatogr B Analyt Technol Biomed Life Sci 2015;978–979:157–62. https://doi.org/10.1016/j.jchromb.2014.12.001 [Epub 2014 Dec 11] 25550191. (b) Fagerholm U, Breuer O, Swedmark S, Hoogstraate J. Pre-clinical pharmacokinetics of the cyclooxygenase-inhibiting nitric oxide donor (CINOD) AZD3582. J Pharm Pharmacol 2005;57(5):587–97. https://doi.org/10.1211/0022357056028. 15901348. (c) Fagerholm U, Björnsson MA. Clinical pharmacokinetics of the cyclooxygenase inhibiting nitric oxide donator (CINOD) AZD3582. J Pharm Pharmacol 2005;57(12):1539–54. https://doi.org/10.1211/jpp.57.12.0004. 16354398.

[182] (a) Ferrer MD, Busquets-Cortés C, Capó X, Tejada S, Tur JA, Pons A, Sureda A. Cyclooxygenase-2 inhibitors as a therapeutic target in Inflammatory diseases. Curr Med Chem 2019;26(18):3225–41. https://doi.org/10.2174/0929867325666180514112124. 29756563. (b) Patrono C. Cardiovascular effects of cyclooxygenase-2 inhibitors: a mechanistic and clinical perspective. Br J Clin Pharmacol 2016;82(4):957–64. https://doi.org/10.1111/bcp.13048. (c) Tacconelli S, Bruno A, Grande R, Ballerini P, Patrignani P. Nonsteroidal anti-inflammatory drugs and cardiovascular safety - translating pharmacological data into clinical readouts. Expert Opin Drug Saf 2017;16(7):791–807. https://doi.org/10.1080/14740338.2017.1338272.

[183] (a) Chegaev K, Lazzarato L, Tosco P, Cena C, Marini E, Rolando B, Carrupt PA, Fruttero R, Gasco A. NO-donor COX-2 inhibitors. New nitrooxy-substituted 1,5-diarylimidazoles endowed with COX-2 inhibitory and vasodilator properties. J Med Chem 2007;50(7):1449–57. https://doi.org/10.1021/jm0607247. [Epub 2007 Mar 3 17335184. (b) Bhardwaj A, Huang Z, Kaur J, Knaus EE. Rofecoxib analogues possessing a nitric oxide donor sulfohydroxamic acid (SO_2NHOH) cyclooxygenase-2 pharmacophore: synthesis, molecular modeling, and biological evaluation as anti-inflammatory agents. ChemMedChem 2012;7(1):62–7. https://doi.org/10.1002/cmdc.201100393 [Epub 2011 Oct 11] 21990143. (c) Bocca C, Bozzo F, Bassignana A, Miglietta A. Antiproliferative effect of a novel nitro-oxy derivative of celecoxib in human colon cancer cells: role of COX-2 and nitric oxide. Anticancer Res 2010;30(7):2659–66. 20682995.

[184] (a) Biava M, Porretta GC, Poce G, Battilocchio C, Alfonso S, Rovini M, Valenti S, Giorgi G, Calderone V, Martelli A, Testai L, Sautebin L, Rossi A, Papa G, Ghelardini C, Di Cesare ML, Giordani A, Anzellotti P, Bruno A, Patrignani P, Anzini M. Novel analgesic/anti-inflammatory agents: diarylpyrrole acetic esters endowed with nitric oxide releasing properties. J Med Chem 2011;54(22):7759–71. https://doi.org/10.1021/jm200715n [Epub 2011 Oct 31] 21992176. (b) Anzini M, Di Capua A, Valenti S, Brogi S, Rovini M, Giuliani G, Cappelli A, Vomero S, Chiasserini L, Sega A, Poce G, Giorgi G, Calderone V, Martelli A, Testai L, Sautebin L, Rossi A, Pace S, Ghelardini C, Di Cesare Mannelli L, Benetti V, Giordani A, Anzellotti P, Dovizio M, Patrignani P, Biava M. Novel analgesic/anti-inflammatory agents: 1,5-diarylpyrrole nitrooxyalkyl ethers and related compounds as cyclooxygenase-2 inhibiting nitric oxide donors. J Med Chem 2013;56(8):3191–206. https://doi.org/10.1021/jm301370e [Epub 2013 Apr 11. Erratum in: J Med Chem. 2013;56(11):4821] 23534442. (c) Consalvi S, Poce G, Ragno R, Sabatino M, La Motta C, Sartini S, Calderone V, Martelli A, Ghelardini C, Di Cesare ML, Biava M. A series of COX-2 inhibitors endowed with NO-releasing properties: synthesis, biological evaluation, and docking analysis. ChemMedChem 2016;11(16):1804–11. https://doi.org/10.1002/cmdc.201600086 [Epub 2016 May 27] 27229194.

[185] Martelli A, Testai L, Anzini M, Cappelli A, Di Capua A, Biava M, Poce G, Consalvi S, Giordani A, Caselli G, Rovati L, Ghelardini C, Patrignani P, Sautebin L, Breschi MC, Calderone V. The novel anti-inflammatory agent VA694, endowed with both NO-releasing and COX2-selective inhibiting properties, exhibits NO-mediated positive effects on blood pressure, coronary flow and endothelium in an experimental model of hypertension and endothelial dysfunction. Pharmacol Res 2013;78:1–9. https://doi.org/10.1016/j.phrs.2013.09.008 [Epub 2013 Sep 29] 24083950.

[186] (a) Hu Y, Xiang J, Su L, Tang X. The regulation of nitric oxide in tumor progression and therapy. J Int Med Res 2020;48(2). https://doi.org/10.1177/0300060520905985. 300060520905985 32090657. PMCID:PMC7110915. (b) Kashfi K. Nitric oxide in cancer and beyond. Biochem Pharmacol 2020;176:114006. https://doi.org/10.1016/j.bcp.2020.114006 [Epub 2020 Apr 28] 32360361. (c) Khan FH, Dervan E, Bhattacharyya DD, McAuliffe JD, Miranda KM, Glynn SA. The role of nitric oxide in cancer: master regulator or NOT? Int J Mol Sci 2020;21(24):9393. https://doi.org/10.3390/ijms21249393. 33321789. PMCID:PMC7763974.

[187] Holotiuk VV, Kryzhanivska AY, Churpiy IK, Tataryn BB, Ivasiutyn DY. Role of nitric oxide in pathogenesis of tumor growth and its possible application in cancer treatment. Exp Oncol 2019;41(3):210–5. https://doi.org/10.32471/exp-oncology.2312-8852.vol-41-no-3.13515. 31569933.

[188] Vannini F, Kashfi K, Nath N. The dual role of iNOS in cancer. Redox Biol 2015;6:334–43. https://doi.org/10.1016/j.redox.2015.08.009 [Epub 2015 Aug 24] 26335399. PMCID:PMC4565017.

[189] (a) Hays E, Bonavida B. Nitric oxide-mediated enhancement and reversal of resistance of anticancer therapies. Antioxidants (Basel) 2019;8(9):407. https://doi.org/10.3390/antiox8090407. 31533363. PMCID:PMC6769868. (b) Jiang W, Dong W, Li M, Guo Z, Wang Q, Liu Y, Bi Y, Zhou H, Wang Y. Nitric oxide induces immunogenic cell death and potentiates cancer immunotherapy. ACS Nano 2022;16(3):3881–94. https://doi.org/10.1021/acsnano.1c09048 [Epub 2022 Mar 3] 35238549.

[190] (a) Kashfi K, Kannikal J, Nath N. Macrophage reprogramming and cancer therapeutics: role of iNOS-derived NO. Cell 2021;10(11):3194. https://doi.org/10.3390/cells10113194. 34831416. PMCID:PMC8624911. (b) Nath N, Kashfi K. Tumor associated macrophages and 'NO'. Biochem Pharmacol 2020;176:113899. https://doi.org/10.1016/j.bcp.2020.113899 [Epub 2020 Mar 4] 32145264. (c) Biswas SK, Mantovani A. Macrophage plasticity and interaction with lymphocyte subsets: cancer as a paradigm. Nat Immunol 2010;11(10):889–96. https://doi.org/10.1038/ni.1937 [Epub 2010 Sep 20] 20856220.

[191] Navasardyan I, Bonavida B. Regulation of T-cells in cancer by nitric oxide. Cell 2021;10(10):2655. https://doi.org/10.3390/cells10102655. 34685635. PMCID:PMC8534057.

[192] (a) Huang Z, Fu J, Zhang Y. Nitric oxide donor-based cancer therapy: advances and prospects. J Med Chem 2017;60(18):7617–35. https://doi.org/10.1021/acs.jmedchem.6b01672 [Epub 2017 May 23] 28505442. (b) Ding QG, Zang J, Gao S, Gao Q, Duan W, Li X, Xu W, Zhang Y. Nitric oxide donor hybrid compounds as promising anticancer agents. Drug Discov Ther 2017;10(6):276–84. https://doi.org/10.5582/ddt.2016.01067 [Epub 2016 Dec 18] 27990006. (c) Alimoradi H, Greish K, Gamble AB, Giles GI. Controlled delivery of nitric oxide for cancer therapy. Pharm Nanotechnol 2019;7(4):279–303. https://doi.org/10.2174/2211738507666190429111306. 31595847. PMCID: PMC6967185.

[193] (a) Gresele P, Momi S. Pharmacologic profile and therapeutic potential of NCX 4016, a nitric oxide-releasing aspirin, for cardiovascular disorders. Cardiovasc Drug Rev 2006;24(2):148–68. https://doi.org/10.1111/j.1527-3466.2006.00148.x. 16961726. (b) Wallace JL, Ignarro LJ, Fiorucci S. Potential cardioprotective actions of no-releasing aspirin. Nat Rev Drug Discov 2002;1(5):375–82. https://doi.org/10.1038/nrd794. 12120413.

[194] (a) Fiorucci S, Del Soldato P. NO-aspirin: mechanism of action and GI safety. Dig Liver Dis 2003;35(Suppl. 2):S9–19. https://doi.org/10.1016/s1590-8658(03)00047-1. 12846439. (b) Wallace JL. Nitric oxide, aspirin-triggered lipoxins and NO-aspirin in gastric protection. Inflamm Allergy Drug Targets 2006;5(2):133. https://doi.org/10.2174/187152806776383116. 7 16613572.

[195] Williams JL, Borgo S, Hasan I, Castillo E, Traganos F, Rigas B. Nitric oxide-releasing nonsteroidal anti-inflammatory drugs (NSAIDs) alter the kinetics of human colon cancer cell lines more effectively than traditional NSAIDs: implications for colon cancer chemoprevention. Cancer Res 2001;61(8):3285–9. 11309281.

[196] (a) Williams JL, Kashfi K, Ouyang N, del Soldato P, Kopelovich L, Rigas B. NO-donating aspirin inhibits intestinal carcinogenesis in min (APC(min/+)) mice. Biochem Biophys Res Commun 2004;313(3):784–8. https://doi.org/10.1016/j.bbrc.2003.12.015. 14697260. (b) Yeh RK, Chen J, Williams JL, Baluch M, Hundley TR, Rosenbaum RE, Kalala S, Traganos F, Benardini F, del Soldato P, Kashfi K, Rigas B. NO-donating nonsteroidal antiinflammatory drugs (NSAIDs) inhibit colon cancer cell growth more potently than traditional NSAIDs: a general pharmacological property? Biochem Pharmacol 2004;67(12):2197–205. https://doi.org/10.1016/j.bcp.2004.02.027. 15163551.

[197] (a) Hundley TR, Rigas B. Nitric oxide-donating aspirin inhibits colon cancer cell growth via mitogen-activated protein kinase activation. J Pharmacol Exp Ther 2006;316(1):25–34. https://doi.org/10.1124/jpet.105.091363 [Epub 2005 Sep 16] 16169935. (b) Selvendiran K, Bratasz A, Tong L, Ignarro LJ, Kuppusamy P. NCX-4016, a nitro-derivative of aspirin, inhibits EGFR and STAT3 signaling and modulates Bcl-2 proteins in cisplatin-

II. Nitric oxide pathway and cancer progression and therapy

resistant human ovarian cancer cells and xenografts. Cell Cycle 2008;7(1):81. https://doi.org/10.4161/cc.7.1.5103. 8. [Epub 2007 Sep 28] 18196976. PMCID: PMC2890223.

[198] Carini M, Aldini G, Orioli M, Piccoli A, Rossoni G, Maffei FR. Nitric oxide release and distribution following oral and intraperitoneal administration of nitroaspirin (NCX 4016) in the rat. Life Sci 2004;74(26):3291–305. https://doi.org/10.1016/j.lfs.2003.11.018. 15094329.

[199] (a) Carini M, Aldini G, Orioli M, Piccoli A, Tocchetti P, Facino RM. Chemiluminescence and LC-MS/MS analyses for the study of nitric oxide release and distribution following oral administration of nitroaspirin (NCX 4016) in healthy volunteers. J Pharm Biomed Anal 2004;35(2):277. https://doi.org/10.1016/S0731-7085(03)00531-4. 87 15063462. (b) Wallace JL. Nitric oxide, aspirin-triggered lipoxins and NO-aspirin in gastric protection. Inflamm Allergy Drug Targets 2006;5(2):133. https://doi.org/10.2174/187152806776383116. 7 16613572.

[200] Ricciotti E, Dovizio M, Di Francesco L, Anzellotti P, Salvatore T, Di Francesco A, Sciulli MG, Pistritto G, Monopoli A, Patrignani P. NCX 4040, a nitric oxide-donating aspirin, exerts anti-inflammatory effects through inhibition of I kappa B-alpha degradation in human monocytes. J Immunol 2010;184(4):2140–7. https://doi.org/10.4049/jimmunol.0903107 [Epub 2010 Jan 11] 20065114.

[201] Kashfi K, Borgo S, Williams JL, Chen J, Gao J, Glekas A, Benedini F, Del Soldato P, Rigas B. Positional isomerism markedly affects the growth inhibition of colon cancer cells by nitric oxide-donating aspirin in vitro and in vivo. J Pharmacol Exp Ther 2005;312(3):978–88. https://doi.org/10.1124/jpet.104.075994 [Epub 2004 Nov 4] 15528453.

[202] Gao J, Kashfi K, Rigas B. In vitro metabolism of nitric oxide-donating aspirin: the effect of positional isomerism. J Pharmacol Exp Ther 2005;312(3):989–97. https://doi.org/10.1124/jpet.104.076190. Mar. [Epub 2004 Nov 4] 15528452.

[203] Gao J, Liu X, Rigas B. Nitric oxide-donating aspirin induces apoptosis in human colon cancer cells through induction of oxidative stress. Proc Natl Acad Sci USA 2005;102(47):17207–12. https://doi.org/10.1073/pnas.0506893102 [Epub 2005 Nov 10] 16282376. PMCID:PMC1287992.

[204] (a) Hulsman N, Medema JP, Bos C, Jongejan A, Leurs R, Smit MJ, de Esch IJ, Richel D, Wijtmans M. Chemical insights in the concept of hybrid drugs: the antitumor effect of nitric oxide-donating aspirin involves a quinone methide but not nitric oxide nor aspirin. J Med Chem 2007;50(10):2424–31. https://doi.org/10.1021/jm061371e [Epub 2007 Apr 19] 17441704. (b) Dunlap T, Chandrasena RE, Wang Z, Sinha V, Wang Z, Thatcher GR. Quinone formation as a chemoprevention strategy for hybrid drugs: balancing cytotoxicity and cytoprotection. Chem Res Toxicol 2007;20(12):1903–12. https://doi.org/10.1021/tx7002257 [Epub 2007 Nov 1] 17975886.

[205] (a) Steele VE, Rao CV, Zhang Y, Patlolla J, Boring D, Kopelovich L, Juliana MM, Grubbs CJ, Lubet RA. Chemopreventive efficacy of naproxen and nitric oxide-naproxen in rodent models of colon, urinary bladder, and mammary cancers. Cancer Prev Res (Phila) 2009;2(11):951–6. https://doi.org/10.1158/1940-6207.CAPR-09-0080. 19892664. PMCID: PMC2774912. (b) Chattopadhyay M, Goswami S, Rodes DB, Kodela R, Velazquez CA, Boring D, Crowell JA, Kashfi K. NO-releasing NSAIDs suppress NF-κB signaling in vitro and in vivo through S-nitrosylation. Cancer Lett 2010;298(2):204. https://doi.org/10.1016/j.canlet.2010.07.006. 11. [Epub 2010 Jul 31] 20674154.

[206] (a) Boschi D, Lazzarato L, Rolando B, Filieri A, Cena C, Di Stilo A, Fruttero R, Gasco A. Nitrooxymethyl-substituted analogues of celecoxib: synthesis and pharmacological characterization. Chem Biodivers 2009;6 (3):369–79. https://doi.org/10.1002/cbdv.200800307. 19319873. (b) Bocca C, Bozzo F, Bassignana A, Miglietta A. Antiproliferative effect of a novel nitro-oxy derivative of celecoxib in human colon cancer cells: role of COX-2 and nitric oxide. Anticancer Res 2010;30(7):2659–66. 20682995.

[207] 4-{{1-[4-(Nitrooxy)methyl]phenyl}-3-(trifluoromethyl)-1H-pyrazol-5-yl}benzyl nitrate.

[208] Ren SZ, Wang ZC, Zhu D, Zhu XH, Shen FQ, Wu SY, Chen JJ, Xu C, Zhu HL. Design, synthesis and biological evaluation of novel ferrocene-pyrazole derivatives containing nitric oxide donors as COX-2 inhibitors for cancer therapy. Eur J Med Chem 2018;157:909–24. https://doi.org/10.1016/j.ejmech.2018.08.048 [Epub 2018 Aug 22] 30149323.

[209] Biava M, Porretta GC, Poce G, Supino S, Forli S, Rovini M, Cappelli A, Manetti M, Botta M, Sautebin L, Rossi A, Pergola C, Ghelardini C, Vivoli E, Makovec F, Anzellotti P, Patrignani P, Anzini M. Cyclooxygenase-2 inhibitors. 1,5-diarylpyrrol-3-acetic esters with enhanced inhibitory activity toward cyclooxygenase-2 and improved cyclooxygenase-2/cyclooxygenase-1 selectivity. J Med Chem 2007;50:5403–11. https://doi.org/10.1021/jm0707525.

[210] Anzini M, Rovini M, Cappelli A, Vomero S, Manetti F, Botta M, Sautebin L, Rossi A, Pergola C, Ghelardini C, Norcini M, Giordani A, Makovec F, Anzellotti P, Patrignani P, Biava M. Synthesis, biological evaluation, and enzyme docking simulations of 1,5-diarylpyrrole-3-alkoxyethyl ethers as selective cyclooxygenase-2 inhibitors

endowed with anti-inflammatory and antinociceptive activity. J Med Chem 2008;5:4476–81. https://doi.org/10.1021/jm800084s.

[211] Biava M, Porretta GC, Poce G, Battilocchio C, Manetti F, Botta M, Forli S, Sautebin L, Rossi A, Pergola C, Ghelardini C, Galeotti N, Makovec F, Giordani A, Anzellotti P, Patrignani P, Anzini M. Novel ester and acid derivatives of the 1,5-diarylpyrrole scaffold as anti-inflammatory and analgesic agents. Synthesis and in vitro and in vivo biological evaluation. J Med Chem 2010;53:723–33. https://doi.org/10.1021/jm901269y.

[212] Biava M, Battilocchio C, Poce G, Alfonso S, Consalvi S, Porretta GC, Schenone S, Calderone V, Martelli A, Testai L, Ghelardini C, Di Cesare ML, Sautebin L, Rossi A, Giordani A, Patrignani P, Anzini M. Improving the solubility of a new class of antiinflammatory pharmacodynamic hybrids, that release nitric oxide and inhibit cycloxygenase-2 isoenzyme. Eur J Med Chem 2012;58:287–98. https://doi.org/10.1016/j.ejmech.2012.10.014.

[213] Biava M, Battilocchio C, Poce G, Alfonso S, Consalvi S, Di Capua A, Calderone V, Martelli A, Testai L, Sautebin L, Rossi A, Ghelardini C, Di Cesare ML, Giordani A, Persiani S, Colovic M, Dovizio M, Patrignani P, Anzini M. Enhancing the pharmacodynamic profile of a class of selective COX-2 inhibiting nitric oxide donors. Bioorg Med Chem 2014;22:772–86. https://doi.org/10.1016/j.bmc.2013.12.008.

[214] Bhardwaj A, Batchu SN, Kaur J, Huang Z, Seubert JM, Knaus EE. Cardiovascular properties of a nitric oxide releasing rofecoxib analogue: beneficial anti-hypertensive activity and enhanced recovery in an ischemic reperfusion injury model. ChemMedChem 2012;7:1365–8. https://doi.org/10.1002/cmdc.201200234.

[215] Abdellatif KRA, Moawad A, Knaus EE. Synthesis of new 1-(4-methane(amino)sulfonylphenyl)-5-(4-substituted-aminomethylphenyl)-3-trifluoromethyl-1H-pyrazoles: a search for novel nitric oxide donor anti-inflammatory agents. Bioorg Med Chem Lett 2014;24:5015–21. https://doi.org/10.1016/j.bmcl.2014.09.024.

[216] Chowdhury MA, Abdellatif KRA, Dong Y, Yu G, Huang Z, Rahman M, Das D, Velázquez CA, Suresh MR, Knaus EE. Celecoxib analogs possessing a N-(4-nitrooxybutyl)piperidin-4-yl or N-(4-nitrooxybutyl)-1,2,3,6-tetrahydropyridin-4-yl nitric oxide donor moiety: synthesis, biological evaluation and nitric oxide release studies. Bioorg Med Chem Lett 2010;20:1324–9. https://doi.org/10.1016/j.bmcl.2010.01.014.

[217] Muley MM, Krustev E, McDougall JJ. Preclinical assessment of Inflammatory pain. CNS Neurosci Ther 2016;22:88–101. https://doi.org/10.1111/cns.12486.

[218] Patil KR, Mahajan UB, Unger BS, Goyal SN, Belemkar S, Surana SJ, Ojha S, Patil CR. Animal models of inflammation for screening of anti-inflammatory drugs: implications for the discovery and development of phytopharmaceuticals. Int J Mol Sci 2019;20:4367. https://doi.org/10.3390/ijms20184367.

[219] (a) Ramsay RR, Popovic-Nikolic MR, Nikolic K, Uliassi E, Bolognesi ML. A perspective on multi-target drug discovery and design for complex diseases. Clin Transl Med 2018;7(1):3. https://doi.org/10.1186/s40169-017-0181-2. 29340951. PMCID:PMC5770353. (b) Amelio I, Lisitsa A, Knight RA, Melino G, Antonov AV. Polypharmacology of approved anticancer drugs. Curr Drug Targets 2017;18(5):534–43. https://doi.org/10.2174/1389450117666160301095233. 26926468.

4

Targeting dimethylarginine dimethylaminohydrolase 1 to suppress vasculogenic mimicry in breast cancer: Current evidence and future directions

Arduino A. Mangoni[a,b], Julie-Ann Hulin[a], Lashika Weerakoon[a], and Sara Tommasi[a,b]

[a]Discipline of Clinical Pharmacology, College of Medicine and Public Health and Flinders Health and Medical Research Institute, Flinders University, Adelaide, SA, Australia [b]Department of Clinical Pharmacology, Flinders Medical Centre, Southern Adelaide Local Health Network, Adelaide, SA, Australia

Abstract

Nitric oxide (NO) plays a critical pathophysiological role in cancer by modulating several processes such as angiogenesis, tumor growth, and metastatic potential. However, the role of NO in vasculogenic mimicry, an alternative neovascularization process involving the formation of vessel-like networks directly by the tumor cells themselves and predicting high metastatic burden and poor survival, is less clear. The pathophysiological and clinical significance of vasculogenic mimicry have been particularly well studied in triple-negative breast cancer (TNBC), a type of breast cancer characterized by aggressive behavior, high relapse rate, poor prognosis, and lack of effective targeted treatments. Recent studies have reported that isoform 1 of the enzyme dimethylarginine dimethylaminohydrolase (DDAH1), responsible for the metabolism of the endogenous NO synthase inhibitors, the methylated arginines asymmetric N^G,N^G-dimethyl-L-arginine and N^G-monomethyl-L-arginine, is essential for TNBC cells to undertake vasculogenic mimicry. Furthermore, treatment with small-molecule arginine analogs with inhibitory activity toward DDAH1 has been shown to significantly reduce vasculogenic mimicry by TNBC cells. This chapter describes the current knowledge regarding the pathophysiological and clinical significance of vasculogenic mimicry, the biology of DDAH1 and methylated arginines, and the role of DDAH1 as a promising "druggable" target to suppress vasculogenic mimicry in cancer, with a focus on TNBC.

Nitric Oxide in Health and Disease
https://doi.org/10.1016/B978-0-443-13342-8.00013-2

Abbreviations

ADMA	asymmetric N^G,N^G-dimethyl-L-arginine
DDAH1	dimethylarginine dimethylaminohydrolase 1
eNOS	endothelial nitric oxide synthase
HIF-1α	hypoxia-inducible factor 1-alpha
iNOS	inducible nitric oxide synthase
NMMA	N^G-monomethyl-L-arginine
nNOS	neuronal nitric oxide synthase
NO	nitric oxide
NOS	nitric oxide synthase
SDMA	symmetric N^G,N^G-dimethyl-L-arginine
TGFβ	transforming growth factor beta
TNBC	triple-negative breast cancer
VEGF-A	vascular endothelial growth factor A

Conflict of interest

No potential conflicts of interest were disclosed.

Introduction

Despite significant advances in diagnosis and treatment, particularly over the last three decades, cancer still represents a significant public health burden worldwide in terms of incidence, disease-related disability, premature mortality, and associated health care costs [1,2]. Therefore, there are ongoing efforts to identify novel "druggable" targets and more effective therapies. In this context, an adequate blood supply of oxygen and nutrients is essential for the growth and the dissemination of cancer cells. Angiogenesis, a type of endothelial cell-driven neovascularization that involves the formation, sprouting, extension, and remodeling of preexisting blood vessels, plays a critical role in the development of intratumoral vascular networks. These networks ensure adequate blood supply to cancer cells and represent an attractive therapeutic target for local and/or systemic antiangiogenic therapies [3–6]. However, despite their theoretical efficacy, antiangiogenic drugs, a class of anticancer agents introduced for routine clinical use in 2004, have generally failed to exert tangible effects on tumor progression and survival in several types of cancer both in clinical trials and in "real-world" patients. The relative lack of efficacy of antiangiogenic drugs is thought to be mainly a consequence of the development of treatment "resistance" [7,8]. One important factor responsible for resistance to traditional antiangiogenic drugs is represented by vasculogenic mimicry, an alternative neovascularization paradigm and an emerging therapeutic target in cancer [9–11]. Vasculogenic mimicry is frequently observed in aggressive types of cancer, e.g., triple-negative breast cancer (TNBC), and is associated with an increased risk of metastasis and adverse outcomes [12,13].

A recently discovered "druggable" target in the quest for new treatments that may suppress vasculogenic mimicry is represented by isoform 1 of the enzyme dimethylarginine dimethylaminohydrolase (DDAH1) [14]. Physiologically, DDAH1 metabolizes the methylated arginines, asymmetric N^G,N^G-dimethyl-L-arginine (ADMA) and N^G-monomethyl-L-arginine (LNMMA), which are endogenous inhibitors of nitric oxide (NO) synthase (NOS) [15]. This chapter describes the pathophysiological and clinical relevance of vasculogenic mimicry with a focus on TNBC, the biology of methylated arginines and DDAH1, and the promising role of DDAH1 as a "druggable" target to suppress vasculogenic mimicry in TNBC.

Vasculogenic mimicry: Molecular mechanisms and pathophysiological significance

Vasculogenic mimicry, a neovascularization paradigm that has been discovered relatively recently, involves the formation of new functional blood vessel–like structures and networks by cancer cells that mimic the vascular endothelium [16,17]. Two types of vasculogenic mimicry have been described: tubular and patterned matrix [18]. The critical involvement of tumor cells and specific extracellular matrix components within the tumor microenvironment in the development of these structures is confirmed by the predominant staining of the newly formed vessels with the periodic acid–Schiff reagent over conventional endothelial cell markers such as CD31 [16]. Vasculogenic mimicry was originally reported in melanoma [16,17]; however, further studies have convincingly demonstrated the occurrence of vasculogenic mimicry in many other solid cancers, e.g., breast, ovary, prostate, and lung cancers, and particularly in association with metastatic behavior [19]. Angiogenesis and vasculogenic mimicry can also coexist in cancer tissues, possibly in an attempt to maximize the supply of oxygen and nutrients to cancer cells [20].

The mechanisms involved in the development of vasculogenic mimicry are complex and not entirely well understood. Briefly, tumor-associated fibroblasts within the tumor microenvironment stimulate vasculogenic mimicry through the secretion of transforming growth factor beta (TGFβ) and stromal cell–derived factor 1. Concomitantly, tumor-associated fibroblasts also favor vasculogenic mimicry by secreting interleukin-6 and TGFβ [21]. Another critical pathophysiological step in vasculogenic mimicry is represented by epithelial-to-mesenchymal transition, which involves the reduced expression of cell adhesion molecules, such as E-cadherin, due to the expression of the transcription factors twist and snail, and the upregulation of specific proteins, e.g., VE cadherin and fibronectin [21]. Epithelial-to-mesenchymal transition is modulated by several signaling pathways, including hypoxia-inducible factor 1-alpha (HIF-1α), TGFβ [22], Wnt [23], and Notch signaling pathways [24], as well as micro-RNA regulatory networks, e.g., miR34-SNAIL1 and miR200-ZEB1 [25]. Additional factors reported to influence vasculogenic mimicry include cyclo-oxygenase-2 [26], sphingosine-1 phosphate receptor 1 [27], anticoagulant proteins Serpine2 and Slpi [28], osteopontin [29], and micro-RNAs miR-141, miR-125a, and miR-490-3p [30–32]. Cancer stem cells have also been shown to be involved in vasculogenic mimicry in studies of TNBC [33], glioblastoma [34], prostate cancer [35], and hepatocellular carcinoma [36]. In this context, hypoxia and HIF-1α signaling pathways and vascular endothelial growth factor A (VEGF-A) have been shown to play a critical role in favoring the transformation of cancer stem cells into endothelial cell–like structures [10].

A better understanding of the molecular mechanisms underpinning vasculogenic mimicry has also stimulated the search for therapeutic strategies that are able to prevent or suppress this neovascularization process. Several approaches have been proposed, which include the combination of cytotoxic drugs with inhibitors of sarcoma family kinases [22], also involved in the regulation of vasculogenic mimicry; the combination of acridine and metals [37], able to induce apoptosis of cancer cells and inhibit both angiogenesis and vasculogenic mimicry; and the natural compounds brucine and hinokitiol [38,39], and 6′-bis (2.3-dimethoxybenzoyl)-a,a-D-trehalose, a derivative of a metabolite identified in actinomycetes [40]. Excellent reviews have been published on the molecular and biochemical mechanisms involved in vasculogenic mimicry and the therapeutic options currently under investigation [10,11,21,22,41,42].

There is good evidence that vasculogenic mimicry represents an important mechanism of resistance to antiangiogenic agents. Neither endogenous inhibitors of angiogenesis, e.g., endostatin, nor conventional antiangiogenic drugs targeting VEGF-A exert any significant inhibitory effect on vasculogenic mimicry [43,44]. Importantly, there is also in vitro and in vivo evidence that the use of anti-VEGF drugs, e.g., sunitinib, or VEGF silencing can paradoxically stimulate some cancer cells, e.g., TNBC and melanoma, to adopt vasculogenic mimicry as an alternate angiogenic strategy. This phenomenon results in an enhanced tumor aggressiveness and might also explain the lack of tangible anticancer effects of anti-VEGF drugs reported in several solid cancers [45–47].

In the context of breast cancer, the pathophysiological and clinical relevance of vasculogenic mimicry is further highlighted by clinical studies reporting a significant association between the presence of this alternative neovascularization process and an increased risk of tumor dissemination, relapse rate, and poor prognosis (hazard ratio for mortality = 2.50, 95% CI 0.85–3.95, $P = .002$) [12,13]. Vasculogenic mimicry appears to be particularly common in specific breast cancer subtypes such as TNBC [41]. TNBC affects 15%–20% of women with breast cancer and is characterized by the lack of expression of the estrogen receptor, progesterone receptor, and human epidermal growth factor receptor 2 [48,49]. When compared to other types of breast cancer, TNBC is associated with a more aggressive behavior and a higher relapse rate and mortality [50–53]. Notably, there are no available targeted treatments for TNBC, except for patients with advanced disease expressing programmed cell death ligand 1 [54]. The relatively high prevalence, poor prognosis, and lack of targeted therapies, particularly for the early stages of the disease, have stimulated the quest for novel "druggable" targets and more effective therapies to combat TNBC.

Dimethylarginine dimethylaminohydrolase 1: Biology and role in vasculogenic mimicry

The signaling molecule nitric oxide (NO) plays a critical role in the regulation of several physiological and pathophysiological processes, e.g., vascular tone, platelet function, inflammation, and immunity [55–58]. NO is synthesized through the conversion of the amino acid L-arginine to L-citrulline and NO by the family of NO synthases, endothelial (eNOS), neuronal (nNOS), and inducible (iNOS) [59,60]. There is increasing evidence that NO also exerts a critical role in the modulation of carcinogenesis and tumor progression [55,61,62]. In particular, the effects of NO on cancer seem to be highly dependent on local NO concentrations, with studies reporting a significant association between excessive local NO synthesis, mainly driven by iNOS, and increased invasiveness and poor prognosis in several cancers, including breast cancer [63–65]. Therefore, the identification of therapeutic strategies that are able to modulate NO synthesis, specifically reducing the excessive synthesis of this endogenous messenger, might exert significant anticancer effects [66].

The isoform 1 of the enzyme dimethylarginine dimethylaminohydrolase (DDAH1) plays a critical role in the conversion of the endogenous methylated arginines, ADMA and NMMA, into L-citrulline and dimethylamine and monomethylamine, respectively (Fig. 1) [15,67,68]. The pathophysiological role of ADMA has been particularly well studied in experimental and human studies of atherosclerosis and cardiovascular disease as this methylated arginine, together with NMMA, is a potent endogenous inhibitor of all three NOS isoforms, with an estimated half-maximal inhibitory concentration of 2–3 μM [15,67–76]. ADMA, NMMA, and another methylated arginine, symmetric N^G,N^G-dimethyl-L-arginine (SDMA), are generated following the methylation of arginine residues in proteins, a reaction mediated by the protein arginine N-methyltransferases type I and II (Fig. 1) [67]. Following proteolysis, ADMA and NMMA are either metabolized by DDAH1 or transported across the cell membrane before undergoing renal elimination. SDMA is also transported across the cell membrane; however, unlike ADMA and NMMA, it is not a substrate for DDAH1 nor does it directly inhibit NOS (Fig. 1) [77].

There is increasing evidence that a dysregulation of the DDAH1/ADMA/NO pathway, secondary to an increased expression and/or activity of DDAH1, with a consequent depletion of ADMA and an increased synthesis of NO, is associated with tumor angiogenesis, growth, invasion, and metastasis [14,78]. An increased expression of DDAH1 has been reported in tumors of the pancreas, breast, colon, ovary, prostate, and glioma, suggesting a potential role of this enzyme as "druggable" target [14,78,79]. In the context of TNBC, Hulin et al. have investigated the expression of DDAH1 and the micro-RNA miR-193b, a known tumor

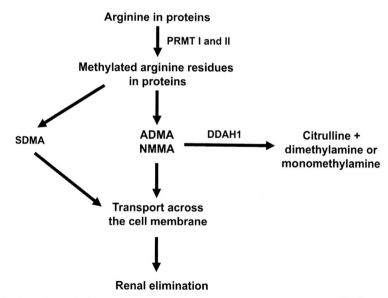

FIG. 1 Synthesis and metabolism of methylated arginines. *ADMA*, asymmetric N^G,N^G-dimethyl-L-arginine; *DDAH1*, dimethylarginine dimethylaminohydrolase 1; *NMMA*, N^G-monomethyl-L-arginine; *PRMT I and II*, type I and type II protein arginine N-methyltransferase; *SDMA*, symmetric N^G,N^G-dimethyl-L-arginine.

suppressor, in immortalized normal human primary mammary epithelial cells (hTERT-MEC), nontumorigenic mammary epithelial cells of fibrocystic disease origin (MCF10A), and the breast cancer cell lines MCF7 (non-TNBC), ZR-75-1 (non-TNBC), MDA-MB-231 (TNBC), MDA-MB-453 (TNBC), and BT549 (TNBC) [80]. The expression of DDAH1 mRNA was significantly higher in MDA-MB-231, BT549, MDA-MB-453, and ZR-75-1 cells than in hTERT-MEC. However, when assessed at the protein level, DDAH1 expression was not detectable in hTERT-MEC and MCF7 cells, despite the abundant mRNA expression. DDAH1 protein was most highly expressed in MDA-MB-231, BT549, and MDA-MB-453 TNBC cells (Fig. 2) [80]. Concomitantly, miR-193b expression was significantly reduced in MDA-MB-231, MDA-MB-453, and BT549 cells compared to hTERT-MEC (Fig. 2) [80]. There was a significant and inverse correlation, for all cell lines assessed, between DDAH1 and miR-193b expression at both the transcript and the protein levels (Fig. 2) [80]. In further analyses using the TCGA-BRCA RNASeq dataset, similar significant negative correlations between DDAH1 and miR-193b expression were observed both in normal breast specimens ($n = 104$) and in TNBC specimens ($n = 109$; Fig. 2) [80].

Using bioinformatics analysis to further investigate the mechanisms underpinning the interaction between miR-193b and DDAH1, Hulin et al. have identified a single predicting binding site for miR-193b at position 300–326 of the *DDAH1* 3′-untranslated region [80]. Transfection of an miR-193b mimic into MDA-MB-231 cells significantly reduced the transcript expression of *DDAH1* and DDAH1 protein expressions compared to cells transfected with the nontargeting NC mimic (Fig. 3) [80]. This was associated with a significant reduction in the conversion of the DDAH1 substrate ADMA to L-citrulline, with concomitant accumulation of intracellular ADMA (Fig. 3) [80]. In further experiments, MDA-MB-231 cells formed an extensive network of tube-like structures, confirming the capacity of TNBC cells to undertake VM (Fig. 4) [80]. Notably, *DDAH1* knockdown with siRNAs significantly reduced (80%) the number of tubes and branches formed compared to control-transfected cells. Furthermore, transfection with miR-193b mimic completely inhibited tube formation compared to the NC mimic (Fig. 4). These effects were associated with a significant reduction in VEGF-A mRNA [80]. miR-193b mimics, but not DDAH1 knockdown with siRNA, affected cell proliferation and viability [80]. Cell migration assessment revealed a significant delay in wound closure time both in *DDAH1*-knockdown cells and miR-193b mimics [80]. These in vitro experiments provide compelling evidence that DDAH1 plays a critical role in favoring TNBC cells to undertake vasculogenic mimicry. Therefore, DDAH1 downregulation might represent a useful strategy to prevent or suppress vasculogenic mimicry in TNBC.

Effects of pharmacological DDAH1 inhibition on vasculogenic mimicry in TNBC

The effects of pharmacological DDAH1 inhibition on vasculogenic mimicry have been investigated using a series of small molecule arginine analogs incorporating carboxylate bioisosteric functions developed by Tommasi et al. Within this series, compound 10a (ZST316), characterized by an acylsulfonamide isosteric replacement of the carboxylate, showed a 13-fold greater inhibitory activity (IC$_{50}$: 3 μM; K$_i$: 1 μM) toward DDAH1 when compared to the known DDAH1 inhibitor, L-257. Another compound, oxadiazolone 14b

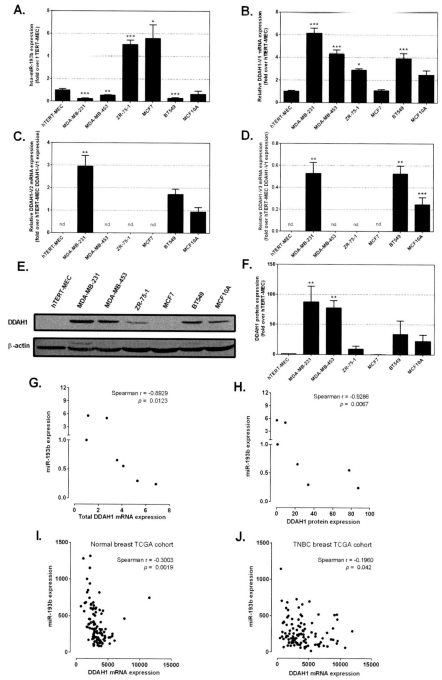

FIG. 2 Expression of miR-193b (A), *DDAH1-V1* (B), *DDAH1-V2* (C), and *DDAH1-V3* (D) in breast cancer cell lines relative to hTERT-MEC cells. (E) Expression of endogenous DDAH1-V1 (full-length protein) in breast cancer cell lines, as shown by a representative Western blot, with ß-actin as a loading control. (F) Quantification of DDAH1 protein expression as in (E), normalized to ß-actin expression and shown relative to DDAH1 expression in hTERT-MEC. Error bars represent SEM. *$P < .05$, **$P < .01$, and ***$P < .001$ relative to expression in hTERT-MEC. (G, H) Spearman's rank-order correlation analysis between mean miR-193b expression and mean total *DDAH1* mRNA (G) and protein (H) expression. (I, J) Spearman's rank-order correlation analysis of The Cancer Genome Atlas (TCGA)/breast carcinoma (BRCA) dataset between DDAH1 and miR-193b in normal breast specimens (I) and TNBC specimens (J). *From Hulin JA, Tommasi S, Elliot D, Hu DG, Lewis BC, Mangoni AA. MiR-193b regulates breast cancer cell migration and vasculogenic mimicry by targeting dimethylarginine dimethylaminohydrolase 1. Sci Rep 2017;7:13996.*

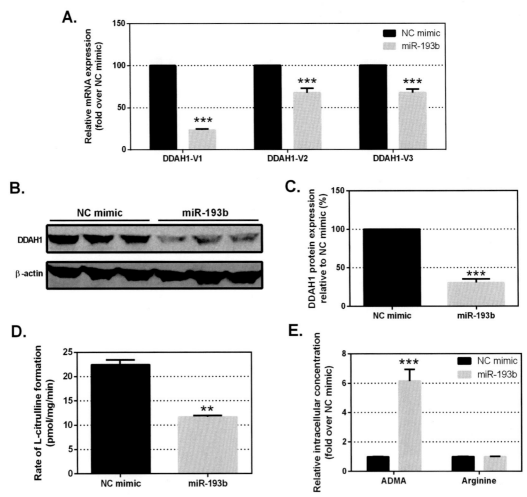

FIG. 3 Effect of an miR-193b mimic on DDAH1 mRNA, protein, and metabolic activity in MDA-MB-231 cells. (A) Expression levels of *DDAH1-V1*, *DDAH1-V2*, and *DDAH1-V3* mRNA in MDA-MB-231 cells following transfection of NC or miR-193b mimic. (B) DDAH1 protein expression assessed by Western blotting 48h post-transfection. ß-Actin expression was used as a control for total protein. (C) Quantification of DDAH1 protein expression as in (B), normalized to ß-actin expression and shown relative to DDAH1 expression in the NC condition. (D) DDAH1 activity in MDA-MB-231 cells transfected with an NC or miR-193b mimic. The activity of DDAH1 in cell lysates is reported as the rate of L-citrulline formation with 200 μM ADMA as substrate. (E) Relative concentrations of intracellular ADMA and arginine quantified in MDA-MB-231 cells transfected with an NC or miR-193b mimic. Error bars represent SEM. **P < .01 and ***P < .001. *From Hulin JA, Tommasi S, Elliot D, Hu DG, Lewis BC, Mangoni AA. MiR-193b regulates breast cancer cell migration and vasculogenic mimicry by targeting dimethylarginine dimethylaminohydrolase 1. Sci Rep 2017;7:13996.*

(ZST152), was also effective (IC$_{50}$: 18 μM; K$_i$: 7 μM; Fig. 5) [81,82]. In experiments using MDA-MB-231 cells, there was no significant degradation of ZST316 and ZST152 from the culture media [83]. Furthermore, cell uptake was demonstrated, with the observed concentrations of ZST316 and ZST152 in the assay cell lysates, 0.32 and 0.28 μM, translating into an average intracellular concentration of 39 and 35 pmol/million cells, respectively [83].

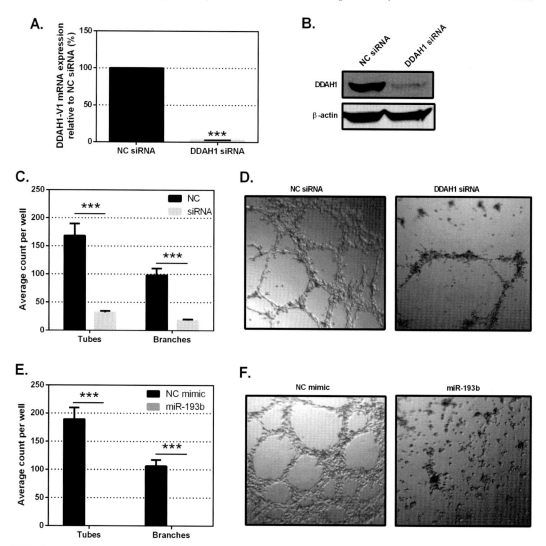

FIG. 4 DDAH1 regulates vasculogenic mimicry by MDA-MB-231 cells. (A, B) Validation of DDAH1 gene knockdown following transfection with DDAH1-targeting or control siRNA (A). DDAH1 protein expression was assessed by Western blotting (B). (C) Number of tubes and branches produced by MDA-MB-231 cells with DDAH1-targeting siRNA or NC. (D) Representative phase-contrast images. (E) Number of tubes and branches produced by MDA-MB-231 cells with miR-193b mimic or NC. (F) Representative phase-contrast images. Error bars represent SEM. ***$P < .001$. *From Hulin JA, Tommasi S, Elliot D, Hu DG, Lewis BC, Mangoni AA. MiR-193b regulates breast cancer cell migration and vasculogenic mimicry by targeting dimethylarginine dimethylaminohydrolase 1. Sci Rep 2017;7:13996.*

In further experiments, compounds ZST316 and ZST152 exerted significant antivasculogenic mimicry effects, as demonstrated by a significant reduction in the number of tubes and branches formed by MDA-MB-231 and BT549 cells (experiments conducted with ZST316 only; Fig. 6) [83]. The significant effects of DDAH1 inhibition on the DDAH1/ADMA/NO axis were confirmed by the observation that the DDAH1 substrate and NOS

II. Nitric oxide pathway and cancer progression and therapy

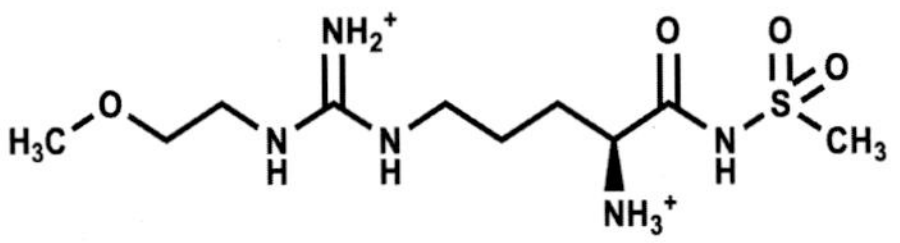

ZST316

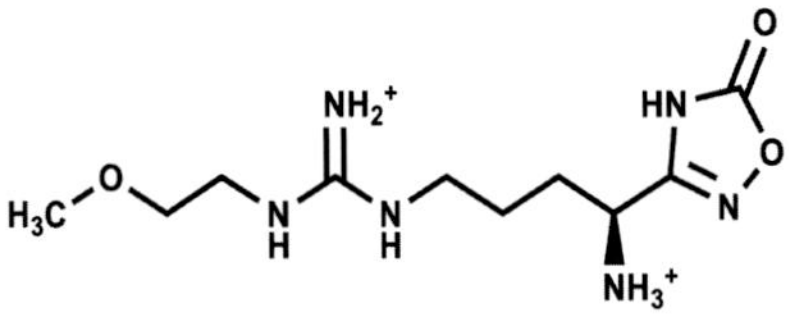

ZST152

FIG. 5   Chemical structures of compounds ZST316 and ZST152.

inhibitor NMMA significantly inhibited the formation of tubes and branches, whereas SDMA, neither a substrate for DDAH1 nor an inhibitor of NOS, did not exert any significant effect on tube formation by MDA-MB-231 cells (Fig. 6) [83]. ZST316 and ZST152 did not influence MDA-MB-231 cell viability or proliferation, ruling out the possibility that a reduction in vasculogenic mimicry was a result of reduced cell survival or proliferation. However, ZST316 and ZST152 significantly reduced MDA-MB-231 cell migration [83]. Treatment of MDA-MB-231 cells with ZST316 or ZST152 significantly increased the concentrations of the DDAH1 substrate, ADMA, and reduced the DDAH1 product L-citrulline, confirming the inhibitory effect of the compounds on enzyme activity (Fig. 7) [83].

Following these in vitro studies, a comprehensive pharmacokinetic characterization, dose optimization, and safety assessment of ZST316 and ZST152 in healthy mice after acute and chronic administration showed that the compound ZST316 has a particularly favorable pharmacokinetic profile with a relatively high bioavailability following intraperitoneal administration, 59%, suitability for once-daily dosing, and excellent safety and tolerability during chronic treatment [84].

General considerations

This chapter has discussed the recent developments in the identification of novel "druggable" targets and therapeutic strategies designed to suppress vasculogenic mimicry in TNBC through the modulation of the DDAH1/ADMA/NO axis. The results of these experiments also highlight the critical pathophysiological role played by NO in the development of vasculogenic mimicry, in addition to the known effects of this endogenous modulator on canonical angiogenesis [14]. Pending the results of in vivo studies, DDAH1 inhibition appears a promising treatment strategy to suppress vasculogenic mimicry, and, potentially, cancer cell invasiveness and metastatic potential in TNBC. As previously described, TNBC is a particularly aggressive breast cancer subtype that is associated with

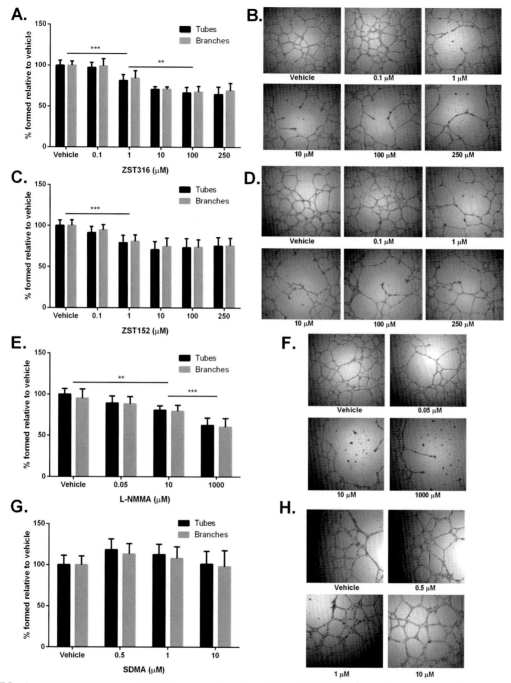

FIG. 6 Effect of ZST316 and ZST152 on vasculogenic mimicry in MDA-MB-231 cells. The number of tubes and branches were counted after treatment with ZST316 (A, B), ZST152 (C, D), NMMA (E, F), and SDMA (G, H) and are expressed as a % relative to vehicle control. Error bars represent SD. **$P < .01$ and ***$P < .001$. *From Hulin JA, Tommasi S, Elliot D, Mangoni AA. Small molecule inhibition of DDAH1 significantly attenuates triple negative breast cancer cell vasculogenic mimicry in vitro. Biomed Pharmacother 2019;111:602–12.*

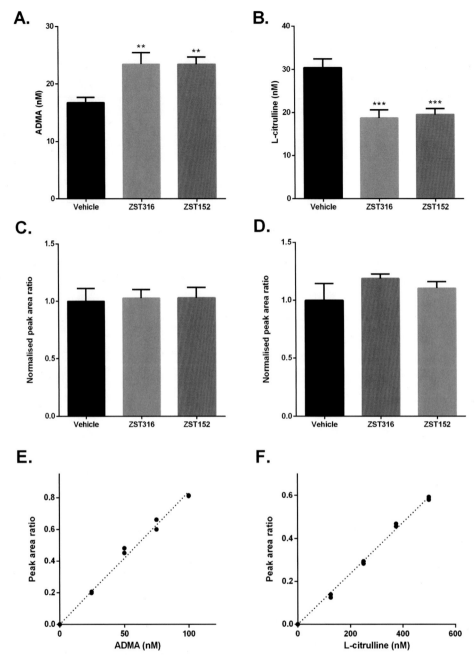

FIG. 7 Effect of ZST316 and ZST152 on intracellular DDAH1 activity in MDA-MB-231 cells. (A) Intracellular ADMA concentration. (B) Intracellular L-citrulline concentration. (C) Relative intracellular arginine concentration, expressed as a fold change-to-the peak area ratio (arginine/d7-ADMA) of vehicle control. (D) Relative intracellular ornithine concentration, expressed as a fold change-to-the peak area ratio (ornithine/d7-ADMA) of vehicle control. Error bars represent SEM. **$P < .01$ and ***$P < .001$ relative to vehicle controls. (E) Representative calibration curve for ADMA. (F) Representative calibration curve for L-citrulline. *From Hulin JA, Tommasi S, Elliot D, Mangoni AA. Small molecule inhibition of DDAH1 significantly attenuates triple negative breast cancer cell vasculogenic mimicry in vitro. Biomed Pharmacother 2019;111:602–12.*

significantly higher 2 year breast cancer specific mortality and overall mortality, more annual hospitalizations, and higher inpatient costs [48–53]. From a pathophysiological point of view, the dissemination of tumor cells is the most significant issue in TNBC patients because it translates into a higher risk of metastasis, relapse, and local recurrence than non-TNBC (estrogen receptor–positive) breast cancers [48–53]. The lack of effective targeted therapies and the poor prognosis associated with the disease strongly justify the urgent need for novel therapeutic targets and effective treatments for TNBC.

A strong experimental and clinical evidence suggest that vasculogenic mimicry is a highly "druggable" pathophysiological process in TNBC. In this context, the significant antivasculogenic mimicry effects observed with pharmacological inhibition of DDAH1 has the potential to lead to a breakthrough in the search for novel, effective therapies in TNBC. Importantly, blocking DDAH1-mediated vasculogenic mimicry might represent a highly effective therapeutic strategy not only to directly suppress TNBC growth, dissemination, and metastasis but also to increase, as an adjuvant treatment, the therapeutic efficacy of antiangiogenic drugs in this type of cancer. This is particularly relevant, given that recent experimental studies have provided convincing evidence that treatment with traditional antiangiogenic agents can paradoxically stimulate the initiation of vasculogenic mimicry by TNBC cells, and a more aggressive cancer phenotype, as a possible mechanism of adaptive resistance to treatment [45–47].

In conclusion, targeting DDAH1 might represent a new, highly effective strategy to suppress vasculogenic mimicry and exert an anticancer effect in TNBC and, possibly, other types of cancer that are characterized by DDAH1 overexpression and overt vasculogenic mimicry. The in vivo confirmation of the effects of DDAH1 inhibition on vasculogenic mimicry, tumor growth, and metastatic burden is essential before a comprehensive preclinical development of the most promising DDAH1 inhibitors and, ultimately, the conduct of human studies are envisaged.

References

[1] Global Burden of Disease 2019 Cancer Collaboration. Cancer incidence, mortality, years of life lost, years lived with disability, and disability-adjusted life years for 29 cancer groups from 2010 to 2019: a systematic analysis for the Global Burden of Disease Study 2019. JAMA Oncol 2022;8:420–44.

[2] Sung H, Ferlay J, Siegel RL, Laversanne M, Soerjomataram I, Jemal A, Bray F. Global cancer statistics 2020: GLOBOCAN estimates of incidence and mortality worldwide for 36 cancers in 185 countries. CA Cancer J Clin 2021;71:209–49.

[3] Lugano R, Ramachandran M, Dimberg A. Tumor angiogenesis: causes, consequences, challenges and opportunities. Cell Mol Life Sci 2020;77:1745–70.

[4] De Palma M, Biziato D, Petrova TV. Microenvironmental regulation of tumour angiogenesis. Nat Rev Cancer 2017;17:457–74.

[5] Giordo R, Wehbe Z, Paliogiannis P, Eid AH, Mangoni AA, Pintus G. Nano-targeting vascular remodeling in cancer: recent developments and future directions. Semin Cancer Biol 2022;86(Pt 2):784–804.

[6] Lopes-Coelho F, Martins F, Pereira SA, Serpa J. Anti-angiogenic therapy: current challenges and future perspectives. Int J Mol Sci 2021;22:3765.

[7] Ribatti D, Solimando AG, Pezzella F. The anti-VEGF(R) drug discovery legacy: improving attrition rates by breaking the vicious cycle of angiogenesis in cancer. Cancers (Basel) 2021;13:3433.

[8] Itatani Y, Kawada K, Yamamoto T, Sakai Y. Resistance to anti-angiogenic therapy in cancer-alterations to anti-VEGF pathway. Int J Mol Sci 2018;19:1232.

[9] Haibe Y, Kreidieh M, El Hajj H, Khalifeh I, Mukherji D, Temraz S, Shamseddine A. Resistance mechanisms to anti-angiogenic therapies in cancer. Front Oncol 2020;10:221.

[10] Wei X, Chen Y, Jiang X, Peng M, Liu Y, Mo Y, Ren D, Hua Y, Yu B, Zhou Y, Liao Q, Wang H, Xiang B, Zhou M, Li X, Li G, Li Y, Xiong W, Zeng Z. Mechanisms of vasculogenic mimicry in hypoxic tumor microenvironments. Mol Cancer 2021;20:7.

[11] Belotti D, Pinessi D, Taraboletti G. Alternative vascularization mechanisms in tumor resistance to therapy. Cancers (Basel) 2021;13:1912.

[12] Mitra D, Bhattacharyya S, Alam N, Sen S, Mitra S, Mandal S, Vignesh S, Majumder B, Murmu N. Phosphorylation of EphA2 receptor and vasculogenic mimicry is an indicator of poor prognosis in invasive carcinoma of the breast. Breast Cancer Res Treat 2020;179:359–70.

[13] Yang JP, Liao YD, Mai DM, Xie P, Qiang YY, Zheng LS, Wang MY, Mei Y, Meng DF, Xu L, Cao L, Yang Q, Yang XX, Wang WB, Peng LX, Huang BJ, Qian CN. Tumor vasculogenic mimicry predicts poor prognosis in cancer patients: a meta-analysis. Angiogenesis 2016;19:191–200.

[14] Hulin JA, Gubareva EA, Jarzebska N, Rodionov RN, Mangoni AA, Tommasi S. Inhibition of dimethylarginine dimethylaminohydrolase (DDAH) enzymes as an emerging therapeutic strategy to target angiogenesis and vasculogenic mimicry in cancer. Front Oncol 2019;9:1455.

[15] Jarzebska N, Mangoni AA, Martens-Lobenhoffer J, Bode-Boger SM, Rodionov RN. The second life of methylarginines as cardiovascular targets. Int J Mol Sci 2019;20:4592.

[16] Maniotis AJ, Folberg R, Hess A, Seftor EA, Gardner LM, Pe'er J, Trent JM, Meltzer PS, Hendrix MJ. Vascular channel formation by human melanoma cells in vivo and in vitro: vasculogenic mimicry. Am J Pathol 1999;155:739–52.

[17] Folberg R, Arbieva Z, Moses J, Hayee A, Sandal T, Kadkol S, Lin AY, Valyi-Nagy K, Setty S, Leach L, Chevez-Barrios P, Larsen P, Majumdar D, Pe'er J, Maniotis AJ. Tumor cell plasticity in uveal melanoma: microenvironment directed dampening of the invasive and metastatic genotype and phenotype accompanies the generation of vasculogenic mimicry patterns. Am J Pathol 2006;169:1376–89.

[18] Folberg R, Maniotis AJ. Vasculogenic mimicry. APMIS 2004;112:508–25.

[19] Shirakawa K, Tsuda H, Heike Y, Kato K, Asada R, Inomata M, Sasaki H, Kasumi F, Yoshimoto M, Iwanaga T, Konishi F, Terada M, Wakasugi H. Absence of endothelial cells, central necrosis, and fibrosis are associated with aggressive inflammatory breast cancer. Cancer Res 2001;61:445–51.

[20] Shirakawa K, Kobayashi H, Heike Y, Kawamoto S, Brechbiel MW, Kasumi F, Iwanaga T, Konishi F, Terada M, Wakasugi H. Hemodynamics in vasculogenic mimicry and angiogenesis of inflammatory breast cancer xenograft. Cancer Res 2002;62:560–6.

[21] Luo Q, Wang J, Zhao W, Peng Z, Liu X, Li B, Zhang H, Shan B, Zhang C, Duan C. Vasculogenic mimicry in carcinogenesis and clinical applications. J Hematol Oncol 2020;13:19.

[22] Li S, Meng W, Guan Z, Guo Y, Han X. The hypoxia-related signaling pathways of vasculogenic mimicry in tumor treatment. Biomed Pharmacother 2016;80:127–35.

[23] Wang Y, Sun H, Zhang D, Fan D, Zhang Y, Dong X, Liu S, Yang Z, Ni C, Li Y, Liu F, Zhao X. TP53INP1 inhibits hypoxia-induced vasculogenic mimicry formation via the ROS/snail signalling axis in breast cancer. J Cell Mol Med 2018;22:3475–88.

[24] Krishna Priya S, Nagare RP, Sneha VS, Sidhanth C, Bindhya S, Manasa P, Ganesan TS. Tumour angiogenesis— origin of blood vessels. Int J Cancer 2016;139:729–35.

[25] Nieto MA, Huang RY, Jackson RA, Thiery JP. Emt: 2016. Cell 2016;166:21–45.

[26] Basu GD, Liang WS, Stephan DA, Wegener LT, Conley CR, Pockaj BA, Mukherjee P. A novel role for cyclooxygenase-2 in regulating vascular channel formation by human breast cancer cells. Breast Cancer Res 2006;8:R69.

[27] Liu S, Ni C, Zhang D, Sun H, Dong X, Che N, Liang X, Chen C, Liu F, Bai J, Lin X, Zhao X, Sun B. S1PR1 regulates the switch of two angiogenic modes by VE-cadherin phosphorylation in breast cancer. Cell Death Dis 2019;10:200.

[28] Wagenblast E, Soto M, Gutierrez-Angel S, Hartl CA, Gable AL, Maceli AR, Erard N, Williams AM, Kim SY, Dickopf S, Harrell JC, Smith AD, Perou CM, Wilkinson JE, Hannon GJ, Knott SR. A model of breast cancer heterogeneity reveals vascular mimicry as a driver of metastasis. Nature 2015;520:358–62.

[29] Shevde LA, Metge BJ, Mitra A, Xi Y, Ju J, King JA, Samant RS. Spheroid-forming subpopulation of breast cancer cells demonstrates vasculogenic mimicry via hsa-miR-299-5p regulated de novo expression of osteopontin. J Cell Mol Med 2010;14:1693–706.

II. Nitric oxide pathway and cancer progression and therapy

[30] Li G, Huang M, Cai Y, Ke Y, Yang Y, Sun X. miR141 inhibits glioma vasculogenic mimicry by controlling EphA2 expression. Mol Med Rep 2018;18:1395–404.

[31] Salinas-Vera YM, Marchat LA, Garcia-Vazquez R, Gonzalez de la Rosa CH, Castaneda-Saucedo E, Tito NN, Flores CP, Perez-Plasencia C, Cruz-Colin JL, Carlos-Reyes A, Lopez-Gonzalez JS, Alvarez-Sanchez ME, Lopez-Camarillo C. Cooperative multi-targeting of signaling networks by angiomiR-204 inhibits vasculogenic mimicry in breast cancer cells. Cancer Lett 2018;432:17–27.

[32] Park Y, Kim J. Regulation of IL-6 signaling by miR-125a and let-7e in endothelial cells controls vasculogenic mimicry formation of breast cancer cells. BMB Rep 2019;52:214–9.

[33] Liu TJ, Sun BC, Zhao XL, Zhao XM, Sun T, Gu Q, Yao Z, Dong XY, Zhao N, Liu N. CD133+ cells with cancer stem cell characteristics associates with vasculogenic mimicry in triple-negative breast cancer. Oncogene 2013;32:544–53.

[34] Mao XG, Xue XY, Wang L, Zhang X, Yan M, Tu YY, Lin W, Jiang XF, Ren HG, Zhang W, Song SJ. CDH5 is specifically activated in glioblastoma stemlike cells and contributes to vasculogenic mimicry induced by hypoxia. Neuro-Oncology 2013;15:865–79.

[35] Wang H, Huang B, Li BM, Cao KY, Mo CQ, Jiang SJ, Pan JC, Wang ZR, Lin HY, Wang DH, Qiu SP. ZEB1-mediated vasculogenic mimicry formation associates with epithelial-mesenchymal transition and cancer stem cell phenotypes in prostate cancer. J Cell Mol Med 2018;22:3768–81.

[36] Zhao X, Sun B, Liu T, Shao B, Sun R, Zhu D, Zhang Y, Gu Q, Dong X, Liu F, Zhao N, Zhang D, Li Y, Meng J, Gong W, Zheng Y, Zheng X. Long noncoding RNA n339260 promotes vasculogenic mimicry and cancer stem cell development in hepatocellular carcinoma. Cancer Sci 2018;109:3197–208.

[37] Perez SA, de Haro C, Vicente C, Donaire A, Zamora A, Zajac J, Kostrhunova H, Brabec V, Bautista D, Ruiz J. New acridine thiourea gold(I) anticancer agents: targeting the nucleus and inhibiting vasculogenic mimicry. ACS Chem Biol 2017;12:1524–37.

[38] Xu MR, Wei PF, Suo MZ, Hu Y, Ding W, Su L, Zhu YD, Song WJ, Tang GH, Zhang M, Li P. Brucine suppresses vasculogenic mimicry in human triple-negative breast cancer cell line MDA-MB-231. Biomed Res Int 2019;2019:6543230.

[39] Tu DG, Yu Y, Lee CH, Kuo YL, Lu YC, Tu CW, Chang WW. Hinokitiol inhibits vasculogenic mimicry activity of breast cancer stem/progenitor cells through proteasome-mediated degradation of epidermal growth factor receptor. Oncol Lett 2016;11:2934–40.

[40] Li S, Zhang Q, Zhou L, Guan Y, Chen S, Zhang Y, Han X. Inhibitory effects of compound DMBT on hypoxia-induced vasculogenic mimicry in human breast cancer. Biomed Pharmacother 2017;96:982–92.

[41] Andonegui-Elguera MA, Alfaro-Mora Y, Caceres-Gutierrez R, Caro-Sanchez CHS, Herrera LA, Diaz-Chavez J. An overview of vasculogenic mimicry in breast cancer. Front Oncol 2020;10:220.

[42] Morales-Guadarrama G, Garcia-Becerra R, Mendez-Perez EA, Garcia-Quiroz J, Avila E, Diaz L. Vasculogenic mimicry in breast cancer: clinical relevance and drivers. Cells 2021;10:1758.

[43] Hendrix MJ, Seftor EA, Hess AR, Seftor RE. Vasculogenic mimicry and tumour-cell plasticity: lessons from melanoma. Nat Rev Cancer 2003;3:411–21.

[44] van der Schaft DW, Seftor RE, Seftor EA, Hess AR, Gruman LM, Kirschmann DA, Yokoyama Y, Griffioen AW, Hendrix MJ. Effects of angiogenesis inhibitors on vascular network formation by human endothelial and melanoma cells. J Natl Cancer Inst 2004;96:1473–7.

[45] Sun H, Zhang D, Yao Z, Lin X, Liu J, Gu Q, Dong X, Liu F, Wang Y, Yao N, Cheng S, Li L, Sun S. Anti-angiogenic treatment promotes triple-negative breast cancer invasion via vasculogenic mimicry. Cancer Biol Ther 2017;18:205–13.

[46] Schnegg CI, Yang MH, Ghosh SK, Hsu MY. Induction of vasculogenic mimicry overrides VEGF-A silencing and enriches stem-like cancer cells in melanoma. Cancer Res 2015;75:1682–90.

[47] Pezzella F, Ribatti D. Vascular co-option and vasculogenic mimicry mediate resistance to antiangiogenic strategies. Cancer Rep (Hoboken) 2022;5(12):e1318.

[48] Marotti JD, de Abreu FB, Wells WA, Tsongalis GJ. Triple-negative breast cancer: next-generation sequencing for target identification. Am J Pathol 2017;187:2133–8.

[49] Borri F, Granaglia A. Pathology of triple negative breast cancer. Semin Cancer Biol 2021;72:136–45.

[50] Baser O, Wei W, Henk HJ, Teitelbaum A, Xie L. Patient survival and healthcare utilization costs after diagnosis of triple-negative breast cancer in a United States managed care cancer registry. Curr Med Res Opin 2012;28:419–28.

[51] Bianchini G, Balko JM, Mayer IA, Sanders ME, Gianni L. Triple-negative breast cancer: challenges and opportunities of a heterogeneous disease. Nat Rev Clin Oncol 2016;13:674–90.

II. Nitric oxide pathway and cancer progression and therapy

[52] Hsu JY, Chang CJ, Cheng JS. Survival, treatment regimens and medical costs of women newly diagnosed with metastatic triple-negative breast cancer. Sci Rep 2022;12:729.

[53] Li X, Yang J, Peng L, Sahin AA, Huo L, Ward KC, O'Regan R, Torres MA, Meisel JL. Triple-negative breast cancer has worse overall survival and cause-specific survival than non-triple-negative breast cancer. Breast Cancer Res Treat 2017;161:279–87.

[54] Kwapisz D. Pembrolizumab and atezolizumab in triple-negative breast cancer. Cancer Immunol Immunother 2021;70:607–17.

[55] Khan FH, Dervan E, Bhattacharyya DD, McAuliffe JD, Miranda KM, Glynn SA. The role of nitric oxide in cancer: master regulator or NOt? Int J Mol Sci 2020;21(24):9393.

[56] Pacher P, Beckman JS, Liaudet L. Nitric oxide and peroxynitrite in health and disease. Physiol Rev 2007;87:315–424.

[57] Coleman JW. Nitric oxide in immunity and inflammation. Int Immunopharmacol 2001;1:1397–406.

[58] Morbidelli L, Donnini S, Ziche M. Role of nitric oxide in the modulation of angiogenesis. Curr Pharm Des 2003;9:521–30.

[59] Iyengar R, Stuehr DJ, Marletta MA. Macrophage synthesis of nitrite, nitrate, and N-nitrosamines: precursors and role of the respiratory burst. Proc Natl Acad Sci U S A 1987;84:6369–73.

[60] Stuehr DJ, Kwon NS, Nathan CF, Griffith OW, Feldman PL, Wiseman J. N omega-hydroxy-L-arginine is an intermediate in the biosynthesis of nitric oxide from L-arginine. J Biol Chem 1991;266:6259–63.

[61] Choudhari SK, Chaudhary M, Bagde S, Gadbail AR, Joshi V. Nitric oxide and cancer: a review. World J Surg Oncol 2013;11:118.

[62] Salimian Rizi B, Achreja A, Nagrath D. Nitric oxide: the forgotten child of tumor metabolism. Trends Cancer 2017;3:659–72.

[63] Jadeski LC, Hum KO, Chakraborty C, Lala PK. Nitric oxide promotes murine mammary tumour growth and metastasis by stimulating tumour cell migration, invasiveness and angiogenesis. Int J Cancer 2000;86:30–9.

[64] Loibl S, von Minckwitz G, Weber S, Sinn HP, Schini-Kerth VB, Lobysheva I, Nepveu F, Wolf G, Strebhardt K, Kaufmann M. Expression of endothelial and inducible nitric oxide synthase in benign and malignant lesions of the breast and measurement of nitric oxide using electron paramagnetic resonance spectroscopy. Cancer 2002;95:1191–8.

[65] Jin Z, Wang W, Jiang N, Zhang L, Li Y, Xu X, Cai S, Wei L, Liu X, Chen G, Zhou Y, Liu C, Li Z, Jin F, Chen B. Clinical implications of iNOS levels in triple-negative breast cancer responding to neoadjuvant chemotherapy. PLoS One 2015;10, e0130286.

[66] Hickok JR, Thomas DD. Nitric oxide and cancer therapy: the emperor has NO clothes. Curr Pharm Des 2010;16:381–91.

[67] Vallance P, Leiper J. Cardiovascular biology of the asymmetric dimethylarginine dimethylarginine:dimethylaminohydrolase pathway. Arterioscler Thromb Vasc Biol 2004;24:1023–30.

[68] Wadham C, Mangoni AA. Dimethylarginine dimethylaminohydrolase regulation: a novel therapeutic target in cardiovascular disease. Expert Opin Drug Metab Toxicol 2009;5:303–19.

[69] Asif M, Soiza RL, McEvoy M, Mangoni AA. Asymmetric dimethylarginine: a possible link between vascular disease and dementia. Curr Alzheimer Res 2013;10:347–56.

[70] Bouteldja N, Woodman RJ, Hewitson CL, Domingo E, Barbara JA, Mangoni AA. Methylated arginines and nitric oxide in end-stage renal disease: impact of inflammation, oxidative stress and haemodialysis. Biomarkers 2013;18:357–64.

[71] Erre GL, Mangoni AA, Castagna F, Paliogiannis P, Carru C, Passiu G, Zinellu A. Meta-analysis of asymmetric dimethylarginine concentrations in rheumatic diseases. Sci Rep 2019;9:5426.

[72] Mangoni AA, Rodionov RN, McEvoy M, Zinellu A, Carru C, Sotgia S. New horizons in arginine metabolism, ageing and chronic disease states. Age Ageing 2019;48:776–82.

[73] Mangoni AA, Tommasi S, Sotgia S, Zinellu A, Paliogiannis P, Piga M, Cauli A, Pintus G, Carru C, Erre GL. Asymmetric dimethylarginine: a key player in the pathophysiology of endothelial dysfunction, vascular inflammation and atherosclerosis in rheumatoid arthritis? Curr Pharm Des 2021;27:2131–40.

[74] Shah RJ, Tommasi S, Faull R, Gleadle JM, Mangoni AA, Selvanayagam JB. Arginine metabolites as biomarkers of myocardial ischaemia, assessed with cardiac magnetic resonance imaging in chronic kidney disease. Biomolecules 2021;11(3):416.

[75] Lee TF, Bersten AD, Heilbronn LK, Zinellu A, Carru C, Sotgia S, Mangoni AA, Burt MG. ADMA and homoarginine independently predict mortality in critically ill patients. Nitric Oxide 2022;122–123:47–53.

[76] Rees DD, Palmer RM, Schulz R, Hodson HF, Moncada S. Characterization of three inhibitors of endothelial nitric oxide synthase in vitro and in vivo. Br J Pharmacol 1990;101:746–52.

[77] Mangoni AA. The emerging role of symmetric dimethylarginine in vascular disease. Adv Clin Chem 2009;48:73–94.

[78] Papaevangelou E, Boult JKR, Whitley GS, Robinson SP, Howe FA. Assessment of the direct effects of DDAH I on tumour angiogenesis in vivo. Angiogenesis 2018;21:737–49.

[79] Reddy KRK, Dasari C, Duscharla D, Supriya B, Ram NS, Surekha MV, Kumar JM, Ummanni R. Dimethylarginine dimethylaminohydrolase-1 (DDAH1) is frequently upregulated in prostate cancer, and its overexpression conveys tumor growth and angiogenesis by metabolizing asymmetric dimethylarginine (ADMA). Angiogenesis 2018;21:79–94.

[80] Hulin JA, Tommasi S, Elliot D, Hu DG, Lewis BC, Mangoni AA. MiR-193b regulates breast cancer cell migration and vasculogenic mimicry by targeting dimethylarginine dimethylaminohydrolase 1. Sci Rep 2017;7:13996.

[81] Tommasi S, Zanato C, Lewis BC, Nair PC, Dall'Angelo S, Zanda M, Mangoni AA. Arginine analogues incorporating carboxylate bioisosteric functions are micromolar inhibitors of human recombinant DDAH-1. Org Biomol Chem 2015;13:11315–30.

[82] Murphy RB, Tommasi S, Lewis BC, Mangoni AA. Inhibitors of the hydrolytic enzyme dimethylarginine dimethylaminohydrolase (DDAH): discovery, synthesis and development. Molecules (Basel, Switzerland) 2016;21(5):615.

[83] Hulin JA, Tommasi S, Elliot D, Mangoni AA. Small molecule inhibition of DDAH1 significantly attenuates triple negative breast cancer cell vasculogenic mimicry in vitro. Biomed Pharmacother 2019;111:602–12.

[84] Mangoni AA, Ceruti T, Frapolli R, Russo M, Fichera S, Zucchetti M, Tommasi S. Pharmacokinetic characterization of the DDAH1 inhibitors ZST316 and ZST152 in mice using a HPLC-MS/MS method. Molecules 2022;27:1017.

Cancer stem cells and nitric oxide

Aysegul Taskiran[a], Aleyna Demir[a], Eda Acikgoz[b], and Gulperi Oktem[a]

[a]Department of Histology and Embryology, Faculty of Medicine, Ege University, Izmir, Turkey
[b]Department of Histology and Embryology, Faculty of Medicine, Van Yuzuncu Yil University, Van, Turkey

Abstract

Cancer stem cells (CSCs) forming the tumor heterogeneity are thought to be the main reason for ineffective and insufficient conventional cancer treatments including surgery, radiotherapy, and chemotherapy and, therefore, causing relapse, metastasis, and multidrug resistance in the long term. CSCs express specific biomarkers on their surface and, thus, differentiate from non-CSCs. The metabolic and signaling activities of CSCs have been shown to be different from those of non-CSCs, and there are still many unknown activities. CSCs share Wnt, Hedgehog, and Notch signaling pathways and many surface markers with embryonic and adult stem cells, indicating that CSCs are the starting point of tumor formation. Deregulation of intrinsic and extrinsic factors of cells induces altered metabolic activities, including the nitric oxide (NO) metabolism, that have a crucial role in the cell fate. CSCs produce high levels of NO and secrete it in the tumor microenvironment involving a wide range of components such as stromal cells, cancer-associated fibroblasts (CAFs), immune cells, nonimmune cells, and blood vessels. Studies have shown that cancer (stem) cell-derived NO promotes chronic inflammation in the tumor microenvironment, pro-tumorigenic activities of CAFs, drug resistance, invasion, and metastasis. These events are reversible by inhibiting cellular NO by NO-releasing drugs or NO donors in cancer therapy either alone or combined with other cytotoxic drugs. Thereby, NO is suggested to be a promising agent for cancer therapy, prevention of the metastatic cascade, and CSC transformation. Further research is needed to elucidate the highly sophisticated activities of NO and CSCs for the advancements of new therapeutic strategies targeting CSCs.

Abbreviations

ALDH	aldehyde dehydrogenase
ASC	adult stem cell
CAF	cancer-associated fibroblast
Cav-1	caveolin-1
CSC	cancer stem cell
CXCL14	chemokine (CXC motif) ligand 14
EMT	epithelial to mesenchymal transition

eNOS	endothelial nitric oxide synthase (NOS3)
ESC	embryonic stem cell
HCC	hepatocellular carcinoma cells
Hh	hedgehog
iNOS	inducible nitric oxide synthase (NOS2)
nNOS	neuronal nitric oxide synthase (NOS1)
NO	nitric oxide
NOS	nitric oxide synthase
Ptch	patched
SC	stem cell
Smo	smoothened
TF	transcription factor
TME	tumor microenvironment

Conflict of interest

No potential conflicts of interest were disclosed.

Introduction

Cancer is a type of disease that can occur in almost any organ or tissue, where abnormal cells have uncontrollable growth capacity and invasion. Metastasis is the main cause of death from cancer. Despite many conventional treatments for cancer recurrence, metastasis, and resistance in the clinic, such as surgery, radiotherapy, chemotherapy, and targeted therapy, the mortality and recurrence rates still need to be improved. Exploring the detailed biological properties of tumors needs further approaches that take into account the biology of CSCs. On the one hand, cancer treatment failures might be elucidated by tumor heterogeneity including the CSC hypothesis. CSCs are believed to be the starting point of tumor formation; therefore, targeting CSCs in cancer treatment is particularly important for effective therapies [1].

Stem cells (SCs) are capable of self-renewal and differentiation. Embryonic stem cells (ESCs) are pluripotent, so they can differentiate into any kind of cell during embryonic development. Adult stem cells (ASCs) are multipotent or unipotent, found in adult tissues, and have limited differentiation capacities. ASCs are important in the renewal and repair of adult tissues. Within tumors, there are cells called CSCs that have both SC and cancer cell properties [2]. CSCs with different gene expression profiles, cancer potential, and metabolism induce different states of the tumor, resulting in the tumor heterogeneity. Among the signaling molecules, NO has a prominent role in proliferation, survival, and mediating tumorigenesis, which has been shown to be upregulated in both cancer cells and cancer SCs. NO is another common stemness molecule between ESCs and CSCs [3]. Depending on high and low doses, NO has critical importance in the regulation of basic biological processes such as pluripotency, cell survival, and differentiation in SCs [4].

For more effective cancer therapies, it is important to understand meticulously about cancer initiation and progression. The concept of CSC is an important issue that demands to be elucidated for improved responses in tumorigenesis and inhibition of carcinogenesis [5]. The Yin Yang role of NO in CSCs is evaluated from different metabolic perspectives, and a critical conclusion emerges as follows: "Like a double-edged sword, the reactions of NO in the cell must be carefully considered in new approaches targeting NO, which are likely to change according to the cell and the state of the cell." In this chapter, we present a comprehensive perspective on the roles and biological outcomes of NO in CSCs from the current literature.

Cancer stem cells

The notion of CSCs was reported for the first time in the 19th century in leukemia [6]. These undifferentiated cells constitute quite a small subpopulation within the heterogeneous tumor aggregations that are responsible for tumor invasion, metastasis, high multidrug resistance, and relapse. These events are based on self-renewal and differentiation capacities. CSCs can divide symmetrically for self-renewal and asymmetrically for differentiated cell generation. With symmetrical division, they give rise to other CSCs, increasing tumor growth, while with the asymmetrical division, one CSC and one daughter cell are formed. During tumorigenesis, there is a tendency toward asymmetric division, and it is more frequent than symmetric division, which is a strategy implemented by CSCs to increase the SC population and tumor aggressiveness [7–9].

CSCs have been detected in most cancer types, including glioblastoma; melanoma; breast, colon, prostate, liver, ovarian, pancreatic cancers; and many others [10]. The quantity of CSCs and the surface biomarker expressions differ from one cancer type to another, between patients having the same cancer type, and within the same tumor sample. They express a vast number of specific surface biomarkers, such as CD24, CD26, CD44, CD133, CD166, aldehyde dehydrogenase (ALDH), and Ep-CAM, changing according to cancer type, which allows the identification of these cells among others [9,11–13]. The separation/isolation using the specific markers is performed by fluorescence-activated cell sorting and magnetic-activated cell sorting, the most used techniques for cell isolation. CSCs express many surface markers in common with normal ESCs and ASCs. This similarity suggests that CSCs arise from normal SCs, with the accumulation of epigenetic and/or genetic alterations. For example, CD133 is a hematopoietic SC marker and is also expressed in CSCs of cancers such as breast, prostate, colon, glioma, liver, lung, and ovary cancers [14,15]. Another example is CXCR4, a surface marker in ASCs but not in ESCs. This chemokine receptor and FDA-approved target is also expressed in CSCs in breast, brain, and pancreatic cancers [16–18]. CD34 is also another ASC surface marker (not expressed on ESC) and functions in cell adhesion. Leukemia and squamous cell carcinoma CSCs express CD34 on their surface [19].

On the contrary, CSCs are controlled by many extrinsic (tumor microenvironment signals) and intrinsic (genetic mutations and epigenetic modifications) factors, so targeting these factors is a promising cancer treatment strategy that focuses on the stem of tumor bulk by preventing self-renewal and proliferation of CSCs (Fig. 1). In addition, CSCs can escape from traditional drug treatments and recurrence through their ability to arrest in the G0 phase, which is the quiescent state [1,10]. CSCs in this state do not show active replication or metabolic activity. This is a genius strategy of CSCs for escaping from any kind of treatment. Chemotherapeutic agents target proliferative active cancer cells, leading CSCs to escape into a quiescent state that supports tumorigenesis. Quiescent CSCs stay in this state for many years until stimulated by a signal, and this activation induces recurrence and metastasis [20]. Cancer cells within the tumor mass are not alone; these cells share a common niche

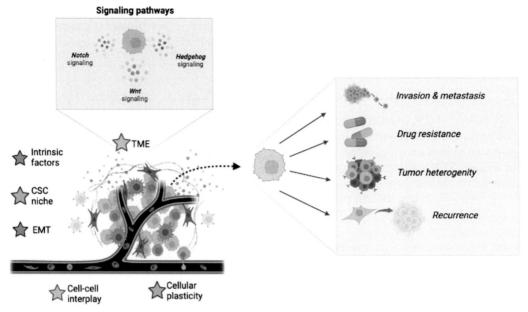

FIG. 1   Overview of the tumor microenvironment (TME) and cancer stem cell (CSC) implication. Cancer and CSC niche, intrinsic factors, EMT, cell-cell interplay, and cellular plasticity are the main players of TME. Notch, Wnt, and Hedgehog signaling pathways regulate CSCs through tumorigenesis. CSCs and their microenvironment are involved in invasion and metastasis, drug resistance, tumor heterogeneity and recurrence.

(microenvironment) with other neighboring cells that regulate their function by coordinating the flow route of stimuli. The tumor microenvironment (TME) can affect tumor characteristics including plasticity, metabolic glycolysis, oxidative phosphorylation, and cell cycle through signaling and epigenetic modifications. Cellular plasticity is a significant cause of intratumoral heterogeneity. Maintaining CSC plasticity is essential for tumor cell survival and ensured by DNA mutations, epigenetic modifications, and microenvironmental signals [21].

CSCs can arise due to epigenetic changes in SCs or differentiated cells, random oncogenic mutations in somatic cells, and activation of the TME. These CSCs have high immune evasion capacity, reduced apoptosis, and high proliferation rates. Continuously occurring mutations can generate various types of cancer from CSCs. CSCs show important plasticity and mobility abilities, also involved in epithelial-to-mesenchymal transition (EMT). Loss of cell adhesion molecules and polarity lead to cell detachment from each other to facilitate free move and invasion; therefore, metastasis occurs. With EMT, non-CSCs can differentiate into CSC-like phenotypes. TWIST1, SNAI1, ZEB1, and TGF-β are the key regulators of the EMT process [7,9,22,23].

CSCs maintaining tumors are defined not only by surface marker expression but also by their gene expression and subsequent signaling pathway activations. The Wnt/β-catenin, Sonic Hedgehog, and Notch signaling pathways are the three major regulators of CSCs and are also present in ESCs. These signaling pathways mediate the process of self-renewal, pluripotency, and differentiation.

First, the Wnt pathway is an essential mechanism that guides cell proliferation, polarity, SC pluripotency, and cell fate decisions throughout embryogenesis and adult tissue homeostasis. Wnt ligands bind to a frizzled family receptor. This binding interrupts and decomposes the β-catenin degradation complex, triggering the cytoplasmic accumulation of β-catenin. Consequently, through nuclear translocation, β-catenin attaches to TCF/LEF transcription factors (TFs) triggering Wnt target gene activation [24,25]. This activation contributes to asymmetric division, generating SCs and differentiated cells. Therefore, this pathway is involved in tumor plasticity. In several cancers, including glioma, colon, ovarian cancers, and others, the Wnt pathway is abnormally activated in CSCs [26–30].

Second, the Sonic Hedgehog signaling is fundamental in normal development and plays a crucial role in adult tissue maintenance. Hedgehog (Hh) proteins act in a concentration- and time-dependent way to induce various mechanisms, including cell survival, proliferation, cell fate determination, and differentiation. Hh proteins start signaling by binding to the receptor patched (Ptch) and coreceptors GAS1, CDON, and BOC. Ptch is a 12-pass transmembrane protein. When there is a lack of Hh ligand, Ptch limits smoothened (Smo) activity by relocalizing it to the cell surface. In mammals, Hh signaling occurs in dormant cilia, where Smo and other downstream elements must travel to activate glioma-associated oncogene (Gli) TFs. This factor translocates into the nucleus and activates Hh target genes. There are three different Gli TFs: Gli1 and Gli2, which act as transcription activators, and Gli3 which functions as a transcriptional repressor [25]. Besides its significant roles during normal embryonic development and adult tissue homeostasis, an abnormal Hh pathway has been implicated in the initiation of numerous malignancies, such as basal cell carcinoma, medulloblastoma, and rhabdomyosarcoma; overactivated Hh signaling plays a role in pancreatic, gastrointestinal, colon, lung, prostate, ovarian, and breast cancers [31–34].

Third, the Notch signaling is another evolutionarily conserved and vital pathway involved in cell fate decision and regulation during development and maintenance of adult tissue homeostasis. In mammals, there are four different transmembrane Notch receptors (Notch 1–4), and all respond to different ligands: Jagged 1 and 2, and delta-like 1, 3, and 4 [25]. Notch receptors are composed of functional extracellular domain (NECD), transmembrane domain, and intracellular domain (NICD). The signaling pathway is triggered by ligand-receptor binding that induces NICD cleavage, which enables its translocation into the cytoplasm and then to the nucleus, leading to recombination signal binding protein 1 for J-kappa activation to express target Notch genes [20,35]. The Notch pathway plays a pivotal role in tumorigenesis depending on the TME. Its abnormal signaling is involved in CSC self-renewal and metastasis promotion in hepatocellular carcinoma, glioblastoma, breast, and ovarian cancers. Also, this pathway participates in the EMT process, boosting the stem-like phenotype of cancer [1,21,36,37].

Nitric oxide

NO is a free radical signaling molecule that is involved in several intracellular and intercellular signaling pathways, as well as regulating angiogenesis, smooth muscle tone, immune response, apoptosis, and synaptic communication [38]. NO is produced by nitric oxide synthase (NOS). On the contrary, overexpressed and uncontrolled NO synthesis has been linked to several pathophysiological conditions, including cancer, as a cause or a contributing factor [39]. Structurally produced NO is essential in revealing the cancer cell phenotype. NO roles in tumorigenesis comprise tumor penetration into surrounding tissues, which allows metastasis, and neovascularization, allowing the increased blood flow for the required resources [40].

NOS converts arginine to citrulline, resulting in NO production [41]. Oxygen and NADPH contribute to this process as cofactors. NOS is divided into three isoforms based on the activity or the tissue type in which they were originally identified. These isoforms are neuronal NOS (nNOS or NOS1), endothelial NOS (eNOS or NOS3), and inducible NOS (iNOS or NOS2). All three isoforms, despite their names, can be found in many tissues and cell types. Fig. 2 shows the general mechanism of NO production by NOS.

nNOS and eNOS are mainly expressed in mammalian cells, and NO is synthesized in response to increased intracellular calcium levels [42]. However, in some cases, cells can also enhance NO production independently of calcium levels in response to stimuli such as stress [43]. iNOS activity is independent of the intracellular calcium level but, as with all NOS isoforms, is dependent on calmodulin binding. Increases in cellular calcium cause an increase in calmodulin levels, which leads to enhanced calmodulin binding to eNOS and nNOS, resulting in a transient elevation in NO production by these enzymes [44]. iNOS,

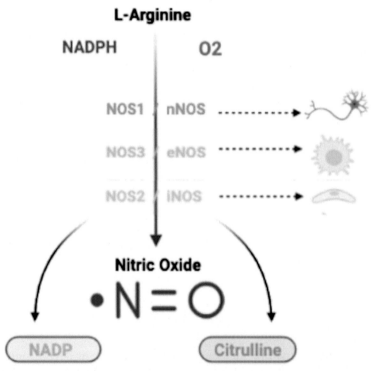

FIG. 2   Nitric oxide (NO) synthesis and the isoforms of nitric oxide synthase (NOS). NO is produced by NOS which converts arginine to citrulline, resulting in NO production. O_2 and NADPH are the cofactors. Based on the activity/tissue, NOS is divided into three: neuronal NOS (nNOS or NOS1), endothelial NOS (eNOS or NOS3), and inducible NOS (iNOS or NOS2).

on the contrary, may bind to calmodulin strongly even at quite low cellular calcium concentrations [45]. In other words, changes in intracellular calcium levels do not affect iNOS activity. Consequently, NO production from iNOS is much more long-lasting than other NOS isoforms and is likely present in higher NO concentrations in the cell [46]. Contrarily, transcription can control NO production from iNOS. iNOS levels are either very low or partially undetectable in most cell types. Even so, cytokines or growth factors may stimulate these cells, resulting in increased iNOS transcription, with an ensuing NO production [47].

Nitric oxide as a modulator of the tumor microenvironment

Cancer tissue, taken together rather than as a single entity, exists as a combination of different cellular phenotypes that contribute significantly to their entire ecosystem, and this environment is termed the tumor microenvironment (TME) [48]. It is clear that cancer cells grow in a complex TME that allows them to invade and metastasize to distant organs. The TME is made up of immune and nonimmune cells, stromal components, and blood vessels, all of which work together to trigger cancer progression [48]. Considering the critical importance of NO in the tumor microenvironment, it assumes a quite significant function in manipulating other cells by cancer cells. In this context, NO released by tumor cells reprograms stromal cells to perform functions that allow tumor growth (Fig. 3). For instance, cancer cell-derived NO

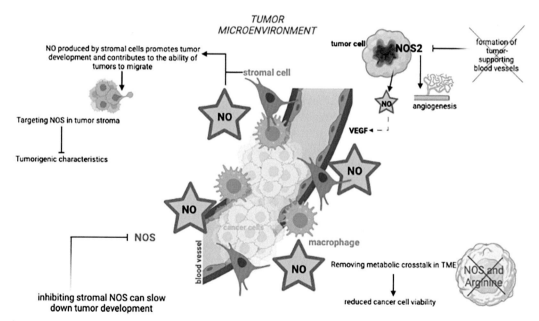

FIG. 3   Tumor microenvironment, NOS and NO interaction. Complex TME that allows cancer cells to invade and metastasize to distant organs is made up of immune and nonimmune cells, stromal components, and blood vessels, all of which work together to trigger cancer progression. Tumor cells release NO that reprograms stromal cells into tumorigenic function. Targeting NOS and its isoforms in tumor stroma have a suppressor effect on tumorigenesis.

promotes chronic inflammation in the TME of melanoma cells, which induces drug resistance; and increasing NO levels in the TME enhances breast cancer migration by upregulating caveolin-1 (Cav-1) expression [49].

Likewise, the induction of NOS in stromal cells contributes to tumor development. NOS1 expression is required for cancer-associated fibroblast (CAF)-supported growth of breast and prostate cancer cells in CAFs, producing C-X-C motif chemokine ligand 14 (CXCL14). Moreover, inhibiting NOS1 expression altered CXCL14-expressing CAFs' pro-tumorigenic functions and decreased tumor growth in mice [50]. NOS1-derived NO promoted CXCL14 activity within CAFs since NOS1 expression did not enhance extracellular NO (Fig. 3) [51]. In colon cancer patients, increased NO in the TME is related to tumorigenic activities. Lymph node metastasis incidence has been raised in colon cancer patients with elevated NOS2 expression, and enhanced NOS2 expression in the upper colon in colitis patients predicts an increased risk of colon cancer [52,53].

Besides the role of NO in regulating metastasis and tumorigenesis, it is the major regulator of angiogenesis [54]. In glioblastoma and hepatoma cells, elevated NO in the TME has been shown to promote vascular endothelial growth factor (VEGF). Also, the effects of NO on angiogenesis have been used to make glioma tumors in mice more sensitive to radiotherapy by suppressing the NOS1 expression [50]. Suppression of NO in glioma conducts normal tumor vascularization, resulting in oxygenation of tumors, which promotes radiotherapy [55].

Expression of nitric oxide synthases in tumors

iNOS was the first NOS isoform associated with the macrophage-mediated tumor-killing mechanism, and as a result, the expression of this isoform has been the focus of NO research in cancer biology [56]. iNOS has been found in macrophages and neutrophils, and also in hepatocytes, cardiac myocytes, chondrocytes, and a variety of nontumorigenic cell types. The absence of iNOS in knock-out mice was recently discovered to increase the risk of intestinal tumorigenesis in the Apc(Min/+) colon cancer mouse model, demonstrating the importance of iNOS in host defense mechanisms [57]. In a panel of 15 invasive breast carcinomas, the first research on iNOS expression in human breast cancer indicated that iNOS activity was increased in less differentiated tumors [58]. iNOS expression is most detectable in peritumoral and intratumoral macrophages. Three recent large-scale research studies revealed that iNOS is expressed in tumor cells as well as stromal cells and macrophages [59–62].

NOS activity was reported by Revenue et al. in 27 of 40 human breast tumors [58]. In a study on invasive breast cancers, carcinomas with both iNOS positive tumor and stromal cells exhibited elevated apoptotic and microvessel density indexes than in situ carcinomas [60]. While none of the benign lesions was positive for iNOS, more than half of the in situ carcinomas exhibited iNOS tumor cell staining. More than half of the invasive lesions of breast carcinoma also showed eNOS expression [61]. Lesions expressing iNOS and eNOS exhibited strong coexpression. It has also been shown that in addition to breast cancer, iNOS is prominently expressed in most human adenomas and 20%–25% of colon carcinomas [63]. On the contrary, the expression is low or absent in surrounding normal tissues [64]. In terms of ovarian cancer, the activity of iNOS has been localized in tumor cells and not found in normal tissue [65]. Brain, head and neck, esophagus, lung, prostate, bladder, and pancreatic cancers and Kaposi's sarcoma are among the tumors that have shown iNOS gene expression [66]. NO has a range of biological activities in the central nervous system, including vasorelaxation and neurotransmission. nNOS has been found in various oligodendroglioma and neuroblastoma cell lines, but further research is needed to fully understand its involvement in tumor pathology [67].

Studies concerning CSCs and NO

While studies on cancer biology and NO have been conducted since the 19th century, specialized studies examining CSCs and NO together are still quite limited. Due to many unknowns of CSC biology, there is still much to investigate and explore in different metabolic pathways, including NO metabolism.

Gliomas are one of the most challenging and aggressive cancer types with still not enlightened molecular mechanisms. The very small subpopulation of CSCs of gliomas showed increased NOS2 levels through NO production. The difference between neural progenitors, CSCs, and non-CSCs is that glioma CSCs need NOS2 to induce aggressive tumor behavior. In vivo experiments in murine models determined low survival rates induced by cell cycle deregulation through high NOS2 expression, and downregulated NOS2 inhibited glioma CSC survival, proliferation, and tumor spheroid formation [68]. In 2013, a study conducted by Kim and colleagues showed an increase in glioma stem-like cells responsible for glioblastoma recurrence and induction of resistance to cisplatin, taxol, or ionizing radiation treatments following radiotherapy, which is one of the conventional cancer therapies. Radiation therapy caused expansion of stem-like cells through iNOS upregulation, thereby increasing NO production. iNOS downregulation by siRNA transfection targeting iNOS reduced expanded glioma stem-like cells and reduced resistance. Therefore, ionizing radiation combined with iNOS targeting might be a new combinational treatment strategy [69].

Lung cancer has the lowest survival rate among other cancers. Nonsmall-cell lung cancer (NSCLC) has the highest incidence among other lung cancer types. H292 and H460 cell lines showed stem-like phenotypes when treated with NO. The aggressive nature of the CSC-like cell effect is reversed after treatment is stopped or by adding NO scavenger into the cell medium shown by CSC markers expressions. In H292 and H460 cells, NO upregulated Cav-1 stimulation, triggering CSCs through a more aggressive phenotype [70]. In lung cancer, NO and NOS are highly activated in TME. Oct-4 is SCs' major regulatory TF, while in cancer cells, it activates stemness and, therefore, the CSC transformation. Maiuthed A. and colleagues showed that there is an Oct-4-Cav-1 complex formation, which is mediated by tyrosine-14 of Cav-1. NO promoted the CSC activity by inducing intracellular Oct-4 expression, leading to Oct-4-Cav-1 complex dissociation. This work elucidated a new molecular mechanism involved in CSCs related to NO, which could be useful for new targeted drug therapies [71]. Zou and colleagues developed two radioresistant cell lines that showed increased invasion, spheroid formation, and CSC phenotype. In addition, these CSC-like resistant cell lines had altered cell cycle phases and decreased DNA damage response. Treatment by the combination of radiotherapy and β-elemene reversed the adverse consequences of radiotherapy on cells in vivo and in vitro. The analyses exhibited high levels of radiosensitivity and low levels of CSCs and EMT marker expression through the Prx-1/NF-kB/iNOS signaling pathway [72].

Puglisi and colleagues investigated the implication of NO on colon cancer initiation and progression concerning CSCs. Both colon cancer cells and CSCs produced increased levels of endogenous NO. The qRT-PCR analysis uncovered similar molecular profiles between NO^{high} cells from colon CSCs and colon cancer cell lines. Firstly, an increase in the expression of SC markers (CD133, LGR5, and BMI) and gene (β-catenin, Twist, and Snail) expressions that play a role in cell growth and epithelial-to-mesenchymal transition is detected compared to NO^{low} cells. Secondly, CSCs with higher levels of NO showed an increase in iNOS expression than NO^{low} cells. These findings suggested distinctive NO synthesis in colon CSCs and colon cancer cells is regulated by the iNOS expression [73].

The CSC-like phenotype is established by highly expressed CSC markers and drug resistance. When oncogenic HRAS-transformed mouse embryonic fibroblast cells were cultured in serum depleted medium, cells produced increased levels of NO, and this led to a change in the oxygen consumption rate. These changes affected cells into a CSC-like phenotype, which was reversible by a NOS inhibitor (SEITU), proposing oxygen consumption rate inhibitors might be used to target CSCs as a treatment [74].

In the Apc-deficient mouse model, where the β-catenin degradation complex was disrupted during Wnt signaling, intestinal tumor organoids showed eNOS overexpression, hyperproliferation behavior, and increased CSC markers expression, which was reversible by NO scavengers (c-PTIO). NO-depleted colorectal CSCs did not show tumor spheroid formation, and CSC-related signaling pathways were disrupted [75].

In vivo experiments showed higher induction of tumorigenesis in CD133 + CD24+ hepatocellular carcinoma cells (HCC) than in CD133 − CD24− HCC when inoculated in NOD/SCID mice. These findings were also supported in vitro by colony and spheroid formation assays, indicating high self-renewal capacity of CSCs. CD133 + CD24+ HCC showed drug resistance against sorafenib and increased stemness-related gene expression profiles including Nanog and Sox2. Immunohistochemical staining and qPCR analysis indicated higher expression of iNOS in CD133+ CD24+ HCC, which was inhibited by shRNA-mediated knockdown. Mice inoculated with knockdown CSCs showed a decreased number and volume of tumors. The increased levels of iNOS expression upregulated Notch signaling through TACE/ADAM17 activity, which induces CSC transformation and poor prognosis in patients [76].

For estrogen-positive breast cancer patients, the resistance to endocrine therapy poses a big problem. Concerning hormonal therapies, NO targeting could be a new additional strategy with tamoxifen to increase treatment efficacy. It is demonstrated that tamoxifen resistance was due to CSCs and high NOS2 expression. NO depleted or NOS2 silenced estrogen receptor-positive breast cancer cells showed, in vivo and in vitro, blocked mammosphere formation capacity and lowered CSC marker expression, leading to higher treatment efficacy of tamoxifen and lower metastasis [77].

In prostate cancer, increased levels of eNOS and NO have been demonstrated according to the stage of cancer. The high expression levels have been linked to high tumorigenicity and metastasis. Especially upregulated eNOS played a significant role in promoting prostate CSCs and antiandrogen-resistant prostate cancer cell growth. This study indicated eNOS-NO signaling as a promising target for prostate cancer treatment targeting CSCs [78].

NO as a novel therapeutic target in cancer

NO may have a dual action, in which growth inhibition and/or apoptosis signaling is triggered when NO levels are above a threshold concentration for tumor growth and survival [39]. These features of NO have been used therapeutically with outstanding outcomes in preclinical tumor models to reduce growth and improve chemotherapy and radiation effectiveness [79]. iNOS gene therapy, iNOS induction, and administration of NO donor drugs [80] are among the options being investigated by researchers for modulating in vivo synthesis and exogenous delivery of this molecule for therapeutic advantage. One of the methods for NO delivery is the transfer of NOS-encoding cDNA sequences into cancer cells [39]. Nevertheless, because retroviral and adenoviral vectors can be harmful to the host, cell-based techniques are being explored [81]. Further research on the exact mechanisms of this process is needed. NO-releasing drugs or NO donors might be used as alternative means for NO delivery. Depending on the dosage of the NO donor, cancer type, and its grade, they can concurrently exhibit a variety of anticancer activities, including an increase in apoptotic stimuli, inhibition of metastasis, inhibition of angiogenesis, and suppression of hypoxia [82].

Numerous promising findings back up the therapeutic use of NO donors in cancer therapy, either alone or combined with other cytotoxic drugs. NO donors have been found to play a biphasic role in tumor cell sensitization to chemotherapy and immunotherapy, as well as in the control and suppression of metastasis [83].

However, possible systemic effects implemented in vivo have restricted the therapeutic utility of NO donors. Vasodilation, which causes severe hypotension, and the formation of hazardous metabolites such as cyanide are among the side effects [84]. NO hybrids were created in response to the necessity to generate the optimized NO donor having maximum antiproliferative characteristics and minimum complications. NO hybrids supply a special environment for antitumor drugs. Supporting NO with other medications, such as NSAIDs or statins, has the advantage of maximizing NO power [76]. NO-drug combinations have shown potential as antitumor drugs in phase I randomized studies supported by the National Cancer Institute (i.e., NO-aspirin in colorectal cancer patients) [85].

Pharmaceutical research has a significant problem with producing molecules that can release optimum NO levels at the proper time and the place. NO donors can be linked to biopolymers or integrated into them to simulate endogenous NO production at a specific location [86,87]. Nanomaterials are being used to charge elevated quantities of NO because of their stability and biological activity. Chemical modifications and optimizations can be made to their surfaces for specialized medical applications. They may make it easier to build systems that can be used for both therapeutic and diagnostic purposes [88]. Physiochemical, chemical, and mechanical methods can be used to produce these nanoparticles [89]. Drug release from particles, on the contrary, may change depending on the polymer used or the encapsulated drug [90]. NO nanocarriers increase the availability of the drug in systemic circulation and enhance targeting as well [88]. In consequence, NO seems to be a hope-inspiring molecule for cancer therapy, metastatic cascade repression, and CSC transformation prevention. Further research is needed to fully comprehend the complicated and wide-ranging activities of NO to ease its therapeutic usage.

Conclusion

NO is involved in several stages of carcinogenesis such as tumor initiation, tumor growth, and metastasis. NOS expression has been detected in a variety of human cancers, thus making NO-dependent metabolic reactions an important therapeutic target. On the contrary, NO has also tumor-killing characteristics and is suggested to have a cytostatic and/or cytotoxic impact on tumors. Additionally, NO seems to have a pro-tumoral effect instead of an antitumor effect in cancer initiation. By contrast, NO capacity to destroy tumors is used to treat cancer. Thus, it may function as a novel potential therapeutic agent and be included in a new therapeutic approach for cancer therapy, making resistant tumors more susceptible to radiation, chemotherapy, and immunotherapy. To sum up, even though NO can be used in cancer therapy because of its tumor prevention property, more confirmation and experimental/clinical trials are necessary to improve NO-based techniques for cancer prevention and treatment.

Acknowledgments

We, as the authors, thank to Dr. Benjamin Bonavida for unconditionally uniting and supporting his wide circle. We are deeply grateful to him for sharing his creativity and scientific superiority with us in the light of science.

References

[1] Yang L, Shi P, Zhao G, Xu J, Peng W, Zhang J, et al. Targeting cancer stem cell pathways for cancer therapy. vol. 5. Springer US; 2020. https://doi.org/10.1038/s41392-020-0110-5.

[2] Liu G, David BT, Trawczynski M, Fessler RG. Advances in pluripotent stem cells: history, mechanisms, technologies, and applications. Stem Cell Rev Rep 2020;16:3–32. https://doi.org/10.1007/s12015-019-09935-x.

[3] Shi X, Zhang Y, Zheng J, Pan J. Reactive oxygen species in cancer stem cells. Antioxid Redox Signal 2012;16: 1215–28. https://doi.org/10.1089/ARS.2012.4529.

[4] Caballano-Infantes E, Cahuana GM, Bedoya FJ, Salguero-Aranda C, Tejedo JR. The role of nitric oxide in stem cell biology. Antioxidants 2022;11:1–20. https://doi.org/10.3390/antiox11030497.

[5] Ayob AZ, Ramasamy TS. Cancer stem cells as key drivers of tumour progression. J Biomed Sci 2018;25:1–18. https://doi.org/10.1186/s12929-018-0426-4.

[6] Lapidot T, Sirard C, Vormoor J, Murdoch B, Hoang T, Caceres-Cortes J, et al. A cell initiating human acute myeloid leukaemia after transplantation into SCID mice. Nature 1994;367(6464):645–8. https://doi.org/10.1038/367645a0.

[7] Batlle E, Clevers H. Cancer stem cells revisited. Nat Med 2017;23:1124–34. https://doi.org/10.1038/nm.4409.

[8] Aponte PM, Caicedo A. Stemness in cancer: stem cells, cancer stem cells, and their microenvironment. Stem Cells Int 2017;2017. https://doi.org/10.1155/2017/5619472.

[9] Najafi M, Farhood B, Mortezaee K. Cancer stem cells (CSCs) in cancer progression and therapy. J Cell Physiol 2019;234:8381–95. https://doi.org/10.1002/jcp.27740.

[10] Prager BC, Xie Q, Bao S, Rich JN. Cancer stem cells: the architects of the tumor ecosystem. Cell Stem Cell 2019;24:41–53. https://doi.org/10.1016/j.stem.2018.12.009.

[11] Marquardt S, Solanki M, Spitschak A, Vera J, Pützer BM. Emerging functional markers for cancer stem cell-based therapies: understanding signaling networks for targeting metastasis. Semin Cancer Biol 2018;53:90–109. https://doi.org/10.1016/j.semcancer.2018.06.006.

[12] Walcher L, Kistenmacher AK, Suo H, Kitte R, Dluczek S, Strauß A, et al. Cancer stem cells—origins and biomarkers: perspectives for targeted personalized therapies. Front Immunol 2020;11:1–33. https://doi.org/10.3389/fimmu.2020.01280.

[13] Girirajan S, Campbell C, Eichler E. 心提取 HHS public access. Physiol Behav 2011;176:139–48. https://doi.org/10.4103/ctm.ctm.

[14] Sundberg M, Jansson L, Ketolainen J, Pihlajamäki H, Suuronen R, Skottman H, et al. CD marker expression profiles of human embryonic stem cells and their neural derivatives, determined using flow-cytometric analysis, reveal a novel CD marker for exclusion of pluripotent stem cells. Stem Cell Res 2009;2:113–24. https://doi.org/10.1016/j.scr.2008.08.001.

[15] Grosse-Gehling P, Fargeas CA, Dittfeld C, Garbe Y, Alison MR, Corbeil D, et al. CD133 as a biomarker for putative cancer stem cells in solid tumours: limitations, problems and challenges. J Pathol 2013;229: 355–78. https://doi.org/10.1002/path.4086.

[16] Zhang L, Hua Q, Tang K, Shi C, Xie X, Zhang R. CXCR4 activation promotes differentiation of human embryonic stem cells to neural stem cells. Neuroscience 2016;337:88–97. https://doi.org/10.1016/j.neuroscience.2016.09.001.

[17] Dubrovska A, Hartung A, Bouchez LC, Walker JR, Reddy VA, Cho CY, et al. CXCR4 activation maintains a stem cell population in tamoxifen-resistant breast cancer cells through AhR signalling. Br J Cancer 2012;107:43–52. https://doi.org/10.1038/bjc.2012.105.

[18] Ahmed MI, Harvey JR, Kirby J, Ali S, Lennard TWJ. Role of the chemokine receptor CXCR4 in breast cancer metastasis. Eur J Cancer Suppl 2007;5:30. https://doi.org/10.1016/s1359-6349(07)71788-3.

[19] Kim WT, Ryu CJ. Cancer stem cell surface markers on normal stem cells. BMB Rep 2017;50:285–98. https://doi.org/10.5483/BMBRep.2017.50.6.039.

[20] Aramini B, Masciale V, Grisendi G, Bertolini F, Mauer M, Guaitoli G, et al. Dissecting tumor growth: the role of cancer stem cells in drug resistance and recurrence. Cancers (Basel) 2022;14:1–28. https://doi.org/10.3390/cancers14040976.

[21] Behavior SC, Kumar VE, Nambiar R, De Souza C, Nguyen A. Targeting epigenetic modifiers of tumor plasticity and cancer stem cell behavior. Cell 2022;11:1–23.

[22] Nakano M, Kikushige Y, Miyawaki K, Kunisaki Y, Mizuno S, Takenaka K, et al. Dedifferentiation process driven by TGF-beta signaling enhances stem cell properties in human colorectal cancer. Oncogene 2019;38:780–93. https://doi.org/10.1038/s41388-018-0480-0.

[23] Chang L, Graham PH, Hao J, Ni J, Bucci J, Cozzi PJ, et al. Acquisition of epithelialmesenchymal transition and cancer stem cell phenotypes is associated with activation of the PI3K/Akt/mTOR pathway in prostate cancer radioresistance. Cell Death Dis 2013;4. https://doi.org/10.1038/cddis.2013.407.

[24] Correia C, Weiskittel TM, Ung CY, Villasboas Bisneto JC, Billadeau DD, Kaufmann SH, et al. Uncovering pharmacological opportunities for cancer stem cells—a systems biology view. Front Cell Dev Biol 2022;10:1–12. https://doi.org/10.3389/fcell.2022.752326.

[25] Aktug H, editor. Hücre Sinyal Yolakları—Temel Yolaklar ve Mekanizmalar. 1st ed; 2021. Istanbul.

[26] Vermeulen L, De Sousa E, Melo F, Van Der Heijden M, Cameron K, De Jong JH, Borovski T, et al. Wnt activity defines colon cancer stem cells and is regulated by the microenvironment. Nat Cell Biol 2010;12:468–76. https://doi.org/10.1038/ncb2048.

[27] Peng Zhao SX, Ge T, Fan J. WNT/β-catenin pathway activation correlates with immune exclusion across human cancers. Physiol Behav 2016;176:139–48. https://doi.org/10.1158/1078-0432.CCR-18-1942.WNT/.

[28] Nguyen VHL, Hough R, Bernaudo S, Peng C. Wnt/β-catenin signalling in ovarian cancer: insights into its hyperactivation and function in tumorigenesis. J Ovarian Res 2019;12:1–17. https://doi.org/10.1186/s13048-019-0596-z.

[29] Virolle T. Cancer stem cells in glioblastoma. Bull Cancer 2017;104:1075–9. https://doi.org/10.1016/j.bulcan.2017.10.012.

[30] Martin-Orozco E, Sanchez-Fernandez A, Ortiz-Parra I, Ayala-San NM. WNT signaling in tumors: the way to evade drugs and immunity. Front Immunol 2019;10:1–21. https://doi.org/10.3389/fimmu.2019.02854.

[31] Regan JL, Schumacher D, Staudte S, Steffen A, Haybaeck J, Keilholz U, et al. Non-canonical hedgehog signaling is a positive regulator of the WNT pathway and is required for the survival of colon cancer stem cells. Cell Rep 2017;21:2813–28. https://doi.org/10.1016/j.celrep.2017.11.025.

[32] Giroux-Leprieur E, Costantini A, Ding VW, He B. Hedgehog signaling in lung cancer: from oncogenesis to cancer treatment resistance. Int J Mol Sci 2018;19:1–17. https://doi.org/10.3390/ijms19092835.

[33] Jeng KS, Chang CF, Lin SS. Sonic hedgehog signaling in organogenesis, tumors, and tumor microenvironments. Int J Mol Sci 2020;21. https://doi.org/10.3390/ijms21030758.

[34] Zhang J, Fan J, Zeng X, Nie M, Luan J, Wang Y, et al. Hedgehog signaling in gastrointestinal carcinogenesis and the gastrointestinal tumor microenvironment. Acta Pharm Sin B 2021;11:609–20. https://doi.org/10.1016/j.apsb.2020.10.022.

II. Nitric oxide pathway and cancer progression and therapy

[35] Toh TB, Lim JJ, Chow EKH. Epigenetics in cancer stem cells. Mol Cancer 2017;16:1–20. https://doi.org/10.1186/s12943-017-0596-9.

[36] Zhang YU, Xie ZY, Guo XT, Xiao XH, Xiong LX. Notch and breast cancer metastasis: current knowledge, new sights and targeted therapy (review). Oncol Lett 2019;18:2743–55. https://doi.org/10.3892/ol.2019.10653.

[37] Seymour T, Nowak A, Kakulas F. Targeting aggressive cancer stem cells in glioblastoma. Front Oncol 2015;5:1–9. https://doi.org/10.3389/fonc.2015.00159.

[38] Mishra D, Patel V, Banerjee D. Nitric oxide and S-nitrosylation in cancers: emphasis on breast cancer. Breast Cancer 2020;14. https://doi.org/10.1177/1178223419882688.

[39] Korde Choudhari S, Chaudhary M, Bagde S, Gadbail AR, Joshi V. Nitric oxide and cancer: a review. World J Surg Oncol 2013;11:118. https://doi.org/10.1186/1477-7819-11-118.

[40] Derici MK, Demirel-Yilmaz E. Nitrik oksitin kanser gelişimi ve metastaz üzerine etkileri [The effects of nitric oxide on cancer development and metastasis]. Turk Hij Den Biyol Derg 2017;74:161–74.

[41] Wijnands KAP, Castermans TMR, Hommen MPJ, Meesters DM, Poeze M. Arginine and citrulline and the immune response in sepsis. Nutrients 2015;7:1426. https://doi.org/10.3390/NU7031426.

[42] Pizzorno JE, Murray MT, Joiner-Bey H. Infertility, male. Clin Handb Nat Med 2016;521–46. https://doi.org/10.1016/B978-0-7020-5514-0.00052-X.

[43] Andrews AM, Jaron D, Buerk DG, Barbee KA. Shear stress-induced NO production is dependent on ATP autocrine signaling and capacitative calcium entry. Cell Mol Bioeng 2014;7:510. https://doi.org/10.1007/S12195-014-0351-X.

[44] Lane P, Gross SS. Disabling a C-terminal autoinhibitory control element in endothelial nitric-oxide synthase by phosphorylation provides a molecular explanation for activation of vascular NO synthesis by diverse physiological stimuli. J Biol Chem 2002;277:19087–94. https://doi.org/10.1074/JBC.M200258200.

[45] Wu PR, Kuo CC, Yet SF, Liou JY, Wu KK, Chen PF. Lobe-specific calcium binding in calmodulin regulates endothelial nitric oxide synthase activation. PLoS One 2012;7. https://doi.org/10.1371/JOURNAL.PONE.0039851.

[46] Okamoto I, Abe M, Shibata K, Shimizu N, Sakata N, Katsuragi T, et al. Evaluating the role of inducible nitric oxide synthase using a novel and selective inducible nitric oxide synthase inhibitor in septic lung injury produced by cecal ligation and puncture. Am J Respir Crit Care Med 2012;162:716–22. https://doi.org/10.1164/AJRCCM.162.2.9907039.

[47] Kleinert H, Art J, Pautz A. Regulation of the expression of inducible nitric oxide synthase. Nitric Oxide 2010;23:211–67. https://doi.org/10.1016/B978-0-12-373866-0.00007-1.

[48] Vedenko A, Panara K, Goldstein G, Ramasamy R, Arora H. Tumor microenvironment and nitric oxide: concepts and mechanisms. Adv Exp Med Biol 2020;1277:143–58. https://doi.org/10.1007/978-3-030-50224-9_10.

[49] Sanuphan A, Chunhacha P, Pongrakhananon V, Chanvorachote P. Long-term nitric oxide exposure enhances lung cancer cell migration. Biomed Res Int 2013;2013. https://doi.org/10.1155/2013/186972.

[50] Salimian Rizi B, Achreja A, Nagrath D. Nitric oxide—the forgotten child of tumor metabolism. Trends Cancer 2017;3:659. https://doi.org/10.1016/J.TRECAN.2017.07.005.

[51] Augsten M, Sjöberg E, Frings O, Vorrink SU, Frijhoff J, Olsson E, et al. Cancer-associated fibroblasts expressing CXCL14 rely upon NOS1-derived nitric oxide signaling for their tumor-supporting properties. Cancer Res 2014;74:2999–3010. https://doi.org/10.1158/0008-5472.CAN-13-2740.

[52] De Oliveira GA, Cheng RYS, Ridnour LA, Basudhar D, Somasundaram V, McVicar DW, et al. Inducible nitric oxide synthase in the carcinogenesis of gastrointestinal cancers. Antioxid Redox Signal 2017;26:1059–77. https://doi.org/10.1089/ARS.2016.6850.

[53] Erdman SE, Rao VP, Poutahidis T, Rogers AB, Taylor CL, Jackson EA, et al. Nitric oxide and TNF-alpha trigger colonic inflammation and carcinogenesis in Helicobacter hepaticus-infected, Rag2-deficient mice. Proc Natl Acad Sci USA 2009;106:1027–32. https://doi.org/10.1073/PNAS.0812347106.

[54] Kimura H, Weisz A, Kurashima Y, Hashimoto K, Ogura T, D'Acquisto F, Addeo R, Makuuchi M, Esumi H. Hypoxia response element of the human vascular endothelial growth factor gene mediates transcriptional regulation by nitric oxide: control of hypoxia-inducible factor-1 activity by nitric oxide. Blood 2000;95:189–97.

[55] Kashiwagi S, Tsukada K, Xu L, Miyazaki J, Kozin SV, Tyrrell JA, et al. Perivascular nitric oxide gradients normalize tumor vasculature. Nat Med 2008;14:255–7. https://doi.org/10.1038/NM1730.

[56] Nathan C. Inducible nitric oxide synthase: what difference does it make? J Clin Invest 1997;100:2417–23. https://doi.org/10.1172/JCI119782.

[57] Scott DJ, Hull MA, Cartwright EJ, Lam WK, Tisbury A, Poulsom R, et al. Lack of inducible nitric oxide synthase promotes intestinal tumorigenesis in the Apc(Min/+) mouse. Gastroenterology 2001;121:889–99. https://doi.org/10.1053/GAST.2001.27994.

[58] Thomsen LL, Miles DW, Happerfield L, Bobrow LG, Knowles RG, Moncada S. Nitric oxide synthase activity in human breast cancer. Br J Cancer 1995;72:41–4. https://doi.org/10.1038/BJC.1995.274.

[59] Bentrari F, Arnould L, Jackson AP, Jeannin J-F, Pance A, Pance A. Progesterone enhances cytokine-stimulated nitric oxide synthase II expression and cell death in human breast cancer cells. Lab Investig 2005;85: 624–32. https://doi.org/10.1038/labinvest.3700267.

[60] Vakkala M, Kahlos K, Lakari E, Pääkkö P, Kinnula V, Soini Y. Inducible nitric oxide synthase expression, apoptosis, and angiogenesis in in situ and invasive breast carcinomas. Clin Cancer Res 2000;6(6):2408–16.

[61] Loibl S, Von Minckwitz G, Weber S, Sinn HP, Schini-Kerth VB, Lobysheva I, et al. Expression of endothelial and inducible nitric oxide synthase in benign and malignant lesions of the breast and measurement of nitric oxide using electron paramagnetic resonance spectroscopy. Cancer 2002;95:1191–8. https://doi.org/10.1002/CNCR.10817.

[62] Reveneau S, Arnould L, Jolimoy G, Hilpert S, Lejeune P, Saint-Giorgio V, Belichard C, Jeannin JF. Nitric oxide synthase in human breast cancer is associated with tumor grade, proliferation rate, and expression of progesterone receptors. Lab Invest 1999;79(10):1215–25.

[63] Ambs S, Merriam WG, Bennett WP, Felley-Bosco E, Ogunfusika MO, Oser SM, Klein S, Shields PG, Billiar TR, Harris CC. Frequent nitric oxide synthase-2 expression in human colon adenomas: implication for tumor angiogenesis and colon cancer progression. Cancer Res 1998;58(2):334–41.

[64] Chhatwal VJS, Ngoi SS, Chan STF, Chia YW, Moochhala SM. Aberrant expression of nitric oxide synthase in human polyps, neoplastic colonic mucosa and surrounding peritumoral normal mucosa. Carcinogenesis 1994;15:2081–5. https://doi.org/10.1093/CARCIN/15.10.2081.

[65] Thomsen LL, Lawton FG, Knowles RG, Beesley JE, Riveros-Moreno V, Moncada S. Nitric oxide synthase activity in human gynecological cancer. Cancer Res 1994;54(5):1352–4.

[66] Xu W, Liu LZ, Loizidou M, Ahmed M, Charles IG. The role of nitric oxide in cancer. Cell Res 2002;12:311–20. https://doi.org/10.1038/sj.cr.7290133.

[67] Cobbs CS, Brenman JE, Aldape KD, Bredt DS, Israel MA. Expression of nitric oxide synthase in human central nervous system tumors. Cancer Res 1995;55:727–30.

[68] Eyler CE, et al. Glioma stem cell proliferation and tumor growth are promoted by nitric oxide synthase-2. Cell 2011;146:53–66. https://doi.org/10.1016/j.cell.2011.06.006.

[69] Kim RK, Suh Y, Cui YH, Hwang E, Lim EJ, Yoo KC, et al. Fractionated radiation-induced nitric oxide promotes expansion of glioma stem-like cells. Cancer Sci 2013;104:1172–7. https://doi.org/10.1111/cas.12207.

[70] Yongsanguanchai N, Pongrakhananon V, Mutirangura A, Rojanasakul Y, Chanvorachote P. Nitric oxide induces cancer stem cell-like phenotypes in human lung cancer cells. Am J Physiol Cell Physiol 2015;308:C89–100. https://doi.org/10.1152/ajpcell.00187.2014.

[71] Maiuthed A, Bhummaphan N, Luanpitpong S, Mutirangura A, Aporntewan C, Meeprasert A, et al. Nitric oxide promotes cancer cell dedifferentiation by disrupting an Oct4:caveolin-1 complex: a new regulatory mechanism for cancer stem cell formation. J Biol Chem 2018;293:13534–52. https://doi.org/10.1074/jbc.RA117.000287.

[72] Zou K, Li Z, Zhang Y, Mu L, Chen M, Wang R, et al. β-Elemene enhances radiosensitivity in non-small-cell lung cancer by inhibiting epithelial–mesenchymal transition and cancer stem cell traits via Prx-1/NF-kB/iNOS signaling pathway. Aging (Albany NY) 2020;13:2575–92. https://doi.org/10.18632/aging.202291.

[73] Puglisi MA, Cenciarelli C, Tesori V, Cappellari M, Martini M, Di Francesco AM, et al. High nitric oxide production, secondary to inducible nitric oxide synthase expression, is essential for regulation of the tumour-initiating properties of colon cancer stem cells. J Pathol 2015;236:479–90. https://doi.org/10.1002/path.4545.

[74] Monji K, Uchiumi T, Hoshizawa S, Yagi M, Matsumoto T, Setoyama D, et al. Serum depletion induced cancer stem cell-like phenotype due to nitric oxide synthesis in oncogenic HRas transformed cells. Oncotarget 2016;7:75221–34. https://doi.org/10.18632/oncotarget.12117.

[75] Peñarando J, López-Sánchez LM, Mena R, Guil-Luna S, Conde F, Hernández V, et al. A role for endothelial nitric oxide synthase in intestinal stem cell proliferation and mesenchymal colorectal cancer. BMC Biol 2018;16:1–14. https://doi.org/10.1186/s12915-017-0472-5.

[76] Wang R, Li Y, Tsung A, Huang H, Du Q, Yang M, et al. INOS promotes CD24+CD133+ liver cancer stem cell phenotype through a TACE/ADAM17-dependent Notch signaling pathway. Proc Natl Acad Sci USA 2018;115:E10127–36. https://doi.org/10.1073/pnas.1722100115.

II. Nitric oxide pathway and cancer progression and therapy

[77] López-Sánchez LM, Mena R, Guil-Luna S, Mantrana A, Peñarando J, Toledano-Fonseca M, et al. Nitric oxide-targeted therapy inhibits stemness and increases the efficacy of tamoxifen in estrogen receptor-positive breast cancer cells. Lab Investig 2021;101:292–303. https://doi.org/10.1038/s41374-020-00507-z.

[78] Gao W, Wang Y, Yu S, Wang Z, Ma T, Chan AML, et al. Endothelial nitric oxide synthase (eNOS)-NO signaling axis functions to promote the growth of prostate cancer stem-like cells. Stem Cell Res Ther 2022;13:1–17. https://doi.org/10.1186/s13287-022-02864-6.

[79] Singh S, Gupta AK. Nitric oxide: role in tumour biology and iNOS/NO-based anticancer therapies. Cancer Chemother Pharmacol 2011;67:1211–24. https://doi.org/10.1007/S00280-011-1654-4.

[80] Aranda E, Lopez-Pedrera C, De La Haba-Rodriguez R, Rodriguez-Ariza A. Nitric oxide and cancer: the emerging role of S-nitrosylation. Curr Mol Med 2011;12:50–67. https://doi.org/10.2174/156652412798376099.

[81] Lehrman S. Virus treatment questioned after gene therapy death. Nature 1999;401:517–8. https://doi.org/10.1038/43977.

[82] Huerta S, Sapna Chilka BB. Nitric oxide donors: novel cancer therapeutics (review). Int J Oncol 2008;33(5):909–27.

[83] Bonavida B, Baritaki S, Huerta-Yepez S, Vega MI, Chatterjee D, Yeung K. Novel therapeutic applications of nitric oxide donors in cancer: roles in chemo- and immunosensitization to apoptosis and inhibition of metastases. Nitric Oxide Biol Chem 2008;19:152–7. https://doi.org/10.1016/J.NIOX.2008.04.018.

[84] Lee DH, Pfeifer GP. Mutagenesis induced by the nitric oxide donor sodium nitroprusside in mouse cells. Mutagenesis 2007;22:63–7. https://doi.org/10.1093/MUTAGE/GEL051.

[85] Rigas B. Novel agents for cancer prevention based on nitric oxide. Biochem Soc Trans 2007;35:1364–8. https://doi.org/10.1042/BST0351364.

[86] Frost MC, Reynolds MM, Meyerhoff ME. Polymers incorporating nitric oxide releasing/generating substances for improved biocompatibility of blood-contacting medical devices. Biomaterials 2005;26:1685–93. https://doi.org/10.1016/J.BIOMATERIALS.2004.06.006.

[87] Seabra AB, Durán, N. Nitric oxide-releasing vehicles for biomedical applications. J Mater Chem 2010;20:1624–1637.

[88] Saraiva J, Marotta-Oliveira SS, Cicillini SA, de Oliveira Eloy J, Marchetti JM. Nanocarriers for nitric oxide delivery. J Drug Deliv 2011;2011:1–16. https://doi.org/10.1155/2011/936438.

[89] Quintanar-Guerrero D, Ganem-Quintanar A, Allémann E, Fessi H, Doelker E. Influence of the stabilizer coating layer on the purification and freeze-drying of poly(D,L-lactic acid) nanoparticles prepared by an emulsion-diffusion technique. J Microencapsul 1998;15:107–19. https://doi.org/10.3109/02652049809006840.

[90] Jain R, Shah NH, Malick AW, Rhodesl CT. Controlled drug delivery by biodegradable poly (ester) devices: different preparative approaches. 1998;24:703–27.

Inducible nitric oxide synthase 2 (NOS2) and antitumor γδ-T cells

Brayden K. Leyva[a] and Benjamin Bonavida[b]

[a]Department of Physiological Sciences, David Geffen School of Medicine, Jonsson Comprehensive Cancer Center, University of California at Los Angeles, Los Angeles, CA, United States
[b]Department of Microbiology, Immunology and Molecular Genetics, David Geffen School of Medicine, Jonsson Comprehensive Cancer Center, University of California at Los Angeles, Los Angeles, CA, United States

Abstract

Several novel immunotherapeutic strategies based on the classical antitumor alpha/beta T (αβ-T) lymphocytes have been developed to treat cancers that are resistant to conventional cytotoxic therapies. Significant clinical responses were achieved in a subset of cancer patients. However, a major subset was unresponsive and in need of a novel approach. Gamma delta T (γδ-T) cells have been considered as these cells have distinct properties from αβ-T cells and can exert their cytotoxic function independent of the MHC complex as well recognizing ligands expressed in the majority of cancers. The antitumor γδ-T cells also mediate their killing effects by both the TCR and NK receptors. The clinical response in vivo by the γδ-T cells has been promising. However, in the TME, γδ-T cells can be modulated and polarized into Th17 cells that are immunosuppressive. This polarization is mediated in large part by the expression of NOS2, which results in the production of IL-17. Consequently, IL-17 attracts PMN/MDSCs, which produce various immunosuppressive factors that inhibit the antitumor CD8 T immune response and T-cell anergy. It is speculated that NOS2/NO inhibitors may reverse the immunosuppression of the γδ-T cells and restore their antitumor activities and the inhibition of tumor growth.

Abbreviations

CAR	chimeric antigen receptor
DNA	deoxyribose nucleic acid
HCC	hepatocellular carcinoma
ICI	immune checkpoint inhibitor
IL	interleukin
mAB	monoclonal antibody
MHC	major histocompatibility complex
NK	natural killer

Nitric Oxide in Health and Disease
https://doi.org/10.1016/B978-0-443-13342-8.00007-7

NOS/iNOS	nitric oxide synthase/inducible nitric oxide synthase
TAA	tumor-associated antigens
TCR	T-cell receptor
Tfh	T follicular helper
TIL	tumor-infiltrating lymphocyte
TLR	toll-like receptor
TME	tumor microenvironment
Γδ/gd	gamma delta

Conflict of interest

No potential conflicts of interest were disclosed.

Introduction

Cancer: General properties

The human body is made up of trillions of cells that divide and multiply through a process known as fission, replacing old cells that die or become damaged. Sometimes, the new cells that are produced are abnormal or already defective and undergo several mutations, which alter their phenotype and properties, leading to the onset of cancer [1]. Cancerous cells acquire invasive and migrating properties and escape and/or become unresponsive to the host antitumor immune response [2]. In addition, cancer cells recruit blood vessels to supply them with oxygen and nutrients, further allowing for alterations within their chromosomes [3]. There are many factors that are involved in the induction of various cancers, including inherited genetics from parents, environmental factors, and virus infections for some cancers (hepatitis, herpes, Epstein-Barr) [4].

Genetic drivers of cancer include the alteration of protooncogenes involved in normal cell division and growth [5] as well as DNA repair genes, which become inflicted with mutations and lead to duplicates and deletions of chromosomes and, thus, the conversion of protooncogenes into oncogenes and the induction of cancer [6]. Genome sequencing technology revealed that tumor cells can contain between 10,000 and 50,000 single-nucleotide variants and that there are over 1000 genes that are linked with cancer, with mutations in the *TP53* gene being the most common [7]. Although cancer is thought to be caused by one's genetic background, new evidence confirms that a small number of cancer cells are capable of tumorigenesis, thus supporting that cancer might actually derive from cancer stem cells as well [8]. Furthermore, the idea of cancer as a metabolic disorder is beginning to take hold as the "Warburg effect" of cancer cells producing a specific phenotypic outcome of increased glucose uptake is being proven with these emerging sequencing technologies [9].

Cancer is the second leading cause of death worldwide and accounts for nearly 1 in every 6 deaths in the United States [10]. There are over 100 different types of cancer categorized by the tissue or organ they are affecting [11]. The stage of cancer, ranging from one to four, also indicates the difficulty of treatment, with stage four suggesting the cancer has metastasized to other parts of the body [12]. Recent advancements in modern medicine have provided a subset of patients diagnosed with cancer a fighting chance of remission with many different therapeutic treatment strategies to choose from depending on the tumor type.

Cancer treatments (surgery, chemotherapy, and radiation)

Cancer treatments are constantly evolving, with research providing new insights into how best to eradicate the body of the aggressive disease as well as how to selectively target certain types of cancer. Common forms of cancer treatment include surgery, chemotherapy, radiation, and immunotherapy.

Surgery

Perhaps the most common and aggressive form of treatment involves the surgical removal of tumors and tumor cells when possible. Surgeons also normally excise additional tissues surrounding the tumor, which may harbor fewer cancer cells or cancer stem cells that can generate tumors after surgery (curative surgery). There are many different types of cancer surgeries depending on the tumor type. Biopsies are taken to determine if a tumor is histologically and morphologically cancerous. Biopsies can be performed either incisional by removing a small portion of the tumor, or excisional by removing the whole cancerous tissue. Staging surgeries remove lymph nodes adjacent to the tumors to help determine the spread of the cancer while debulking only a portion of the tumor as to not damage an organ. Other subsets of surgeries include (a) palliative, using surgery to treat masses that are not responding to medication; (b) supportive, making quality of life a little better and providing easier access to cancer treatment (catheter for medication); and (c) reconstructive to repair damage (breast augmentation); and lastly preventative [13]. Although much success has been found with surgery to treat certain accessible cancers, they are costly and require downtime for recovery.

Chemotherapy

Chemotherapy for the most part utilizes pharmaceuticals to target the cancerous cells and kill them, slowing their growth and division [14]. By systemically targeting cells undergoing mitosis, chemotherapy destroys the internucleon genes, inhibiting the cell from being able to divide. Chemotherapy prevents the cancer from spreading, shrinking the tumor, and, in some cases, completely removing it. It is administered orally, intravenously, or via injection (intrathecal, intraperitoneal, or intraarterial). Through its targeting of *all* cells undergoing fission, however, chemotherapy also stops healthy cells from dividing including hair, bone marrow, and skin, resulting in damage and adverse side effects like hair loss and other body toxic effects. By disrupting the DNA, RNA, or protein syntheses of neoplastic cells or macromolecular syntheses, chemotherapy can initiate apoptosis, which leads to cell death [15]. Antibiotics, antimetabolites, antimicrotubular, and alkylating agents are all examples of chemotherapeutic agents. Alkylating agents attack the DNA by producing an unstable alkyl group, affecting DNA replication and transcription, whereas antimetabolites go directly into the DNA, affecting DNA methyltransferases or DNA polymerases [15]. Antimicrotubular agents impact DNA and RNA syntheses, and antibiotics generate single- and double-strand DNA breaks. Aside from its overall toxicity and side effects, chemotherapy is only effective in certain cancers, and among these cancers, not all patients respond the same. There exists a subset of patients who are inherently resistant to chemotherapy, and there is also a subset of patients who initially respond but become refractory to further treatments. Hence, chemo-resistance is a major drawback of chemotherapy; however, combination treatments have resulted in additional responses [15].

Radiation

Radiation therapy has come a long way since Marie Curie began her research of radium and serves as a low-cost option for treating selective cancers [16]. Radiation is the process of destroying cancer cells via high-dose energy rays called radiation [17]. Low doses of ionizing radiation (forms ions) are present in X-rays; however, at high doses, it impacts the cancerous DNA by killing the cell and helping to shrink the tumor. Radiation therapy is divided into two subsets: external beam radiation therapy, which employs a machine to send radiation to a specific part of one's body, and internal radiation therapy, where radiation is delivered inside of one's body. Internal radiation therapy with a solid source like a capsule is called brachytherapy and disperses the radiation over time, whereas a liquid-sourced internal radiation therapy is known as systemic therapy and sends radiation through the bloodstream to the affected tissues [17]. There are a plethora of radiation therapy delivery techniques, including fractionation delivering radiation in a fractionated regime, intensity-modulated ration therapy (IMRT), which give the oncologist the ability to administer doses in a shape that conforms to the tumor, as well as stereotactic body radiation therapy (SBRT), which targets well-defined tumors via small high doses of radiation [17]. Radiation causes nausea and oral sores, making it difficult to eat and hard to maintain weight and further complicating this treatment plan.

Although effective, these types of cancer treatments are invasive and bring with them devastating side effects. The advancement of targeted biological medicines has allowed a new form of cancer treatment, immunotherapy, to emerge as a promising anticancer treatment.

Cancer immunotherapies

Immunotherapy for cancer has evolved significantly during the last decade, with several new milestones and novel means targeting the cancer cells selectively with significant clinical responses in many cancers [18]. The therapeutic strategies for immunotherapy mainly consist of boosting the immune response in vivo by various means and by the ex vivo development of antitumor immune T or NK cells, or specific monoclonal antitumor antibodies. These ex vivo cells/antibodies are administered to the cancer patients targeting the cancer cells.

T-cell-mediated immunotherapies

T-cell-mediated cancer immunotherapy centers around the activation and increased production of the body's natural anticancer cytotoxic CD8 T cells. Cancer cells contain surface MHC-peptide complexes that the cancer-specific T cells can bind to and destroy. In order to activate these cells, however, antigen peptides must be processed from antigen-presenting cells and displayed with human leukocyte antigen (HLA) molecules for recognition by the TCR of T cells [19]. Additionally, the surface molecules B7 and CD28 must be bound to antigen-presenting cells as well as T cells. If and when these criteria are met, T cells become activated and cancer-specific, helping to kill the cancer cells [20].

T-cell transfer therapy focuses on enhancing these activated T cells to fight against cancer and has proven effective in reducing malignancies from proliferating throughout the body. Several approaches have been made to generate ex vivo antitumor T cells.

Tumor-infiltrating lymphocytes

These are generated by harvesting biopsies from the patient cancer and processing these cells in vitro by the addition of growth factors and their significant expansion by proliferation. These activated cells are then administered to the cancer patient and normally with exogenous low dose of IL-2 to maintain their activities and survival in vivo [21].

Genetically engineered antitumor T cells

In an effort to generate more specific antitumor CD8 T cells, a patient's normal blood T cells are transfected with tumor-specific T-cell receptors (isolated from a responding cancer patient) and grown in culture in large quantities. These tumor-specific T cells are then administered back to the same patient for treatment [22].

CAR T cells

CAR T-cell therapy adds a chimeric antigen receptor (CAR) to make them better able to recognize the cancer. Basically, normal T cells from the patient are transduced with a specific antitumor antibody fragment linked to activating intracellular chains. Once these cells interact with cancer cells via the antibody recognition, they are activated to become cytotoxic and secrete immune cytokines. These CAR T cells, therefore, mediate their recognition independent of the T-cell receptors [23]. The CAR T cells have been approved for use in hematological malignancies only and, thus far, not effective in solid tumors [24].

Despite its seemingly harmless nature, T-cell transfer therapy brings with it its own set of limitations that require it to be further studied before widespread use is adopted. CAR T-cell therapy has been known to cause cytokine release syndrome, which can be life-threatening as large quantities of cytokines are released into the bloodstream. CAR T cells have mistakenly recognized noncancerous cells as toxic ones which leads to organ failure. Tumor-infiltrating lymphocyte (TIL) therapy sometimes causes dangerously low blood pressure due to capillary leak syndrome [25]. Also, a major limitation of TILs and CAR T cells is that they should recognize a specific antigen on the cancer cells. Ideally, one would like universal T cells, which can recognize antigens expressed in the majority of cancers and also can be used across allogeneic patients without the harmful effects of GVH or HVG [26]. A newer focus of T-cell therapy, gamma delta T cells provides a seemingly safe and effective foundation for allogeneic cancer cell therapies as they have shown great promise in the treatment of a variety of cancers sharing the antigens recognized by the cells without harmful side effects.

Immune checkpoint inhibitors

Immune checkpoint inhibitors (ICIs) and immune system modulators both allow for a more robust immune response by blocking the immune system's natural checkpoints and allowing for an increased overall enhancement of immunity [27]. ICIs involve a drug that is administered with the intention of blocking an immune system checkpoint protein's ability to limit immune response. The immunotherapeutic consequence is an enhanced T-cell recruitment that aids in the fight against cancer and other diseases [28]. Although proven to be effective, side effects can include mild symptoms such as fatigue, nausea, and bowel irritation, as well as more severe symptoms like life-threatening immune attacks [25].

Vaccines

Cancer vaccines have become an attractive option for prevention and treatment and are divided into four different types: immune cell-based vaccines, peptide-based vaccines, viral vector-based vaccines, and nucleic acid-based vaccines [29]. DNA and RNA vaccines are becoming increasingly popular due to their easy manufacturing ability, successful antigen processing, and induction of CD4+ and CD8+ T cells [30]. Cancer vaccines target three types of antigens that are expressed by tumor cells. Overexpressed antigens include proteins that demonstrate increased expression levels in mRNA, DNA, or protein within the tumor cells. Cancer testis antigens are ignored by the immune system due to their location within the body and are recognized in most tumor types. Finally, oncofetal antigens involve fetal antigens that, during development, are turned off; however, due to cancer, they are turned back on [31]. Specific examples of cancer vaccines include the use of granulocyte-macrophage colony-stimulating factor-engineered tumor cells to improve immunogenicity [31].

Cytokines: IL-2

Interleukin-2 (IL-2) is a cytokine primarily produced by CD4+ T cells; however, it can also be produced by natural killer (NK) cells and is responsible for the growth and differentiation of B-, T-, and NK cell types [32]. Thus, IL-2 also plays a direct role in the activation of T cells, making it an interesting target for cancer immunotherapy. In fact, when complexing IL-2 with anti-IL-2 mAbs, IL-2 can potentiate signaling via the intermediate affinity CD122/CD132 receptor and has been proven to cause CD8+ T-cell division and proliferation in vivo [32]. In fact, upon its discovery and use in clinical trials of patients with metastatic renal cancer, administration of high doses of IL-2 demonstrated tumor regression monotherapeutically. Further research is being devoted to increased IL-2 efficacy, especially in combination with other cytokines like HD, as well as T and NK cells [33]. Other uses of IL-2 include combining it with chemotherapeutic agents, peptide vaccines, and immune checkpoint inhibitors [34].

Monoclonal antibodies

To help the immune system recognize cancer cells, antitumor antibodies are generated in vivo in several cancer patients. These polyclonal antibodies participate in the elimination of cancer cells [35]. Accordingly, antitumor monoclonal antibodies that recognize a tumor-specific antigen have been produced ex vivo and used to treat many cancers. Today, there exists a large number of FDA-approved antitumor mAbs (over 60) [36]. Monoclonal antibodies are B-cell-secreted glycoproteins made up of two heavy and two light chains that are grouped into different isotypes dependent on these heavy chains [37]. This new form of cancer treatment is becoming as common as chemotherapy, radiation, and surgery and helps the body to flag cancer cells, block cell growth by preventing recruitment of blood vessels, trigger cell membrane destruction, and directly attack the cancer cell by the use of antibody-drug/radiation conjugates [36]. Monoclonal antibodies can be conjugated to chemotherapeutic drugs and target cancer cell destruction with a higher potency than antibodies alone while reducing drug toxicity [38]. Additionally, they can be radiolabeled to target cancer cell destruction by radiation.

Gamma delta T (γδ-T) cells

General properties

γδ-T cells have emerged as a key immunotherapeutic tool in the treatment and prevention of cancer due to their unique ability to identify the majority of malignant tumor cells and produce a cytotoxic immune response [39]. They interact with other cells to secrete cytokines, chemokines, and growth factors; provide support for helper B cells; trigger dendritic cell maturation; induce antitumor cytotoxic αβ CD8 T cells; and recruit macrophages [40]. They have also been discovered to display cytolytic activity and efficiency in αβ-T-cell processing [40]. Perhaps the reason γδ-T cells are such an attractive objective for adoptive cell immunotherapy, however, revolves around their nonspecific biology and independence of the MHC-peptide complex. Although γδ-T cells make up only 5% of T lymphocytes, their broad antigen specificity and unique ability to migrate to peripheral tissues play a critical role in antitumor immunosurveillance and cytotoxic cytokine secretion. γδ-T cells contribute to approximately 5% of the total CD3+ cells; however, unlike their αβ-T cell counterpart, which comprises the other 95%, they do not express CD4 or CD8 lineage markers, allowing for an MHC molecule independence and the ability to evade the immune system when transplanted into an allogeneic host [41]. This provides γδ-T cells the unique ability to recognize a variety of malignancies without being confined to a single antigen receptor. γδ-T cells also express functional NK receptors of innate immune cells, which directly trigger cytotoxic activity such as the activating NK receptors NKG2D, NKp30, and NKp44. With their ability to differentiate into Th1, Th2, Th9, and Th17, they produce cytokines such as IFN-γ, IL-4, IL-10, and IL-17. They also have toll-like receptors and costimulatory molecules, which aid in their robust anticancer immunity and trigger a pro-inflammatory cascade [42]. The difficulty that lies in the expansion of their diverse clones, their simultaneous promotion of γδ-T-cell suppressive function, and the 21% average response rate, which are among the factors that limit their immunotherapeutic benefits [43]. Current research is focused on expanding their therapeutic efficacy, and with their direct activation via phosphoantigens, their enrichment as a clinically scalable tool is very feasible.

Subsets and phenotypes and ligands

Human γδ-T cells are divided into two major distinguished subsets: Vδ1 and Vδ2, dependent on their surface antigen and γδ heterodimeric T-cell receptor (TCRγδ). Overall, 50%–95% of the γδ-T cells in human blood express the Vδ2 chain coexpressed with the Vγ9 chain [44]. Upon activation, Vγ9γδ2 T cells act as a source of pro-inflammatory cytokines like IFN-γ and TNF-α and recognize nonpeptidic phosphoantigens. Additionally, Vγ9γδ2 T cells inhibit T-cell proliferation, are resilient to programmed cell death 1 (PD-1), and express TGF-β, IL-4, and IL-10. Their development primarily takes place in humans in the fetal thymus from around 8–15 weeks old and are exclusively activated by phosphoantigens, which solely bind to the specific proteins, rather than TCR recognition [45]. Known phosphorylated antigen receptor recognition markers for Vγ9γδ2 T-cell activation include F1_ATPase expressed by tumor cells and butyrophilin 3A1. Toll-like receptors (TLRs) and natural killer receptors (NKRs) costimulate Vγ9γδ2 T cells with TCRs via a pathogen-associated molecular pattern cascade that involves Vγ9γδ2 T-cell activation of TLRs, triggering cytokine and chemokine production [45].

Making up the majority of tissue-associated γδ-T cells (gut epithelia, dermis, spleen, and liver), Vδ1+ T cells protect epithelial tissue against tissue degradation or infection and their TCR gene rearrangement occurs 4–6 months after birth [45]. This subset of γδ-T cells display potent antitumor ability and defend against epithelial cancers secreting IL-17 and transforming growth factor-β (TGF-β) [46]. Their antiviral immunity is highlighted with the inversion of the normal γδ2/γδ1 ratio with an increase of γδ1 in HIV-infected patients. Although their ligand recognition is still uncharacterized, CD1 family proteins like CD1c and CD1d are recognized. Additionally, γδ1-T-cell activation recognizes B7-H6, an NKp30-secreted B7 family member expressed on tumor cells [45]. The Vδ1 chain can interact with various γ chains, allowing for a wide range of possible γδ-T cells; however, the Vδ2 chain is only able to interact and combine with the Vγ9. There is a third extremely small γδ-T-cell subset, Vδ3, that exists mostly in the blood, liver, and gut and makes up for only 0.2% of circulating T cells. Vδ3 that are expressed with Vγ2 or Vγ3 cells not only respond to CD1d but also express the degranulation marker CD107a (Table 1).

Functional activities and mechanisms of activation

The γδ-T-cell histocompatibility complex (MHC) independence allows them to use TCRγδ and natural killer cell receptors (NKRs) like NKG2D to trigger cytotoxic activity and toll-like receptors (TLRs), initiating a pro-inflammatory cascade. They use these receptors to detect tumor-associated antigens (TAAs), including nonpeptidic prenyl-pyrophosphate antigens (PAg) and stress proteins [47]. With the ability to positively impact a multitude of solid and hematopoietic malignancies, γδ-T cells have become a very promising target for cancer immunotherapy.

TABLE 1 Subsets of gamma delta T cells.

Gamma delta T cells			
Subset/ chain		**Ligand**	**Tissue distribution**	**Expression/recognition**
Vγ1	Vγ9	Uncharacterized	Skin, small intestine, liver, spleen	IL-17, TGF-β, IFN-γ, TNFα, perforin, granzyme, TRAIL, FASL CD1c, CD1d, B7-H6
Vγ2	Vγ2 Vγ3 Vγ4 Vγ5 Vγ8 Vγ10	Pyrsophosphate molecules Bromohydrin pyrophosphate (BrHPP) Isopentyl pyrophosphate (IPP)	Peripheral blood	TGF-β, IL-4, IL-10, IFN-γ, TNFα, perforin, granzyme, TRAIL, FASL F1_ATPase, butyrophilin 3A1, TLR, NKR
Vγ3	N/A	Uncharacterized	Peripheral blood, liver, small intestine	Degranulation marker CD107a CD1c, CD1d

γδ-T cells interact with our immune cells and activate the release of cytokines like IL-2, 4, and 10 to provide helper signals, which activate B cells to differentiate and produce antibody-secreting plasma cells via various pathways, including the CD40/CD40 ligand, inducible T-cell costimulatory (ICOS) ligand, and CD86/CD28 ligand [41]. Other γδ-T cell interactions can result in the release of, via the receptor-mediated signal transduction pathways, ligand acting glycoproteins. These include (a) wnt molecules which help to promote CD4+ T-cells into T follicular helper (Tfh) cells, (b) CX3CL13 to localize B cells into the germinal center, and (c) presenting antigens to B cells or activating other antigens to develop Tfhs [48]. It has also been shown that Vδ3+ T cells help upregulate CD40-, CD86-, and HLA-DR-producing IgM B cells.

This process however is reciprocal and B cells can also influence the activation of γδ-T cells. More specifically, Vδ1+ T cells can become activated by the expression of B-cell markers B7 and CD39 appearing more TCR ligand-dependent [48]. B cells interact with γδ-T cells via butrophilins (BTNs), which are members of the B7 family, including B7.1 (CD80) and B7.2 (CD86), by helping to select γδ-T cells like Skint1 for tissue epithelium immune homeostasis [49]. BTNs also behave as direct ligands of human γδ TCRs (Vγ9$^+$Vδ2$^+$ T cells and Vγ4$^+$ T cells) [50].

INOS/NOS2 expression

General properties of INOS

Inducible nitric oxide synthase (iNOS or NOS2) is an enzyme that helps the body destroy pathogens and produces one of the 10 smallest natural molecules, the free radical nitric oxide (NO), from L-arginine [51]. NO serves an important role in cellular signaling as it holds implications in several physiologic functions, such as immunity, neurotransmission, and vasodilation [51]. An abundance or disruption of NO, therefore, results in disruption of said systems and has been linked to neurodegeneration and cancer [52]. iNOS differs from the other isoforms of nitric oxide in that it is only expressed when activated, most commonly by pro-inflammatory cytokines [51]. iNOS has also been known to be activated by bacteria Lipopolysaccharide (LPS) [51]. iNOS serves as an important therapeutic target and has generated scientific interest due to the potentially helpful or harmful effects of NO overproduction. High volumes of NO could result in a higher immune response, and therefore, a more robust immunity; however, it can also pose toxic conditions to the host [53]. Nitric oxide synthase exists in three isoforms, two of which neuronal NO synthase (nNOS) and endothelial NO synthase (eNOS) are calcium-dependent, and their production of NO is minimal lasting no more than a few minutes. The third isoform, inducible NO synthase (iNOS), is calcium-independent and can generate NO lasting for hours or even days [51] (See Fig. 1).

Structure

iNOS is made up of over 1153 amino acids, forming a C-terminal reductase subdomain and a N-terminal oxygenase that creates a homodimeric quaternary structure, giving it the ability to convert L-arginine to L-citrulline [51]. This process is calmodulin-mediated as binding between the reductase and oxygenase with the help of the electron transport chain, and other cofactors

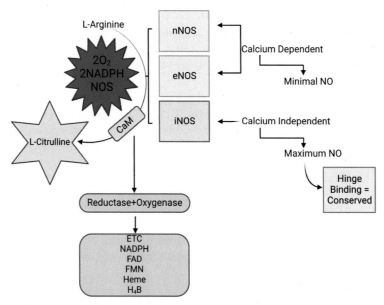

FIG. 1   Nitric oxide synthase (NOS) exists in three forms. L-Arginine is converted to L-citrulline via the use of 2 oxygen molecules and 2 NADPH molecules. iNOS is calcium-independent and produces maximal nitric oxide, which lasts for hours due to its well-conserved hinge binding. NOS is CaM-mediated; the reaction between reductase and oxygenase utilizes ETC, NADPH, FAD, FMN, heme, and H_4B. Neuronal nitric oxide synthase and endothelial nitric oxide synthase are calcium-dependent, and the production of nitric oxide dissipates in minutes.

including nicotinamide adenine dinucleotide phosphate (NADPH), flavin adenine dinucleotide (FAD), flavin mononucleotide (FMN), heme, and $(6R)$-5,6,7,8-tetrahydrobiopterin (H_4B) occur [54]. This hinge binding in iNOS is well conserved and, therefore, allows for reactions to occur without the need for high levels of calcium. Additionally, amino acids play a critical role in the enzymes' activity as further analysis has identified Glu546-mutated asparagine to lower the electron transfer between the hem in the oxygenase and the FMN. As a result, interdomain binding affinity was decreased and so was the rate constant [55]. The H4B cofactor-binding resulting in dimerization and proper function is directly linked with Arg375 (which also mediates H4B redox modulation), TRP455, TRP457, and Phe470 [56]. Through the mutation of Ser562 and Cys563, calmodulin binding is destabilized [57].

Biological role in cancer

As mentioned, iNOS helps the body destroy invaders, mostly harmful bacteria and pathogens by producing NO and increasing inflammation as an immune response [58]. Overexpression of iNOS has been positively linked with anticancer effects as an increase in NO has been found to consequently cause an enhanced sensitivity to radiation therapy [59]. Additionally, increased iNOS production coupled with other cytokines like INF-y has slowed tumor growth and progression and given rise to the idea that iNOS could be an anticancer therapeutic [55]. On the contrary, however, iNOS production and overexpression have also been linked with tumors and their progression to metastasis [60].

The role of iNOS in cancer and other diseases is, as mentioned, one of controversy. In some cancers, iNOS serves as a detriment, almost fueling the cancer cells to become more potent and untreatable, whereas in other types, iNOS serves as a "putative biomarker of immune response," even serving as a protective measure against some malignancies [61]. It was found that several factors determine if the iNOS would result in suppression or progression including the tumor microenvironment (TME), timing, concentration, cancer cell type, and the genetic background [62]. Prostate cancer cells and colon cancer have been shown to demonstrate a higher sensitivity to radiation therapy due to an upregulation of iNOS [63]. On the contrary, iNOS also negatively impacts the ability of M1 macrophages to differentiate, causing a reduced function and an increase in inflammatory diseases and cytokines [64]. These stromal host cells are constantly in contact with the tumor cells, and therefore, their relationship is also important in determining how iNOS contributes to that tumors demise or success.

General regulation

The regulation of expressed iNOS has several regulatory factors, including the availability of substrate and cofactors, protein interaction, and auto-inactivation [51].

Substrate and cofactor availability

iNOS and the urea cycle compete for the same substrate as L-arginine helps remove ammonia by converting arginine to ornithine and urea during the urea cycle [51]. L-Arg's availability largely depends on its amino acid transporters CAT1, CAT2, and CAT3 [65]. iNOS inductive conditions aid in arginine transporter expression and, thus, arginine uptake as evidenced by increased iNOS production and increased CATs, and reduced iNOS production and reduced CATs [51]. L-citrulline, which converts iNOS into L-Arg, also impacts the enzyme as it can be converted back to arginine via arginosuccinate synthase. This process of arginine reversal is vital as it provides the necessary arginine for iNOS-mediated homeostasis [51]. H4B, as a cofactor, aids in iNOS dimerization, and therefore, its availability is essential as cells producing little H4B also produce low levels of iNOS [56].

Protein-protein interactions

Protein-protein interactions are known mediators of iNOS production and regulation. Notably, within the central nervous system (CNS), the relationship between iNOS and the cytosolic protein Kalirin, low levels of which has been linked with increased iNOS production in Alzheimer patients' hippocampi, has been observed [51]. Briefly, studies involving LPS-treated mice demonstrated Kalirin interacts only with iNOS monomers and not its dimers, but in Kalirin-expressing cells, iNOS exists as a heterodimer with minimal monomeric iNOS, giving rise to the idea that Kalirin regulates iNOS via reduced homodimerization [51]. Additionally, iNOS interacts with Rho GTPase Rac 2 in neutrophils, playing a role in antimicrobial defense [51].

Auto-inactivation

The addition of the NO scavenger hemoglobin increases iNOS production, while adding NO donors S-nitrosoacetylpenicillamine, or S-nitroso glutathione, decreases its production, indicating an auto-inactivation domain [51]. Furthermore, irreversible binding of NO to iNOS is demonstrated as iNOS activity cannot be returned in cells that have been activated after NO removal.

iNOS impacts

The autocrine and paracrine capabilities of NO and its implications in immunoregulation such as B-cell survival and alpha beta T-cell differentiation makes it a target for γδ-T-cell function and efficiency, especially in the context of cancer biology. Inducible nitric oxide synthase (iNOS) can be found in many cell types, including tumor cells, and is necessary for the survival of antibody-secreting plasma cells, where γδ-T cells are responsible for promoting [66]. Although little is known regarding the direct relationship between γδ-T cells and iNOS production/expression, we can infer the importance of such factors that suggest interplay occurrence. For example, it was reported that in mice, when an injury like a burn occurred, iNOS expression would increase 18-fold as well as other pro-inflammatory cytokines such as TNF-α, Il-1β, G-CSF, and Il-6; however, in mice with δ $TCR^{-/-}$, that expression was significantly reduced [67]. This finding suggests that the γδ TCR lineage allows for the upregulation of iNOS perhaps by the upregulation of cytokines responsible for the iNOS in the first place. Herein lies the controversy regarding whether iNOS is a necessary part of the immune response, or detrimental: whether the cytokines TNF-α and IFN-y, which are extremely potent and antitumor, are more helpful or just help stimulate the overproduction of iNOS. Additionally, based on the impacts iNOS has on αβ-T cells, one can infer the effect it would have on γδ-T cells.

T cells expressing either an αβ TCR or γδ TCR are different from T cells expressing the 2 antigen-binding subunits TCR-α/TCR-β, or TCR-γ/TCR-δ heterodimers [68]. During development, the four different chains are divided into two subunits, a constant C and a variable V. The V regions are very similar, being formed from somatic recombination of RAG1/2 recombinase gene segments. This region composes the membrane-distal immunoglobulin-like domain with the antigen-binding site. The C regions, however, differ greatly and are made up of the membrane-proximal immunoglobulin-like domain, the connecting peptide, the transmembrane region, and the cytoplasmic tail (CT) [68]. The C region differences that are at fault for biochemical contrasts include a longer distance in the disulfide bond in the CT of the γδ TCR, a conserved FG loop in the C region of the TCR-β in comparison to the TCR-γ (which is thought to play a part in αβ TCR-induced signaling), as well as shape and charge distribution differences on their surfaces [69]. Regulation of iNOS expression is done at the transcriptional level by cytokines (IFN-γ, IL-1β, and TNF-α), bacterial endotoxins, and oxidative stress/hypoxia [69].

NOS2 and γδ-T cells

In the report by Douguet et al. [66], they showed that NOS2 was involved in γδ-T cells and its protumorigenic activities. NOS2 mediated the production of IL-17, which resulted in the recruitment of PMN-MDSCs and subsequently in metastasis formation. They demonstrated in melanoma mouse models that the infiltration of γδ-T cells produced NOS2 to attract the PMN-MDSC immunosuppressive cells in the TME. In another report by Douguet et al. [70], they have reported that γδ-T cells express NOS2 and have a reduced ability to produce IL-2. To underline the mechanism of the NOS2-mediated effect on γδ-T cells, they demonstrated that NOS2 inactivation reduced cell proliferation and glycolysis metabolism, both of which can be restored by the addition of IL-2. The induction of NOS2 in γδ-T cells is via triggering the TCR activation. Endogenous NOS2 enhanced glycolysis of γδ-T cells, which is important for their efficient proliferation. Overall, the metabolic regulations of immune cells are closely linked to their functions, and changes in metabolism have been shown to enhance or suppress T-cell functions and fate [71].

MDSCs play an important immunosuppressive role in the TME. They produce various immunosuppressive mediators, such as arginase 1 (ARG1), indoleamine 2,3 dioxygenase (IDO), and NOS2, all of which induce T-cell anergy [72]. MDSCs inhibit IFN-γ production by activated γδ-T cells and suppress their cytotoxic function [73].

In a subsequent report by Douguet et al. [74], they examined the molecular mechanism underlying the expression of NOS2 in tumor-induced γδ-T cells. Using a spontaneous model of murine metastatic melanoma, they have found that IL-1β and IL-6 were responsible for the induction of NOS2 in γδ-T cells. Previous reports have demonstrated that IL-1β and IL-6 induced NOS2 expression in immune cells including macrophages, plasma cells, and Th-17 cells [75–78]. Nitric oxide is required for the induction and stability of human Th-17 responses [75]. Hence, chronic inflammation in the TME is a hallmark of cancer that promotes tumorigenesis and metastasis [79,80]. Supporting these findings, Faye et al. [81] reviewed the interplay between the innate and adaptive immune systems by γδ-T cells. The γδ-T cells modulate inflammation and are sensitive to the levels of cytokines in the milieu caused by chronic inflammation. Importantly, while the cytokines produced by γδ-T cells are necessary for the health of the tissues and cells, in high levels, these cytokines can cause chronic inflammation.

It has been reported that the metabolism of L-arginine is involved in the regulation of immune responses and tumor progression. Multiple enzyme isoforms metabolize arginine [82]. NOS-mediated arginine metabolism yields NO, which also has immunomodulatory activities. Corsale et al. [83] have reviewed the metabolic changes that take place in the TME and affect the properties of γδ-T cells. Hence, lipids, amino acids, hypoxia, prostaglandins, and several other metabolic changes occurring in the TME reduce the efficacy of γδ-T cells and polarize these cells toward IL-17-producing cells and that play a protumor role. Targeting some of these metabolites may enhance the immunotherapeutic effectiveness of the γδ-T cells.

Gocher et al. [84] have reviewed the role of IFN-γ in gamma delta T cells. These cells produce IFNg upon activation. In the TME, the duration and the extent of IFNg signaling are dependent on the tumor burden and the immune cell infiltrates, respectively. At the onset, the exposure to IFN-γ recruits cells equipped for antigen presentation, T-cell priming, and activation, leading to tumor cell killing. However, prolonged exposure to IFN-γ will revert these features and promote protumorigenic effects mediated by immunosuppression and angiogenesis in which INOS2 participates, and resulting in tumor cell proliferation [85].

II. Nitric oxide pathway and cancer progression and therapy

γδ-T cells in cancer immunotherapy

Several recent reports have described the therapeutic role of gamma delta γδ-T cells in cancer. In the following text, several examples are briefly described on the immunotherapeutic application of γδ-T cells in the treatment of various cancers. As discussed before, γδ-T cells have several unique properties in comparison with the αβ-T cells, like having no MHC restrictions, recognizing syngeneic and allogeneic tumors sharing ligands, and their ability to act as antigen-presenting cells. Jhita and Raikar [86] reviewed the application of γδ-T cells in the immunotherapy of hematologic malignancies. Interestingly, γδ-T cells, in comparison with αβ-T cells, are superior antileukemic effector cells without causing GVH reactions [87]. Several clinical studies are now investigating the adoptive transfer of allogeneic donor-derived γδ-T cells in the posttransplant setting. Hematologic malignancies are more suited for targeted cellular therapies. Most current cellular therapies utilize autologous patient-derived αβ-T cells that are expanded ex vivo and adoptively transferred to the cancer patient, though with a failure in most patients. Hence, efforts are focused on the "off-the-shelf" allogeneic cellular therapies using healthy donors as the source of the effector cells [88,89]. Clinical trials evaluating the use of γδ-T cells in hematologic malignancies were distinguished in their preparations, namely, in vivo stimulation of autologous γδ-T cells, adoptive transfer of ex vivo-expanded autologous cells, and adoptive transfer of ex vivo expanded allogeneic cells. Jita and Raikar [86] have reviewed these clinical studies. γδ-T cells are also ideal to develop allogeneic CAR T-cell therapies [90,91]. Lee et al. [92] have reviewed the role of γδ-T-cell subsets in cancer immunotherapy (Fig. 2).

Macek [93] have reported the potential use of γδ-T cells in the treatment of hepatocellular carcinoma (HCC). It was recently reported that the intrinsic γδ-T cells in HCC patients had undergone several phenotypic and molecular changes compared to normal cells [94]. There was also a shift in the Vδ1 to Vδ2 T-cell subpopulation in HCC liver tissue. Thus, the authors suggested that the adoptive transfer of allogeneic Vδ2+ γδ-T cells that had been expanded from the peripheral blood mononuclear cells of healthy donors could complement the in vivo loss observed in the intertumoral γδ-T cells as a new therapeutic strategy for HCC patients.

Ko et al. [95] have reported the potential use of adoptively transferred ex vivo-expanded γδ-T cells in the treatment of patients with osteosarcoma. The expanded γδ-T cells exhibited potent in vitro cytotoxicity against OS in a ratio- and time-dependent manner. Also, the combination with chemotherapy enhanced the in vitro cytotoxicity against OS cells. The authors suggested that γδ-T cells in combination with chemotherapy is a novel strategy for the treatment of patients with OS.

The current use of autologous CAR T cells against hematologic malignancies expressing CD19 have led to significant clinical responses and high remission rates [96,97]. However, several patients do not respond to CAR T cells, and many experience relapses [98,99]. A potential solution for these limitations is the use of donor-derived γδ-T cells as a CAR backbone [91]. These investigators validated their hypothesis in in vitro and in vivo animal models. They demonstrated that expanded γδ CAR T cells targeting CD19 were effective against CD19 tumor cell lines and on CD19—clones which were CAR-independent. They also suggest that γδ CAR T cells may also be used in the allogeneic setting and target

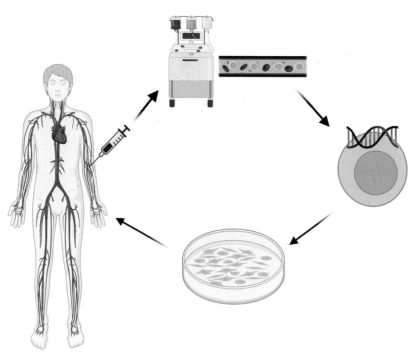

FIG. 2 CAR T-cell therapy. Removal of blood and isolation of T cells, which are then transduced with a specific antitumor antibody fragment in vitro (chimeric antigen receptor). Once activated to be cytotoxic, they are infused back into the patient.

antigen-negative clones. Wawrzyniecka et al. [100] demonstrated that the engineered γδ CAR T cells can kill malignant γδ T tumor cell malignancies in which there are no available effective therapies. Like CAR T cells, γδ TILs can also be generated and administered to cancer patients (Fig. 3).

In a recent clinical study in patients with late-stage lung or liver cancer, Xue et al. [101] have reported both the safety and efficacy of allogeneic Vγ9Vδ2 T-cell immunotherapy. Among the 132 cancer patients, only 8 liver and 10 lung patients received >−5 cell infusions, and among those, prolongation of survival was in seven out of 8 liver cancer and 8 out of 10 lung cancer patients, all of whom were late-stage cancer patients. Further validations are needed in future clinical studies. Importantly, these studies emphasized the therapeutic role of allogenic γδ-T cells in solid cancers.

Perspectives

We are currently witnessing new milestones in the treatment of various cancers, resistant to conventional therapies, with the advent of various novel targeted immunotherapeutics that have resulted in significant clinical responses and prolongation of survivals. These immunotherapeutics primarily consisted of both the development of numerous specific

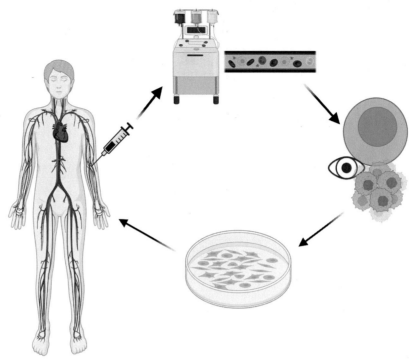

FIG. 3 Tumor-infiltrating lymphocytes. Collecting biopsies of cancer patients to culture tumor-infiltrating lympho-cytes. In vitro processing involves the addition of growth factors to expand these cells to be more effective in their anticancer capabilities. These activated cells, once proliferated, are then administered to the cancer patient (normally with exogenous low dose of IL-2 to maintain their activities and survival).

and FDA-approved antitumor monoclonal antibodies and various T-cell-mediated antitumor responses. While these immune therapies have been successful in many cancer types, however, various cancers were not responding as a result of the inherent resistance of the cancer cells and/or the unresponsiveness of initially responding cells. One mechanism of unresponsiveness to T-cell-mediated immunotherapy was the induction of anergy of the antitumor αβ-T cells in the TME.

Hence, the advantages of using γδ-T antitumor T cells in comparison with the αβ-T cells was envisaged and validated in both preclinical and clinical findings. Also, it was observed, under certain conditions, in the TME that the infiltrating γδ-T cells were polarized into Th17 cells and secrete IL-17, which recruits immunosuppressive PMN/MDSCs and inhibit both the antitumor γδ-T and αβ-T cells. The activation of the γδ-T cells by the tumor cells induces the expression of NOS2, which is responsible for the production of the immunosuppressive IL-17. Therefore, a potential strategy to inhibit the polarization of γδ-T cells into Th-17cells is possible via the inhibition of NOS2/NO by various inhibitors. Several reviews have summarized the various NOS2/NO inhibitors in various cancer models [51,102–107]. While such inhibitors are not specific since NOS2/NO plays important roles in the physiology of both normal and cancer tissues, it will be possible to monitor the doses, schedules of administration, and their use, alone or in combination with other therapies, in experimental preclinical models prior to their clinical applications.

Acknowledgments

We acknowledge the assistance provided by the Department of Microbiology, Immunology & Molecular Genetics and the David Geffen School of Medicine at UCLA.

References

[1] Sarkar S, Horn G, Moulton K, Oza A, Byler S, Kokolus S, Longacre M. Cancer development, progression, and therapy: an epigenetic overview. Int J Mol Sci 2013;14(10):21087–113. https://doi.org/10.3390/ijms141021087.

[2] Wang JH. Why the outcome of anti-tumor immune responses is heterogeneous: a novel idea in the context of immunological heterogeneity in cancers. Bioessays 2020;42(10):e2000024. https://doi.org/10.1002/bies.202000024.

[3] Hausman DM. What is cancer? Perspect Biol Med 2019;62(4):778–84. https://doi.org/10.1353/pbm.2019.0046.

[4] Liao W, Lin JX, Leonard WJ. Interleukin-2 at the crossroads of effector responses, tolerance, and immunotherapy. Immunity 2013;38(1):13–25. https://doi.org/10.1016/j.immuni.2013.01.004.

[5] Hnisz D, Weintraub AS, Day DS, Valton AL, Bak RO, Li CH, Goldmann J, Lajoie BR, Fan ZP, Sigova AA, Reddy J, Borges-Rivera D, Lee TI, Jaenisch R, Porteus MH, Dekker J, Young RA. Activation of proto-oncogenes by disruption of chromosome neighborhoods. Science 2016;351(6280):1454–8. https://doi.org/10.1126/science.aad9024.

[6] Chen M, Chen X, Li S, Pan X, Gong Y, Zheng J, Xu J, Zhao C, Zhang Q, Zhang S, Qi L, Wang Z, Shi K, Ding BS, Xue Z, Chen L, Yang S, Wang Y, Niu T, Dai L, Lowe SW, Chen C, Liu Y. An epigenetic mechanism underlying chromosome 17p deletion-driven tumorigenesis. Cancer Discov 2021;11(1):194–207. https://doi.org/10.1158/2159-8290.CD-20-0336.

[7] Lee W, Jiang Z, Liu J, Haverty PM, Guan Y, Stinson J, Yue P, Zhang Y, Pant KP, Bhatt D, Ha C, Johnson S, Kennemer MI, Mohan S, Nazarenko I, Watanabe C, Sparks AB, Shames DS, Gentleman R, de Sauvage FJ, Stern H, Pandita A, Ballinger DG, Drmanac R, Modrusan Z, Seshagiri S, Zhang Z. The mutation spectrum revealed by paired genome sequences from a lung cancer patient. Nature 2010;465(7297):473–7. https://doi.org/10.1038/nature09004.

[8] Yin W, Wang J, Jiang L, James KY. Cancer and stem cells. Exp Biol Med (Maywood) 2021;246(16):1791–801. https://doi.org/10.1177/15353702211005390.

[9] Li C, Zhang G, Zhao L, et al. Metabolic reprograming in cancer cells: glycolysis, glutaminolysis, and Bcl-2 proteins as novel therapeutic targets for cancer. World J Surg Oncol 2015;14:15. https://doi.org/10.1186/s12957-016-0769-9.

[10] Bray F, Laversanne M, Weiderpass E, Soerjomataram I. The ever-increasing importance of cancer as a leading cause of premature death worldwide. Cancer 2021;127(16):3029–30. https://doi.org/10.1002/cncr.33587.

[11] Chalmers ZR, Connelly CF, Fabrizio D, Gay L, Ali SM, Ennis R, Schrock A, Campbell B, Shlien A, Chmielecki J, Huang F, He Y, Sun J, Tabori U, Kennedy M, Lieber DS, Roels S, White J, Otto GA, Ross JS, Garraway L, Miller VA, Stephens PJ, Frampton GM. Analysis of 100,000 human cancer genomes reveals the landscape of tumor mutational burden. Genome Med 2017;9(1):34. https://doi.org/10.1186/s13073-017-0424-2.

[12] Mupparapu M, Shanti RM. Evaluation and staging of oral cancer. Dent Clin N Am 2018;62(1):47–58. https://doi.org/10.1016/j.cden.2017.08.003.

[13] Hübner N, Shariat SF. Palliative Chirurgie beim metastasierten Urothelkarzinom. Palliative surgery for metastatic urothelial cancer. Aktuelle Urol 2018;49(5):412–6. German https://doi.org/10.1055/a-0659-9827.

[14] Fujita S, Kotake K. Chemotherapy. Nihon Rinsho 2014;72(1):102–7. Japanese 24597356.

[15] Amjad MT, Chidharla A, Kasi A. Cancer chemotherapy. In: StatPearls. Treasure Island, FL: StatPearls Publishing; 2022 March 3. [Internet]. 2022.

[16] Fellag AC. Marie Curie, the international radium standard and the BIPM. Appl Radiat Isot 2021;168:109528. https://doi.org/10.1016/j.apradiso.2020.109528.

II. Nitric oxide pathway and cancer progression and therapy

[17] Baskar R, Lee KA, Yeo R, Yeoh KW. Cancer and radiation therapy: current advances and future directions. Int J Med Sci 2012;9(3):193–9. https://doi.org/10.7150/ijms.3635.

[18] Riley RS, June CH, Langer R, Mitchell MJ. Delivery technologies for cancer immunotherapy. Nat Rev Drug Discov 2019;18(3):175–96. https://doi.org/10.1038/s41573-018-0006-z.

[19] Palucka K, Banchereau J. Cancer immunotherapy via dendritic cells. Nat Rev Cancer 2012;12(4):265–77. https://doi.org/10.1038/nrc3258.

[20] Wang M, Yin B, Wang HY, Wang RF. Current advances in T-cell-based cancer immunotherapy. Immunotherapy 2015;6(12):1265–78. https://doi.org/10.2217/imt.14.86.

[21] Paijens ST, Vledder A, de Bruyn M, Nijman HW. Tumor-infiltrating lymphocytes in the immunotherapy era. Cell Mol Immunol 2021;18(4):842–59. https://doi.org/10.1038/s41423-020-00565-9.

[22] Xie G, Dong H, Liang Y, Ham JD, Rizwan R, Chen J. CAR-NK cells: a promising cellular immunotherapy for cancer. EBioMedicine 2020;59:102975. https://doi.org/10.1016/j.ebiom.2020.102975.

[23] Hong M, Clubb JD, Chen YY. Engineering CAR-T cells for next-generation cancer therapy. Cancer Cell 2020;38(4):473–88. https://doi.org/10.1016/j.ccell.2020.07.005.

[24] Depil S, Duchateau P, Grupp SA, Mufti G, Poirot L. 'Off-the-shelf' allogeneic CAR T cells: development and challenges. Nat Rev Drug Discov 2020;19(3):185–99. https://doi.org/10.1038/s41573-019-0051-2.

[25] Immunotherapy for Cancer—NCI. Immunotherapy for cancer—NCI (nciglobal, ncienterprise), 2015. (2015, April 29). [CgvArticle] https://www.cancer.gov/about-cancer/treatment/types/immunotherapy.

[26] Ye Y, Yang L, Yuan X, Huang H, Luo Y. Optimization of donor lymphocyte infusion for AML relapse after Allo-HCT in the era of new drugs and cell engineering. Front Oncol 2022;11:790299. https://doi.org/10.3389/fonc.2021.790299.

[27] Benci JL, Xu B, Qiu Y, Wu TJ, Dada H, Twyman-Saint Victor C, Cucolo L, Lee DSM, Pauken KE, Huang AC, Gangadhar TC, Amaravadi RK, Schuchter LM, Feldman MD, Ishwaran H, Vonderheide RH, Maity A, Wherry EJ, Minn AJ. Tumor interferon signaling regulates a multigenic resistance program to immune checkpoint blockade. Cell 2016;167(6):1540–1554.e12. https://doi.org/10.1016/j.cell.2016.11.022.

[28] Franzin R, Netti GS, Spadaccino F, Porta C, Gesualdo L, Stallone G, Castellano G, Ranieri E. The use of immune checkpoint inhibitors in oncology and the occurrence of AKI: where do we stand? Front Immunol 2020;11:574271. https://doi.org/10.3389/fimmu.2020.574271.

[29] Faghfuri E, Pourfarzi F, Faghfouri AH, Abdoli Shadbad M, Hajiasgharzadeh K, Baradaran B. Recent developments of RNA-based vaccines in cancer immunotherapy. Expert Opin Biol Ther 2021;21(2):201–18. https://doi.org/10.1080/14712598.2020.1815704.

[30] Saini AS, Shenoy GN, Rath S, Bal V, George A. Inducible nitric oxide synthase is a major intermediate in signaling pathways for the survival of plasma cells. Nat Immunol 2014;15:275–82. https://doi.org/10.1038/ni.2806.

[31] Butterfield LH. Cancer vaccines. BMJ 2015;350:h988. https://doi.org/10.1136/bmj.h988.

[32] Kamimura D, Bevan MJ. Naive CD8+ T cells differentiate into protective memory-like cells after IL-2-anti-IL-2 complex treatment in vivo. J Exp Med 2007;204(8):1803–12. https://doi.org/10.1084/jem.20070543.

[33] Wrangle JM, Patterson A, Johnson CB, Neitzke DJ, Mehrotra S, Denlinger CE, Paulos CM, Li Z, Cole DJ, Rubinstein MP. IL-2 and beyond in cancer immunotherapy. J Interferon Cytokine Res 2018;38(2):45–68. https://doi.org/10.1089/jir.2017.0101.

[34] Boyman O, Sprent J. The role of interleukin-2 during homeostasis and activation of the immune system. Nat Rev Immunol 2012;12(3):180–90. https://doi.org/10.1038/nri3156.

[35] Kimiz-Gebologlu I, Gulce-Iz S, Biray-Avci C. Monoclonal antibodies in cancer immunotherapy. Mol Biol Rep 2018;45(6):2935–40. https://doi.org/10.1007/s11033-018-4427-x.

[36] Singh S, Kumar NK, Dwiwedi P, Charan J, Kaur R, Sidhu P, Chugh VK. Monoclonal antibodies: a review. Curr Clin Pharmacol 2018;13(2):85–99. https://doi.org/10.2174/1574884712666170809124728.

[37] Buss NA, Henderson SJ, McFarlane M, Shenton JM, de Haan L. Monoclonal antibody therapeutics: history and future. Curr Opin Pharmacol 2012;12(5):615–22. https://doi.org/10.1016/j.coph.2012.08.001.

[38] Leung D, Wurst JM, Liu T, Martinez RM, Datta-Mannan A, Feng Y. Antibody conjugates-recent advances and future innovations. Antibodies (Basel) 2020;9(1):2. https://doi.org/10.3390/antib9010002.

[39] Zou C, Zhao P, Xiao Z, Han X, Fu F, Fu L. γδ T cells in cancer immunotherapy. Oncotarget 2017;8(5):8900–9. https://doi.org/10.18632/oncotarget.13051.

[40] Wu YL, Ding YP, Tanaka Y, Shen LW, Wei CH, Minato N, Zhang W. γδ T cells and their potential for immunotherapy. Int J Biol Sci 2014;10(2):119–35. https://doi.org/10.7150/ijbs.7823.

[41] Kabelitz D, Serrano R, Kouakanou L, Peters C, Kalyan S. Cancer immunotherapy with γδ T cells: many paths ahead of us. Cell Mol Immunol 2020;17(9):925–39. https://doi.org/10.1038/s41423-020-0504-x.

[42] Coffelt SB, Kersten K, Doornebal CW, Weiden J, Vrijland K, Hau CS, Verstegen NJM, Ciampricotti M, Hawinkels LJAC, Jonkers J, de Visser KE. IL-17-producing γδ T cells and neutrophils conspire to promote breast cancer metastasis. Nature 2015;522(7556):345–8. https://doi.org/10.1038/nature14282.

[43] Zhao Y, Niu C, Cui J. Gamma-delta (γδ) T cells: friend or foe in cancer development? J Transl Med 2018;16 (1):3. https://doi.org/10.1186/s12967-017-1378-2.

[44] Pistoia V, Tumino N, Vacca P, Veneziani I, Moretta A, Locatelli F, Moretta L. Human γδ T-cells: from surface receptors to the therapy of high-risk leukemias. Front Immunol 2018;9:984. https://doi.org/10.3389/fimmu.2018.00984.

[45] Wu D, Wu P, Qiu F, Wei Q, Huang J. Human γδT-cell subsets and their involvement in tumor immunity. Cell Mol Immunol 2017;14(3):245–53. https://doi.org/10.1038/cmi.2016.55.

[46] Li Y, Li G, Zhang J, Wu X, Chen X. The dual roles of human γδ T cells: anti-tumor or tumor-promoting. Front Immunol 2021;11:619954. https://doi.org/10.3389/fimmu.2020.619954.

[47] Yazdanifar M, Barbarito G, Bertaina A, Airoldi I. γδ T cells: the ideal tool for cancer immunotherapy. Cells 2020;9(5):1305. https://doi.org/10.3390/cells9051305.

[48] Rampoldi F, Ullrich L, Prinz I. Revisiting the interaction of γδ T-cells and B-cells. Cells 2020;9(3):743. https://doi.org/10.3390/cells9030743.

[49] Rhodes DA, Reith W, Trowsdale J. Regulation of immunity by butyrophilins. Annu Rev Immunol 2016;34:151–72. https://doi.org/10.1146/annurev-immunol-041015-055435.

[50] Di Marco BR, Roberts NA, Dart RJ, Vantourout P, Jandke A, Nussbaumer O, Deban L, Cipolat S, Hart R, Iannitto ML, Laing A, Spencer-Dene B, East P, Gibbons D, Irving PM, Pereira P, Steinhoff U, Hayday A. Epithelia use butyrophilin-like molecules to shape organ-specific γδ T cell compartments. Cell 2016;167(1):203–218. e17. https://doi.org/10.1016/j.cell.2016.08.030.

[51] Cinelli MA, Do HT, Miley GP, Silverman RB. Inducible nitric oxide synthase: regulation, structure, and inhibition. Med Res Rev 2020;40(1):158–89. https://doi.org/10.1002/med.21599.

[52] Liy PM, Puzi NNA, Jose S, Vidyadaran S. Nitric oxide modulation in neuroinflammation and the role of mesenchymal stem cells. Exp Biol Med (Maywood) 2021;246(22):2399–406. https://doi.org/10.1177/1535370221997052.

[53] Lind M, Hayes A, Caprnda M, Petrovic D, Rodrigo L, Kruzliak P, Zulli A. Inducible nitric oxide synthase: good or bad? Biomed Pharmacother 2017;93:370–5. https://doi.org/10.1016/j.biopha.2017.06.036.

[54] Le X, Wei D, Huang S, Lancaster Jr JR, Xie K. Nitric oxide synthase II suppresses the growth and metastasis of human cancer regardless of its up-regulation of protumor factors. Proc Natl Acad Sci USA 2005;102(24):8758–63. https://doi.org/10.1073/pnas.0409581102.

[55] Li W, Chen L, Lu C, Elmore BO, Astashkin AV, Rousseau DL, Yeh SR, Feng C. Regulatory role of Glu546 in flavin mononucleotide-heme electron transfer in human inducible nitric oxide synthase. Inorg Chem 2013;52(9):4795–801. https://doi.org/10.1021/ic3020892.

[56] Ghosh S, Wolan D, Adak S, Crane BR, Kwon NS, Tainer JA, Getzoff ED, Stuehr DJ. Mutational analysis of the tetrahydrobiopterin-binding site in inducible nitric-oxide synthase. J Biol Chem 1999;274(34):24100–12. https://doi.org/10.1074/jbc.274.34.24100.

[57] Li W, Fan W, Chen L, Elmore BO, Piazza M, Guillemette JG, Feng C. Role of an isoform-specific serine residue in FMN-heme electron transfer in inducible nitric oxide synthase. J Biol Inorg Chem 2012;17(5):675–85. https://doi.org/10.1007/s00775-012-0887-y.

[58] Chakravortty D, Hensel M. Inducible nitric oxide synthase and control of intracellular bacterial pathogens. Microbes Infect 2003;5(7):621–7. https://doi.org/10.1016/s1286-4579(03)00096-0.

[59] Chung P, Cook T, Liu K, Vodovotz Y, Zamora R, Finkelstein S, Billiar T, Blumberg D. Overexpression of the human inducible nitric oxide synthase gene enhances radiation-induced apoptosis in colorectal cancer cells via a caspase-dependent mechanism. Nitric Oxide 2003;8(2):119–26. https://doi.org/10.1016/s1089-8603(02)00147-7.

[60] Zhang L, Liu J, Wang X, Li Z, Zhang X, Cao P, She X, Dai Q, Tang J, Liu Z. Upregulation of cytoskeleton protein and extracellular matrix protein induced by stromal-derived nitric oxide promotes lung cancer invasion and metastasis. Curr Mol Med 2014;14(6):762–71. https://doi.org/10.2174/1566524014666140724103147.

[61] Giatromanolaki A, Tsolou A, Daridou E, Kouroupi M, Chlichlia K, Koukourakis MI. iNOS expression by tumor-infiltrating lymphocytes, PD-L1 and prognosis in non-small-cell lung cancer. Cancers (Basel) 2020;12 (11):3276. https://doi.org/10.3390/cancers12113276.

II. Nitric oxide pathway and cancer progression and therapy

[62] Navasardyan I, Bonavida B. Regulation of T cells in cancer by nitric oxide. Cells 2021;10(10):2655. https://doi.org/10.3390/cells10102655.

[63] Adams C, McCarthy HO, Coulter JA, Worthington J, Murphy C, Robson T, Hirst DG. Nitric oxide synthase gene therapy enhances the toxicity of cisplatin in cancer cells. J Gene Med 2009;11(2):160–8. https://doi.org/10.1002/jgm.1280.

[64] Xue Q, Yan Y, Zhang R, Xiong H. Regulation of iNOS on immune cells and its role in diseases. Int J Mol Sci 2018;19(12):3805. https://doi.org/10.3390/ijms19123805.

[65] Schmidlin A, Wiesinger H. Transport of L-arginine in cultured glial cells. Glia 1994;11(3):262–8. https://doi.org/10.1002/glia.440110307.

[66] Douguet L, Cherfils-Vicini J, Bod L, Lengagne R, Gilson E, Prévost-Blondel A. Nitric oxide synthase 2 improves proliferation and glycolysis of peripheral γδ T cells. PLoS One 2016;11(11):e0165639. https://doi.org/10.1371/journal.pone.0165639.

[67] Oppeltz RF, Rani M, Zhang Q, Schwacha MG. Gamma delta (γδ) T-cells are critical in the up-regulation of inducible nitric oxide synthase at the burn wound site. Cytokine 2012;60(2):528–34. https://doi.org/10.1016/j.cyto.2012.07.003.

[68] Morath A, Schamel WW. αβ and γδ T cell receptors: similar but different. J Leukoc Biol 2020;107(6):1045–55. https://doi.org/10.1002/JLB.2MR1219-233R.

[69] Aktan F. iNOS-mediated nitric oxide production and its regulation. Life Sci 2004;75:639–53. https://doi.org/10.1016/j.lfs.2003.10.042.

[70] Douguet L, Bod L, Lengagne R, Labarthe L, Kato M, Avril MF, Prévost-Blondel A. Nitric oxide synthase 2 is involved in the pro-tumorigenic potential of γδ17 T cells in melanoma. Oncoimmunology 2016;5(8), e1208878. https://doi.org/10.1080/2162402X.2016.1208878.

[71] MacIver NJ, Michalek RD, Rathmell JC. Metabolic regulation of T lymphocytes. Annu Rev Immunol 2013;31:259–83. https://doi.org/10.1146/annurev-immunol-032712-095956.

[72] Fleming V, Hu X, Weber R, Nagibin V, Groth C, Altevogt P, Utikal J, Umansky V. Targeting myeloid-derived suppressor cells to bypass tumor-induced immunosuppression. Front Immunol 2018;9:398. https://doi.org/10.3389/fimmu.2018.00398.

[73] Sacchi A, Tumino N, Sabatini A, Cimini E, Casetti R, Bordoni V, Grassi G, Agrati C. Myeloid-derived suppressor cells specifically suppress IFN-γ production and antitumor cytotoxic activity of Vδ2 T cells. Front Immunol 2018;9:1271. https://doi.org/10.3389/fimmu.2018.01271.

[74] Douguet L, Bod L, Labarthe L, Lengagne R, Kato M, Couillin I, Prévost-Blondel A. Inflammation drives nitric oxide synthase 2 expression by γδ T cells and affects the balance between melanoma and vitiligo associated melanoma. Onco Targets Ther 2018;7(9):e1484979. https://doi.org/10.1080/2162402X.2018.1484979.

[75] Obermajer N, Wong JL, Edwards RP, Chen K, Scott M, Khader S, Kolls JK, Odunsi K, Billiar TR, Kalinski P. Induction and stability of human Th17 cells require endogenous NOS2 and cGMP-dependent NO signaling. J Exp Med 2013;210:1433–45. https://doi.org/10.1084/jem.20121277.

[76] Saini AS, Shenoy GN, Rath S, Bal V, George A. Inducible nitric oxide synthase is a major intermediate in signaling pathways for the survival of plasma cells. Nat Immunol 2014;15:275–82. https://doi.org/10.1038/ni.2806.

[77] Yang J, Gonon AT, Sjoquist PO, Lundberg JO, Pernow J. Arginase regulates red blood cell nitric oxide synthase and export of cardio-protective nitric oxide bioactivity. Proc Natl Acad Sci USA 2013;110:15049–54. https://doi.org/10.1073/pnas.1307058110.

[78] Lima-Junior DS, Costa DL, Carregaro V, Cunha LD, Silva AL, Mineo TW, Gutierrez FR, Bellio M, Bortoluci KR, Flavell RA, et al. Inflammasome-derived IL-1beta production induces nitric oxide-mediated resistance to Leishmania. Nat Med 2013;19:909–15. https://doi.org/10.1038/nm.3221.

[79] Coussens LM, Werb Z. Inflammation and cancer. Nature 2002;420:860–7. https://doi.org/10.1038/nature01322.

[80] Hanahan D, Weinberg RA. Hallmarks of cancer: the next generation. Cell 2011;144(5):646–74. https://doi.org/10.1016/j.cell.2011.02.013.

[81] Fay NS, Larson EC, Jameson JM. Chronic inflammation and γδ T cells. Front Immunol 2016;7:210. https://doi.org/10.3389/fimmu.2016.00210.

[82] Caldwell RW, Rodriguez PC, Toque HA, Narayanan SP, Caldwell RB. Arginase: a multifaceted enzyme important in health and disease. Physiol Rev 2018;98(2):641–65. https://doi.org/10.1152/physrev.00037.2016.

[83] Corsale AM, Di Simone M, Lo Presti E, Picone C, Dieli F, Meraviglia S. Metabolic changes in tumor microenvironment: how could they affect γδ T cells functions? Cells 2021;10(11):2896. https://doi.org/10.3390/cells10112896.

[84] Gocher AM, Workman CJ, Vignali DAA. Interferon-γ: teammate or opponent in the tumour microenvironment? Nat Rev Immunol 2022;22(3):158–72. https://doi.org/10.1038/s41577-021-00566-3.

[85] Benci JL, Xu B, Qiu Y, Wu TJ, Dada H, Twyman-Saint Victor C, Cucolo L, Lee DSM, Pauken KE, Huang AC, Gangadhar TC, Amaravadi RK, Schuchter LM, Feldman MD, Ishwaran H, Vonderheide RH, Maity A, Wherry EJ, Minn AJ. Tumor interferon signaling regulates a multigenic resistance program to immune checkpoint blockade. Cell 2016;167(6):1540–1554.e12. https://doi.org/10.1016/j.cell.2016.11.022.

[86] Raikar SS, Jhita N. Allogeneic gamma delta T cells as adoptive cellular therapy for hematologic malignancies. Explor Immunol 2022;2(3):334–50. https://doi.org/10.37349/ei.2022.00054.

[87] Gertner-Dardenne J, Castellano R, Mamessier E, Garbit S, Kochbati E, Etienne A, Charbonnier A, Collette Y, Vey N, Olive D. Human Vγ9Vδ2 T cells specifically recognize and kill acute myeloid leukemic blasts. J Immunol 2012;188(9):4701–8. https://doi.org/10.4049/jimmunol.1103710.

[88] Kunzmann V, Wilhelm M. Anti-lymphoma effect of gammadelta T cells. Leuk Lymphoma 2005;46(5):671–80. https://doi.org/10.1080/10428190500051893.

[89] Benyamine A, Le Roy A, Mamessier E, Gertner-Dardenne J, Castanier C, Orlanducci F, Pouyet L, Goubard A, Collette Y, Vey N, Scotet E, Castellano R, Olive D. BTN3A molecules considerably improve Vγ9Vδ2T cells-based immunotherapy in acute myeloid leukemia. Onco Targets Ther 2016;5(10):e1146843. https://doi.org/10.1080/2162402X.2016.1146843.

[90] Deniger DC, Switzer K, Mi T, Maiti S, Hurton L, Singh H, Huls H, Olivares S, Lee DA, Champlin RE, Cooper LJ. Bispecific T-cells expressing polyclonal repertoire of endogenous γδ T-cell receptors and introduced CD19-specific chimeric antigen receptor. Mol Ther 2013;21(3):638–47. https://doi.org/10.1038/mt.2012.267.

[91] Rozenbaum M, Meir A, Aharony Y, Itzhaki O, Schachter J, Bank I, Jacoby E, Besser MJ. Gamma-Delta CAR-T cells show CAR-directed and independent activity against Leukemia. Front Immunol 2020;11:1347. https://doi.org/10.3389/fimmu.2020.01347.

[92] Park JH, Lee HK. Function of γδ T cells in tumor immunology and their application to cancer therapy. Exp Mol Med 2021;53(3):318–27. https://doi.org/10.1038/s12276-021-00576-0.

[93] Macek JZ. Gamma delta T cells in hepatocellular carcinoma: sunrise of new therapy based on Vδ2 T cells? Clin Transl Med 2022;12(4), e834. https://doi.org/10.1002/ctm2.834.

[94] He W, Hu Y, Chen D, Li Y, Ye D, Zhao Q, Lin L, Shi X, Lu L, Yin Z, He X, Gao Y, Wu Y. Hepatocellular carcinoma-infiltrating γδ T cells are functionally defected and allogenic Vδ2+ γδ T cell can be a promising complement. Clin Transl Med 2022;12(4), e800. https://doi.org/10.1002/ctm2.800.

[95] Ko Y, Jeong YH, Lee JA. Therapeutic potential of ex vivo expanded γδ T cells against osteosarcoma cells. Cells 2022;11(14):2164. https://doi.org/10.3390/cells11142164.

[96] Jacoby E, Shahani SA, Shah NN. Updates on CAR T-cell therapy in B-cell malignancies. Immunol Rev 2019;290:39–59. https://doi.org/10.1111/imr.12774.

[97] Salter AI, Pont MJ, Riddell SR. Chimeric antigen receptor modified T cells: CD19 and the road beyond. Blood 2018;131:2621–9. https://doi.org/10.1182/blood-2018-01-785840.

[98] Hamieh M, Dobrin A, Cabriolu A, van der Stegen SJC, Giavridis T, Mansilla- Soto J, et al. CAR T cell trogocytosis and cooperative killing regulate tumour antigen escape. Nature 2019;568:112–6. https://doi.org/10.1038/s41586-019-1054-1.

[99] Shah NN, Fry TJ. Mechanisms of resistance to CAR T cell therapy. Nat Rev Clin Oncol 2019;16:372–85. https://doi.org/10.1038/s41571-019-0184-6.

[100] Wawrzyniecka PA, Ibrahim L, Gritti G, Pule MA, Maciocia PM. Chimeric antigen receptor T cells for gamma-delta T cell malignancies. Leukemia 2022;36(2):577–9. https://doi.org/10.1038/s41375-021-01385-0.

[101] Xue Q, Yan Y, Zhang R, Xiong H. Regulation of iNOS on immune cells and its role in diseases. Int J Mol Sci 2018;19(12):3805. https://doi.org/10.3390/ijms19123805.

[102] Basudhar D, Somasundaram V, de Oliveira GA, Kesarwala A, Heinecke JL, Cheng RY, Glynn SA, Ambs S, Wink DA, Ridnour LA. Nitric oxide synthase-2-derived nitric oxide drives multiple pathways of breast cancer progression. Antioxid Redox Signal 2017;26(18):1044–58. https://doi.org/10.1089/ars.2016.6813.

[103] Özenver N, Efferth T. Small molecule inhibitors and stimulators of inducible nitric oxide synthase in cancer cells from natural origin (phytochemicals, marine compounds, antibiotics). Biochem Pharmacol 2020;176:113792. https://doi.org/10.1016/j.bcp.2020.113792.

II. Nitric oxide pathway and cancer progression and therapy

[104] Mintz J, Vedenko A, Rosete O, Shah K, Goldstein G, Hare JM, Ramasamy R, Arora H. Current advances of nitric oxide in cancer and anticancer therapeutics. Vaccines (Basel) 2021;9(2):94. https://doi.org/10.3390/vaccines9020094.

[105] Navasardyan I, Bonavida B. Regulation of T cells in cancer by nitric oxide. Cells 2021;10(10):2655. https://doi.org/10.3390/cells10102655.

[106] Omidkhah N, Ghodsi R. NO-HDAC dual inhibitors. Eur J Med Chem 2022;227:113934. https://doi.org/10.1016/j.ejmech.2021.113934.

[107] Doman AJ, Tommasi S, Perkins MV, McKinnon RA, Mangoni AA, Nair PC. Chemical similarities and differences among inhibitors of nitric oxide synthase, arginase and dimethylarginine dimethylaminohydrolase-1: implications for the design of novel enzyme inhibitors modulating the nitric oxide pathway. Bioorg Med Chem 2022;72:116970. https://doi.org/10.1016/j.bmc.2022.116970.

The regulation of the programmed death ligand 1 (PD-L1) by nitric oxide in breast cancer: Immunotherapeutic implication

Katie Lin and Benjamin Bonavida

Department of Microbiology, Immunology and Molecular Genetics, David Geffen School of Medicine, Jonsson Comprehensive Cancer Center, University of California at Los Angeles, Los Angeles, CA, United States

Abstract

Several milestones have been accomplished in the last two decades on the treatment of various drug-resistant cancers with immunotherapy. Several FDA-approved immunotherapeutic regimens are currently in use clinically, including targeted monoclonal antibodies and CD8 T-cell–mediated cytotoxic therapies. In the TME, the interaction of tumor-specific CD8 T cells with cancer cells results in tumor destruction. However, often this interaction results in the inactivation of the CD8 T cells via the expression on the tumor cells of an inhibitory ligand, such as programmed death ligand 1 (PD-L1), with the corresponding receptor, PD-1, on the surface of the CD8 T cells. The use of the FDA-approved monoclonal antibodies (mAbs) directed against PD-L1 or PD-1 to block the inactivation of CD8 T cells resulted in significant killing of tumor cells and tumor inhibition. Such blocking antibodies or checkpoint inhibitors (CPIs) are effective in many, but not all, cancer types. Thus, another approach to prevent the inactivation of CD8 T cells is to inhibit the expression of PD-L1 on the tumor cells. Interestingly, the expression of inducible nitric oxide synthase (NOS2) in tumor cells plays a role in the regulation of PD-L1 expression. Thus, the inhibition of NOS2 will result in the downregulation of PD-L1 expression and restoration of the antitumor cytotoxic activity of the CD8 T cells. In this review, we examined human breast cancer cells, as a cancer example, expressing PD-L1 and NOS2 and their roles in immunosuppression. We also discussed the role of NO inhibitors in restoring the activity of the antitumor CD8 T cells.

Abbreviations

ACT	adoptive cellular therapy
CD8 T cells/CTLs	cytotoxic T lymphocytes
CPI	checkpoint inhibitor

CTLA-4	cytotoxic T-lymphocyte–associated protein 4
ER	estrogen receptor
FDA	Food and Drug Administration
gMDSCs	granulocytic myeloid–derived suppressor cells
HER-2	human epidermal growth factor receptor 2
HIF	hypoxia-inducible factor
ICI	immune checkpoint inhibitors
IFN	interferon
IL	interleukin
JAK/STAT	Janus kinase/signal transducer and activator of transcription proteins
L-NAME	L-NG-nitroarginine methyl ester
mAb	monoclonal antibody
MAPK	mitogen-activated protein kinase
MDSCs	myeloid-derived suppressor cells
mTOR	mammalian target of rapamycin
NF-kB	nuclear factor kappa–light-chain enhancer of activated B cells
NO	nitric oxide
NOS2/INOS	inducible nitric oxide synthase
NSCLC	non-squamous non–small-cell lung cancer
ORR	overall response rate
PD-1	programmed death 1
PD-L1	programmed death ligand 1
PI3K	phosphoinositide 3-kinase
TME	tumor microenvironment
TNBC	triple-negative breast cancer
TNF	tumor necrosis factor
YY1	Yin Yang 1

Conflict of interest

No potential conflicts of interest were disclosed.

Introduction

   Breast cancer is the leading cause of cancer death in women throughout the world [1]. There exist different treatment options for breast cancer, such as surgery, chemotherapy, hormonal therapy, radiation therapy, molecular treatments, and immunotherapy [2–5]. Several antibody-targeted therapies have been FDA-approved, such as mAbs and antibody conjugates that are directed against HER-2-overexpressing subsets of cancer cells [6,7]. While these therapies were effective in some patients, a large subset of patients were initially unresponsive [7–9] or became unresponsive following the initial treatments [7,10–13].

   Cell-mediated immune responses to breast cancer have been investigated as it has been discovered that breast cancer cells can be immunogenic [14]. As a result, cell-mediated immunotherapy has been integrated into breast cancer treatment [14]. In cell-mediated immunotherapy, the induction and activation of specific CD8 cytotoxic T lymphocytes (CTLs) play a major role in the recognition and elimination of cancer cells under optimal conditions [15–17].

Evasion of cancer cells from CD8 T-cell–mediated immunotherapy: Role of PD-L1/PD-1 interactions

Tumor cells have developed many mechanisms to evade the immune response. Among these is the expression of inhibitory ligands (e.g., PD-L1 and B7-1/2) that enable the tumor cells to inhibit the cytotoxic activity of CD8 T cells via their interactions with corresponding inhibitory receptors (e.g., PD-1 and CTLA-4) [18] (Fig. 1). Hence, investigations were undertaken in experimental animal model systems. These investigations tested whether or not the interference with inhibitory ligand-receptor interactions could rescue CD8 T-cell activity and, therefore, inhibit tumor growth. Indeed, mAbs were generated against either the ligand (such as PD-L1 and B7-1/2) or the inhibitor receptor (such as PD-1 and CTLA-4) and were tested in vivo in tumor-bearing mice. Noteworthy, these experiments demonstrated that injection of either of such blocking antibodies resulted in both the significant inhibition of tumor growth and the prolongation of survival [19–22]. These findings were the basis for the development of FDA-approved therapeutic blocking antibodies for cancer patients, called checkpoint inhibitors (CPIs). These CPIs were tested for effectiveness in clinical trials [23–25] (Fig. 2).

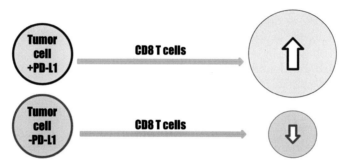

FIG. 1 Expression of PD-L1 in tumor cells and response to CD8 T-cell–mediated effect. The top figure illustrates that tumor cells expressing PD-L1 will evade the cytotoxic effect of the CD8 T cells and will continue to grow. By contrast, the bottom figure illustrates that when tumor cells express low levels or no PD-L1, they respond to the cytotoxic activity of the CD8 T cells, leading to the inhibition of tumor growth.

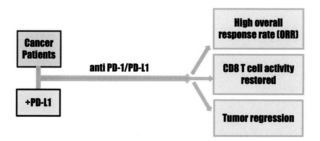

FIG. 2 Response of tumors to anti-PD-1/PD-L1 antibody treatment. For patients with certain cancers that express PD-L1, the treatment with CPIs, like anti-PD-1/PD-L1 mAbs, results in the restoration of the antitumor activity of CD8 T cells, leading to tumor regression and a high ORR in this patient population.

II. Nitric oxide pathway and cancer progression and therapy

Programmed death ligand 1

Programmed death ligand 1 (PD-L1) is the ligand of programmed death 1 (PD-1) [26]. In humans, PD-L1 is found at position 24.1 on chromosome 9 [26,27]. PD-L1 is a member of the B7 protein family and consists of seven exons [26,28]. Sun et al. reported that PD-L1 has been shown to be overexpressed in breast cancer cells [29].

PD-1 has been found to be expressed on activated CD8 cytotoxic T cells [30–32]. When PD-L1 binds to PD-1, it results in the inhibition of T-cell receptor activity, inhibiting their antitumor immune response [30–32]. Noguchi et al. found that TNBC has the highest expression of the PD-L1 gene and protein when compared with other breast cancer subtypes such as HER-2 and ER [33–35]. Therefore, clinical trials of PD-L1 and PD-1 checkpoint inhibitor therapy have been focusing on the TNBC subtype [35].

PD-L1 and PD-1 checkpoint inhibitor therapy uses monoclonal antibodies (mAbs) to block either the ligand PD-L1 or the inhibitory receptor PD-1, which results in the activation of CD8 T cells and their antitumor immune response [36]. However, in TNBC, it was reported that the anti-PD-L1 and anti-PD-1 therapies had a low overall response rate (ORR) of around 5%–20% [35,37–42]. Saleh et al. discovered that the response to ICIs was dependent on PD-L1 expression levels by testing the breast cancer cell lines MDA-MB-231 (low levels of PD-L1) and MDA-MB-468 (high levels of PD-L1) [43]. Saleh et al. found that MDA-MB-231 cells had a greater response to anti-PD-L1 than MDA-MB-468 cells [43]. They suggested that blocking the PD-L1 ligand would rescue the CD8 T-cell activity via PD-1 interaction with PD-L1 [43].

Currently, the US Food and Drug Administration (FDA) has approved the PD-L1-targeted mAb atezolizumab [44]. However, in many cancer types, there exists an innate resistance against the PD-1/PD-L1 blockade [44,45]. This innate resistance could be a result of constitutive oncogenic signaling [44,45] (Fig. 3). There also exists an adaptive immune resistance to the PD-1/PD-L1 blockade [44,46]. In adaptive immune resistance, there is local PD-L1 expression by tumor cells, allowing it to escape the immune response [44,46]. Wang and Wu proposed that to combat this resistance, it might be useful to combine PD-1/PD-L1 blockade therapy with other treatments such as radiotherapy and chemotherapy [44].

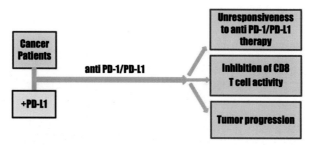

FIG. 3 Response of tumors to anti-PD-1/PD-L1 antibody treatment. For patients with other forms of cancers overexpressing PD-L1, the treatment with CPIs, like PD-1/PD-L1 mAbs, will not be effective in restoring the antitumor activity of CD8 T cells. This will lead to tumor progression.

Reversal of resistance to CMI by checkpoint inhibitors

To combat the PD-1/PD-L1 resistance to blockade therapy, one study reported on the use of adoptive cell therapy (ACT) [32,47–49]. ACT involves generating CD8 T cells that target specific tumor antigens [32,47–49]. The mechanism behind generating CD8 T cells involves an ex vivo modification of low-frequency CD8 T cells that are specific to certain antigens and are infused back into the patient [32,50,51]. For instance, Robbins et al. generated CD8 T cells against the antigen MART-1 in melanoma [32,47–49]. Another method in generating CD8 T cells involves ex vivo modifying peripheral mononuclear blood cells [32,49]. The mechanism involves the transduction of T-cell receptors (TCRs) that are directed against specific tumor antigens into these peripheral mononuclear blood cells, where these cells are then injected into patients [32,49]. Furthermore, to combat the PD-L1/PD-1 resistance is the injection of tumor vaccines into cancer patients [32,52]. In this case, neoantigens are injected into the body to stimulate an immune response through the activation of dendritic cells to generate T cells against tumor antigens [32,53,54]. To generate a greater overall response rate (ORR), ACT and tumor vaccines must be implemented as a treatment method in combination with PD-L1/PD-1 blockade therapy [32]. These methods are more effective because they partially restore the activity of CD8 T cells that was once blocked by PD-1/PD-L1 [32]. Sun et al. found that anti-PD-L1 therapy in combination with transforming growth factor β (TGFβ) blocking agent promoted tumor regression by increasing T-cell activity [55].

Another way to combat the resistance is through the use of PD-L1-based chemotherapy [56]. Yi et al. analyzed clinical trials in nonsquamous non-small-cell lung cancer (NSCLC) and TNBC patients [56]. Yi et al. reported that patients who received atezolizumab in addition to chemotherapy had a higher efficacy than those who received chemotherapy or atezolizumab alone [56]. This is due to chemotherapy's ability to stimulate an antitumor response in the immune system [56–58].

Radiotherapy has been shown to have abscopal effects, eliciting a systemic antitumor response [56]. Specifically, Yi et al. found that radiotherapy resulted in T-cell infiltration, increased tumor-infiltrating lymphocytes, and expansion of the TCR repertoire in the tumor microenvironment (TME) [56]. Thus, radiotherapy relieves the PD-1/PD-L1 resistance and aids in restoring the cytotoxicity in the TME to promote tumor regression [56]. Therefore, Yi et al. reported a possible enhancement of efficacy through the combination of both radiotherapy and anti-PD-L1 immunotherapy [56].

Regulation of PD-L1 expression on cancer cells

The regulation of PDL1 is achieved via inflammatory conditions that are mediated by cytokines such as IFNγ. Several signaling pathways are involved in the induction of PD-L1, including NF-kB, MAPK, PI3K, mTOR, and JAK/STAT pathways. In addition, the tumor suppressors PTEN and Lkb1 and EMT gene products are involved in the regulation of PD-L1 expression and the involvement of transcription factors HIF-1, STAT3, NF-kB, and AP-1 [59].

Signal transduction via PAMPs and IFNγ results in the phosphorylation of NF-kB, MAPK, mTOR, and STAT. Downstream, these molecules lead to the translocation of the various transcription factors. These NF-kB, NFAT, and STAT/IRF factors bind to the PD-L1 promoter and induce the transcription and translation of PD-L1 [60]. We describe a few examples in the following text.

One mechanism of cancer immune escape is via hypoxia. Barsoum et al. reported that exposure of cancer cells to hypoxia resulted in the upregulation of PD-L1 (also known as B7-H1) [61]. This upregulation was dependent on the transcription factor HIF-1-alpha. There was also a colocalization of PD-L1 and HIF-1-alpha within in vivo derived cancer tissues. The upregulation of PD-L1 was, in part, responsible for the resistance of the cancer cells to CTL-mediated cytotoxicity. Barsoum et al. then used glyceryl trinitrate (GTN), an agonist of NO signaling that blocks HIF-1-alpha accumulation in hypoxic cells, which resulted in the inhibition of PD-L1 expression and the sensitization of the cells to CTL-mediated lysis. Barsoum et al. suggested that the use of NO mimetics, such as GTN, or small-molecule inhibitors, could lead to novel immunotherapeutic strategies. Recent data also suggested that the combination of HIF inhibitors and ICIs gives rise to synergism and inhibits tumor development by potentiating antitumor immunity [62].

Doi et al. reported that in pancreatic tumor cell lines, the JAK/STAT pathway regulates PD-L1 expression [63]. Treatment of these cell lines with various chemotherapeutic drugs upregulated PD-L1 expression. STAT-1 was also phosphorylated, with an increase in the total STAT-1 expression. An inhibitor of JAK2 reduced the level of PD-L1 expression in the treated cells. Furthermore, the JAK/STAT pathway has been reported to regulate PD-L1 expression in many cancers [64]. The Wnt/beta catenin pathway is also involved in the regulation of PD-L1 expression. The inhibition of the Wnt pathway in glioblastomas resulted in the inhibition of tumor growth and the potentiation of the response to PD-1 ICI immunotherapy [65].

In a review by Zerdes et al., these authors discussed the regulation of PD-L1 that occurs at different levels [66]. Several signaling pathways are involved, including RAS/RAF/MEK, MAPK-ERK, and PI3K/PTEN/Akt/mTOR. Their activation by oncogenic and/or loss-of-function mutations can lead to either direct action on target genes or the activation of transcription factors. Molecules such as STAT3, STAT1, cJun, HIFs, or NF-κB can shuttle into the nucleus, bind to specific sites on the PD-L1 gene promoter, and induce its expression. PD-L1 is also regulated posttranscriptionally by microRNAs, which bind to mRNA, leading to its translational repression or enhancement. MiR-513 was shown to increase PD-L1 expression [66,67], whereas mutation in the 3'-UTR of PD-L1 mRNA led to the overexpression of the protein by preventing miR-570 binding in gastric cancer. PD-L1 is subject to posttranscriptional regulation by several miRNAs, CSN5, CMTM6, CDK4, and other possible unknown mechanisms.

Ju et al. reported that NF-kB is involved in the regulation of PD-L1 in gastric cancer. In this case, they found that the infiltrated macrophages release cytokines IL-6 and TNFα, which induce PDL1 expression through TLR and NF-kB signaling [68].

Hays and Bonavida have reported that the transcription factor Yin Yang 1 (YY1), which is overexpressed in many cancers, is involved in the pathogenesis of cancers, including cell proliferation, cell invasion, EMT, metastasis, and resistance to both chemo- and immunotherapeutics [69]. Hence, Hays, and Bonavida hypothesized that YY1 may also be involved in the regulation of PD-L1 expression. They suggested that indeed, several crosstalk signaling pathways—reported in the literature—existed between the regulations of both YY1 and

PD-L1. These included p53, STAT3, NFkB, and PI3k/AKT/mTOR pathways, and c-Myc, COX2, and miR34a. Thus, targeting YY1 may result in multiple hits on the properties of the cancer cells, as well as restoration of the antitumor immune response.

Atsaves et al. reviewed the role of the transcription factor AP-1 in the regulation of various immune responses in cancer [70]. They also viewed the role of AP-1 in the regulation of PD-L1 in various cancers. For example, in Hodgkin's lymphoma (HL), AP-1 response elements were identified. Both cJun and JunB were found to bind to an enhancer region of the PD-L1 promoter, facilitating the PD-L1 expression [71]. In addition, in the nasopharyngeal carcinoma (NPC), the EBV-induced latent membrane protein 1 (LMP1) and IFNγ upregulated PD-L1 expression through AP-1, STAT3, and NF-κB pathways [72].

Li et al. examined the regulation of PD-L1 expression in colorectal cancer (CRC) [64]. They investigated fibroblast growth factor receptor 2 (FGFR2), which initiates a cascade of intracellular signals by binding to FGF. They found that FGFR2 is coexpressed with PD-L1 in CRC. Li et al. reported that tumor-derived activated GFGR2 induced PD-L1 expression via the JAK/STAT pathway [64].

Regulation of PD-L1 expression by nitric oxide (NO)

In non-small-cell lung cancer (NSCLC), Lamberti et al. reviewed the regulation of PD-L1 expression and found that genomic alterations that activated *KRAS, EGFR, ALK*, and *PTEN* were associated with increased PD-L1 expression [73].

Wang et al. investigated the role of IL17 in the regulation of the immune response in the TME [74]. Primarily, they focused on the mesenchymal/stromal cells (MSCs) in the TME. They found that IFNγ and TNF-alpha induce the expression of PD-L1 in the MSCs. IL-17 had synergistic activity with IFNγ and TNFa in enhancing PD-L1 expression. Interestingly, the upregulation of PD-L1 expression in MSCs was mediated by the accumulation of NO. NO donors mimicked the IL-17 effect on MSCs. Overall, these findings demonstrated that IL-17 increased PD-L1 expression in MSCs through the induction of iNOS. Nafea et al. have investigated the role of noncoding RNAs on NO-mediated effects in TNBC patients [75]. They found that mIR-939-5p and lncRNA HEIH were involved in the modulation of NO effects in TNBC. MiR-939-5p has an inhibitory effect on NOS2 and NOS3 transcripts. They characterized MiR-939-5p as a tumor suppressor and HEIH—upregulated in TNBC—as a novel oncogenic lncRNA in TNBC. Nafea et al. found that the knockdown of HEIH induced MICA/B and inhibited PD-L1 expression.

Kiriyama et al. investigated the regulation of PDL1 expression in glioblastoma cells [76]. They examined the effect of the NO donor, NOOC-18, on the tumor cells and found that it increased the level of PD-L1 expression. This increase was mediated by the c-Jun kinase pathway. Kang et al. reported that the nuclear factor erythroid 2-related factor 2 (Nrf12)–knockout—or 17-beta-estradiol (E2)–treated mice—reduced PD-L1 expression in colon tissues in the AOM/DSS model of colitis-associated cancer [77]. The PD-L1 expression in colon tissues correlated positively with iNOS and COX2 expressions. Kang et al. suggested that the antitumorigenic effect of E2 is associated with the immune microenvironment and cooperates with Nrf2 deficiency.

PD-L1 expression on cancer cells is regulated by hypoxia [29,78], which, in turn, is regulated by NO via the ubiquitous transcription factors Yin Yang 1 (YY1) and HIF-1α [69,79–82]. The effects of NO on PD-L1 expression were investigated recently [76,83]. Sung et al. revealed

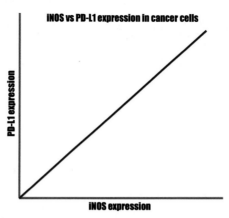

FIG. 4 Correlation between tumors expressing iNOS and the expression of PD-L1. This figure illustrates the direct correlation between the expression of iNOS in the tumors and the expression of PD-L1.

that NO-releasing NPs ($>5\mu M$) regulated the activity of transcription factor SP1 in vitro, which led to the suppression of the PD-L1 expression on hepatocellular carcinoma cells in vitro in a dose-dependent manner [83]. However, the opposite results were also reported, with DETA-NONOate ($>200\mu M$) upregulating PD-L1 expression on A172 glioblastoma cells in vitro via c-Jun N-terminal kinase (JNK) pathways [76]. These results imply that the expression of PD-L1 can depend on the cancer cell type, concentration, and type of NO donor or delivery system.

Overall, these findings strongly support that there is a positive correlation between the expression of NOS2 and the expression of PD-L1 (Fig. 4).

Inhibitors of NO and inhibition of PD-L1: Restoration of cancer cell response to CD8 T-cell–mediated immunotherapy

We have previously discussed that NOS2 is involved in the regulation of PD-L1 expression in cancer cells, thus hampering the antitumor PD-1-expressing CD8 T cells to mediate their cytotoxic activity and eliminate cancer cells [74,76,77,83]. Therefore, the selective inhibition of NOS2 in cancer cells—or the inhibition of NO in the TME—may result in the inhibition of PD-L1 expression in cancer cells and the relief of PD-L1 inhibitory activity on CD8 T cells (Fig. 5).

It is clear that the interference of NO production by NOS2 is an emerging strategy for the treatment of several inflammatory diseases. There have been several reports on various inhibitors of NOS2 that are briefly summarized later. Minhas et al. have reviewed in detail the structure of numerous inhibitors of NOS2 [84]. They briefly describe natural NOS2 inhibitors such as phenolic compounds, various terpenes, and various synthetic inhibitors. These include arginine analogs as arginine is the natural substrate of NOS2. Also, nonarginine analogs have been classified into two groups: amidinic compounds and heterocyclic compounds—5-and 6-membered compounds. Likewise, several natural and synthetic

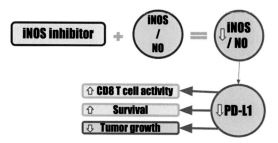

FIG. 5 Effect of treatment with iNOS inhibitors in cancer patients. This figure illustrates that the treatment of cancer patients, who are unresponsive to treatment with anti-PD-1/PD-L1 mAbs, with an iNOS inhibitor will result in the inhibition of PD-L1 expression and restoration of the antitumor CD8 T-cell activity, leading to tumor regression and prolongation of survival.

flavonoids and thioflavones have been reported to inhibit NO production as well as the expression of NOS2. In addition, steroidal compounds and chalcone derivatives have been reported as NOS2 inhibitors.

Kaneguchi et al. have reviewed the NOS2 inhibitor L-NG-nitroarginine methyl ester (L-NAME) in inflammation [85]. Their study deals with the underlying mechanism of joint remobilization-induced inflammation. They hypothesized that the induction of hypoxia/reoxygenation initiates inflammation through the induction of NO from NOS2. In experimental rats, they tested the administration of the NOS inhibitor L-NAME and demonstrated that the inflammation was reduced by the inhibitor.

Krol and Kepinska have reviewed the general properties of human NOS in inflammation, diabetes, and cardiovascular diseases and also the use of various NOS inhibitors in clinical trials [86]. These included tilarginine (L-NMMA), L-NAME, asymmetric dimethylarginine (ADMA), 7-nitroindazole (7-NI), and aminoguanidine. However, the clinical findings were not encouraging.

Abiko et al. reviewed the role of iNOS in breast cancer [87]. Specifically, they found that myeloid-derived suppressor cells (MDSCs) are found to be increased in the TME of ovarian cancer patients [87,88]. There are two categories of MDSCs: monocytic MDSCs (M-MDSCs) and polymorphonuclear MDSCs (PM-MDSCs) [87,89]. In the TME, they found that MDSCs suppress cytotoxic T-cell activity [87,88]. Abiko et al. found that the mechanism behind this suppression was through the production of iNOS and arginase [87,88]. In these same ovarian cancer cells, they also found overexpression of PD-L1 [87,88]. Abiko et al. reported that it has been found that inhibition of MDSCs resulted in decreased tumor growth in ovarian cancer mouse models [87,88]. This inhibition was through the use of the anti-VEGF drug bevacizumab, which targets MDSCs and results in the increase of T-cell activity through the inhibition of iNOS [87,90–92]. Abiko et al. also reported that MDSCs were involved in the NF-kB pathway [87,93]. In this pathway, NF-kB expresses the CXCL1/2-CXCR2 axis, which is the axis that activates MSDC migration in ovarian cancer [87,93]. But NF-kB was also found to induce PD-L1 in ovarian cancer [87,94]. As a result, they reported that iNOS and PD-L1 were indirectly correlated, where inhibition of the NF-kB pathway could result in the inhibition of iNOS and PD-L1. This inhibition could result in the promotion of T-cell activity, which could restore the ovarian cancer cell responses to CMI [87].

II. Nitric oxide pathway and cancer progression and therapy

Furthermore, Davis et al. analyzed the reversal of T-lymphocyte suppression through the use of granulocytic MDSCs (gMDSCs) [95]. Specifically, they studied head and neck squamous cell carcinomas (HNSCCs). They reported that MDSCs are drivers of immune suppression in HNSCCs [95–104]. They also found that P13K in the isoforms of p110δ and p110γ is frequently overexpressed in hematopoietic cells [95,105]. These isoforms have been shown to have immunosuppressive effects in the TME [95,106]. The PI3K pathway is involved in the regulation of MDSC function [95]. IPI-145 is an inhibitor of P13K isoforms p110δ and p110γ [95,107,108]. When giving IPI-145, it was found that the immunosuppressive effects of the PD-L1 pathway were abrogated [95]. The mechanism behind this was that IPI-145 suppressed gMDSCs, which resulted in the inhibition of arginase and iNOS production [95]. This was performed in murine oral cancer cells MOC1 and MOC2 [95].

Davis et al. found that the inhibition of gMDSCs resulted in the partial restoration of T-lymphocyte proliferation through the inhibition of iNOS and arginase [95]. It also resulted in the enhancement of CD8 cytotoxic T-cell activity. This restored the response to PD-L1 mAb therapy, aiding in the reversal of the resistance against PD-L1 blockade therapy. Therefore, this displays that in MOC1 and MOC2, iNOS contributes to the regulation of PD-L1 in the TME, whereby the inhibition of iNOS resulted in the inhibition of PD-L1 [95].

Ekmekcioglu et al. reported that iNOS plays a significant role in the resistance against adoptive T-cell therapies in many cancers [109–113]. Specifically, iNOS has been shown to increase malignancy in pancreatic cancers [113,114]. In CSF1/CSF1R blockade therapy, the inhibition of iNOS resulted in a greater ORR to the blockade therapy [113]. This study concluded that further research must be conducted to confirm the role of inhibiting iNOS in improving checkpoint inhibitor therapies. This could inform whether or not inhibiting iNOS would improve the ORR to PD-L1 blockade therapy in cancers [113].

Liu et al. found that interferons (IFNs) are involved in inhibiting MDSC T-cell suppression [115,116]. Specifically, STAT-1 is a protein that mediates IFNγ signaling [116,117]. When STAT-1 was knocked out in mice, MDSCs no longer could inhibit T-cell activation [116,117]. This is because MDSCs could no longer produce iNOS and arginase [116–118]. As a result, indirectly inhibiting iNOS activity resulted in the restoration of T-cell activity [116,117]. They also found that PD-L1 is upregulated by MDSCs [116,119]. Therefore, when STAT-1 activates IFNγ signaling, it inhibits both iNOS and PD-L1 upregulation, which results in combating the resistance against PD-L1 blockade therapy [116].

Yin et al. investigated the effects of the serine/threonine kinase Aurora A on iNOS in breast cancer [120–123]. They conducted their experiment through the use of the in vitro 4T1 murine mammary tumor cell line [123]. Specifically, they used the drug alisertib, which is a small-molecule inhibitor of Aurora A kinase [123–128]. When they treated the cancer cells with alisertib, they found that apoptosis was simulated in the MDSCs. The mechanism behind this was that alisertib inhibits STAT3, which is a key transcription factor in MDSCs [123,129]. As a result, alisertib inhibits the mRNA levels of iNOS in the cancer cells, resulting in the increase in CD8 T lymphocyte activity. This activity restores the immunosuppression caused by PD-L1.

In breast cancer, the application of CPIs was examined [130]. Santa-Maria and Nanda reported that different subtypes of breast cancer had different overall response rates (ORRs) to immunotherapy [130–132]. They conducted their review on PD-L1-positive patients [130]. They found that triple-negative breast cancer (TNBC) has been reported to show the greatest ORR of 18.5% to immune checkpoint inhibitors (ICIs) such as PD-1 inhibitors [37,130]. ER breast cancer had a lower ORR of 12% to PD-1 ICIs [130,133]. In HER-2-positive breast cancer, it was found to have an ORR of 15% to PD-1 ICIs [130,134]. However, in PD-L1-positive patients, immunotherapy in combination with therapies such as chemotherapy and radiation therapy has had greater overall survival rates than immunotherapy alone [130,135,136]. This is a result of PD-L1-positive patients showing a resistance to immunotherapy [137,138]. In combination with PD-L1 blockade therapy, Aurora A allows for novel therapies to enhance the efficacy of anti-PD-L1 therapy in breast cancer [123].

A major challenge that we face is in obtaining clinically potent NOS2 inhibitors that are highly selective and with targeting specificity. While significant therapeutic effects with NOS2 inhibitors were shown in animal models, it remains their proof in clinical trials [139,140].

Remarks and perspectives

We have witnessed significant milestones in cancer treatment with targeted immunotherapies. These new treatment modalities have been reported to exert significant clinical responses in many resistant cancer types. However, there remains a large subset of cancer patients who are resistant to various immunotherapeutic regimens and require alternative interventions to reverse the resistance. Among the approaches that have been used clinically, the treatment with the FDA-approved CPIs resulted in significant clinical responses in many cancers [141]. But not all CPIs—for example, mAbs directed against PD-1 or PD-L1—blocked the inactivation of the anti-CD8 T cells via the PD-1 and PD-L1 interactions. In many cancers, CPIs were not effective in reversing resistance. Thus, if PD-L1 expression in cancer cells is inhibited, it will result in the restoration of the antitumor activity of CD8 T cells, which will inhibit tumor growth and prolong survival.

In this review, we have addressed the role of NOS2/NO in tumor cells in regulating the expression of PD-L1. We have also suggested that the treatment of PD-L1 expressing cancer cells with NO inhibitors will result in the inhibition of PD-L1 and will reduce/eliminate the inactivation of the antitumor CD8 T cells. Clearly, while this approach appears reasonable, the inhibition of NOS2/NO may have consequential effects. This is because NOS2/NO is also involved in other activities that are antitumorigenic, such as the antitumor cytotoxic activity of macrophages mediated by NO. NO has also been reported to sensitize tumor cells to both chemo- and immunotherapeutic drugs [142–145]. Thus, a more targeted inhibition of solely NOS2/NO in cancer cells may be an approach to circumvent other anticancer activities mediated by NO derived from other cells in the TME. It is possible to use conjugates of, for example, tumor-specific antibody fragments coupled with the NO inhibitor either directly [146,147] or in nanospheres [148,149]. Preclinical studies are recommended to test these therapeutics for their effectiveness and tumor specificity.

Acknowledgments

We acknowledge the Department of Microbiology, Immunology and Molecular Genetics and the Jonsson Comprehensive Cancer Center at UCLA for their assistance and support.

References

[1] García-Aranda M, Redondo M. Immunotherapy: a challenge of breast cancer treatment. Cancers 2019;11 (12):1822. https://doi.org/10.3390/cancers11121822.

[2] Peart O. Breast intervention and breast cancer treatment options. Radiol Technol 2015;86(5):535M–58M. quiz 559–562.

[3] Tong CWS, Wu M, Cho WCS, To KKW. Recent advances in the treatment of breast cancer. Front Oncol 2018;8:227.

[4] Łukasiewicz S, Czeczelewski M, Forma A, Baj J, Sitarz R, Stanisławek A. Breast cancer—epidemiology, risk factors, classification, prognostic markers, and current treatment strategies—an updated review. Cancers 2021;13(17):4287. https://doi.org/10.3390/cancers13174287.

[5] Maqbool M, Bekele F, Fekadu G. Treatment strategies against triple-negative breast cancer: an updated review. Breast Cancer (Dove Med Press) 2022;14:15–24. https://doi.org/10.2147/BCTT.S348060.

[6] Kaufman B, Mackey JR, Clemens MR, Bapsy PP, Vaid A, Wardley A, Tjulandin S, Jahn M, Lehle M, Feyereislova A, Révil C, Jones A. Trastuzumab plus anastrozole versus anastrozole alone for the treatment of postmenopausal women with human epidermal growth factor receptor 2-positive, hormone receptor-positive metastatic breast cancer: results from the randomized phase III TAnDEM study. J Clin Oncol 2009;27(33):5529–37. https://doi.org/10.1200/JCO.2008.20.6847.

[7] Higgins MJ, Baselga J. Targeted therapies for breast cancer. J Clin Invest 2011;121(10):3797–803. https://doi.org/10.1172/JCI57152.

[8] Chandarlapaty S, Sawai A, Scaltriti M, Rodrik-Outmezguine V, Grbovic-Huezo O, Serra V, Majumder PK, Baselga J, Rosen N. AKT inhibition relieves feedback suppression of receptor tyrosine kinase expression and activity. Cancer Cell 2011;19(1):58–71. https://doi.org/10.1016/j.ccr.2010.10.031.

[9] Serra V, Markman B, Scaltriti M, Eichhorn PJA, Valero V, Guzman M, Botero ML, Llonch E, Atzori F, Di Cosimo S, Maira M, Garcia-Echeverria C, Parra JL, Arribas J, Baselga J. NVP-BEZ235, a dual PI3K/MTOR inhibitor, prevents PI3K signaling and inhibits the growth of cancer cells with activating PI3K mutations. Cancer Res 2008;68(19):8022–30. https://doi.org/10.1158/0008-5472.CAN-08-1385.

[10] Berns K, Horlings HM, Hennessy BT, Madiredjo M, Hijmans EM, Beelen K, Linn SC, Gonzalez-Angulo AM, Stemke-Hale K, Hauptmann M, Beijersbergen RL, Mills GB, van de Vijver MJ, Bernards R. A functional genetic approach identifies the PI3K pathway as a major determinant of trastuzumab resistance in breast cancer. Cancer Cell 2007;12(4):395–402. https://doi.org/10.1016/j.ccr.2007.08.030.

[11] Mittendorf EA, Wu Y, Scaltriti M, Meric-Bernstam F, Hunt KK, Dawood S, Esteva FJ, Buzdar AU, Chen H, Eksambi S, Hortobagyi GN, Baselga J, Gonzalez-Angulo AM. Loss of HER2 amplification following trastuzumab-based neoadjuvant systemic therapy and survival outcomes. Clin Cancer Res 2009;15(23): 7381–8. https://doi.org/10.1158/1078-0432.CCR-09-1735.

[12] Wong ST, Goodin S. Overcoming drug resistance in patients with metastatic breast cancer. Pharmacotherapy 2009;29(8):954–65. https://doi.org/10.1592/phco.29.8.954.

[13] Scaltriti M, Eichhorn PJ, Cortés J, Prudkin L, Aura C, Jiménez J, Chandarlapaty S, Serra V, Prat A, Ibrahim YH, Guzmán M, Gili M, Rodríguez O, Rodríguez S, Pérez J, Green SR, Mai S, Rosen N, Hudis C, Baselga J. Cyclin E amplification/overexpression is a mechanism of trastuzumab resistance in HER2+ breast cancer patients. Proc Natl Acad Sci U S A 2011;108(9):3761–6. https://doi.org/10.1073/pnas.1014835108.

[14] Disis ML, Stanton SE. Immunotherapy in breast cancer: an introduction. Breast 2018;37:196–9. https://doi.org/10.1016/j.breast.2017.01.013.

[15] Roybal KT, Rupp LJ, Morsut L, Walker WJ, McNally KA, Park JS, Lim WA. Precision tumor recognition by T cells with combinatorial antigen-sensing circuits. Cell 2016;164(4):770–9. https://doi.org/10.1016/j.cell.2016.01.011.

[16] Durgeau A, Virk Y, Corgnac S, Mami-Chouaib F. Recent advances in targeting CD8 T-cell immunity for more effective cancer immunotherapy. Front Immunol 2018;9:14.

[17] Raskov H, Orhan A, Christensen JP, Gögenur I. Cytotoxic CD8+ T cells in cancer and cancer immunotherapy. Br J Cancer 2021;124(2):359–67. https://doi.org/10.1038/s41416-020-01048-4.

[18] Buchbinder EI, Desai A. CTLA-4 and PD-1 pathways. Am J Clin Oncol 2016;39(1):98–106. https://doi.org/10.1097/COC.0000000000000239.

[19] Strome SE, Dong H, Tamura H, Voss SG, Flies DB, Tamada K, Salomao D, Cheville J, Hirano F, Lin W, Kasperbauer JL, Ballman KV, Chen L. B7-H1 blockade augments adoptive T-cell immunotherapy for squamous cell carcinoma. Cancer Res 2003;63(19):6501–5.

[20] John LB, Devaud C, Duong CPM, Yong CS, Beavis PA, Haynes NM, Chow MT, Smyth MJ, Kershaw MH, Darcy PK. Anti-PD-1 antibody therapy potently enhances the eradication of established tumors by gene-modified T cells. Clin Cancer Res 2013;19(20):5636–46. https://doi.org/10.1158/1078-0432.CCR-13-0458.

[21] Mayor M, Yang N, Sterman D, Jones DR, Adusumilli PS. Immunotherapy for non-small cell lung cancer: current concepts and clinical trials. Eur J Cardiothorac Surg 2016;49(5):1324–33. https://doi.org/10.1093/ejcts/ezv371.

[22] Cherkassky L, Morello A, Villena-Vargas J, Feng Y, Dimitrov DS, Jones DR, Sadelain M, Adusumilli PS. Human CAR T cells with cell-intrinsic PD-1 checkpoint blockade resist tumor-mediated inhibition. J Clin Invest 2016;126(8):3130–44. https://doi.org/10.1172/JCI83092.

[23] FDA. FDA approves atezolizumab for BRAF V600 unresectable or metastatic melanoma. FDA; 2020.

[24] Hodi FS, Chiarion-Sileni V, Gonzalez R, Grob J-J, Rutkowski P, Cowey CL, Lao CD, Schadendorf D, Wagstaff J, Dummer R, Ferrucci PF, Smylie M, Hill A, Hogg D, Marquez-Rodas I, Jiang J, Rizzo J, Larkin J, Wolchok JD. Nivolumab plus ipilimumab or nivolumab alone versus ipilimumab alone in advanced melanoma (CheckMate 067): 4-year outcomes of a multicentre, randomised, phase 3 trial. Lancet Oncol 2018;19(11):1480–92. https://doi.org/10.1016/S1470-2045(18)30700-9.

[25] Willsmore ZN, Harris RJ, Crescioli S, Hussein K, Kakkassery H, Thapa D, Cheung A, Chauhan J, Bax HJ, Chenoweth A, Laddach R, Osborn G, McCraw A, Hoffmann RM, Nakamura M, Geh JL, MacKenzie-Ross A, Healy C, Tsoka S, Spicer JF, Papa S, Barber L, Lacy KE, Karagiannis SN. B cells in patients with melanoma: implications for treatment with checkpoint inhibitor antibodies. Front Immunol 2021;11:622442.

[26] Kythreotou A, Siddique A, Mauri FA, Bower M, Pinato DJ. Pd-L1. J Clin Pathol 2018;71(3):189–94. https://doi.org/10.1136/jclinpath-2017-204853.

[27] Salmaninejad A, Valilou SF, Shabgah AG, Aslani S, Alimardani M, Pasdar A, Sahebkar A. PD-1/PD-L1 pathway: basic biology and role in cancer immunotherapy. J Cell Physiol 2019;234(10):16824–37. https://doi.org/10.1002/jcp.28358.

[28] Dong H, Zhu G, Tamada K, Chen L. B7-H1, a third member of the B7 family, co-stimulates T-cell proliferation and interleukin-10 secretion. Nat Med 1999;5(12):1365–9. https://doi.org/10.1038/70932.

[29] Sun C, Mezzadra R, Schumacher TN. Regulation and function of the PD-L1 checkpoint. Immunity 2018;48(3):434–52. https://doi.org/10.1016/j.immuni.2018.03.014.

[30] Hui E, Cheung J, Zhu J, Su X, Taylor MJ, Wallweber HA, Sasmal DK, Huang J, Kim JM, Mellman I, Vale RD. T cell costimulatory receptor CD28 is a primary target for PD-1-mediated inhibition. Science 2017;355(6332):1428–33. https://doi.org/10.1126/science.aaf1292.

[31] Kamphorst AO, Wieland A, Nasti T, Yang S, Zhang R, Barber DL, Konieczny BT, Daugherty CZ, Koenig L, Yu K, Sica GL, Sharpe AH, Freeman GJ, Blazar BR, Turka LA, Owonikoko TK, Pillai RN, Ramalingam SS, Araki K, Ahmed R. Rescue of exhausted CD8 T cells by PD-1-targeted therapies is CD28-dependent. Science 2017;355(6332):1423–7. https://doi.org/10.1126/science.aaf0683.

[32] Nowicki TS, Hu-Lieskovan S, Ribas A. Mechanisms of resistance to PD-1 and PD-L1 blockade. Cancer J 2018;24(1):47–53. https://doi.org/10.1097/PPO.0000000000000303.

[33] Mittendorf EA, Philips AV, Meric-Bernstam F, Qiao N, Wu Y, Harrington S, Su X, Wang Y, Gonzalez-Angulo AM, Akcakanat A, Chawla A, Curran M, Hwu P, Sharma P, Litton JK, Molldrem JJ, Alatrash G. PD-L1 expression in triple-negative breast cancer. Cancer Immunol Res 2014;2(4):361–70. https://doi.org/10.1158/2326-6066.CIR-13-0127.

[34] Kitano A, Ono M, Yoshida M, Noguchi E, Shimomura A, Shimoi T, Kodaira M, Yunokawa M, Yonemori K, Shimizu C, Kinoshita T, Fujiwara Y, Tsuda H, Tamura K. Tumour-infiltrating lymphocytes are correlated with higher expression levels of PD-1 and PD-L1 in early breast cancer. ESMO Open 2017;2(2), e000150. https://doi.org/10.1136/esmoopen-2016-000150.

[35] Noguchi E, Shien T, Iwata H. Current status of PD-1/PD-L1 blockade immunotherapy in breast cancer. Jpn J Clin Oncol 2021;51(3):321–32. https://doi.org/10.1093/jjco/hyaa230.

[36] Johnson DB, Chandra S, Sosman JA. Immune Checkpoint Inhibitor Toxicity in 2018. JAMA 2018;320(16):1702–3. https://doi.org/10.1001/jama.2018.13995.

[37] Nanda R, Chow LQM, Dees EC, Berger R, Gupta S, Geva R, Pusztai L, Pathiraja K, Aktan G, Cheng JD, Karantza V, Buisseret L. Pembrolizumab in patients with advanced triple-negative breast cancer: phase Ib KEYNOTE-012 study. J Clin Oncol 2016;34(21):2460–7. https://doi.org/10.1200/JCO.2015.64.8931.

[38] Dirix LY, Takacs I, Jerusalem G, Nikolinakos P, Arkenau H-T, Forero-Torres A, Boccia R, Lippman ME, Somer R, Smakal M, Emens LA, Hrinczenko B, Edenfield W, Gurtler J, von Heydebreck A, Grote HJ, Chin K, Hamilton EP. Avelumab, an anti-PD-L1 antibody, in patients with locally advanced or metastatic

II. Nitric oxide pathway and cancer progression and therapy

breast cancer: a phase 1b JAVELIN Solid Tumor Study. Breast Cancer Res Treat 2018;167(3):671–86. https://doi.org/10.1007/s10549-017-4537-5.

[39] Rugo HS, Loi S, Adams S, Schmid P, Schneeweiss A, Barrios CH, Iwata H, Dieras VC, Winer EP, Kockx M, Peeters D, Chui SY, Lin JC, Nguyen Duc A, Viale G, Molinero L, Emens LA. LBA20 – performance of PD-L1 immunohistochemistry (IHC) assays in unresectable locally advanced or metastatic triple-negative breast cancer (MTNBC): post-hoc analysis of IMpassion130. Ann Oncol 2019;30:v858–9. https://doi.org/10.1093/annonc/mdz394.009.

[40] Adams S, Loi S, Toppmeyer D, Cescon DW, De Laurentiis M, Nanda R, Winer EP, Mukai H, Tamura K, Armstrong A, Liu MC, Iwata H, Ryvo L, Wimberger P, Rugo HS, Tan AR, Jia L, Ding Y, Karantza V, Schmid P. Pembrolizumab monotherapy for previously untreated, PD-L1-positive, metastatic triple-negative breast cancer: cohort B of the phase II KEYNOTE-086 study. Ann Oncol 2019;30(3):405–11. https://doi.org/10.1093/annonc/mdy518.

[41] Adams S, Schmid P, Rugo HS, Winer EP, Loirat D, Awada A, Cescon DW, Iwata H, Campone M, Nanda R, Hui R, Curigliano G, Toppmeyer D, O'Shaughnessy J, Loi S, Paluch-Shimon S, Tan AR, Card D, Zhao J, Karantza V, Cortés J. Pembrolizumab monotherapy for previously treated metastatic triple-negative breast cancer: cohort A of the phase II KEYNOTE-086 study. Ann Oncol 2019;30(3):397–404. https://doi.org/10.1093/annonc/mdy517.

[42] Emens LA, Cruz C, Eder JP, Braiteh F, Chung C, Tolaney SM, Kuter I, Nanda R, Cassier PA, Delord J-P, Gordon MS, ElGabry E, Chang C-W, Sarkar I, Grossman W, O'Hear C, Fassò M, Molinero L, Schmid P. Long-term clinical outcomes and biomarker analyses of atezolizumab therapy for patients with metastatic triple-negative breast cancer: a phase 1 study. JAMA Oncol 2019;5(1):74–82. https://doi.org/10.1001/jamaoncol.2018.4224.

[43] Saleh R, Toor SM, Khalaf S, Elkord E. Breast cancer cells and PD-1/PD-L1 blockade upregulate the expression of PD-1, CTLA-4, TIM-3 and LAG-3 immune checkpoints in CD4+ T cells. Vaccines 2019;7(4):149. https://doi.org/10.3390/vaccines7040149.

[44] Wang Q, Wu X. Primary and acquired resistance to PD-1/PD-L1 blockade in cancer treatment. Int Immunopharmacol 2017;46:210–9. https://doi.org/10.1016/j.intimp.2017.03.015.

[45] Jiang X, Zhou J, Giobbie-Hurder A, Wargo J, Hodi FS. The activation of MAPK in melanoma cells resistant to BRAF inhibition promotes PD-L1 expression that is reversible by MEK and PI3K inhibition. Clin Cancer Res 2013;19(3):598–609. https://doi.org/10.1158/1078-0432.CCR-12-2731.

[46] Teng MWL, Ngiow SF, Ribas A, Smyth MJ. Classifying cancers based on T-cell infiltration and PD-L1. Cancer Res 2015;75(11):2139–45. https://doi.org/10.1158/0008-5472.CAN-15-0255.

[47] Robbins PF, Morgan RA, Feldman SA, Yang JC, Sherry RM, Dudley ME, Wunderlich JR, Nahvi AV, Helman LJ, Mackall CL, Kammula US, Hughes MS, Restifo NP, Raffeld M, Lee C-CR, Levy CL, Li YF, El-Gamil M, Schwarz SL, Laurencot C, Rosenberg SA. Tumor regression in patients with metastatic synovial cell sarcoma and melanoma using genetically engineered lymphocytes reactive with NY-ESO-1. J Clin Oncol 2011;29(7):917–24. https://doi.org/10.1200/JCO.2010.32.2537.

[48] Chodon T, Comin-Anduix B, Chmielowski B, Koya RC, Wu Z, Auerbach M, Ng C, Avramis E, Seja E, Villanueva A, McCannel TA, Ishiyama A, Czernin J, Radu CG, Wang X, Gjertson DW, Cochran AJ, Cornetta K, Wong DJL, Kaplan-Lefko P, Hamid O, Samlowski W, Cohen PA, Daniels GA, Mukherji B, Yang L, Zack JA, Kohn DB, Heath JR, Glaspy JA, Witte ON, Baltimore D, Economou JS, Ribas A. Adoptive transfer of MART-1 T-cell receptor transgenic lymphocytes and dendritic cell vaccination in patients with metastatic melanoma. Clin Cancer Res 2014;20(9):2457–65. https://doi.org/10.1158/1078-0432.CCR-13-3017.

[49] Robbins PF, Kassim SH, Tran TLN, Crystal JS, Morgan RA, Feldman SA, Yang JC, Dudley ME, Wunderlich JR, Sherry RM, Kammula US, Hughes MS, Restifo NP, Raffeld M, Lee C-CR, Li YF, El-Gamil M, Rosenberg SA. A pilot trial using lymphocytes genetically engineered with an NY-ESO-1-reactive T-cell receptor: long-term follow-up and correlates with response. Clin Cancer Res 2015;21(5):1019–27. https://doi.org/10.1158/1078-0432.CCR-14-2708.

[50] Hunder NN, Wallen H, Cao J, Hendricks DW, Reilly JZ, Rodmyre R, Jungbluth A, Gnjatic S, Thompson JA, Yee C. Treatment of metastatic melanoma with autologous CD4+ T cells against NY-ESO-1. N Engl J Med 2008;358(25):2698–703. https://doi.org/10.1056/NEJMoa0800251.

[51] Pollack SM, Jones RL, Farrar EA, Lai IP, Lee SM, Cao J, Pillarisetty VG, Hoch BL, Gullett A, Bleakley M, Conrad EU, Eary JF, Shibuya KC, Warren EH, Carstens JN, Heimfeld S, Riddell SR, Yee C. Tetramer guided, cell sorter assisted production of clinical grade autologous NY-ESO-1 specific CD8(+) T cells. J Immunother Cancer 2014;2(1):36. https://doi.org/10.1186/s40425-014-0036-y.

[52] Somaiah N, Block MS, Kim JW, Shapiro G, Hwu P, Eder JP, Jones RL, Gnjatic S, Lu H, Hsu FJ, Pollack S. Phase I, first-in-human trial of LV305 in patients with advanced or metastatic cancer expressing NY-ESO-1. JCO 2015;33 (15_suppl):3021. https://doi.org/10.1200/jco.2015.33.15_suppl.3021.

[53] Ott PA, Hu Z, Keskin DB, Shukla SA, Sun J, Bozym DJ, Zhang W, Luoma A, Giobbie-Hurder A, Peter L, Chen C, Olive O, Carter TA, Li S, Lieb DJ, Eisenhaure T, Gjini E, Stevens J, Lane WJ, Javeri I, Nellaiappan K, Salazar AM, Daley H, Seaman M, Buchbinder EI, Yoon CH, Harden M, Lennon N, Gabriel S, Rodig SJ, Barouch DH, Aster JC, Getz G, Wucherpfennig K, Neuberg D, Ritz J, Lander ES, Fritsch EF, Hacohen N, Wu CJ. An immunogenic personal neoantigen vaccine for patients with melanoma. Nature 2017;547(7662):217–21. https://doi.org/10.1038/nature22991.

[54] Sahin U, Derhovanessian E, Miller M, Kloke B-P, Simon P, Löwer M, Bukur V, Tadmor AD, Luxemburger U, Schrörs B, Omokoko T, Vormehr M, Albrecht C, Paruzynski A, Kuhn AN, Buck J, Heesch S, Schreeb KH, Müller F, Ortseifer I, Vogler I, Godehardt E, Attig S, Rae R, Breitkreuz A, Tolliver C, Suchan M, Martic G, Hohberger A, Sorn P, Diekmann J, Ciesla J, Waksmann O, Brück A-K, Witt M, Zillgen M, Rothermel A, Kasemann B, Langer D, Bolte S, Diken M, Kreiter S, Nemecek R, Gebhardt C, Grabbe S, Höller C, Utikal J, Huber C, Loquai C, Türeci Ö. Personalized RNA mutanome vaccines mobilize poly-specific therapeutic immunity against cancer. Nature 2017;547(7662):222–6. https://doi.org/10.1038/nature23003.

[55] Sun J-Y, Zhang D, Wu S, Xu M, Zhou X, Lu X-J, Ji J. Resistance to PD-1/PD-L1 blockade cancer immunotherapy: mechanisms, predictive factors, and future perspectives. Biomark Res 2020;8(1):35. https://doi.org/10.1186/s40364-020-00212-5.

[56] Yi M, Zheng X, Niu M, Zhu S, Ge H, Wu K. Combination strategies with PD-1/PD-L1 blockade: current advances and future directions. Mol Cancer 2022;21(1):28. https://doi.org/10.1186/s12943-021-01489-2.

[57] Obeid M, Tesniere A, Ghiringhelli F, Fimia GM, Apetoh L, Perfettini J-L, Castedo M, Mignot G, Panaretakis T, Casares N, Métivier D, Larochette N, van Endert P, Ciccosanti F, Piacentini M, Zitvogel L, Kroemer G. Calreticulin exposure dictates the immunogenicity of cancer cell death. Nat Med 2007;13(1):54–61. https://doi.org/10.1038/nm1523.

[58] Zhu H, Shan Y, Ge K, Lu J, Kong W, Jia C. Oxaliplatin induces immunogenic cell death in hepatocellular carcinoma cells and synergizes with immune checkpoint blockade therapy. Cell Oncol 2020;43(6):1203–14. https://doi.org/10.1007/s13402-020-00552-2.

[59] Beenen AC, Sauerer T, Schaft N, Dörrie J. Beyond cancer: regulation and function of PD-L1 in health and immune-related diseases. Int J Mol Sci 2022;23(15):8599. https://doi.org/10.3390/ijms23158599.

[60] Ritprajak P, Azuma M. Intrinsic and extrinsic control of expression of the immunoregulatory molecule PD-L1 in epithelial cells and squamous cell carcinoma. Oral Oncol 2015;51(3):221–8. https://doi.org/10.1016/j.oraloncology.2014.11.014.

[61] Barsoum IB, Smallwood CA, Siemens DR, Graham CH. A mechanism of hypoxia-mediated escape from adaptive immunity in cancer cells. Cancer Res 2014;74(3):665–74. https://doi.org/10.1158/0008-5472.CAN-13-0992.

[62] You L, Wu W, Wang X, Fang L, Adam V, Nepovimova E, Wu Q, Kuca K. The role of hypoxia-inducible factor 1 in tumor immune evasion. Med Res Rev 2021;41(3):1622–43. https://doi.org/10.1002/med.21771.

[63] Doi T, Ishikawa T, Okayama T, Oka K, Mizushima K, Yasuda T, Sakamoto N, Katada K, Kamada K, Uchiyama K, Handa O, Takagi T, Naito Y, Itoh Y. The JAK/STAT pathway is involved in the upregulation of PD-L1 expression in pancreatic cancer cell lines. Oncol Rep 2017;37(3):1545–54. https://doi.org/10.3892/or.2017.5399.

[64] Li P, Huang T, Zou Q, Liu D, Wang Y, Tan X, Wei Y, Qiu H. FGFR2 promotes expression of PD-L1 in colorectal cancer via the JAK/STAT3 signaling pathway. J Immunol 2019;202(10):3065–75. https://doi.org/10.4049/jimmunol.1801199.

[65] Galluzzi L, Spranger S, Fuchs E, López-Soto A. WNT signaling in cancer immunosurveillance. Trends Cell Biol 2019;29(1):44–65. https://doi.org/10.1016/j.tcb.2018.08.005.

[66] Zerdes I, Matikas A, Bergh J, Rassidakis GZ, Foukakis T. Genetic, transcriptional and post-translational regulation of the programmed death protein ligand 1 in cancer: biology and clinical correlations. Oncogene 2018;37 (34):4639–61. https://doi.org/10.1038/s41388-018-0303-3.

[67] Gong A-Y, Zhou R, Hu G, Li X, Splinter PL, O'Hara SP, LaRusso NF, Soukup GA, Dong H, Chen X-M. MicroRNA-513 regulates B7-H1 translation and is involved in IFN-gamma-induced B7-H1 expression in cholangiocytes. J Immunol 2009;182(3):1325–33. https://doi.org/10.4049/jimmunol.182.3.1325.

[68] Ju X, Zhang H, Zhou Z, Chen M, Wang Q. Tumor-associated macrophages induce PD-L1 expression in gastric cancer cells through IL-6 and TNF-α signaling. Exp Cell Res 2020;396(2), 112315. https://doi.org/10.1016/j.yexcr.2020.112315.

II. Nitric oxide pathway and cancer progression and therapy

[69] Hays E, Bonavida B. YY1 regulates cancer cell immune resistance by modulating PD-L1 expression. Drug Resist Updat 2019;43:10–28. https://doi.org/10.1016/j.drup.2019.04.001.

[70] Atsaves V, Leventaki V, Rassidakis GZ, Claret FX. AP-1 transcription factors as regulators of immune responses in cancer. Cancers 2019;11(7):1037. https://doi.org/10.3390/cancers11071037.

[71] Green MR, Rodig S, Juszczynski P, Ouyang J, Sinha P, O'Donnell E, Neuberg D, Shipp MA. Constitutive AP-1 activity and EBV infection induce PD-L1 in Hodgkin lymphomas and posttransplant lymphoproliferative disorders: implications for targeted therapy. Clin Cancer Res 2012;18(6):1611–8. https://doi.org/10.1158/1078-0432.CCR-11-1942.

[72] Fang W, Zhang J, Hong S, Zhan J, Chen N, Qin T, Tang Y, Zhang Y, Kang S, Zhou T, Wu X, Liang W, Hu Z, Ma Y, Zhao Y, Tian Y, Yang Y, Xue C, Yan Y, Hou X, Huang P, Huang Y, Zhao H, Zhang L. EBV-driven LMP1 and IFN-γ up-regulate PD-L1 in nasopharyngeal carcinoma: implications for oncotargeted therapy. Oncotarget 2014;5(23):12189–202.

[73] Lamberti G, Sisi M, Andrini E, Palladini A, Giunchi F, Lollini P-L, Ardizzoni A, Gelsomino F. The mechanisms of PD-L1 regulation in non-small-cell lung cancer (NSCLC): which are the involved players? Cancers 2020;12(11):3129. https://doi.org/10.3390/cancers12113129.

[74] Wang S, Wang G, Zhang L, Li F, Liu K, Wang Y, Shi Y, Cao K. Interleukin-17 promotes nitric oxide-dependent expression of PD-L1 in mesenchymal stem cells. Cell Biosci 2020;10(1):73. https://doi.org/10.1186/s13578-020-00431-1.

[75] Nafea H, Youness RA, Abou-Aisha K, Gad MZ. LncRNA HEIH/MiR-939-5p interplay modulates triple-negative breast cancer progression through NOS2-induced nitric oxide production. J Cell Physiol 2021;236(7):5362–72. https://doi.org/10.1002/jcp.30234.

[76] Kiriyama Y, Tani A, Kadoya M, Okamoto R, Nochi H. Induction of PD-L1 by nitric oxide *via* JNK activation in A172 glioblastoma cells. Biol Pharm Bull 2020;43(6):1020–2. https://doi.org/10.1248/bpb.b20-00087.

[77] Kang C, Song C-H, Kim N, Nam RH, Choi SI, Yu JE, Nho H, Choi JA, Kim JW, Na HY, Lee H-N, Surh Y-J. The enhanced inhibitory effect of estrogen on PD-L1 expression following Nrf2 deficiency in the AOM/DSS model of colitis-associated cancer. Front Oncol 2021;11, 679324. https://doi.org/10.3389/fonc.2021.679324.

[78] Lequeux A, Noman MZ, Xiao M, Sauvage D, Van Moer K, Viry E, Bocci I, Hasmim M, Bosseler M, Berchem G, Janji B. Impact of hypoxic tumor microenvironment and tumor cell plasticity on the expression of immune checkpoints. Cancer Lett 2019;458:13–20. https://doi.org/10.1016/j.canlet.2019.05.021.

[79] Mateo J, García-Lecea M, Cadenas S, Hernández C, Moncada S. Regulation of hypoxia-inducible factor-1α by nitric oxide through mitochondria-dependent and -independent pathways. Biochem J 2003;376(2):537–44. https://doi.org/10.1042/bj20031155.

[80] Bonavida B, Baritaki S, Huerta-Yepez S, Vega MI, Chatterjee D, Yeung K. Novel therapeutic applications of nitric oxide donors in cancer: roles in chemo- and immunosensitization to apoptosis and inhibition of metastases. Nitric Oxide 2008;19(2):152–7. https://doi.org/10.1016/j.niox.2008.04.018.

[81] Dai X, Pi G, Yang S, Chen GG, Liu L, Dong H-H. Association of PD-L1 and HIF-1α coexpression with poor prognosis in hepatocellular carcinoma. Transl Oncol 2018;11(2):559–66. https://doi.org/10.1016/j.tranon.2018.02.014.

[82] Hays E, Bonavida B. Nitric oxide-mediated enhancement and reversal of resistance of anticancer therapies. Antioxidants 2019;8(9):407. https://doi.org/10.3390/antiox8090407.

[83] Sung Y-C, Jin P-R, Chu L-A, Hsu F-F, Wang M-R, Chang C-C, Chiou S-J, Qiu JT, Gao D-Y, Lin C-C, Chen Y-S, Hsu Y-C, Wang J, Wang F-N, Yu P-L, Chiang A-S, Wu AY-T, Ko JJ-S, Lai CP-K, Lu T-T, Chen Y. Delivery of nitric oxide with a nanocarrier promotes tumour vessel normalization and potentiates anti-cancer therapies. Nat Nanotechnol 2019;14(12):1160–9. https://doi.org/10.1038/s41565-019-0570-3.

[84] Minhas R, Bansal Y, Bansal G. Inducible nitric oxide synthase inhibitors: a comprehensive update. Med Res Rev 2020;40(3):823–55. https://doi.org/10.1002/med.21636.

[85] Kaneguchi A, Ozawa J, Minamimoto K, Yamaoka K. Nitric oxide synthase inhibitor L-NG-nitroarginine methyl ester (L-NAME) attenuates remobilization-induced joint inflammation. Nitric Oxide 2020;96:13–9. https://doi.org/10.1016/j.niox.2020.01.003.

[86] Król M, Kepinska M. Human nitric oxide synthase—its functions, polymorphisms, and inhibitors in the context of inflammation, diabetes and cardiovascular diseases. Int J Mol Sci 2021;22(1):56. https://doi.org/10.3390/ijms22010056.

[87] Abiko K, Hamanishi J, Matsumura N, Mandai M. Dynamic host immunity and PD-L1/PD-1 blockade efficacy: developments after "IFN-γ from lymphocytes induces PD-L1 expression and promotes progression of ovarian cancer". Br J Cancer 2022;1–7. https://doi.org/10.1038/s41416-022-01960-x.

II. Nitric oxide pathway and cancer progression and therapy

[88] Horikawa N, Abiko K, Matsumura N, Hamanishi J, Baba T, Yamaguchi K, Yoshioka Y, Koshiyama M, Konishi I. Expression of vascular endothelial growth factor in ovarian cancer inhibits tumor immunity through the accumulation of myeloid-derived suppressor cells. Clin Cancer Res 2017;23(2):587–99. https://doi.org/10.1158/1078-0432.CCR-16-0387.

[89] Abiko K, Hayashi T, Yamaguchi K, Mandai M, Konishi I. Potential novel ovarian cancer treatment targeting myeloid-derived suppressor cells. Cancer Investig 2021;39(4):310–4. https://doi.org/10.1080/07357907.2020.1871487.

[90] Perren TJ, Swart AM, Pfisterer J, Ledermann JA, Pujade-Lauraine E, Kristensen G, Carey MS, Beale P, Cervantes A, Kurzeder C, Bois Ad, Sehouli J, Kimmig R, Stähle A, Collinson F, Essapen S, Gourley C, Lortholary A, Selle F, Mirza MR, Leminen A, Plante M, Stark D, Qian W, Parmar MKB, Oza AM. A phase 3 trial of bevacizumab in ovarian cancer. N Engl J Med 2011;365(26):2484–96. https://doi.org/10.1056/NEJMoa1103799.

[91] Aghajanian C, Blank SV, Goff BA, Judson PL, Teneriello MG, Husain A, Sovak MA, Yi J, Nycum LR. OCEANS: a randomized, double-blind, placebo-controlled phase III trial of chemotherapy with or without bevacizumab in patients with platinum-sensitive recurrent epithelial ovarian, primary peritoneal, or fallopian tube cancer. J Clin Oncol 2012;30(17):2039–45. https://doi.org/10.1200/JCO.2012.42.0505.

[92] Poveda AM, Selle F, Hilpert F, Reuss A, Savarese A, Vergote I, Witteveen P, Bamias A, Scotto N, Mitchell L, Pujade-Lauraine E. Bevacizumab combined with weekly paclitaxel, pegylated liposomal doxorubicin, or topotecan in platinum-resistant recurrent ovarian cancer: analysis by chemotherapy cohort of the randomized phase III AURELIA trial. J Clin Oncol 2015;33(32):3836–8. https://doi.org/10.1200/JCO.2015.63.1408.

[93] Taki M, Abiko K, Baba T, Hamanishi J, Yamaguchi K, Murakami R, Yamanoi K, Horikawa N, Hosoe Y, Nakamura E, Sugiyama A, Mandai M, Konishi I, Matsumura N. Snail promotes ovarian cancer progression by recruiting myeloid-derived suppressor cells via CXCR2 ligand upregulation. Nat Commun 2018;9(1):1685. https://doi.org/10.1038/s41467-018-03966-7.

[94] Peng J, Hamanishi J, Matsumura N, Abiko K, Murat K, Baba T, Yamaguchi K, Horikawa N, Hosoe Y, Murphy SK, Konishi I, Mandai M. Chemotherapy induces programmed cell death-ligand 1 overexpression via the nuclear factor-κB to foster an immunosuppressive tumor microenvironment in ovarian cancer. Cancer Res 2015;75(23):5034–45. https://doi.org/10.1158/0008-5472.CAN-14-3098.

[95] Davis RJ, Moore EC, Clavijo PE, Friedman J, Cash H, Chen Z, Silvin C, Van Waes C, Allen C. Anti-PD-L1 efficacy can be enhanced by inhibition of myeloid-derived suppressor cells with a selective inhibitor of PI3Kδ/γ. Cancer Res 2017;77(10):2607–19. https://doi.org/10.1158/0008-5472.CAN-16-2534.

[96] Pak AS, Wright MA, Matthews JP, Collins SL, Petruzzelli GJ, Young MR. Mechanisms of immune suppression in patients with head and neck cancer: presence of CD34(+) cells which suppress immune functions within cancers that secrete granulocyte-macrophage colony-stimulating factor. Clin Cancer Res 1995;1(1):95–103.

[97] Young MRI, Petruzzelli GJ, Kolesiak K, Achille N, Lathers DMR, Gabrilovich DI. Human squamous cell carcinomas of the head and neck chemoattract immune suppressive CD34+ progenitor cells. Hum Immunol 2001;62(4):332–41. https://doi.org/10.1016/S0198-8859(01)00222-1.

[98] Gabrilovich DI, Bronte V, Chen S-H, Colombo MP, Ochoa A, Ostrand-Rosenberg S, Schreiber H. The terminology issue for myeloid-derived suppressor cells. Cancer Res 2007;67(1):425. author reply 426 https://doi.org/10.1158/0008-5472.CAN-06-3037.

[99] Gabrilovich DI, Nagaraj S. Myeloid-derived suppressor cells as regulators of the immune system. Nat Rev Immunol 2009;9(3):162–74. https://doi.org/10.1038/nri2506.

[100] Gabitass RF, Annels NE, Stocken DD, Pandha HA, Middleton GW. Elevated myeloid-derived suppressor cells in pancreatic, esophageal and gastric cancer are an independent prognostic factor and are associated with significant elevation of the Th2 cytokine interleukin-13. Cancer Immunol Immunother 2011;60(10):1419–30. https://doi.org/10.1007/s00262-011-1028-0.

[101] Vasquez-Dunddel D, Pan F, Zeng Q, Gorbounov M, Albesiano E, Fu J, Blosser RL, Tam AJ, Bruno T, Zhang H, Pardoll D, Kim Y. STAT3 regulates arginase-I in myeloid-derived suppressor cells from cancer patients. J Clin Invest 2013;123(4):1580–9. https://doi.org/10.1172/JCI60083.

[102] Arina A, Schreiber K, Binder DC, Karrison TG, Liu RB, Schreiber H. Adoptively transferred immune T cells eradicate established tumors despite cancer-induced immune suppression. J Immunol 2014;192(3):1286–93. https://doi.org/10.4049/jimmunol.1202498.

[103] Weed DT, Vella JL, Reis IM, De la Fuente AC, Gomez C, Sargi Z, Nazarian R, Califano J, Borrello I, Serafini P. Tadalafil reduces myeloid-derived suppressor cells and regulatory T cells and promotes tumor immunity in patients with head and neck squamous cell carcinoma. Clin Cancer Res 2015;21(1):39–48. https://doi.org/10.1158/1078-0432.CCR-14-1711.

II. Nitric oxide pathway and cancer progression and therapy

[104] Davis RJ, Van Waes C, Allen CT. Overcoming barriers to effective immunotherapy: MDSCs, TAMs, and Tregs as mediators of the immunosuppressive microenvironment in head and neck cancer. Oral Oncol 2016;58:59–70. https://doi.org/10.1016/j.oraloncology.2016.05.002.

[105] Vanhaesebroeck B, Guillermet-Guibert J, Graupera M, Bilanges B. The emerging mechanisms of isoform-specific PI3K signalling. Nat Rev Mol Cell Biol 2010;11(5):329–41. https://doi.org/10.1038/nrm2882.

[106] Ali K, Soond DR, Pineiro R, Hagemann T, Pearce W, Lim EL, Bouabe H, Scudamore CL, Hancox T, Maecker H, Friedman L, Turner M, Okkenhaug K, Vanhaesebroeck B. Inactivation of PI(3)K P110δ breaks regulatory T-cell-mediated immune tolerance to cancer. Nature 2014;510(7505):407–11. https://doi.org/10.1038/nature13444.

[107] Winkler DG, Faia KL, DiNitto JP, Ali JA, White KF, Brophy EE, Pink MM, Proctor JL, Lussier J, Martin CM, Hoyt JG, Tillotson B, Murphy EL, Lim AR, Thomas BD, Macdougall JR, Ren P, Liu Y, Li L-S, Jessen KA, Fritz CC, Dunbar JL, Porter JR, Rommel C, Palombella VJ, Changelian PS, Kutok JL. PI3K-δ and PI3K-γ inhibition by IPI-145 abrogates immune responses and suppresses activity in autoimmune and inflammatory disease models. Chem Biol 2013;20(11):1364–74. https://doi.org/10.1016/j.chembiol.2013.09.017.

[108] Flinn I, Oki Y, Patel M, Horwitz SM, Foss FM, Sweeney J, Allen K, Douglas M, Steelman L, Dunbar J, Stern HM, Kelly P, Kahl B. A Phase 1 evaluation of duvelisib (IPI-145), a PI3K-δ,γ inhibitor, in patients with relapsed/refractory INHL. Blood 2014;124(21):802. https://doi.org/10.1182/blood.V124.21.802.802.

[109] Cianchi F, Cortesini C, Fantappiè O, Messerini L, Schiavone N, Vannacci A, Nistri S, Sardi I, Baroni G, Marzocca C, Perna F, Mazzanti R, Bechi P, Masini E. Inducible nitric oxide synthase expression in human colorectal cancer: correlation with tumor angiogenesis. Am J Pathol 2003;162(3):793–801. https://doi.org/10.1016/S0002-9440(10)63876-X.

[110] Ekmekcioglu S, Ellerhorst JA, Prieto VG, Johnson MM, Broemeling LD, Grimm EA. Tumor INOS predicts poor survival for stage III melanoma patients. Int J Cancer 2006;119(4):861–6. https://doi.org/10.1002/ijc.21767.

[111] Grimm EA, Ellerhorst J, Tang C-H, Ekmekcioglu S. Constitutive intracellular production of INOS and NO in human melanoma: possible role in regulation of growth and resistance to apoptosis. Nitric Oxide 2008;19(2):133–7. https://doi.org/10.1016/j.niox.2008.04.009.

[112] Granados-Principal S, Liu Y, Guevara ML, Blanco E, Choi DS, Qian W, Patel T, Rodriguez AA, Cusimano J, Weiss HL, Zhao H, Landis MD, Dave B, Gross SS, Chang JC. Inhibition of INOS as a novel effective targeted therapy against triple-negative breast cancer. Breast Cancer Res 2015;17:25. https://doi.org/10.1186/s13058-015-0527-x.

[113] Ekmekcioglu S, Grimm EA, Roszik J. Targeting INOS to increase efficacy of immunotherapies. Hum Vaccin Immunother 2017;13(5):1105–8. https://doi.org/10.1080/21645515.2016.1276682.

[114] Bailey P, Chang DK, Forget M-A, Lucas FAS, Alvarez HA, Haymaker C, Chattopadhyay C, Kim S-H, Ekmekcioglu S, Grimm EA, Biankin AV, Hwu P, Maitra A, Roszik J. Exploiting the neoantigen landscape for immunotherapy of pancreatic ductal adenocarcinoma. Sci Rep 2016;6:35848. https://doi.org/10.1038/srep35848.

[115] Greifenberg V, Ribechini E, Rössner S, Lutz MB. Myeloid-derived suppressor cell activation by combined LPS and IFN-gamma treatment impairs DC development. Eur J Immunol 2009;39(10):2865–76. https://doi.org/10.1002/eji.200939486.

[116] Liu Y, Wei G, Cheng WA, Dong Z, Sun H, Lee VY, Cha S-C, Smith DL, Kwak LW, Qin H. Targeting myeloid-derived suppressor cells for cancer immunotherapy. Cancer Immunol Immunother 2018;67(8):1181–95. https://doi.org/10.1007/s00262-018-2175-3.

[117] Kusmartsev S, Gabrilovich DI. STAT1 signaling regulates tumor-associated macrophage-mediated T cell deletion. J Immunol 2005;174(8):4880–91. https://doi.org/10.4049/jimmunol.174.8.4880.

[118] Gallina G, Dolcetti L, Serafini P, De Santo C, Marigo I, Colombo MP, Basso G, Brombacher F, Borrello I, Zanovello P, Bicciato S, Bronte V. Tumors induce a subset of inflammatory monocytes with immunosuppressive activity on CD8+ T cells. J Clin Invest 2006;116(10):2777–90. https://doi.org/10.1172/JCI28828.

[119] Noman MZ, Desantis G, Janji B, Hasmim M, Karray S, Dessen P, Bronte V, Chouaib S. PD-L1 is a novel direct target of HIF-1α, and its blockade under hypoxia enhanced MDSC-mediated T cell activation. J Exp Med 2014;211(5):781–90. https://doi.org/10.1084/jem.20131916.

[120] Nikonova AS, Astsaturov I, Serebriiskii IG, Dunbrack RL, Golemis EA. Aurora A kinase (AURKA) in normal and pathological cell division. Cell Mol Life Sci 2013;70(4):661–87. https://doi.org/10.1007/s00018-012-1073-7.

[121] D'Assoro AB, Haddad T, Galanis E. Aurora-A kinase as a promising therapeutic target in cancer. Front Oncol 2015;5:295. https://doi.org/10.3389/fonc.2015.00295.

[122] Damodaran AP, Vaufrey L, Gavard O, Prigent C. Aurora A kinase is a priority pharmaceutical target for the treatment of cancers. Trends Pharmacol Sci 2017;38(8):687–700. https://doi.org/10.1016/j.tips.2017.05.003.

[123] Yin T, Zhao Z-B, Guo J, Wang T, Yang J-B, Wang C, Long J, Ma S, Huang Q, Zhang K, Ma X, Liu C, Liu S, Lian Z-X, Yang Z. Aurora A inhibition eliminates myeloid cell–mediated immunosuppression and enhances the efficacy of anti–PD-L1 therapy in breast cancer. Cancer Res 2019;79(13):3431–44. https://doi.org/10.1158/0008-5472.CAN-18-3397.

[124] Cervantes A, Elez E, Roda D, Ecsedy J, Macarulla T, Venkatakrishnan K, Roselló S, Andreu J, Jung J, Sanchis-Garcia JM, Piera A, Blasco I, Maños L, Pérez-Fidalgo J-A, Fingert H, Baselga J, Tabernero J. Phase I pharmacokinetic/pharmacodynamic study of MLN8237, an investigational, oral, selective Aurora a kinase inhibitor, in patients with advanced solid tumors. Clin Cancer Res 2012;18(17):4764–74. https://doi.org/10.1158/1078-0432.CCR-12-0571.

[125] Dees EC, Cohen RB, von Mehren M, Stinchcombe TE, Liu H, Venkatakrishnan K, Manfredi M, Fingert H, Burris HA, Infante JR. Phase I study of Aurora A kinase inhibitor MLN8237 in advanced solid tumors: safety, pharmacokinetics, pharmacodynamics, and bioavailability of two oral formulations. Clin Cancer Res 2012;18 (17):4775–84. https://doi.org/10.1158/1078-0432.CCR-12-0589.

[126] Matulonis UA, Sharma S, Ghamande S, Gordon MS, Del Prete SA, Ray-Coquard I, Kutarska E, Liu H, Fingert H, Zhou X, Danaee H, Schilder RJ. Phase II study of MLN8237 (alisertib), an investigational Aurora A kinase inhibitor, in patients with platinum-resistant or -refractory epithelial ovarian, fallopian tube, or primary peritoneal carcinoma. Gynecol Oncol 2012;127(1):63–9. https://doi.org/10.1016/j.ygyno.2012.06.040.

[127] Melichar B, Adenis A, Lockhart AC, Bennouna J, Dees EC, Kayaleh O, Obermannova R, DeMichele A, Zatloukal P, Zhang B, Ullmann CD, Schusterbauer C. Safety and activity of alisertib, an investigational Aurora kinase A inhibitor, in patients with breast cancer, small-cell lung cancer, non-small-cell lung cancer, head and neck squamous-cell carcinoma, and gastro-oesophageal adenocarcinoma: a five-arm phase 2 study. Lancet Oncol 2015;16(4):395–405. https://doi.org/10.1016/S1470-2045(15)70051-3.

[128] Liewer S, Huddleston A. Alisertib: a review of pharmacokinetics, efficacy and toxicity in patients with hematologic malignancies and solid tumors. Expert Opin Investig Drugs 2018;27(1):105–12. https://doi.org/10.1080/13543784.2018.1417382.

[129] Diaz-Montero CM, Salem ML, Nishimura MI, Garrett-Mayer E, Cole DJ, Montero AJ. Increased circulating myeloid-derived suppressor cells correlate with clinical cancer stage, metastatic tumor burden, and doxorubicin-cyclophosphamide chemotherapy. Cancer Immunol Immunother 2009;58(1):49–59. https://doi.org/10.1007/s00262-008-0523-4.

[130] Santa-Maria CA, Nanda R. Immune checkpoint inhibitor therapy in breast cancer. J Natl Compr Cancer Netw 2018;16(10):1259–68. https://doi.org/10.6004/jnccn.2018.7046.

[131] Perou CM, Sørlie T, Eisen MB, van de Rijn M, Jeffrey SS, Rees CA, Pollack JR, Ross DT, Johnsen H, Akslen LA, Fluge Ø, Pergamenschikov A, Williams C, Zhu SX, Lønning PE, Børresen-Dale A-L, Brown PO, Botstein D. Molecular portraits of human breast tumours. Nature 2000;406(6797):747–52. https://doi.org/10.1038/35021093.

[132] Tobin NP, Harrell JC, Lövrot J, Egyhazi Brage S, Frostvik Stolt M, Carlsson L, Einbeigi Z, Linderholm B, Loman N, Malmberg M, Walz T, Fernö M, Perou CM, Bergh J, Hatschek T, Lindström LS, Hatschek T, Fernö M, Lindström LS, Hedenfalk I, Brandberg Y, Carstensen J, Egyhazy S, Stolt MF, Skoog L, Hellström M, Maliniemi M, Svensson H, Åström G, Bergh J, Bjöhle J, Lidbrink E, Rotstein S, Wallberg B, Einbeigi Z, Carlsson P, Linderholm B, Walz T, Loman N, Malmström P, Söderberg M, Malmberg M, Carlsson L, Umeå, Lindh B, Sundqvist M, Malmberg L. Molecular subtype and tumor characteristics of breast cancer metastases as assessed by gene expression significantly influence patient post-relapse survival. Ann Oncol 2015;26(1):81–8. https://doi.org/10.1093/annonc/mdu498.

[133] Rugo H, Delord J-P, Im S-A, Ott P, Piha-Paul S, Bedard P, Sachdev J, Le Tourneau C, van Brummelen E, Varga A, Saraf S, Pietrangelo D, Karantza V, Tan A. Abstract S5-07: preliminary efficacy and safety of pembrolizumab (MK-3475) in patients with PD-L1–positive, estrogen receptor-positive (ER+)/HER2-negative advanced breast cancer enrolled in KEYNOTE-028. Cancer Res 2016;76(4_Supplement). https://doi.org/10.1158/1538-7445.SABCS15-S5-07. S5-07.

[134] Loi S, Giobbie-Hurder A, Gombos A, Bachelot T, Hui R, Curigliano G, Campone M, Biganzoli L, Bonnefoi H, Jerusalem G, Bartsch R, Rabaglio-Poretti M, Kammler R, Maibach R, Smyth MJ, Di Leo A, Colleoni M, Viale G, Regan MM, André F. International Breast Cancer Study Group and the Breast International Group.

II. Nitric oxide pathway and cancer progression and therapy

Pembrolizumab plus trastuzumab in trastuzumab-resistant, advanced, HER2-positive breast cancer (PANA-CEA): a single-arm, multicentre, phase 1b-2 trial. Lancet Oncol 2019;20:371–82.

[135] Zeng J, See AP, Phallen J, Jackson CM, Belcaid Z, Ruzevick J, Durham N, Meyer C, Harris TJ, Albesiano E, Pradilla G, Ford E, Wong J, Hammers H-J, Mathios D, Tyler B, Brem H, Tran PT, Pardoll D, Drake CG, Lim M. Anti-PD-1 blockade and stereotactic radiation produce long-term survival in mice with intracranial gliomas. Int J Radiat Oncol Biol Phys 2013;86(2):343–9. https://doi.org/10.1016/j.ijrobp.2012.12.025.

[136] Emens LA, Adams S, Loi S, Schneeweiss A, Rugo HS, Winer EP, Barrios CH, Dieras V, de la Haba-Rodriguez J, Gianni L, Chui SY, Schmid P. IMpassion130: a phase III randomized trial of atezolizumab with nab-paclitaxel for first-line treatment of patients with metastatic triple-negative breast cancer (MTNBC). JCO 2016;34 (15_suppl). https://doi.org/10.1200/JCO.2016.34.15_suppl.TPS1104. TPS1104.

[137] Zhang J, Fang W, Qin T, Yang Y, Hong S, Liang W, Ma Y, Zhao H, Huang Y, Xue C, Huang P, Hu Z, Zhao Y, Zhang L. Co-expression of PD-1 and PD-L1 predicts poor outcome in nasopharyngeal carcinoma. Med Oncol 2015;32(3):86. https://doi.org/10.1007/s12032-015-0501-6.

[138] Ren D, Hua Y, Yu B, Ye X, He Z, Li C, Wang J, Mo Y, Wei X, Chen Y, Zhou Y, Liao Q, Wang H, Xiang B, Zhou M, Li X, Li G, Li Y, Zeng Z, Xiong W. Predictive biomarkers and mechanisms underlying resistance to PD1/PD-L1 blockade cancer immunotherapy. Mol Cancer 2020;19(1):19. https://doi.org/10.1186/s12943-020-1144-6.

[139] Özenver N, Efferth T. Small molecule inhibitors and stimulators of inducible nitric oxide synthase in cancer cells from natural origin (phytochemicals, marine compounds, antibiotics). Biochem Pharmacol 2020;176, 113792. https://doi.org/10.1016/j.bcp.2020.113792.

[140] Gage MC, Thippeswamy T. Inhibitors of Src family kinases, inducible nitric oxide synthase, and NADPH oxidase as potential CNS drug targets for neurological diseases. CNS Drugs 2021;35(1):1–20. https://doi.org/10.1007/s40263-020-00787-5.

[141] Kaushik I, Ramachandran S, Zabel C, Gaikwad S, Srivastava SK. The evolutionary legacy of immune checkpoint inhibitors. Semin Cancer Biol 2022. https://doi.org/10.1016/j.semcancer.2022.03.020. S1044-579X(22) 00076-1.

[142] Wink DA, Cook JA, Christodoulou D, Krishna MC, Pacelli R, Kim S, DeGraff W, Gamson J, Vodovotz Y, Russo A, Mitchell JB. Nitric oxide and some nitric oxide donor compounds enhance the cytotoxicity of cisplatin. Nitric Oxide 1997;1(1):88–94. https://doi.org/10.1006/niox.1996.0108.

[143] Huerta S, Baay-Guzman G, Gonzalez-Bonilla CR, Livingston EH, Huerta-Yepez S, Bonavida B. In vitro and in vivo sensitization of SW620 metastatic colon cancer cells to CDDP-induced apoptosis by the nitric oxide donor DETANONOate: involvement of AIF. Nitric Oxide 2009;20(3):182–94. https://doi.org/10.1016/j.niox.2008.11.006.

[144] Huerta-Yepez S, Baritaki S, Baay-Guzman G, Hernandez-Luna MA, Hernandez-Cueto A, Vega MI, Bonavida B. Contribution of either YY1 or BclXL-induced inhibition by the NO-Donor DETANONOate in the reversal of drug resistance, both in vitro and in vivo. YY1 and BclXL are overexpressed in prostate cancer. Nitric Oxide 2013;29:17–24. https://doi.org/10.1016/j.niox.2012.12.001.

[145] Bonavida B, Garban H. Nitric oxide-mediated sensitization of resistant tumor cells to apoptosis by chemoimmunotherapeutics. Redox Biol 2015;6:486–94. https://doi.org/10.1016/j.redox.2015.08.013.

[146] Thomas A, Teicher BA, Hassan R. Antibody–drug conjugates for cancer therapy. Lancet Oncol 2016;17(6): e254–62. https://doi.org/10.1016/S1470-2045(16)30030-4.

[147] Alibakhshi A, Abarghooi Kahaki F, Ahangarzadeh S, Yaghoobi H, Yarian F, Arezumand R, Ranjbari J, Mokhtarzadeh A, de la Guardia M. Targeted cancer therapy through antibody fragments-decorated nanomedicines. J Control Release 2017;268:323–34. https://doi.org/10.1016/j.jconrel.2017.10.036.

[148] Liang Y, Liu J, Liu T, Yang X. Anti-c-Met antibody bioconjugated with hollow gold nanospheres as a novel nanomaterial for targeted radiation ablation of human cervical cancer cell. Oncol Lett 2017;14(2): 2254–60. https://doi.org/10.3892/ol.2017.6383.

[149] del Solar V, Contel M. Metal-based antibody drug conjugates. Potential and challenges in their application as targeted therapies in cancer. J Inorg Biochem 2019;199, 110780. https://doi.org/10.1016/j.jinorgbio.2019.110780.

Pepper fruit, as a nutraceutical food, shows antiproliferative activity against tumor cells and it is potentiatied by nitric oxide (NO)

José M. Palma[a], José Pérez del Palacio[b], Marta Rodríguez-Ruiz[a], Salvador González-Gordo[a], Caridad Díaz[b], Carmen Ramos[b], Bastien Cautain[b,c], Francisca Vicente[b], and Francisco J. Corpas[a]

[a]Group of Antioxidants, Free Radicals and Nitric Oxide in Biotechnology, Food and Agriculture, Estación Experimental del Zaidín, CSIC, Granada, Spain [b]Department of Screening and Target Validation, Fundación MEDINA, Granada, Spain [c]Evotec – University Paul Sabatier Toulouse III, Toulouse, France

Abstract

Fruits and vegetables have provided human nutrition with a plethora of bioactive compounds, whose specific roles and identification have not yet been totally deciphered. This group of molecules includes vitamins A, C, and E, which can be obtained through the intake of plant products, but also polyphenols and derived metabolites (flavonoids like quercetin, anthocyanins, tannins, etc.), carotenoids, terpernoids, and alkaloids, among others. The majority of them are potent antioxidants in plant metabolism, but their requirement in the human diet is very low and their role in our metabolism is mostly regulatory. A number of studies have attributed to these compounds therapeutic potentialities in diverse pathologies and disorders, with cancer being one of their main targets. Many of these metabolites are present in pepper fruits, and their content is, in most cases, improved during ripening or through the treatment of fruits with exogenous nitric oxide (NO) gas. Additionally, the antiproliferative activity of crude extracts from pepper fruits was reported against seven tumor cell lines. This chapter reviews the potential therapeutic uses of crude extracts from pepper fruits according to their chemical compositions and proposes that, based on those potentialities against cancer and perhaps other pathologies, this horticultural product could be considered not only a nutritional vehicle but also a nutraceutical food.

Nitric Oxide in Health and Disease
https://doi.org/10.1016/B978-0-443-13342-8.00012-0

Abbreviations

AP-1	activation of protein 1
APX	ascorbate peroxidase
AsA	ascorbic acid
CAT	catalase
DMSO	dimethyl sulfoxide
ERK	extracellular signal-regulated kinase
FAD	flavin-adenine dinucleotide
FAs	fatty acids
GSH	reduced glutathione
GSNOR	*S*-nitrosoglutathione reductase
HPLC-HRMS	high-performance liquid chromatography coupled to high-resolution mass spectrometry
JNK	N-terminal c-Jun kinase
MAPK	mitogen-activated protein kinase
MTT	3-(4,5-dimethylthiazol-2-yl)-2,5-diphenyltetrazolium bromide
NF-κB	nuclear factor κB
NO	nitric oxide
PI3K/Akt	phosphatidylinositol 3-kinase/serine-threonine protein kinase
PPARγ	peroxisomal proliferator-activated receptors
PUFA	polyunsaturated fatty acid
RDA	recommended dietary allowance
RNS	reactive nitrogen species
ROS	reactive oxygen species
TNF-α	tumor necrosis factor-α
TPA	12-*O*-tetradecanoylphorbol-13-acetate
Trp	tryptophan
TRPV1	transient receptor potential vanilloid type-1

Conflict of interest

No potential conflicts of interest were disclosed.

Introduction

Since humans started cultivating plants in the dawn of Neolithic, the majority of species of plant origin were considered sources not only of macronutrients (basically fiber, carbohydrates, lipids, and proteins) but also of micronutrients with bioactive potentialities. Macronutrients are mainly derived for the provision of energy and as architectural pieces for structural purposes to promote growth and development. On the other hand, micronutrients are compounds which are essential in lower amounts to activate/deactivate chemical reactions and regulate metabolic processes. Vitamins can be considered the paradigm of this group of molecules, being necessary for very little quantities.

In this scenario, fruits and vegetables have provided human nutrition with a plethora of bioactive compounds, whose specific roles and identification have not yet been totally deciphered. In fact, plants contain a huge number of analytes from the secondary metabolism, many of them exclusive of certain species and with a still unidentified nature. This group of compounds includes vitamins A, C, and E that can be obtained through the intake of plant products but also polyphenols and derived metabolites (flavonoids, anthocyanins, tannins, etc.), carotenoids, terpernoids, and alkaloids, among others. Most of them participate as potent antioxidants in plant metabolism, but their requirement in the human diet is very low and their role in our physiology is mostly regulatory, acting as drivers/triggers of metabolic reactions [1].

A clear example of this kind of molecule is capsaicin (8-methyl-N-vanillyl-*trans*-6-nonenamide), an alkaloid with a phenyl-propanoid nature which is exclusive of hot *Capsicum* (pepper) species. Fig. 1A shows the chemical structure of capsaicin. This compound, responsible for the pungency trait of hot peppers, has been shown to behave as an antioxidant, functioning as an analgesic, and participating in the cardiovascular, nervous, and immune systems against infectious diseases, inflammation, obesity, and cancer (Fig. 1B) [2–6]. In particular, the proapoptotic activity of capsaicin is promoted by the transient receptor potential vanilloid type-1 (TRPV1) in many cancers. Additionally, capsaicin seems to induce phosphorylation of the tumor suppressor protein p53, thus leading to its activation [4,7–10]. Works in this field allowed David Julius to be awarded Nobel Prize 2021 in Physiology and Medicine. In fact, Julius' team showed, with the help of capsaicin, the existence of a sensorial neurone, called nociceptor, which responds to physical and chemical stimuli whose intensities provoke pain in human beings. Julius identified the TRPV1 channel as the neuronal receptor for harmful stimuli. Through this channel, it is possible to issue treatment for chronic pains, neuronal inflammatory syndromes, and those associated with arthritis, asthma and, even, cancer [11,12].

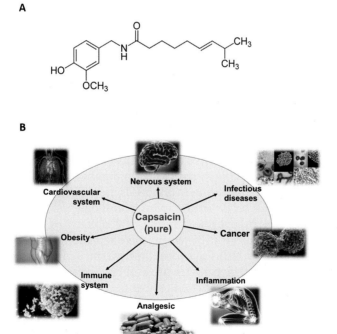

FIG. 1 Capsaicin and its functions in human physiology. (A) Molecular structure of capsaicin (8-methyl-N-vanillyl-trans-6-nonenamide). (B) Functions of pure capsaicin as an analgesic, in cardiovascular, nervous, and immune systems, and in some pathologies including obesity, infectious diseases, inflammation, and cancer.

Pepper fruit as a potential source of antitumoral compounds

Pepper (*Capsicum annuum* L.) is a herbaceous plant species originally from Central/South America belonging to Solanaceae, a family where other relevant crops are framed, including tomato (*Lycopersicum esculentum*), potato (*Solanum tuberosum*), and aubergine (*Solanum melongena*) [13–15]. Nowadays, due to its wide distribution, pepper fruit is one of the most representative horticultural products in the human diet worldwide. This makes this food gain relevance at nutritional and economical levels and many agro-companies are using their newest varieties as attraction issues. Fruits from *Solanaceae* show a great diversity of shapes, sizes, colors, and flavors among species, but also among varieties within each species [5]. The fruit color, perhaps the main claiming feature for growers, agro-companies, and consumers, is a consequence of their chemical composition, basically, that which refers to the combination of carotenoids, chlorophyll, flavonoids, and anthocyanins, as molecules of plant's secondary metabolism with a wide range of absorbance at the visible scale [15–17]. Regarding pepper fruits, a great number of varieties are being cultivated throughout the world, with a diversity of colors such as red, yellow, orange, purple, white, and others. Thus, a large number of local names are used to designate hot and sweet pepper fruit varieties [13,18–20]. Pepper fruits are also classified according to their culinary uses. Thus, pepper fruits can be consumed raw or cooked (either fried, roasted, or boiled), as a powder, as a spice, or as jarred food. This great versatility of culinary uses and the increasing production over the last year justify the relevance and economic importance of the cultivation of pepper. Not only that but due to the great and diverse consumption of pepper fruits and their molecular compositions, they could be envisaged as vehicles of bioactive compounds with therapeutic potential.

Pepper fruit is one of the richest vitamin C (ascorbic acid, ascorbate, AsA) sources in our diet (Table 1), but it also contains high levels of pro-vitamin A, with β-carotene as its precursor. In fact, according to the recommended dietary allowance (RDA) of both vitamin C and A, 50–80 g of pepper fruits may provide 100% (about 80 mg) and 25% (about 200 out of 800 μg), respectively, to our diet [18–26]. The high ascorbate content in pepper fruits has led to proposal that this compound rather than acting as a typical antioxidant may function as a redox buffer to balance and stabilize the huge number of redox and transforming reactions which take place during the ripening of fruits. This role would allow the fruit survival and successful seed dispersal to ensure the next generation [18,27]. Vitamin C is one of the most powerful low-molecular-weight antioxidants and in mammals is essential since it takes part in a number of metabolic processes and in preventing many pathologies. Thus, enzymes involved in the biosynthesis of cholesterol, collagen, L-carnitine, catecholamines, and amino acids, as well as in the phagocytosis by leukocytes, histamine detoxification, and hormonal activation, among others, are stimulated by AsA. Likewise, the incidence of several pathologies associated with immunity dysfunction, blood pressure and cardiovascular diseases, tissue regeneration, nervous system disorders, and even cancer is somehow reduced by vitamin C. In contrast, the lack of vitamin C provokes scurvy and this undergoes more fragile blood vessels and damaged connective tissues. These symptoms, which derive from a failure of collagen production and general collapse, may end in death [1,28–31].

Primates, including humans, along with guinea pigs, bats, and some birds, unlike the majority of living beings, are unable to synthesize ascorbate. In the case of humans, the absence of

TABLE 1   Ascorbate content in the main fruits and vegetables.

Fruits	Vitamin C (Ascorbate, mg/100 g FW)
Apple	6–60
Banana	10–11
Grape	2–3
Grapefruit	36
Kiwi	59
Lemon	58
Tangerine	20
Mango	37
Orange	46–54
Peach	6
Pear	3–6
Pineapple	12
Plum	4–5
Raspberry	26
Strawberry	61–77

Vegetables	Vitamin C (Ascorbate, mg/100 g FW)
Aubergine	22
Broccoli	45–87
Cauliflower	15–43
Cabbage	49
Celery	8
Leek	16
Lettuce	<2–3
Onion	5–6
Pea	22
Pepper (green)	140
Pepper (red)	157
Spinach	7
Tomato	17–18

Values are given as mg of ascorbate per 100 g fresh weight (FW).
Modified from Palma JM, Sevilla F, Jiménez A, del Río LA, Corpas FJ, Álvarez de Morales P, Camejo DM. Physiology of pepper fruits and the metabolism of antioxidants: chloroplasts, mitochondria and peroxisomes. Ann Bot 2015;116:627–36.

the last enzyme of its biosynthetic pathway, the L-gulono-1,4-lactone oxidase [32], makes us be strictly dependent on an external vitamin C provision, basically plant products [1].

Vitamin A is obtained from β-carotene, once this polyisoprenoid is assimilated by our metabolism, with each carotene molecule giving rise to two vitamin A molecules. β-carotene is highly important in plants for the photosynthesis and as an antioxidant, while in humans, vitamin A is crucial for the regulation of redox homeostasis in several physiological episodes associated with vision, growth and development, skeletal muscle dysfunction, but also to protect the epithelium and the mucus integrity in some systems like respiratory, urinary, and gastrointestinal tracts [1,32–36]. Although little amounts of β-carotene are necessary to carry out its role in humans, as with any other vitamin, excessive intake may provoke unwanted redox imbalances which may lead to some disorders. Thus, the use of vitamin A as a diet complement is sometimes under debate.

Pepper fruits also contain other carotenoids including capsanthin, capsorubin, and lutein. Capsanthin is the main carotenoid in pepper fruits and is basically present at the ripe stage being responsible for the red color [13,25,37]. This compound is well known for its anticarcinogenic potential as well as for its preventive effect against atherosclerosis and obesity [38,39]. Conversely, lutein is the main carotenoid in unripened green fruits. This pigment prevents macular degeneration associated with age and lowers the risk of apoplexy, cardiovascular disorders, and cancer [38,40,41].

Likewise, pepper fruits also contain other bioactive compounds whose content fluctuates according to the climate, culture conditions, variety, ripening stage, part of the fruit (either pericarp, placenta, or seeds), and harvesting, processing, and storage practices [13,25]. Within this group of bioactive compounds, it can be highlighted phenolics since they show beneficial health effects due to their protective role against damage produced by oxidizing agents. This group includes flavonoids such as anthocyanidins, isoflavones, chalcones, and anthocyanins. Globally, flavonoids display antibacterial, antifungal, antioxidant, and anticancer effects [25,42–46]. The phenolic profiles from diverse pepper varieties have been reported [13,20,25,47–50]. Very recently, by using high-performance liquid chromatography coupled with high-resolution mass spectrometry (HPLC-HRMS) and data processing against diverse metabolic databases, 12 bioactive compounds were identified in sweet pepper fruits. These include quercetin and a set of its derivatives, phytosphingosine, FAD, gingerglycolipid A, tetrahydropentoxylin, blumenol C glucoside, colnelenic acid and capsoside A, and L-trypto-phan. It was observed that the abundance of these metabolites varied depending on the ripening stage of the fruits, either immature green or ripe red, and this metabolite profile was also supported by the transcriptomic analysis of the genes involved in the biosynthesis of these compounds [5].

Quercetin has a great ability to scavenge reactive oxygen and nitrogen species (ROS and RNS, respectively) due to its great antioxidant capacity. This potentiality of quercetin has been attributed to the number of free hydroxyl groups in the molecule [51,52]. Quercetin in food is often in the form of quercetin glycoside [53], but it can be also taken as a dietary supplement with recommended daily doses of 200–1200 mg [51,54]. The bioavailability of quercetin is relatively low, mainly because of its low absorption, extensive metabolism, and rapid elimination [51]. The absorption of quercetin depends on the type of sugar and the conjugation site of these groups [43,51,53], and some studies have suggested that this flavonoid is absorbed in the upper segment of the small intestine [43].

In in vitro assays with animal models, quercetin has displayed a great range of biological actions such as antiviral, antiinflammatory, and antitumoral activities [44,52,55,56]. In addition, due to its antioxidant capacity, it has been shown that quercetin reduces capillary permeability and platelet aggregation [44]. Quercetin also inhibits cyclooxygenases and lipoxygenases, thus interfering with inflammation episodes [54]. But this flavonoid also participates in inflammation processes in different ways: one is mediated by tumor necrosis factor-α (TNF-α) directly activating the N-terminal c-Jun kinase (JNK), extracellular signal-regulated kinase (ERK), and nuclear factor κB (NF-κB), which are potent inflammation inducers. On the other hand, quercetin can indirectly prevent inflammation by increasing the activity of peroxisomal proliferator-activated receptors (PPARγ). In this way, it antagonizes the transcription of inflammatory genes by the activation of protein 1 (AP-1). Likewise, quercetin decreases clinical signs of arthritis in adjuvant-induced chronic arthritis rats, as compared to untreated controls [43].

The mechanisms of action of quercetin against tumors depend on its concentration and the type of cancer [57]. At high concentrations, it operates as a pro-oxidant and, accordingly, can produce chemotherapeutic effects [44]. Most of the anticancer effects of quercetin are due to its ability to halt the cell cycle by acting on cyclins and cyclin-dependent kinases. It also interferes with the mitogen-activated protein kinase (MAPK) and PI3K/Akt pathways [57]. In breast cancer, quercetin inhibits the production of metalloproteases, thus causing cell cycle arrest and apoptosis by the regulation of Akt and Bax signaling pathways (proapoptotic proteins of the Bcl family-2) [52].

On the other hand, phytosphingosine has been found in many mammalian tissues where it is linked to some types of cancer cells [58,59]. This compound activates the p38 MAPK pathway and suppresses the ERK1/2 pathway. This dual role is associated with the concomitant induction of the Bax translocation from the cytosol to the mitochondria. This leads to an intracellular signaling cascade which terminates with caspase-dependent cellular apoptosis [60]. Lately, phytosphingosine has been found to function as an anticancer agent whose targets are the nutrient transport systems and cell vacuolation [61]. Other roles have been reported for phytosphingosine. Thus, in hairless mouse skin, it inhibits the inflammatory epidermal hyperplasia induced by 12-O-tetradecanoylphorbol-13-acetate (TPA), and in human keratinocytes, it stimulates differentiation [62]. Likewise, the interaction of phytosphingosine with the CD300b receptor promotes nitric oxide (NO)-dependent neutrophil recruitment induced by zymosan [63].

Tryptophan (Trp) is obtained by humans from the diet and then is absorbed in the intestine and metabolized by the microbiota in the colon. Trp and related metabolites are essential in several metabolic processes, including protein biosynthesis and the coordination of organism responses to environmental stimuli through neurotransmitters and other signaling molecules. Imbalances in the tryptophan levels are associated with diverse human pathologies, like depression, schizophrenia, autoimmunity, and also cancer [64]. Derivatives from the tryptophan metabolism also play key roles in the activation of cells of the immune system. A very important cue is that tryptophan is the necessary precursor for the synthesis in the mitochondria of the neurotransmitter serotonin, first, and then melatonin and other neuromodulators like triptamin [64,65]. In animals, melatonin participates in sleep regulation, modulation of circadian rhythms, immunity, and as an anticancer agent. On the other hand, this Trp-derived compound preserves its capacity to lower oxidative stress through processes that are mainly receptor-independent [66].

As a whole, all the above data provide a scenario where a notable number of molecules with potential therapeutic properties, including antitumoral or antiproliferative activity against tumor cells, are part of the secondary metabolism of pepper fruits. A screening of pepper varieties containing the highest contents of these compounds in fruits along with in vitro analyses of the potential antitumoral activity of these varieties are complementary strategies which may be helpful to address future nutraceutical studies, not only in pepper fruits but also with other agronomic products commonly used in our daily diet.

Ripening and NO boost the nutritional properties of pepper fruits

It has been demonstrated that the levels of most bioactive compounds reported above, namely ascorbate, carotenoids, quercetin, phytosphingosine, and tryptophan are modulated by the maturation process and also by NO and derived RNS in sweet pepper fruits. Additionally, the content of other functional molecules such as fatty acids (FAs) is also influenced by the ripening of pepper fruits. Thus, it was found that the polyunsaturated α-linoleic (C18:2) and α-linolenic (C18:3) acids and the saturated palmitic (C16) and stearic (C18) acids were the most abundant FAs in sweet pepper fruits [67]. As shown in Fig. 2, α-linolenic and stearic

II. Nitric oxide pathway and cancer progression and therapy

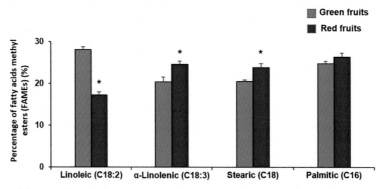

FIG. 2   Content of the main fatty acids, expressed as fatty acid methyl esters (FAMEs), in immature green and ripe red pepper fruits from type California. *t*-student was used to compare each fatty acid (linoleic, α-linolenic, stearic, and palmitic) at the two ripening stages. *$P < .05$. *Data taken from González-Gordo S, Bautista R, Claros MG, Cañas A, Palma JM, Corpas FJ. Nitric oxide-dependent regulation of sweet pepper fruit ripening. J Exp Bot 2019;70:4557–70.*

acids were significantly increased in ripe fruits, whereas α-linoleic acid was decreased. Similar data were also reported in pepper fruits from diverse origins [68–71] and also in tomatoes [72].

An overall view of how ripening proceeds in pepper fruits at the metabolic level is depicted in Fig. 3. Globally, at ripening, decreases in NO, glutathione (GSH), and α-linoleic acid contents were reported, and this was accompanied by lower S-nitrosoglutathione reductase (GSNOR), catalase (CAT), and ascorbate peroxidase (APX) activities. Ascorbic acid was also slightly increased once pepper fruits ripened, as it is observed in Table 1. In contrast, an enhancement of lipid peroxidation and lipoxygenase activity takes place, along with a rise in the contents of H_2S, proline, α-linolenic, lauric, and myristic acids. During this physiological event, higher levels of protein nitration and protein S-nitrosation, two posttranslational modifications promoted by NO/RNS, were also detected [67]. It has to remark the pattern followed by α-linolenic acid since this is a very important polyunsaturated fatty acid (PUFA), framed within the ω-3 series, which is essential to prevent cardiovascular diseases and protect against cardiac arrhythmias and macular degeneration, and it also shows a neuroprotecting effect [73–77].

Regarding NO, it is well known that this radical gas exerts diverse roles in the cardiovascular, nervous, and immune systems, as well as in a series of disorders and pathologies including cancer (Fig. 4A) [78–84]. Likewise, in plants, NO is involved in many physiological functions including root and nodule formation, seed and pollen germination, senescence, the response against biotic and abiotic stresses, and also in fruit ripening (Fig. 4B) [27,85–88]. Thus, the effect of NO on the content of the above-reported metabolites was investigated in pepper fruits subjected to exogenous NO gas (5 ppm) for 1 h. Thus, besides NO provoking a 3-day delay in the ripening process of sweet pepper fruits [27,89], this treatment exerted a positive influence on ascorbate metabolism. Pepper fruits treated with NO increased 40% of their ascorbate content, and this correlated with a higher gene expression and enzyme activity of the L-galactono-1,4-lactone dehydrogenase, the last enzyme of the main ascorbate biosynthetic pathway reported in plants [26,27,90]. This effect promoted by NO in the ascorbate level

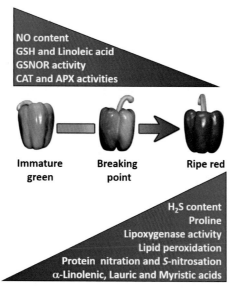

FIG. 3   Working model of pepper fruit metabolism during ripening. Immature green fruits ripen till the red stage in a process which takes 3–8 days depending on the variety. An intermediate stage is involved (breaking point) from which the ripening event is irreversible. During the whole process, decreases of the nitric oxide (NO) and reduction of glutathione (GSH) and linoleic acid contents and S-nitrosoglutathione reductase (GSNOR), catalase (CAT), and ascorbate peroxidase (APX) enzyme activities occur. This is accompanied by an enhancement of the contents of hydrogen sulfide (H₂S), proline, α-linolenic, lauric, and myristic acids, and lipoxygenase activity and increasing levels of protein nitration, protein S-nitrosation, and lipid peroxidation. *Modified from González-Gordo S, Bautista R, Claros MG, Cañas A, Palma JM, Corpas FJ. Nitric oxide-dependent regulation of sweet pepper fruit ripening. J Exp Bot 2019;70:4557–70.*

was also observed in tomato fruits treated with NO, where other regulating points in the biosynthesis pathway were proposed [91].

Preliminary results on the influence of NO in the profile of carotenoids in pepper fruits indicate that these pigments are boosted by this chemical species [92]. Conversely, NO-treated tomato fruits underaccumulated lycopene, phytoene, and phytofluene, and showed similar amounts of β-carotene and other carotenoids. Overall, the total carotenoid content in tomato fruits treated with NO was approximately 70% lower than in control fruits, although this reactive species participates at several levels in the modulation of genes involved in the biosynthesis of carotenoids [91].

The content of flavonoids in pepper fruits is also altered by the ripening process and the treatment with NO (Table 2). Quercetin and its derivatives accumulate in immature fruits with respect to red fruits, and their content was also favored by NO. Furthermore, the biosynthetic reactions' cascade which leads to all forms of quercetin was also proved to be regulated by NO [5]. Similarly, flavonoids displayed 60% of overaccumulation in tomato fruits subjected to NO treatment [91]. This pattern agrees with the observed symptoms which support that NO mimics the immature stage of fruits and delays ripening [27]. Interestingly, Trp abundance was stimulated by both ripening and NO, contradicting the bahavior of flavonoids [5].

II. Nitric oxide pathway and cancer progression and therapy

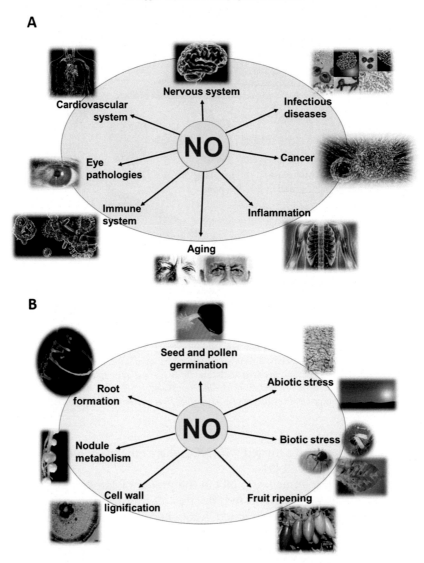

FIG. 4 Role of NO in human (A) and plant (B) physiology and pathologies. (A) In humans NO is involved in the functioning of the cardiovascular, nervous, and immune systems, as well as in some processes related to infectious diseases, eye pathologies, aging, inflammation, and cancer. (B) In plants NO participates in several events including seed and pollen germination, root formation, nodule metabolism, cell wall lignification, senescence, fruit ripening, and in response against abiotic and biotic stresses. *(B) Modified from Corpas FJ, Barroso JB, Palma JM, del Río LA. Peroxisomes as cell generators of reactive nitrogen species (RNS) signal molecules. Subcell Biochem 2013;69:283–98.*

TABLE 2 Tentatively identified metabolites from green and red sweet pepper fruits, treated or untreated with nitric oxide (NO).

Metabolite	Formula	m/z	Retention time	Adduct	Error ppm	Ripening stage/ +/− NO	P-value
Colnelenic acid	$C_{18}H_{28}O_3$	293.2121	10.69	H^+	3	PV	6.72e-12
Capsoside A	$C_{33}H_{58}O_{15}$	677.3754	9.54	$-H_2O^+/$ H^+	0	PV	1.049e-7
Quercetin	$C_{15}H_{10}O_7$	303.0507	5.40	H^+	2	PV/PE+NO	1.68e-13/ 1.13e-16
Quercitrin (Quercetin rhamnoside)	$C_{21}H_{20}O_{11}$	449.1074	5.38	H^+	0	PV/PE+NO	2.278e-13/ 3.92e-18
Quercitrin	$C_{21}H_{20}O_{11}$	471.0892	5.4	Na^+	0	PV/PE+NO	3.65e-16/ 5.47e-14
Gingerglycolipid A	$C_{33}H_{56}O_{14}$	694.4012	9.51	NH_4^+	0	PV/PE+NO	1.402e-8/ 0.025
Quercetin 3-(2Gal-apiosylrobinobioside)	$C_{32}H_{38}O_{20}$	743.2052	3.74	H^+	3	PV/PE+NO	7.396e-7/ 2.454e-9
Phytosphingosin	$C_{18}H_{39}O_3$	318.3004	8.26	H^+	0	PR	1.34e-10
FAD	$C_{27}H_{33}N_9O_{15}P_2$	786.1624	4.97	H_+	2	PR	1.453e-12
L-Tryptophan	$C_{11}H_{12}N_2O_2$	205.0959	3.23	H^+	3	PR/PE+NO	8.01e-14/ 3.53e-5
Tetrahydropentoxylin	$C_{17}H_{22}N_2O_7$	367.1509	3.01	H^+	2	PR/PE+NO	5.21e-5/ 0.0492
Blumenol C glucoside	$C_{19}H_{32}O_7$	373.2216	5.35	H^+	1	PR/PE+NO	1.8697e-10/ 0.00189
Quercetin 3-(3-glucosylrutinoside)	$C_{33}H_{40}O_{21}$	773.2133	3.69	H^+	0	PR/PE−NO	1.14e-10/ 1.42e-7

The name of each compound, its chemical formula, the mass/charge (m/z) value, and the retention time obtained from the metabolomic analysis are indicated. The associated adduct to each metabolite and its ppm error are also given. Additionally, the ripening stage (PV, green/PR, red) and the NO treatment (PE+NO, treated with NO/PE−NO, untreated) in which each metabolite was found differentially more abundant are indicated, along with the corresponding P-values.

Adapted from Guevara L, Domínguez-Anaya MA, Ortigosa A, González-Gordo S, Díaz C, Vicente F, Corpas FJ, Pérez del Palacio J, Palma JM. Identification of compounds with potential therapeutic uses from sweet pepper (Capsicum annuum L.) *fruits and their modulation by nitric oxide (NO). Int J Mol Sci 2021;22:4476.*

Fig. 5 summarizes how, through the impact of ripening and NO, the metabolome of pepper fruits can be influenced by modulating the levels of compounds with bioactive activity, including ascorbate, FAs (mainly α-linolenic acid), carotenoids, flavonoids (quercetin), tryptophan and, perhaps, others. It means that many roles that these molecules play in human physiology (as indicated above) can be, somehow, tuned by practices applied during the ripening process but also under postharvest conditions (NO treatment).

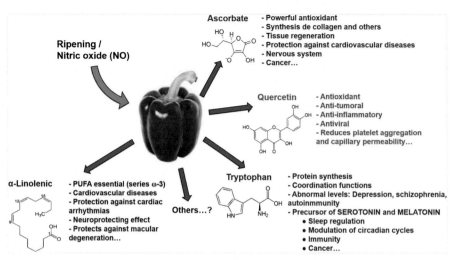

FIG. 5 Working model on how practices involving the handling of ripening and treatment of pepper fruits with NO influence the levels of bioactive molecules (ascorbate, quercetin, tryptophan, and α-linolenic, among others) and, consequently, their potential therapeutic uses.

Pepper fruits show antiproliferative activity on tumor cells

According to the presence/absence of (the capacity to synthesize) capsaicin, pepper fruits are classified as hot and sweet. The classification of thousands of pepper varieties according to their pungency is based on the so-called Scoville scale which attributes a value 0 to the total absence of capsaicin and $16 \cdot 10^6$ to the pure compound. The mark given to each variety according to that scale is assigned by a panel of experts although, at present, the content of capsaicin in pepper fruits can easily be determined by HPLC-MS [19]. Capsaicin is synthesized in the vacuole of the placenta cells and then is distributed through the pericarp and seeds. As indicated above, this phenylpropanoid shows activity against cancer and, accordingly, it could be assumed that hot pepper fruits could have the potential to provoke the same effect of pure capsaicin, although many other secondary metabolites that are present in fruits may act either synergistically or antagonistically.

To address this issue, a set of experiments was carried out in our laboratory where crude extracts of fruits from four pepper varieties with different capsaicin content were assayed against several tumor cell lines, and the antiproliferative activity was recorded. Thus, pericarp and placenta from pepper fruits of the varieties Melchor (type California), Padrón, Piquillo, and Alegría riojana were used at both immature green and ripe red stages (Fig. 6A). Plant material was powdered under liquid N_2 with the help of a mortar and pestle, and then homogenates were prepared in DMSO 20% (v/v). For the assays, the following tumor cell lines were tested: lung, A549; melanoma (skin), A2058; hepatoma (liver), Hep-G2; colon, HT-29; breast, MCF-7; pancreas, MIA PaCa-2; and prostate, PC-3. To assay the antiproliferative activity, the MTT test was used after 72h incubation of cells (10,000) with

A

Pepper varieties (code in the abscisas)	Ripening stage of fruits (code in the abscisas)	Tissue (code in the abscisas)
California (C)	Green (g) Red (r)	Placenta (PL) Pericarp (PE)
Padrón (P)	Green (g) Red (r)	Placenta (PL) Pericarp (PE)
Alegría riojana (AR)	Green (g) Red (r)	Placenta (PL) Pericarp (PE)
Piquillo (Pi)	Green (g) Red (r)	Placenta (PL) Pericarp (PE)

Cell lines	Type of cancer
A549	Lung
A2058	Melanoma
Hep-G2	Hepatoma
HT-29	Colon
MCF-7	Breast
Mia PaCa-2	Pancreas
PC-3	Prostate

B

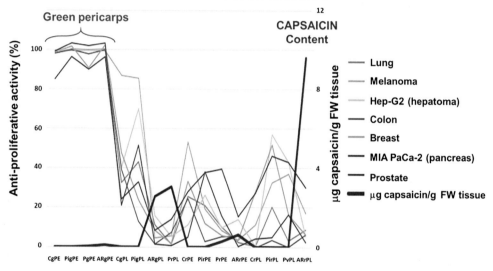

FIG. 6   Antiproliferative activity of diverse crude extracts from fruits of four pepper varieties against seven tumor cell lines. (A) Plant materials and tumor cell lines used in this experiment. They include placenta (PL) and pericarp (PL) from green (g) and red (r) pepper fruits from the varieties California (C), Padrón (P), Alegría riojana (AR), and Piquillo (Pi). The cell lines used corresponded to tumors from lung (A549), melanoma (A2058), hepatoma (Hep-G2), colon (HT-29), breast (MCF-7), pancreas (MIA PaCa-2), and prostate (PC-3). (B) Antiproliferative activity (%) of pepper fruit samples on seven tumor cell lines, and capsaicin content, expressed as mg/g fresh weight (FW), determined in the samples of pepper fruits used in the assays.

diverse concentrations of the pepper fruit extracts [93]. The concentration of capsaicin in the pepper fruit samples was achieved by HPLC-MS, using commercial capsaicin as standard [19].

As shown in Fig. 6B, the greatest antiproliferative activity in all tumor cell lines was shown by the pericarp of green fruits of the four pepper varieties. Surprisingly, this tissue was the one which contained the lowest amount of capsaicin, while the tissue with the highest capsaicin level, mainly placentas, displayed null activity [94]. This research opens new windows on the pepper fruit's bioactive compounds with nutraceutical and biomedical potentialities, as well as on their possible mechanism of action in the tumor cells.

Conclusions

Fruits and vegetables are sources, in some cases unique, of many bioactive compounds which, in plant physiology, are part of secondary metabolism. Among them, ascorbate (vitamin C), carotenoids (previtamin A), fatty acids, polyphenols, and flavonoids are the most important. By different approaches, it has been reported that most of them exert health benefits for humans and animals, including tumor pathologies. But other molecules with specific presence in plant species, such as capsaicin that is exclusive of pepper fruits, are also important for therapeutic purposes related to cancer and other disorders and diseases. Much of the research which has been conducted to this beneficial perspective has been performed with pure compounds, and less is known when plant products enriched in those molecules are directly intaken. Then, some contradiction may be observed, as the one shown here where samples from pepper fruits with the highest capsaicin content do not display the greatest antiproliferative activity against cancer cells, while pure capsaicin has been proved to be anticarcinogenic. It implies that other compounds present in the green fruits, as part of the crude extract, seem to be responsible for such an activity, either individually or synergistically. Research targeted at the identification of such metabolites has to be addressed by combining in vitro assays along with metabolomic approaches for the real characterization of such analytes. Overall, and considering the wide view of the chemical composition provided in this chapter, it can be proposed that pepper fruits, besides providing color, taste, flavor, and some nutrients to our dishes, can be considered a nutraceutical food, as they supply us a mix of bioactive compounds that can impact our welfare.

Acknowledgments

This research was supported by the European Regional Development Fund (ERDF)-co-financed grants from the Ministry of Science and Innovation (PID2019-103924GB-I00) and Junta de Andalucía (P18-FR-1359), Spain. Authors from the Fundación MEDINA acknowledge the financial support from this public-private partnership of Merck Sharp & Dohme de España S.A. with the University of Granada and the Andalusian Regional Government (PIN-0474-2016).

References

[1] Palma JM, Seiquer I. To be or not be … an antioxidant? That is the question. Antioxidants 2020;9:1234.
[2] Sancho R, Lucena C, Macho A, Calzado MA, Blanco-Molina M, Minassi A, Appendino G, Muñoz E. Immunosuppressive activity of capsaicinoids: capsiate derived from sweet peppers inhibits NF-kappa activation and is a potent antiinflammatory compound in vivo. Eur J Immunol 2002;32:1753–63.

[3] Materska M, Perucka I. Antioxidant activity of the main phenolic compounds isolated from hot pepper fruit (*Capsicum annuum* L). J Agric Food Chem 2005;53:1750–6.

[4] Clark R, Lee SH. Anticancer properties of capsaicin against human cancer. Anticancer Res 2016;36:837–44.

[5] Guevara L, Domínguez-Anaya MA, Ortigosa A, González-Gordo S, Díaz C, Vicente F, Corpas FJ, Pérez del Palacio J, Palma JM. Identification of compounds with potential therapeutic uses from sweet pepper (*Capsicum annuum* L.) fruits and their modulation by nitric oxide (NO). Int J Mol Sci 2021;22:4476.

[6] Merritt JC, Richbart SD, Moles EG, Cox AJ, Brown KC, Miles SL, Finch PT, Hess JA, Tirona MT, Valentovic MA, Dasgupta P. Anti-cancer activity of sustained release capsaicin formulations. Pharmacol Ther 2022;238, 108177.

[7] Chapa-Oliver AM, Mejía-Teniente L. Capsaicin: from plants to a cancer-suppressing agent. Molecules 2016;21:931.

[8] Georgescu SR, Sârbu MI, Matei C, Ilie MA, Caruntu C, Constantin C, Neagu M, Tampa M. Capsaicin: friend or foe in skin cancer and other related malignancies? Nutrients 2017;9:1365.

[9] Tabrizi MA, Baraldi PG, Baraldi S, Gessi S, Merighi S, Borea PA. Medicinal chemistry, pharmacology, and clinical implications of TRPV1 receptor antagonists. Med Res Rev 2017;37:936–83.

[10] Yang F, Zheng J. Understand spiciness: mechanism of TRPV1 channel activation by capsaicin. Protein Cell 2017;8:169–77.

[11] Cao E, Cordero-Morales JF, Liu BY, Qin F, Julis D. TRPV1 channels are intrinsically heat sensitive and negatively regulated by phosphoinositide lipids. Neuron 2013;77:667–79.

[12] Zhang KH, Julis D, Cheng YF. Structural snapshots of TRPV1 reveal mechanism of polymodal functionality. Cell 2021;184:5138–50.

[13] Baenas N, Belović N, Ilicb N, Moreno DA, García-Viguera C. Industrial use of pepper (*Capsicum annum* L.) derived products: technological benefits and biological advantages. Food Chem 2019;274:872–85.

[14] Gebhardt C. The historical role of species from the Solanaceae plant family in genetic research. Theor Appl Genet 2016;129:2281–94.

[15] Li W, Li J, Zhao J, He C. Evolutionary developmental genetics of fruit morphological variation within the Solanaceae. Front Plant Sci 2015;6:248.

[16] Karasawa MMG, Mohan C. Fruits as prospective reserves of bioactive compounds: a review. Nat Prod Bioprospecting 2018;8:335–46.

[17] Yoshida Y, Koyama N, Tamura H. Color and anthocyanin composition of strawberry fruit: changes during fruit development and differences among cultivars, with special reference to the occurrence of pelargonidin 3-malonylglucoside. J Jpn Soc Hortic Sci 2020;7:3155–361.

[18] Palma JM, Sevilla F, Jiménez A, del Río LA, Corpas FJ, Álvarez de Morales P, Camejo DM. Physiology of pepper fruits and the metabolism of antioxidants: chloroplasts, mitochondria and peroxisomes. Ann Bot 2015;116:627–36.

[19] Palma JM, Terán F, Contreras-Ruiz A, Rodríguez-Ruiz M, Corpas FJ. Antioxidant profile of pepper (*Capsicum annuum* L.) fruits containing diverse levels of capsaicinoids. Antioxidants 2020;9:878.

[20] Fratianni F, d'Acierno A, Cozzolino A, Spigno P, Riccardi R, Raimo F, Pane C, Zaccardelli M, Tranchida LV, Tucci M, et al. Biochemical characterization of traditional varieties of sweet pepper (*Capsicum annuum* L.) of the Campania region, southern Italy. Antioxidants 2020;9:556.

[21] Howard LR, Talcott ST, Brenes CH, Villalon B. Changes in phytochemical and antioxidant activity of selected pepper cultivars (*Capsicum* species) as influenced by maturity. Food Chem 2000;48:1713–20.

[22] Proteggente AR, Pannala AS, Paganga G, Van Buren L, Wagner E, Wiseman S, Van De Put F, Dacombe C, Rice-Evans CA. The antioxidant activity of regularly consumed fruit and vegetables reflects their phenolic and vitamin C composition. Free Radic Res 2002;36:217–33.

[23] Mariko N, Hassimoto A, Genovese MI, Lajolo FM. Antioxidant capacity of Brazilian fruit, vegetables and commercially-frozen fruit pulps. J Food Compos Anal 2009;22:394–6.

[24] Mateos RM, Jiménez A, Román P, Romojaro F, Bacarizo S, Leterrier M, Gómez M, Sevilla F, del Río LA, Corpas FJ, et al. Antioxidant systems from pepper (*Capsicum annuum* L.): involvement in the response to temperature changes in ripe fruits. Int J Mol Sci 2013;14:9556–80.

[25] Wahyuni Y, Ballester A-R, Sudarmonowati E, Bino RJ, Bovy AG. Secondary metabolites of *Capsicum* species and their importance in the human diet. J Nat Prod 2013;76:783–93.

[26] Rodríguez-Ruiz M, Mateos RM, Codesido V, Corpas FJ, Palma JM. Characterization of the galactono-1,4-lactone dehydrogenase from pepper fruits and its modulation in the ascorbate biosynthesis. Role of nitric oxide. Redox Biol 2017;12:171–81.

[27] Palma JM, Freschi L, Rodríguez-Ruiz M, González-Gordo S, Corpas FJ. Nitric oxide in the physiology and quality of fleshy fruits. J Exp Bot 2019;70:4405–17.

II. Nitric oxide pathway and cancer progression and therapy

[28] Grosso G, Bei R, Mistretta A, Marventano S, Calabrese G, Masuelli L, Giganti MG, Modesti A, Galvano F, Gazzolo D. Effects of vitamin C on health: a review of evidence. Front Biosci 2013;18:1017–29.

[29] Gordon DS, Rudinsky AJ, Guillaumin J, Parker VJ, Creighton KJ. Vitamin C in health and disease: a companion animal focus. Top Companion Anim Med 2020;39, 100432.

[30] Rowe S, Carr AC. Global vitamin C status and prevalence of deficiency: a cause for concern? Nutrients 2020;2:2008.

[31] Hujoel PP, Hujoel MLA. Vitamin C and scar strength: analysis of a historical trial and implications for collagen-related pathologies. Am J Clin Nutr 2022;115:8–17.

[32] Granger M, Eck P. Dietary vitamin C in human health. Adv Food Nutr Res 2018;83:281–310.

[33] Huang Z, Liu Y, Qi G, Brand D, Zheng SG. Role of vitamin A in the immune system. J Clin Med 2018;7:258.

[34] Marzęda P, Łuszczki JJ. Role of vitamin A in health and illness. J Pre-Clin Clin Res 2019;13:137–42.

[35] Awasthi S, Awasthi A. Role of vitamin A in child health and nutrition. Clin Epidem Glob Health 2020;8:1039–42.

[36] Russo C, Valle MS, Casabona A, Spicuzza L, Sambataro G, Malaguarnera L. Vitamin D impacts on skeletal muscle dysfunction in patients with COPD promoting mitochondrial health. Biomedicines 2022;10:898.

[37] Jeong HB, Kang MY, Jung A, Han K, Lee JH, Jo J, Lee HY, An JW, Kim S, Kang BC. Single-molecule real-time sequencing reveals diverse allelic variations in carotenoid biosynthetic genes in pepper (Capsicum spp.). Plant Biotechnol J 2018;1:1–13.

[38] Fernández-Bedmar Z, Alonso-Moraga A. In vivo and in vitro evaluation for nutraceutical purposes of capsaicin, capsanthin, lutein and four pepper varieties. Food Chem Toxicol 2016;98:89–99.

[39] Wu T, Gao Y, Hao J, Geng J, Zhang J, Yin J, Liu R, Sui W, Gong L, Zhang M. Capsanthin extract prevents obesity, reduces serum TMAO levels and modulates the gut microbiota composition in high-fat-diet induced obese C57BL/6J mice. Food Res Int 2020;128, 108774.

[40] Chung RWS, Leanderson P, Lundberg AK, Jonasson L. Lutein exerts anti-inflammatory effects in patients with coronary artery disease. Atherosclerosis 2017;262:87–93.

[41] Jia JP, Sun L, Yu HS, Liang LP, Li W, Ding H, Song XB, Zhang LJ. The pharmacological effects of lutein and zeaxanthin on visual disorders and cognition diseases. Molecules 2017;22:610.

[42] Batiha GES, Alqahtani A, Oluwafemi AO, Shaheen HM, Wasef L, Elzeiny M, Ismail M, Shalaby M, Murata T, Zaragoza-Bastida A, et al. Biological properties, bioactive constituents, and pharmacokinetics of some Capsicum spp. and capsaicinoids. Int J Mol Sci 2020;21:5179.

[43] Li Y, Yao J, Han C, Yang J, Chaudhry MT, Wang S, Liu H, Yin Y. Quercetin, inflammation and immunity. Nutrients 2016;8:167.

[44] Reyes-Farias M, Carrasco-Pozo C. The anti-cancer effect of quercetin: molecular implications in cancer metabolism. Int J Mol Sci 2019;20:3177.

[45] Metsämuuronen S, Sirén H. Bioactive phenolic compounds, metabolism and properties: a review on valuable chemical compounds in Scots pine and Norway spruce. Phytochem Rev 2019;18:623–64.

[46] Dessalegn E, Bultosa G, Haki GD, Chen F, Rupasinghe HPV. Antioxidant and cytotoxicity to liver cancer HepG2 cells in vitro of Korarima (Aframomum corrorima (Braun) PCM Jansen) seed extracts. Int J Food Prop 2022;25:1–10.

[47] Ribes-Moya AM, Adalid AM, Raigón MD, Hellín P, Fita A, Rodríguez-Burruezo A. Variation in flavonoids in a collection of peppers (Capsicum sp.) under organic and conventional cultivation: effect of the genotype, ripening stage, and growing system. J Sci Food Agric 2020;100:2208–23.

[48] Morales-Soto A, Gómez-Caravaca AM, García-Salas P, Segura-Carretero A, Fernández-Gutiérrez A. High-performance liquid chromatography coupled to diode array and electrospray time-of-flight mass spectrometry detectors for a comprehensive characterization of phenolic and other polar compounds in three pepper (Capsicum annuum L.) samples. Food Res Int 2013;51:977–84.

[49] Ashokkumar K, Pandian A, Murugan M, Dhanya MK, Sathyan T, Sivakumar P, Raj S, Warkentin TD. Profiling bioactive flavonoids and carotenoids in select south Indian spices and nuts. Nat Prod Res 2020;34:1306–10.

[50] Pascale R, Acquavia MA, Cataldi TRI, Onzo A, Coviello D, Bufo SA, Scrano L, Ciriello R, Guerrieri A, Bianco G. Profiling of quercetin glycosides and acyl glycosides in sun-dried peperoni di Senise peppers (Capsicum annuum L.) by a combination of LC-ESI(−)-MS/MS and polarity prediction in reversed-phase separations. Anal Bioanal Chem 2020;412:3005–15.

[51] Lesjak M, Beara I, Simin N, Pintać D, Majkić T, Bekvalac K, Orčić D, Mimica-Dukić N. Antioxidant and anti-inflammatory activities of quercetin and its derivatives. J Funct Foods 2018;40:68–75.

[52] Davoodvandi A, Varkani MS, Clark CCT, Jafarnejad S. Quercetin as an anticancer agent: focus on esophageal cancer. J Food Biochem 2020;44, e13374.

[53] Costa LG, Garrick JM, Roquè PJ, Pellacani C. Mechanisms of neuroprotection by quercetin: counteracting oxidative stress and more. Oxidative Med Cell Longev 2016;2986796.

[54] Chen W, Wang S, Wu Y, Shen S, Xu S, Guo Z, Zhang R, Xing D. The physiologic activity and mechanism of quercetin-like natural plant flavonoids. Curr Pharm Biotechnol 2020;8:654–8.

[55] Li KK, Zang XL, Meng XJ, Li YF, Xie Y, Chen XH. Targeted delivery of quercetin by biotinylated mixed micelles for non-small cell lung cancer treatment. Drug Deliv 2022;29:970–85.

[56] Gokbilen SO, Vatansever HS. Senescence-mediated anticancer effects of quercetin. Nutr Res 2022;10h4:82–90.

[57] Rauf A, Imran M, Khan IA, Ur-Rehman M, Gilani SA, Mehmood Z, Mubarak MS. Anticancer potential of quercetin: a comprehensive review. Phytother Res 2018;32:2109–30.

[58] Kim BM, Choi YJ, Han Y, Yun YS, Hong SH. N,N-dimethyl phytosphingosine induces caspase-8-dependent cytochrome *c* release and apoptosis through ROS generation in human leukemia cells. Toxicol Appl Pharmacol 2009;239:87–97.

[59] Sun RL, Gu JF, Chang XW, Liu FY, Liang Y, Yang XY, Liang L, Tang DC. Metabonomics study on orthotopic transplantion mice model of colon cancer treated with Astragalus membranaceus-Curcuma wenyujin in different proportions via UPLC-Q-TOF/MS. J Pharm Biomed Anal 2021;193, 113708.

[60] Kim S, Hong I, Hwang JS, Choi JK, Rho HS, Kim DH, Chang I, Lee SH, Lee MO, Hwang JS. Phytosphingosine stimulates the differentiation of human keratinocytes and inhibits TPA-induced inflammatory epidermal hyperplasia in hairless mouse skin. Mol Med 2006;12:17–24.

[61] Garsi JB, Sernissi L, Vece V, Hanessian S, McCracken AN, Simitian G, Edinger AL. In search of constrained FTY720 and phytosphingosine analogs as dual acting anticancer agents targeting metabolic and epigenetic pathways. Eur J Med Chem 2018;159:217–42.

[62] Takahashi M, Izawa K, Urai M, Yamanishi Y, Maehara A, Isobe M, Matsukawa T, Kaitani A, Takamori A, Uchida S, et al. The phytosphingosine-CD300b interaction promotes zymosan-induced, nitric oxide–dependent neutrophil recruitment. Sci Signal 2019;12:eaar5514.

[63] Sebela M, Radova A, Angelini R, Tavladoraki P, Frébort IP. FAD-containing polyamine oxidases: a timely challenge for researchers in biochemistry and physiology of plants. Plant Sci 2001;160:197–207.

[64] Platten P, Nollen EAA, Röhrig UF, Fallarino F, Opitz CA. Tryptophan metabolism as a common therapeutic target in cancer, neurodegeneration and beyond. Nat Rev Drug Discov 2019;18:379–401.

[65] Sorgdrager FJH, Naudé PJW, Kema IP, Nollen EA, De Deyn PD. Tryptophan metabolism in inflammaging: from biomarker to therapeutic target. Front Immunol 2019;10:2565.

[66] Celenza JL. Metabolism of tyrosine and tryptophan—new genes for old pathways. Curr Opin Plant Biol 2001;4:234–40.

[67] González-Gordo S, Bautista R, Claros MG, Cañas A, Palma JM, Corpas FJ. Nitric oxide-dependent regulation of sweet pepper fruit ripening. J Exp Bot 2019;70:4557–70.

[68] Pérez-Gálvez A, Garrido-Fernández J, Mínguez-Mosquera MI, Lozano-Ruiz M, Montero-de-Espinosa V. Fatty acid composition of two new pepper varieties (*Capsicum annuum* L. cv. Jaranda and Jariza). Effect of drying process and nutritional aspects. J Am Oil Chem Soc 1999;76:205–8.

[69] Sora GT, Haminiuk CW, da Silva MV, Zielinski AA, Gonçalves GA, Bracht A, Peralta RM. A comparative study of the capsaicinoid and phenolic contents and in vitro antioxidant activities of the peppers of the genus *Capsicum*: an application of chemometrics. J Food Sci Technol 2015;52:8086–94.

[70] Ananthan R, Subhash K, Longvah T. Capsaicinoids, amino acid and fatty acid profiles in different fruit components of the world hottest Naga king chilli (*Capsicum chinense* Jacq). Food Chem 2018;238:51–7.

[71] Saini RK, Keum Y-S. GC–MS and HPLC–DAD analysis of fatty acids and tocopherols in sweet peppers (*Capsicum annuum* L.). J Food Meas Charact 2016;10:685–9.

[72] Saini RK, Zamany AJ, Keum YS. Ripening improves the content of carotenoid, α-tocopherol, and polyunsaturated fatty acids in tomato (*Solanum lycopersicum* L.) fruits. 3 Biotech 2017;7:43.

[73] Morya S, Menaa F, Jimenez-Lopez C, Lourenco-Lopes C, BinMowyna MN, Alqahtani A. Nutraceutical and pharmaceutical behavior of bioactive compounds of miracle oilseeds: an overview. Foods 2022;11:1824.

[74] Gogna S, Kaur J, Sharma K, Bhadariya V, Singh J, Kumar V, Rasane P, Vipasha V. A systematic review on the role of alpha linolenic acid (ALA) in combating non-communicable diseases (NCDs). Nutr Food Sci 2022. https://doi.org/10.1108/NFS-01-2022-0023.

II. Nitric oxide pathway and cancer progression and therapy

[75] Pertiwi K, Kupers LK, de Goede J, Zock PL, Kromhout D, Geleijnse JM. Dietary and circulating long-chain omega-3 polyunsaturated fatty acids and mortality risk after myocardial infarction: a long-term follow-up of the alpha omega cohort. J Am Heart Assoc 2021;10, 022617.

[76] Elmore A, Harris WS, Mu LN, Brady WE, Hovey KM, Mares JA, Espeland MA, Haan MN, Millen AE. Red blood cell fatty acids and age-related macular degeneration in postmenopausal women. Eur J Nutr 2022;61:1585–94.

[77] Pomponi M, Di Gioia A, Bria P, Pomponi MFL. Fatty aspirin: a new perspective in the prevention of dementia of Alzheimer's type? Curr Alzheimer Res 2008;5:422–31.

[78] McIntyre M, Dominiczak AF. Nitric oxide and cardiovascular disease. Postgrad Med J 1997;73:630–4.

[79] Ignarro LJ, Napoli C, Loscalzo J. Nitric oxide donors and cardiovascular agents modulating the bioactivity of nitric oxide – an overview. Circ Res 2022;90:21–8.

[80] Boycott HE, Nguyen MN, Vrellaku B, Gehmlich K, Robinson P. Nitric oxide and mechano-electrical transduction in cardiomyocytes. Front Physiol 2020;11, 606740.

[81] Cyr AR, Huckaby LV, Shiva SS, Zuckerbraun BS. Nitric oxide and endothelial dysfunction. Crit Care Clin 2020;36:307–21.

[82] Coulter JA, McCarthy HO, Xiang J, Roedl W, Wagner E, Robson T, Hirst DG. Nitric oxide – a novel therapeutic for cancer. Nitric Oxide Biol Chem 2008;19:192–8.

[83] Ridnour LA, Thomas DD, Switzer C, Flores-Santana W, Isenberg JS, Ambs S, Roberts DD, Wink DA. Molecular mechanisms for discrete nitric oxide levels in cáncer. Nitric Oxide Biol Chem 2008;19:73–6.

[84] Terwoord JD, Beyer AM, Gutterman DD. Endothelial dysfunction as a complication of anti-cancer therapy. Pharmacol Ther 2022;237, 108116.

[85] Corpas FJ, Barroso JB, Palma JM, del Río LA. Peroxisomes as cell generators of reactive nitrogen species (RNS) signal molecules. Subcell Biochem 2013;69:283–98.

[86] Corpas FJ, Barroso JB. Nitric oxide from a "green" perspective. Nitric Oxide Biol Chem 2015;45:15–9.

[87] Kolbert Z, Barroso JB, Brouquisse R, Corpas FJ, Gupta KJ, Lindermayr C, Loake GJ, Palma JM, Petrivalsky M, Wendehenne D, Hancock JT. A forty year journey: the generation and roles of NO in plants. Nitric Oxide 2019;93:53–70.

[88] Gupta KJ, Kolbert Z, Durner J, Lindermayr C, Corpas FJ, Brouquisse R, Barroso JB, Umbreen S, Palma JM, Hancock JT, Petrivalsky M, Wendehenne D, Loake GJ. Regulating the regulator: nitric oxide control of post-translational modifications. New Phytol 2020;227:1319–25.

[89] Chaki M, Álvarez de Morales P, Ruiz C, Begara-Morales JC, Barroso JB, Corpas FJ, Palma JM. Ripening of pepper (Capsicum annuum) fruit is characterized by an enhancement of protein tyrosine nitration. Ann Bot 2015;116:637–47.

[90] Agius F, Gonzalez-Lamothe R, Caballero JL, Muñoz-Blanco J, Botella MA, Valpuesta V. Engineering increased vitamin C levels in plants by overexpression of a D-galacturonic acid reductase. Nat Biotechnol 2003;21:177–81.

[91] Zuccarelli R, Rodríguez-Ruiz M, Lopes-Oliveira PJ, Pascoal GB, Andrade SCS, Furlan CM, Purgatto E, Palma JM, Corpas FJ, Rossi M, Freschi L. Multifaceted roles of nitric oxide in tomato fruit ripening: NO-induced metabolic rewiring and consequences for fruit quality traits. J Exp Bot 2021;72:941–58.

[92] Codesido V, Ruiz-Torres C, Corpas FJ, Palma JM. Garlic mimicks nitric oxide (NO) effects on ripening of pepper (Capsicum annuum L.) fruits and improves their commercial and nutritional properties. The First International Electronic Conference on Agronomy-IECAG 2021; https://sciforum.net/paper/view/10012.

[93] Mao Z, Liu Z, Chen L, Yang J, Zhao B, Jung YM, Wang X, Zhao C. Predictive value of the surface-enhanced resonance raman scattering-based MTT assay: a rapid and ultrasensitive method for cell viability in situ. Anal Chem 2013;2013(85):7361–8.

[94] Palma JM, Pérez Del Palacio J, Rodríguez-Ruiz M, González-Gordo S, Díaz C, Ramos C, Vicente F, Corpas FJ. Does nitric oxide (NO) potentiate the anti-tumoral activity of pepper fruit extracts? In: Second international conference on therapeutic applications of nitric oxide in cancer and inflammatory-related diseases; 2022.

PART III

Nitric oxide donors and cardiovascular and metabolic diseases

Nitric oxide (NO) donors in kidney damage and diseases

Gabriel Tavares do Vale[a], Bruna Pinheiro Pereira[b], Simone Regina Potje[a], and Carla Speroni Ceron[c]

[a]Minas Gerais State University (UEMG), Passos, Minas Gerais, Brazil [b]Federal University of Alfenas (UNIFAL), Alfenas, Minas Gerais, Brazil [c]Department of Biological Sciences, Institute of Exact and Biological Sciences, Federal University of Ouro Preto (UFOP), Ouro Preto, Minas Gerais, Brazil

Abstract

Nitric oxide (NO) is a free radical that participates in renal hemodynamics and deregulation of its synthetic pathway in the kidneys has been observed in several renal diseases. These observations led to the use of NO donors and in addition, their clinical limitations have been observed in a variety of clinical and experimental studies of kidney injuries or diseases. The objective of this book chapter is to review the physiological role of NO in the kidneys, present a brief review of mostly used NO donors with some advantages of their use and their main limitations, and discuss the use/role of NO donors in models of kidney damage or diseases. In addition, we address the application of NO donors in other human diseases. Thus, this review contributes to the understanding of the therapeutic potential of this class of drugs and encouraging the development of new NO donors.

Abbreviations

ARF	acute renal failure
BH$_4$	tetrahydrobiopterin
CKD	chronic kidney disease
DM1	type 1 diabetes mellitus
DM2	type 2 diabetes mellitus
eNOS	endothelial NOS
ET-1	endothelin-1
Fe-NTA	ferric nitrilotriacetic acid
GNT	organic nitrate and nitroglycerin
GSH	glutathione
IL	interleukin

iNOS	inducible NOS
L-NAME	L-NG-nitro arginine methyl ester
LPS	lipopolysaccharide
MAPK	mitogen-activated protein kinase
MIP	macrophage inflammatory protein
NAPQI	N-acetyl-p-benzoquinone imine
NF-κB	nuclear factor-κB
nNOS	neuronal NOS
NO	nitric oxide
NOS	nitric oxide synthases
ONOO	peroxynitrite
PDE	phosphodiesterase
PKG	protein kinase G
sGC	soluble guanylyl cyclase
SIN-1	3-morpholinosydnonimine
SNAP	S-nitroso-n-acetylpenicillamine
TNF	tumor necrosis factor
V-PYRRO/NO	O2-vinyl-1-(pyrrolidin-1-yl)diazen-1-ium-1,2-diolate

Conflict of interest

No potential conflicts of interest were disclosed.

Introduction

Nitric oxide (NO) is a gaseous molecule that has lipophilic capacity; therefore, it can easily diffuse in the biological systems and cross the cell membranes and lipoproteins. The mechanism of action of NO has been investigated in several ways regarding its physiological, pathological, and pharmacological roles in different diseases. As NO has a short half-life, the development of a class of compounds that exogenously release NO and stabilize the radical until its release allowed a better understanding of the potential of NO in the treatment of diseases [1].

It is well known that NO has an essential role in renal hemodynamics, such as controlling natriuresis and diuresis, maintaining medullar perfusion, and controlling tubuloglomerular feedback [2–4]. Thereby, the understanding that an impairment of the NO synthetic pathway in the kidneys could imbalance the renal hemodynamics and may be associated with the progression of renal disease has led to the investigation of the benefits of NO donors in experimental models of kidney damage or diseases.

In this report, we review the physiological role of NO in the kidneys—we also address the mostly used NO donors, such as organic nitrates, sodium nitroprusside, diazeniumdiolate, ruthenium compounds, hybrid NO drugs, and S-nitrosothiols in clinical and experimental studies—and some of the advantages of their use and their main limitations, and we also discuss the use/role of NO donors in kidney damage or disease models. In addition, we briefly discuss the application of NO donors in other human diseases.

Physiological role of nitric oxide in the kidneys

NO is a molecule present in low quantities in the atmosphere that contains an unpaired electron, which promotes its high reactivity [3]. Its synthesis occurs by the L-arginine-nitric-oxide pathway, in which nitric oxide synthases (NOS) catalyze the conversion of L-arginine in NO and L-citrulline, in the presence of NADPH and tetrahydrobiopterin (BH_4) [3,5].

There are three main NOS isoforms that promote NO formation: neuronal (nNOS), endothelial (eNOS), and inducible (iNOS) [6]. In the kidneys, the isoform most expressed in the macula densa is nNOS, as well as in specialized neurons, renal arteries of the hilus, arcuate and interlobular arteries, outer medullary collecting duct, cortical collecting duct, and the inner medullary thin limb [2]. Considering the synthase eNOS, its expression is mostly detected in the renal vascular endothelium of arteries and arterioles, glomerular capillaries, medullary descending vasa recta, the tubules present in the inner medullary collecting duct, the thick ascending limb of the loop of Henle, and the proximal convoluted tubule; however, it is not seen in the cortical capillaries or venous endothelium [3]. Lastly, iNOS is induced by renal damage and it contributes to the pathophysiology of septic shock and inflammatory diseases [7].

NO has several functions in the kidneys, including the control of natriuresis and diuresis by regulating renal hemodynamics, maintaining medullary perfusion, and also controlling the tubuloglomerular feedback by inhibiting sodium reabsorption by renal tubules and increasing sodium excretion and urinary flow, which enables to demonstrate its essential role in kidney hemodynamics [2,3]. Since NO is also known as an "endothelial-derived relaxing factor," it has a significant contribution to the maintenance of low vascular resistance and renal blood flow [8,9].

NO exerts its main functions through the NO/cGMP pathway, and in the kidneys, the main NO producer is eNOS, which through the NO/sGC/cGMP pathway produces vasodilation (Fig. 1) [2,6]. When there is an increase in intracellular calcium due to bradykinin and

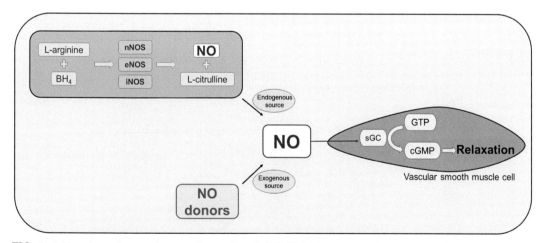

FIG. 1 NO pathway in vascular smooth muscle cells (VSMCs). The nitric oxide (NO) molecule is synthesized endogenously from the conversion of L-arginine to L-citrulline by isoforms of nitric oxide synthases (NOS) in the presence of different cofactors, including tetrahydrobiopterin (BH_4). Furthermore, the NO molecule can be obtained from an exogenous source through its release from compounds known as NO donors. NO is essential for vascular homeostasis. In this way, NO produced endogenously or obtained from an exogenous source diffuses through the cell membranes reaching vascular smooth muscle cells (VSMCs) in blood vessels. Thus, NO activates the enzyme soluble guanylate cyclase (sGC), which converts guanosine triphosphate (GTP) into cyclic guanosine monophosphate (cGMP), promoting activation of protein kinase G (PKG) and reduction of intracellular calcium, all these actions promote vasodilation.

III. Nitric oxide donors and cardiovascular and metabolic diseases

acetylcholine (vasodilator agonists), eNOS is activated and NO is produced in endothelial cells [6]. NO diffuses into the vascular smooth muscle activating soluble guanylyl cyclase (sGC), producing cyclic guanosine monophosphate (cGMP), which increases vasorelaxation [6]. There is a balance that determines the level of cGMP, and it occurs between the sGC synthesis and the enzyme phosphodiesterase (PDE) catabolism, promoting the metabolism of cGMP to 5'-GMP, which is its biologically inactive metabolite [6].

Due to the lower rate of cGMP synthesis when compared to the PDE hydrolysis rate (10-fold lower), PDE has become a considerable therapeutic target for several pathological conditions, such as erectile dysfunction [6]. A second possible therapeutic target is protein kinase G (PKG), which is activated by cGMP stimulation and promotes the phosphorylation of different target proteins that are involved in vasodilation, neutrophil activation, modulation of smooth muscle cell tone, and matrix expansion [6].

One of the important NO actions is in renal autoregulation, which is the kidney's capacity to maintain blood pressure and glomerular filtration constant despite the alterations in systemic blood pressure (Fig. 2) [3]. The process of tubuloglomerular feedback is extremely significant in this process, releasing sodium in the loop of Henle when there is an increase in glomerular filtration, promoting the vasoconstriction of the afferent arteriole and the decrease of the glomerular filtration [3]. In this process, NO derived from nNOS promotes the regulation through sGC stimuli, producing cGMP and activating the kinase cGMP-dependent protein among the cells in the macula densa [9].

Considering the renal tubules, NO has the capacity to inhibit sodium reabsorption, promoting natriuretic and diuretic effects [2]. Previous studies demonstrated that the use of an L-arginine analog (L-NAME) decreased 40% of the renal medullary flow, indicating that NO has the capacity to influence the renal vases in the renal medulla [10]. In addition, NO in the renal medulla opposes noradrenaline, vasopressin, and angiotensin II vasoconstriction effects, which maintains a normal medullary flow and prevents the development of hypertension [2].

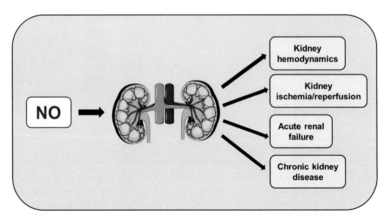

FIG. 2   Effects of NO on the kidneys. Nitric oxide (NO) promotes several effects on renal metabolism, playing an important role in modulating renal hemodynamics, which is the kidney capacity to maintain the blood pressure and glomerular filtration constant despite the alterations in the systemic blood pressure. In addition, NO protects the renal tissues from damages derived from renal ischemia/reperfusion, acute renal failure, and chronic kidney disease.

Applicability and limitations of NO donors

As NO in nNOS has a biological half-life of several seconds, this could limit the study of the chemical characteristics of the NO molecule and its endogenous mechanism of action in the cardiovascular and renal systems. In addition, some pathologies are associated with an impairment of NO synthesis; in this way, the possibility of creating a compound that releases NO exogenously became attractive. Furthermore, it is important that these NO donors stabilize the radical until the moment when its release is required [1]. In this context, a number of NO donors stand out, such as organic nitrates, sodium nitroprusside, diazeniumdiolate, ruthenium compounds, hybrid NO drugs, and S-nitrosothiols.

Since the NO molecule is present in the chemical structure of NO donors, these compounds have the ability to release the NO molecule independent of the enzymatic action of NOS [11]. Each NO donor presents different singularities according to its structure, presenting an optimized NO delivery strategy [12], being able to release intra- or extracellular NO [13] and even release NO quickly or slowly and constantly [14]. In addition, some NO donors may need some activation such as pH change [15], light [16] or redox activation [17], thus releasing NO in a controlled manner.

NO donors have different applications and we are highlighting them in kidney damage or diseases (Fig. 3).

NO donors in kidney hemodynamics

A variety of studies have consolidated that NO plays an important role in renal hemodynamics and excretory functions. Its formation and release can be enhanced by the effects of some endogenous agonists such as acetylcholine, bradykinin, and others. In addition, nitrovasodilators that are characterized as NO donors can also ameliorate NO levels systemically or in the tissues [18]. Accordingly, Majid et al. [18] observed that intra-arterial infusion of an NO donor S-nitroso-n-acetylpenicillamine (SNAP) at a constant rate (2 µg/kg/min) in dogs resulted in the amelioration of intrarenal arterial pressure as a result of kidney vasodilation and also an increase of natriuresis, reinforcing the beneficial effects of NO.

According to Nielsen et al. [19] the renal effect of sodium nitroprusside is associated with its capacity to increase the production of cGMP in the kidneys. In their study, healthy volunteers received an infusion of sodium nitroprusside (0.7 µg/kg/min) for 90 min, which resulted in a significant decrease of mean arterial blood pressure, urinary output, and free water clearance, in parallel to an increase in the tubular transport of cGMP, as an effect of its higher production.

NO donors and kidney ischemia/reperfusion

Ischemia-reperfusion is strongly associated with renal inflammation, characterized by the increase of leukocyte infiltration, especially neutrophils, and high levels of chemokines. Chemokines work in association with adhesion molecules and act as a guide to direct leukocyte migration. Ischemia is also related to increased expression and activity of MAPK which results in renal damage [20]. Based on this, Martinez-Mier et al. [20] evaluated the effect of an

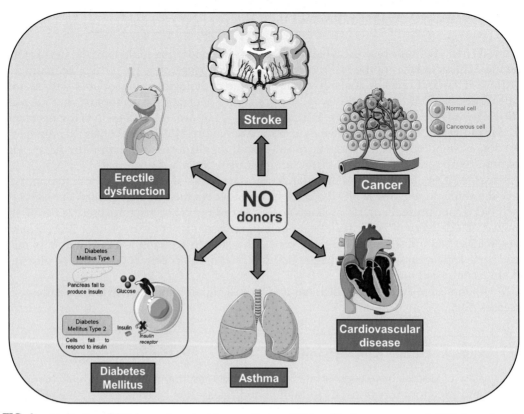

FIG. 3   Application of NO donors in several human diseases. Nitric oxide donor compounds (NO donors) can be used as a main or adjunct therapeutic alternative in the treatment of cardiovascular diseases, including arterial hypertension, pulmonary hypertension, atherosclerosis, stroke, and angina pectoris, causing direct vasodilation and recovering tissue perfusion. In addition, NO donors demonstrate beneficial effects as an adjuvant treatment of other pathologies such as erectile dysfunction, cancer, diabetes mellitus, and asthma.

NO donor in the ischemia-reperfusion-induced inflammation in the kidneys. The authors treated ischemic rats with sodium nitroprusside (5 mg/kg) 15 min prior to the restoration of blood flow. The study demonstrated that NO donor prevented renal inflammation by reducing the levels of chemokines (such as MIP-2 and MIP-1α) and decreasing leukocyte infiltration. Sodium nitroprusside also caused prevention of higher activity of the MAPK p44/42 signaling pathway, which resulted in amelioration of kidney function [20].

Ischemia/reperfusion injury is also associated with other pro-inflammatory characteristics such as increased leukocyte adhesion and migration, thrombocyte-leukocyte aggregation, the flow of higher levels of albumin, mast cell degranulation, and epithelial hyperpermeability. Thus, NO donors present beneficial effects in ischemia/reperfusion cases by decreasing albumin flow, mast cell degranulation, and leukocyte accumulation, preventing epithelial hyperpermeability, and increasing vasodilatation. These responses are associated with NO-induced reduction of superoxide anion levels and antineutrophil aggregative properties [21]. Considering this finding, Kucuk et al. [21] evaluated the effect of glyceryl trinitrate, an

NO donor, in a rat model of kidney ischemia-reperfusion. The animals were submitted to right nephrectomy and received two weeks later an isotonic solution (0.9% NaCl) for 30 min using the cannulated right iliac vein, followed by the left renal pedicle clamp for 45 min using a bulldog clamp. One group of rats received an infusion of glyceryl trinitrate (75 or 150 μg/kg/min) 30 min before the surgery. Overall, glyceryl trinitrate resulted in amelioration of renal function, and its response was related to the reduction in tubular necrosis and kidney damage [21].

It is important to mention that the renal ischemia/reperfusion pathogenesis is related to NO deficiency since NO causes a diversity of positive effects, such as vasodilation, antiplatelet aggregation, prevention of neutrophil recruitment, and scavenging of reactive oxygen species [22]. In agreement, Katsumi et al. [22] evaluated the effect of a novel NO donor called S-nitrosylated Ser-PAMAM (SNO-Ser-PAMAM) in ischemia/reperfusion-induced renal damage. The authors induced renal ischemia by occluding the right renal artery and vein of mice for 30 min. A group of these animals received SNO-Ser-PAMAM intravenously at doses 0.08, 0.4, or 2 μmol SNO/kg immediately before reperfusion. As a result, SNO-Ser-PAMAM prevented ischemia/reperfusion-induced kidney damage and dysfunction showing a promising drug for this specific clinical case [22].

Endothelin-1 is an important vasoactive agent that causes vasoconstriction and plays a crucial role in hypertension, atherosclerosis, and ischemia/reperfusion damage. It has been demonstrated that the endothelin-1 content and mRNA expression are elevated in the kidneys after ischemia, reinforcing their participation in ischemic acute renal failure [23]. Hence, Kurata et al. [23] evaluated the effect of an NO donor FK409 in the involvement of endothelin-1 in ischemia/reperfusion-induced renal injury. A group of rats were submitted to surgery of right kidney removal and after 2 weeks these animals had their renal arteries and veins occluded by a nontraumatic clamp for 45 min. Another group of rats received an infusion of FK409 (1 mg/kg) 5 min before the ischemic period. After the end of the procedure, NO donor treatment resulted in reduced endothelin-1 overproduction in parallel to the prevention of renal dysfunction and histological damage. These results suggest that FK409 plays a suppressive effect on endothelin-1 overproduction that must be associated with its renal benefits [23].

On the other hand, renal warm ischemia is inevitable during some procedures such as partial nephrectomy, renal vascular surgery, and renal transplantation [24]. Male Sprague-Dawley rats were submitted to right nephrectomy while the left renal vascular artery was occluded with an atraumatic vascular clip for 60 min. One group of nephrectomized rats received one dose of molsidomine (30 mg/kg) 2 days before surgery. The NO donor molsidomine reduced increased levels of serum creatinine and renal histological damage, showing that NO protects the kidneys from the deleterious effects of renal warm ischemia [24].

Following this finding, it is known that abdominal aortic aneurysm surgery is a clinical practice that may result in a systemic inflammatory response, which is associated with ischemia/reperfusion due to the need of implementing a clamp to introduce a prosthesis. In parallel, hemorrhagic shock is also related to systemic inflammatory response, and one of the worst consequences is the development of kidney failure [25]. To evaluate the tissue effects of an NO donor on abdominal aortic aneurysm induced-renal damage, Lozano et al. [25] submitted rats to a suprarenal aortoiliac clamping during 30 min followed by an aortic bypass.

Another group was also submitted to hemorrhage after clamping (40% of total blood volume). There were also two more parallel groups that received molsidomine 4 mg/kg, intravenously, but the first group received it before aortic clamping and the second immediately after the aortic clamping and bleeding. Thus, molsidomine caused a reduction of inflammatory response in the kidneys, by decreasing pro-inflammatory cells and cytokines, as well as ameliorating the antioxidant defense that resulted in normalization of renal function, showing that the administration of an NO donor minimizes kidney damage in abdominal aortic aneurysm surgery case [25].

Edaravone is a new free radical scavenger which neutralizes free radicals by a one-electron transfer in polar media. This molecule presents a variety of benefits, such as a neuroprotective effect during acute brain infarction, protective response in patients with acute myocardial infarction, and protective factor for acute kidney injury development induced by renal ischemia/reperfusion [26]. Thus, Chiazza et al. [26] evaluated the possibility of an edaravone derivative NO donor named furoxan (NO-edaravone) to enhance the positive effects of edaravone in the ischemia/reperfusion-induced renal damage. Rats were submitted to bilateral renal occlusion for 45 min using nontraumatic artery clamps to clamp renal pedicles, followed by reperfusion for 6 h. An animal group received a dose-dependently infusion of edaravone (1.2, 6, and 30 µmol/kg) at the beginning of reperfusion and again after 30 min of reperfusion. Another group received the NO donor (NO-edaravone) at the same dose and time as the last group. By the end of the procedure, the NO edaravone caused a reduction of lipid peroxidation and increased the expression of SOD in the renal tissues. The NO donor also decreased the levels of pro-inflammatory cytokines such as IL-1β, IL-18, IL-6, and TNF-α, inhibiting iNOS and NF-κB activation. Therefore, the results showed that the edaravone derivative presents important effects leading to the prevention of renal damage [26].

NO donors and acute renal failure

Acute renal failure (ARF) is present in several hospitalized patients and in 15% of patients that need intensive care worldwide [4]. Its mortality rate exceeds 50% and most survivors become dependent of special care, such as hemodialysis. In this sense, ischemia/reperfusion is the most important cause of renal failure, but sepsis, hypotension, and nephrotoxic drugs are also associated with this kidney dysfunction. Oxidative stress is an immediate response after ischemia/reperfusion, caused by excessive generation of reactive oxygen species (ROS) from infiltrating inflammatory cells. ROS must react with endogenous vasodilators, antithrombotic, and antiinflammatory agents, as well as NO, which results in the loss of its beneficial effects and production of peroxynitrite (ONOO$^-$) that is extremely deleterious to the kidneys [27]. In this context, Zhang et al. [27] evaluated a new molecule (N-hydroxyguanidine), an NO donor that was protected against spontaneous NO release. This NO donor (100 µM) was tested in isolated kidneys of rats, homogenates of the renal cortex and medulla, and also in the aorta. The drug promoted renal vasodilation and increased the levels of NO in this tissue, demonstrating that it could be essential in acute renal failure cases [27].

On the other hand, rhabdomyolysis is characterized by disintegration of skeletal muscles, leading to the release of intracellular constituents into the extracellular fluids and circulation.

This condition can cause complications, including myoglobinuric acute renal failure. The most widely used model of myoglobinuric ARF is by subcutaneous or intramuscular injection of hypertonic glycerol. Subcutaneous or intramuscular injection of hypertonic glycerol causes muscle cell necrosis and myoglobinuria and provokes local fluid accumulation [28]. Hence, Chander and Chopra [28] administered an intramuscular injection of 8 mL/kg hypertonic glycerol to induce rhabdomyolysis in rats. In parallel, another group of rats was orally treated with molsidomine 5 or 10 mg/kg, 60 min prior to glycerol injection. A third group received L-arginine 125 mg/kg orally, 60 min before glycerol administration. By the end of the procedure, it was observed that the glycerol treatment caused a reduction in tissue and urine nitric oxide levels, increased renal oxidative stress, and resulted in significant kidney dysfunction along with deterioration of tissue morphology. Pretreatment of animals with molsidomine (10 mg/kg) and L-arginine 60 min before glycerol administration attenuated the decrease of nitric oxide levels, renal dysfunction, and morphological alterations; it normalized TBARS concentration and restored the depleted renal antioxidant enzymes. It was demonstrated that NO donors are an important option for treatment during a rhabdomyolysis case.

In addition, Samuvel et al. [29] treated lipopolysaccharide (LPS)-induced sepsis rats with NO donor S-nitrosoglutathione (GSNO). The authors found that GSNO treatment decreased kidney levels of caspase-3, iNOS, and TNF-a, as well as tissue T-lymphocyte infiltration. GSNO also increased kidney levels of GSH, IL-10, and PPAR-c and increased NO, creatinine, and blood urea nitrogen (BUN) levels after LPS induction.

NO donors and chronic kidney disease

The end-stage of renal failure is the most common pathway of many types of glomerular disease independently of the first stimulus for this injury. Thus, renal mass reduction is used to mimic this condition by right nephrectomy and ligation of two or three branches of the left renal artery under anesthesia [30]. The animals received molsidomine in the drinking water at a dose of 120 mg/L from day 21 after surgery, when rats had hypertension and proteinuria until the death of the vehicle-treated rats. Molsidomine normalized systemic hypertension, only partially reducing proteinuria and serum creatinine levels, but significantly prolonging animal survival, particularly in the early stage of the disease. Increased levels of endothelin-1 (ET-1) in the kidneys of animals with renal failure were reduced by molsidomine, which is probably associated with prolongation of survival by the NO donor and, in turn, may limit the smooth muscle cell proliferation and matrix accumulation responsible for organ fibrosis and dysfunction. The limitation of this study was the administration of molsidomine in the drinking water and not by gavage, which could be responsible for less efficacy in the renal damage observed in the results [30].

Considering these aspects, chronic kidney disease (CKD) is generally related to cardiovascular dysfunction, which includes left ventricular hypertrophy, systolic dysfunction, and heart failure. The prognosis of patients with CKD in association with heart failure is worse, increasing the risk of death. This coexistence of cardiac and renal failure was designated as (severe) cardiorenal syndrome [31]. An animal model was created to mimic this disease, in which rats were submitted to a 5/6th nephrectomy, followed by 8 weeks of nitric oxide synthase inhibitor treatment N^{ω}-nitro-L-arginine (L-NNA) 20 mg/L in drinking water, for

8 weeks, resulting in reduced ejection fraction. After this diagnosis, a group of these rats received molsidomine 120 mg/L in the drinking water during the following 5 weeks. Thus, the NO donor caused an increase in the ejection fraction and stroke volume. Molsidomine also ameliorated cardiac hypertrophy, reduced tubulointerstitial injury in the kidneys, and improved creatinine clearance. Therefore, this study suggests that NO can modulate cardiac function in individuals with CKD, even though there was an absence of significant effects on systemic arterial pressure and peripheral resistance [31].

In addition, Tsuchiya et al. [32] have shown that long-term exposure to L-NAME induces hypertension in rats and that the model is able to induce progressive kidney damage related to CKD. Moreover, administration of sodium nitrite orally was the source of NO and reduced L-NAME-induced proteinuria and kidney tissue damage. In this sense, Kemmner et al. exerted a supplementation nitrate (beetroot juice) in the diet of CKD caused by hypertensive or diabetic nephropathy in patients. The oral nitrate decreased blood pressure, increased plasma nitrite levels, and reduced the renal resistive index, a marker of the progression of renal disease and cardiovascular mortality, measured by Doppler ultrasonography [33].

On the other hand, Cogan et al. [34] evaluated the effect of nitroprusside, an NO donor, in 9 patients with severe congestive heart failure. After this infusion of sodium nitroprusside, total renal resistance decreased and renal blood flow (RBF) significantly increased, while the distribution of cardiac output to the kidney remained depressed. The glomerular filtration rate (GFR) did not change significantly with this NO donor, although increases in GFR were seen in selected patients in whom RBF increased by more than 10% when compared to the control. The fraction of plasma filtered decreased toward the normal rate with nitroprusside infusion, and the excretion of total cations was significantly increased. These changes all represent improvements in systemic and renal hemodynamic abnormalities occurring in patients with CKD. It is important to mention that this study used only one administration of NO donor, demonstrating that long-term therapy could bring more positive results in this group of patients [34].

NO donors and nephrotoxic substances

Cyclosporine is a commonly used drug for the treatment of autoimmune diseases and for transplantation, even though this drug can cause nephrotoxicity and hypertension. Cyclosporine nephrotoxicity is related to renal vasoconstriction, leading to a decrease in renal plasma flow and glomerular filtration rate. Vasoconstriction in the kidneys is associated with an imbalance in the release of vasoactive substances, such as high levels of thromboxane, angiotensin II, and endothelin, which are vasoconstrictors. On the other hand, a reduction of vasodilators was observed, such as NO and prostacyclin [35]. In this sense, Chander and Chopra [35] administered subcutaneously cyclosporine 20 mg/kg for 21 days in rats. Another group of animals received molsidomine 5 mg/kg orally for 21 days, in parallel to cyclosporine. Cyclosporine caused renal dysfunction, oxidative stress, and alteration in renal morphology. Molsidomine promoted an improvement in renal dysfunction by preventing oxidative stress and morphological damage. These positive results were associated with increased levels of NO in the kidneys. It is also important to mention that treatment with L-NAME in parallel to molsidomine blocked the positive effects of NO donor, demonstrating that NO plays an important role in renoprotective effects against cyclosporine nephrotoxicity [35].

On the other hand, Potier et al. [36] evaluated the effect of another NO donor during cyclosporine treatment. For this, renal superficial glomeruli or mesangial cells were isolated from rats, and cultures were prepared. Both cultures of cells were incubated with cyclosporine (10–6 mol/L) for 30 min. Another group of cells was incubated with an NO donor 3-morpholinosydnonimine (SIN-1) at variable nontoxic concentrations ranging from 10^{-4} to 10^{-9} mol/L 10 min prior to cyclosporine incubation. This study demonstrated that SIN-1 prevented the constrictive effect of cyclosporine on isolated mesangial and glomeruli cells, suggesting that NO may play a beneficial effect on this immunosuppressive renal damage agent-induced [36].

Furthermore, ferric-nitrilotriacetic acid (Fe-NTA) is a common water pollutant which is found in drinking water and in water from the wash-off of detergents used in soaps and laundry, besides the fact that it may act as a nephrotoxic agent and renal tumor promoter. Fe-NTA intoxication results in increased levels of iron at the luminal side of the proximal tubules leading to higher generation of ROS and consequently oxidative stress, characterized by lipid peroxidation, DNA damage, and reduced levels of tissue glutathione (GSH) [37]. Rahman et al. [37] evaluated the effect of an NO donor, glyceryl trinitrate, on Fe-NTA-induced nephrotoxicity. The authors treated a group of rats with a single dose of Fe-NTA (9 mg/kg) intraperitoneally and another group also received glyceryl trinitrate (3 or 6 mg/kg) 1 h after Fe-NTA administration. The NO donor caused a reduction in renal oxidative stress, as observed by the recovery of GSH levels, reduction of lipid peroxidation, and a decrease of DNA alteration, which promoted a decrease in the pathological damage to kidneys [37].

Paracetamol is a drug widely used as an analgesic and antipyretic. Its use is considered safe in therapeutically used doses but the overdose may cause hepatotoxicity and nephrotoxicity. Paracetamol-induced renal damage is caused by its metabolic activation that leads to formation of N-acetyl-p-benzoquinone imine (NAPQI) which reacts directly with glutathione (GSH). The depletion of GSH results in lipid peroxidation and protein dysfunction, leading to kidney dysfunction [38]. Li et al. [38] evaluated the ability of a novel NO donor O2-vinyl-1-(pyrrolidin-1-yl)diazen-1-ium-1,2-diolate (V-PYRRO/NO) to protect the renal tissues with an overdose of paracetamol. To test this hypothesis, the authors administered one overdose of paracetamol (600 mg/kg) intraperitoneally in rats. Another group was submitted to an implant of an osmotic pump containing V-PYRRO/NO (5.4 mg/mL), 4 h before the administration of paracetamol. The study showed that V-PYRRO/NO prevented paracetamol-induced nephrotoxicity, as observed by reduced renal damage, increased levels of GSH, and decreased lipid peroxidation, which demonstrates that this NO donor is a valuable possible drug in this case of renal damage [38].

NO donors and anesthesia

Sodium nitroprusside is commonly used to induce hypotension during anesthesia because of its rapid effect and short duration of action. However, it is very established that hypotension may compromise renal function once the renal blood flow decreases significantly [39]. Ohmura et al. [39] evaluated the effect of sodium nitroprusside infusion in dogs during halothane anesthesia. NO donor was infused at a dose of 0.2 mg/mL while the administration of halothane was continued. During the procedure, renal blood flow was well maintained, showing the security of sodium nitroprusside use during anesthesia.

As mentioned before, NO plays an important role in the regulation of renal vascular tone and renal tubular reabsorption of sodium and water during the anesthesia period [40]. Thus, Urabe et al. [40] evaluated the effect of FK409, an NO donor in the anesthesia-induced renal alterations in hemodynamics and excretory responses. The authors injected thiobutabarbital (100 mg/kg) intraperitoneally to induce rats to anesthesia. After the stabilization period, a group of animals received an infusion of FK409 (3 or 10 μg/kg) for 20 min. By the end of the procedure, FK409 caused renal vasodilation and an increase in urinary flow and natriuresis and ameliorated the glomerular filtration rate. The results reinforce that the NO donor presents positive effects in the kidneys during anesthesia, improving hemodynamics and sodium excretion.

NO donors and hypercholesterolemia

Hypercholesterolemia is responsible for decreasing NO bioavailability causing podocyte activation and renal injury [41]. Attia et al. [41] submitted female rats to a diet with 0 or 1% of cholesterol for 24 weeks; in parallel, another group received oral treatment with molsidomine in drinking water (120 mg/kg). Hypercholesterolemia resulted in a dose-dependent increase of proteinuria with reduced renal NO synthesis. This response was associated with decreased eNOS activity and higher levels of superoxide anion generation. The drug molsidomine prevented all these renal injuries, demonstrating that NO deficiency must be an important pathway leading to podocyte activation and proteinuria. Although there are positive effects of NO donor, the study has a significant limitation, which is the administration of the drug in the drinking water and not by gavage, decreasing the accuracy of the administered dose.

Below, we address the application of NO donors in other human diseases.

NO donors and diabetes mellitus

The number of people living with diabetes worldwide is approximately 463 million; it is estimated that 90% of these individuals have type 2 diabetes mellitus (DM2) and approximately 10% have type 1 diabetes mellitus (DM1) [42]. Type 1 diabetes (DM1) is an autoimmune disease that presents depletion and the progressive destruction of pancreatic β cells, resulting in a deficiency in endogenous insulin secretion under the stimulus of chronic hyperglycemia, with impairment of the function of glucagon-producing α cells [43]. Type 2 diabetes (DM2) is characterized by impaired glucose homeostasis due to insulin insensitivity because of insulin resistance and, subsequently, there is decreased insulin production and eventual failure of the pancreatic beta cells [44]. In these patients, there is an impairment of the vascular endothelium and deficiency of NO signaling, compromising the functioning of the vascular system; therefore, the major cause of mortality is associated with cardiovascular complications [45].

Chronic administration of NCX4016, an aspirin derivative that releases nitric oxide in diabetic rats with streptozotocin, reduced the incidence of ventricular tachycardia and also promoted a protective effect on the heart [46]. In addition, treatment of rats with diabetic nephropathy with NO donors alleviates extracellular matrix accumulation, further preventing diabetes-mediated oxidative and nitrostatic stress and restoring downregulation of endothelial NO synthase expression [47]. Fibroblasts cultured with NO hydrogels (NO covalently coupled to the polymer) showed higher production of extracellular matrix compared to cells cultured without NO hydrogels. Furthermore, diabetic mice used as a wound healing model that received hydrogel dressing showed greater modulation of wound healing [48]. However, insulin-dependent patients with diabetes mellitus had reduced forearm blood flow in response to donor SNP infusion compared to age-matched healthy controls [49]. Due to NO deficiency signaling, it is important to emphasize the role of NO donors as a therapeutic potential to circumvent NO resistance.

NO donors to treat cardiovascular diseases

NO is one of the most important vasodilator molecules produced by the vascular endothelium and participates in vascular homeostasis [50]. NO acts on vascular smooth muscle cells (VSMCs) by binding it with soluble guanylate cyclase, promoting its activation, and increasing intracellular cyclic guanosine monophosphate (cGMP), which stimulates protein kinase G (PKG). Activation of the NO/cGMP/PKG pathway in VSMCs promotes vasodilation [51]. The reduced bioavailability of NO compromises its signaling pathway, which is demonstrated in pathophysiological mechanisms of several cardiovascular diseases, such as arterial hypertension, pulmonary hypertension, atherosclerosis, and angina pectoris.

The oldest class of NO donors is organic nitrate, and nitroglycerin (GNT) is the best known, which has been used clinically. GNT is primarily used for the acute relief of pain associated with angina, while other slow-release derivative compounds, such as isosorbide mononitrate, are used for the treatment of chronic angina [1]. In addition, 20 patients with pulmonary hypertension undergoing mitral valve replacement surgery were treated with inhaled GNT and a reduction in mean arterial pressure and systemic vascular resistance was observed [52]. However, the limitation of organic nitrates is the development of tolerance when these drugs are used chronically, which requires larger doses to achieve the desired effect [53]. To avoid the phenomenon of tolerance, a nitrate-free interval is necessary during the therapeutic regimen, which can compromise the management of chronic treatments [1]. In addition, tolerance may be associated with endothelial dysfunction and increased oxidative stress [54], which can worsen cardiovascular diseases.

The other NO donor used clinically in hypertensive crisis is sodium nitroprusside (SNP), with the aim of reducing blood pressure quickly, with a short depressor effect [1]. However, when SNP is metabolized to release NO, it also releases five cyanide groups incorporated into its structure, which promotes cytotoxicity [55]. In addition, SNP-induced hypotension is often associated with reflex tachycardia, which is not desirable in hypertensive patients.

Diazeniumdiolates (NONOates) are compounds bound to a nucleophile adduct via a nitrogen atom that release NO spontaneously and induce vasodilation. A number of NONOates have been described with half-lives ranging from seconds to hours, which favors chronic study. In the porcine model of acute lung injury that received intratracheally NONOates there was a reduction in pulmonary hypertension [56]. In addition, pulmonary vasodilatory properties were observed without causing significant systemic toxicity [57]. An attractive feature of NONOates is the controlled rate of NO release. However, NONOates are unstable free radicals and there are no data from human clinical trials [58].

NO donors to treat stroke

Stroke affects thousands of people every year, being the leading cause of death worldwide. Differentiating between ischemic stroke and intracerebral hemorrhage requires a complete diagnosis, including clinical features and brain imaging [59]. Neurodegeneration in Parkinson's disease is associated with oxidative stress that promotes damage to neurons in the substantia nigra. In Alzheimer's disease, the redox action of active metal ions that bind to β-amyloid promotes the generation of reactive oxygen species, leading to neuronal death [60].

The administration of a nitric oxide donor NONOate to young adult rats subjected to embolic middle cerebral artery occlusion increased cell proliferation and migration in the subventricular zone and the dentate gyrus, and these rats showed improvements in neurological outcome during recovery from ischemic stroke [61]. L-Arginine and NO donors reduced total cerebral infarct volume in permanent and transient models of ischemia. Furthermore, NO donors increased cortical cerebral blood flow in the permanent model [62].

Godinez-Rubi [63] reports a series of studies in a review that demonstrated the neuroprotective effect and antioxidant action of NO donors in the brain of Parkinson's disease models. In addition, NO inhibited lipid peroxidation from oxidation of low-density lipoproteins, preventing oxidative stress and aggravating Alzheimer's disease [63]. NO donors appear to be suitable for clinical use in neurosurgical procedures involving transient arterial occlusions and in the treatment of acute ischemic stroke. In addition, NO donors can be a complementary option in the treatment of neurodegenerative diseases such as Parkinson's or Alzheimer's, where oxidative stress is exacerbated and causes cellular damage [63].

NO donors to treat erectile dysfunction

Penile erection is mediated mainly by the NO molecule, which induces vasodilation of the cavernosal smooth muscle. Erectile dysfunction is a chronic condition associated with NO deficiency that leads to a commonly treated sexual disorder, but it reduces the quality of life in middle-aged and elderly men and represents a challenge for physicians and research experts in this field [64].

Gur et al. [64] reported in a review different NO donors such as sodium nitrate, SNAP, SNP, SIN-1, NONOate, BAY 41-2272, and BAY 60-2770 and their actions on the corpus cavernosum of humans, monkeys, rats, and mice. NO donors were effective in promoting relaxation associated with potassium channels, increasing intracavernous pressure, thus improving penile erection. A limitation of using NO donors to treat erectile dysfunction is that some NO donors do not release NO to specific tissues, which can lead to hypotension and consequently cause tachycardia reflex.

NO donors to treat lung disease

Asthma is a common lung condition that causes occasional breathing difficulties due to chronic inflammatory airway disease associated with allergen-induced airway hyperresponsiveness, inflammation, and airway remodeling [65]. Increased synthesis of NO from an endogenous source or application of exogenous NO may improve the asthmatic condition.

SNP and GNT promoted in vitro relaxation of isolated guinea pig trachealis muscle [66]. NO administered by inhalation also promoted relaxation of smooth muscle from the trachea and airway and reduced methacholine-induced bronchoconstriction in guinea pigs and rabbits [67,68]. In addition, NO-releasing drugs decreased cell proliferation from smooth muscle cells in human airways [69]. Moreover, a nitrosyl-ruthenium compound [cis-[Ru(bpy)2(2-MIM)(NO)](PF6)3] abbreviated as FOR811A, promoted bronchial smooth muscle relaxation, thus improving respiratory mechanics during asthma and providing a protective effect [70]. In this way, NO donors can be used as the main treatment or adjunctive therapies for the treatment of asthma or chronic lung disease.

NO donors and cancer

Two review articles excellently reported NO signaling in cancer [71,72]. NO has an antagonistic effect on cancer biology since at low concentrations of NO (pico to nanomolar) angiogenic and antiapoptotic effects were observed, promoting tumor progression and growth. On the other hand, the highest concentration of NO (micro to millimolar) is associated with nitrosative and oxidative stress, leading to cellular apoptosis and tumor suppression.

The NO molecule linked to nonsteroidal antiinflammatory drugs (NSAIDs) known as NO-NSAIDs has shown significant potency in cancers of diverse tissue origins by inhibiting the growth of cancer cells. Although the chemotherapeutic action of NO-NSAIDs is undeniable, a limitation of their use is due to side effects since all NSAIDs can eventually cause some degree of gastrointestinal erosion and eventually develop ulcers, but most NSAIDs have side effects in cardiovascular and renal systems [71].

Conclusions

Several pieces of evidence support the roles of NO and NO donors as antihypertensive and renoprotective agents in models of kidney damage or kidney diseases, besides their clinical limitations. Thus, because of the promising therapeutic potential of this class of drugs, the development of new NO donors, as well as a better understanding of the roles of the existing NO donors in new experimental and clinical studies are still necessary and also very important in the scenario of renal diseases.

Acknowledgments

The authors thank the Coordenação de Aperfeiçoamento de Pessoal de Nível Superior (CAPES, Brazil), the Conselho Nacional de Desenvolvimento Científico e Tecnológico (CNPq, grant number 302076/222-0, Brazil), the Fundação de Amparo à Pesquisa do Estado de Minas Gerais (FAPEMIG, grant number PPM-00383-18, Brazil) and the Minas Gerais State University (UEMG). The figures/graphical abstract were created using Smart Servier (https://smart.servier.com/).

References

[1] Miller MR, Megson IL. Recent developments in nitric oxide donor drugs. Br J Pharmacol 2007;151(3):305–21.
[2] Mount PF, Power DA. Nitric oxide in the kidney: functions and regulation of synthesis. Acta Physiol (Oxford) 2006;187(4):433–46.

[3] Pereira BP, do Vale GT, Ceron CS. The role of nitric oxide in renovascular hypertension: from the pathophysiology to the treatment. Naunyn Schmiedeberg's Arch Pharmacol 2022;395(2):121–31.

[4] Pieretti JC, et al. H2S- and NO-releasing gasotransmitter platform: a crosstalk signaling pathway in the treatment of acute kidney injury. Pharmacol Res 2020;161, 105121.

[5] Carlstrom M. Nitric oxide signalling in kidney regulation and cardiometabolic health. Nat Rev Nephrol 2021;17 (9):575–90.

[6] Ahmad A, et al. Role of nitric oxide in the cardiovascular and renal systems. Int J Mol Sci 2018;19(9):1–23.

[7] Tessari P. Nitric oxide in the normal kidney and in patients with diabetic nephropathy. J Nephrol 2015;28 (3):257–68.

[8] Bauer V, Sotnikova R. Nitric oxide—the endothelium-derived relaxing factor and its role in endothelial functions. Gen Physiol Biophys 2010;29(4):319–40.

[9] Majid DS, Navar LG. Nitric oxide in the control of renal hemodynamics and excretory function. Am J Hypertens 2001;14(6 Pt 2):74S–82S.

[10] Cowley Jr AW, et al. Role of renal NO production in the regulation of medullary blood flow. Am J Physiol Regul Integr Comp Physiol 2003;284(6):R1355–69.

[11] Ignarro LJ, Napoli C, Loscalzo J. Nitric oxide donors and cardiovascular agents modulating the bioactivity of nitric oxide: an overview. Circ Res 2002;90(1):21–8.

[12] Saraiva J, et al. Nanocarriers for nitric oxide delivery. J Drug Deliv 2011;2011:936438.

[13] Patel S, et al. Nitric oxide donors release extracellular traps from human neutrophils by augmenting free radical generation. Nitric Oxide 2010;22(3):226–34.

[14] Yang T, Zelikin AN, Chandrawati R. Progress and promise of nitric oxide-releasing platforms. Adv Sci 2018;5 (6):1701043.

[15] Thomson MJ, Stevanin TM, Moir JW. Measuring nitric oxide metabolism in the pathogen Neisseria meningitidis. Methods Enzymol 2008;437:539–60.

[16] Blangetti M, et al. A nonmetal-containing nitric oxide donor activated with single-photon green light. Chemistry 2017;23(38):9026–9.

[17] Stamler JS, Singel DJ, Loscalzo J. Biochemistry of nitric oxide and its redox-activated forms. Science 1992;258 (5090):1898–902.

[18] Majid DS, et al. Renal responses to intra-arterial administration of nitric oxide donor in dogs. Hypertension 1993;22(4):535–41.

[19] Nielsen CB. Sodium nitroprusside increases renal synthesis of cGMP and reduces free water clearance in human. Nephron 1994;68(2):273.

[20] Martinez-Mier G, et al. Exogenous nitric oxide downregulates MIP-2 and MIP-1alpha chemokines and MAPK p44/42 after ischemia and reperfusion of the rat kidney. J Investig Surg 2002;15(5):287–96.

[21] Kucuk HF, et al. Role of glyceryl trinitrate, a nitric oxide donor, in the renal ischemia-reperfusion injury of rats. Eur Surg Res 2006;38(5):431–7.

[22] Katsumi H, et al. S-nitrosylated l-serine-modified dendrimer as a kidney-targeting nitric oxide donor for prevention of renal ischaemia/reperfusion injury. Free Radic Res 2020;54(11–12):841–7.

[23] Kurata H, et al. Protective effect of nitric oxide on ischemia/reperfusion-induced renal injury and endothelin-1 overproduction. Eur J Pharmacol 2005;517(3):232–9.

[24] Ozturk H, et al. The effects of the nitric oxide donor molsidomine prevent in warm ischemia-reperfusion injury of the rat renal—a functional and histophatological study. Int Urol Nephrol 2001;32(4):601–7.

[25] Lozano FS, et al. Exogenous nitric oxide modulates the systemic inflammatory response and improves kidney function after risk-situation abdominal aortic surgery. J Vasc Surg 2005;42(1):129–39.

[26] Chiazza F, et al. A nitric oxide-donor furoxan moiety improves the efficacy of edaravone against early renal dysfunction and injury evoked by ischemia/reperfusion. Oxidative Med Cell Longev 2015;2015:804659.

[27] Zhang Q, et al. Development and characterization of glutamyl-protected N-hydroxyguanidines as reno-active nitric oxide donor drugs with therapeutic potential in acute renal failure. J Med Chem 2013;56(13):5321–34.

[28] Chander V, Chopra K. Molsidomine, a nitric oxide donor and L-arginine protects against rhabdomyolysis-induced myoglobinuric acute renal failure. Biochim Biophys Acta 2005;1723(1–3):208–14.

[29] Samuvel DJ, et al. S-Nitrosoglutathione ameliorates acute renal dysfunction in a rat model of lipopolysaccharide-induced sepsis. J Pharm Pharmacol 2016;68(10):1310–9.

[30] Benigni A, et al. Renoprotection by nitric oxide donor and lisinopril in the remnant kidney model. Am J Kidney Dis 1999;33(4):746–53.

[31] Bongartz LG, et al. The nitric oxide donor molsidomine rescues cardiac function in rats with chronic kidney disease and cardiac dysfunction. Am J Physiol Heart Circ Physiol 2010;299(6):H2037–45.

[32] Tsuchiya K, et al. Dietary nitrite ameliorates renal injury in L-NAME-induced hypertensive rats. Nitric Oxide 2010;22(2):98–103.

[33] Kemmner S, et al. Dietary nitrate load lowers blood pressure and renal resistive index in patients with chronic kidney disease: a pilot study. Nitric Oxide 2017;64:7–15.

[34] Cogan JJ, et al. Renal effects of nitroprusside and hydralazine in patients with congestive heart failure. Circulation 1980;61(2):316–23.

[35] Chander V, Chopra K. Effect of molsidomine and L-arginine in cyclosporine nephrotoxicity: role of nitric oxide. Toxicology 2005;207(3):463–74.

[36] Potier M, Winicki J, Cambar J. Nitric oxide (NO) donor 3-morpholinosydnonimine antagonizes cyclosporin A-induced contraction in two in vitro glomerular models. Cell Biol Toxicol 1996;12(4–6):335–9.

[37] Rahman A, et al. Glyceryl trinitrate, a nitric oxide donor, suppresses renal oxidant damage caused by potassium bromate. Redox Rep 1999;4(6):263–9.

[38] Li C, et al. The nitric oxide donor, V-PYRRO/NO, protects against acetaminophen-induced nephrotoxicity in mice. Toxicology 2003;189(3):173–80.

[39] Ohmura A, et al. Effects of halothane and sodium nitroprusside on renal function and autoregulation. Br J Anaesth 1982;54(1):103–8.

[40] Urabe K, et al. Renal hemodynamic and excretory responses in anesthetized rats to FK409, a novel nitric oxide donor. Eur J Pharmacol 1997;321(2):195–200.

[41] Attia DM, et al. Proteinuria is preceded by decreased nitric oxide synthesis and prevented by a NO donor in cholesterol-fed rats. Kidney Int 2002;61(5):1776–87.

[42] Federation ID. Latest figures show 463 million people now living with diabetes worldwide as numbers continue to rise. Diabetes Res Clin Pract 2019;157:107932.

[43] Katsarou A, et al. Type 1 diabetes mellitus. Nat Rev Dis Primers 2017;3:17016.

[44] DeFronzo RA, et al. Type 2 diabetes mellitus. Nat Rev Dis Primers 2015;1:15019.

[45] McCarthy O, et al. Supplementary nitric oxide donors and exercise as potential means to improve vascular health in people with type 1 diabetes: yes to NO? Nutrients 2019;11(7):1–18.

[46] Burke SG, et al. The effect of NCX4016 [2-acetoxy-benzoate 2-(2-nitroxymethyl)-phenyl ester] on the consequences of ischemia and reperfusion in the streptozotocin diabetic rat. J Pharmacol Exp Ther 2006;316 (3):1107–14.

[47] Hsu YC, et al. Nitric oxide donors rescue diabetic nephropathy through oxidative-stress-and nitrosative-stress-mediated Wnt signaling pathways. J Diabetes Investig 2015;6(1):24–34.

[48] Masters KS, et al. Effects of nitric oxide releasing poly(vinyl alcohol) hydrogel dressings on dermal wound healing in diabetic mice. Wound Repair Regen 2002;10(5):286–94.

[49] Calver A, Collier J, Vallance P. Inhibition and stimulation of nitric oxide synthesis in the human forearm arterial bed of patients with insulin-dependent diabetes. J Clin Invest 1992;90(6):2548–54.

[50] Moncada S, Higgs EA. Nitric oxide and the vascular endothelium. Handb Exp Pharmacol 2006;176 Pt 1:213–54.

[51] Francis SH, et al. cGMP-dependent protein kinases and cGMP phosphodiesterases in nitric oxide and cGMP action. Pharmacol Rev 2010;62(3):525–63.

[52] Yurtseven N, et al. Effect of nitroglycerin inhalation on patients with pulmonary hypertension undergoing mitral valve replacement surgery. Anesthesiology 2003;99(4):855–8.

[53] Rutherford JD. Nitrate tolerance in angina therapy. How to avoid it. Drugs 1995;49(2):196–9.

[54] Munzel T, et al. Effects of long-term nitroglycerin treatment on endothelial nitric oxide synthase (NOS III) gene expression, NOS III-mediated superoxide production, and vascular NO bioavailability. Circ Res 2000;86(1):E7–E12.

[55] Bates JN, et al. Nitric oxide generation from nitroprusside by vascular tissue. Evidence that reduction of the nitroprusside anion and cyanide loss are required. Biochem Pharmacol 1991;42(Suppl):S157–65.

[56] Brilli RJ, et al. Intratracheal instillation of a novel NO/nucleophile adduct selectively reduces pulmonary hypertension. J Appl Physiol (1985) 1997;83(6):1968–75.

[57] Jacobs BR, et al. Aerosolized soluble nitric oxide donor improves oxygenation and pulmonary hypertension in acute lung injury. Am J Respir Crit Care Med 1998;158(5 Pt 1):1536–42.

[58] Li B, et al. Recent developments in pharmacological effect, mechanism and application prospect of diazeniumdiolates. Front Pharmacol 2020;11:923.

[59] Campbell BCV, Khatri P. Stroke. Lancet 2020;396(10244):129–42.

III. Nitric oxide donors and cardiovascular and metabolic diseases

[60] Lin MT, Beal MF. Mitochondrial dysfunction and oxidative stress in neurodegenerative diseases. Nature 2006;443(7113):787–95.

[61] Zhang R, et al. A nitric oxide donor induces neurogenesis and reduces functional deficits after stroke in rats. Ann Neurol 2001;50(5):602–11.

[62] Willmot M, et al. A systematic review of nitric oxide donors and L-arginine in experimental stroke; effects on infarct size and cerebral blood flow. Nitric Oxide 2005;12(3):141–9.

[63] Godinez-Rubi M, Rojas-Mayorquin AE, Ortuno-Sahagun D. Nitric oxide donors as neuroprotective agents after an ischemic stroke-related inflammatory reaction. Oxidative Med Cell Longev 2013;2013:297357.

[64] Gur S, Chen AL, Kadowitz PJ. Nitric oxide donors and penile erectile function. In: Seabra AB, editor. Nitric oxide donors—novel biomedical applications and perspectives. Academic Press; 2017. p. 121–40.

[65] Prado CM, Martins MA, Tiberio IF. Nitric oxide in asthma physiopathology. ISRN Allergy 2011;2011:832560.

[66] Kishen R, Pleuvry BJ. Some actions of sodium nitroprusside and glyceryl trinitrate on guinea-pig isolated trachealis muscle. J Pharm Pharmacol 1985;37(7):502–4.

[67] Dupuy PM, et al. Bronchodilator action of inhaled nitric oxide in guinea pigs. J Clin Invest 1992;90(2):421–8.

[68] Hogman M, et al. Inhalation of nitric oxide modulates methacholine-induced bronchoconstriction in the rabbit. Eur Respir J 1993;6(2):177–80.

[69] Patel HJ, et al. Constitutive expressions of type I NOS in human airway smooth muscle cells: evidence for an antiproliferative role. FASEB J 1999;13(13):1810–6.

[70] Costa PPC, et al. Anti-asthmatic effect of nitric oxide metallo-donor FOR811A [cis-[Ru(bpy)2(2-MIM)(NO)](PF6) 3] in the respiratory mechanics of Swiss mice. PLoS One 2021;16(3):e0248394.

[71] Kashfi K, Duvalsaint PL. Nitric oxide donors and therapeutic applications in cancer. In: Seabra AB, editor. Nitric oxide donors—novel biomedical applications and perspectives. Academic Press; 2017. p. 75–119.

[72] Seabra AB, Duran N. Nitric oxide donors for prostate and bladder cancers: current state and challenges. Eur J Pharmacol 2018;826:158–68.

Nitric oxide resistance in type 2 diabetes: Potential implications of HNO donors

Zahra Bahadoran[a], Parvin Mirmiran[b], Khosrow Kashfi[c], and Asghar Ghasemi[d]

[a]Nutrition and Endocrine Research Center, Research Institute for Endocrine Sciences, Shahid Beheshti University of Medical Sciences, Tehran, Iran [b]Department of Clinical Nutrition and Dietetics, Faculty of Nutrition Sciences and Food Technology, National Nutrition and Food Technology Research Institute, Shahid Beheshti University of Medical Sciences, Tehran, Iran [c]Department of Molecular, Cellular, and Biomedical Sciences, Sophie Davis School of Biomedical Education, City University of New York School of Medicine, New York, NY, United States [d]Endocrine Physiology Research Center, Research Institute for Endocrine Sciences, Shahid Beheshti University of Medical Sciences, Tehran, Iran

Abstract

Nitric oxide (NO•) resistance syndrome refers to a state of decreased NO• bioavailability and/or impaired responsiveness to NO•. Excessive production of reactive oxygen species (ROS) scavenging NO• from the environment, oxidation of its intracellular receptor soluble guanylate cyclase (sGC), or impairing the main physiologically relevant NO• signaling cascade (i.e., NO•/cyclic guanosine 5′-monophosphate (cGMP)/cGMP-dependent protein kinase (PKG) pathway) are the leading causes of NO• resistance. The state of NO• resistance in type 2 diabetes mellitus (T2DM), manifested by a decreased responsiveness of the myocardium, vasculature, platelets, skeletal muscle, and vascular smooth muscle to endogenous and exogenous NO•, is associated with future risk of cardiovascular events. Nitroxyl (HNO), a recently highlighted nitrogen oxide species, can effectively circumvent NO• resistance by bypassing the pathways that become relatively nonresponsive to NO• in T2DM.

Abbreviations

ACh	acetylcholine
ADP	adenosine diphosphate
BH$_4$	tetrahydrobiopterin
cAMP	cyclic adenosine 5'-monophosphate
cGMP	cyclic guanosine 5'-monophosphate
CGRP	calcitonin gene–related peptide
CREB	cAMP response element–binding protein
Cu$^+$	cuprous copper
Cu^{2+}	cupric copper
CVD	cardiovascular disease
DAG	diacylglycerol
DEA-NO	diethylamine-NONOate
EDRF	endothelium-derived relaxing factor
eNOS	endothelial NO• synthase
ERKs	extracellular signal–related kinases
Fe^{2+}	ferrous iron
Fe^{3+}	ferric iron
GAPDH	glyceraldehyde-3-phosphate dehydrogenase
GK	Goto-Kakizaki
GSH	reduced glutathione
GTN	glyceryl trinitrate
GTP	guanosine triphosphate
H$_2$NCN	cyanamide
HbA1c	glycosylated hemoglobin
HFD	high-fat diet
HNO	nitroxyl
HXC	hydroxycobalamin
L-NAME	N^G-nitro-L-arginine methyl ester
met-Hb	methemoglobin
met-Mb	metmyoglobin
N$_2$O	nitrous oxide
NADPH	reduced nicotinamide adenine dinucleotide phosphate
NH$_2$OH	hydroxylamine
NH$_3$	ammonia
NO•	nitric oxide
NO$_2^-$	nitrite
NO$_3^-$	nitrate
NOHA	N-hydroxy-L-arginine
NOX	NADPH oxidase
ODQ	1H-[1,2,4]oxadiazolo[4,3-a]quinoxalin-1-one
oxy-Hb	oxyhemoglobin
PDE	cyclic nucleotide phosphodiesterase
ONOO$^-$	peroxynitrite
PIP$_2$	phosphatidylinositol 4,5-bisphosphate
PKA	protein kinase A
PKCε	protein kinase Cε
PKG	cGMP-dependent protein kinase
PLC-β1	phospholipase C-β1
ROS	reactive oxygen species
SERCA$_{2a}$	sarco-/endoplasmic reticulum Ca^{2+} adenosine triphosphatase-$_{2a}$
sGC	soluble guanylate cyclase
SNP	sodium nitroprusside

SOD	superoxide dismutase
STZ	streptozotocin
T1DM	type 1 diabetes
T2DM	type 2 diabetes
XOD	xanthine oxidase

Conflict of interest

No potential conflicts of interest were disclosed.

Introduction

The term "nitric oxide (NO•) resistance syndrome," initially coined by Gladwin in 2006 [1], describes a state of decreased NO• bioavailability and/or impaired responsiveness to NO•. NO• is now considered an endocrine hormone [2]. Thus, NO• resistance can be analogized to insulin resistance, a state of preserved/overproduction of insulin with a general resistance to insulin at the receptor level [3], or other endocrinopathies, like thyroid hormone resistance, manifested with elevated thyroid hormone levels along with reduced end-organ responsiveness to the hormones [4]. NO• resistance has been documented in heart failure [5], stable angina pectoris, acute coronary syndrome [6], sickle cell disease vasculopathy [7], polycystic ovary syndrome [8], metabolic syndrome [9], chronic kidney diseases [10], insulin resistance [11], and type 2 diabetes mellitus (T2DM) [12–15].

NO• resistance, as a multifaceted disorder, mainly occurs due to (1) overproduction of reactive oxygen species (ROS, e.g., superoxide anion and hydrogen peroxide); (2) oxidative reactions with cell-free plasma hemoglobin, which scavenges NO• from the environment; or (3) oxidation and (reversible) inactivation of its intracellular receptor soluble guanylate cyclase (sGC) [7,11]. Impairment of the main physiologically relevant NO• signaling cascade, i.e., NO•/cyclic guanosine 5′-monophosphate (cGMP)/cGMP-dependent protein kinase (PKG) pathway, is a well-documented cause of NO• resistance; this occurs at both receptor level (i.e., binding of NO• to sGC) and postreceptor level (i.e., cGMP generation by sGC, cGMP degradation by cyclic nucleotide phosphodiesterase (PDE), and cGMP-induced protein kinase activation) [11,16]. The binding of NO• to reduced ferrous (Fe^{2+}) heme residue of sGC increases its catalytic activity and increases the production of cGMP from guanosine triphosphate (GTP); high levels of ROS can oxidize the sGC heme iron to the ferric form (Fe^{3+}), rendering sGC insensitive to normal levels of NO• and developing the NO• resistance state [17,18].

Several agents may attenuate the NO• resistance state, including angiotensin-converting enzyme inhibitors (e.g., ramipril and perindopril), the antianginal agent perhexiline, insulin (following acute but not long-term administration, by decreasing oxidative stress and superoxide production), and statins (by upregulating endothelial NO• synthase (eNOS) expression and activity) [16,19]. Furthermore, nitrite (NO_2^-), sGC activators, and nitroxyl (HNO) donors overcome NO• resistance [19]. HNO not only escapes from ROS-related reactions, quenching NO• under oxidative conditions, but also exerts antioxidant properties [19,20]. Administration of HNO donors (e.g., Angeli's salt) is one strategy for overcoming NO• resistance in T2DM [19]. Here, we discuss NO• resistance in T2DM and the potential therapeutic application of HNO donors to circumvent this problem.

Evidence of NO• resistance in T2DM

NO• resistance is associated with a loss in the vaso- and cardioprotective effects of either endogenous or exogenous NO• [16] and predicts the risk of adverse cardiovascular events [21]. For example, decreased platelet responsiveness to the antiaggregatory effects of NO•, a phenomenon termed "platelet NO• resistance," contributes to an increased propensity toward thrombosis [22]. In addition, vascular NO• resistance, exhibited as impaired vasodilator function in both the peripheral and coronary circulation, was associated with future cardiovascular events (i.e., myocardial infarction, definite angina, coronary revascularization, stroke, resuscitated cardiac arrest, and cardiovascular disease (CVD) mortality), independent of the well-known risk factors [21,23].

NO• resistance syndrome in diabetes has been documented in the myocardium, vasculature, platelets, skeletal muscle, and vascular smooth muscle [5,11,13,16,24]. The first reports of NO• resistance in the myocardium in diabetic conditions (either streptozotocin (STZ)-induced diabetes and high-fat diet, or low-dose STZ–induced diabetes, representing models of type 1 diabetes (T1DM) and T2DM, respectively) have been published by Qin et al. [25] and Velagic et al. [26]. In the isolated hearts of rats with T2DM, inotropic (increase in the force of heart muscle contraction) and lusitropic (increase in the rate of the heart muscle relaxation) responses to diethylamine-NONOate (DEA-NO), a NO• donor, are markedly reduced [26]. In addition, the coronary flow response to exogenous NO• was reduced, while a dose-dependent increase in the heart rate (positive chronotropic) was evident in diabetic rats [26]. Upregulation of p22phox expression (critical mediator of superoxide production by reduced nicotinamide adenine dinucleotide phosphate (NADPH) oxidase enzymes 1 and 2, NOX1, 2) in the left ventricles from diabetic hearts and a reduced level of GSH/GSSG support this hypothesis that diabetes-induced imbalance in the reduced versus the oxidized form of sGC contributes to developing NO• resistance in the diabetic myocardium and coronary vasculature [26].

In the T1DM model, the inotropic response to DEA-NO decreased in severely hyperglycemic rat hearts compared with normal hearts; in addition, the dose-dependent increases in the heart rate that was seen with DEA-NO in nondiabetic rats were somewhat attenuated in the hearts isolated from diabetic rats [25]. An upregulated NOX2 subunit p22, an elevated NOX4 protein expression, and NOX2 gene expression, concomitant with increased ROS and nitrotyrosine levels, were observed in severely diabetic hearts [25]. The diabetes-induced myocardial NO• resistance was accompanied by progressively diminished sGC-mediated components of these responses in parallel with increased blood glucose and glycosylated hemoglobin (HbA1c) [25].

The existence of vascular NO• resistance in T2DM is supported by evidence indicating reduced vascular responses to exogenous NO• donors [26,27] or those demonstrating impaired NO•-dependent vasorelaxation in the presence of eNOS-derived NO• [28]. Isolated resistance arteries from female spontaneous T2DM rats (Goto-Kakizaki rats, GK) displayed decreased responsiveness to acetylcholine (ACh) and sodium nitroprusside (SNP) and increased sensitivity to sildenafil, a PDE5 inhibitor, an enzyme that catalyzes the breakdown of cGMP to 5'-GMP. Furthermore, the vasodilatory response to both heme-dependent sGC activation (using BAY 41-2272, an sGC stimulator, which binds directly to the reduced-form of heme-containing sGC) and heme-independent sGC activation (using BAY 58-2667, an sGC activator, which binds directly to oxidized form of heme-containing sGC) was reduced in mesenteric arteries from diabetic rats compared with normal ones [27]. This diabetes-induced hyporesponsiveness to the sGC activator in the mesenteric arteries was negligible (5% vs 10% compared with the sGC stimulator) and compensated by ODQ (1H-[1,2,4]oxadiazolo[4,3-a] quinoxalin-1-one, which makes sGC unavailable for NO• binding due to oxidation of the sGC heme); likewise, other vascular beds, e.g., aorta derived from diabetic GK rats and isolated vessels from T2DM humans, exhibited a preserved and enhanced relaxation response to sGC activators (i.e., heme-independent activator protoporphyrin-IX and BAY 58–2667, respectively) [29,30]. These data suggest that in an oxidative state (e.g., in conditions like hyperglycemia), in which sGC can mainly exist in an oxidized (heme-free) form, the enzyme preferentially responds to activators that bind to heme-Fe^{3+} containing sGC. Indeed, sGC activators and stimulators seem to competitively activate the enzyme in a hyperglycemic state [27]. sGC bioactivity seems redox-regulated and oxidative stress shifts intracellular levels of native sGC toward the oxidized, heme-free form, which is insensitive to NO•.

Although it seems vasculature type–specific, reduced relaxation response to NO• has been attributed to NO• resistance at the receptor level, rather than at the cGMP-PKG level [27] since cGMP-induced relaxation response and PKG expression remained unchanged in mesenteric arteries derived from T2DM rats [27]. Since the expression of sGC was preserved [29] or even increased in the vasculature of diabetic animals [27], it can be assumed that the reduced sGC response to NO• is due to a reduction in the enzyme's heme content and/or oxidation of the heme iron.

In another animal model of T2DM that was induced by a high-fat diet and low-dose STZ, significantly impaired SNP-induced endothelium-independent vasorelaxation was documented in mesenteric arteries [26]; relaxation response to the exogenous NO• donor, DEA-NO was also reduced in arteries from diabetic rats [26]. Vascular sensitivity to DEA-NO was significantly impaired, but no impact on maximum relaxation was observed in mesenteric arteries of severely diabetic rats [25]. Similar to animal models, a subphenotype of endothelial dysfunction, characterized by NO• resistance at the receptor level, has been identified in the human blood vessels of patients with T2DM [30].

NO• is a physiological inhibitor of platelet aggregation, and its antiaggregatory effect is likely to be impaired in T2DM [22,31]. Evidence of platelet NO• resistance in T2DM has been provided by experimental studies [31,32]. T2DM patients exhibited a reduced platelet response to NO• donors, SNP, and glyceryl trinitrate (GTN) compared with normal subjects; inhibited adenosine diphosphate (ADP)–induced aggregation was $15.4 \pm 7\%$ and $19.5 \pm 8.2\%$ in patients with T2DM vs $73.1 \pm 5.9\%$ and $50.3 \pm 7.7\%$ in healthy controls [32]. In addition, the magnitude of platelet hyporesponsiveness to NO• was related to the degree of patient glycemic control and reversed by insulin therapy [31].

Nitroxyl (HNO)

Nitroxyl (HNO) or nitroxide anion (NO^-) (also named nitrosyl hydride, nitroso hydrogen, or azanone), the one-electron reduced and protonated congener of NO•, is the most enigmatic and misunderstood of the nitrogen oxide species with unique biological properties and discrete behavior compared with NO• [33–35]. Within the nitrogen oxide redox spectrum, referring to the oxidation states of the nitrogen atom (ranging from +5 to −3, from nitrate (NO_3^-) to ammonia (NH_3)), HNO is an intermediate species with an oxidation state of +1 [33,36].

Although HNO was thought to be a good acid that should primarily exist in its anionic form, it actually behaves as a very poor acid ($pK_a = 11.4$) and at physiological pH (~7) exists almost exclusively as HNO (equilibrium concentrations being about 25,000 to 1, HNO compared with NO^-) [37] as predicted from the Henderson-Hasselbalch equation; however, formation of NO^- would be significant in alkaline solutions [38]:

$$pH = pK_a + Log\frac{[NO^-]}{[HNO]}$$
$$7.0 = 11.4 + Log\frac{[NO^-]}{[HNO]}$$
$$Log\frac{[NO^-]}{[HNO]} = -4.4$$
$$\frac{[HNO]}{[NO^-]} = 25,119$$

HNO metabolism

NO• is primarily synthesized through oxidation of L-arginine by NOS enzymes in the presence of NADPH and molecular O_2 requiring calmodulin and tetrahydrobiopterin (BH_4) as cofactors; it may also be synthesized by enzymatic and nonenzymatic reduction of NO_3^-/NO_2^- [39,40]. Endogenous biosynthetic pathways for HNO have remained debatable [33,41]; this lack of certainty concerning endogenous production of HNO is due to its unstable nature and the difficulties of quantitative detection, especially where NO• is present [42]. The following pathways have been proposed for HNO production (Fig. 1): (1) L-arginine-NOS pathway via oxidation of N-hydroxy-L-arginine (NOHA), which is an intermediate in the L-arginine-NO• pathway by uncoupled NOS, i.e., BH_4-free NOS [43], or in an oxidative environment [44]. HNO may also be produced by peroxidation of hydroxylamine (NH_2OH), by the NOS system [45], or by the heme-containing peroxidases (i.e., myeloperoxidase, myoglobin, hemoglobin) [46]; (2) the transnitrosation reaction of S-nitrosothiols with thiol species [47,48]; (3) mitochondrial reduction of NO• [49,50] (in prokaryotes), and its reduction by metalloenzymes, e.g., manganese- and iron-containing superoxide dismutase (Mn- and Fe-SOD) [51] and xanthine oxidase (XOD) [52], or through reactions with reductants such as ubiquinol [53]; and (4) drug metabolism (e.g., alcohol-sensitizing drug cyanamide (H_2NCN) [54] and hydroxyurea used to reduce the complications of sickle cell disease [55]). Although redox conversion of NO• to HNO (and vice versa) occurs in vitro and seems to be feasible in vivo, similar to other biological agents interacting with redox siblings through outer-sphere electron transfer, the observed orthogonal properties of these nitrogen oxides imply that the HNO-NO• redox interplay is not facile in vivo [35,41,56]. Furthermore, the reduction potential of this process ($E^{0'}$ NO• → NO^-/HNO, i.e., ~−0.68 V at pH 7) is outside

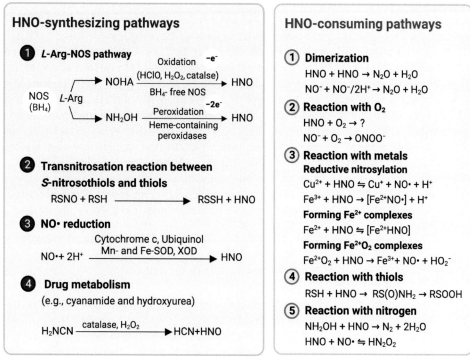

FIG. 1 A summary of nitroxyl (HNO)-synthesizing (A) and consuming pathways (B). The proposed mechanisms of HNO synthesis are (1) oxidation of N-hydroxy-L-arginine (NOHA) by uncoupled nitric oxide (NO•) synthase (NOS) and oxidative agents, or peroxidation of hydroxylamine (NH_2OH) by some heme-containing peroxidases (i.e., myeloperoxidase, myoglobin, and hemoglobin); (2) reaction of S-nitrosothiols (RSNO) with thiol (RSH) species; (3) mitochondrial reduction of NO•, and its reduction by metalloenzymes, e.g., manganese- and iron-containing superoxide dismutase (Mn- and Fe-SOD), and xanthine oxidase (XOD); (4) drug metabolism (e.g., cyanamide (H_2NCN) and hydroxyurea). HNO may be consumed by several mechanisms, including dimerization, and reaction with O_2, metals (metal-containing proteins, e.g., SOD, met-Hb, met-Mb, deoxy-Hb, and soluble guanylyl cyclase), thiols, and nitrogen (e.g., nucleophilic nitrogen oxides such as hydroxylamine, NO•, and nitrite). HCN, hydrogen cyanide; N_2O, dinitrogen monoxide or nitrous oxide; $ONOO^-$, peroxynitrite; Cu^+, cuprous copper; Cu^{2+}, cupric copper; Fe^{2+}, ferrous iron; Fe^{3+}, ferric iron; HO_2^-, hydroperoxyl radical or protonated form of superoxide (O_2^-).

the biological range, and a substantial thermodynamic barrier for the conversion of NO• to HNO makes it improbable to a significant extent under physiological conditions [57]. The historically discarded possibility of NO• conversion to HNO has been reconsidered by evidence of a possible biochemically and biologically relevant HNO source resulting from the reaction of NO• with aromatic or pseudoaromatic alcohols (i.e., tyrosine, ascorbic acid, and hydroquinone) [58]. This is not a simple thermodynamically unfavorable outer sphere reduction coupled to proton release/uptake; this reaction involves a nucleophilic addition of ROH/ RO^- to NO•, coupled to a proton transfer, resulting in an RO-N(H)O• intermediate, which decays by O–N bond cleavage, producing HNO [58].

Depending on the reaction conditions, HNO may also be consumed by some mechanisms, including (1) rapid dimerization and dehydration to form nitrous oxide (N_2O, $k = 8 \times 10^6 \, m^{-1} \, s^{-1}$), (2) oxidation to peroxynitrite (with a rate constant, $k = 1.8–2 \times 10^4 \, m^{-1} \, s^{-1}$ at pH 7.4), (3) reaction with metal complexes (e.g., Fe^{3+} or Cu^{2+}-containing complexes, Fe^{2+}-containing complexes, and $Fe^{2+}O_2$-containing complexes), (4) reaction with thiols, and reaction with nitrogen oxides, e.g., hydroxylamine, NO•, and NO_2^- [59]. In exposure to metal complexes, HNO reacts with oxyhemoglobin (oxy-Hb, with a rate constant of about $1 \times 10^7 \, M^{-1} \, s^{-1}$, to form methemoglobin, met-Hb, NO•, and peroxide), and met-Hb to form Hb-NO• (with a rate constant of $8 \times 10^5 \, M^{-1} \, s^{-1}$) [35]. The affinity of HNO (the relative reactivity) to biomolecules is oxy-Mb > reduced glutathione (GSH) > N-acetylcysteine > Cu/Zn-SOD > Mn-SOD > metmyoglobin (met-Mb) ≈ catalase > ferricytochrome c > O_2 [35]. HNO can also be converted to NO• by various ubiquitous biological oxidants, e.g., oxygen, Cu^{2+} (Cu^{2+}-containing SOD), met-Hb, and flavins [60,61]. For more comprehensive and detailed discussions about HNO chemistry and its differences from NO• chemistry, some useful references are available [33,59,62].

Physiological effects of HNO

HNO has been speculated to have an orthogonal relationship with NO• [41,56]. This term refers to the fact that they use different second messenger systems. Although their physiological effects can, at times, overlap, HNO targets calcitonin gene–related peptide (CGRP), while NO• modulates sGC [41]. HNO was originally a candidate for the endothelium-derived relaxing factor (EDRF) [63]; however, it was largely ignored once NO• was identified as this species. In sham rats, ACh-induced relaxation decreased in the presence of both a selective NO• scavenger (hydroxycobalamin, HXC) and a selective HNO scavenger (L-cysteine), indicating the contribution of both NO• and HNO in the endothelium-dependent relaxation of carotid arteries [64].

The physiological effects of HNO have been reviewed extensively [36,65,66]. In brief, HNO directly interacts with thiol residues in target proteins (e.g., sarco-/endoplasmic reticulum Ca^{2+}-adenosine triphosphatase-$_{2a}$ (SERCA$_{2a}$), phospholamban, ryanodine receptors, and myofilament proteins in cardiomyocytes) and causes reversible posttranslational modifications (i.e., nitrosylation). It increases the release of CGRP, exhibits antioxidant properties (via donation of its hydrogen and induction of expression/activity of the antioxidant protein heme oxygenase), inhibits platelet aggregation, and improves cardiovascular function [36,65,66]. HNO seems to dictate its effects in the cardiovascular system independent of NO•, cGMP, and β-adrenergic signaling. It increases CGRP (an agonist of calcitonin receptor–like receptor) but not cGMP and subsequently activates adenylate cyclase, increases intracellular cyclic adenosine monophosphate (cAMP), and activates protein kinase A (PKA) [67]; in an animal model of cardiac failure, Angeli's salt, an HNO donor, increased contractility by twofold; enhanced relaxation; and decreased cardiac preload and afterload without altering plasma cGMP, independent of and additive to β-adrenergic stimulation and by releasing CGRP (enhanced plasma CGRP by threefold) [67]. Likewise, infusion of Angeli's salt resulted in elevated CGRP levels in the arterial, venous, and coronary sinus, while plasma cGMP was not altered [35].

Potential target molecules that undergo CGRP-induced cAMP-PKA-dependent phosphorylation are L-type Ca^{2+} channels and ATP-dependent K^+ channels involved in vasodilatation [68]. Furthermore, PKA can phosphorylate and activate NOS, cAMP response element–binding protein (CREB), and extracellular signal–related kinases (ERKs) [68]. PKA targets phospholipase C-β1 (PLC-β1), which cleaves phosphatidylinositol 4,5-bisphosphate (PIP_2), ultimately leading to an increase of the intracellular Ca^{2+} and activation of the diacylglycerol (DAG)-mediated upregulation of protein kinase Cε (PKCε) [68].

Although previous attempts had failed to differentiate biological actions resulting from endogenous production of HNO and those due to its sibling, using pharmacological approaches, HNO has been shown to act with NO• together as the EDRF-mediated component of dilatation in resistance arteries [69,70]. Furthermore, the biological effects of HNO are mainly distinct and sometimes are in contrast to NO•; the biochemical rationale for the discrete behavior of these nitrogen oxides is their differential reactivity toward metals and thiols (e.g., HNO preferentially reacts with thiols and ferric complexes, while NO• prefers radicals and ferrous complexes), which leads to differential alteration of cAMP and cGMP levels [35,71]. Furthermore, it has been suggested that the fundamental difference in the biological activity of HNO compared with NO• is related to its greater propensity to react with thiols [42].

Mechanisms of action of HNO

Despite the previously well-argued assumptions that established NO• as the only biologically relevant nitrogen oxide species that activated sGC [72], or those that suggested HNO-induced sGC activation and the involvement of HNO in the cGMP signaling pathway was solely due on its conversion to NO• [60,73], there is now strong evidence supporting the notion that HNO has a direct and NO•-independent effect on sGC signaling. Angeli's salt, a *bona fide* HNO donor, can elicit cGMP-dependent effects in the presence of NO• scavengers [74,75]. HNO-regulating sGC activity is mediated via its interactions with both the regulatory ferrous (or probably ferric [35]) heme and cysteine thiols of the enzyme [76]. Evidence of preferential binding of HNO to ferric versus ferrous heme-containing proteins (e.g., metmyoglobin and catalase) initially suggested that HNO can interact with the oxidized form of sGC to give the ferrous nitrosyl adduct (i.e., the same product of NO• reaction with the ferrous form of the enzyme) [35,77,78]. However, this concept was not supported by evidence showing that HNO can only activate the reduced form of sGC [76]. The initial concept that HNO interacts with the oxidized form of sGC was from the experiments that indicated exposing ferric-heme–containing proteins (five-coordinate heme-containing proteins, e.g., horseradish peroxidase, met-Mb, and met-Hb) to Angeli's salt resulted in reductive nitrosylation of the ferric center and formation of a stable complex of ferrous heme-nitrosyl [Fe(III) + HNO → Fe(II)NO]. By contrast, the NO• donor DEA/NO resulted in the formation of an unstable ferric-nitrosyl complex [Fe(III) + NO• ↔ Fe(III)NO]. Furthermore, in contrast to NO•, which reacted with ferrous-heme–containing proteins to generate a stable complex of ferrous heme-nitrosyl, the association of HNO with deoxy-hemes would be transitory [79]. Assuming HNO would interact with sGC (a five-coordinate heme-containing protein) similarly, it is accepted that HNO would react predominately with the oxidized form of sGC, rather than its native form [35,79].

III. Nitric oxide donors and cardiovascular and metabolic diseases

HNO donation, Angeli's salt, and NO• resistance in T2DM

A frequently used source of aqueous HNO/NO$^-$ is trioxodinitrate or Angeli's salt (salt of nitrohydroxylaminic acid, $Na_2N_2O_3$), which decomposes at physiological pH to yield HNO and NO_2^-, with a rate constant of about 6×10^{-4} s^{-1} [38,80]. HNO donors have been used clinically since the 1950s in antialcoholism therapy [81].

HNO has remained effective where NO• resistance occurs in the vasculature, platelets, and myocardium [25,26,28]. In an STZ-induced model of diabetes, Angeli's salt–mediated vasorelaxation remained unaffected in either femoral or mesenteric arteries and did not change in the presence of NO• scavenger (HXC, 100 μM) but was reduced by up to fourfold in the presence of L-cysteine, a well-known HNO scavenger. Surprisingly, HXC increased the sensitivity of femoral arteries to Angeli's salt by approximately fivefold in diabetic rats; the relaxant response of either mesenteric and femoral arteries to Angeli's salt tended to be zero in the presence of ODQ, an sGC inhibitor [28]. These findings suggest that Angeli's salt can effectively compensate for the impaired-NO• signaling and alleviate diabetes-induced vascular dysfunction by releasing HNO, which acts predominantly via the sGC-cGMP pathway [28], providing further support that HNO only affects the reduced form of sGC. The augmented Angeli's salt-induced relaxation of femoral arteries in the presence of L-NAME (N^G-nitro-L-arginine methyl ester, an eNOS inhibitor) and NO• scavenger (in both control and diabetic animals) may indicate that endogenous NO• downregulates the response to exogenous HNO, probably via S-nitrosylation and reducing the sensitivity of sGC to HNO [28]. In diabetic rats (HFD and two low doses of STZ), L-cysteine but not HXC decreased ACh-induced relaxation, indicating that in diabetic rats, NO-mediated, but not HNO-mediated, relaxation is impaired; basal release of endogenous NO is reduced by diabetes, while the basal release of HNO is preserved [64].

The reduced responsiveness to NO• in the myocardium of diabetic rats (both T1DM and T2DM), documented recently by Velagic and Qin et al., is circumvented by the HNO donors [25,26]. In contrast to exogenous NO•, Angeli's salt effectively restored a diabetes-induced decrease in inotropic and lusitropic responses in diabetic hearts [26]. Moreover, vasorelaxation to Angeli's salt was enhanced in diabetic mesenteric arteries, which were hyporesponsive to the vasodilatory effects of exogenous NO• [26]. These findings imply that HNO donors like Angeli's salt may be clinically efficient for preventing adverse cardiovascular outcomes such as myocardial infarction in patients with T2DM because they can improve cardiac contraction and relaxation and promote vasodilation through circumvention of NO• resistance in both myocardium and vasculature [26]. These beneficial effects of Angeli's salt are attributed to the HNO's ability to maintain its effectiveness in the oxidative environment because, unlike NO•, it does not react with ROS to form superoxide anions and, therefore, is not scavenged from the environment [82]. The HNO-induced vasodilation remained sustained in diabetic hearts, regardless of the degree of hyperglycemia, and surprisingly, the positive inotropic and lusitropic effects of HNO were enhanced in T1DM rat hearts [25].

In contrast to that observed in NO• experiments, the contribution of sGC to HNO-induced vasodilation and cardiac function remained unaffected by diabetes and the severity of hyperglycemia; these findings suggest that the effects of HNO within the cardiovascular system not only are mediated through circumventing the scavenging effects of ROS but also extend to maintenance of responsiveness of partially inactivated, redox-affected sGC [25]. Furthermore, compared with NO•, HNO has unique and distinct cardioprotective properties; e.g., NO• donors (e.g., SNAP, S-nitroso-N-acetylpenicillamine) induced weak-positive and -negative inotropic effects at low and high doses, respectively [83], whereas the HNO donor Angeli's salt consistently induced load-independent positive inotropic and lusitropic effects through both sGC-cGMP–dependent and predominantly independent mechanisms (i.e., interaction with thiol-containing proteins like sarcoplasmic ryanodine receptors and SERCA), to enhance Ca^{2+} cycling and increase myocardial contractility [84,85]. These HNO-induced cardioprotective effects, which were enhanced, rather than impaired, in hyperglycemic conditions, make Angeli's salt a candidate therapeutic agent in managing cardiovascular disorders in diabetes [25].

Conclusion and perspectives

Although HNO signaling pathways and their underlying mechanisms to circumvent NO• resistance in T2DM have not yet been fully elucidated, it seems that HNO is an important and neglected nitrogen oxide species with potential endogenous production and various relevant physiological actions, including vasorelaxation, antiplatelet activity, and the positive inotropic effect. Furthermore, targeting alternative biological molecules (e.g., CGRP and thiol residues) and distinct pathways (i.e., cAMP-PKA vs cGMP-PKG) enables HNO to bypass the pathways that become relatively nonresponsive to NO• in T2DM (Fig. 2). These potentials make HNO a good candidate for managing NO•-related cardiovascular complications in T2DM, where NO•-releasing drugs do not act effectively.

However, definitive proof of this hypothesis awaits further studies because several pressing and important questions remain to be answered: (1) Is HNO just a Janus face of NO•, or should it be considered an independent molecule with unique properties distinct from NO•? (2) Among the mechanisms proposed as endogenous routes of HNO production, which one is physiologically relevant? Moreover, is endogenous production of HNO quantitatively meaningful and comparable with that of NO•? (3) Which pathways are common for both NO• and HNO, and how does HNO cross-talk with NO• to handle similar physiological pathways in health or diseases? (4) Dose HNO alternate NO• signaling and actions in pathologic conditions like T2DM? (5) Which biological players (e.g., O_2, NO• availability, the environment's redox state, and pH) dictate HNO behavior and its downstream signaling pathways? Answering these questions awaits further studies and paves the way for both HNO-based therapeutic approaches and understanding endogenous HNO biology.

Acknowledgments

This study has been supported by the Shahid Beheshti University of Medical Sciences, Tehran, Iran.

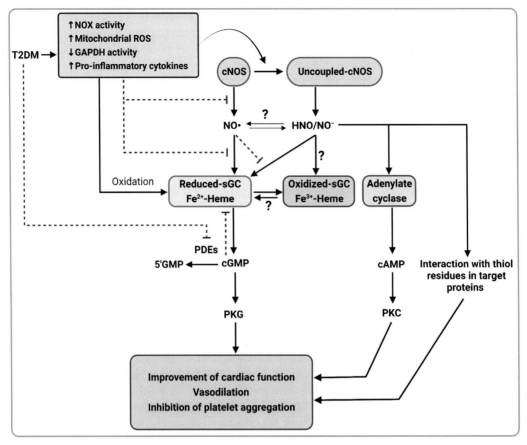

FIG. 2   A proposed summary of underlying mechanisms of nitric oxide (NO•) resistance in type 2 diabetes mellitus (T2DM) and the potential role of nitroxyl (HNO) in overcoming this state. Hyperglycemia-induced oxidative stress impairs NO• signaling by increasing nicotinamide adenine dinucleotide phosphate (NADPH) oxidase (NOX) enzymes and superoxide generation. In mitochondria, hyperglycemia increases reactive oxygen species (ROS) production, resulting in the maturation and secretion of the proinflammatory cytokines (e.g., interleukin-1β and interleukin-18). Furthermore, decreased glyceraldehyde-3 phosphate dehydrogenase (GAPDH) activity (due to ROS-induced DNA breaking and activation of poly-ADP ribose polymerase) leads to activation of the hexosamine pathway, upregulation of protein kinase C (PKC), elevated glucose flux through the polyol pathway, and overproduction of advanced glycation end-products (AGEs). Upregulation of these pathways results in impaired NO• production, NO• scavenging from the environment, oxidation of soluble guanylyl cyclase (sGC), and finally, NO• resistance. PDEs, cyclic nucleotide phosphodiesterase; cNOS, constitutive NO• synthase (i.e., endothelial NOS and neural NOS).

References

[1] Gladwin MT. Deconstructing endothelial dysfunction: soluble guanylyl cyclase oxidation and the NO resistance syndrome. J Clin Invest 2006;116(9):2330–2.
[2] Bahadoran Z, Carlström M, Mirmiran P, Ghasemi A. Nitric oxide: to be or not to be an endocrine hormone? Acta Physiol 2020;229(1), e13443.
[3] Wilcox G. Insulin and insulin resistance. Clin Biochem Rev 2005;26(2):19–39.

[4] Weiss RE, Dumitrescu A, Refetoff S. Approach to the patient with resistance to thyroid hormone and pregnancy. J Clin Endocrinol Metab 2010;95(7):3094–102.

[5] Anderson R, Ellis G, Chirkov Y, Holmes A, Payne N, Blackman D, et al. Determinants of platelet responsiveness to nitric oxide in patients with chronic heart failure. Eur J Heart Fail 2004;6(1):47–54.

[6] Chirkov YY, Holmes AS, Willoughby SR, Stewart S, Wuttke RD, Sage PR, et al. Stable angina and acute coronary syndromes are associated with nitric oxide resistance in platelets. J Am Coll Cardiol 2001;37(7):1851–7.

[7] Wood KC, Hsu LL, Gladwin MT. Sickle cell disease vasculopathy: a state of nitric oxide resistance. Free Radic Biol Med 2008;44(8):1506–28.

[8] Tarkun I, Arslan BÇ, Cantürk Z, Turemen E, Şahin T, Duman C. Endothelial dysfunction in young women with polycystic ovary syndrome: relationship with insulin resistance and low-grade chronic inflammation. J Clin Endocrinol Metab 2004;89(11):5592–6.

[9] Wagenmakers AJ, Frisbee JC, Delp MD. Vascular function in the metabolic syndrome and the effects on skeletal muscle perfusion: lessons from the obese Zucker rat. Essays Biochem 2006;42:145–60.

[10] Geenen IL, Kolk FF, Molin DG, Wagenaar A, Compeer MG, Tordoir JH, et al. Nitric oxide resistance reduces arteriovenous fistula maturation in chronic kidney disease in rats. PLoS One 2016;11(1), e0146212.

[11] Russo I, Del Mese P, Doronzo G, Mattiello L, Viretto M, Bosia A, et al. Resistance to the nitric oxide/cyclic guanosine 5'-monophosphate/protein kinase G pathway in vascular smooth muscle cells from the obese Zucker rat, a classical animal model of insulin resistance: role of oxidative stress. Endocrinology 2008;149(4):1480–9.

[12] McVeigh GE, Brennan GM, Johnston GD, McDermott BJ, McGrath LT, Henry WR, et al. Impaired endothelium-dependent and independent vasodilation in patients with type 2 (non-insulin-dependent) diabetes mellitus. Diabetologia 1992;35(8):771–6.

[13] Williams SB, Cusco JA, Roddy MA, Johnstone MT, Creager MA. Impaired nitric oxide-mediated vasodilation in patients with non-insulin-dependent diabetes mellitus. J Am Coll Cardiol 1996;27(3):567–74.

[14] van Etten RW, de Koning EJ, Verhaar MC, Gaillard CA, Rabelink TJ. Impaired NO-dependent vasodilation in patients with Type II (non-insulin-dependent) diabetes mellitus is restored by acute administration of folate. Diabetologia 2002;45(7):1004–10.

[15] Okon EB, Chung AW, Rauniyar P, Padilla E, Tejerina T, McManus BM, et al. Compromised arterial function in human type 2 diabetic patients. Diabetes 2005;54(8):2415–23.

[16] Chirkov YY, Horowitz JD. Impaired tissue responsiveness to organic nitrates and nitric oxide: a new therapeutic frontier? Pharmacol Ther 2007;116(2):287–305.

[17] Shah RC, Sanker S, Wood KC, Durgin BG, Straub AC. Redox regulation of soluble guanylyl cyclase. Nitric Oxide 2018;76:97–104.

[18] Stuehr DJ, Misra S, Dai Y, Ghosh A. Maturation, inactivation, and recovery mechanisms of soluble guanylyl cyclase. J Biol Chem 2021;296, 100336.

[19] Velagic A, Qin C, Woodman OL, Horowitz JD, Ritchie RH, Kemp-Harper BK. Nitroxyl: a novel strategy to circumvent diabetes associated impairments in nitric oxide signaling. Front Pharmacol 2020;11:727.

[20] Lopez BE, Shinyashiki M, Han TH, Fukuto JM. Antioxidant actions of nitroxyl (HNO). Free Radic Biol Med 2007;42(4):482–91.

[21] Schächinger V, Britten MB, Zeiher AM. Prognostic impact of coronary vasodilator dysfunction on adverse long-term outcome of coronary heart disease. Circulation 2000;101(16):1899–906.

[22] Chirkov YY, Nguyen TH, Horowitz JD. Impairment of anti-aggregatory responses to nitric oxide and prostacyclin: mechanisms and clinical implications in cardiovascular disease. Int J Mol Sci 2022;23(3):1042.

[23] Halcox JP, Schenke WH, Zalos G, Mincemoyer R, Prasad A, Waclawiw MA, et al. Prognostic value of coronary vascular endothelial dysfunction. Circulation 2002;106(6):653–8.

[24] Young ME, Leighton B. Evidence for altered sensitivity of the nitric oxide/cGMP signalling cascade in insulin-resistant skeletal muscle. Biochem J 1998;329(Pt 1):73–9.

[25] Qin CX, Anthonisz J, Leo CH, Kahlberg N, Velagic A, Li M, et al. Nitric oxide resistance, induced in the myocardium by diabetes, is circumvented by the nitric oxide redox sibling, nitroxyl. Antioxid Redox Signal 2020;32(1):60–77.

[26] Velagic A, Li JC, Qin CX, Li M, Deo M, Marshall SA, et al. Cardioprotective actions of nitroxyl donor Angeli's salt are preserved in the diabetic heart and vasculature in the face of nitric oxide resistance. Br J Pharmacol 2022;179(16):4117–35.

[27] Goulopoulou S, Hannan JL, Matsumoto T, Ogbi S, Ergul A, Webb RC. Reduced vascular responses to soluble guanylyl cyclase but increased sensitivity to sildenafil in female rats with type 2 diabetes. Am J Physiol Heart Circ Physiol 2015;309(2):H297–304.

III. Nitric oxide donors and cardiovascular and metabolic diseases

[28] Tare M, Kalidindi RS, Bubb KJ, Parkington HC, Boon WM, Li X, et al. Vasoactive actions of nitroxyl (HNO) are preserved in resistance arteries in diabetes. Naunyn Schmiedeberg's Arch Pharmacol 2017;390(4):397–408.

[29] Witte K, Jacke K, Stahrenberg R, Arlt G, Reitenbach I, Schilling L, et al. Dysfunction of soluble guanylyl cyclase in aorta and kidney of Goto-Kakizaki rats: influence of age and diabetic state. Nitric Oxide 2002;6(1):85–95.

[30] Stasch JP, Schmidt PM, Nedvetsky PI, Nedvetskaya TY, HS AK, Meurer S, et al. Targeting the heme-oxidized nitric oxide receptor for selective vasodilatation of diseased blood vessels. J Clin Invest 2006;116(9):2552–61.

[31] Worthley MI, Holmes AS, Willoughby SR, Kucia AM, Heresztyn T, Stewart S, et al. The deleterious effects of hyperglycemia on platelet function in diabetic patients with acute coronary syndromes mediation by superoxide production, resolution with intensive insulin administration. J Am Coll Cardiol 2007;49(3):304–10.

[32] Anderson RA, Ellis GR, Evans LM, Morris K, Chirkov YY, Horowitz JD, et al. Platelet nitrate responsiveness in fasting and postprandial type 2 diabetes. Diab Vasc Dis Res 2005;2(2):88–93.

[33] Miranda KM, Ridnour L, Esprey M, Citrin D, Thomas D, Mancardi D, et al. Comparison of the chemical biology of NO and HNO: an inorganic perspective. In: Karlin KD, editor. Progress in inorganic chemistry. John Wiley & Sons, Inc.; 2005. p. 349–84.

[34] Paolocci N, Jackson MI, Lopez BE, Miranda K, Tocchetti CG, Wink DA, et al. The pharmacology of nitroxyl (HNO) and its therapeutic potential: not just the Janus face of NO. Pharmacol Ther 2007;113(2):442–58.

[35] Miranda KM, Paolocci N, Katori T, Thomas DD, Ford E, Bartberger MD, et al. A biochemical rationale for the discrete behavior of nitroxyl and nitric oxide in the cardiovascular system. Proc Natl Acad Sci 2003;100 (16):9196–201.

[36] Fukuto JM, Bartberger MD, Dutton AS, Paolocci N, Wink DA, Houk KN. The physiological chemistry and biological activity of nitroxyl (HNO): the neglected, misunderstood, and enigmatic nitrogen oxide. Chem Res Toxicol 2005;18(5):790–801.

[37] Shafirovich V, Lymar SV. Nitroxyl and its anion in aqueous solutions: spin states, protic equilibria, and reactivities toward oxygen and nitric oxide. Proc Natl Acad Sci U S A 2002;99(11):7340–5.

[38] Miranda KM, Dutton AS, Ridnour LA, Foreman CA, Ford E, Paolocci N, et al. Mechanism of aerobic decomposition of Angeli's salt (sodium trioxodinitrate) at physiological pH. J Am Chem Soc 2005;127(2):722–31.

[39] Weitzberg E, Lundberg JON. Nonenzymatic nitric oxide production in humans. Nitric Oxide 1998;2(1):1–7.

[40] Babu BR, Frey C, Griffith OW. l-arginine binding to nitric-oxide synthase: the role of H-bonds to the nonreactive guanidinium nitrogens. J Biol Chem 1999;274(36):25218–26.

[41] Fukuto JM, Dutton AS, Houk KN. The chemistry and biology of nitroxyl (HNO): a chemically unique species with novel and important biological activity. ChemBioChem 2005;6(4):612–9.

[42] Fukuto JM, Cisneros CJ, Kinkade RL. A comparison of the chemistry associated with the biological signaling and actions of nitroxyl (HNO) and nitric oxide (NO). J Inorg Biochem 2013;118:201–8.

[43] Adak S, Wang Q, Stuehr DJ. Arginine conversion to nitroxide by tetrahydrobiopterin-free neuronal nitric-oxide synthase: IMPLICATIONS FOR MECHANISM*. J Biol Chem 2000;275(43):33554–61.

[44] Pufahl RA, Wishnok JS, Marletta MA. Hydrogen peroxide-supported oxidation of NG-hydroxy-L-arginine by nitric oxide synthase. Biochemistry 1995;34(6):1930–41.

[45] Schmidt HH, Hofmann H, Schindler U, Shutenko ZS, Cunningham DD, Feelisch M. No .NO from NO synthase. Proc Natl Acad Sci U S A 1996;93(25):14492–7.

[46] Donzelli S, Espey MG, Flores-Santana W, Switzer CH, Yeh GC, Huang J, et al. Generation of nitroxyl by heme protein-mediated peroxidation of hydroxylamine but not N-hydroxy-L-arginine. Free Radic Biol Med 2008;45 (5):578–84.

[47] Wong PS, Hyun J, Fukuto JM, Shirota FN, DeMaster EG, Shoeman DW, et al. Reaction between S-nitrosothiols and thiols: generation of nitroxyl (HNO) and subsequent chemistry. Biochemistry 1998;37(16):5362–71.

[48] Arnelle DR, Stamler JS. NO+, NO, and NO− donation by S-nitrosothiols: implications for regulation of physiological functions by S-nitrosylation and acceleration of disulfide formation. Arch Biochem Biophys 1995;318 (2):279–85.

[49] Clarkson RB, Norby SW, Smirnov A, Boyer S, Vahidi N, Nims RW, et al. Direct measurement of the accumulation and mitochondrial conversion of nitric oxide within Chinese hamster ovary cells using an intracellular electron paramagnetic resonance technique. Biochim Biophys Acta 1995;1243(3):496–502.

[50] Sharpe MA, Cooper CE. Reactions of nitric oxide with mitochondrial cytochrome c: a novel mechanism for the formation of nitroxyl anion and peroxynitrite. Biochem J 1998;332(Pt 1):9–19.

[51] Niketić V, Stojanović S, Nikolić A, Spasić M, Michelson AM. Exposure of Mn and FeSODs, but not Cu/ZnSOD, to NO leads to nitrosonium and nitroxyl ions generation which cause enzyme modification and inactivation: an in vitro study. Free Radic Biol Med 1999;27(9–10):992–6.

[52] Saleem M, Ohshima H. Xanthine oxidase converts nitric oxide to nitroxyl that inactivates the enzyme. Biochem Biophys Res Commun 2004;315(2):455–62.

[53] Poderoso JJ, Carreras MC, Schöpfer F, Lisdero CL, Riobó NA, Giulivi C, et al. The reaction of nitric oxide with ubiquinol: kinetic properties and biological significance. Free Radic Biol Med 1999;26(7–8):925–35.

[54] Nagasawa HT, DeMaster EG, Redfern B, Shirota FN, Goon DJ. Evidence for nitroxyl in the catalase-mediated bioactivation of the alcohol deterrent agent cyanamide. J Med Chem 1990;33(12):3120–2.

[55] Kim-Shapiro DB, King SB, Bonifant CL, Kolibash CP, Ballas SK. Time resolved absorption study of the reaction of hydroxyurea with sickle cell hemoglobin. Biochim Biophys Acta 1998;1380(1):64–74.

[56] Wink DA, Miranda KM, Katori T, Mancardi D, Thomas DD, Ridnour L, et al. Orthogonal properties of the redox siblings nitroxyl and nitric oxide in the cardiovascular system: a novel redox paradigm. Am J Physiol Heart Circ Physiol 2003;285(6):H2264–76.

[57] Bartberger MD, Liu W, Ford E, Miranda KM, Switzer C, Fukuto JM, et al. The reduction potential of nitric oxide (NO) and its importance to NO biochemistry. Proc Natl Acad Sci 2002;99(17):10958–63.

[58] Suarez SA, Neuman NI, Muñoz M, Álvarez L, Bikiel DE, Brondino CD, et al. Nitric oxide is reduced to HNO by proton-coupled nucleophilic attack by ascorbate, tyrosine, and other alcohols. A new route to HNO in biological media? J Am Chem Soc 2015;137(14):4720–7.

[59] Miranda KM. The chemistry of nitroxyl (HNO) and implications in biology. Coord Chem Rev 2005;249(3): 433–55.

[60] Fukuto JM, Hobbs AJ, Ignarro LJ. Conversion of nitroxyl (HNO) to nitric oxide (NO) in biological systems: the role of physiological oxidants and relevance to the biological activity of HNO. Biochem Biophys Res Commun 1993;196(2):707–13.

[61] Murphy ME, Sies H. Reversible conversion of nitroxyl anion to nitric oxide by superoxide dismutase. Proc Natl Acad Sci U S A 1991;88(23):10860–4.

[62] Bianco CL, Toscano JP, Bartberger MD, Fukuto JM. The chemical biology of HNO signaling. Arch Biochem Biophys 2017;617:129–36.

[63] Fukuto JM, Chiang K, Hszieh R, Wong P, Chaudhuri G. The pharmacological activity of nitroxyl: a potent vasodilator with activity similar to nitric oxide and/or endothelium-derived relaxing factor. J Pharmacol Exp Ther 1992;263(2):546–51.

[64] Li JC, Velagic A, Qin CX, Li M, Leo CH, Kemp-Harper BK, et al. Diabetes attenuates the contribution of endogenous nitric oxide but not nitroxyl to endothelium dependent relaxation of rat carotid arteries. Front Pharmacol 2020;11, 585740.

[65] Irvine JC, Ritchie RH, Favaloro JL, Andrews KL, Widdop RE, Kemp-Harper BK. Nitroxyl (HNO): the Cinderella of the nitric oxide story. Trends Pharmacol Sci 2008;29(12):601–8.

[66] Felker GM, Borentain M, Cleland JG, DeSouza MM, Kessler PD, O'Connor CM, et al. Rationale and design for the development of a novel nitroxyl donor in patients with acute heart failure. Eur J Heart Fail 2019;21(8):1022–31.

[67] Paolocci N, Katori T, Champion HC, St John ME, Miranda KM, Fukuto JM, et al. Positive inotropic and lusitropic effects of HNO/NO− in failing hearts: independence from beta-adrenergic signaling. Proc Natl Acad Sci U S A 2003;100(9):5537–42.

[68] Doctorovich F, Farmer PJ, Marti MA. The chemistry and biology of nitroxyl (HNO). Elsevier; 2016.

[69] Andrews KL, Irvine JC, Tare M, Apostolopoulos J, Favaloro JL, Triggle CR, et al. A role for nitroxyl (HNO) as an endothelium-derived relaxing and hyperpolarizing factor in resistance arteries. Br J Pharmacol 2009;157(4):540–50.

[70] Martin W. Nitroxyl anion—the universal signalling partner of endogenously produced nitric oxide? Br J Pharmacol 2009;157(4):537–9.

[71] Flores-Santana W, Salmon DJ, Donzelli S, Switzer CH, Basudhar D, Ridnour L, et al. The specificity of nitroxyl chemistry is unique among nitrogen oxides in biological systems. Antioxid Redox Signal 2011;14(9):1659–74.

[72] Dierks EA, Burstyn JN. Nitric oxide (NO), the only nitrogen monoxide redox form capable of activating soluble guanylyl cyclase. Biochem Pharmacol 1996;51(12):1593–600.

[73] Zeller A, Wenzl MV, Beretta M, Stessel H, Russwurm M, Koesling D, et al. Mechanisms underlying activation of soluble guanylate cyclase by the nitroxyl donor Angeli's salt. Mol Pharmacol 2009;76(5):1115–22.

[74] Wanstall JC, Jeffery TK, Gambino A, Lovren F, Triggle CR. Vascular smooth muscle relaxation mediated by nitric oxide donors: a comparison with acetylcholine, nitric oxide and nitroxyl ion. Br J Pharmacol 2001;134(3):463–72.

[75] Favaloro JL, Kemp-Harper BK. The nitroxyl anion (HNO) is a potent dilator of rat coronary vasculature. Cardiovasc Res 2007;73(3):587–96.

III. Nitric oxide donors and cardiovascular and metabolic diseases

[76] Miller TW, Cherney MM, Lee AJ, Francoleon NE, Farmer PJ, King SB, et al. The effects of nitroxyl (HNO) on soluble guanylate cyclase activity: interactions at ferrous heme and cysteine thiols. J Biol Chem 2009;284 (33):21788–96.

[77] Shi Y, Zhang Y. Mechanisms of HNO reactions with ferric heme proteins. Angew Chem Int Ed Engl 2018;57 (51):16654–8.

[78] Doctorovich F, Bikiel D, Pellegrino J, Suárez SA, Larsen A, Martí MA. Nitroxyl (azanone) trapping by metalloporphyrins. Coord Chem Rev 2011;255(23):2764–84.

[79] Miranda KM, Nims RW, Thomas DD, Espey MG, Citrin D, Bartberger MD, et al. Comparison of the reactivity of nitric oxide and nitroxyl with heme proteins. A chemical discussion of the differential biological effects of these redox related products of NOS. J Inorg Biochem 2003;93(1–2):52–60.

[80] He X, Azarov I, Jeffers A, Presley T, Richardson J, King SB, et al. The potential of Angeli's salt to decrease nitric oxide scavenging by plasma hemoglobin. Free Radic Biol Med 2008;44(7):1420–32.

[81] Ferguson JK. A new drug for the treatment of alcoholism. Can Med Assoc J 1956;74(10):793–5.

[82] Leo CH, Joshi A, Hart JL, Woodman OL. Endothelium-dependent nitroxyl-mediated relaxation is resistant to superoxide anion scavenging and preserved in diabetic rat aorta. Pharmacol Res 2012;66(5):383–91.

[83] González DR, Fernández IC, Ordenes PP, Treuer AV, Eller G, Boric MP. Differential role of S-nitrosylation and the NO-cGMP-PKG pathway in cardiac contractility. Nitric Oxide 2008;18(3):157–67.

[84] Chin KY, Qin C, Cao N, Kemp-Harper BK, Woodman OL, Ritchie RH. The concomitant coronary vasodilator and positive inotropic actions of the nitroxyl donor Angeli's salt in the intact rat heart: contribution of soluble guanylyl cyclase-dependent and -independent mechanisms. Br J Pharmacol 2014;171(7):1722–34.

[85] Solaro RJ. Nitroxyl effects on myocardium provide new insights into the significance of altered myofilament response to calcium in the regulation of contractility. J Physiol 2007;580(Pt 3):697.

11

Inhaled nitric oxide (iNO) administration in intubated and nonintubated patients: Delivery systems, interfaces, dose administration, and monitoring techniques

Stefano Gianni[a], Lorenzo Berra[b,c,d,], and Emanuele Rezoagli[e,f,*]*

[a]Department of Anesthesia and Intensive Care Medicine, Niguarda Ca' Granda Hospital, Milan, Italy [b]Harvard Medical School, Boston, MA, United States [c]Department of Anesthesia, Critical Care and Pain Medicine, Massachusetts General Hospital, Boston, MA, United States [d]Respiratory Care Department, Massachusetts General Hospital, Boston, MA, United States [e]School of Medicine and Surgery, University of Milano-Bicocca, Monza, Italy [f]Department of Emergency and Intensive Care, San Gerardo Hospital, Monza, Italy

Abstract

Inhaled nitric oxide (iNO) is a drug used to treat neonates with persistent pulmonary hypertension and as a rescue strategy for the treatment of severe hypoxemia. The clinical administration of iNO is challenging since the patient population is heterogeneous, ranging from critically ill patients intubated and mechanically ventilated to patients with chronic pulmonary hypertension receiving iNO at home [8]. In the intubated mechanically ventilated patients, airways are sealed by a cuffed endotracheal tube. Therefore, it is possible to precisely reach and maintain the target iNO concentration. Conversely, in nonintubated spontaneously breathing

*Co-senior authors.

patients, the patient airways are not sealed by a cuffed endotracheal tube, so the instantaneous delivered dose cannot be accurately determined. A snug-fitting mask can be used to deliver NO as a patient interface in hospitalized patients with acute bacterial or viral pneumonia. In patients requiring long-term iNO administration, nasal cannula can be a suitable patient interface, which is also often used for long-term oxygen administration. To safely administer iNO, the continuous monitoring of the delivered NO and nitrogen dioxide (NO_2) concentrations is recommended to avoid excessive NO_2 delivery that is irritant for the airways. Further, blood oxygenation and methemoglobin concentration monitoring have to be considered during iNO administration to ensure an adequate tissue oxygenation.

Abbreviations

C_{NOset}	target NO dose
$C_{NOsource}$	NO gas concentration of the NO source
COVID 19	coronavirus disease 2019
CPU	central processing unit
FDA	Food and Drug Administration
FiO_2	oxygen-inspired fraction
HFNC	high-flow nasal cannula
ICU	intensive care unit
iNO	inhaled nitric oxide
MetHb	methemoglobin
NO_2	nitrogen dioxide
OSHA	Occupational Safety and Health Administration
PPHN	persistent pulmonary hypertension of the neonate
Q_{atm}	gas flow flowing directly from the atmosphere into the patient airways
Q_{NO}	instantaneous gas flow from the NO source
Q_{tot}	total gas flowing into the airways
Q_{vent}	gas flow delivered by the mechanical ventilator into the patient airways
SARS-CoV-2	severe acute respiratory syndrome coronavirus 2

Conflict of interest

Lorenzo Berra receives salary support from K23 HL128882/NHLBI NIH as principal investigator for his work on hemolysis and nitric oxide; receives technologies and devices from iNO Therapeutics LLC, Praxair Inc., Masimo Corp; receives grants from "Fast Grants for COVID-19 research" at Mercatus Center of George Mason University and from iNO Therapeutics LLC; receives Reginald Jenney Endowment Chair at Harvard Medical School to LB, by LB Sundry Funds at Massachusetts General Hospital, and by laboratory funds of the Anesthesia Center for Critical Care Research of the Department of Anesthesia, Critical Care and Pain Medicine at Massachusetts General Hospital. LB has filed a patent application on June 7, 2021 for NO delivery in COVID-19 disease: PCT application number: PCT/US2021/036269. Stefano Gianni and Emanuele Rezoagli have not potential conflicts of interest.

Inhaled nitric oxide in intubated patients

Patient interface

Since its approval by the Food and Drug Administration (FDA) in 1999 for the persistent pulmonary hypertension of the neonate (PPHN) [1], inhaled nitric oxide (iNO) is considered a rescue strategy for the treatment of severe hypoxemia [2]. iNO can be administered in critically ill adult patients under mechanical ventilation admitted to the intensive care unit (ICU). Mechanical ventilation is provided by using a mechanical ventilator connected to a cuffed endotracheal tube. The endotracheal tube serves as the conduit to deliver tidal ventilation.

Consequently, the gas mixture that includes NO flows into patient airways, and iNO is measured and titrated by using delivery systems working within the mechanical ventilator.

Inhaled nitric oxide delivery systems

The administration of iNO has some safety issues to be addressed. Since the reaction between oxygen and NO generates NO_2, which is an irritant gas of the airway mucosa, its concentration must be continuously monitored. In the United States, the Occupational Safety and Health Administration (OSHA) requires to keep NO_2 levels below 5 ppm. As for NO_2, the delivered NO and O_2 concentrations must be continuously monitored. Moreover, the target NO dose must be accurately administered through the respiratory cycle by avoiding excessive oscillations of NO concentration. Furthermore, since the reaction between NO and hemoglobin generates methemoglobin (MetHb), its concentration must be monitored since an increase in the MetHb concentration beyond 20%–30% can impair the oxygen delivery to peripheral tissues [3]. Generally MetHb is maintained below 5%–10% when iNO is administered in clinical practice.

A NO delivery system is composed of

1. a NO source,
2. a control system of the delivered NO dose, and
3. a gas monitoring system for the delivered NO, O_2, and NO_2 concentration.

The accurate delivery of the target NO dose is an essential characteristic of any NO delivery system. The delivered NO concentration must be as close as possible to the set the NO dose, and it should aim to be constant throughout the entire respiratory cycle [4].

To reach and maintain the set NO concentration, the instantaneous gas flow from the NO source (Q_{NO}) is as follows:

$$Q_{NO} = [C_{NOset}/(C_{NOsource} - C_{NOset})]^*(Q_{vent} + Q_{atm}) = [C_{NOset}/(C_{NOsource} - C_{NOset})]^*(Q_{tot})$$

(1)

where C_{NOset} is the target NO dose; $C_{NOsource}$ is the NO gas concentration of the NO source (i.e., the NO concentration of the NO pressurized cylinder); Q_{vent} is the gas flow delivered by the mechanical ventilator into the patient airways; and Q_{atm} is the gas flow flowing directly from the atmosphere into the patient airways. Q_{vent} and Q_{atm} together form the total gas flowing into the airways (Q_{tot}).

In the intubated mechanically ventilated patient, the airways are sealed by the cuffed endotracheal tube, so Q_{atm} is zero. Consequently, in this subset of patients, Q_{NO} and Q_{tot} are proportional: $Q_{NO}/Q_{vent} = [C_{NOset}/(C_{NOsource} - C_{NOset})]$. According to this relationship, a delivery system can reach and maintain the desired NO concentration precisely by adjusting two variables: Q_{NO}/Q_{vent} ratio and $C_{NOsource}$. For example, delivery systems that use NO pressurized cylinders as a NO source regulate the delivered NO concentration by altering the Q_{NO}/Q_{vent} ratio. When chemical or electric NO generators are used, $C_{NOsource}$ is the altered variable (different types of NO sources are discussed elsewhere in another chapter).

The easiest way to administer iNO from a pressurized cylinder is by injecting the NO gas at a constant flow rate directly into the inspired limb of the ventilator breathing circuit [5]. Q_{NO} is obtained from Eq. (1). The main drawback of this method is that the NO concentration delivered to the patient can vary widely during the tidal ventilation. This phenomenon is due to the constant Q_{NO} that creates a bolus of high-concentration gas in the inspiratory limb of the breathing circuit during the expiratory phase, when there is no ventilator gas flow.

To overcome the limitation of the continuous flow administration, NO from the pressurized cylinder can be premixed with air using a gas blender. The gas mixture is then supplied to the air inlet port on the ventilator. This approach enables a constant concentration of NO that is delivered to the patient as the oxygen and NO gas flow are kept proportional by the internal flow control valves of the ventilator. NO concentration delivered to the patient remains at the set value in a wide range of ventilator modes [6]. Since the target NO concentration that will be achieved depends on the setting of the external NO/air blender and on the set oxygen inspiratory fraction on the ventilator, complex nomograms are required to adequately set the target iNO concentration. Moreover, since NO and air are mixed before entering the ventilator, a higher concentration of NO_2 can be produced since its production depends on NO and O_2 partial pressure and the contact time between NO and O_2 [7]. A scavenger containing calcium hydroxide should be added to the ventilator circuit to keep the delivered NO_2 concentration below 5 ppm and, ideally, not higher than 1 ppm.

Novel and complex delivery systems of NO have been developed since the approval of inhaled NO from the US FDA for PPHN. These delivery systems are integrated systems that include all the components required to deliver iNO:

1. a NO source (i.e., NO/N_2 pressurized cylinders);
2. a gas-monitoring system for the delivered NO, NO_2, and O_2 concentration;
3. and a central processing unit (CPU) to regulate NO delivery in real time.

These systems can deliver the NO gas into the inspiratory limb of the ventilator circuit synchronously and proportionally to the ventilator gas flow. The N_2/NO pressurized cylinder is connected to a fast response flow injector that delivers a set NO flow into the inspiratory arm of the respiratory circuit. A CPU continuously measures the gas flow delivered to the patient and regulates the NO flow from the pressurized cylinder in real time. The target NO concentration can be calculated according to Eq. (1). The NO flow from the NO source can be continuous throughout the entire respiratory cycle, or it can be synchronized with the ventilation (Fig. 1).

Inhaled nitric oxide in nonintubated patients

Patient interface

Despite iNO is more commonly administered in mechanically ventilated patients with hypoxemia [2], its use in spontaneously breathing patients is a growing field of interest. Moreover, most of NO delivery systems are bulky and difficult to move outside the ICU. Only the development of newer and more portable NO delivery systems allowed the use of iNO in the spontaneously breathing nonintubated patients.

The administration of iNO to spontaneously breathing nonintubated patients is challenging for clinicians since the patient population is heterogeneous and include different etiologies of hypoxia, ranging from chronic pulmonary hypertension receiving iNO at home [8]

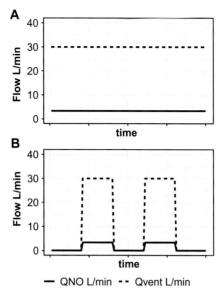

FIG. 1 Nitric oxide flow (QNO) necessary to obtain a delivered concentration of 80 ppm from a 800 ppm N_2/NO pressurized cylinder with different gas flows (Qvent). Q_{NO} is obtained from Eq. (1). C_{NOset} is 80 ppm; $C_{NOsource}$ is 800 ppm. Q is the total gas flow (L/min). In panel A, a continuous gas flow is represented (i.e., by a nasal cannula or a high-flow nasal cannula). In panel B, the flow generated by a mechanical ventilator is shown (i.e., in a volume-controlled mode).

to hospitalized patients with acute bacterial or viral pneumonia receiving antibacterial/virucidal high dose of iNO [9,10]. Consequently, many different ventilatory interfaces should be adapted to deliver iNO in different clinical settings.

Snug fitting mask

As discussed earlier in this chapter, the NO flow necessary to reach the desired NO concentration can be obtained by the previously described Eq. (1):

$$Q_{NO} = [C_{NOset}/(C_{NOsource} - C_{NOset})]^* (Q_{vent} + Q_{atm}) = [C_{NOset}/(C_{NOsource} - C_{NOset})]^* (Q_{tot})$$

In nonintubated patients, since the patient airways are not sealed by the cuffed endotracheal tube, Q_{atm} is not zero. Consequently, the instantaneous delivered dose cannot be accurately determined since it is not possible to accurately measure Q_{atm}.

The use of snug fitting masks as patient interface—like the mask used for noninvasive mechanical ventilation—may be a strategy to reduce Q_{atm}. A snug fitting mask, which is adequately positioned on the patient face, can effectively reduce Q_{atm} to negligible value. This allows the precise delivery of the target NO concentration.

A snug fitting mask can be used to deliver iNO with a mechanical ventilator. The NO—usually delivered from a N_2/NO pressurized cylinders—is blended with air and enters into the air inlet of the ventilator as previously described. This system has been successfully used to deliver both low- and high-dose NO [11,12]. However, pressurized cylinders are bulky and difficult to move. Moreover, its use is confined to the hospital environment with the need of trained healthcare providers to ensure safe and effective delivery.

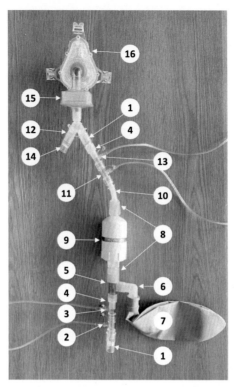

FIG. 2 System for delivering inhaled nitric oxide (NO) during spontaneous breathing. (1) Inspiratory one-way valve; (2) gas connector for medical air; (3) gas connector for NO; (4) two-step adapter; (5) T adaptor; (6) elbow adaptor; (7) reservoir bag (3 L); (8) silicone adapter; (9) NO_2 scavenger; (10) flex connector; (11) gas connector for O_2; (12) Y-piece; (13) gas sample port for NO and NO_2 analyzers; (14) expiratory one-way valve; (15) HEPA filter; (16) snug fitting full-face mask. *Reproduced from Gianni S, Morais CCA, Larson G, Pinciroli R, Carroll R, Yu B, et al. Ideation and assessment of a nitric oxide delivery system for spontaneously breathing subjects. Nitric Oxide 2020;104–105:29–35. doi:10.1016/j.niox.2020.08.004, with permission from the publisher.*

During the coronavirus disease 2019 (COVID 19) pandemic [13], many investigators and institutions explored the antiviral effects of high-dose NO on severe acute respiratory syndrome coronavirus 2 (SARS-CoV-2), the virus responsible for the COVID-19 pandemic [14–16]. Our group put a lot of effort to develop a system easy to use and without the need of a mechanical ventilator to successfully administer high-dose NO to many patients during the pandemic. We developed a non-rebreathing circuit (Fig. 2). Medical air, O_2, and NO are delivered from regular flow meters into the circuit. Since this delivery system does not rely on a mechanical ventilator and is able to generate bias flow immediately ready to match the patient inspiratory flow, the delivered iNO concentration may significantly oscillate during tidal ventilation. The addition of a 3-L reservoir bag on the inspiratory branch of the circuit minimized the NO intratidal oscillation. The addition of a reservoir bag together with the relatively low fresh gas flow leads to increased NO_2 delivery due to an increased contact time between NO and O_2. The NO_2 increase becomes relevant when a high concentration of iNO is delivered. The addition of a NO_2 scavenger–containing calcium hydroxide reduces the delivered NO_2 concentration to acceptable levels (<5 ppm) [17].

In conclusion, a snug fitting mask may be a promising interface to deliver an accurate NO dose in nonintubated patients since it minimizes Q_{atm}. Despite this advantage, a snug fitting mask may be uncomfortable for patients and not aimed for a long-term use.

Different interfaces should be considered in patients requiring long-term NO administration, in particular outside the hospital.

Nasal cannula and high-flow nasal cannula

In patients with chronic pulmonary hypertension, the administration of iNO improves exercise tolerance [8]. Since these patients may need iNO outside the hospital for many hours/days, the use of a snug fitting mask may be inappropriate. In this subset of patients, a suitable patient interface is the nasal cannula, which is often used for long-term oxygen administration.

The continuous NO flow needed to reach the target NO concentration using nasal cannulas can be obtained by Eq. (1). In this clinical condition, Q_{atm} is not measurable or predictable, and the NO delivered concentration is highly dependent from the respiratory pattern [18]. Despite this limitation, iNO administered by a nasal cannula showed a reduction of pulmonary vascular resistance in patients with acute right ventricle dysfunction [19].

An alternative for iNO administration in hospitalized patients is a high-flow nasal cannula (HFNC). An HFNC is a humidified nasal cannula able to administer up to 60 L/min of gas flow, which is much higher than the 1–8 L/min of gas flow delivered by using a regular nasal cannula. This system could theoretically increase the accuracy of the delivered concentration, thus increasing the Q_{vent}/Q_{atm} ratio (see Eq. 1), and has been extensively used to deliver iNO either in patients with COVID-19 or acute right ventricle dysfunction [19,20].

Pulsed NO administration may play a key role in reducing the NO concentration variability because of the unpredictable Q_{atm} during the administration of iNO with a nasal cannula. As opposed to the continuous administration of iNO—when a mixture of NO and air/oxygen is administered according to Eq. (1)—NO can be administered as a set pulsed volume of NO at the onset of each breath. Consequently, the delivered NO dose—which can be expressed in mcg/kg/h—is constant and independent on minute ventilation and inspiratory flow. Another potential advantage of pulsed NO administration is that the brief pulse of NO minimizes the amount of drug dispersed, and it reduces the environmental exhaust of NO [21,22].

Inhaled nitric oxide administration in clinical practice

Dose selection

The iNO target concentration mainly depends on the clinical indication of iNO use. In neonates with pulmonary hypertension, an iNO concentration of 5–20 ppm is usually recommended [23]. Evidence is lacking for the benefit of doses above 20 ppm.

In patients with acute respiratory distress syndrome, an iNO concentration of 5–80 ppm has been used, while most of clinical trials describing the use of iNO in acute respiratory distress syndrome reports a concentration between 5 and 20 ppm [24]. Further, in patients with pulmonary hypertension after cardiac surgery, reported doses of iNO concentration range from 5 to 80 ppm [25,26].

Of note, the administration of high-concentration iNO showed promising results against bacterial and viral infections, despite that the antibacterial/antiviral properties of iNO are still under investigation [2,27]. The antibacterial/antiviral effect of iNO was described by using a concentration of 160–200 ppm [28–30]. As continuous administration of high-dose iNO would lead to a unsustainable increase in methemoglobin, intermittent administration of iNO is suggested (i.e., usually two to six times a day, with a cycle duration of iNO administration of 15–30 min).

Dose titration

Rebound pulmonary hypertension is a potential drawback to consider during iNO titration and after its discontinued. Nitric oxide is a potent selective pulmonary vasodilator, and its rapid withdrawal after prolonged use may lead to an increase in pulmonary vascular resistance [31,32]. The proposed mechanism behind this phenomenon is a transient increase of endothelin-1 [33] together with a decrease in nitric oxide synthase activity [34].

To avoid rebound pulmonary hypertension and the possible reduction in arterial oxygenation, abrupt discontinuation of iNO is discouraged. A gradual decrease in the delivered iNO concentration with the continuous monitoring of the arterial oxygenation can reduce the risk of rebound pulmonary hypertension. Interestingly, this phenomenon is observed more frequently at the end of iNO withdrawal, when iNO administration is discontinued [35] after continuous and prolonged (days) of iNO therapy.

When rebound pulmonary hypertension occurs, an increase in oxygen inspired fraction (FiO_2) can usually ameliorate hypoxemia [36]. Moreover, case studies and case series have reported some benefits by using phosphodiesterase 5 inhibitors, such as sildenafil, to attenuate rebound pulmonary hypertension when iNO is discontinued [37,38].

Monitoring of NO concentration during iNO administration

During iNO administration, the continuous monitoring of the delivered NO, NO_2, and FiO_2 concentrations is recommended. The available approved NO delivery systems use electro-chemical cells to measure the concentrations of iNO, NO_2, and FiO_2 [39]. The delivered gas mixture is sampled from the inspiratory limb of the delivery system downstream from the site of injection. The distance between the gas sampling port and the patient interface should be less than 15 cm to avoid underestimation of the delivered NO_2 concentration [39].

Moreover, blood oxygenation and methemoglobin concentration monitoring are highly relevant. Blood oxygenation, in clinical practice, is continuously monitored through peripheral oxygen saturation (SpO_2). The measurement of the methemoglobin concentration is usually measured from an arterial blood sample since the methemoglobin concentration is usually embedded in the point-of-care arterial blood gas analyzers. In the past years, the non-invasive measurement of methemoglobin concentration has been proposed, and it is embedded in a carbon monoxide (CO)-oxymeter device available on the market (Masimo rainbow SET, Irvine, CA 92618) [40]. This portable CO-oxymeter can continuously measure both SpO_2 and peripheral methemoglobin concentration.

References

[1] Barrington KJ, Finer N, Pennaforte T, Altit G. Nitric oxide for respiratory failure in infants born at or near term. Cochrane Database Syst Rev 2017. https://doi.org/10.1002/14651858.CD000399.pub3.

[2] Redaelli S, Magliocca A, Malhotra R, Ristagno G, Citerio G, Bellani G, et al. Nitric oxide: clinical applications in critically ill patients. Nitric Oxide Biol Chem 2022;121:20–33. https://doi.org/10.1016/j.niox.2022.01.007.

[3] Rehman HU. Methemoglobinemia. West J Med 2001;175:193–6.

[4] Montgomery FJ, Berssenbrugge AD. Inhaled nitric oxide delivery and monitoring. J Clin Monit Comput 1999;15:325–35. https://doi.org/10.1023/a:1009920724708.

[5] Berra L, Rodriguez-Lopez J, Rezoagli E, Yu B, Fisher DF, Semigran MJ, et al. Electric plasma–generated nitric oxide: hemodynamic effects in patients with pulmonary hypertension. Am J Respir Crit Care Med 2016;194:1168–70. https://doi.org/10.1164/rccm.201604-0834LE.

[6] Putensen C, Räsänen J, Thomson MS, Braman RS. Method of delivering constant nitric oxide concentrations during full and partial ventilatory support. J Clin Monit 1995;11:23–31. https://doi.org/10.1007/BF01627416.

[7] Nishimura M, Hess D, Kacmarek RM, Ritz R, Hurford WE. Nitrogen dioxide production during mechanical ventilation with nitric oxide in adults. Effects of ventilator internal volume, air versus nitrogen dilution, minute ventilation, and inspired oxygen fraction. Anesthesiology 1995;82:1246–54. https://doi.org/10.1097/00000542-199505000-00020.

[8] Nathan SD, Flaherty KR, Glassberg MK, Raghu G, Swigris J, Alvarez R, et al. A randomized, double-blind, placebo-controlled study of pulsed, inhaled nitric oxide in subjects at risk of pulmonary hypertension associated with pulmonary fibrosis. Chest 2020;158:637–45. https://doi.org/10.1016/j.chest.2020.02.016.

[9] Hedenstierna G, Chen L, Hedenstierna M, Lieberman R, Fine DH. Nitric oxide dosed in short bursts at high concentrations may protect against Covid 19. Nitric Oxide 2020;103:1–3. https://doi.org/10.1016/j.niox.2020.06.005.

[10] Wiegand SB, Traeger L, Nguyen HK, Rouillard KR, Fischbach A, Zadek F, et al. Antimicrobial effects of nitric oxide in murine models of Klebsiella pneumonia. Redox Biol 2021;39, 101826. https://doi.org/10.1016/j.redox.2020.101826.

[11] Marrazzo F, Spina S, Zadek F, Lama T, Xu C, Larson G, et al. Protocol of a randomised controlled trial in cardiac surgical patients with endothelial dysfunction aimed to prevent postoperative acute kidney injury by administering nitric oxide gas. BMJ Open 2019;9, e026848. https://doi.org/10.1136/bmjopen-2018-026848.

[12] Bartley BL, Gardner KJ, Spina S, Hurley BP, Campeau D, Berra L, et al. High-dose inhaled nitric oxide as adjunct therapy in cystic fibrosis targeting *Burkholderia multivorans*. Case Rep Pediatr 2020;2020:1–6. https://doi.org/10.1155/2020/1536714.

[13] Rezoagli E, Magliocca A, Bellani G, Pesenti A, Grasselli G. Development of a critical care response – experiences from Italy during the coronavirus disease 2019 pandemic. Anesthesiol Clin 2021;39:265–84. https://doi.org/10.1016/j.anclin.2021.02.003.

[14] Akaberi D, Krambrich J, Ling J, Luni C, Hedenstierna G, Järhult JD, et al. Mitigation of the replication of SARS-CoV-2 by nitric oxide in vitro. Redox Biol 2020;, 101734. https://doi.org/10.1016/j.redox.2020.101734.

[15] Safaee Fakhr B, Di Fenza R, Gianni S, Wiegand SB, Miyazaki Y, Araujo Morais CC, et al. Inhaled high dose nitric oxide is a safe and effective respiratory treatment in spontaneous breathing hospitalized patients with COVID-19 pneumonia. Nitric Oxide 2021;116:7–13. https://doi.org/10.1016/j.niox.2021.08.003.

[16] Safaee Fakhr B, Wiegand SB, Pinciroli R, Gianni S, Morais CCA, Ikeda T, et al. High concentrations of nitric oxide inhalation therapy in pregnant patients with severe coronavirus disease 2019 (COVID-19). Obstet Gynecol 2020;136:1109–13. https://doi.org/10.1097/AOG.0000000000004128.

[17] Gianni S, Morais CCA, Larson G, Pinciroli R, Carroll R, Yu B, et al. Ideation and assessment of a nitric oxide delivery system for spontaneously breathing subjects. Nitric Oxide 2020;104–105:29–35. https://doi.org/10.1016/j.niox.2020.08.004.

[18] Pillay K, Chen JZ, Finlay WH, Martin AR. Inhaled nitric oxide: in vitro analysis of continuous flow noninvasive delivery via nasal cannula. Respir Care 2021;66:228–39. https://doi.org/10.4187/respcare.07737.

[19] Tremblay J-A, Couture ÉJ, Albert M, Beaubien-Souligny W, Elmi-Sarabi M, Lamarche Y, et al. Noninvasive administration of inhaled nitric oxide and its hemodynamic effects in patients with acute right ventricular dysfunction. J Cardiothorac Vasc Anesth 2019;33:642–7. https://doi.org/10.1053/j.jvca.2018.08.004.

[20] Chandel A, Patolia S, Ahmad K, Aryal S, Brown AW, Sahjwani D, et al. Inhaled nitric oxide via high-flow nasal cannula in patients with acute respiratory failure related to COVID-19. Clin Med Insights Circ Respir Pulm Med 2021;15. https://doi.org/10.1177/11795484211047065. 11795484211047064.

III. Nitric oxide donors and cardiovascular and metabolic diseases

[21] Heinonen E, Högman M, Meriläinen P. Theoretical and experimental comparison of constant inspired concentration and pulsed delivery in NO therapy. Intensive Care Med 2000;26:1116–23. https://doi.org/10.1007/s001340051326.

[22] Hajian B, de Backer J, Vos W, van Holsbeke C, Ferreira F, Quinn D, et al. Pulmonary vascular effects of pulsed inhaled nitric oxide in COPD patients with pulmonary hypertension. Int J Chron Obstruct Pulmon Dis 2016;11:1533–41. https://doi.org/10.2147/COPD.S106480.

[23] Kinsella JP, Parker TA, Galan H, Sheridan BC, Halbower AC, Abman SH. Effects of inhaled nitric oxide on pulmonary edema and lung neutrophil accumulation in severe experimental hyaline membrane disease. Pediatr Res 1997;41:457–63. https://doi.org/10.1203/00006450-199704000-00002.

[24] Gebistorf F, Karam O, Wetterslev J, Afshari A. Inhaled nitric oxide for acute respiratory distress syndrome (ARDS) in children and adults. Cochrane Database Syst Rev 2016;CD002787. https://doi.org/10.1002/14651858.CD002787.pub3.

[25] Sardo S, Osawa EA, Finco G, Gomes Galas FRB, de Almeida JP, Cutuli SL, et al. Nitric oxide in cardiac surgery: a meta-analysis of randomized controlled trials. J Cardiothorac Vasc Anesth 2018;32:2512–9. https://doi.org/10.1053/j.jvca.2018.02.003.

[26] Lei C, Berra L, Rezoagli E, Yu B, Dong H, Yu S, et al. Nitric oxide decreases acute kidney injury and stage 3 chronic kidney disease after cardiac surgery. Am J Respir Crit Care Med 2018;198:1279–87. https://doi.org/10.1164/rccm.201710-2150OC.

[27] Signori D, Magliocca A, Hayashida K, Graw JA, Malhotra R, Bellani G, et al. Inhaled nitric oxide: role in the pathophysiology of cardio-cerebrovascular and respiratory diseases. Intensive Care Med Exp 2022;10:28. https://doi.org/10.1186/s40635-022-00455-6.

[28] Miller CC, Hergott CA, Rohan M, Arsenault-Mehta K, Döring G, Mehta S. Inhaled nitric oxide decreases the bacterial load in a rat model of Pseudomonas aeruginosa pneumonia. J Cyst Fibros 2013;12:817–20. https://doi.org/10.1016/j.jcf.2013.01.008.

[29] Miller C, McMullin B, Ghaffari A, Stenzler A, Pick N, Roscoe D, et al. Gaseous nitric oxide bactericidal activity retained during intermittent high-dose short duration exposure. Nitric Oxide Biol Chem 2009;20:16–23. https://doi.org/10.1016/j.niox.2008.08.002.

[30] Tal A, Greenberg D, Av-Gay Y, Golan-Tripto I, Feinstein Y, Ben-Shimol S, et al. Nitric oxide inhalations in bronchiolitis: a pilot, randomized, double-blinded, controlled trial. Pediatr Pulmonol 2018;53:95–102. https://doi.org/10.1002/ppul.23905.

[31] Miller OI, Tang SF, Keech A, Celermajer DS. Rebound pulmonary hypertension on withdrawal from inhaled nitric oxide. Lancet Lond Engl 1995;346:51–2. https://doi.org/10.1016/s0140-6736(95)92681-x.

[32] Lavoie A, Hall JB, Olson DM, Wylam ME. Life-threatening effects of discontinuing inhaled nitric oxide in severe respiratory failure. Am J Respir Crit Care Med 1996;153:1985–7. https://doi.org/10.1164/ajrccm.153.6.8665066.

[33] Pearl JM, Nelson DP, Raake JL, Manning PB, Schwartz SM, Koons L, et al. Inhaled nitric oxide increases endothelin-1 levels: a potential cause of rebound pulmonary hypertension. Crit Care Med 2002;30:89–93. https://doi.org/10.1097/00003246-200201000-00014.

[34] Black SM, Heidersbach RS, McMullan DM, Bekker JM, Johengen MJ, Fineman JR. Inhaled nitric oxide inhibits NOS activity in lambs: potential mechanism for rebound pulmonary hypertension. Am J Phys 1999;277:H1849–56. https://doi.org/10.1152/ajpheart.1999.277.5.H1849.

[35] Sokol GM, Van Meurs KP, Wright LL, Rivera O, Thorn WJ, Chu PM, et al. Nitrogen dioxide formation during Inhaled nitric oxide therapy. Clin Chem 1999;45:382–7. https://doi.org/10.1093/clinchem/45.3.382.

[36] Aly H, Sahni R, Wung JT. Weaning strategy with inhaled nitric oxide treatment in persistent pulmonary hypertension of the newborn. Arch Dis Child Fetal Neonatal Ed 1997;76:F118–22. https://doi.org/10.1136/fn.76.2.f118.

[37] Behrends M, Beiderlinden M, Peters J. Combination of sildenafil and bosentan for nitric oxide withdrawal. Eur J Anaesthesiol 2005;22:155–7. https://doi.org/10.1017/s0265021505220288.

[38] Atz AM, Wessel DL. Sildenafil ameliorates effects of inhaled nitric oxide withdrawal. Anesthesiology 1999;91:307–10. https://doi.org/10.1097/00000542-199907000-00041.

[39] DiBlasi RM, Myers TR, Hess DR. Evidence-based clinical practice guideline: inhaled nitric oxide for neonates with acute hypoxic respiratory failure. Respir Care 2010;55:1717–45.

[40] Shamir MY, Avramovich A, Smaka T. The current status of continuous noninvasive measurement of total, carboxy, and methemoglobin concentration. Anesth Analg 2012;114:972–8. https://doi.org/10.1213/ANE.0b013e318233041a.

III. Nitric oxide donors and cardiovascular and metabolic diseases

12

Inhaled nitric oxide (iNO): Clinical applications in critical care medicine, delivery devices, and measuring techniques

Bijan Safaee Fakhr[a], Lorenzo Berra[b,c,d,*], and Emanuele Rezoagli[a,e,*]

[a]Department of Emergency and Intensive Care, San Gerardo Hospital, Monza, Italy [b]Harvard Medical School, Boston, MA, United States [c]Department of Anesthesia, Critical Care and Pain Medicine, Massachusetts General Hospital, Boston, MA, United States [d]Respiratory Care Department, Massachusetts General Hospital, Boston, MA, United States [e]School of Medicine and Surgery, University of Milano-Bicocca, Monza, Italy

Abstract

Inhaled nitric oxide (iNO) is widely available for the treatment of multiple conditions such as hypoxemia due to pulmonary hypertension of the newborn (i.e., >34 weeks of gestational age), acute respiratory distress syndrome, myocardial infarction, and it is under investigation as an antimicrobial agent. Other uses of iNO can be observed in the perioperative management of pulmonary hypertension in cardiac and transplantation surgery.

With a wide range of doses from 1 up to 200 ppm reported in the clinical setting, the care of the patient receiving iNO must include the monitoring of nitrogen dioxide (NO_2) levels delivered to the patients and the methemoglobin concentration reached during the treatment together with the evaluation of the heart and the kidney functions.

The methods primarily used to measure the amount of iNO delivered to the patient include absorbance, fluorescence, chemiluminescence-based approaches, electron paramagnetic resonance (EPR), and electrochemistry.

Because of the cost and the organizational complexity of using NO stored in cylinders, iNO treatment is not available worldwide. However, a growing amount of evidence is exploring other methods to produce iNO (e.g., electric NO generators, chemical NO generators, NO-releasing solutions, and nanoparticles), making it more cost-efficient and potentially more available worldwide.

*Co-senior authors.

Nitric Oxide in Health and Disease
https://doi.org/10.1016/B978-0-443-13342-8.00016-8

Abbreviations

AKI	acute kidney injury
ARDS	acute respiratory distress syndrome
CI	confidence interval
CPB	cardiopulmonary bypass
ECMO	extracorporeal membrane oxygenation
EPR	electron paramagnetic resonance
FDA	Food and Drug Administration
FiO2	fraction of inspired oxygen
HEPA	high-efficiency particulate air filter
ICU	intensive care unit
iNO	inhaled nitric oxide
MetHb	methemoglobin
PaO2	arterial partial pressure of oxygen
PCI	percutaneous coronary intervention
ppb	parts per billion
PPHN	primary pulmonary hypertension
ppm	parts per million
PPV	positive predictive value
RCT	randomized controlled trial
SaO2	peripheral saturation of oxygen
SpMet	peripheral saturation of methemoglobin
UV	ultraviolet

Conflict of interest

Lorenzo Berra: L.B. receives salary support from K23 HL128882/NHLBI NIH as principal investigator for his work on hemolysis and nitric oxide; receives technologies and devices from iNO Therapeutics LLC, Praxair Inc., Masimo Corp; receives grants from "Fast Grants for COVID-19 research" at Mercatus Center of George Mason University and from iNO Therapeutics LLC; receives Reginald Jenney Endowment Chair at Harvard Medical School to LB, by LB Sundry Funds at Massachusetts General Hospital, and by laboratory funds of the Anesthesia Center for Critical Care Research of the Department of Anesthesia, Critical Care and Pain Medicine at Massachusetts General Hospital. L.B. has filed a patent application on June 7, 2021 for NO delivery in COVID-19 disease: PCT application number: PCT/US2021/036269.

  Emanuele Rezoagli: Dr. Rezoagli is supported by the Bicocca Starting grant 2020 from the University of Milano-Bicocca with the project titled: "Functional Residual Capacity Assessment using a Wash-In/Wash-Out technique based on a fast main-stream O2 Sensor with nanofluorescent geometry for severe lung injury (FAST) – COVID and beyond"; by the International Young Investigator Award 2018 from European Society of Intensive Care Medicine (ESICM) with the project titled: "Role of the exhaled breath condensate as non-invasive monitoring of the lung inflammation during ARDS: a prospective cohort study"; and by the National Merck Sharp & Dohme Corporation Research Award 2017 from the Società Italiana di Anestesia Analgesia Rianimazione e Terapia Intensiva (SIAARTI) with the project titled: "Studio della concentrazione di ossido nitrico nell'esalato espiratorio come marcatore di danno polmonare acuto in pazienti adulti con ARDS sottoposti a ventilazione meccanica. Dr. Rezoagli received lecturing fees from Draeger Italia Spa."

Introduction

iNO indications and use in critical care medicine: State-of-the-art

Thirty years went by since Warren M. Zapol and Claes Frostell started to explore the therapeutic effects of inhaled nitric oxide (iNO) by demonstrating its beneficial effects on newborns with congenital heart diseases and adult patients with acute respiratory distress syndrome (ARDS). The great advantage of NO gas in the clinical setting is that it selectively dilates the pulmonary vessels of ventilated regions and is annihilated by a rapid deoxygenation reaction with circulating hemoglobin, avoiding systemic vasodilation [1,2].

In December 1999, after a long series of studies verifying the effectiveness of NO treatment, the Food and Drug Administration (FDA) approved iNO as a drug for the treatment of hypoxemia related to primary pulmonary hypertension of the newborns. Since then, approximately 150,000 babies have inhaled NO in the United States, and 350,000 adults and children have inhaled NO for off-label use.

To date, iNO is used to treat multiple conditions carrying out multiple beneficial effects through different mechanisms [3–6].

Inhaled NO improves systemic oxygenation in newborns with pulmonary hypertension

The substantial evidence about the effectiveness of inhaled NO in improving systemic oxygenation led to the FDA's approval to treat hypoxic newborns (i.e., >34 weeks of gestational age) with pulmonary hypertension [7–9]. Inhaled NO beneficial effects were observed at different concentrations, ranging from 5 to 80 parts per million (ppm). The physiological effects of NO gas on oxygenation translated into an improved clinical outcome in hypoxemic newborns with primary pulmonary hypertension, as highlighted in different studies reporting a decreased need for Extracorporeal Membrane Oxygenation (ECMO) [7–9]. Several trials further investigated the effects of iNO in preterm infants with respiratory failure showing a reduction in bronchopulmonary dysplasia in children <1000 g and overall risk of brain injury [10,11]. However, despite some studies showed benefits on systemic oxygenation in this population, most trials failed to demonstrate a clear survival benefit of iNO in the preterm population [10–15].

Inhaled NO improves oxygenation in acute respiratory distress syndrome

Preclinical and clinical studies on acute respiratory distress syndrome (ARDS) have demonstrated the physiological benefit of inhaling NO at 5 to 80 ppm by producing selective pulmonary vasodilation of the aerated lung areas, decreasing pulmonary capillary pressure and pulmonary transvascular albumin flux, and determining an overall improvement in systemic oxygenation [2,16]. This physiological effect was not confirmed in a significant improvement in survival, as shown by pooled data from different clinical trials [17]. However, thanks to its ability to improve oxygenation and to facilitate the right heart function by decreasing pulmonary vascular resistance, NO gas is still considered as a rescue treatment in hypoxemic patients with ARDS [18,19]. Furthermore, the trials investigating the role of iNO on survival in ARDS were performed before the era of protective lung ventilation, which may play as a confounder.

Inhaled NO improves perioperative pulmonary hypertension in adult and pediatric patients after cardiac surgery

Inhaled NO is routinely used to test pulmonary vasoreactivity in pediatric and adult patients with pulmonary arterial hypertension [20]. This helps to select the most suitable surgical strategy for heart and lung transplantation [21,22].

The selective pulmonary vascular resistance reduction induced by iNO plays a key role in the management of perioperative pulmonary hypertension, which is a common feature in pediatric patients undergoing cardiac surgery [23]. James et al. reported a reduced incidence of low cardiac output syndrome when NO gas is delivered intraoperatively through the cardiopulmonary bypass machine [24]. Despite that evidence, different randomized clinical trials did not confirm any hemodynamic or survival benefit [25–29].

In the setting of heart transplantation, when reperfusion generates acute-onset pulmonary hypertension and right heart failure, breathing NO reduces pulmonary pressure and improves heart function. Inhaled NO significantly decreased pulmonary vascular resistance in right ventricle dysfunction in the presence of a left ventricular assist device [30,31]. However, this benefit was not confirmed in a more recent larger trial comparing 40 ppm NO to placebo [32,33].

Inhaled NO reduces ischemia/reperfusion injury

Many preclinical studies demonstrated the efficacy of inhaled NO in preventing organ damage and improving survival in models of myocardial infarction, ischemic stroke, and cardiac arrest [34–37]. Lang et al. tested the ability of 80 ppm NO gas to enhance postoperative allograft function and reduce hepatobiliary complication rates after liver transplantation [38]. Those beneficial effects were confirmed in a later study by Janssens and colleagues who observed an improvement in left ventricular function recovery 4 months after myocardial infarction by administering NO at 80 ppm starting before PCI up to 4 h after reperfusion. However, iNO decreased the infarction size only in a subgroup of patients who did not receive intraarterial nitroglycerin (i.e., a systemic NO donor) (i.e., ratio of myocardial infarction size to left ventricular mass: 17.0% vs 22.4; iNO vs control; $P = .044$) [39].

Inhaled NO protects the kidney during hemolysis

During hemolysis, circulating heme reacts with endothelial NO, transforming oxyhemoglobin into methemoglobin by the deoxygenation reaction leading to the change of iron chemical structure from ferrous (Fe^{++}) to ferric (Fe^{+++}) state. In a preclinical study, Minneci and coworkers demonstrated the beneficial effects of iNO at 80 ppm in attenuating hemolysis-induced renal dysfunction by preventing the consumption of endogenous NO [40]. Based on their observations, it has been proposed that NO inhalation may attenuate the state of vasoconstriction characteristic of intravascular hemolysis.

Acute intravascular hemolysis plays a crucial role in developing acute kidney injury (AKI) after cardiopulmonary bypass (CPB) [41,42]. Lei and colleagues hypothesized that exposure to NO during and after CPB protects the kidney by three possible mechanisms: (1) selective vasodilation of the pulmonary circulation, leading to improved left ventricular preload and cardiac output; (2) reduction of ischemia/reperfusion renal injury; (3) oxidation of plasma hemoglobin to methemoglobin, which cannot scavenge endogenous NO. This hypothesis was verified in a prospective RCT showing that iNO 80 ppm compared to control (i.e., N_2) reduced the incidence of postoperative AKI from 63% to 50% ($P = .04$) and reduced transition to stage III chronic kidney disease at 90 days from 33% to 21% ($P = .024$) [41]. This hypothesis has been further confirmed in other trials showing the applicability and the beneficial effects of NO on kidney protection in cardiac surgery [42–44].

Inhaled NO exerts antimicrobial effects

Preclinical studies reported that iNO may have antimicrobial properties. In a murine model of *Klebsiella pneumoniae*, Wiegand and colleagues showed how the administration of 300 ppm of NO for 12 min every 3 h reduced *K. pneumoniae* colony-forming units in lung tissues compared to controls [45].

An innovative human study tested 160 ppm twice daily as adjunctive therapy in a cystic fibrosis patient with chronic lung infection by a multidrug-resistant *Burkholderia multivorans*. The study evidenced that the treatment appeared to improve the antibiotic resistance pattern of the *B. multivorans*. The proposed mechanism included: (1) direct toxic effect of NO on bacteria and (2) bacterial biofilm dispersal [46–49].

Nitric oxide has been widely tested in vitro for its antiviral effects showing activity against multiple viruses such as Influenza A viruses, HSV-1, Coxsackie virus, coronavirus (SARS-CoV-1 and 2), and Dengue virus through the inhibition of protein synthesis or viral replication in a dose-dependent fashion [50–52].

Inhaled NO at 160 ppm for 30 min 5 times daily was tested in a multicenter RCT involving 43 infants with viral bronchiolitis and showed improved oxygenation and a reduced hospital length of stay [53]. Antiviral effects of iNO have further been verified in patients with SARS-CoV-1 and COVID-19 [54]. Different studies explored the effects of 160 ppm NO gas for 30 min twice daily in nonintubated patients with COVID-19 ranging from a mild-to-severe respiratory failure showing an improvement in respiratory rate and systemic oxygenation in tachypneic and hypoxemic patients, respectively. None of the treated patients was readmitted after hospital discharge [55,56]. Valsecchi and colleagues further evaluated the clinical effects of inhaled NO at 200 ppm for 30 min twice daily in nonintubated pregnant patients with severe COVID-19 respiratory failure. The treatment group showed a reduction in oxygen requirement (oxygen supplementation free days NO vs standard of care 24 [23–26] vs 22 [14–24] days, $P = .01$) and a shorter ICU (59.7% shorter ICU length of stay; 95%CI: 36.2–95.4%, $P < .001$) and hospital (63.6% shorter hospital length of stay, 95%CI: 55.1–70.8%; $P < .001$) length of stay, as compared to patients in the control group [57].

Despite preliminary promising results, more studies will be required to assess the efficacy of high-dose NO in treating COVID-19. A large multicenter clinical trial (NCT04306393) to test the effect of 80 ppm NO inhalation for 48 h in mechanically ventilated COVID-19 ARDS patients is currently in progress [58].

Low dose vs high dose (>80 ppm)

The US FDA approves inhaled NO at a dose up to 20 ppm with several trials that tasted its safety up to 80 ppm [3,59,60]. However, evidence is expanding on the off-label high-dose (>80 ppm) iNO treatment for its potential antimicrobial effects.

In the newborns with PPHN, at doses of iNO <80 ppm, the increase in oxygenation is directly proportional to the degree of hypoxia before inhalation. An inhaled concentration of 5 to 20 ppm was enough to increase arterial oxygen levels above those measured in the controls, although the maximum increase in systemic oxygenation was reported with a concentration of 80 ppm [9,61].

In 2006, Gerlach and colleagues performed a dose-response study in adult patients with ARDS and showed how incremental steps of iNO (0.01, 0.1, 1, 10, 100 ppm) affected PaO_2/FiO_2 ratio and pulmonary vascular resistance. Gerlach's study evidenced that the peak level of oxygenation improvement was obtained at 10 ppm.

However, the off-label antimicrobial properties of NO are dose-dependent. Unfortunately, iNO at a dose >80 ppm for prolonged periods might be dangerous because of the production of NO_2—with the subsequent risk of chemical lung injury—and the increase in methemoglobin levels—which decrease the oxygen transport. Accordingly, different groups hypothesized and tested that a few breaths or short intermittent pulses of antimicrobial high NO concentrations might be better tolerated than continuous inhalation of the standard dose because of the highest peak concentration reached during the treatment [45,51,62]. Based on that rationale, high-dose inhaled NO is being tested in multiple clinical scenarios [46,53].

Despite that, high dose NO gas is still off-label as an antimicrobial, and more studies will be required to assess its efficacy in treating bacterial or viral infections. To date, the increasing amount of literature is encouraging about the safety and efficacy of high dose iNO as an antimicrobial agent. However, since most in vitro studies were performed testing NO donors in an aqueous solution, the exact antiviral dose of iNO is still under investigation [63].

NO measuring techniques

The NO measurement is critical to achieve an accurate delivery in the clinical setting. Unfortunately, analytical assays for monitoring NO are challenged by its unique chemical and physical properties, such as its instability, rapid diffusion, and extremely short half-life (i.e., a few seconds). Since the effects of NO are mediated by a broad range of concentrations, the techniques used to measure it need a wide linear response range.

The methods aimed at detecting NO in clinical setting include absorbance, fluorescence, chemiluminescence-based approaches, electron paramagnetic resonance (EPR), and electrochemistry. Other approaches mostly involved in preclinical and environmental field include mass spectrometry, X-ray photoelectron spectroscopy, infrared and UV lasers, quartz crystal microbalance, photoluminescent porous silicon and cadmium selenide, gas chromatography, and Raman spectroscopy [64]. This section will emphasize the techniques used to evaluate the concentration of the delivered NO gas in the clinical setting, focusing on concentrations ranging within parts per million range.

Spectroscopic methods:

(1) Absorbance-based measurements:
   a. Metalloprotein-based assay: This assay is based on hemoglobin or hemoglobin-derived-proteins and involves the reaction of oxyhemoglobin (HbO_2) and NO to produce Methemoglobin (MetHb) and nitrate:

$$Hemoglobin - Fe(II) - O_2 + NO \rightarrow Hemoglobin - Fe(III) + NO_3^-.$$

   This reaction determines a spectral shift which is analyzed by spectrophotometry. The interaction between NO and hemoglobin is nearly diffusion-limited and 26 times faster than the reaction between NO and O_2, allowing NO measurement which is not influenced by O_2. Although other nitrogen oxides do not interfere, factors that interfere with this technique include fluctuation in temperature, the presence of other heme-containing proteins, and changes in pH due to their effect on the absorbance spectrum of the MetHb.

Heme-containing proteins other than hemoglobin (e.g., tetramethylorthosilicate (TMOS) xerogel) are also suitable for quantitative NO detection based on absorbance changes after reacting with NO. They have been used to create a sensor capable of generating a linear response to NO from 1 to 25 ppm. While O_2, nitrogen gas, or carbon monoxide did not influence the measurement of NO, the introduction of NO_2 at 10–1000 ppm did interfere with NO measurement [64,65].

b. Other assays with metal-based indicators: metal-based indicators different from the previously described metalloproteins have also gained attention in monitoring NO's gaseous concentrations. An example is a copper-eriochrome cyanine R complex [Cu(II)-ECR] which is suitable for monitoring NO gas within a range between 0.23 and 6 ppm. The sensor response is reversible and selective for NO over O_2, NO_2, and CO [66].

c. Diazotization assay (Griess reaction): it measures nitrite deriving from the reaction of NO with oxygenated media via three different reactions:

(1) $2NO + O_2 \rightarrow 2NO_2$
(2) $NO + NO_2 \rightarrow N_2O_3$
(3) $N_2O_3 + H_2O \rightarrow 2NO_2^- + 2H^+$

The nitrite reacts with sulfanilamide and N-(1-naphtyl)ethylenesiamine (NED), producing an azo dye. The azo dye concentration is then used as an indirect indicator of nitrite and NO concentration by comparing it with a calibration curve via a fluorescence spectrophotometer. The Griess assay is unsuitable for real-time monitoring of NO for different reasons: (1) it detects a byproduct of NO; (2) it needs control experiments to distinguish basal nitrite levels from those due to changes in NO concentrations; and (3) it is influenced by the nitrates (NO_3^-) concentration. However, in 2007, a new method for monitoring NO gas via diazotization assay was validated with a limit of detection of the NO microanalysis system between 7 ppb and 1 ppm. However, NO concentrations as high as 50 ppm may be determined by including a multipoint calibration [67].

(2) Chemiluminescence: among the chemiluminescent methods that selectively detect NO gas, the one using NO's reaction with ozone (O_3) is the most important in clinical practice. This reaction produces an excited state of nitrogen dioxide (NO_2^*), which emits a photon upon relaxation to the ground state:

$$NO + O_3 \rightarrow NO_2^* + O_2; NO_2^* \rightarrow NO_2 + hv,$$
$$hv = \text{photon}.$$

A photomultiplier tube then measures the emitted light with intensity proportional to the amount of NO in the reaction cell. For more technical information about this technique, we redirect from an explanatory video from Di Fenza et al. [68]. The ozone-based chemiluminescent reaction is specific for NO, although NO_2^- and NO_3^- may interfere through their reduction to NO. However, this measurement mode is susceptible to carrier flow rate changes and is only suited for detecting gaseous NO. With a detection limit of 0.5 ppb up to 500 ppm, an excellent sensitivity, and near-real-time monitoring of NO, chemiluminescence is the gold standard for NO detection to date.

III. Nitric oxide donors and cardiovascular and metabolic diseases

Electrochemical technique

It is the most used analytical method for monitoring NO in physiology/biology due to specific inherent advantages, such as

- real-time monitoring
- amenability to miniaturization
- ability to enhance selectivity and sensitivity via electrode modification and/or the applied potential
- excellent spatial resolution with extraordinarily low limits of detection

However, this technique has a certain degree of interference from O_2.

Electrochemical monitors use a simple electrochemical principle based on the oxidation of NO to nitrite. The electrodes are modified to reduce interference from other redox-active species and facilitate selective detection of NO. The electrolyte solution contains the sensing electrode (anode), a counter electrode (cathode), and a reference electrode. The voltage between the anode and cathode is kept constant, and the current flowing through the sensor is proportional to the amount of NO reacting.

Nitric oxide detection is possible thanks to the following reactions occurring at the sensor and counter electrode, respectively:

$$(NO + 2H_2) \rightarrow HNO_3^- + 3H^+ + 3e^- \text{ (i.e., sensor electrode)}$$
$$O_2 + 4H^+ + 4e^- \rightarrow 2H_2O \text{ (i. e., counter electrode)}.$$

The current is proportional to NO concentration because each NO molecule consumes three electrons at the sensor electrode. The reference electrode in the NO cell provides a bias voltage by applying an external potential to keep the sensing electrode at the correct operating voltage. Purtz et al. showed that different electrochemical analyzers performed better at NO gas concentrations ≤ 20 ppm [64,69,70].

To date, the gold standard for evaluating the clinical monitoring of inhaled NO is ozone-based chemiluminescence, which requires a bigger, more expensive, and challenging device that it might make it unsuitable for clinical use. Many studies have shown that the electrochemical method has an accuracy as comparable to the chemiluminescence technique, despite being smaller, less expensive, and easier to use [69].

Nitric oxide safety monitoring

Methemoglobin

The reaction between oxyhemoglobin and NO generates methemoglobin (metHb) by oxidizing the ferrous (Fe^{2+}) iron of the heme group to its ferric (Fe^{3+}) state. In healthy subjects, cyanosis does not appear until metHb levels reach 15%–20%, and clinical symptoms of hypoxia—such as fatigue and dyspnea—become significant in the presence of metHb levels >30% [6]. The impact of methemoglobin on tissue oxygenation is significant in subjects with impaired lung (e.g., ARDS patients) or heart (e.g., congenital heart diseases) functions. Thus, it is crucial to monitor the methemoglobin levels adequately. The gold standard to quantify the methemoglobin level is by using a laboratory multiwavelength oximeter [71]. Recently, an alternative pulse oximeter-like device has become available for the continuous and noninvasive measurement of the percentage of methemoglobin (SpMet) using multiple LED wavelengths, allowing a dynamic assessment of metHb.

A study evaluating the accuracy of the SpMet reading compared to the gold standard blood gas analyzer showed that when a reading error is defined as an absolute bias over 5% compared to the one measured with the blood gas analysis, SpMet reading accuracy appeared best at $SaO_2 > 95\%$, with an increasing trend to overestimate %MetHb as the SaO_2 decreases ($P < .05$) [72]. Considering a threshold of 10% metHb, the positive predictive value seemed to suffer from its tendency to overestimate significantly %metHb as the SaO_2 decreases. In the normal $SaO_2 > 95\%$ range, PPV was 90% but decreased to <10% at ranges of $SaO_2 < 85\%$ [72]. When NO gas is administered, this false-positive result would not be a patient safety issue, whereas a false negative could be of greater concern because it would delay the gas administration interruption. In case of a concern, a blood sample would help to clarify the accurate metHb level and should be performed in a patient with significant hypoxemia.

The management of NO-induced metHb includes reducing the amount of gas delivered to the patient until treatment discontinuation. The enzyme metHb reductase in the red blood cells rapidly converts methemoglobin to hemoglobin. However, a reduced methemoglobin reductase activity must be taken into account in the neonates as they are more prone to develop methemoglobinemia.

Nitrogen dioxide (NO₂)

Nitrogen dioxide is a toxic free-radical gas derived from the reaction of NO and O_2. Nitrogen dioxide is rapidly converted to nitric acid (pH 1.0) in aqueous solutions and can be highly toxic by directly injuring the respiratory tract mucosa. Increased airway reactivity has been reported in humans after exposures to as low as 1.5 ppm NO_2 [6]. Occupational Safety and Health Administration Permissible Exposure Limits order to maintain the levels of this toxic compound below 5 ppm [73]. The National Institute for Occupational Safety and Health recommends to breath levels below 1 ppm to avoid any possible side effects [74].

Nitrogen dioxide can be measured by chemiluminescence, cavity-attenuated phase shift, electrochemically and infrared/UV lasers (which has the advantage of having the possibility of monitor simultaneously and dynamically the concentration of NO and NO_2 [75]). As compared with the chemiluminescence—which is the technique with the highest sensibility—both the cavity attenuated phase shift and the electrochemical technique have a high reliability and are suitable methods for clinical monitoring of NO_2 [69,76].

In a large number of adults and newborn patients pooled from several clinical trials, significant methemoglobinemia or NO_2 formation was uncommon in patients breathing NO at doses ranging from 1.25 to 80 ppm.

When approaching the use of NO gas at doses >80 ppm, attention has been focused on the possibility of delivering a high dose of NO_2 and on the possible accumulation of metHb. To avoid that, regimens based on high dose inhaled NO intervals for a limited time have been established. Miller et al. evaluated the safety of 160 ppm NO gas delivered 5 times a day for 5 consecutive days in a phase 1 trial in nonintubated healthy subjects. In a total of 250 treatments, NO_2 level always remained <5 ppm (i.e., highest level 2.8; mean 2.3 with a 95% CI 2.2–2.5 ppm); metHb reached the highest level of 2.5% with an average increase during the treatment of ~1% and return to baseline levels within 3 h (Fig. 1).

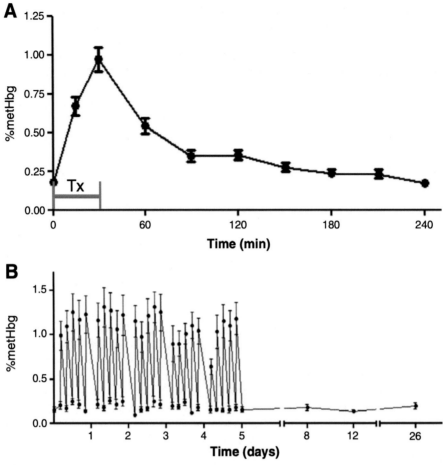

FIG. 1   Panel A: Methemoglobin (MetHb) values across the inhalation of nitric oxide (NO) at 160 ppm for 30 min 5 times daily in healthy subjects ($n = 250$ treatments). Panel B: MetHb values before and after the treatment during the 5 days, showing that MetHb returned to baseline values after each treatment. *Reproduced from Miller C, Miller M, McMullin B, Regev G, Serghides L, Kain K, Road J, Av-Gay Y. A phase I clinical study of inhaled nitric oxide in healthy adults. J Cyst Fibros 2012;11:324–31. doi:10.1016/j.jcf.2012.01.003, after granting permission from the publisher.*

The safety of NO gas administered at doses of 160–200 ppm with regard to NO_2 delivery, and metHb concentration was evaluated also in patients with viral pneumonia during the COVID-19 pandemic, and it was confirmed in infant and pregnant patients [56,57,77].

Left heart failure

Inhaled NO-related pulmonary vasodilation increases the intrathoracic volume, which may overwhelm a failing left ventricle, thereby increasing the risk of pulmonary edema. Specific attention should be focused on patients with heart failure, including clinical signs of acute congestive heart failure (e.g., dyspnea, desaturation, hypotension, and tachycardia) and an echocardiographic evaluation before and after initiating the treatment with NO [6].

Acute kidney injury

Controversial is the effect of NO gas on kidney function. A metaanalysis published in 2016 pointed out an increased risk of renal impairment in ARDS patients receiving NO gas (RR 1.59, 95%CI 1.17 to 2.16), although no pathophysiological explanation was provided [17]. Meanwhile, the nephroprotective effect of NO treatment was observed in a separate meta-analysis, including 579 cardiac surgical patients [78]. The rationale behind this protective has been previously described in the paragraph "Inhaled NO protects the kidney during hemolysis."

NO sources

Nitric oxide gas represents one of the most expensive drugs used in neonatal medicine, costing about 14,000 $ for each treatment [6]. To date, NO therapy is available on the market by cylinder production and distribution network; by a complex delivery and monitoring device to regulate NO, NO_2, and O_2 concentrations; and requires highly trained personnel. Because of the cost and the organizational complexity, NO treatment is not available worldwide. Several methods are being tested to produce NO for biomedical purposes and are still under investigation [79].

Cylinders

Pressurized NO cylinders at various concentrations buffered in nitrogen (NO/N_2 to avoid the generation of toxic compounds such as NO_2 by using O_2) represent most of the commercially available NO delivery systems [79]. This modality is safe and reliable and can efficiently deliver a wide range of NO concentrations. To date, more than 350,000 patients have been treated worldwide [80]. The delivery of NO from the cylinders is adjusted using a flow-regulated injector that modulates the NO flow targeting the desired concentration of NO in the inspiratory limb of the respiratory circuit. The processing unit regulates the NO flow from the pressurized cylinder in real-time, considering the total gas flow delivered to the patients. The NO gas administration can be continuous throughout the respiratory cycle, or it can be synchronized with the patient ventilation. All the commercially available NO delivery systems continuously measure NO and NO_2 concentrations by using an electrochemical sensor cell [69,79].

Electric NO generators

In 2015, Yu and colleagues reported that therapeutic doses of NO gas could be produced by a novel, lightweight, portable device to serve as a simple and economical method for producing pure NO from the air using high-voltage electrical discharge [79,81]. An electric potential between 2 electrodes ionizes the air, causing an electron flow from the cathode to the anode.

The frequent electron collisions due to the high current intensity raise the temperature between the electrodes and determine the dissociation of N_2 and O_2 into a plasma state, generating NO, NO_2, and O_3. The NO and NO_2 production increase proportionally with the frequency of the sparking pulse while decreases by increasing the airflow. As described by Yu et al., an electrical NO generator combines a gas pump, a NO generation chamber containing an iridium spark plug, an 18-g scavenger containing calcium hydroxide, and a High-Efficiency Particulate Air filter (HEPA) filter [82]. The calcium hydroxide filter (Ca $(OH)_2$) has the aim of selectively removing toxic compounds such as

(1) NO_2, through the following reaction: $Ca(OH)_2 + NO_2 + NO \rightarrow Ca(NO_2)_2 + H_2O$, that reduces the NO_2 levels by 70%–90%.
(2) O_3 can be detected in the output arm of the NO generator ranging from 18 ppb to 10 ppm— with an environmental safety limit of 70 ppb. A calcium hydroxide filter removes O_3, reaching O_3 levels <0.1 ppb.
(3) The etching of the electrodes releases metals such as brass and platinum during electric discharge. The HEPA filters aims to remove these metal particles from the generated NO.

The opportunity to generate NO from the air without needing cylinders is promising and could make NO widely available. However, it has 2 potential limitations: (1) NO production decreases when the air flow through the sparker increases, and it may not be sufficient to maintain the targeted NO concentration (e.g., patients receiving high minute tidal ventilation); (2) the high risk of safety issues related to the possible delivery of toxic compounds such as metal particles and ozone.

However, in 2016, Berra et al. evidenced in a first-in-human study in 6 patients with chronic pulmonary hypertension that 25 ppm NO for 10 minutes delivered through an electric NO generator was safe and determined an acute improvement in pulmonary vascular resistance that was equivalent to the one obtained by the commercially available cylinders [83].

Chemical NO generators ($N_2O4 \rightarrow NO_2$-(ascorbic acid) $\rightarrow$ NO)

In 2011, Lovich and colleagues defined and validated a process to generate purified NO by passing a gas mixture of NO_2, N_2, and O_2 through an ascorbic acid-silica gel cartridge that reduces NO_2 to pure NO [84,85]. This method entirely avoids the dilution and mixing of NO with O_2 and allows NO gas generation free of NO_2. Furthermore, the presence of a silica gel matrix absorbs potential volatile contaminants.

The device is composed of a thermoplastic structure containing a porous tube made of ascorbic acid and silica. In this cartridge, the ascorbic acid protonates NO_2 in a concentrated, high-efficient reaction as follows:

$$NO_2 + \text{Ascorbic Acid} \rightarrow \text{Dehydroascorbic acid} + NO + H_2O.$$

This reaction generates water and NO that are delivered to the patient. The cartridge can convert 80 ppm NO_2 into NO with an output NO_2 concentration <1 ppm (i.e., 0.6– 0.8 ppm using 1 cartridge with FiO_2 of 1). The cartridges are designed for use in a ventilator or an anesthesia machine where flow rates can be as high as 100 L/min and where a low-pressure drop is essential to minimize the work of breathing. The measured pressure drop across this cartridge is less than 0.1 cm H_2O at 5 L/min. The NO_2 needed for the process can be obtained from a small volume of liquid dinitrogen tetraoxide (2 mL of N_2O_4 contained in an evaporation chamber), which is vaporized to NO_2 gas. This sequence of physical-chemical reactions aimed to miniaturize the source of an NO increasing its potential for ambulatory use without the need for pressurized gas cylinders of NO_2. With this system, NO production is regulated only by the evaporating chamber temperature; the cross-sectional area; and length of the capillary tube linking the N_2O_4 reservoir to the manifold.

To date, the only FDA-approved NO delivery system using the Lovich technology can deliver NO at a concentration of up to 20 ppm with NO_2 concentration < 3 ppm [59]. The main advantage of this device is the reduced size and weight compared to cylinder-based delivery systems. However, this device still depends on an extensive production and supply chain.

NO-releasing solutions (SaNOtize) and nanoparticles

In 2015, Stenzler and colleagues patented the use of a NO-releasing solution—composed of sodium nitrite—and capable of releasing NO depending on pH changes [86]:

- with pH > 4, the production of NO is negligible.
- with pH < 4, NO production increases as pH decreases.

The solution is stored dormant and must be activated by adding a defined substance (e.g., citric acid monohydrate) that drops the solution's pH below 4. Once activated, the reaction is self-maintaining, keeping the pH < 4 by the reaction of NO with O_2 to generate NO_2 that reacts with water to generate nitric acid. These NO-releasing solutions can produce up to 300 ppm NO gas in the presence of a continuous flow of 3 L/min from 64 mL of a 60 mM $NaNO_2$ sodium nitrite. Targeted clinical uses under investigation include topical cutaneous infections, COVID-19, and chronic bacterial sinusitis.

NO-releasing nanoparticles consist of small particles containing either NO or an inactive NO precursor in a stable form capable of releasing NO to a target tissue in a controlled manner. Friedman et al. reported that NO could be efficiently generated by converting nitrites enclosed in a solid matrix when exposed to moisture [87]. The pattern of NO released from the nanoparticle depends on the matrix's composition. A glassy matrix releases NO more rapidly than a hydrogel/glass matrix. Like NO-releasing solutions, the nanoparticles could be used to administer antimicrobial doses of NO topically. Furthermore, due to their small diameter, the nanoparticles could potentially be delivered through an aerosol directly into the lung.

References

[1] Frostell CG, Blomqvist H, Hedenstierna G, Lundberg J, Zapol WM. Inhaled nitric oxide selectively reverses human hypoxic pulmonary vasoconstriction without causing systemic vasodilation. Anesthesiology 1993;78:427–35. https://doi.org/10.1097/00000542-199303000-00005.
[2] Rossaint R, Falke KJ, López F, Slama K, Pison U, Zapol WM. Inhaled nitric oxide for the adult respiratory distress syndrome. N Engl J Med 1993;328:399–405. https://doi.org/10.1056/NEJM199302113280605.

[3] Redaelli S, Magliocca A, Malhotra R, Ristagno G, Citerio G, Bellani G, Berra L, Rezoagli E. Nitric oxide: clinical applications in critically ill patients. Nitric Oxide 2022;121:20–33. https://doi.org/10.1016/j.niox.2022.01.007.

[4] Signori D, Magliocca A, Hayashida K, Graw JA, Malhotra R, Bellani G, Berra L, Rezoagli E. Inhaled nitric oxide: role in the pathophysiology of cardio-cerebrovascular and respiratory diseases. Intensive Care Med Exp 2022;10:28. https://doi.org/10.1186/s40635-022-00455-6.

[5] Alvarez RA, Berra L, Gladwin MT. Home NO therapy for COVID-19. Am J Respir Crit Care Med 2020. https://doi.org/10.1164/rccm.202005-1906ED.

[6] Ignarro LJ, Freeman B. Nitric oxide: biology and pathobiology. Academic Press; 2017.

[7] Roberts JD, Fineman JR, Morin FC, Shaul PW, Rimar S, Schreiber MD, Polin RA, Zwass MS, Zayek MM, Gross I, Heymann MA, Zapol WM. Inhaled nitric oxide and persistent pulmonary hypertension of the newborn. The inhaled nitric oxide study group. N Engl J Med 1997;336:605–10. https://doi.org/10.1056/NEJM199702273360902.

[8] The Neonatal Inhaled Nitric Oxide Study Group (NINOS). Inhaled nitric oxide and hypoxic respiratory failure in infants with congenital diaphragmatic hernia. The Neonatal Inhaled Nitric Oxide Study Group (NINOS). Pediatrics 1997;99:838–45. https://doi.org/10.1542/peds.99.6.838.

[9] Clark RH, Kueser TJ, Walker MW, Southgate WM, Huckaby JL, Perez JA, Roy BJ, Keszler M, Kinsella JP. Low-dose nitric oxide therapy for persistent pulmonary hypertension of the newborn. N Engl J Med 2000;342:469–74. https://doi.org/10.1056/NEJM200002173420704.

[10] Kinsella JP, Cutter GR, Walsh WF, Gerstmann DR, Bose CL, Hart C, Sekar KC, Auten RL, Bhutani VK, Gerdes JS, George TN, Southgate WM, Carriedo H, Couser RJ, Mammel MC, Hall DC, Pappagallo M, Sardesai S, Strain JD, Baier M, Abman SH. Early inhaled nitric oxide therapy in premature newborns with respiratory failure. N Engl J Med 2006;355:354–64. https://doi.org/10.1056/NEJMoa060442.

[11] Ballard RA, Truog WE, Cnaan A, Martin RJ, Ballard PL, Merrill JD, Walsh MC, Durand DJ, Mayock DE, Eichenwald EC, Null DR, Hudak ML, Puri AR, Golombek SG, Courtney SE, Stewart DL, Welty SE, Phibbs RH, Hibbs AM, Luan X, Wadlinger SR, Asselin JM, Coburn CE. Inhaled nitric oxide in preterm infants undergoing mechanical ventilation. N Engl J Med 2006;355:343–53. https://doi.org/10.1056/NEJMoa061088.

[12] Kinsella JP, Walsh WF, Bose CL, Gerstmann DR, Labella J, Sardesai S, Walsh-Sukys MC, McCaffrey MJ, Cornfield DN, Bhutani VK, Cutter GR, Baier M, Abman SH. Inhaled nitric oxide in premature neonates with severe hypoxaemic respiratory failure: a randomised controlled trial. Lancet 1999;354:1061–5. https://doi.org/10.1016/S0140-6736(99)03558-8.

[13] Field D, Elbourne D, Truesdale A, Grieve R, Hardy P, Fenton AC, Subhedar N, Ahluwalia J, Halliday HL, Stocks J, Tomlin K, Normand C, On behalf of the INNOVO Trial Collaborating Group. Neonatal ventilation with inhaled nitric oxide versus ventilatory support without inhaled nitric oxide for preterm infants with severe respiratory failure: the INNOVO multicentre randomised controlled trial (ISRCTN 17821339). Pediatrics 2005;115:926–36. https://doi.org/10.1542/peds.2004-1209.

[14] Van Meurs KP, Wright LL, Ehrenkranz RA, Lemons JA, Ball MB, Poole WK, Perritt R, Higgins RD, Oh W, Hudak ML, Laptook AR, Shankaran S, Finer NN, Carlo WA, Kennedy KA, Fridriksson JH, Steinhorn RH, Sokol GM, Konduri GG, Aschner JL, Stoll BJ, D'Angio CT, Stevenson DK. Inhaled nitric oxide for premature infants with severe respiratory failure. N Engl J Med 2005;353:13–22. https://doi.org/10.1056/NEJMoa043927.

[15] Mercier J-C, Hummler H, Durrmeyer X, Sanchez-Luna M, Carnielli V, Field D, Greenough A, Van Overmeire B, Jonsson B, Hallman M, Baldassarre J, EUNO Study Group. Inhaled nitric oxide for prevention of bronchopulmonary dysplasia in premature babies (EUNO): a randomised controlled trial. Lancet 2010;376:346–54. https://doi.org/10.1016/S0140-6736(10)60664-2.

[16] Benzing A, Geiger K. Inhaled nitric oxide lowers pulmonary capillary pressure and changes longitudinal distribution of pulmonary vascular resistance in patients with acute lung injury. Acta Anaesthesiol Scand 1994;38:640–5. https://doi.org/10.1111/j.1399-6576.1994.tb03970.x.

[17] Gebistorf F, Karam O, Wetterslev J, Afshari A. Inhaled nitric oxide for acute respiratory distress syndrome (ARDS) in children and adults. Cochrane Database Syst Rev 2016;CD002787. https://doi.org/10.1002/14651858.CD002787.pub3.

[18] Fan E, Del Sorbo L, Goligher EC, Hodgson CL, Munshi L, Walkey AJ, Adhikari NKJ, Amato MBP, Branson R, Brower RG, Ferguson ND, Gajic O, Gattinoni L, Hess D, Mancebo J, Meade MO, McAuley DF, Pesenti A, Ranieri VM, Rubenfeld GD, Rubin E, Seckel M, Slutsky AS, Talmor D, Thompson BT, Wunsch H, Uleryk E, Brozek J, Brochard LJ. An Official American Thoracic Society/European Society of Intensive Care Medicine/Society of Critical Care Medicine clinical practice guideline: mechanical ventilation in adult patients with acute respiratory distress syndrome. Am J Respir Crit Care Med 2017;195:1253–63. https://doi.org/10.1164/rccm.201703-0548ST.

[19] Griffiths MJD, McAuley DF, Perkins GD, Barrett N, Blackwood B, Boyle A, Chee N, Connolly B, Dark P, Finney S, Salam A, Silversides J, Tarmey N, Wise MP, Baudouin SV. Guidelines on the management of acute respiratory distress syndrome. BMJ Open Respir Res 2019;6:e000420. https://doi.org/10.1136/bmjresp-2019-000420.

[20] Malhotra R, Hess D, Lewis GD, Bloch KD, Waxman AB, Semigran MJ. Vasoreactivity to inhaled nitric oxide with oxygen predicts long-term survival in pulmonary arterial hypertension. Pulm Circ 2011;1:250–8. https://doi.org/10.4103/2045-8932.83449.

[21] Balzer DT, Kort HW, Day RW, Corneli HM, Kovalchin JP, Cannon BC, Kaine SF, Ivy DD, Webber SA, Rothman A, Ross RD, Aggarwal S, Takahashi M, Waldman JD. Inhaled nitric oxide as a preoperative test (INOP test I). Circulation 2002;106:I76. https://doi.org/10.1161/01.cir.0000032875.55215.cb.

[22] Haraldsson A, Kieler-Jensen N, Nathorst-Westfelt U, Bergh CH, Ricksten SE. Comparison of inhaled nitric oxide and inhaled aerosolized prostacyclin in the evaluation of heart transplant candidates with elevated pulmonary vascular resistance. Chest 1998;114:780–6. https://doi.org/10.1378/chest.114.3.780.

[23] Checchia PA, Bronicki RA, Goldstein B. Review of inhaled nitric oxide in the pediatric cardiac surgery setting. Pediatr Cardiol 2012;33:493–505. https://doi.org/10.1007/s00246-012-0172-4.

[24] James C, Millar J, Horton S, Brizard C, Molesworth C, Butt W. Nitric oxide administration during paediatric cardiopulmonary bypass: a randomised controlled trial. Intensive Care Med 2016;42:1744–52. https://doi.org/10.1007/s00134-016-4420-6.

[25] Miller OI, Tang SF, Keech A, Celermajer DS. Rebound pulmonary hypertension on withdrawal from inhaled nitric oxide. Lancet 1995;346:51–2. https://doi.org/10.1016/s0140-6736(95)92681-x.

[26] Morris K, Beghetti M, Petros A, Adatia I, Bohn D. Comparison of hyperventilation and inhaled nitric oxide for pulmonary hypertension after repair of congenital heart disease. Crit Care Med 2000;28:2974–8.

[27] Russell IAM, Zwass MS, Fineman JR, Balea M, Rouine-Rapp K, Brook M, Hanley FL, Silverman NH, Cahalan MK. The effects of inhaled nitric oxide on postoperative pulmonary hypertension in infants and children undergoing surgical repair of congenital heart disease. Anesth Analg 1998;87:46–51. https://doi.org/10.1213/00000539-199807000-00011.

[28] Day RW, Hawkins JA, McGough EC, Crezeé KL, Orsmond GS. Randomized controlled study of inhaled nitric oxide after operation for congenital heart disease. Ann Thorac Surg 2000;69:1907–12. https://doi.org/10.1016/S0003-4975(00)01312-6.

[29] Bizzarro M, Gross I, Barbosa FT. Inhaled nitric oxide for the postoperative management of pulmonary hypertension in infants and children with congenital heart disease. Cochrane Database Syst Rev 2014. https://doi.org/10.1002/14651858.CD005055.pub3.

[30] Macdonald PS, Keogh A, Mundy J, Rogers P, Nicholson A, Harrison G, Jansz P, Kaan AM, Spratt P. Adjunctive use of inhaled nitric oxide during implantation of a left ventricular assist device. J Heart Lung Transplant 1998;17:312–6.

[31] Argenziano M, Choudhri AF, Moazami N, Rose EA, Smith CR, Levin HR, Smerling AJ, Oz MC. Randomized, double-blind trial of inhaled nitric oxide in LVAD recipients with pulmonary hypertension. Ann Thorac Surg 1998;65:340–5. https://doi.org/10.1016/S0003-4975(97)01307-6.

[32] Potapov E, Meyer D, Swaminathan M, Ramsay M, El Banayosy A, Diehl C, Veynovich B, Gregoric ID, Kukucka M, Gromann TW, Marczin N, Chittuluru K, Baldassarre JS, Zucker MJ, Hetzer R. Inhaled nitric oxide after left ventricular assist device implantation: a prospective, randomized, double-blind, multicenter, placebo-controlled trial. J Heart Lung Transplant 2011;30:870–8. https://doi.org/10.1016/j.healun.2011.03.005.

[33] Schlapbach LJ, Gibbons KS, Horton SB, Johnson K, Long DA, Buckley DHF, Erickson S, Festa M, d'Udekem Y, Alphonso N, Winlaw DS, Delzoppo C, van Loon K, Jones M, Young PJ, Butt W, Schibler A, NITRIC Study Group, the Australian and New Zealand Intensive Care Society Clinical Trials Group (ANZICS CTG), and the ANZICS Paediatric Study Group (PSG). Effect of nitric oxide via cardiopulmonary bypass on ventilator-free days in young children undergoing congenital heart disease surgery: the NITRIC randomized clinical trial. JAMA 2022;328:38–47. https://doi.org/10.1001/jama.2022.9376.

[34] Derwall M, Ebeling A, Nolte KW, Weis J, Rossaint R, Ichinose F, Nix C, Fries M, Brücken A. Inhaled nitric oxide improves transpulmonary blood flow and clinical outcomes after prolonged cardiac arrest: a large animal study. Crit Care 2015;19:328. https://doi.org/10.1186/s13054-015-1050-2.

[35] Liu X, Huang Y, Pokreisz P, Vermeersch P, Marsboom G, Swinnen M, Verbeken E, Santos J, Pellens M, Gillijns H, Van de Werf F, Bloch KD, Janssens S. Nitric oxide inhalation improves microvascular flow and decreases infarction size after myocardial ischemia and reperfusion. J Am Coll Cardiol 2007;50:808–17. https://doi.org/10.1016/j.jacc.2007.04.069.

III. Nitric oxide donors and cardiovascular and metabolic diseases

[36] Minamishima S, Kida K, Tokuda K, Wang H, Sips PY, Kosugi S, Mandeville JB, Buys ES, Brouckaert P, Liu PK, Liu CH, Bloch KD, Ichinose F. Inhaled nitric oxide improves outcomes after successful cardiopulmonary resuscitation in mice. Circulation 2011;124:1645–53. https://doi.org/10.1161/CIRCULATIONAHA.111.025395.

[37] Hayashida K, Bagchi A, Miyazaki Y, Hirai S, Seth D, Silverman MG, Rezoagli E, Marutani E, Mori N, Magliocca A, Liu X, Berra L, Hindle AG, Donnino MW, Malhotra R, Bradley MO, Stamler JS, Ichinose F. Improvement in outcomes after cardiac arrest and resuscitation by inhibition of S-nitrosoglutathione reductase. Circulation 2019;139:815–27. https://doi.org/10.1161/CIRCULATIONAHA.117.032488.

[38] Lang Jr JD, Smith AB, Brandon A, Bradley KM, Liu Y, Li W, Crowe DR, Jhala NC, Cross RC, Frenette L, Martay K, Vater YL, Vitin AA, Dembo GA, DuBay DA, Bynon JS, Szychowski JM, Reyes JD, Halldorson JB, Rayhill SC, Dick AA, Bakthavatsalam R, Brandenberger J, Broeckel-Elrod JA, Sissons-Ross L, Jordan T, Chen LY, Siriussawakul A, Eckhoff DE, Patel RP. A randomized clinical trial testing the anti-inflammatory effects of preemptive inhaled nitric oxide in human liver transplantation. PLoS One 2014;9:e86053. https://doi.org/10.1371/journal.pone.0086053.

[39] Janssens SP, Bogaert J, Zalewski J, Toth A, Adriaenssens T, Belmans A, Bennett J, Claus P, Desmet W, Dubois C, Goetschalckx K, Sinnaeve P, Vandenberghe K, Vermeersch P, Lux A, Szelid Z, Durak M, Lech P, Zmudka K, Pokreisz P, Vranckx P, Merkely B, Bloch KD, Van de Werf F, NOMI Investigators. Nitric oxide for inhalation in ST-elevation myocardial infarction (NOMI): a multicentre, double-blind, randomized controlled trial. Eur Heart J 2018;39:2717–25. https://doi.org/10.1093/eurheartj/ehy232.

[40] Minneci PC, Deans KJ, Zhi H, Yuen PST, Star RA, Banks SM, Schechter AN, Natanson C, Gladwin MT, Solomon SB. Hemolysis-associated endothelial dysfunction mediated by accelerated NO inactivation by decompartmentalized oxyhemoglobin. J Clin Invest 2005;115:3409–17. https://doi.org/10.1172/JCI25040.

[41] Lei C, Berra L, Rezoagli E, Yu B, Dong H, Yu S, Hou L, Chen M, Chen W, Wang H, Zheng Q, Shen J, Jin Z, Chen T, Zhao R, Christie E, Sabbisetti VS, Nordio F, Bonventre JV, Xiong L, Zapol WM. Nitric oxide decreases acute kidney injury and stage 3 chronic kidney disease after cardiac surgery. Am J Respir Crit Care Med 2018;198:1279–87. https://doi.org/10.1164/rccm.201710-2150OC.

[42] Hu J, Rezoagli E, Zadek F, Bittner EA, Lei C, Berra L. Free hemoglobin ratio as a novel biomarker of acute kidney injury after on-pump cardiac surgery: secondary analysis of a randomized controlled trial. Anesth Analg 2021;132:1548–58. https://doi.org/10.1213/ANE.0000000000005381.

[43] Kamenshchikov NO, Anfinogenova YJ, Kozlov BN, Svirko YS, Pekarskiy SE, Evtushenko VV, Lugovsky VA, Shipulin VM, Lomivorotov VV, Podoksenov YK. Nitric oxide delivery during cardiopulmonary bypass reduces acute kidney injury: a randomized trial. J Thorac Cardiovasc Surg 2022;163:1393–1403.e9. https://doi.org/10.1016/j.jtcvs.2020.03.182.

[44] Kamenshchikov NO, Mandel IA, Podoksenov YK, Svirko YS, Lomivorotov VV, Mikheev SL, Kozlov BN, Shipulin VM, Nenakhova AA, Anfinogenova YJ. Nitric oxide provides myocardial protection when added to the cardiopulmonary bypass circuit during cardiac surgery: randomized trial. J Thorac Cardiovasc Surg 2019;157:2328–2336.e1. https://doi.org/10.1016/j.jtcvs.2018.08.117.

[45] Wiegand SB, Traeger L, Nguyen HK, Rouillard KR, Fischbach A, Zadek F, Ichinose F, Schoenfisch MH, Carroll RW, Bloch DB, Zapol WM. Antimicrobial effects of nitric oxide in murine models of Klebsiella pneumonia. Redox Biol 2021;39:101826. https://doi.org/10.1016/j.redox.2020.101826.

[46] Bartley BL, Gardner KJ, Spina S, Hurley BP, Campeau D, Berra L, Yonker LM, Carroll RW. High-dose inhaled nitric oxide as adjunct therapy in cystic fibrosis targeting Burkholderia multivorans. Case Rep Pediatr 2020;2020:1536714. https://doi.org/10.1155/2020/1536714.

[47] Barraud N, Schleheck D, Klebensberger J, Webb JS, Hassett DJ, Rice SA, Kjelleberg S. Nitric oxide signaling in Pseudomonas aeruginosa biofilms mediates phosphodiesterase activity, decreased cyclic Di-GMP levels, and enhanced dispersal. J Bacteriol 2009;191:7333–42. https://doi.org/10.1128/JB.00975-09.

[48] Howlin RP, Cathie K, Hall-Stoodley L, Cornelius V, Duignan C, Allan RN, Fernandez BO, Barraud N, Bruce KD, Jefferies J, Kelso M, Kjelleberg S, Rice SA, Rogers GB, Pink S, Smith C, Sukhtankar PS, Salib R, Legg J, Carroll M, Daniels T, Feelisch M, Stoodley P, Clarke SC, Connett G, Faust SN, Webb JS. Low-dose nitric oxide as targeted anti-biofilm adjunctive therapy to treat chronic Pseudomonas aeruginosa infection in cystic fibrosis. Mol Ther 2017;25:2104–16. https://doi.org/10.1016/j.ymthe.2017.06.021.

[49] Ahonen MJR, Dorrier JM, Schoenfisch MH. Antibiofilm efficacy of nitric oxide-releasing alginates against cystic fibrosis bacterial pathogens. ACS Infect Dis 2019;5:1327–35. https://doi.org/10.1021/acsinfecdis.9b00016.

[50] Regev-Shoshani G, Vimalanathan S, McMullin B, Road J, Av-Gay Y, Miller C. Gaseous nitric oxide reduces influenza infectivity in vitro. Nitric Oxide 2013;31:48–53. https://doi.org/10.1016/j.niox.2013.03.007.

[51] Miller C, McMullin B, Ghaffari A, Stenzler A, Pick N, Roscoe D, Ghahary A, Road J, Av-Gay Y. Gaseous nitric oxide bactericidal activity retained during intermittent high-dose short duration exposure. Nitric Oxide 2009;20:16–23. https://doi.org/10.1016/j.niox.2008.08.002.

[52] Akaberi D, Krambrich J, Ling J, Luni C, Hedenstierna G, Järhult JD, Lennerstrand J, Lundkvist Å. Mitigation of the replication of SARS-CoV-2 by nitric oxide in vitro. Redox Biol 2020;101734. https://doi.org/10.1016/j.redox.2020.101734.

[53] Goldbart A, Golan-Tripto I, Pillar G, Livnat-Levanon G, Efrati O, Spiegel R, Lubetzky R, Lavie M, Carmon L, Nahum A. Inhaled nitric oxide therapy in acute bronchiolitis: a multicenter randomized clinical trial. Sci Rep 2020;10:9605. https://doi.org/10.1038/s41598-020-66433-8.

[54] Chen L, Liu P, Gao H, Sun B, Chao D, Wang F, Zhu Y, Hedenstierna G, Wang CG. Inhalation of nitric oxide in the treatment of severe acute respiratory syndrome: a rescue trial in Beijing. Clin Infect Dis 2004;39:1531–5. https://doi.org/10.1086/425357.

[55] Safaee Fakhr B, Di Fenza R, Gianni S, Wiegand SB, Miyazaki Y, Araujo Morais CC, Gibson LE, Chang MG, Mueller AL, Rodriguez-Lopez JM, Ackman JB, Arora P, Scott LK, Bloch DB, Zapol WM, Carroll RW, Ichinose F, Berra L, Nitric Oxide Study Investigators. Inhaled high dose nitric oxide is a safe and effective respiratory treatment in spontaneous breathing hospitalized patients with COVID-19 pneumonia. Nitric Oxide 2021;116:7–13. https://doi.org/10.1016/j.niox.2021.08.003.

[56] Wiegand SB, Safaee Fakhr B, Carroll RW, Zapol WM, Kacmarek RM, Berra L. Rescue treatment with high-dose gaseous nitric oxide in spontaneously breathing patients with severe coronavirus disease 2019. Crit Care Explor 2020;2:e0277. https://doi.org/10.1097/CCE.0000000000000277.

[57] Valsecchi C, Winterton D, Safaee Fakhr B, Collier AY, Nozari A, Ortoleva J, Mukerji S, Gibson LE, Carroll RW, Shaefi S, Pinciroli R, La Vita C, Ackman JB, Hohmann E, Arora P, Barth WHJ, Kaimal A, Ichinose F, Berra L, DELiverly oF iNO (DELFiNO) Network Collaborators. High-dose inhaled nitric oxide for the treatment of spontaneously breathing pregnant patients with severe coronavirus disease 2019 (COVID-19) pneumonia. Obstet Gynecol 2022. https://doi.org/10.1097/AOG.0000000000004847.

[58] Lei C, Su B, Dong H, Bellavia A, Di Fenza R, Safaee Fakhr B, Gianni S, Grassi LG, Kacmarek R, Araujo Morais CC, Pinciroli R, Vassena E, Berra L. Protocol of a randomized controlled trial testing inhaled nitric oxide in mechanically ventilated patients with severe acute respiratory syndrome in COVID-19 (SARS-CoV-2). MedRxiv 2020. https://doi.org/10.1101/2020.03.09.20033530.

[59] Drugs@FDA: FDA-approved drugs; n.d. https://www.accessdata.fda.gov/scripts/cder/daf/index.cfm?event=BasicSearch.process (Accessed 31 July 2022).

[60] Gerlach H, Keh D, Semmerow A, Busch T, Lewandowski K, Pappert DM, Rossaint R, Falke KJ. Dose-response characteristics during long-term inhalation of nitric oxide in patients with severe acute respiratory distress syndrome: a prospective, randomized, controlled study. Am J Respir Crit Care Med 2003;167:1008–15. https://doi.org/10.1164/rccm.2108121.

[61] Roberts JD, Chiche JD, Weimann J, Steudel W, Zapol WM, Bloch KD. Nitric oxide inhalation decreases pulmonary artery remodeling in the injured lungs of rat pups. Circ Res 2000;87:140–5. https://doi.org/10.1161/01.res.87.2.140.

[62] Hedenstierna G, Chen L, Hedenstierna M, Lieberman R, Fine DH. Nitric oxide dosed in short bursts at high concentrations may protect against Covid 19. Nitric Oxide 2020;103:1–3. https://doi.org/10.1016/j.niox.2020.06.005.

[63] Ignarro LJ. Inhaled NO and COVID-19. Br J Pharmacol 2020;177:3848–9. https://doi.org/10.1111/bph.15085.

[64] Hetrick EM, Schoenfisch MH. Analytical chemistry of nitric oxide. Annu Rev Anal Chem (Palo Alto, Calif) 2009;2:409–33. https://doi.org/10.1146/annurev-anchem-060908-155146.

[65] Aylott JW, Richardson DJ, Russell DA. Optical biosensing of gaseous nitric oxide using spin-coated sol−gel thin films. Chem Mater 1997;9:2261–3. https://doi.org/10.1021/cm970324v.

[66] Dacres H, Narayanaswamy R, Dacres H, Narayanaswamy R. Evaluation of copper(ii) eriochrome cyanine R (ECR) complex immobilized in anion exchange membrane as a potential nitric oxide optical sensor. Aust J Chem 2008;61:189–96. https://doi.org/10.1071/CH07281.

[67] Toda K, Hato Y, Ohira S, Namihira T. Micro-gas analysis system for measurement of nitric oxide and nitrogen dioxide: respiratory treatment and environmental mobile monitoring. Anal Chim Acta 2007;603:60–6. https://doi.org/10.1016/j.aca.2007.09.052.

[68] Fenza RD, Yu B, Carroll RW, Berra L. Chemiluminescence-based assays for detection of nitric oxide and its derivatives from autoxidation and nitrosated compounds. J Vis Exp 2022;e63107. https://doi.org/10.3791/63107.

III. Nitric oxide donors and cardiovascular and metabolic diseases

[69] Purtz EP, Hess D, Kacmarek RM. Evaluation of electrochemical nitric oxide and nitrogen dioxide analyzers suitable for use during mechanical ventilation. J Clin Monit 1997;13:25–34. https://doi.org/10.1023/a:1007301912697.

[70] Baysal A. Nitric oxide I: advances in the measurements for clinical applications. Turk J Med Sci 2001;31:471–6.

[71] Zaouter C, Zavorsky GS. The measurement of carboxyhemoglobin and methemoglobin using a non-invasive pulse CO-oximeter. Respir Physiol Neurobiol 2012;182:88–92. https://doi.org/10.1016/j.resp.2012.05.010.

[72] Feiner JR, Bickler PE, Mannheimer PD. Accuracy of methemoglobin detection by pulse CO-oximetry during hypoxia. Anesth Analg 2010;111:143–8. https://doi.org/10.1213/ANE.0b013e3181c91bb6.

[73] 1988 OSHA PEL Project—Nitrogen Dioxide. NIOSH. CDC; 2020. https://www.cdc.gov/niosh/pel88/10102-44.html. [Accessed 11 June 2020].

[74] 1988 OSHA PEL Project—Nitrogen Dioxide. NIOSH. CDC; 2020. https://www.cdc.gov/niosh/pel88/10102-44.html. [Accessed 8 May 2022].

[75] Cueto R, Pryor WA. Cigarette smoke chemistry: conversion of nitric oxide to nitrogen dioxide and reactions of nitrogen oxides with other smoke components as studied by Fourier transform infrared spectroscopy. Vib Spectrosc 1994;7:97–111. https://doi.org/10.1016/0924-2031(94)85045-3.

[76] Kebabian PL, Herndon SC, Freedman A. Detection of nitrogen dioxide by cavity attenuated phase shift spectroscopy. Anal Chem 2005;77:724–8. https://doi.org/10.1021/ac048715y.

[77] Safaee Fakhr B, Wiegand SB, Pinciroli R, Gianni S, Morais CCA, Ikeda T, Miyazaki Y, Marutani E, Di Fenza R, Larson GM, Parcha V, Gibson LE, Chang MG, Arora P, Carroll RW, Kacmarek RM, Ichinose F, Barth WH, Kaimal A, Hohmann EL, Zapol WM, Berra L. High concentrations of nitric oxide inhalation therapy in pregnant patients with severe coronavirus disease 2019 (COVID-19). Obstet Gynecol 2020;136:1109–13. https://doi.org/10.1097/AOG.0000000000004128.

[78] Hu J, Spina S, Zadek F, Kamenshchikov NO, Bittner EA, Pedemonte J, Berra L. Effect of nitric oxide on postoperative acute kidney injury in patients who underwent cardiopulmonary bypass: a systematic review and meta-analysis with trial sequential analysis. Ann Intensive Care 2019;9:129. https://doi.org/10.1186/s13613-019-0605-9.

[79] Gianni S, Carroll RW, Kacmarek RM, Berra L. Inhaled nitric oxide delivery systems for mechanically ventilated and nonintubated patients: a review. Respir Care 2021;66:1021–8. https://doi.org/10.4187/respcare.08856.

[80] Zapol WM. Nitric oxide story. Anesthesiology 2019;130:435–40. https://doi.org/10.1097/ALN.0000000000002579.

[81] Yu B, Muenster S, Blaesi AH, Bloch DB, Zapol WM. Producing nitric oxide by pulsed electrical discharge in air for portable inhalation therapy. Sci Transl Med 2015;7:294ra107. https://doi.org/10.1126/scitranslmed.aaa3097.

[82] Yu B, Blaesi AH, Casey N, Raykhtsaum G, Zazzeron L, Jones R, Morrese A, Dobrynin D, Malhotra R, Bloch DB, Goldstein LE, Zapol WM. Detection and removal of impurities in nitric oxide generated from air by pulsed electrical discharge. Nitric Oxide 2016;60:16–23. https://doi.org/10.1016/j.niox.2016.08.005.

[83] Berra L, Rodriguez-Lopez J, Rezoagli E, Yu B, Fisher DF, Semigran MJ, Bloch DB, Channick RN, Zapol WM. Electric plasma-generated nitric oxide: hemodynamic effects in patients with pulmonary hypertension. Am J Respir Crit Care Med 2016;194:1168–70. https://doi.org/10.1164/rccm.201604-0834LE.

[84] Lovich MA, Bruno NK, Plant CP, Wei AE, Vasquez GB, Johnson BJ, Fine DH, Gilbert RJ. Use of ultra pure nitric oxide generated by the reduction of nitrogen dioxide to reverse pulmonary hypertension in hypoxemic swine. Nitric Oxide 2011;24:204–12. https://doi.org/10.1016/j.niox.2011.04.006.

[85] Lovich MA, Fine DH, Denton RJ, Wakim MG, Wei AE, Maslov MY, Gamero LG, Vasquez GB, Johnson BJ, Roscigno RF, Gilbert RJ. Generation of purified nitric oxide from liquid N2O4 for the treatment of pulmonary hypertension in hypoxemic swine. Nitric Oxide 2014;37:66–72. https://doi.org/10.1016/j.niox.2014.02.001.

[86] Stenzler A. Compositions and methods for treating diseases or disorders using extended release nitric oxide releasing solutions, US20150328256A1., 2015, https://patents.google.com/patent/US20150328256A1/en. [Accessed 13 May 2022].

[87] Friedman AJ, Han G, Navati MS, Chacko M, Gunther L, Alfieri A, Friedman JM. Sustained release nitric oxide releasing nanoparticles: characterization of a novel delivery platform based on nitrite containing hydrogel/glass composites. Nitric Oxide 2008;19:12–20. https://doi.org/10.1016/j.niox.2008.04.003.

Mechanistic insights on the role of nitric oxide in ischemia-reperfusion injury

Bhaskar Arora, Heena Khan, Amarjot Kaur Grewal, and Thakur Gurjeet Singh

Chitkara College of Pharmacy, Chitkara University, Rajpura, Punjab, India

Abstract

Cerebral ischemia is a major cause of acute brain damage due to decreased blood supply to the brain. Excitotoxicity, intracellular calcium accumulation, reactive oxygen species generation, membrane lipid breakdown, and DNA damage are undesirable processes that impair cellular homeostasis and cause structural damage to ischemic tissue. Ischemia also generates acute inflammation, which worsens the primary organ damage. As potential treatments for ischemic stroke, lowering oxidative stress and regulating the inflammatory response are crucial features to be investigated. As there are now no clinically effective drugs and no specific therapies for stroke, chemicals that can affect both features will provide intriguing alternative treatments. Because of their ability to regulate both oxidative stress and inflammation, the role of nitric oxide donors in the pathophysiology of ischemia-reperfusion injury has garnered considerable interest. In this chapter, the possible protective effects of nitric oxide donors and inhibitors in ischemia/reperfusion therapy are discussed.

Abbreviations

AKT	Ak strain transforming
AMPK	AMP-activated protein kinase
CBF	cerebral blood flow
cGMP	cyclic guanosine monophosphate
CREB	cyclic AMP-response element binding protein
eNOS	endothelial nitric oxide synthase
ERK	extracellular signal-regulated kinases
GSNO	*S*-nitroso glutathione
GTN	glyceryl trinitrate
IFN-γ	interferon gamma
IGL-1	Institut Georges Lopez-1

Nitric Oxide in Health and Disease
https://doi.org/10.1016/B978-0-443-13342-8.00004-1

IL-1	interleukin-1
iNOS	inducible nitric oxide synthase
IRI	ischemic reperfusion injury
JNK	c-Jun N-terminal kinases
L-NAME	N(G)-nitro-L-arginine methyl ester
L-NMMA	N(G)-methyl-L-arginine acetate
L-NNA, L-NOARG	N(G)-nitro-L-arginine
LPS	lipopolysaccharides
MAPK	mitogen-activated protein kinases
MCAO	middle cerebral artery occlusion
NMDA	N-methyl-D-aspartate
nNOS	neuronal nitric oxide synthase
NO	nitric oxide
NOD	nitric oxide donors
ROS	reactive oxygen species
SGC	soluble guanylate cyclase
SIN1	SAPK-interacting protein 1
SNP	sodium nitroprusside
TBI	traumatic brain injury
TNF	tumor necrosis factor

Conflict of interest

No potential conflicts of interest were disclosed.

Introduction

Nitric oxide (NO) is a gas produced by the enzyme nitric oxide synthase (NOS) from L-arginine. NO functions as an inter- and intracellular messenger in a variety of cell types, including articular chondrocytes and induces apoptosis in several cell systems [1]. As a neurotransmitter, it is a component of the signaling pathways that operate between blood vessels, neurons, and glial cells of the brain. NOS has three isoforms: neuronal nitric oxide synthase (nNOS), endothelial nitric oxide synthase (eNOS), and inducible nitric oxide synthase (iNOS). When the NO pathway is interrupted, numerous mechanisms responsible for brain injury are disrupted, and the NO released from each of the three isoforms has a different effect on the progression of brain damage [2].

Nitric oxide regulates numerous physiological and pathological processes, including cell division, proliferation, and inflammation [3]. Pharmacologically active substances that secrete NO in vivo or in vitro are known as NO donors. Nitroglycerin (glyceryl trinitrate), isosorbide dinitrate, isosorbide mononitrate, and isoamyl nitrite are examples of nitric oxide donors. The identification of nitric oxide as an endothelium-derived relaxing agent has provided a pharmacological basis for the role of NO donors [4]. NO synthase inhibitors are a well-studied class of drugs that may be useful for treating diseases characterized by excessive NO production. L-NMMA and L-NAME are specific NOS inhibitors [5]. The action of NO is not confined to vasodilation alone (Table 1). NO, on the other hand, has several activities, including the secretion of prostanoids in infarcted myocardium, suppression of platelet aggregation and leukocyte adhesion, maintenance of vascular impermeability, an influence on angiogenesis, and the reaction with oxygen and generating free radicals [14].

TABLE 1 Nitric oxide donors in ischemic reperfusion injury.

S. no.	Nitric oxide donor	Species	Model use	Dose	Effects	References
1.	GSNO	Rat	MCAO	1 mg/kg	Decreased infarct size Increase in CBF Inhibition of monocyte/macrophage infiltration Downregulates adhesion molecules (ICAM-1, LFA-1)	[6]
2.	ZJM-289	Rat	MCAO	0.1 and 0.2 mmol/kg	Healing in neurological impairment (motor function) Decrease of the infarct size Reduction in brain water content	[7]
3.	Sodium nitrate	Rat	MCAO	480 nmol	Decreased infarct size Improvement in motor function Reduction of microhypoxic areas	[8]
4.	SIN-1	Rat	Permanent MCAO	3 mg/kg	Reduction in infarct size Increase in CBF	[9]
5.	SNP	Rat	4-VO	5 mg/kg	Elevation of Akt and Bad phosphorylation, preventing the release of cytochrome c within mitochondria	[10]
6.	Inhaled NO	Mice	TBI	50 ppm	Decreased lesion volume and improved neurological function	[11]
7.	L-Arginine	Rat	MCAO	300 mg/kg	Decreased infarct volume by 35%	[12]
8.	ProliNO/ NONO- ate	Rabbit and rat	MCAO	Rabbit: 10–6 mol/L Rat: 10–5 mol/L	Decrease in free reactive oxygen species and infarct size	[13]

Ischemia restricts blood flow to the brain, heart, liver, lungs, and kidneys, resulting in decreased glucose and oxygen delivery to these organs [15]. The secondary treatment for an ischemia-reperfusion injury (IRI) is to restore blood flow to the affected tissue. IRI is characterized by an increase in the generation of reactive oxygen species and pro-inflammatory chemicals, which cause significant tissue damage [16].

The cellular oxidative status of NO donors influences the neuroprotective effects of NO donors at various stages of cerebral ischemia-reperfusion injury. SNP and NONOate, when administered early after transient focal cerebral ischemia, can help reduce the extent of the infarct [17]. On the other hand, S-nitrosothiols (GSNO and SNAP) and SIN-1 decreased the size of the infarct and enhanced neurological function [18]. SNP, GSNO, and SNAP improve CBF in the penumbral region when delivered at the commencement of reperfusion [19].

III. Nitric oxide donors and cardiovascular and metabolic diseases

Nitric oxide derivatives

Nitric oxide donors

Nitric oxide donors are pharmacologically active substances that secrete NO in vivo or in vitro. NO has multiple roles, including the synthesis of prostanoids, suppression of platelets, angiogenesis, and generation of oxygen free radicals. In preclinical and clinical research, a variety of NO donors have been employed to replenish NO levels depleted by ischemia and reperfusion. Nitroglycerin and sodium nitroprusside (SNP) are NO donors in addition to glyceryl trinitrate (GTN) and isosorbide-5-mononitrate. Multiple studies have proven a neuroprotective effect of NO donors on experimental stroke, following the early success of NO donors in ameliorating kidney and liver damage in rats exposed to IRI settings [20,21]. Regarding myocardial IRI, NO donors have demonstrated positive effects in animal research, but clinical trials have been less clear [22]. It has been discovered that plasma NO levels in patients with acute myocardial infarction are much lower. Based on this finding, a study was carried out using an SNP pad to raise systemic NO levels in cancer patients, who typically have a higher chance of death from an acute myocardial infarction than the overall population. After several years of utilizing SNP pads, the plasma NO concentration was returned to baseline, preventing the death of individuals who sustained an acute myocardial infarction [23,24]. However, sodium nitrite had little effect on the infarction's severity. In a trial with patients who had an acute ST-elevation myocardial infarction, administering sodium nitrite intravenously before reperfusion did not decrease infarction [25] (Table 1).

Nitric oxide inhibitors (see Table 2)

In animal models of severe diseases where significant levels of iNOS-derived NO have been detected, either as a source or as a result of the disease, NO inhibitors are frequently administered. L-Arginine-derived analogs, such as L-NMMA and L-NAME, have been

TABLE 2 Nitric oxide inhibitors in ischemic reperfusion injury.

S. no.	Nitric oxide inhibitors	Species	Model use	Dose	Effects	References
1.	L-NNA	Dog	In vivo	360 μg/kg	Decrease in regional myocardial function assessed as a decrease in wall thickening	[26]
2.	L-NMMA	Rabbit	In vitro	1 μM	An increase in left ventricular developed pressure	[27]
3.	L-NAME	Rat	In vivo	100 μM	Decrease in cardiac output	[28]
4.	L-NOARG	Rat	In vitro	10 μM	Decrease in left ventricular developed pressure	[29]
5.	L-NAME	Dog	In vivo	20 μg/kg	Increase in regional myocardial function was assessed as an increase in wall thickening	[30]

synthesized and identified as competitive NOS inhibitors. All of these early inhibitors exhibited the property of nonselectivity concerning the NO source (i.e., isoforms of NOS) [31].

Selective NOS inhibitors: There is a large number of "isoform selective" NOS inhibitors available, which solely inhibit the neuronal isoform of the enzyme. 7-Nitroindazole and its analogs are examples of nNOS inhibitors, while aminoguanidine and *S*-alkylated isothiourea derivatives are examples of iNOS inhibitors [32]. Because NO produced by iNOS is crucial in mediating the cardiovascular disturbances that are characteristic of septic shock, researchers are focusing their efforts on identifying an iNOS inhibitor (Table 2). Remarkably, nonselective NOS inhibitors employed in prior trials have shown diverse results [33].

Nonselective NOS inhibitors: Individuals with septic shock are treated with N(G)-methyl-L-arginine hydrochloride, a nonselective NOS inhibitor. N(G)-methyl-L-arginine hydrochloride can restore the balance of vasomotor tone. Other synthetic nonselective NOS inhibitors, such as L-NAME and L-NNA, are associated with drug abuse since they decrease the symptoms of opioid withdrawal in rats [31].

Nitric oxide pathophysiology in ischemic reperfusion injury

NO can pass through cell membranes being a gaseous molecule with a short half-life. In biological tissues, endothelial NO synthase (eNOS or NOS3), neuronal NO synthase (nNOS or NOS1), and inducible NO synthase (iNOS or NOS2) generate NO from L-arginine. This causes a general rise in NO levels when constitutively expressed. Once activated, iNOS is capable of releasing a substantial amount of NO, but it is particularly effective at producing NO in inflammatory cells such as macrophages and astrocytes [34]. NO synthesis by iNOS is induced by an increase in the levels of tumor necrosis factor (TNF), interleukin-1 (IL-1), and lipopolysaccharides (LPS) [35].

NO performs its function in part by interacting directly with specific proteins. Consequently, cysteine and glutathione may form disulfide bonds [36]. NO has also been demonstrated to increase cell signaling by boosting cyclic guanosine monophosphate (cGMP) production. In addition to its involvement in normal physiological function, NO is an important mediator in cellular disorders induced by inflammation and a defective oxygen supply (Fig. 1). eNOS activity was observed to be reduced during IRI, resulting in decreased NO generation [37]. Ischemia in the brain tissue of stroke patients modifies NO levels. eNOS and nNOS activities have been reported to decrease significantly in cases of ischemia [38]. As a result, by occluding middle cerebral artery, it has been revealed that the ischemic brain's NO level decreased significantly following reperfusion [39]. Due to the pathophysiology of NO in IRI, numerous studies have been conducted to determine the impact of NO on tissue injury protection. According to the studied literature, during the initial phases of cerebral ischemia, it is advantageous to provide the patient with nitric oxide. The protective effect could be attributed to an improvement in CBF to the ischemic region, most likely the ischemic penumbra. These data show that NO donors may provide a novel therapeutic technique for acute stroke treatment (Fig. 1).

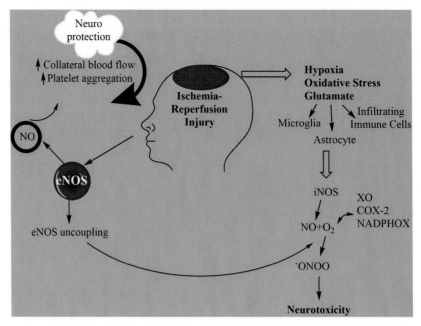

FIG. 1 Overview of nitric-oxide pathway. Brain ischemia and reperfusion lead to stimulation of endothelial NOS (eNOS), resulting in brief increases in endothelial NO generation, associated with neuroprotective actions. Energy depletion and oxidant production trigger the release of glutamate, which results in upregulated inducible NOS (iNOS) in astrocytes, microglia, and infiltrating inflammatory cells. iNOS activation also occurs in response to the release of inflammatory cytokines such as TNFα and IFNβ, and cellular signaling pathways responsible for the response to hypoxia. During the same period of time, superoxide production is enhanced due to uncoupling of eNOS, mitochondrial dysfunction, and the stimulated activity of NADPH oxidase, xanthine oxidase (XO), and cyclooxygenase-2 (COX-2).

Signaling pathways mediated by nitric oxide involved in ischemia-reperfusion injury

As reported in Fig. 2, the various pathways involved in NO cellular actions are presented:

a. **MAPK pathway**: NO appears to be an important modulator of mitogen-activated protein kinases (MAPKs) [40]. MAPKs can transduce signals into cellular responses by modulating gene and protein expression involved in cell differentiation, proliferation, survival, and death [41]. Some of the MAPKs include extracellular signal-regulated kinases (ERK), c-Jun N-terminal kinases (JNK), and p38 kinases [42]. These MAPKs are activated due to early events of I/R, including the activation of TNF-α and other proteins. ERK, p38 MAPK, and JNK are activated by NO-related species and participate in NO signal transduction. NO influences downstream MAPK activation through the nitrosylation of critical thiol residues, which possibly activates specific protein kinase C (PKC) isoforms [43].

   A mechanism was investigated by which NO exerts beneficial effects. NO can induce preconditioning of hepatocytes by promoting the sequential activation of guanylate cyclase, cGK, and p38 MAPK [44]. A study was sought to investigate the role of the p38

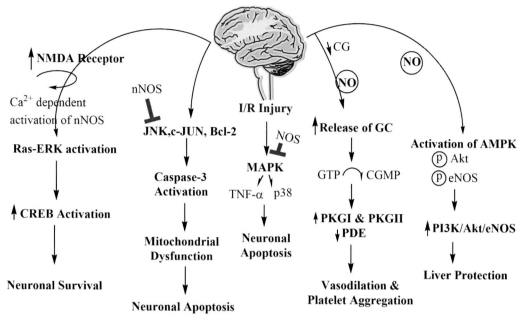

FIG. 2 Schematic representation of how modulation of nitric oxide leads to neuronal survival and apoptosis. Activation of NMDA receptor causes activation of Ras-ERK and CREB activation leading to neuronal survival; nNOS inhibits MAPK and JNK, c-JUN, Bcl-2 which will further hinder TNF-α, caspase-3 activation, mitochondrial dysfunction and neuronal apoptosis; NO stimulates the release of cGMP produced by guanyl cyclase (GC) which further decreases PDE and increases PKG I and PKG II activation, leading to vasodilation and platelet aggregation; Activation of AMPK stimulates PI3K/Akt/eNOS pathway providing the organ protection.

MAPK signal transduction pathway on apoptosis induced by NO. It was demonstrated the p38 signal transduction pathway of NO-induced articular chondrocyte apoptosis in a rabbit model [45,46]. It has also been suggested that MAPKs can intensify inflammatory signaling and that the appropriate inhibition of MAPKs could potentially help ameliorate the ischemic response [47,48].

b. **JNK3 pathway**: Cerebral ischemia-reperfusion boosts nNOS activity, which improves its NO synthesis. This NO can react with free radicals to produce $ONOO^-$ and also activates the JNK3 pathway. The result is c-Jun phosphorylation and mitochondrial dysfunction, with an increase in Bcl2 phosphorylation and cytochrome C release into the cytoplasm. In addition, this activates caspase-3 and leads to neuronal apoptosis [49,50]. Nitric oxide donors-derived NO downregulates neuronal apoptosis by inhibiting increased phosphorylation of JNK, c-Jun, and Bcl-2. This is achieved by S-nitrosylation of nNOS, which interferes with its NO production [51]. It was demonstrated that the S-nitrosylation of cysteine 116 in the macrophage JNK1 follows the IFN-γ induced production of NO and that this modification causes significant inhibition of JNK1 activity. It was also reported that the IFN-γ-induced production of NO could inhibit the activation of ASK1 through a thiol redox mechanism [52]. A recent study demonstrated that after global cerebral ischemia, endogenous NO produced by NOS enhanced S-nitrosylation of JNK3, which leads to the activation of JNK3. However, exogenous NO decreases the level of S-nitrosylation and phosphorylation of JNK3 via inhibiting NOS. Thus, exogenous NO provides a neuroprotective role on ischemia/reperfusion-induced brain injury [10,53].

c. **NO-cGMP pathway**: The major target of NO in the cardiovascular system is the soluble guanylyl cyclase [54]. Activation of the guanylyl cyclase results in the conversion of GTP to the cGMP. cGMP activates two specific cGMP-dependent protein kinases (PKG I and II), PKG I being the most important for vasodilation and inhibition of platelet aggregation [55]. CGMP also inhibits the activity of PDE II and III; inhibition of PDE III elevates the concentration of cyclic adenosine monophosphate (cAMP), thereby subsequently increasing the activity of protein kinase A [56]. During ischemia, the ensuing acidosis reduces the guanylyl cyclase activity in isolated rat cardiomyocytes [57,58], thereby potentially counterbalancing the increased NO concentration during early ischemia [59,60]. According to reported studies, cGMP dose-dependently inhibits PDE or activates PKG, thereby mediating its effects on the vasculature, platelets, and myocytes. NO has also been shown to activate sGC, which leads to an elevation of cGMP. cGMP, through downstream effectors, has been shown to regulate neurotransmission, cell migration, proliferation, differentiation, survival, axon outgrowth and guidance, and visual signal transduction [61].

d. **ERK pathway**: Stimulation of the NMDA receptor activates the Ras-ERK pathway via calcium-dependent activation of nNOS and NO generation [62]. NMDA-stimulated phosphorylation of cAMP-response element binding protein (CREB), a downstream effector of ERK, is also NO-dependent [63]. Activation of the Ras/ERK pathway by NO may be mediated by direct activation of Ras GTPase activity presumably by nitrosylation of cysteine through a redox-sensitive interaction. Calcium-dependent activation of the Ras-MAPK pathway is thought to be a major pathway of neural activity-dependent long-term changes in the nervous system [64]. NO may be a key mediator linking activity to gene expression and long-term plasticity. NO donors activate all three types of MAPKs (ERK, JNK/SAPK, p38 MAPK). It is also known that the ERK pathways are implicated in neuronal survival [65].

e. **PI3K-eNOS/NO pathway**: PI3K is a heterodimer composed of the catalytic subunit p10 and regulatory subunit p85 and is also a lipid second messenger. PI3K can phosphorylate the serine/threonine of its downstream signal kinase Akt, which may further phosphorylate eNOS to promote an increase in endogenous NO generation [66]. The protective effect of rHuEPO in IR injury is mediated via the activation of the PI3K/Akt/eNOS signaling pathway, at least in part, by increasing p-Akt and p-eNOS, which leads to the maintenance of an elevated level of NO [67,68]. It has been also reported that IGL-1 solution results in better liver preservation and protection against hepatic ischemic reperfusion injury by activating Akt and AMPK, which are concomitant with increased eNOS expression and nitrite/nitrate levels [69].

Conclusion

During ischemic reperfusion injury, NO plays a complex role. NO can participate in immunological modulation, suppresses the inflammatory cascade, prevents the production of the p53 gene and the accumulation of proinflammatory cytokines and chemokines, reduces ROS by blocking the mitochondrial respiratory chain, and has antiinflammatory characteristics. Additionally, NO triggers the NO/cGMP pathway as the first messenger to prevent [Na^+] from entering the cells. Ischemic reperfusion injury may be prevented and treated by effectively increasing NO levels, such as by using exogenous NO donors or increasing NO availability. It has been demonstrated that NO modulators are neuroprotective and effective in preventing subsequent brain injury in animals, possibly by mimicking a few of the actions of endogenous NO produced by eNOS. As a result, iNOS inhibitors may show promise as prospective neurotherapeutic targets. For future perspective, "stratified medicine" is a new way of regularly finding the most suitable and cost-effective treatment for different patients. It is the classification of patients based on illness risk or therapeutic response utilizing diagnostic tests or procedures. In stratified medicine, a clinical biomarker is analyzed to connect a patient with a certain treatment.

References

[1] Fukuo K, Hata S, Suhara T, Nakahashi T, Shinto Y, Tsujimoto Y, Morimoto S, Ogihara T. Nitric oxide induces upregulation of Fas and apoptosis in vascular smooth muscle. Hypertension 1996;27(3):823–6.
[2] Toda N, Ayajiki K, Okamura T. Cerebral blood flow regulation by nitric oxide: recent advances. Pharmacol Rev 2009;61(1):62–97.
[3] Ghimire K, Altmann HM, Straub AC, Isenberg JS. Nitric oxide: what's new to NO? Am J Physiol Cell Physiol 2017;312(3):C254–62.
[4] Ignarro LJ, Lippton HO, Edwards JC, Baricos WH, Hyman AL, Kadowitz PJ, Gruetter CA. Mechanism of vascular smooth muscle relaxation by organic nitrates, nitrites, nitroprusside and nitric oxide: evidence for the involvement of S-nitrosothiols as active intermediates. J Pharmacol Exp Ther 1981;218(3):739–49.
[5] Palmer RM, Rees DD, Ashton DS, Moncada S. L-arginine is the physiological precursor for the formation of nitric oxide in endothelium-dependent relaxation. Biochem Biophys Res Commun 1988;153(3):1251–6.
[6] Khan M, Sekhon B, Giri S, Jatana M, Gilg AG, Ayasolla K, Elango C, Singh AK, Singh I. S-Nitrosoglutathione reduces inflammation and protects brain against focal cerebral ischemia in a rat model of experimental stroke. J Cereb Blood Flow Metab 2005;25(2):177–92.
[7] Zhuang P, Ji H, Zhang YH, Min ZL, Ni QG, You R. ZJM-289, a novel nitric oxide donor, alleviates the cerebral ischaemic–reperfusion injury in rats. Clin Exp Pharmacol Physiol 2010;37(3):e121–7.
[8] Jung KH, Chu K, Lee ST, Park HK, Kim JH, Kang KM, Kim M, Lee SK, Roh JK. Augmentation of nitrite therapy in cerebral ischemia by NMDA receptor inhibition. Biochem Biophys Res Commun 2009;378(3):507–12.
[9] Zhang F, White JG, Iadecola C. Nitric oxide donors increase blood flow and reduce brain damage in focal ischemia: evidence that nitric oxide is beneficial in the early stages of cerebral ischemia. J Cereb Blood Flow Metab 1994;14(2):217–26.
[10] Pei DS, Song YJ, Yu HM, Hu WW, Du Y, Zhang GY. Exogenous nitric oxide negatively regulates c-Jun N-terminal kinase activation via inhibiting endogenous NO-induced S-nitrosylation during cerebral ischemia and reperfusion in rat hippocampus. J Neurochem 2008;106(4):1952–63.
[11] Terpolilli NA, Kim SW, Thal SC, Kuebler WM, Plesnila N. Inhaled nitric oxide reduces secondary brain damage after traumatic brain injury in mice. J Cereb Blood Flow Metab 2013;33(2):311–8.
[12] Morikawa E, Moskowitz MA, Huang Z, Yoshida T, Irikura K, Dalkara T. L-arginine infusion promotes nitric oxide-dependent vasodilation, increases regional cerebral blood flow, and reduces infarction volume in the rat. Stroke 1994;25(2):429–35.
[13] Pluta RM, Rak R, Wink DA, Woodward JJ, Khaldi A, Oldfield EH, Watson JC. Effects of nitric oxide on reactive oxygen species production and infarction size after brain reperfusion injury. Neurosurgery 2001;48(4):884–93.
[14] Yamamoto T, Kakar NR, Vina ER, Johnson PE, Bing RJ. The effect of aspirin and two nitric oxide donors on the infarcted heart in situ. Life Sci 2000;67(7):839–46.
[15] Kerrigan CL, Stotland MA. Ischemia reperfusion injury: a review. Microsurgery 1993;14(3):165–75.
[16] Wu MY, Yiang GT, Liao WT, Tsai AP, Cheng YL, Cheng PW, Li CY, Li CJ. Current mechanistic concepts in ischemia and reperfusion injury. Cell Physiol Biochem 2018;46(4):1650–67.
[17] Salom JB, Ortí M, Centeno JM, Torregrosa G, Alborch E. Reduction of infarct size by the NO donors sodium nitroprusside and spermine/NO after transient focal cerebral ischemia in rats. Brain Res 2000;865(2):149–56.

[18] Khan M, Jatana M, Elango C, Paintlia AS, Singh AK, Singh I. Cerebrovascular protection by various nitric oxide donors in rats after experimental stroke. Nitric Oxide 2006;15(2):114–24.

[19] Zhang F, Iadecola C. Reduction of focal cerebral ischemic damage by delayed treatment with nitric oxide donors. J Cereb Blood Flow Metab 1994;14(4):574–80.

[20] Willmot M, Gray L, Gibson C, Murphy S, Bath PM. A systematic review of nitric oxide donors and L-arginine in experimental stroke; effects on infarct size and cerebral blood flow. Nitric Oxide 2005;12(3):141–9.

[21] Saklani P, Khan H, Gupta S, Kaur A, Singh TG. Neuropeptides: potential neuroprotective agents in ischemic injury. Life Sci 2022;288:120186.

[22] Schulz R, Kelm M, Heusch G. Nitric oxide in myocardial ischemia/reperfusion injury. Cardiovasc Res 2004;61(3):402–13.

[23] Ghosh R, Ray U, Jana P, Bhattacharya R, Banerjee D, Sinha A. Reduction of death rate due to acute myocardial infarction in subjects with cancers through systemic restoration of impaired nitric oxide. PLoS One 2014;9(2): e88639.

[24] Thapa K, Khan H, Kanojia N, Singh TG, Kaur A, Kaur G. Therapeutic insights on ferroptosis in Parkinson's disease. Eur J Pharmacol 2022;175133.

[25] Siddiqi N, Neil C, Bruce M, MacLennan G, Cotton S, Papadopoulou S, Feelisch M, Bunce N, Lim PO, Hildick-Smith D, Horowitz J. Intravenous sodium nitrite in acute ST-elevation myocardial infarction: a randomized controlled trial (NIAMI). Eur Heart J 2014;35(19):1255–62.

[26] Hasebe N, Shen YT, Vatner SF. Inhibition of endothelium-derived relaxing factor enhances myocardial stunning in conscious dogs. Circulation 1993;88(6):2862–71.

[27] Depré C, Vanoverschelde JL, Goudemant JF, Mottet I, Hue L. Protection against ischemic injury by nonvasoactive concentrations of nitric oxide synthase inhibitors in the perfused rabbit heart. Circulation 1995;92(7):1911–8.

[28] Luo Z, Diaco M, Murohara T, Ferrara N, Isner JM, Symes JF. Vascular endothelial growth factor attenuates myocardial ischemia-reperfusion injury. Ann Thorac Surg 1997;64(4):993–8.

[29] Bereęsewicz A, Karwatowska-Prokopczuk E, Lewartowski B, Cedro-Ceremużyńska K. A protective role of nitric oxide in isolated ischaemic/reperfused rat heart. Cardiovasc Res 1995;30(6):1001–8.

[30] Mori E, Haramaki N, Ikeda H, Imaizumi T. Intra-coronary administration of L-arginine aggravates myocardial stunning through production of peroxynitrite in dogs. Cardiovasc Res 1998;40(1):113–23.

[31] Wong V, Lerner E. Nitric oxide inhibition strategies. Future Sci OA 2015;1(1):FSO35.

[32] Moore PK, Handy RL. Selective inhibitors of neuronal nitric oxide synthase—is no NOS really good NOS for the nervous system? Trends Pharmacol Sci 1997;18(4):204–11.

[33] Muscará MN, Wallace JL. V. Therapeutic potential of nitric oxide donors and inhibitors. Am J Physiol Gastrointest Liver Physiol 1999;276(6):G1313–6.

[34] Förstermann U, Sessa WC. Nitric oxide synthases: regulation and function. Eur Heart J 2012;33(7):829–37.

[35] Jiang WW, Kong LB, Li GQ, Wang XH. Expression of iNOS in early injury in a rat model of small-for-size liver transplantation. Hepatobiliary Pancreat Dis Int 2009;8(2):146–51.

[36] Cohen RA, Adachi T. Nitric-oxide-induced vasodilatation: regulation by physiologic S-glutathiolation and pathologic oxidation of the sarcoplasmic endoplasmic reticulum calcium ATPase. Trends Cardiovasc Med 2006;16(4):109–14.

[37] Köken T, İnal M. The effect of nitric oxide on ischemia–reperfusion injury in rat liver. Clin Chim Acta 1999;288(1–2):55–62.

[38] Kader A, Frazzini VI, Solomon RA, Trifiletti RR. Nitric oxide production during focal cerebral ischemia in rats. Stroke 1993;24(11):1709–16.

[39] Sugimura T, Sako K, Tohyama Y, Yonemasu Y. Consecutive in vivo measurement of nitric oxide in transient forebrain ischemic rat under normothermia and hypothermia. Brain Res 1998;808(2):313–6.

[40] Boyd CS, Cadenas E. Nitric oxide and cell signaling pathways in mitochondrial-dependent apoptosis. Biol Chem 2002;383(3–4):411–23.

[41] Carreras MC, Poderoso JJ. Mitochondrial nitric oxide in the signaling of cell integrated responses. Am J Physiol Cell Physiol 2007;292(5):C1569–80.

[42] Yong T, Meijia Z, Haiyan H, Guoliang X. Regulation between nitric oxide and MAPK signal transduction in mammals. Prog Nat Sci 2005;15(1):1–9.

[43] Rakhit RD, Kabir AN, Mockridge JW, Saurin A, Marber MS. Role of G proteins and modulation of p38 MAPK activation in the protection by nitric oxide against ischemia–reoxygenation injury. Biochem Biophys Res Commun 2001;286(5):995–1002.

[44] Carini R, De Cesaris MG, Splendore R, Domenicotti C, Nitti MP, Pronzato MA, Albano E. Signal pathway responsible for hepatocyte preconditioning by nitric oxide. Free Radic Biol Med 2003;34(8):1047–55.

[45] Shen YH, Wang XL, Wilcken DE. Nitric oxide induces and inhibits apoptosis through different pathways. FEBS Lett 1998;433(1–2):125–31.

[46] Prabhakar NK, Khan H, Grewal AK, Singh TG. Intervention of neuroinflammation in the traumatic brain injury trajectory: in vivo and clinical approaches. Int Immunopharmacol 2022;108:108902.

[47] Toledo-Pereyra LH, Toledo AH, Walsh J, Lopez-Neblina F. Molecular signaling pathways in ischemia/reperfusion. Exp Clin Transplant 2004;2(1):174–7.

[48] Khan H, Bangar A, Grewal AK, Bansal P, Singh TG. Caspase-mediated regulation of the distinct signaling pathways and mechanisms in neuronal survival. Int Immunopharmacol 2022;110:108951.

[49] Lok J, Gupta P, Guo S, Kim WJ, Whalen MJ, van Leyen K, Lo EH. Cell–cell signaling in the neurovascular unit. Neurochem Res 2007;32(12):2032–45.

[50] Khan H, Singh TG, Dahiya RS, Abdel-Daim MM. α-Lipoic acid, an organosulfur biomolecule a novel therapeutic agent for neurodegenerative disorders: an mechanistic perspective. Neurochem Res 2022;21:1–2.

[51] Lu D, Maulik NI, Moraru II, Kreutzer DL, Das DK. Molecular adaptation of vascular endothelial cells to oxidative stress. Am J Physiol Cell Physiol 1993;264(3):C715–22.

[52] Hall JP, Merithew E, Davis RJ. c-Jun N-terminal kinase (JNK) repression during the inflammatory response? Just say NO. Proc Natl Acad Sci 2000;97(26):14022–4.

[53] Saklani P, Khan H, Singh TG, Gupta S, Grewal AK. Demethyleneberberine, a potential therapeutic agent in neurodegenerative disorders: a proposed mechanistic insight. Mol Biol Rep 2022;3:1–3.

[54] Friebe A, Koesling D. Regulation of nitric oxide-sensitive guanylyl cyclase. Circ Res 2003;93(2):96–105.

[55] Gewaltig MT, Kojda G. Vasoprotection by nitric oxide: mechanisms and therapeutic potential. Cardiovasc Res 2002;55(2):250–60.

[56] Kojda G, Kottenberg K. Regulation of basal myocardial function by NO. Cardiovasc Res 1999;41(3):514–23.

[57] Agullo L, Garcia-Dorado D, Escalona N, Ruiz-Meana M, Inserte J, Soler-Soler J. Effect of ischemia on soluble and particulate guanylyl cyclase-mediated cGMP synthesis in cardiomyocytes. Am J Physiol Heart Circ Physiol 2003;284(6):H2170–6.

[58] Khan H, Kashyap A, Kaur A, Singh TG. Pharmacological postconditioning: a molecular aspect in ischemic injury. J Pharm Pharmacol 2020;72(11):1513–27.

[59] Du Toit EF, Meiring J, Opie LH. Relation of cyclic nucleotide ratios to ischemic and reperfusion injury in nitric oxide-donor treated rat hearts. J Cardiovasc Pharmacol 2001;38(4):529–38.

[60] Khan H, Singh A, Thapa K, Garg N, Grewal AK, Singh TG. Therapeutic modulation of the phosphatidylinositol 3-kinases (PI3K) pathway in cerebral ischemic injury. Brain Res 2021;1761:147399.

[61] Madhusoodanan KS, Murad F. NO-cGMP signaling and regenerative medicine involving stem cells. Neurochem Res 2007;32(4):681–94.

[62] Lander HM, Ogiste JS, Pearce SF, Levi R, Novogrodsky A. Nitric oxide-stimulated guanine nucleotide exchange on p21ras (*). J Biol Chem 1995;270(13):7017–20.

[63] Yun HY, Dawson VL, Dawson TM. Glutamate-stimulated calcium activation of Ras/Erk pathway mediated by nitric oxide. Diabetes Res Clin Pract 1999;45(2–3):113–5.

[64] Finkbeiner S, Greenberg ME. Ca2+-dependent routes to Ras: mechanisms for neuronal survival, differentiation, and plasticity? Neuron 1996;16(2):233–6.

[65] Xia Z, Dickens M, Raingeaud J, Davis RJ, Greenberg ME. Opposing effects of ERK and JNK-p38 MAP kinases on apoptosis. Science 1995;270(5240):1326–31.

[66] Zhang C, Liao Y, Li Q, Chen M, Zhao Q, Deng R, Wu C, Yang A, Guo Z, Wang D, He X. Recombinant adiponectin ameliorates liver ischemia reperfusion injury via activating the AMPK/eNOS pathway. PLoS One 2013;8(6):e66382.

[67] Fu W, Liao X, Ruan J, Li X, Chen L, Wang B, Wang K, Zhou J. Recombinant human erythropoietin preconditioning attenuates liver ischemia reperfusion injury through the phosphatidylinositol-3 kinase/AKT/endothelial nitric oxide synthase pathway. J Surg Res 2013;183(2):876–84.

[68] Tiwari P, Khan H, Singh TG, Grewal AK. Poly (ADP-ribose) polymerase: an overview of mechanistic approaches and therapeutic opportunities in the management of stroke. Neurochem Res 2022;18:1–23.

[69] Tabka D, Bejaoui M, Javellaud J, Roselló-Catafau J, Achard JM, Abdennebi HB. Effects of Institut Georges Lopez-1 and Celsior preservation solutions on liver graft injury. World J Gastroenterol 2015;21(14):4159.

III. Nitric oxide donors and cardiovascular and metabolic diseases

PART IV

Nitric oxide derivatives in ocular diseases

Effect of nitric oxide inhibitors in retinitis pigmentosa

*Antolín Cantó, Javier Martínez-González, Rosa López-Pedraja,
Amparo Sánchez-Fideli, and María Miranda*

Department of Biomedical Sciences, Faculty of Health Sciences, Institute of Biomedical Sciences,
Cardenal Herrera-CEU University, CEU Universities, Valencia, Spain

Abstract

Nitric oxide (NO) is an essential signaling molecule. In the retina, NO modulates visual transduction and maintains a normal visual function. NO has been shown to stimulate guanylate cyclase (GC) production, which leads to the formation of cyclic guanosine monophosphate (cGMP). In the vertebrate retina, cGMP is a critical molecule in the phototransduction cascade. In addition, NO acts as an immediate vascular endothelial relaxant and is implicated in ocular blood flow control under normal situations.

Although NO is beyond doubt employed in the retina to maintain usual ocular function, it has also been found to be related to different visual diseases. In this context, the importance of NO in our visual system must be confirmed because its underproduction is related to several eye diseases, particularly to glaucoma. On the other hand, an excess of NO is deleterious for the eye. One of the eye diseases that can be related to an increase in NO is retinitis pigmentosa (RP). RP is a retinal hereditary and neurodegenerative disease and is characterized by rod degeneration followed by cone degeneration. RP has been related with accumulation in cGMP, glutamate, and calcium. All of these molecules may stimulate NO production which can contribute to photoreceptor death. Herein, we review studies that have used NO inhibitors as neuroprotective agents in RP.

Abbreviations

1400W	*N*-(3-(aminomethyl)benzyl)acetamidine
adRP	autosomal-dominant retinitis pigmentosa
cGMP	cyclic guanosine monophosphate
Cnga3	cone photoreceptor cyclic nucleotide-gated channel
Cngb1	cyclic nucleotide gated channel beta 1
eNOS or NOS III	endothelial nitric oxide synthase
ETPI	*S*-ethyl-*N*-[4-(trifluoromethyl)phenyl]isothiourea hydrochloride
GC	guanylate cyclase
GSH	glutathione

iNOS or NOS II	inducible nitric oxide synthase
KO	knockout
L-NAME	HL-Nω-alkylated arginines methyl ester
L-NMMA	L-NG-monomethyl arginine acetate
L-NNA	L-Nω-nitroarginine
MNU	N-methyl-N-nitrosourea
NADPH	nicotinamide adenine dinucleotide phosphate
nNOS or NOS-I	neuronal nitric oxide synthase
NO	nitric oxide
NOS	nitric oxide synthase
ONL	outer nuclear cell layer
PDE	phosphodiesterase
Prph2	peripheral protein 2
Rcd1	rod-cone dysplasia type 1
rd1	retinal degeneration 1
rd10	retinal degeneration 10
rds	slow retinal degeneration
RP	retinitis pigmentosa

Conflict of interest

No potential conflicts of interest were disclosed.

Nitric oxide (NO) in the retina

NO is an essential signaling molecule, with gaseous nature, that allows it to diffuse through cell membranes [1]. It is one of the smallest and most ubiquitous molecules known. Though NO has been discovered in the retina only 25 years ago [2], it has been shown to have important functions in retinal physiology.

NO is synthesized by the conversion of L-arginine to L-citrulline. This reaction is catalyzed by the enzyme nitric oxide synthase (NOS), in the presence of O_2 and nicotinamide adenine dinucleotide phosphate (NADPH) [3]. There are three NOS isoforms, in which two of them are calcium-dependent: the neuronal (nNOS or NOS-I) and endothelial (eNOS or NOS III) isoforms. The third one is the inducible (iNOS or NOS II), a calcium-independent isoform [4]. iNOS is responsible for the release of NO during the immune and inflammatory responses. Although all of the three isoforms are expressed in the retina, nNOS is the main one regarding the different visual responses [4]. Indeed, in the rat retina, NO has been found in the photoreceptor inner segments, amacrine cells, bipolar cells, inner plexiform layer, and ganglion cells. Interestingly, no NO synthesis has been detected in cell bodies and outer segments of the photoreceptors [4] (Fig. 1).

NO is an essential molecule recognized because of its important role in neurotransmission, in cellular defense mechanisms, and as a potent vasodilator. NO is also a free radical [2]. In the retina, NO modulates visual transduction and maintains a normal visual function. NO has been shown to stimulate GC (a target enzyme for the action of NO) production, which leads to the formation of cGMP. In the vertebrate retina, cGMP modulates photoreceptor signal transduction and regulates ion channel and gap junction function [5]. cGMP is a critical molecule in the phototransduction cascade. These series of reactions in rods are initiated by rhodopsin. Light or photoexcitation converts 11-cis retinal to the retinal trans-isomer. This leads

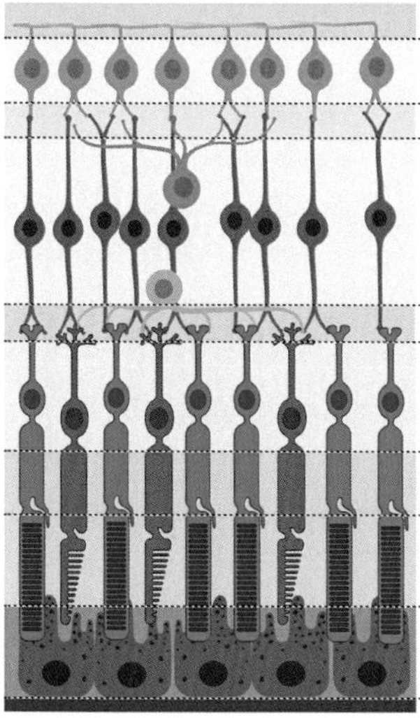

Layer	nNOS	iNOS	eNOS
GCL	X		X
IPL	X		
INL	X	X	X
OPL	X		
ONL			
IS			
OS		X	
EPR			

FIG. 1   The three nitric oxide synthases have been shown to be expressed in different retinal layers. Neuronal nitric oxide synthase (nNOS); inducible nitric oxide synthase (iNOS); endothelial nitric oxide synthase (eNOS); ganglion cell layer (GCL); inner plexiform layer (IPL); inner nuclear layer (INL); outer plexiform layer (OPL); outer nuclear layer (ONL); inner photoreceptor segments (IS); outer photoreceptor segments (OS); retinal epithelium pigment (EPR).

to the activation of transducin, a G-protein, that activates a phosphodiesterase (PDE) which hydrolyzes cGMP (previously formed because of NO) to 5′-GMP. This decrease in cGMP induces cGMP-gated cation channels in the outer segment membrane to close [6]. Consequently, there is an alteration in calcium influx and the cell is now hyperpolarized. Then, glutamate release in the synaptic region of the photoreceptors is decreased, and an electric signal in the downstream neuron of the photoreceptor is generated and sent to the visual cortex [7] (Fig. 2).

In addition, endothelial-derived NO acts as an immediate vascular relaxant and is implicated in ocular blood flow control under normal situations, and it mediates the vasodilator responses of several substances including acetylcholine, bradykinin, histamine, substance P, or insulin [8]. Apart from light stimulation, the synthesis of retinal NO is also regulated by acetylcholine, melatonin, dopamine, and glutamate. Acetylcholine, dopamine, and glutamate (the main excitatory retinal neurotransmitter) receptors activate retinal NOS, while melatonin inhibits NOS activity [4].

Although NO is beyond doubt employed in the retina to maintain usual ocular function, it has also been found to be related to different visual diseases. In this regard, the importance of NO in our visual system may be confirmed because its underproduction is related to several eye diseases, particularly to glaucoma. It is known that changes in the anterior segment of the eye, and specifically in the trabecular meshwork, responsible for most of the aqueous humor drainage, are directly related to variations in intraocular pressure that occur in the glaucoma patient [9]. Different studies associate polymorphisms in the eNOS gene with increased risk of

IV. Nitric oxide derivatives in ocular diseases

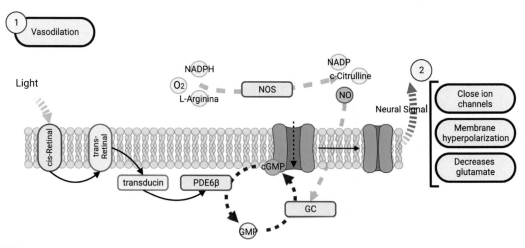

FIG. 2   Nitric oxide (NO) retinal functions. 1; NO acts as a vascular relaxant and is implicated in ocular blood flow control. 2; The visual transduction pathway starts when light changes cis-Retinal to trans-Retinal. Trans-Retinal activates PDE6β through transducin. PDE6β change cGMP to GMP and with this, ion channels in photoreceptors are closed, the bipolar membrane gets hyperpolarized, and the neural signal is transmitted by decreasing the amount of released glutamate. NO can modulate visual transduction by stimulation of GC activity that increases cGMP.

glaucoma. eNOS may produce high NO values. In response to this increased NO concentrations, the cells of the trabecular meshwork relax and change volume, which implies an increase in the flow output of the aqueous humor. For this reason, some studies indicate that NO deficiency or an alteration in its signaling cascade may be one of the pathological mechanisms that underlie glaucoma and that topical ophthalmic administration of NO-donor compounds provides a marked and sustained decrease in intraocular pressure in experimental models of glaucoma and in subjects with ocular hypertension [9].

On the other hand, an excess of NO is deleterious for the eye. As stated before, iNOS is induced under pathological and inflammatory responses and leads to NO excess that is converted into NO_2, nitrite, peroxynitrite, and free radicals [2]. Increased levels of NO have been associated with ocular disease states involving ischemia, oxidative stress, and inflammation (such as diabetic retinopathy, age-related macular degeneration, and RP) [10–13]. In all the mentioned diseases, increased levels of NO are associated with negative disease states.

The relation of ischemia and increase in NO is due to the increase in glutamate and aspartate metabolisms. The excess in glutamate and aspartate leads to increases in intracellular calcium, which is related to cell death. And because nNOS is calcium-dependent, this causes nNOS to produce NO [5].

NO is also highly associated with oxidative stress. Although NO itself is a radical, its reactivity is low compared to the potentially damaging oxidative products that it generates. N_2O_3 and peroxynitrite are produced by the reaction of NO with O_2 or superoxide [14]. Normally, NO is quickly removed from tissues by diffusion and the superoxide concentration is low with the help of superoxide dismutases, but when the oxidative stress increases, peroxynitrite is easily formed [12]. The potent oxidant peroxynitrite can react with biomolecules and nitrates and oxidizes proteins, inferring a considerable impact on cellular functions including cell death [15]. The antioxidant capacity of the cell is due to the existence of molecules such as glutathione (GSH). NO can react with GSH and produces S-nitrosoglutathione, decreasing GSH bioavailability. Peroxynitrite can also react with tyrosine residues in proteins to form nitrotyrosine, which induces damage in different tissues (including the retina) by protein inactivation, lipid peroxidation, or DNA damage [10]. Finally, inflammation is related with an excess of NO as it induces iNOS.

We conclude that NO can have protective or toxic effects, depending on the situation and the decreased or increased concentration. Accordingly, inducers or inhibitors of NOS can be used to treat or even prevent eye diseases. In this review, we will focus on the use of NOS inhibitors as potential pharmacological RP treatments.

Retinitis pigmentosa

Retinitis pigmentosa (RP) is a retinal hereditary and neurodegenerative disease and is characterized by pigment deposits in the mid periphery, which gives the name to the pathology [16]. This inherited disorder was first introduced by an ophthalmologist called Franciscus Cornelius Donders in the Netherlands in 1857, and since then, a further 59 genes are known to be related to different RP subtypes, making it a very heterogeneous disease [17].

RP is a rare disease with a prevalence of about 1 in 4000 and a variable age of onset, from childhood to adulthood [16]. According to Hartong et al. [18], in 2006, more than one million people were affected worldwide by retinitis pigmentosa, constituting 85%–90% of all retinal degenerative diseases. A fundamental characteristic of RP is its unpredictable behavior. As such, the first symptoms' onset age, the speed of symptoms' appearance, and the severity of the symptoms are extremely variable characteristics that do not only depend on a person's genetic predisposition. There are plenty of unknown factors that influence disease development [18].

During RP progression, patients progressively lose their peripheric distant vision, developing a "tunnel vision." As time passes and the degeneration progresses, there is a loss of the central vision too and patients become blind at the age of 60 generally [18]. In most cases, the pathology starts with rod degeneration, whose role is to allow achromatic vision in dark conditions, followed by cone degeneration, which provides color vision and light condition details. This degenerative sequence would explain why patients develop dark blindness in the first term and is only in elderly patients when daylight blindness consolidates [19].

Many different genes are related to the appearance of the disease, and this makes RP a very complex pathology. Apart from the large number of genes involved, different mutations located in the same gene can cause different RP variants, and the same gene mutation can lead to a huge familiar phenotypic variability [20].

All these factors show how extremely challenging is to find a truly effective and suitable treatment for any RP patient nowadays.

Nitric oxide and retinitis pigmentosa

To understand the role of NO in RP, two important concepts must be considered. The first one is the role of the cGMP axis in cones and rods, and the second one is that there are different variants of the human RP and different animal RP models with different mutations.

The consequence is that the role of NO may not be the same in rods and cones and in the several types of human RP or animal models.

Cones and rods respond differently to the NO-cGMP pathway

In adult photoreceptors, cGMP is a key signaling molecule for the transduction of light. Cone and rod photoreceptors do not react in a similar way to activation or inhibition of NO-cGMP signaling. In cone cells, reduction in cGMP or NO synthesis decreases growth. Increases in cGMP result in increased growth when stimulation is moderate; higher levels of cGMP, however, cause a reversion to normal growth [21]. Differently, in rod photoreceptors, NO-cGMP pathway activation prompts a reduction in growth. Reduction in cGMP or NO causes either no change or an increase in growth. It is possible that the differences between cones and rods are due to the fact that rods' intracellular levels of cGMP are intrinsically higher than in cones [22].

RP animal models and changes in NO

Despite that the retina of mice has certain structural differences with respect to the human retina, such as the absence of a macula or the smaller percentage of cones, mice have been widely used to study RP. Different mouse models have been used with gene defects that cause different forms of RP. Keeler in 1924 described the first mouse RP model [22]. The mutation found by Keeler was the retinal degeneration 1 (rd1) mutation or PDE6βrd1 [23]. This mutation is located in the chromosome 5 of the gene encoding for PDE6β [24] and is due to the insertion of a murine virus that introduces a nonsense mutation in the exon 7 of the gene [25]. Two characteristics result from the mutation: a deficiency in PDE6β activity and the subsequent accumulation of cGMP [26]. The PDE6β mutation is also found in humans and has been linked to cases of autosomal recessive RP, which accounts for approximately 5% of RP cases in humans [27].

Other mouse strains show retinal degeneration and abnormalities in the PDE6β gene sequence, such as mice with retinal degeneration 10 (rd10) or PDE6βrd10 and the nmf137 or PDE6βnmf137 mouse, among others [28]. Mutation in rd10 mice is also located on chromosome 5 and is caused by a missense mutation in exon 13 of the gene; in nmf137 mice, the mutation occurs in exon 16 [28]. The rate of photoreceptor loss in rd10 mice is slower than that seen in the retina of rd1 mice. This is because retinal degeneration in the rd10 mouse model is not caused by the absence of the PDE6β protein, but by an insufficient expression and/or low activity of this enzyme, which could lead to a cGMP accumulation, similar but slower to that found in the retina of rd1 mice, with eventual cell death [28].

It makes sense to relate these two animal models with alterations in NO. In the retina of both types of mice, rd1 and rd10, there is a cGMP accumulation that leads to alteration in calcium influx, and probably, an increase in glutamate and NO. Indeed, our group has demonstrated an increase in retinal glutamate concentrations both in rd1 and rd10 mice [29,30]. We have also been able to demonstrate an increase in nNOS expression in rd1 retina (unpublished results) and in rd10 retina [30]. Interestingly, the observed increases in glutamate or nNOS expression occurred at different postnatal days and were observed earlier in rd1 mice than in rd10 mice. These results are in accordance with the fact that the degeneration in rd10 mice is slower because the decrease in retinal PDE6β is also lower. The main conclusion may be that, as suggested by others, the expression of NOS (in that case iNOS but may be the same for nNOS) is regulated in a time-dependent manner due to degeneration [31]. Metabolomics have also helped to detect high nitrosoproline concentrations in rd10 retinas, suggesting that nitrosative stress is involved in this RP mouse model [32].

However, RP is not always caused by mutations in PDE6β. There are other mutations in other genes not so closely related with the visual cycle that also induce RP. In those cases, the relation with NO alterations is more difficult to understand. However, in this review, we will try to explain why NO may also be altered in those RP caused by other mutations. We will focus only on rat or mouse models with mutations that may parallel RP mutations in humans.

There are rat models with mutations in the rhodopsin genes. The P23H rats contain a rhodopsin-mutant transgene and had a proline to histidine substitution at codon 23 [33,34]. This was the first and most common rhodopsin mutation identified in patients with autosomal dominant RP (adRP) [35] and accounts for approximately 12% of adRP cases in the United States [36]. Another animal model for RP is the S334ter rat with a mouse opsin transgene bearing a termination codon at residue S334 (S334ter), resulting in a C-terminal truncated opsin protein lacking the last 15 residues [33]. The P23H mutation results in a defective rhodopsin folding in the endoplasmic reticulum, and the S334ter mutation results in defective rhodopsin trafficking and mis-localization of the protein [33]. Excitingly, a significant increase in nNOS protein concentrations in the S334ter has been previously reported [37], although the exact mechanism that leads to this induced nNOS levels is unknown; it has been postulated that dying rods release excessive glutamate, which allows an increase in calcium influx that stimulates nNOS [37].

Another animal model widely used to study RP is the rd2 retinal degeneration model or slow retinal degeneration (rds) and has a dominant spontaneous mutation in the peripheral protein 2 (Prph2). The photoreceptor cells in these mutants lack outer segments that should start developing at 7 days of age. At 2 weeks, the outer nuclear cell layer (ONL) begins to slowly degenerate in mutant animals. ONL disappears by 9 months of age in the peripheral retina and by 12 months in the central retina [38]. The mutation is an insertion of foreign DNA into an exon of Prph2, causing transcription of an abnormally large mRNA [39]. Prph2 encodes a membrane protein found in the outer segment of photoreceptor cells that is involved in photoreceptor disc morphogenesis. The Prph2 null mutation is naturally occurring in the mouse and was found to be the cause of retinal degeneration in mice before its connection to human disease was demonstrated. Diverse Prph2 disease-causing mutations have been found in humans and have been associated with dominant inherited RP [39]. Most of the Prph2 associated RP presents in the third to fifth decades of life, although some cases manifest as early as the first decade [40]. Though cGMP accumulation is not a direct consequence of the peripherin mutation, significant cGMP accumulation has been observed in cell bodies as well as in photoreceptor inner/outer segment of rds retina [40]. Therefore, this increase in cGMP retinal concentration may also cause alterations in calcium influx, glutamate increase, and NO metabolism abnormalities.

This cGMP accumulation has also been reported in other RP animal models with different mutations, including the cone photoreceptor cyclic nucleotide-gated channel (Cnga3), cyclic nucleotide gated channel beta 1 (Cngb1) knockout (KO), and Rho KO mice [41]. Mutations in the human Cnga3 have been associated with achromatopsia, cone dystrophy, Leber's congenital amaurosis, and oligo cone trichromacy [42]. Mutations in Cngb1 result in a retinal degeneration that resembles human RP [42]. Cyclic nucleotide-gated channels are important mediators in the transduction pathways of rod and cone photoreceptors. In mice lacking Cngb1, rods show a slow-progressing degeneration and cones degenerate in later stages [43]. Differently to other RP animal models, cGMP accumulation has been observed mainly in inner/outer photoreceptor segments in Cngb1 KO mice [40]. Homozygous Rho KO mice carry a mutation in exon 2 of the rhodopsin gene. The main consequence is that these mice have a complete absence of rhodopsin and are not able to form rod outer segments [44] with reduced ONL thickness and the virtually complete rod by 3 months of age [45].

Alternative models of higher mammals have been proposed as models of autosomal dominant RP. One example is the rod-cone dysplasia type 1 (rcd1) dogs, a large animal model of naturally occurring PDE6β deficiency [46]. In this animal model, the proper mutation may lead to increases in NO concentration. Indeed, recent research reported increased levels of nNOS and iNOS, resulting in increased NO levels in mutant retinas, not only in rcd1 dogs but also in other two dog animal models with different mutations: the cone rode dystrophy 2 that is a genetic model that affects the pit bull terriers and X-linked PRA2 that represents a spontaneous animal model of X-linked retinal degeneration [47]. We can also find transgenic pigs with a mutation in the rhodopsin gene, the P23H mutation [48]. Though, there is no study relating alterations in NO and this pig animal model, we can conclude that in the mice model with rhodopsin mutations, there is a cGMP accumulation, and the same may occur in the pig retina.

Nitric oxide inhibitors

If NO is increased in RP, a good therapeutic strategy could be to control excessive NO production. At present, potential pharmacological inhibition of NO is mainly achieved because of NOS inhibition. NOS inhibitors can be classified according to different points of view. The most common way of classification is according to the activity on the enzyme. In this sense, it is possible to distinguish between reversible inhibitors, irreversible inhibitors, and inhibitors of the enzymatic reaction [49]. Another possible classification is based on the binding site of the inhibitor on the NOS enzyme.

The multiplicity of binding sites on NOS for the substrate (L-arginine), the cofactors NADPH, flavin adenine dinucleotide, flavin mononucleotide, calmodulin, stabilizer (tetrahydrobiopterin), and the heme prosthetic moiety has provided with a wide range of inhibitors acting at each of these sites [50]. According to the binding-site of the NOS inhibitors classification, we can find four different categories: (i) inhibitors that interact with the arginine binding site, some of them are inhibitors based on the reaction since they need the enzyme NOS to be activated and NADPH for inhibition to occur; (ii) compounds that mimic the cofactor tetrahydrobiopterin; (iii) inhibitors that act directly on the heme group; and (iv) inhibitors that act on the cofactors calmodulin and flavin [49]. Finally, NOS inhibitors can be classified from a structural point of view into two groups: based or not on amino acids [49].

There is a great number of NOS inhibitors described in the literature and in use with pharmacological purposes. Of these, the most widely used have been N-(3-(aminomethyl)benzyl)acetamidine (1400W), L-NG-monomethyl arginine acetate (L-NMMA), L-Nω-nitroarginine (L-NNA), and HL-Nω-alkylated arginines methyl ester (L-NAME), S-ethyl-N-[4-(trifluoromethyl) phenyl]isothiourea hydrochloride(ETPI), aminoguanidine, and 7-nitroindazole. 1400W is a nonpeptidic small heterocyclic molecule and a slow, tight binding inhibitor of human iNOS [51]. The protective action of the iNOS inhibitor 1400W has already been demonstrated in ischemic retinopathy [52].

L-NMMA, L-NNA, and L-NAME are arginine derivatives. L-NMMA is a nonspecific NO synthase inhibitor; it inhibits iNOS, nNOS, and eNOS and is one of the most potent vasocon-strictors known [49]. L-NNA is one of the first synthetic competitive NOS. L-NNA selectively inhibits eNOS and nNOS isoforms and not the iNOS isoform, because the interaction with the inducible isoform is noncovalent and reversible [49]. L-NAME is a weak NOS inhibitor; how-ever, it is much more soluble in aqueous media than L-NNA. ETPI is a selective inhibitor nNOS.

One well-known nonamino acid inhibitor is aminoguanidine. Aminoguanidine contains a guanidino moiety and a hydrazine group in its structure. Aminoguanidine has been classi-cally defined as a selective iNOS inhibitor. However, some studies affirm that this selectivity is limited and that it can inhibit iNOS, nNOS, and even eNOS [53]. The mechanism by which aminoguanidine induces NOS inactivation is not known.

7-Nitroindazole, the endogenous precursor of NO-L-arginine, is a heterocyclic small mol-ecule that contains an indazole ring nitrated at position 7. Nitroindazole acts as a selective inhibitor for neuronal nitric oxide synthase.

Finally, in traditional medicine, many plants used because of their antiinflammatory ac-tions are reported to act by inhibiting NOS. One example is the well-known resveratrol.

Nitric oxide inhibitors in retinitis pigmentosa

There are not many studies that use NO inhibitors in RP, some of them are summarized in Table 1. Among these studies, we can distinguish those that use known NOS inhibitors and those that use molecules not known by their NOS inhibition properties but are found to act inhibiting NOS or reducing NO retinal concentrations.

The first study reported in Table 1 [54] uses N-methyl-N-nitrosourea (MNU) to induce a model of RP because this substance is an alkylating agent with selective toxicity to photore-ceptor cells because of apoptosis. In this model, an intracellular accumulation of Ca^{2+} is also observed. This increase in Ca^{2+} may be responsible for the activation of nNOS and eNOS and the consequent increase in retinal NO concentration. Indeed, this work reported an increased in nNOS immunoreactivity in the inner segments of photoreceptor after MNU adminis-tration. The researchers also demonstrated that the ocular administration of a nNOS-specific inhibitor such as ETPI (immediately after MNU administration) suppressed photoreceptor cell death after 5 days [54]. Similar results are observed also after 3 days of ETPI administration [55].

Other works compare the efficacy of different compounds. In a study by Vargas et al., the effect of clusterin and L-NAME, a classical NOS inhibitor, was compared [37]. Clusterin and L-NAME were intravitreally administered, and L-NMAE was also intraperitoneally adminis-tered to S334ter albino Sprague-Dawley rats (rhodopsin transgenic model of RP). Clusterin is a chaperone protein that was able to preserve rod photoreceptors in these RP rats. Clusterin treatment was also able to suppress the upregulated nNOS. Intraocular administration of

TABLE 1 Nitric oxide (NO) inhibitors or substances that decreases NO used in the treatment of different animal models of retinitis pigmentosa.

Animal model	Substance used to ameliorate rp	Type nitric oxide inhibitor	Dose, time	Result	Article
MNU-induced retinal degeneration in mice	ETPI	Specific nNOS inhibitor	ETPI (400 nM/eye) was intraocularly injected	Treatment with ETPI increased ONL thickness and photoreceptor cell death 5 days after MNU treatment	[54]
S334ter-line3 albino Sprague-Dawley rat	Clusterin L-NAME	Clusterin: chaperone protein L-NAME: arginine derivative NOS inhibitor	Clusterin (10 μg/mL in PBS) (intravitreal administration at postnatal day 15) L NAME (2 μL, 25 mM) (intravitreal administration at postnatal day 15) L-NAME (100 mg/kg) (intraperitoneal administration at postnatal day 15)	Clusterin increases rod survival and modulates nNOS L-NAME, suppresses nNOS expression, and increases rod survival	[37]
rd1 mice	Mixture of L-NNA, L-NAME, L-NMMA, and aminoguanidine Aminoguanidine 7-Nitroindazole	L-NNA, L-NAME, L-NMMA: arginine derivative NOS inhibitors Aminoguanidine used as iNOS inhibitor 7-Nitroindazole used as nNOS inhibitor	Twice daily intraperitoneal injections of L-NNA (400 mg/kg), L-NAME (400 mg/kg), L-NMMA, (200 mg/kg), and aminoguanidine (400 mg/kg) between postnatal day 18 and 30 Twice daily intraperitoneal injections of aminoguanidine (1250 mg/kg) or 7-nitroindazole (30 mg/kg) between postnatal day 18 and 30	Treatment with 4 NOS inhibitors reduced nitrosocysteine and nitrotyrosine staining and increased cone survival. Treatment with 7-nitroindazole, a specific nNOS inhibitor, reduced cone cell death. Aminoguanidine, a relatively specific iNOS, did not	[12]
MNU-induced retinal degeneration in mice	ETPI	Specific nNOS inhibitor	ETPI (400 nM/eye) was intraocularly injected	Treatment with ETPI increased ONL thickness and photoreceptor cell death 3 days after MNU treatment	[55]

TABLE 1 Nitric oxide (NO) inhibitors or substances that decreases NO used in the treatment of different animal models of retinitis pigmentosa—Cont'd

Animal model	Substance used to ameliorate rp	Type nitric oxide inhibitor	Dose, time	Result	Article
P23H and S334ter rats	L-NAME	L-NAME: arginine derivative NOS inhibitors (used as a nNOS-specific inhibitor)	Intraperitoneal injections of L-NAME (100 mg/kg body) before light exposure. One group of mice was exposed to damaging bright light and another group was maintained in dim cyclic light L-NAME administered intraperitoneally or in water to P23H and S334ter rats	L-NAME provided structural protection of photoreceptor from light damage and no protective effect in P23H or S334ter rats	[56]
Rd10 mice	Metipranolol	For hypertension and glaucoma treatment	Daily subcutaneous injections of 40 mg/kg of metipranolol between postnatal day 14 and 65 0.06% solution of metipranolol in water topically applied three times a day from postnatal day 14 to 65	Reduced nitrosative damage and rescue of functional loss of photoreceptors in rd10 mice	[57]
Rd10 mice	Progesterone	Steroid gonadal hormones	Progesterone oral treatment was administered from postnatal day 15 to 21	Decreased nNOS expression	[30]
Rds mice	Minocycline	Long-acting tetracycline	Minocycline (50 mg/kg) was injected intra-peritoneally daily from the second postnatal day until 14, 17, 21, and 28	Reduced iNOS expression and initial photoreceptor apoptosis did not provide long-term protection	[31]

ETPI, *ethyl[4-(trifluoromethyl) phenyl]carbamimidothioate*; iNOS, *inducible nictric oxide synthase*; MNU, *N-methyl-N-nitrosourea*; L-NAME, HL-Nω-alkylated arginines methyl ester; L-NMMA, *L-NG-monomethyl arginine acetate*; L-NNA, *L-Nω-Nitroarginine*; nNOS, *neuronal nitric oxide synthase*; NOS, *nitric oxide synthase*; ONL, *outer nuclear cell layer.*

L-NAME also decreased nNOS. The results from this study revealed that intraperitoneal L-NAME treatment prolonged rod survival in RP retinas, though they did not study the effect of ocular L-NAME administration on photoreceptor cell death.

Komeima et al. investigated the role of different NOS inhibitors specifically on cone cell death rather than in rod death [12]. Their results demonstrated that the treatment of rd1 mice with a mixture of NOS inhibitors (including L-NNA, L-NAME, L-NMMA, and aminoguanidine) reduced S-nitrosocysteine and nitrotyrosine staining and improved cone survival [12]. In this study, a specific inhibitor of neuronal NOS, such as7-nitroindazole, was also able to decrease cone cell death, but aminoguanidine (supposed to be a specific inhibitor of iNOS) was not able to increase cone survival [12].

However, other studies have found that some drugs, such as L-NAME, that protect against light damage, are not effective in preventing inherited degenerations related to rhodopsin mutations [56]. The animal RP models used were P23H and S334ter rats, and L-NAME was administered intraperitoneally or orally. The authors of this work postulated that this differential drug effect may provide some information regarding the mechanism of cell death in specific mutations [56].

Metipranolol, an antiglaucoma and antihypertensive drug, slowed the rod and cone cells death in the rd10 model of RP [57]. This drug has not been described as a classical NOS inhibitor but it has been demonstrated that its effect in rd10 may be related to its ability to inhibit nitrosative stress [57]. This effect was achieved when metipranolol was administered subcutaneously from postnatal day 14 to 65, but also when it was administered in the form of eye drops.

Other two drugs that have not been classically identified as NOS inhibitors are progesterone and minocycline. Progesterone is a steroid gonadal hormone that has demonstrated to be protective in rd10 mice [30]. It has not been established if progesterone protective action is due to its effect on NOS but it is able to inhibit nNOS in the retina of rd10 mice. Nevertheless, the authors suggested that progesterone is pleiotropic, and several other action mechanisms may also be important in delaying photoreceptor cell death in this animal model [30]. Minocycline is a semisynthetic tetracycline derivative that penetrates the blood-brain barrier with neuroprotective properties [31]. It has been demonstrated that minocycline treatment decreased the expression of iNOS in rds mice [31].

The findings in most of these studies are that by inhibiting NO production, we can at least delay photoreceptor cell death in RP. However, the molecules, concentrations, type of administration (intraperitoneally, orally, etc.), and type of RP animal models differ from one study to other. Therefore, new studies trying to unify all these aspects are needed to demonstrate that NO may be a good therapeutic target in RP.

Conclusion

Different studies have reported the important role of NO in the healthy and disease retina. In addition, some of the works reviewed have demonstrated that administration of NOS inhibitors to animal models of RP increases the survival of photoreceptor cells. Most of these articles demonstrate that there is an increase in nitrosative stress in RP retina and that, therefore, NOS inhibitors decrease this stress and delay cell death in RO. These results prove that

NO modulation can be used as a therapeutic target in retinopathies, and particularly, in RP. However, most of the studies regarding retinal degeneration and NO use the most common NOS inhibitors, and most of them use L-NAME as a specific nNOS inhibitor. Future works are needed to study the effect of other NOS inhibitors, such as 7-nitroindazole or new molecules, with more specific and potent NO inhibition action. We also propose to investigate the effect of NOS inhibitors over GC activity, glutamate release, and hyperpolarization in retina.

Furthermore, all the research works reviewed in this manuscript examine the effect of NOS inhibitors in RP animal models. Further studies are needed to contemplate the possible toxic effects of this type of molecules in human retinas, as well as studies to decide which administration and dose may be the most effective in human visual system.

Acknowledgments

This research was funded by Consolidación de Indicadores CEU-UCH 2021-2022 INDI21/39 y Proyectos Precompetitivos CEU 2020-2021 FUSP-BS-PPC19-19F1741D and the grants ACIF/199/2019 and FPU 20/06277.

References

[1] Nathan C. Nitric oxide as a secretory product of mammalian cells. FASEB J 1992;6:3051–64.
[2] Erdinest N, London N, Ovadia H, Levinger N. Nitric oxide interaction with the eye. Vision (Basel) 2021;5:29.
[3] Alderton WK, Cooper CE, Knowles RG. Nitric oxide synthases: structure, function and inhibition. Biochem J 2001;357:593–615.
[4] Vielma AH, Retamal MA, Schmachtenberg O. Nitric oxide signaling in the retina: what have we learned in two decades? Brain Res 2012;1430:112–25.
[5] Stringham JM, Stringham NT. Nitric oxide and lutein: function, performance, and protection of neural tissue. Foods 2015;4:678–89.
[6] Kennan A, Aherne A, Humphries P. Light in retinitis pigmentosa. Trends Genet 2005;21:103–10.
[7] Torre V, Matthews HR, Lamb TD. Role of calcium in regulating the cyclic GMP cascade of phototransduction in retinal rods. Proc Natl Acad Sci USA 1986;83:7109–13.
[8] Schmetterer L, Polak K. Role of nitric oxide in the control of ocular blood flow. Prog Retin Eye Res 2001;20:823–47.
[9] Andrés-Guerrero V, García-Feijoo J. Nitric oxide-donating compounds for IOP lowering in glaucoma. Donadores de óxido nítrico como hipotensores en glaucoma. Arch Soc Esp Oftalmol (Engl Ed) 2018;93:290–9.
[10] Opatrilova R, Kubatka P, Caprnda M, et al. Nitric oxide in the pathophysiology of retinopathy: evidences from preclinical and clinical researches. Acta Ophthalmol 2018;96:222–31.
[11] Toma C, De Cillà S, Palumbo A, Garhwal DP, Grossini E. Oxidative and nitrosative stress in age-related macular degeneration: a review of their role in different stages of disease. Antioxidants (Basel) 2021;10:653.
[12] Komeima K, Usui S, Shen J, Rogers BS, Campochiaro PA. Blockade of neuronal nitric oxide synthase reduces cone cell death in a model of retinitis pigmentosa. Free Radic Biol Med 2008;45:905–12.
[13] Cantó A, Olivar T, Romero FJ, Miranda M. Nitrosative stress in retinal pathologies: review. Antioxidants (Basel) 2019;8:543.
[14] Moncada S. Nitric oxide and cell respiration: physiology and pathology. Verh K Acad Geneeskd Belg 2000;62:171–81.
[15] Hancock JT, Neill SJ. Nitric oxide: its generation and interactions with other reactive signaling compounds. Plants (Basel) 2019;8:41.
[16] Fahim A. Retinitis pigmentosa: recent advances and future directions in diagnosis and management. Curr Opin Pediatr 2018;30:725–33.
[17] Neveling K, Collin RW, Gilissen C, et al. Next-generation genetic testing for retinitis pigmentosa. Hum Mutat 2012;33:963–72.
[18] Hartong DT, Berson EL, Dryja TP. Retinitis pigmentosa. Lancet 2006;368:1795–809.
[19] Hamel C. Retinitis pigmentosa. Orphanet J Rare Dis 2006;1:40.

[20] Ferrari S, Di Iorio E, Barbaro V, Ponzin D, Sorrentino FS, Parmeggiani F. Retinitis pigmentosa: genes and disease mechanisms. Curr Genomics 2011;12(4):238–49.

[21] Zhang N, Beuve A, Townes-Anderson E. The nitric oxide-cGMP signaling pathway differentially regulates presynaptic structural plasticity in cone and rod cells. J Neurosci 2005;25:2761–70.

[22] Keeler CE. The inheritance of a retinal abnormality in white mice. Proc Natl Acad Sci USA 1924;10:329–33.

[23] Pittler SJ, Keeler CE, Sidman RL, Baehr W. PCR analysis of DNA from 70-year-old sections of rodless retina demonstrates identity with the mouse rd defect. Proc Natl Acad Sci USA 1993;90:9616–9.

[24] Sidman RL, Green MC. Retinal degeneration in the mouse: location of the rd locus in linkage group XVII. J Hered 1965;56:23–9.

[25] Pittler SJ, Baehr W. The molecular genetics of retinal photoreceptor proteins involved in cGMP metabolism. Prog Clin Biol Res 1991;362:33–66.

[26] Acosta ML, Fletcher EL, Azizoglu S, Foster LE, Farber DB, Kalloniatis M. Early markers of retinal degeneration in rd/rd mice. Mol Vis 2005;11:717–28.

[27] Danciger M, Blaney J, Gao YQ, Zhao DY, Heckenlively JR, Jacobson SG, Farber DB. Mutations in the PDE6B gene in autosomal recessive retinitis pigmentosa. Genomics 1995;30:1–7.

[28] Chang B, Hawes NL, Pardue MT, German AM, Hurd RE, Davisson MT, Nusinowitz S, Rengarajan K, Boyd AP, Sidney SS, Phillips MJ, Stewart RE, Chaudhury R, Nickerson JM, Heckenlively JR, Boatright JH. Two mouse retinal degenerations caused by missense mutations in the beta-subunit of rod cGMP phosphodiesterase gene. Vis Res 2007;47:624–33.

[29] Sánchez-Vallejo V, Benlloch-Navarro S, Trachsel-Moncho L, López-Pedrajas R, Almansa I, Romero FJ, Miranda M. Alterations in glutamate cysteine ligase content in the retina of two retinitis pigmentosa animal models. Free Radic Biol Med 2016;96:245–54.

[30] Benlloch-Navarro S, Trachsel-Moncho L, Fernández-Carbonell Á, Olivar T, Soria JM, Almansa I, Miranda M. Progesterone anti-inflammatory properties in hereditary retinal degeneration. J Steroid Biochem Mol Biol 2019;189:291–301.

[31] Yang LP, Li Y, Zhu XA, Tso MO. Minocycline delayed photoreceptor death in rds mice through iNOS-dependent mechanism. Mol Vis 2007;13:1073–82.

[32] Weiss ER, Osawa S, Xiong Y, et al. Broad spectrum metabolomics for detection of abnormal metabolic pathways in a mouse model for retinitis pigmentosa. Exp Eye Res 2019;184:135–45.

[33] LaVail MM, Nishikawa S, Steinberg RH, et al. Phenotypic characterization of P23H and S334ter rhodopsin transgenic rat models of inherited retinal degeneration. Exp Eye Res 2018;167:56–90.

[34] Acosta ML, Shin YS, Ready S, Fletcher EL, Christie DL, Kalloniatis M. Retinal metabolic state of the proline-23-histidine rat model of retinitis pigmentosa. Am J Physiol Cell Physiol 2010;298:C764–74.

[35] Dryja TP, McGee TL, Reichel E, Hahn LB, Cowley GS, Yandell DW, Sandberg MA, Berson EL. A point mutation of the rhodopsin gene in one form of retinitis pigmentosa. Nature 1990;343:364–6.

[36] Berson EL, Sandberg MA, Dryja TP. Autosomal dominant retinitis pigmentosa with rhodopsin, valine-345-methionine. Trans Am Ophthalmol Soc 1991;89:117–30.

[37] Vargas A, Yamamoto KL, Craft CM, Lee EJ. Clusterin enhances cell survival by suppressing neuronal nitric-oxide synthase expression in the rhodopsin S334ter-line3 retinitis pigmentosa model. Brain Res 2021;1768:147575.

[38] Chang B, Hawes NL, Hurd RE, Davisson MT, Nusinowitz S, Heckenlively JR. Retinal degeneration mutants in the mouse. Vis Res 2002;42:517–25.

[39] Loewen CJ, Molday RS. Disulfide-mediated oligomerization of Peripherin/Rds and Rom-1 in photoreceptor disk membranes. Implications for photoreceptor outer segment morphogenesis and degeneration. J Biol Chem 2000;275:5370–8.

[40] Stuck MW, Conley SM, Naash MI. PRPH2/RDS and ROM-1: historical context, current views and future considerations. Prog Retin Eye Res 2016;52:47–63.

[41] Arango-Gonzalez B, Trifunović D, Sahaboglu A, Kranz K, Michalakis S, Farinelli P, Koch S, Koch F, Cottet S, Janssen-Bienhold U, Dedek K, Biel M, Zrenner E, Euler T, Ekström P, Ueffing M, Paquet-Durand F. Identification of a common non-apoptotic cell death mechanism in hereditary retinal degeneration. PLoS One 2014;9:e112142.

[42] Shaikh RS, Reuter P, Sisk RA, et al. Homozygous missense variant in the human CNGA3 channel causes cone-rod dystrophy. Eur J Hum Genet 2015;23:473–80.

[43] Hüttl S, Michalakis S, Seeliger M, et al. Impaired channel targeting and retinal degeneration in mice lacking the cyclic nucleotide-gated channel subunit CNGB1. J Neurosci 2005;25:130–8.

[44] de Gooyer TE, Stevenson KA, Humphries P, et al. Rod photoreceptor loss in Rho−/− mice reduces retinal hypoxia and hypoxia-regulated gene expression. Invest Ophthalmol Vis Sci 2006;47:5553–60.

[45] Jaissle GB, May CA, Reinhard J, et al. Evaluation of the rhodopsin knockout mouse as a model of pure cone function. Invest Ophthalmol Vis Sci 2001;42:506–13.

[46] Pichard V, Provost N, Mendes-Madeira A, et al. AAV-mediated gene therapy halts retinal degeneration in PDE6β-deficient dogs. Mol Ther 2016;24:867–76.

[47] Badiei A, Beltran WA, Aguirre GD. Altered transsulfuration pathway enzymes and redox homeostasis in inherited retinal degenerative diseases. Exp Eye Res 2022;215:108902.

[48] Ross JW, Fernandez de Castro JP, Zhao J, et al. Generation of an inbred miniature pig model of retinitis pigmentosa. Invest Ophthalmol Vis Sci 2012;53:501–7.

[49] Víteček J, Lojek A, Valacchi G, Kubala L. Arginine-based inhibitors of nitric oxide synthase: therapeutic potential and challenges. Mediat Inflamm 2012;2012:318087.

[50] Moore PK, Handy RL. Selective inhibitors of neuronal nitric oxide synthase—is no NOS really good NOS for the nervous system? Trends Pharmacol Sci 1997;18:204–11.

[51] Garvey EP, Oplinger JA, Furfine ES, Kiff RJ, Laszlo F, Whittle BJ, Knowles RG. 1400W is a slow, tight binding, and highly selective inhibitor of inducible nitric-oxide synthase in vitro and in vivo. J Biol Chem 1997;272:4959–63.

[52] Schnichels S, Joachim SC. The inducible nitric oxide synthase-inhibitor 1400W as a potential treatment for retinal diseases. Neural Regen Res 2021;16:1221–2.

[53] Jianmongkol S, Vuletich JL, Bender AT, Demady DR, Osawa Y. Aminoguanidine-mediated inactivation and alteration of neuronal nitric-oxide synthase. J Biol Chem 2000;275:13370–6.

[54] Koriyama Y, Hisano S, Ogai K, Sugitani K, Furukawa A, Kato S. Involvement of neuronal nitric oxide synthase in N-methyl-N-nitrosourea-induced retinal degeneration in mice. J Pharmacol Sci 2015;127:394–6.

[55] Hisano S, Koriyama Y, Ogai K, Sugitani K, Kato S. Nitric oxide synthase activation as a trigger of N-methyl-N-nitrosourea-induced photoreceptor cell death. Adv Exp Med Biol 2016;854:379–84.

[56] Káldi I, Dittmar M, Pierce P, Anderson RE. L-NAME protects against acute light damage in albino rats, but not against retinal degeneration in P23H and S334ter transgenic rats. Exp Eye Res 2003;76:453–61.

[57] Kanan Y, Khan M, Lorenc VE, Long D, Chadha R, Sciamanna J, Green K, Campochiaro PA. Metipranolol promotes structure and function of retinal photoreceptors in the rd10 mouse model of human retinitis pigmentosa. J Neurochem 2019;148:307–18.

Advances in the discovery of novel agents for the treatment of glaucoma: The role of nitric oxide donors

Claudiu T. Supuran

University of Florence, Neurofarba Department, Section of Pharmaceutical and Nutraceutical Chemistry, Florence, Italy

Abstract

Glaucoma is a neuropathic disease characterized by increased intraocular pressure (IOP). Reducing this parameter is the only therapeutic approach available so far. Drugs interfering with aqueous humor secretion (e.g., adrenergic agonists/antagonists and carbonic anhydrase inhibitors) and with its outflow from the eye (e.g., prostaglandin (PG) analogs, rho kinase inhibitors, nitric oxide (NO) donors) are in clinical use. The field experienced relevant developments in the last years with the approval of three new drugs belonging to two novel pharmacological classes: the prostaglandin-nitric oxide donor hybrids (such as latanoprostene bunod) and the rho kinase inhibitors. Eye drops containing combinations of several different such drugs are available too, allowing for effective IOP control. NO donors played a relevant role in developing novel antiglaucoma agents belonging, due to the involvement of this gas-transmitter in relevant ocular physiological processes, affording thus interesting new opportunities for the pharmacological management of this disease.

Abbreviations

AH aqueous humor
CA carbonic anhydrase
CAI carbonic anhydrase inhibitor
IOP intraocular pressure
PG prostaglandin
TM trabecular meshwork

Conflict of interest

No potential conflicts of interest were disclosed.

Nitric Oxide in Health and Disease
https://doi.org/10.1016/B978-0-443-13342-8.00003-X

Introduction

Glaucoma is a frequent ophthalmologic disease, which affects the aging population, with millions of patients suffering of this chronic condition worldwide [1–6]. The hallmark of this disease is the increased intraocular pressure (IOP), which, being an asymptomatic condition with no relevant clinical signs or suffering, progressively leads to visual impairment and blindness if no adequate cures are furnished [5–7]. Glaucoma is classified nowadays as a multifactorial neuropathic disease, due to retinal ganglion cell death, which induces damage to the optic nerve, and ultimately blindness [1–3]. IOP is easy to monitor, being thus the only clinically modifiable risk factor for control, progression, and cure of the diseases [3–7]. Thus, all antiglaucoma drugs in clinical use have an effect on IOP either by interfering with the production of aqueous humor (AH) or with its outflow from the anterior segment of the eye [1–5]. AH is a bicarbonate rich fluid which is produced within the ciliary body mainly by the activity of the metalloenzyme carbonic anhydrase (CA, EC 4.2.1.1) which hydrates CO_2 to bicarbonate and protons [8–10]. There are, on the other hand, two outflow pathways of the ocular fluid: (i) the conventional one, which drains the fluid through the trabecular meshwork (TM), the Schlemm's canal, and then to the episcleral veins (being responsible of the drainage of around 80% of the total AH) [1,3]; (ii) the unconventional outflow pathway, comprising the ciliary muscle, together with the supraciliary and suprachoroidal spaces [1,3].

There are several classes of pharmacological agents in clinical use or in clinical development for the management of this disease: (i) classical drugs interfering with the formation of AH, i.e., adrenergic drugs (the β-adrenergic blockers and the α-adrenergic agonists) as well as the carbonic anhydrase inhibitors (CAIs), which can be systemically or topically acting agents [11–13]; and (ii) drugs interfering with the outflow of AH, among which the cholinergic agonists (now with few applications due to the many side effects and the availability of more effective drugs) [2], prostaglandin analogs [14], rho kinase inhibitors [15], nitric oxide (NO)-donating agents [16,17], adenosine receptor modulators, some kinase inhibitors, and natriuretic peptide analogs, etc. [2–4,18]. Here, I will review the latest developments in the discovery of novel antiglaucoma agents belonging to these classes mentioned earlier, mainly emphasizing on the role that NO donors played in this process.

Carbonic anhydrase inhibitors as antiglaucoma agents

CAs are widespread metalloenzymes in all life forms, acting as efficient catalysts for the hydration of CO_2 to bicarbonate and protons [19,20]. Their physiological role is in the pH regulation and homeostasis, due to the bicarbonate acting as a buffer and the protons which may acidify various cell compartments, tissues, and organs [21–26]. However, these enzymes are also involved in metabolic processes [27,28]. As a consequence, the CA inhibitors (CAIs) have a place in therapy as diuretics [29], antiglaucoma drugs [10–12], antiepileptics [30,31], agents for the treatment of obesity [19,32], and some such compounds are in advanced clinical stages as antitumor agents [33–36].

The heterocyclic sulfonamides acetazolamide 1, methazolamide 2, and ethoxzolamide 3 and the aromatic derivative, the bis-sulfonamide dichlorophenamide 4 (Fig. 1), constitute

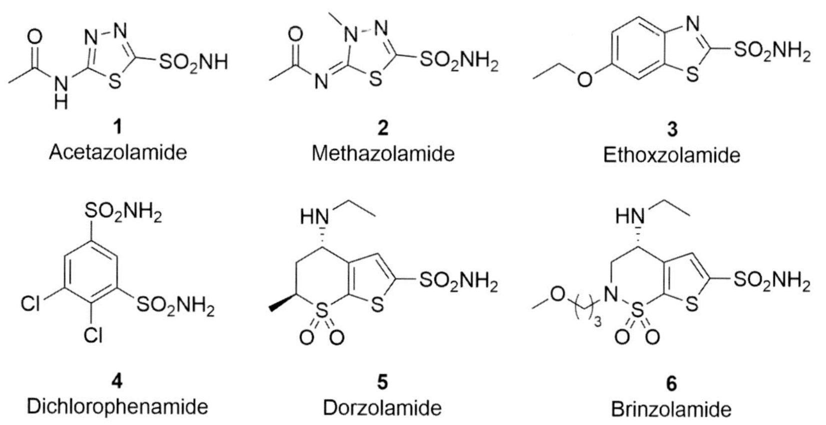

FIG. 1   First generation (compounds 1–4) and second generation (derivatives 5 and 6) CAIs used as antiglaucoma agents.

the first generation of CAIs in clinical use for various conditions [36], including for the management of glaucoma, for several decades [10–12,37]. They act as highly effective (in the low nanomolar range) inhibitors of CA isoforms involved in glaucoma, i.e., CA II, IV, and XII [10,12,19]. Compounds 15–18 are systemically acting CAIs, which by inhibiting the CAs present in the ciliary body, reduce the formation of bicarbonate in the AH and, as a consequence, the formation of the ocular fluid [9,10]. This constitutes the basis for their use as antiglaucoma agents since the 50s [38]. At doses of 50–250 mg/day, acetazolamide and methazolamide effectively reduce IOP by 25%–30%, but these systemic drugs have a range of side effects due to the inhibition of CA isoforms from other organs than the eye [10,11,38]. The adverse effects include metabolic acidosis, depression, numbness and tingling of extremities, fatigue, malaise, metallic taste, weight loss, decreased libido, gastrointestinal irritation, renal stones, transient myopia, and they are due to the fact that there are 15 CA isoforms present in humans, with a very diverse and widespread distribution in many tissues and organs [19–26]. Thus, nowadays, the systemic acting CAIs are used only in glaucoma forms which are reluctant to other therapeutic agents.

In order to avoid problems associated with the systemic use of sulfonamide CAIs, the second-generation compounds, among which dorzolamide 5 and brinzolamide 6 (Fig. 1), are in clinical use [19,39,40], and were designed in such a way as to act topically, being directly administered into the eye. This was not as easy to achieve as initially thought, due to the fact that sulfonamides are poorly water soluble compounds. In fact, as seen from Fig. 3, in contrast to the first-generation CAIs, the second-generation one incorporates bicyclic ring systems and water-solubilizing moieties of the secondary/tertiary amine and sulfone type. Both compounds 19 and 20 show effective inhibition of CA isoforms involved in glaucoma (CA II, IV, and XII) [19,40] and also possess an acceptable water solubility, being sufficiently liposoluble to penetrate through the cornea. They are administered topically, as a 2% water solution for dorzolamide, as hydrochloride salt, and as a 1% suspension, for brinzolamide as hydrochloride salt, 2 times daily [10,12,40].

IV. Nitric oxide derivatives in ocular diseases

The third-generation CAIs were developed starting with 1999, by using the tail approach [42]. By attaching water-solubilizing functionalities to derivatizable moieties of amino, imino, or hydroxyl types present in structurally simple aromatic/heterocyclic sulfonamides, a large collection of water-soluble sulfonamides acting as effective CAIs was obtained [42–49]. Many such derivatives, incorporating among others picolinoyl, isonicotinoyl, perfluoroalkyl/ perfluoroaryl-sulfonyl/carbonyl, carboxypyridine-carboxamido, quinolinesulfonamido, amino acyl, oligopeptidyl, and many other tail functionalities, showed excellent IOP lowering activity in animal models of glaucoma superior to those of the clinically used agent dorzolamide [42–49]. Apart from compounds incorporating one tail, more recently, derivatives with two [48] and respectively three tails [49] have been designed, which incorporate a multitude of lipophilic and/or hydrophilic moieties, and which exploit various binding pockets in the hydrophilic and hydrophobic halves of the CA active site [48,49]. The hybrids incorporating CAIs and other chemotypes, such as NO-donating moieties or fragments acting on the prostaglandin receptors agonists, which will be dealt with in a different section of the chapter, were in fact designed and obtained by using the tail approach originally discovered more than two decades ago [38,50].

Carbonic anhydrase inhibitor: NO donor hybrids

The sulfonamide CAIs are the classical antiglaucoma agents (see discussion above and Fig. 1), and as thus, several approaches to enhance their efficacy were developed, by inserting NO-donating moieties in their molecules, in the form of nitrate esters or other NO-donating groups [17,18,41,51,52] (Figs. 2 and 3).

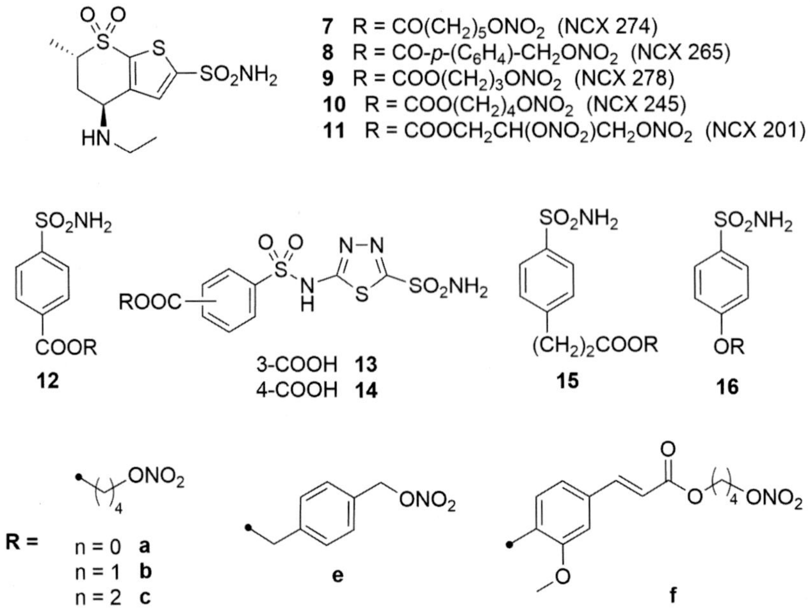

7   R = CO(CH$_2$)$_5$ONO$_2$ (NCX 274)
8   R = CO-p-(C$_6$H$_4$)-CH$_2$ONO$_2$ (NCX 265)
9   R = COO(CH$_2$)$_3$ONO$_2$ (NCX 278)
10   R = COO(CH$_2$)$_4$ONO$_2$ (NCX 245)
11   R = COOCH$_2$CH(ONO$_2$)CH$_2$ONO$_2$ (NCX 201)

12

3-COOH **13**
4-COOH **14**

15

16

R =
n = 0   **a**
n = 1   **b**
n = 2   **c**

e

f

FIG. 2   CAIs incorporating NO-donating moieties of types **7–16**.

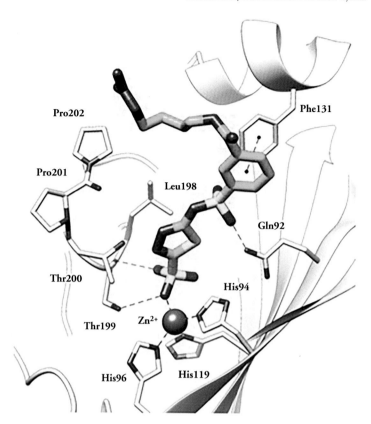

FIG. 3 hCA II in adduct with a sulfonamide incorporating the NO-donating moiety (**13b**) as determined by X-ray crystallography [41]. The zinc ion from the enzyme active site (*gray sphere*), its three His ligands (His94, 96, and 119), and the inhibitor (*in cyan*) are shown as stick model. The protein backbone is shown as *white ribbon*. Amino acid residues involved in the binding of the inhibitor (Thr199, Thr200, Pro201, Pro202, Gln92, and Phe131) are also shown.

The first CAI-NO donor hybrids, of types **7–11**, incorporated the dorzolamide **5** scaffold and aliphatic/aromatic mono- and polynitrate moieties [51]. These derivatives were more effective than dorzolamide **5** as IOP-lowering agents in a rabbit model of glaucoma [51]. Derivatives (**12–16**)(**a-f**) were thereafter obtained by derivatizing simple sulfonamides incorporating carboxylic (**12–15**) or phenolic (**16**) moieties by means of aliphatic (**a-c**) or aromatic (**e,f**) nitrate ester functionalities [52]. The most effective IOP lowering agents among these potent CAIs were **12b** (NCX-250) [16] and **13b**, for which the X-ray crystal structure, bound to the isoform hCA II, was also resolved (Fig. 2) [52].

As seen from Fig. 3, the inhibitor **13b** was observed intact within the enzyme active cavity, with the sulfonamide moiety coordinated to the catalytic metal ion, and the scaffold participating in a multitude of favorable interactions with the protein (i.e., with residues Thr199, Thr200, Pro201, Pro202, Gln92, and Phe131), which explains its high affinity, in the nanomolar range, for the enzyme. Furthermore, the nitrate functionality was observed intact, not being yet hydrolyzed when the inhibitor was bound to the enzyme [52].

IV. Nitric oxide derivatives in ocular diseases

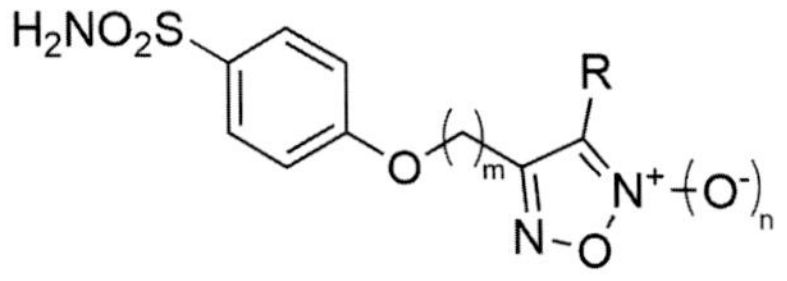

17 X = Br, R = Ph, n = 0, m = 1   25 R = Ph, n = 0, m = 1
18 X = Br, R = Ph, n = 1, m = 1   26 R = Ph, n = 1, m = 1
19 X = Br, R = $CONH_2$, n = 0, m = 1   27 R = $CONH_2$, n = 0, m = 1
20 X = Br, R = $CONH_2$, n = 1, m = 1   28 R = $CONH_2$, n = 1, m = 1
21 X = Br, R = CN, n = 0, m = 1   29 R = CN, n = 0, m = 1
22 X = Br, R = CN, n = 1, m = 1   30 R = CN, n = 1, m = 1
23 X = SO_2Ph, R = SO_2Ph, n = 0, m = 0   31 R = SO_2Ph, n = 0, m = 0
24 X = SO_2Ph, R = SO_2Ph, n = 1, m = 0   32 R = SO_2Ph, n = 1, m = 0

FIG. 4   Furazan/furoxan-sulfonamide CAI hybrids of types 17–32.

Furazan/furoxan-sulfonamide hybrids possessing efficient CA Inhibitory properties of types 17–32 (Fig. 4) were also reported [41]. In this case, the NO donor is constituted by the furazan ring [41]. These sulfonamides acted as low nanomolar inhibitors of isoforms hCA I, II, IX, and XII involved in glaucoma, and showed significant reduction of IOP in various animal models of glaucoma, making them attractive candidates for more detailed pharmacological evaluation [41].

Detailed pharmacological experiments (in vitro and in vivo) showed that the nitrate ester releases NO in vivo, and the IOP lowering is thus due both to the gas-transmitter (together with the well-known vaso-relaxation) as well as due to the inhibition of CAs by the sulfonamide part of the hybrid [16,41,51–53]. Overall, the CAI-NO donor hybrids were among the most effective IOP lowering agents at the moment in which they have been reported [53], and it is pity that they were not considered for clinical development, whereas the PG analogs, which will be treated in the next sections, were preferred instead of them.

Prostaglandin receptor agonists as antiglaucoma agents

Among the many prostaglandins (PGs) known to date, PGD_2, PGE_2, and $PGF_{2\alpha}$ are involved in ocular physiology [14,54]. Diverse PG receptors are expressed in various tissues including the eye, where they are involved in a host of physiological processes including chemotaxis, inflammation, immune response, etc. [54]. PGD_2 was demonstrated to decrease ocular aqueous flow in 1988 [55], but this autacoid is involved in immune responses and other essential processes, and it also provoked a strong reddening of the eye due to its pro-inflammatory action, and for such reasons, subsequent studies focused on PGF_2, PGE_2, and their agonists, which should not elicit immune responses and such strong adverse effects as PGD_2 [54–57]. These autacoids exert their action through G-protein-coupled receptors. There are four PGE_2 receptors (EP1-EP4) and one $PGF_{2\alpha}$ receptor (FP), which are widely expressed in various eye tissues, such as the cornea, conjunctiva, ciliary body, TM, iris, and retina [56]. EP/FP receptor agonists constitute an interesting class of antiglaucoma

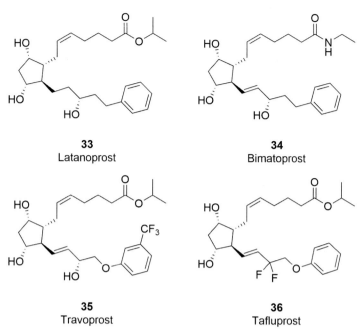

33
Latanoprost

34
Bimatoprost

35
Travoprost

36
Tafluprost

FIG. 5   PGF2$_\alpha$ agonists **33–36** used clinically for the management of glaucoma [62–64].

agents, as these compounds activate TM and ciliary muscle cells, increasing thus the aqueous outflow, both by the nonconventional pathway [14,54,56,57]. Nowadays, at least four drugs belonging to the PG receptors agonists are in clinical use as antiglaucoma agents: latanoprost **33** [58], bimatoprost **34** [59], travoprost **35** [60], and tafluprost **36** [61] (Fig. 5).

These derivatives induce a potent IOP lowering of around 30%, being more effective than the adrenergic drugs and the CAIs, and in addition are administered only once a day [1,56]. As a consequence, they became the most important first line antiglaucoma medication, also because their side effects are uncommon and usually only local. In fact, rarely, ocular inflammation may occur as well as pigmentation problems of light-colored (blue) eyes [56–61].

PG agonists: NO donor hybrids

Considering the effective antiglaucoma activity of the CAI-NO donors [6,16,17], a large number of PG derivatives incorporating NO donating moieties of the nitrate ester type have also been reported and assayed as IOP lowering agents [14,65–68] (Figs. 6 and 7).

These latanoprost NO-donating derivatives (compounds **37–39**, Fig. 6) showed a dual-action in effectively lowering IOP, as measured by the formation of cyclic guanosine-3′,5′-monophosphate (cGMP) in the eye in addition to the tonometric pressure measurements. The high levels of cGMP led to decreased AH formation and the reduction of IOP, in addition to the effects of the PG derivative in the outflow of the AH. These compounds were much

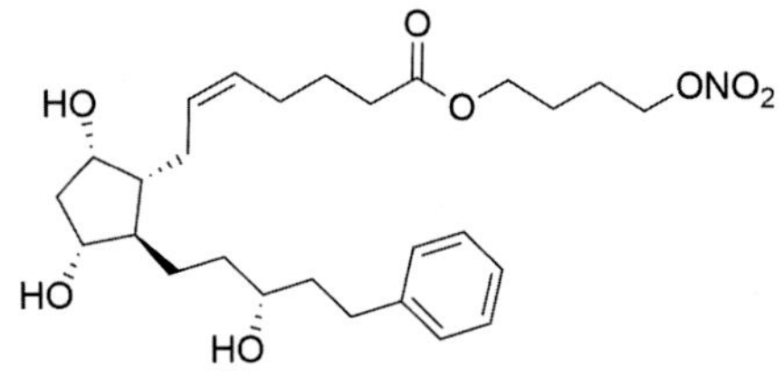

37 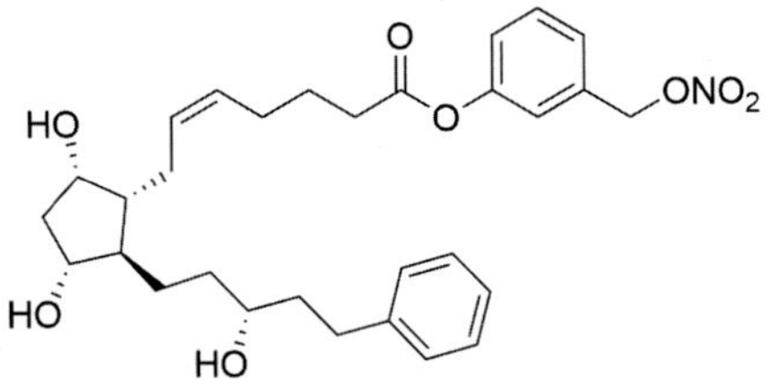   **38**

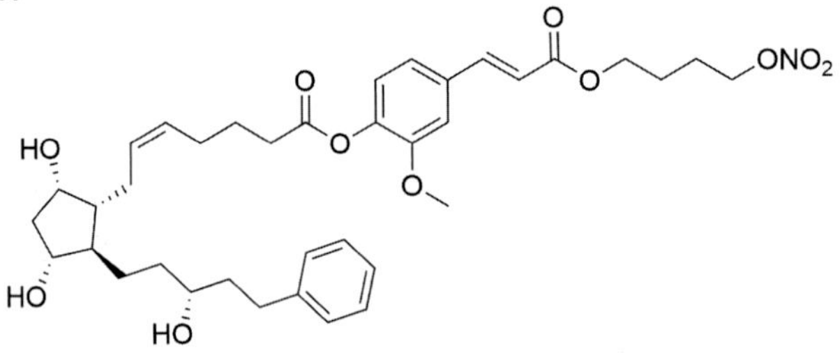

39

FIG. 6   PG derivatives **37–39** incorporating NO donating moieties.

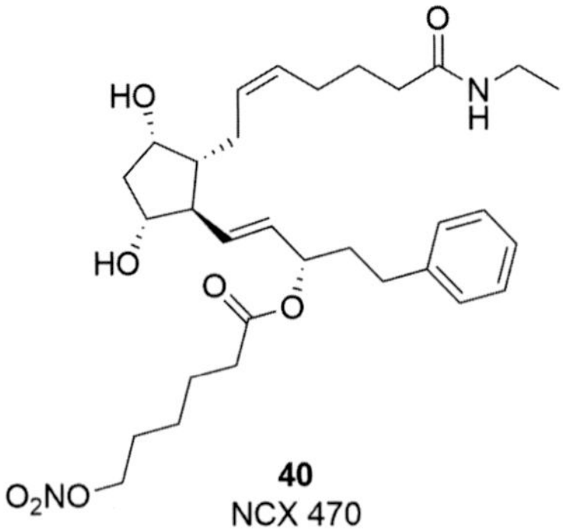

40
NCX 470

FIG. 7   Compound **40** (NCX 470), bimatoprost-NO in phase III clinical development as an antiglaucoma agent.

more effective than latanoprost as IOP lowering agents [65–68]. Compound **37**, known as latanoprostene bunod, was approved for clinical use in 2017 as an antiglaucoma agent which acts by targeting TM outflow both via the PG and NO components (NO is formed in vivo by the reduction of the nitrate prodrug) [6,68]. The drug is well tolerated with some hyperemia reported by few patients [62,69,70].

There are many other PG agonist-NO donors reported in the literature [14] but the one which seems to be the most interesting is the bimatoprost derivative **40**, NCX 470 (bimatoprost-NO), which advanced to phase III clinical trials as an antiglaucoma agent [14,65].

Nitric oxide donors per se

NO is a gas-transmitter possessing free radical character, it is highly unstable, and is produced by the enzyme nitric oxide synthase (NOS). NO has been shown to be involved in AH outflow within the eye, as well as in the local modulation of ocular blood flow, and RGCs death by apoptosis [17,65–68]. Furthermore, patients with glaucoma or ocular hypertension were observed to possess a decreased NO/cGMP content in their AH [65], whereas compounds acting as NO donors were documented to decrease IOP in normal and pathological conditions [16,17,65–68]. Thus, the idea to use NO-donating agents (as NO itself cannot be used due to its low stability and very short half-life) started to be considered as a novel therapeutic approach for glaucoma in the early 2000s [16,17,65–68]. Furthermore, as simple nitrate esters such as isosorbide mono- or dinitrate showed relatively scarce IOP lowering effects [16], the idea to combine the NO donating moiety with another pharmacophore endowed of antiglaucoma activity was very attractive and led to interesting developments which were discussed above for the CAI-NO donor and PG analog-NO donor hybrids.

Conclusions

For almost two decades, no new antiglaucoma drugs were available, probably also due to the fact that the PG analogs, introduced in the late 90s in clinical use, were highly efficient in controlling IOP, and in addition, many fixed combinations of classical drugs (mainly adrenergic agonists/antagonists in combination with CAIs and PG analogs) became available in the first years of the new century [1–3,6]. However, most such drugs must be administered two times a day. As a consequence, one of the first fixed combination to achieve a wide use and clinical success was Cosopt, a combination of timolol and dorzolamide, which is still one of the main eye drops used for the long-term management of glaucoma [1–3]. The PG receptors agonists, such as latanoprost, bimatoprost, travoprost, and tafluprost, decrease IOP by increasing AH outflow through the unconventional pathway, being the first agents to possess this antiglaucoma mechanism [14]. Furthermore, these were the first agents to be administered once a day, which meant an important improvement for the patient compliance. Together with Cosopt, these are first-line drugs for the treatment of the disease, and intense research efforts are dedicated to obtain new such derivatives with improved efficacy and less side effects compared to the agents already in use [1–3,6,14].

An exciting development was the approval of the rho kinase inhibitors, the first new class of antiglaucoma agents to emerge after many years, which act by enhancing the conventional AH outflow [15,71,72]. Two drugs are already available (ripasudil and netarsudil), and many others are in clinical development, but they are not discussed in detail here as there is no connection with NO, at least for the moment. Although their side effects are more relevant compared to other antiglaucoma drug classes, they provide the important advantage of acting also as neuroprotective agents in addition to their IOP lowering effects.

The latest class of antiglaucoma agents to arrive in clinical use was the NO donor, which exert their antiglaucoma action by increasing conventional AH outflow, considering the well-known biological activity of the gas transmitter NO. Furthermore, such agents also incorporate a classical antiglaucoma chemotype of the CAI- or PG-analog-type. In fact, the first agent of the class to be approved was latanoprostene bunod, which is a latanoprost derivative incorporating a nitrate ester as NO-donating moiety [14].

The drug design panorama of antiglaucoma drugs has been considerably enriched over the last decade, with the emergence of new drug targets as well as new approaches, mainly the hybrid drug one, for combining in the same molecule two different chemotypes with such an action. CAIs were the first reported drugs which incorporated in their molecules NO-donating agents, of the nitrate ester or furazan/furoxan type, and aromatic/heterocyclic sulfonamides as CA inhibitory components [6,16,17]. Such hybrids were highly effective as IOP lowering agents, and their action was longer compared to the individual agents. Extensive drug design studies have been reported for sulfonamide CAIs, with many such derivatives available to date, which show considerably better enzyme inhibitory activity and IOP lowering effects after topical administration, compared to the clinically used drugs dorzolamide and brinzolamide [37–40,42]. Furthermore, sulfonamides seem to have an additional beneficial effect as antiglaucoma agents apart their IOP lowering activity due to the ciliary processes CA inhibition [63]. Indeed, Eysteinsson et al. demonstrated that CAIs such as dorzolamide and other sulfonamide CAIs act as potent vasodilators of retinal arteries, through a mechanism of action not completely understood, but which may have a positive effect for this disease, as more blood may arrive to the optical nerve and, thus, exerts positive effects in addition to the lowered pressure [63]. This study demonstrated that the membrane-associated isoform CA IV is mainly responsible for these additional effects of the sulfonamide CAIs but did not exclude that other CAs may be involved [63].

Among the other chemotypes endowed with antiglaucoma action, the PG receptor agonists were also highly investigated, with many such new derivatives reported [54–61]. Many of the new derivatives reported also ultimately incorporate NO-donating moieties of the nitrate ester type, which in fact led to the latest antiglaucoma drug approved so far, latanoprostene bunod. Several other such derivatives are in various phases of clinical development, as these hybrids show highly effective IOP lowering properties.

Overall, a highly relevant progress has been achieved in designing new antiglaucoma agents both belonging to already well-investigated classes of drugs but also in finding alternative targets, for which interesting compounds are already available, some of which constitute totally new classes of drugs useful for the treatment of this chronic disease, and the NO hybrids were of crucial relevance. However, no diagnostic markers for glaucoma apart IOP measurements are available so far [64], and our hypothesis is that probably NO levels in the eye tissues might constitute a valid such alternative, although no such data are available in the literature, and this hypothesis needs to be verified.

References

[1] Lusthaus J, Goldberg I. Current management of glaucoma. Med J Aust 2019;210:180–7.
[2] Guglielmi P, Carradori S, Campestre C, Poce G. Novel therapies for glaucoma: a patent review (2013-2019). Expert Opin Ther Pat 2019;29:769–80.
[3] Supuran CT. The management of glaucoma and macular degeneration. Expert Opin Ther Pat 2019;29:745–7.
[4] Cheng KJ, Hsieh CM, Nepali K, Liou JP. Ocular disease therapeutics: design and delivery of drugs for diseases of the eye. J Med Chem 2020;63:10533–93.

[5] Mietzner R, Breunig M. Causative glaucoma treatment: promising targets and delivery systems. Drug Discov Today 2019;24:1606–13.

[6] Mincione F, Nocentini A, Supuran CT. Advances in the discovery of novel agents for the treatment of glaucoma. Expert Opin Drug Discovery 2021;16:1209–25.

[7] Cvenkel B, Kolko M. Current medical therapy and future trends in the management of glaucoma treatment. J Ophthalmol 2020;2020:6138132.

[8] Friedenwald JS. The formation of the intraocular fluid. Am J Ophthalmol 1949;32:9–27.

[9] Wistrand PJ. Carbonic anhydrase in the anterior uvea of the rabbit. Acta Physiol Scand 1951;24:144–8.

[10] Masini E, Carta F, Scozzafava A, Supuran CT. Antiglaucoma carbonic anhydrase inhibitors: a patent review. Expert Opin Ther Pat 2013;23:705–16.

[11] Nocentini A, Ceruso M, Bua S, et al. Discovery of β-adrenergic receptors blocker-carbonic anhydrase inhibitor hybrids for multitargeted antiglaucoma therapy. J Med Chem 2018;61:5380–94.

[12] Nocentini A, Supuran CT. Adrenergic agonists and antagonists as antiglaucoma agents: a literature and patent review (2013-2019). Expert Opin Ther Pat 2019;29:805–15.

[13] Supuran CT, Altamimi ASA, Carta F. Carbonic anhydrase inhibition and the management of glaucoma: a literature and patent review 2013-2019. Expert Opin Ther Pat 2019;29:781–92.

[14] Angeli A, Supuran CT. Prostaglandin receptor agonists as antiglaucoma agents (a patent review 2013-2018). Expert Opin Ther Pat 2019;29:793–803.

[15] Berrino E, Supuran CT. Rho-kinase inhibitors in the management of glaucoma. Expert Opin Ther Pat 2019;29:817–27.

[16] Fabrizi F, Mincione F, Somma T, et al. A new approach to antiglaucoma drugs: carbonic anhydrase inhibitors with or without NO donating moieties. Mechanism of action and preliminary pharmacology. J Enzyme Inhib Med Chem 2012;27:138–47.

[17] Supuran CT. Carbonic anhydrase inhibitor—NO donor hybrids and their pharmacologic applications. In: Bonavida B, Morbidelli L, editors. Therapeutic applications of nitric oxide in cancer and inflammatory-related disorders. New York: Elsevier; 2019. p. 229–42.

[18] Garhöfer G, Schmetterer L. Nitric oxide: a drug target for glaucoma revisited. Drug Discov Today 2019;24:1614–20.

[19] Supuran CT. Carbonic anhydrases: novel therapeutic applications for inhibitors and activators. Nat Rev Drug Discov 2008;7:168–81.

[20] Supuran CT. Structure and function of carbonic anhydrases. Biochem J 2016;473:2023–32.

[21] Supuran CT, Scozzafava A. Carbonic anhydrase inhibitors and their therapeutic potential. Expert Opin Ther Pat 2000;10:575–600.

[22] Nocentini A, Angeli A, Carta F, et al. Reconsidering anion inhibitors in the general context of drug design studies of modulators of activity of the classical enzyme carbonic anhydrase. J Enzyme Inhib Med Chem 2021;36:561–80.

[23] Supuran CT. Carbonic anhydrase inhibitors and their potential in a range of therapeutic areas. Expert Opin Ther Pat 2018;28:709–12.

[24] Supuran CT. Applications of carbonic anhydrases inhibitors in renal and central nervous system diseases. Expert Opin Ther Pat 2018;28:713–21.

[25] Supuran CT. How many carbonic anhydrase inhibition mechanisms exist? J Enzyme Inhib Med Chem 2016;31:345–60.

[26] Supuran CT. Exploring the multiple binding modes of inhibitors to carbonic anhydrases for novel drug discovery. Expert Opin Drug Discovery 2020;15:671–86.

[27] Supuran CT. Carbonic anhydrases and metabolism. Metabolites 2018;8:25.

[28] Angeli A, Carta F, Nocentini A, et al. Carbonic anhydrase inhibitors targeting metabolism and tumor microenvironment. Metabolites 2020;10:412.

[29] Carta F, Supuran CT. Diuretics with carbonic anhydrase inhibitory action: a patent and literature review (2005–2013). Expert Opin Ther Pat 2013;23:681–91.

[30] Bibi D, Shusterman B, Nocentini A, et al. Stereoselective pharmacokinetic and pharmacodynamic analysis of a CNS-active sulphamoylphenyl carbamate derivative. J Enzyme Inhib Med Chem 2019;34:1078–82.

[31] Supuran CT. An update on drug interaction considerations in the therapeutic use of carbonic anhydrase inhibitors. Expert Opin Drug Metab Toxicol 2020;16:297–307.

[32] Mishra CB, Tiwari M, Supuran CT. Progress in the development of human carbonic anhydrase inhibitors and their pharmacological applications: where are we today? Med Res Rev 2020;40:2485–565.

[33] McDonald PC, Chia S, Bedard PL, et al. A phase 1 study of SLC-0111, a novel inhibitor of carbonic anhydrase IX, in patients with advanced solid tumors. Am J Clin Oncol 2020;43:484–90.

[34] Supuran CT. Carbonic anhydrase inhibitors as emerging agents for the treatment and imaging of hypoxic tumors. Expert Opin Investig Drugs 2018;27:963–70.

[35] McDonald PC, Chafe SC, Supuran CT, Dedhar S. Cancer therapeutic targeting of hypoxia induced carbonic anhydrase IX: from bench to bedside. Cancers (Basel) 2022;14(14):3297.

[36] Supuran CT. Emerging role of carbonic anhydrase inhibitors. Clin Sci (Lond) 2021;135(10):1233–49.

[37] Scozzafava A, Supuran CT. Glaucoma and the applications of carbonic anhydrase inhibitors. Subcell Biochem 2014;75:349–59.

[38] Maren TH. Carbonic anhydrase: chemistry, physiology, and inhibition. Physiol Rev 1967;47:595–781.

[39] Maren TH, Jankowska L, Sanyal G, Edelhauser HF. The transcorneal permeability of sulfonamide carbonic anhydrase innhibitors and their effect on aqueous humor secretion. Exp Eye Res 1983;36:457–80.

[40] Sugrue MF. Pharmacological and ocular hypotensive properties of topical carbonic anhydrase inhibitors. Prog Retin Eye Res 2000;19:87–112.

[41] Chegaev K, Lazzarato L, Tamboli Y, et al. Furazan and furoxan sulfonamides are strong α-carbonic anhydrase inhibitors and potential antiglaucoma agents. Bioorg Med Chem 2014;22:3913–21.

[42] Scozzafava A, Menabuoni L, Mincione F, et al. Carbonic anhydrase inhibitors: synthesis of water-soluble, topically effective intraocular pressure lowering aromatic/heterocyclic sulfonamides containing cationic or anionic moieties: is the tail more important than the ring? J Med Chem 1999;42:2641–50.

[43] Scozzafava A, Briganti F, Mincione G, et al. Carbonic anhydrase inhibitors. Synthesis of water-soluble, amino acyl/dipeptidyl sulfonamides possessing long lasting-intraocular pressure lowering properties via the topical route. J Med Chem 1999;42:3690–700.

[44] Scozzafava A, Menabuoni L, Mincione F, Supuran CT. Carbonic anhydrase inhibitors. A general approach for the preparation of water soluble sulfonamides incorporating polyamino-polycarboxylate tails and of their metal complexes possessing long lasting, topical intraocular pressure lowering properties. J Med Chem 2002;45:1466–76.

[45] Fares M, Eldehna WM, Bua S, et al. Discovery of potent dual-tailed benzenesulfonamide inhibitors of human carbonic anhydrases implicated in glaucoma and in vivo profiling of their intraocular pressure-lowering action. J Med Chem 2020;63:3317–26.

[46] Ferraroni M, Lucarini L, Masini E, et al. 1,3-Oxazole-based selective picomolar inhibitors of cytosolic human carbonic anhydrase II alleviate ocular hypertension in rabbits: potency is supported by X-ray crystallography of two leads. Bioorg Med Chem 2017;25:4560–5.

[47] Nocentini A, Ferraroni M, Carta F, et al. Benzenesulfonamides incorporating flexible triazole moieties are highly effective carbonic anhydrase inhibitors: synthesis and kinetic, crystallographic, computational, and intraocular pressure lowering investigations. J Med Chem 2016;59:10692–704.

[48] Tanpure RP, Ren B, Peat TS, et al. Carbonic anhydrase inhibitors with dual-tail moieties to match the hydrophobic and hydrophilic halves of the carbonic anhydrase active site. J Med Chem 2015;58:1494–501.

[49] Bonardi A, Nocentini A, Bua S, et al. Sulfonamide inhibitors of human carbonic anhydrases designed through a three-tails approach: improving ligand/isoform matching and selectivity of action. J Med Chem 2020;63:7422–44.

[50] Kumar A, Siwach K, Supuran CT, Sharma PK. A decade of tail-approach based design of selective as well as potent tumor associated carbonic anhydrase inhibitors. Bioorg Chem 2022;126:105920.

[51] Steele RM, Batugo MR, Benedini F, et al. Nitric oxide-donating carbonic anhydrase inhibitors for the treatment of open-angle glaucoma. Bioorg Med Chem Lett 2009;19:6565–70.

[52] Mincione F, Benedini F, Biondi S, et al. Synthesis and crystallographic analysis of new sulfonamides incorporating NO-donating moieties with potent antiglaucoma action. Bioorg Med Chem Lett 2011;21:3216–21.

[53] Mincione F, Scozzafava A, Supuran CT. Antiglaucoma carbonic anhydrase inhibitors as ophthalomologic drugs. In: Supuran CT, Winum JY, editors. Drug design of zinc-enzyme inhibitors: functional, structural, and disease applications. Hoboken, NJ: Wiley; 2009. p. 139–54.

[54] Carta F, Supuran CT. Prostaglandins with carboxylic functionalities for the treatment of glaucoma. In: Dinges JJ, Lamberth C, editors. Bioactive carboxylic compound classes. New York: Wiley; 2016. p. 271–9.

[55] Goh Y, Nakajima M, Azuma I, Hayaishi O. Prostaglandin D2 reduces intraocular pressure. Br J Ophthalmol 1988;72:461–4.

[56] Mukhopadhyay P, Geoghegan TE, Patil RV, et al. Detection of EP2, EP4, and FP receptors in human ciliary epithelial and ciliary muscle cells. Biochem Pharmacol 1997;53:1249–55.

[57] Lee PY, Shao H, Xu LA, Qu CK. The effect of prostaglandin F2 alpha on intraocular pressure in normotensive human subjects. Invest Ophthalmol Vis Sci 1988;29:1474–7.

[58] Camras CB, Siebold EC, Lustgarten JS, et al. Maintained reduction of intraocular pressure by prostaglandin F2 alpha-1-isopropyl ester applied in multiple doses in ocular hypertensive and glaucoma patients. Ophthalmology 1989;96:1329–36.

[59] Brubaker RF. Mechanism of action of bimatoprost (Lumigan). Surv Ophthalmol 2001;45(Suppl. 4):S347–51.

[60] Netland PA, Landry T, Sullivan EK, et al. Travoprost compared with latanoprost and timolol in patients with open-angle glaucoma or ocular hypertension. Am J Ophthalmol 2001;132:472–84.

[61] Takagi Y, Nakajima T, Shimazaki A, et al. Pharmacological characteristics of AFP-168 (tafluprost), a new prostanoid FP receptor agonist, as an ocular hypotensive drug. Exp Eye Res 2004;78:767–76.

[62] Addis VM, Miller-Ellis E. Latanoprostene bunod ophthalmic solution 0.024% in the treatment of open-angle glaucoma: design, development, and place in therapy. Clin Ophthalmol 2018;12:2649–57.

[63] Eysteinsson T, Gudmundsdottir H, Hardarson AO, et al. Carbonic anhydrase inhibitors of different structures dilate pre-contracted porcine retinal arteries. Int J Mol Sci 2019;20:467.

[64] Bua S, Supuran CT. Diagnostic markers for glaucoma: a patent and literature review (2013-2019). Expert Opin Ther Pat 2019;29:829–39.

[65] Impagnatiello F, Bastia E, Almirante N, et al. Prostaglandin analogues and nitric oxide contribution in the treatment of ocular hypertension and glaucoma. Br J Pharmacol 2019;176:1079–89.

[66] Galassi F, Masini E, Giambene B, et al. A topical nitric oxide-releasing dexamethasone derivative: effects on intraocular pressure and ocular haemodynamics in a rabbit glaucoma model. Br J Ophthalmol 2006;90:1414–9.

[67] Impagnatiello F, Borghi V, Gale DC, et al. A dual acting compound with latanoprost amide and nitric oxide releasing properties, shows ocular hypotensive effects in rabbits and dogs. Exp Eye Res 2011;93:243–9.

[68] Krauss AH, Impagnatiello F, Toris CB, et al. Ocular hypotensive activity of BOL-303259-X, a nitric oxide donating prostaglandin F2α agonist, in preclinical models. Exp Eye Res 2011;93:250–5.

[69] Weinreb RN, Liebmann JM, Martin KR, et al. Latanoprostene bunod 0.024% in subjects with open-angle glaucoma or ocular hypertension: pooled phase 3 study findings. J Glaucoma 2018;27:7–15.

[70] Okeke CO, Burstein ES, Trubnik V, et al. Retrospective chart review on real-world use of Latanoprostene bunod 0.024% in treatment-naïve patients with open-angle glaucoma. Ophthalmol Therapy 2020;9:1041–53.

[71] Schehlein EM, Robin AL. Rho-associated kinase inhibitors: evolving strategies in glaucoma treatment. Drugs 2019;79:1031–6.

[72] Mueller BK, Mack H, Teusch N. Rho kinase, a promising drug target for neurological disorders. Nat Rev Drug Discov 2005;4:387–98.

IV. Nitric oxide derivatives in ocular diseases

Conclusions and future perspectives

Book "Therapeutic applications of nitric oxide and derivatives"

Nitric oxide (NO) is a small and gaseous signaling molecule that is essential for homeostasis of living beings, and its disturbance leads to different pathologies, such as cardiovascular dysfunctions, sensorial system disturbances, and cancer. The development of different strategies involving NO generation would have important physiological and clinical applications [1,2]. NO is a key vascular mediator that allows adequate functional homeostasis of all organs and tissues. In particular, NO dysfunction is associated with cardiovascular dysfunctions [3] and chronic renal diseases [4], diabetes, and persistent pulmonary hypertension [5,6], brain damage [7], and ocular-related diseases [8,9].

NO has a great impact on tumor induction or progression. The tumor microenvironment results from the pivotal cross-talks among the tumor and cancer stem cells, the stromal cells, and the altered extracellular matrix, which functionally impact the induction or progression of cancer cells. The molecular constructs NO donor-COX-2 inhibitors can be an effective therapeutic agent for cancer treatment, either in combination with immune checkpoint (PD-1/PD-L1) inhibitors or with standard chemotherapy [10]. Nutraceuticals have been shown to be useful as antitumoral agents [11]. The reduction of intratumoral NO generation can be a suitable approach for regulating chronic inflammation, reducing the polarization of T cells from immunosuppressive to pro-tumorigenic activities, and the impact of cancer stem cells in tumor progression, drug resistance, invasion, and metastasis [12–15].

There are several approaches to designing NO donors that are more specific and offer more precise targeting. For instance, Paul et al. [2] have reviewed the use of polymeric NO donors as more advantageous than molecular NO donors. Several polymeric NO donors have overcome the limitations of target-specific delivery and shown their effectiveness in various biomedical applications, being controllable for NO release. These polymeric NO donors also offer the establishment of complexes with drugs and the simultaneous release of NO and drugs. Clearly, their therapeutic applications still require additional study. Giordani et al. [10] reported on the use of Coxib-NO-releasing hybrids in cancer. They proposed that NO-releasing COX-2 selective inhibitors may be useful when used in combination with ICIs for cancer treatment.

Mangoni et al. [12] described drugs targeting TNBC that suppress vasculogenic mimicry via the modulation of the DDAH1/ADAM/NO axis. They propose that targeting DDAH1 is a novel strategy to suppress vasculogenic mimicry and can lead to anticancer effects in TNBC and other cancers that overexpress DDAH1. Further in vivo confirmation of the effects of DDAH1 inhibition on cancer growth and metastasis are still to be validated. Leyva and Bonavida [14] reported on the potential effectiveness of NOS-2/NO inhibitors to inhibit the immunosuppressive role of Gamma delta T cells that invade the TME. Their inhibition should restore antitumor immune rejection. Bahadoran et al. [3] reported on the role of HNO donors in the management of NO-related cardiovascular complications in T2 diabetes. This suggestion is premature and awaits experimental validation. Bijan et al. [6] reported on the use of inhaled NO in medicine. They describe various methods to generate NO that are cost-efficient and could be made available worldwide. Supuran [9] discusses the use of NO donors in the treatment of glaucoma, as no other drugs are available and effective. He reviews the various treatments and proposes that NO hybrids are a potential new class of drugs of clinical relevance.

In conclusion, the field of NO and derivatives has been the subject of investigations for many decades. There have been FDA-approved NO-based drugs for the treatment of various cardiovascular and heart diseases. However, as for their applications in cancer and other inflammatory diseases, there have been no new FDA-approved NO donors or inhibitors for any disease to date. There also existed a controversy on the role of NO and the utility of NO-derived compounds, since it has been reported to lead to contrasting findings. However, this controversy has been resolved in large part by the findings that the concentration/dose of NO dictates the pro- and antiintracellular and functional activities. Therefore, based on those findings, and under the appropriate conditions, the applications of both NO donors/inhibitors in the treatment of various diseases can now be clearly understood and can be pursued effectively for treatments. The topics treated in this book are paving the way for new therapies and/or drug combinations in different pathologies suffering the lack of effective and safe treatments.

References

[1] Ledesma B, Firdaus F, Mosquera S, Campbell K, Farah Rahman MPH, Reddy R, Arora H. Nitric oxide and derivatives: molecular insights and translational opportunities.

[2] Paul S, Kumar M, Mukherjee A, De P. Biomedical applications of polymeric nitric oxide (NO) donors.

[3] Bahadoran Z, Mirmiran P, Kashfi K, Ghasemi A. Nitric oxide resistance in type 2 diabetes: potential implications of HNO donors.

[4] Do Vale GT, Pinheiro Pereira B, Regina Potje S, Speroni Ceron C. Nitric oxide (NO) donors in kidney damage and diseases.

[5] Stefano G, Berra L, Emanuele R. Inhaled nitric oxide (iNO) administration in intubated and non-intubated patients: delivery systems, interfaces, dose administration, and monitoring techniques.

[6] Bijan SF, Berra L, Emanuele R. Inhaled nitric oxide (iNO): clinical applications in critical care medicine, delivery devices and measuring techniques.

[7] Arora B, Khan H, Kaur Grewal A, Gurjeet Singh T. Mechanistic insights on role of nitric oxide in ischemia-reperfusion injury.

[8] Cantó A, Martínez-González J, López-Pedraja R, Sánchez-Fideli A, Miranda M. Effect of nitric oxide inhibitors in retinitis pigmentosa.

[9] Supuran CT. Advances in the discovery of novel agents for the treatment of glaucoma: the role of nitric oxide donors.

[10] Giordani A, Poce G, Consalvi S, Maramai S, Saletti M, Rossi A, Patrignani P, Biava M, Anzini M. Therapeutic potential for coxib-nitric oxide releasing hybrids in cancer treatment..

[11] Palma JM, del Palacio JP, Rodríguez-Ruiz M, González-Gordo S, Díaz C, Ramos C, Cautain B, Vicente F, Corpas FJ. Pepper fruit as a nutraceutical food with anti-proliferative activity against tumor cells potentiated by nitric oxide (NO).

[12] Mangoni AA, Hulin J-A, Weerakoon L, Tommasi S. Targeting dimethylarginine dimethylaminohydrolase-1 to suppress vasculogenic mimicry in breast cancer: current evidence and future directions.

[13] Taskiran A, Demir A, Acikgoz E, Oktem G. Cancer stem cells and nitric oxide.

[14] Leyva BK, Bonavida B. Inducible nitric oxide synthase 2 (NOS2) and anti-tumor γδ-T cells.

[15] Lin K, Bonavida B. The regulation of the programmed death ligand 1 (PD-L1) by nitric oxide in breast cancer: immuno-therapeutic implication.

Index

Note: Page numbers followed by *f* indicate figures and *t* indicate tables.